SECOND EDITION

Python for Finance
Mastering Data-Driven Finance

Yves Hilpisch

Beijing · Boston · Farnham · Sebastopol · Tokyo

Python for Finance

by Yves Hilpisch

Copyright © 2019 Yves Hilpisch. All rights reserved.

Published by O'Reilly Media, Inc., 1005 Gravenstein Highway North, Sebastopol, CA 95472.

O'Reilly books may be purchased for educational, business, or sales promotional use. Online editions are also available for most titles (*http://oreilly.com*). For more information, contact our corporate/institutional sales department: 800-998-9938 or *corporate@oreilly.com*.

Editors: Susan Conant and Jeff Bleiel	**Indexer:** Judith McConville
Production Editor: Kristen Brown	**Interior Designer:** David Futato
Copyeditor: Rachel Head	**Cover Designer:** Karen Montgomery
Proofreader: Kim Cofer	**Illustrator:** Rebecca Demarest

December 2014:   First Edition
December 2018:   Second Edition

Revision History for the Second Edition

2018-11-29:   First Release
2019-01-18:   Second Release
2019-05-31:   Third Release
2019-12-13:   Fourth Release
2020-03-20:   Fifth Release
2020-07-31:   Sixth Release
2020-10-23:   Seventh Release

See *http://oreilly.com/catalog/errata.csp?isbn=9781492024330* for release details.

978-1-492-02433-0

[LSI]

Table of Contents

Part I.   Python and Finance

Part II. Mastering the Basics

Part III. Financial Data Science

Part IV. Algorithmic Trading

Part V.   Derivatives Analytics

Preface

These days, Python is undoubtedly one of the major strategic technology platforms in the financial industry. When I started writing the first edition of this book in 2013, I still had many conversations and presentations in which I argued relentlessly for Python's competitive advantages in finance over other languages and platforms. Toward the end of 2018, this is not a question anymore: financial institutions around the world now simply try to make the best use of Python and its powerful ecosystem of data analysis, visualization, and machine learning packages.

Beyond the realm of finance, Python is also often the language of choice in introductory programming courses, such as in computer science programs. Beyond its readable syntax and multiparadigm approach, a major reason for this is that Python has also become a first class citizen in the areas of artificial intelligence (AI), machine learning (ML), and deep learning (DL). Many of the most popular packages and libraries in these areas are either written directly in Python (such as scikit-learn for ML) or have Python wrappers available (such as TensorFlow for DL).

Finance itself is entering a new era, and two major forces are driving this evolution. The first is the programmatic access to basically all the financial data available—in general, this happens in real time and is what leads to *data-driven finance*. Decades ago, most trading or investment decisions were driven by what traders and portfolio managers could read in the newspaper or learn through personal conversations. Then came terminals that brought financial data in real time to the traders' and portfolio managers' desks via computers and electronic communication. Today, individuals (or teams) can no longer keep up with the vast amounts of financial data generated in even a single minute. Only machines, with their ever-increasing processing speeds and computational power, can keep up with the volume and velocity of financial data. This means, among other things, that most of today's global equities trading volume is driven by algorithms and computers rather than by human traders.

The second major force is the increasing importance of AI in finance. More and more financial institutions try to capitalize on ML and DL algorithms to improve operations and their trading and investment performances. At the beginning of 2018, the first dedicated book on "financial machine learning" was published, which underscores this trend. Without a doubt, there are more to come. This leads to what might be called *AI-first finance*, where flexible, parameterizable ML and DL algorithms replace traditional financial theory—theory that might be elegant but no longer very useful in the new era of data-driven, AI-first finance.

Python is the right programming language and ecosystem to tackle the challenges of this era of finance. Although this book covers basic ML algorithms for unsupervised and supervised learning (as well as deep neural networks, for instance), the focus is on Python's data processing and analysis capabilities. To fully account for the importance of AI in finance—now and in the future—another book-length treatment is necessary. However, most of the AI, ML, and DL techniques require such large amounts of data that mastering data-driven finance should come first anyway.

This second edition of *Python for Finance* is more of an upgrade than an update. For example, it adds a complete part (Part IV) about algorithmic trading. This topic has recently become quite important in the financial industry, and is also quite popular with retail traders. It also adds a more introductory part (Part II) where fundamental Python programming and data analysis topics are presented before they are applied in later parts of the book. On the other hand, some chapters from the first edition have been deleted completely. For instance, the chapter on web techniques and packages (such as Flask) was dropped because there are more dedicated and focused books about such topics available today.

For the second edition, I tried to cover even more finance-related topics and to focus on Python techniques that are particularly useful for financial data science, algorithmic trading, and computational finance. As in the first edition, the approach is a practical one, in that implementation and illustration come before theoretical details and I generally focus on the big picture rather than the most arcane parameterization options of a certain class, method, or function.

Having described the basic approach for the second edition, it is worth emphasizing that this book is neither an introduction to Python programming nor to finance in general. A vast number of excellent resources are available for both. This book is located at the intersection of these two exciting fields, and assumes that the reader has some background in programming (not necessarily Python) as well as in finance. Such readers learn how to apply Python and its ecosystem to the financial domain.

The Jupyter Notebooks and codes accompanying this book can be accessed and executed via our Quant Platform. You can sign up for free at *http://py4fi.pqp.io*.

My company (The Python Quants) and myself provide many more resources to master Python for financial data science, artificial intelligence, algorithmic trading, and computational finance. You can start by visiting the following sites:

- Our company website (*http://tpq.io*)
- My private website (*http://hilpisch.com*)
- Our Python books website (*http://books.tpq.io*)
- Our online training website (*http://training.tpq.io*)
- The Certificate Program website (*http://certificate.tpq.io*)

From all the offerings that we have created over the last few years, I am most proud of our *Certificate Program in Python for Algorithmic Trading*. It provides over 150 hours of live and recorded instruction, over 1,200 pages of documentation, over 5,000 lines of Python code, and over 50 Jupyter Notebooks. The program is offered multiple times per year and we update and improve it with every cohort. The online program is the first of its kind, in that successful delegates obtain an official university certificate in cooperation with htw saar University of Applied Sciences (*http://htwsaar.de*).

In addition, I recently started The AI Machine (*http://aimachine.io*), a new project and company to standardize the deployment of automated, algorithmic trading strategies. With this project, we want to implement in a systematic and scalable fashion what we have been teaching over the years in the field, in order to capitalize on the many opportunities in the algorithmic trading field. Thanks to Python—and data-driven and AI-first finance—this project is possible these days even for a smaller team like ours.

I closed the preface for the first edition with the following words:

> I am really excited that Python has established itself as an important technology in the financial industry. I am also sure that it will play an even more important role there in the future, in fields like derivatives and risk analytics or high performance computing. My hope is that this book will help professionals, researchers, and students alike make the most of Python when facing the challenges of this fascinating field.

When I wrote these lines in 2014, I couldn't have predicted how important Python would become in finance. In 2018, I am even happier that my expectations and hopes have been so greatly surpassed. Maybe the first edition of the book played a small part in this. In any case, a big thank you is in order to all the relentless open source developers out there, without whom the success story of Python couldn't have been written.

Conventions Used in This Book

The following typographical conventions are used in this book:

Italic
  Indicates new terms, URLs, and email addresses.

Constant width

> Used for program listings, as well as within paragraphs to refer to software packages, programming languages, file extensions, filenames, program elements such as variable or function names, databases, data types, environment variables, statements, and keywords.

Constant width italic

> Shows text that should be replaced with user-supplied values or by values determined by context.

 This element signifies a tip or suggestion.

 This element signifies a general note.

 This element indicates a warning or caution.

Using Code Examples

Supplemental material (in particular, Jupyter Notebooks and Python scripts/modules) is available for usage and download at *http://py4fi.pqp.io*.

This book is here to help you get your job done. In general, if example code is offered with this book, you may use it in your programs and documentation. You do not need to contact us for permission unless you're reproducing a significant portion of the code. For example, writing a program that uses several chunks of code from this book does not require permission. Selling or distributing a CD-ROM of examples from O'Reilly books does require permission. Answering a question by citing this book and quoting example code does not require permission. Incorporating a significant amount of example code from this book into your product's documentation does require permission.

We appreciate, but do not require, attribution. An attribution usually includes the title, author, publisher, and ISBN. For example: "*Python for Finance*, 2nd Edition, by Yves Hilpisch (O'Reilly). Copyright 2019 Yves Hilpisch, 978-1-492-02433-0."

If you feel your use of code examples falls outside fair use or the permission given above, feel free to contact us at *permissions@oreilly.com*.

O'Reilly Online Learning

 For more than 40 years, *O'Reilly Media* has provided technology and business training, knowledge, and insight to help companies succeed.

Our unique network of experts and innovators share their knowledge and expertise through books, articles, and our online learning platform. O'Reilly's online learning platform gives you on-demand access to live training courses, in-depth learning paths, interactive coding environments, and a vast collection of text and video from O'Reilly and 200+ other publishers. For more information, visit *http://oreilly.com*.

How to Contact Us

Please address comments and questions concerning this book to the publisher:

O'Reilly Media, Inc.
1005 Gravenstein Highway North
Sebastopol, CA 95472
800-998-9938 (in the United States or Canada)
707-829-0515 (international or local)
707-829-0104 (fax)

We have a web page for this book, where we list errata, examples, and any additional information. You can access this page at *http://bit.ly/python-finance-2e*.

To comment or ask technical questions about this book, send email to *bookquestions@oreilly.com*.

For news and more information about our books and courses, see our website at *http://www.oreilly.com*.

Find us on Facebook: *http://facebook.com/oreilly*

Follow us on Twitter: *http://twitter.com/oreillymedia*

Watch us on YouTube: *http://www.youtube.com/oreillymedia*

Acknowledgments

I want to thank all those who helped to make this book a reality—in particular, the team at O'Reilly, who really improved my manuscript in many ways. I would like to thank the tech reviewers, Hugh Brown and Jake VanderPlas. The book benefited from their valuable feedback and their many suggestions. Any remaining errors, of course, are mine.

Michael Schwed, with whom I have been working closely for more than ten years, deserves a special thank you. Over the years, I have benefited in innumerable ways from his work, support, and Python know-how.

I also want to thank Jason Ramchandani and Jorge Santos of Refinitiv (formerly Thomson Reuters) for their continued support not only of my work but also of the open source community in general.

As with the first edition, the second edition of this book has tremendously benefited from the dozens of "Python for finance" talks I have given over the years, as well as the hundreds of hours of "Python for finance" trainings. In many cases the feedback from participants helped to improve my training materials, which often ended up as chapters or sections in this book.

Writing the first edition took me about a year. Overall, writing and upgrading the second edition also took about a year, which was quite a bit longer than I expected. This is mainly because the topic itself keeps me very busy travel- and business-wise, which I am very grateful for.

Writing books requires many hours in solitude and such hours cannot be spent with the family. Therefore, thank you to Sandra, Lilli, Henry, Adolf, Petra, and Heinz for all your understanding and support—not only with regard to writing this book.

I dedicate the second edition of this book, as the first one, to my lovely, strong, and compassionate wife Sandra. She has given new meaning over the years to what family is really about. Thank you.

— Yves
Saarland, November 2018

## PART I

Python and Finance

This part introduces Python for finance. It consists of two chapters:

- Chapter 1 briefly discusses Python in general and argues in some detail why Python is well suited to addressing the technological challenges in the financial industry as well as in financial data analytics.

- Chapter 2 is about Python infrastructure; it provides a concise overview of important aspects of managing a Python environment to get you started with interactive financial analytics and financial application development in Python.

## CHAPTER 1

Why Python for Finance

Banks are essentially technology firms.

—Hugo Banziger

The Python Programming Language

Python is a high-level, multipurpose programming language that is used in a wide range of domains and technical fields. On the Python website (*https://www.python.org/doc/essays/blurb*) you find the following executive summary:

> Python is an interpreted, object-oriented, high-level programming language with dynamic semantics. Its high-level built in data structures, combined with dynamic typing and dynamic binding, make it very attractive for Rapid Application Development, as well as for use as a scripting or glue language to connect existing components together. Python's simple, easy to learn syntax emphasizes readability and therefore reduces the cost of program maintenance. Python supports modules and packages, which encourages program modularity and code reuse. The Python interpreter and the extensive standard library are available in source or binary form without charge for all major platforms, and can be freely distributed.

This pretty well describes *why* Python has evolved into one of the major programming languages today. Nowadays, Python is used by the beginner programmer as well as by the highly skilled expert developer, at schools, in universities, at web companies, in large corporations and financial institutions, as well as in any scientific field.

Among other features, Python is:

Open source
Python and the majority of supporting libraries and tools available are open source and generally come with quite flexible and open licenses.

Interpreted

The reference CPython implementation is an interpreter of the language that translates Python code at runtime to executable byte code.

Multiparadigm

Python supports different programming and implementation paradigms, such as object orientation and imperative, functional, or procedural programming.

Multipurpose

Python can be used for rapid, interactive code development as well as for building large applications; it can be used for low-level systems operations as well as for high-level analytics tasks.

Cross-platform

Python is available for the most important operating systems, such as Windows, Linux, and macOS. It is used to build desktop as well as web applications, and it can be used on the largest clusters and most powerful servers as well as on such small devices as the Raspberry Pi (*http://www.raspberrypi.org*).

Dynamically typed

Types in Python are in general inferred at runtime and not statically declared as in most compiled languages.

Indentation aware

In contrast to the majority of other programming languages, Python uses indentation for marking code blocks instead of parentheses, brackets, or semicolons.

Garbage collecting

Python has automated garbage collection, avoiding the need for the programmer to manage memory.

When it comes to Python syntax and what Python is all about, Python Enhancement Proposal 20—i.e., the so-called "Zen of Python"—provides the major guidelines. It can be accessed from every interactive shell with the command `import this`:

```
In [1]: import this
        The Zen of Python, by Tim Peters

        Beautiful is better than ugly.
        Explicit is better than implicit.
        Simple is better than complex.
        Complex is better than complicated.
        Flat is better than nested.
        Sparse is better than dense.
        Readability counts.
        Special cases aren't special enough to break the rules.
        Although practicality beats purity.
        Errors should never pass silently.
        Unless explicitly silenced.
```

```
In the face of ambiguity, refuse the temptation to guess.
There should be one-- and preferably only one --obvious way to do it.
Although that way may not be obvious at first unless you're Dutch.
Now is better than never.
Although never is often better than *right* now.
If the implementation is hard to explain, it's a bad idea.
If the implementation is easy to explain, it may be a good idea.
Namespaces are one honking great idea -- let's do more of those!
```

A Brief History of Python

Although Python might still have the appeal of something *new* to some people, it has been around for quite a long time. In fact, development efforts began in the 1980s by Guido van Rossum from the Netherlands. He is still active in Python development and has been awarded the title of *Benevolent Dictator for Life* by the Python community. In July 2018, van Rossum stepped down from this position after decades of being an active driver of the Python core development efforts. The following can be considered milestones in the development of Python (*http://bit.ly/2DYWqCW*):

- **Python 0.9.0** released in 1991 (first release)
- **Python 1.0** released in 1994
- **Python 2.0** released in 2000
- **Python 2.6** released in 2008
- **Python 3.0** released in 2008
- **Python 3.1** released in 2009
- **Python 2.7** released in 2010
- **Python 3.2** released in 2011
- **Python 3.3** released in 2012
- **Python 3.4** released in 2014
- **Python 3.5** released in 2015
- **Python 3.6** released in 2016
- **Python 3.7** released in June 2018

It is remarkable, and sometimes confusing to Python newcomers, that there are two major versions available, still being developed and, more importantly, in parallel use since 2008. As of this writing, this will probably keep on for a little while since tons of code available and in production is still Python 2.6/2.7. While the first edition of this book was based on Python 2.7, this second edition uses Python 3.7 throughout.

The Python Ecosystem

A major feature of Python as an ecosystem, compared to just being a programming language, is the availability of a large number of packages and tools. These packages and tools generally have to be *imported* when needed (e.g., a plotting library) or have to be started as a separate system process (e.g., a Python interactive development environment). Importing means making a package available to the current namespace and the current Python interpreter process.

Python itself already comes with a large set of packages and modules that enhance the basic interpreter in different directions, known as the *Python Standard Library* (*https://docs.python.org/3/library/index.html*). For example, basic mathematical calculations can be done without any importing, while more specialized mathematical functions need to be imported through the math module:

```
In [2]: 100 * 2.5 + 50
Out[2]: 300.0

In [3]: log(1)  ❶

          ---------------------------------------------------------------
          NameError                              Traceback (most recent call last)
          <ipython-input-3-74f22a2fd43b> in <module>
          ----> 1 log(1)  ❶

          NameError: name 'log' is not defined

In [4]: import math  ❷

In [5]: math.log(1)  ❷
Out[5]: 0.0
```

❶ Without further imports, an error is raised.

❷ After importing the math module, the calculation can be executed.

While math is a standard Python module available with any Python installation, there are many more packages that can be installed optionally and that can be used in the very same fashion as the standard modules. Such packages are available from different (web) sources. However, it is generally advisable to use a Python package manager that makes sure that all libraries are consistent with each other (see Chapter 2 for more on this topic).

The code examples presented so far use interactive Python environments: IPython (*http://www.ipython.org*) and Jupyter (*http://jupyter.org*), respectively. These are probably the most widely used interactive Python environments at the time of this writing. Although IPython started out as just an enhanced interactive Python shell, it today has many features typically found in integrated development environments (IDEs), such as support for profiling and debugging. Those features missing in IPython are typically provided by advanced text/code editors, like Vim (*http://vim.org*), which can also be integrated with IPython. Therefore, it is not unusual to combine IPython with one's text/code editor of choice to form the basic toolchain for a Python development process.

IPython enhances the standard interactive shell in many ways. Among other things, it provides improved command-line history functions and allows for easy object inspection. For instance, the help text (`docstring`) for a function is printed by just adding a ? before or after the function name (adding ?? will provide even more information).

IPython originally came in two popular versions: a *shell* version and a *browser-based* version (the *Notebook*). The Notebook variant proved so useful and popular that it evolved into an independent, language-agnostic project now called Jupyter. Given this background, it is no surprise that Jupyter Notebook inherits most of the beneficial features of IPython—and offers much more, for example when it comes to visualization.

Refer to VanderPlas (2016, Chapter 1) for more details on using IPython.

The Python User Spectrum

Python does not only appeal to professional software developers; it is also of use for the casual developer as well as for domain experts and scientific developers.

Professional software developers find in Python all they might require to efficiently build large applications. Almost all programming paradigms are supported; there are powerful development tools available; and any task can, in principle, be addressed with Python. These types of users typically build their own frameworks and classes, also work on the fundamental Python and scientific stack, and strive to make the most of the ecosystem.

Scientific developers or *domain experts* are generally heavy users of certain packages and frameworks, have built their own applications that they enhance and optimize over time, and tailor the ecosystem to their specific needs. These groups of users also generally engage in longer interactive sessions, rapidly prototyping new code as well as exploring and visualizing their research and/or domain data sets.

Casual programmers like to use Python generally for specific problems they know that Python has its strengths in. For example, visiting the gallery page of `matplotlib`, copying a certain piece of visualization code provided there, and adjusting the code to their specific needs might be a beneficial use case for members of this group.

There is also another important group of Python users: *beginner programmers*, i.e., those that are just starting to program. Nowadays, Python has become a very popular language at universities, colleges, and even schools to introduce students to programming.[1] A major reason for this is that its basic syntax is easy to learn and easy to understand, even for the non-developer. In addition, it is helpful that Python supports almost all programming styles.[2]

The Scientific Stack

There is a certain set of packages that is collectively labeled the *scientific stack*. This stack comprises, among others, the following packages:

NumPy *(http://www.numpy.org)*
> NumPy provides a multidimensional array object to store homogeneous or heterogeneous data; it also provides optimized functions/methods to operate on this array object.

SciPy *(http://www.scipy.org)*
> SciPy is a collection of subpackages and functions implementing important standard functionality often needed in science or finance; for example, one finds functions for cubic splines interpolation as well as for numerical integration.

matplotlib *(http://www.matplotlib.org)*
> This is the most popular plotting and visualization package for Python, providing both 2D and 3D visualization capabilities.

pandas *(http://pandas.pydata.org)*
> pandas builds on NumPy and provides richer classes for the management and analysis of time series and tabular data; it is tightly integrated with matplotlib for plotting and PyTables for data storage and retrieval.

scikit-learn *(http://scikit-learn.org)*
> scikit-learn is a popular machine learning (ML) package that provides a unified application programming interface (API) for many different ML algorithms, such as for estimation, classification, or clustering.

PyTables *(http://www.pytables.org)*
> PyTables is a popular wrapper for the HDF5 *(http://www.hdfgroup.org/HDF5/)* data storage package; it is a package to implement optimized, disk-based I/O operations based on a hierarchical database/file format.

---

1 Python, for example, is a major language used in the Master of Financial Engineering Program (*http://mfe.baruch.cuny.edu*) at Baruch College of the City University of New York. The first edition of this book is in use at a large number of universities around the world to teach Python for financial analysis and application building.

2 See *http://wiki.python.org/moin/BeginnersGuide*, where you will find links to many valuable resources for both developers and non-developers getting started with Python.

Depending on the specific domain or problem, this stack is enlarged by additional packages, which more often than not have in common that they build on top of one or more of these fundamental packages. However, the *least common denominator* or *basic building blocks* in general are the NumPy ndarray class (see Chapter 4) and the pandas DataFrame class (see Chapter 5).

Taking Python as a programming language alone, there are a number of other languages available that can probably keep up with its syntax and elegance. For example, Ruby is a popular language often compared to Python. The language's website (*http://www.ruby-lang.org*) describes Ruby as:

> A dynamic, open source programming language with a focus on simplicity and productivity. It has an elegant syntax that is natural to read and easy to write.

The majority of people using Python would probably also agree with the exact same statement being made about Python itself. However, what distinguishes Python for many users from equally appealing languages like Ruby is the availability of the scientific stack. This makes Python not only a good and elegant language to use, but also one that is capable of replacing domain-specific languages and tool sets like Matlab or R. It also provides by default anything that you would expect, say, as a seasoned web developer or systems administrator. In addition, Python is good at interfacing with domain-specific languages such as R, so that the decision usually is not about *either Python or something else*—it is rather about which language should be the major one.

Technology in Finance

With these "rough ideas" of what Python is all about, it makes sense to step back a bit and to briefly contemplate the role of technology in finance. This will put one in a position to better judge the role Python already plays and, even more importantly, will probably play in the financial industry of the future.

In a sense, technology per se is *nothing special* to financial institutions (as compared, for instance, to biotechnology companies) or to the finance function (as compared to other corporate functions, like logistics). However, in recent years, spurred by innovation and also regulation, banks and other financial institutions like hedge funds have evolved more and more into technology companies instead of being *just* financial intermediaries. Technology has become a major asset for almost any financial institution around the globe, having the potential to lead to competitive advantages as well as disadvantages. Some background information can shed light on the reasons for this development.

Technology Spending

Banks and financial institutions together form the industry that spends the most on technology on an annual basis. The following statement therefore shows not only that technology is important for the financial industry, but that the financial industry is also really important to the technology sector:

> FRAMINGHAM, Mass., June 14, 2018 – Worldwide spending on information technology (IT) by financial services firms will be nearly $500 billion in 2021, growing from $440 billion in 2018, according to new data from a series of Financial Services IT Spending Guides from International Data Corporation (IDC).
>
> —IDC (*http://bit.ly/2RUAV8Y*)

In particular, banks and other financial institutions are engaging in a race to make their business and operating models digital:

> Bank spending on new technologies was predicted to amount to 19.9 billion U.S. dollars in 2017 in North America.
>
> The banks develop current systems and work on new technological solutions in order to increase their competitiveness on the global market and to attract clients interested in new online and mobile technologies. It is a big opportunity for global fintech companies which provide new ideas and software solutions for the banking industry.
>
> —Statista (*http://bit.ly/2Q04KYr*)

Large multinational banks today generally employ thousands of developers to maintain existing systems and build new ones. Large investment banks with heavy technological requirements often have technology budgets of several billion USD per year.

Technology as Enabler

The technological development has also contributed to innovations and efficiency improvements in the financial sector. Typically, projects in this area run under the umbrella of *digitalization.*

> The financial services industry has seen drastic technology-led changes over the past few years. Many executives look to their IT departments to improve efficiency and facilitate game-changing innovation—while somehow also lowering costs and continuing to support legacy systems. Meanwhile, FinTech start-ups are encroaching upon established markets, leading with customer-friendly solutions developed from the ground up and unencumbered by legacy systems.
>
> —PwC 19th Annual Global CEO Survey 2016 (*https://pwc.to/1OYTO2d*)

As a side effect of the increasing efficiency, competitive advantages must often be looked for in ever more complex products or transactions. This in turn inherently increases risks and makes risk management as well as oversight and regulation more and more difficult. The financial crisis of 2007 and 2008 tells the story of potential dangers resulting from such developments. In a similar vein, "algorithms and computers gone wild" represent a potential risk to the financial markets; this materialized dramatically in the so-called *flash crash* of May 2010 (*http://en.wikipedia.org/wiki/2010_Flash_Crash*), where automated selling led to large intraday drops in certain stocks and stock indices. Part IV covers topics related to the algorithmic trading of financial instruments.

Technology and Talent as Barriers to Entry

On the one hand, technology advances reduce cost over time, *ceteris paribus*. On the other hand, financial institutions continue to invest heavily in technology to both gain market share and defend their current positions. To be active today in certain areas in finance often brings with it the need for large-scale investments in both technology and skilled staff. As an example, consider the derivatives analytics space:

> Aggregated over the total software lifecycle, firms adopting in-house strategies for OTC [derivatives] pricing will require investments between $25 million and $36 million alone to build, maintain, and enhance a complete derivatives library.
>
> —Ding (2010)

Not only is it costly and time-consuming to build a full-fledged derivatives analytics library, but you also need to have *enough experts* to do so. And these experts have to have the right tools and technologies available to accomplish their tasks. With the development of the Python ecosystem, such efforts have become more efficient and budgets in this regard can be reduced significantly today compared to, say, 10 years ago. Part V covers derivatives analytics and builds a small but powerful and flexible derivatives pricing library with Python and standard Python packages alone.

Another quote about the early days of Long-Term Capital Management (LTCM), formerly one of the most respected quantitative hedge funds—which, however, went bust in the late 1990s—further supports this insight about technology and talent:

> Meriwether spent $20 million on a state-of-the-art computer system and hired a crack team of financial engineers to run the show at LTCM, which set up shop in Greenwich, Connecticut. It was risk management on an industrial level.
>
> —Patterson (2010)

The same computing power that Meriwether had to buy for millions of dollars is today probably available for thousands or can be rented from a cloud provider based on a flexible fee plan. Chapter 2 shows how to set up an infrastructure in the cloud for interactive financial analytics, application development, and deployment with Python. The budgets for such a professional infrastructure start at a few USD per month. On the other hand, trading, pricing, and risk management have become so complex for larger financial institutions that today they need to deploy IT infrastructures with tens of thousands of computing cores.

Ever-Increasing Speeds, Frequencies, and Data Volumes

The one dimension of the finance industry that has been influenced most by technological advances is the *speed and frequency* with which financial transactions are decided and executed. Lewis (2014) describes so-called *flash trading*—i.e., trading at the highest speeds possible—in vivid detail.

On the one hand, increasing data availability on ever-smaller time scales makes it necessary to react in real time. On the other hand, the increasing speed and frequency of trading makes the data volumes further increase. This leads to processes that reinforce each other and push the average time scale for financial transactions systematically down. This is a trend that had already started a decade ago:

> Renaissance's Medallion fund gained an astonishing 80 percent in 2008, capitalizing on the market's extreme volatility with its lightning-fast computers. Jim Simons was the hedge fund world's top earner for the year, pocketing a cool $2.5 billion.
>
> —Patterson (2010)

Thirty years' worth of daily stock price data for a single stock represents roughly 7,500 closing quotes. This kind of data is what most of today's finance theory is based on. For example, modern or mean-variance portfolio theory (MPT), the capital asset pricing model (CAPM), and value-at-risk (VaR) all have their foundations in daily stock price data.

In comparison, on a typical trading day during a single trading hour the stock price of Apple Inc. (AAPL) may be quoted around 15,000 times—roughly twice the number of quotes compared to available end-of-day closing quotes over 30 years (see the example in "Data-Driven and AI-First Finance" on page 24). This brings with it a number of challenges:

Data processing
It does not suffice to consider and process end-of-day quotes for stocks or other financial instruments; "too much" happens during the day, and for some instruments during 24 hours for 7 days a week.

Analytics speed
Decisions often have to be made in milliseconds or even faster, making it necessary to build the respective analytics capabilities and to analyze large amounts of data in real time.

Theoretical foundations
Although traditional finance theories and concepts are far from being perfect, they have been well tested (and sometimes well rejected) over time; for the millisecond and microsecond scales important as of today, consistent financial concepts and theories in the traditional sense that have proven to be somewhat robust over time are still missing.

All these challenges can in general only be addressed by modern technology. Something that might also be a little bit surprising is that the lack of consistent theories often is addressed by technological approaches, in that high-speed algorithms exploit market microstructure elements (e.g., order flow, bid-ask spreads) rather than relying on some kind of financial reasoning.

The Rise of Real-Time Analytics

There is one discipline that has seen a strong increase in importance in the finance industry: *financial and data analytics*. This phenomenon has a close relationship to the insight that speeds, frequencies, and data volumes increase at a rapid pace in the industry. In fact, real-time analytics can be considered the industry's answer to this trend.

Roughly speaking, "financial and data analytics" refers to the discipline of applying software and technology in combination with (possibly advanced) algorithms and methods to gather, process, and analyze data in order to gain insights, to make decisions, or to fulfill regulatory requirements, for instance. Examples might include the estimation of sales impacts induced by a change in the pricing structure for a financial product in the retail branch of a bank, or the large-scale overnight calculation of credit valuation adjustments (CVA) for complex portfolios of derivatives trades of an investment bank.

There are two major challenges that financial institutions face in this context:

Big data
> Banks and other financial institutions had to deal with massive amounts of data even before the term "big data" was coined; however, the amount of data that has to be processed during single analytics tasks has increased tremendously over time, demanding both increased computing power and ever-larger memory and storage capacities.

Real-time economy
> In the past, decision makers could rely on structured, regular planning as well as decision and (risk) management processes, whereas they today face the need to take care of these functions in real time; several tasks that have been taken care of in the past via overnight batch runs in the back office have now been moved to the front office and are executed in real time.

Again, one can observe an interplay between advances in technology and financial/ business practice. On the one hand, there is the need to constantly improve analytics approaches in terms of speed and capability by applying modern technologies. On the other hand, advances on the technology side allow new analytics approaches that were considered impossible (or infeasible due to budget constraints) a couple of years or even months ago.

One major trend in the analytics space has been the utilization of parallel architectures on the central processing unit (CPU) side and massively parallel architectures on the general-purpose graphics processing unit (GPGPU) side. Current GPGPUs have computing cores in the thousands, making necessary a sometimes radical rethinking of what parallelism might mean to different algorithms. What is still an obstacle in this regard is that users generally have to learn new programming paradigms and techniques to harness the power of such hardware.

Python for Finance

The previous section described selected aspects characterizing the role of technology in finance:

- Costs for technology in the finance industry
- Technology as an enabler for new business and innovation
- Technology and talent as barriers to entry in the finance industry
- Increasing speeds, frequencies, and data volumes
- The rise of real-time analytics

This section analyzes how Python can help in addressing several of the challenges these imply. But first, on a more fundamental level, a brief analysis of Python for finance from a language and syntax point of view.

Finance and Python Syntax

Most people who make their first steps with Python in a finance context may attack an algorithmic problem. This is similar to a scientist who, for example, wants to solve a differential equation, evaluate an integral, or simply visualize some data. In general, at this stage, little thought is given to topics like a formal development process, testing, documentation, or deployment. However, this especially seems to be the stage where people fall in love with Python. A major reason for this might be that Python syntax is generally quite close to the mathematical syntax used to describe scientific problems or financial algorithms.

This can be illustrated by a financial algorithm, namely the valuation of a European call option by Monte Carlo simulation. The example considers a Black-Scholes-Merton (BSM) setup in which the option's underlying risk factor follows a geometric Brownian motion.

Assume the following numerical *parameter values* for the valuation:

- Initial stock index level $S_0 = 100$
- Strike price of the European call option $K = 105$
- Time to maturity $T = 1$ year
- Constant, riskless short rate $r = 0.05$

- Constant volatility $\sigma = 0.2$

In the BSM model, the index level at maturity is a random variable given by Equation 1-1, with z being a standard normally distributed random variable.

Equation 1-1. Black-Scholes-Merton (1973) index level at maturity

$$S_T = S_0 \exp\left(\left(r - \frac{1}{2}\sigma^2\right)T + \sigma\sqrt{T}z\right)$$

The following is an algorithmic description of the Monte Carlo valuation procedure:

1. Draw I pseudo-random numbers $z(i), i \in \{1, 2, \ldots, I\}$, from the standard normal distribution.
2. Calculate all resulting index levels at maturity $S_T(i)$ for given $z(i)$ and Equation 1-1.
3. Calculate all inner values of the option at maturity as $h_T(i) = \max\left(S_T(i) - K, 0\right)$.
4. Estimate the option present value via the Monte Carlo estimator as given in Equation 1-2.

Equation 1-2. Monte Carlo estimator for European option

$$C_0 \approx e^{-rT}\frac{1}{I}\sum_I h_T(i)$$

This problem and algorithm must now be translated into Python. The following code implements the required steps:

```
In [6]: import math
        import numpy as np      ❶

In [7]: S0 = 100.      ❷
        K = 105.       ❷
        T = 1.0        ❷
        r = 0.05       ❷
        sigma = 0.2    ❷

In [8]: I = 100000     ❷

In [9]: np.random.seed(1000)    ❸

In [10]: z = np.random.standard_normal(I)    ❹

In [11]: ST = S0 * np.exp((r - sigma ** 2 / 2) * T + sigma * math.sqrt(T) * z)    ❺
```

```
In [12]: hT = np.maximum(ST - K, 0)   ❻

In [13]: C0 = math.exp(-r * T) * np.mean(hT)   ❼

In [14]: print('Value of the European call option: {:5.3f}.'.format(C0))   ❽
         Value of the European call option: 8.019.
```

❶   NumPy is used here as the main package.

❷   The model and simulation parameter values are defined.

❸   The seed value for the random number generator is fixed.

❹   Standard normally distributed random numbers are drawn.

❺   End-of-period values are simulated.

❻   The option payoffs at maturity are calculated.

❼   The Monte Carlo estimator is evaluated.

❽   The resulting value estimate is printed.

Three aspects are worth highlighting:

Syntax
> The Python syntax is indeed quite close to the mathematical syntax, e.g., when it comes to the parameter value assignments.

Translation
> Every mathematical and/or algorithmic statement can generally be translated into a *single* line of Python code.

Vectorization
> One of the strengths of NumPy is the compact, vectorized syntax, e.g., allowing for 100,000 calculations within a single line of code.

This code can be used in an interactive environment like IPython or Jupyter Notebook. However, code that is meant to be reused regularly typically gets organized in so-called *modules* (or *scripts*), which are single Python files (technically text files) with the suffix *.py*. Such a module could in this case look like Example 1-1 and could be saved as a file named *bsm_mcs_euro.py*.

Example 1-1. Monte Carlo valuation of European call option

```python
#
# Monte Carlo valuation of European call option
# in Black-Scholes-Merton model
# bsm_mcs_euro.py
#
# Python for Finance, 2nd ed.
# (c) Dr. Yves J. Hilpisch
#
import math
import numpy as np

# Parameter Values
S0 = 100.  # initial index level
K = 105.  # strike price
T = 1.0  # time-to-maturity
r = 0.05  # riskless short rate
sigma = 0.2  # volatility

I = 100000  # number of simulations

# Valuation Algorithm
z = np.random.standard_normal(I)  # pseudo-random numbers
# index values at maturity
ST = S0 * np.exp((r - 0.5 * sigma ** 2) * T + sigma * math.sqrt(T) * z)
hT = np.maximum(ST - K, 0)  # payoff at maturity
C0 = math.exp(-r * T) * np.mean(hT)  # Monte Carlo estimator

# Result Output
print('Value of the European call option %5.3f.' % C0)
```

The algorithmic example in this subsection illustrates that Python, with its very syntax, is well suited to complement the classic duo of scientific languages, English and mathematics. It seems that adding Python to the set of scientific languages makes it more well rounded. One then has:

- **English** for *writing and talking* about scientific and financial problems, etc.
- **Mathematics** for *concisely, exactly describing and modeling* abstract aspects, algorithms, complex quantities, etc.
- **Python** for *technically modeling and implementing* abstract aspects, algorithms, complex quantities, etc.

Mathematics and Python Syntax

There is hardly any programming language that comes as close to mathematical syntax as Python. Numerical algorithms are therefore in general straightforward to translate from the mathematical representation into the Pythonic implementation. This makes prototyping, development, and code maintenance in finance quite efficient with Python.

In some areas, it is common practice to use *pseudo-code* and therewith to introduce a fourth language family member. The role of pseudo-code is to represent, for example, financial algorithms in a more technical fashion that is both still close to the mathematical representation and already quite close to the technical implementation. In addition to the algorithm itself, pseudo-code takes into account how computers work in principle.

This practice generally has its cause in the fact that with most (compiled) programming languages the technical implementation is quite "far away" from its formal, mathematical representation. The majority of programming languages make it necessary to include so many elements that are only technically required that it is hard to see the equivalence between the mathematics and the code.

Nowadays, Python is often used in a *pseudo-code way* since its syntax is almost analogous to the mathematics and since the technical "overhead" is kept to a minimum. This is accomplished by a number of high-level concepts embodied in the language that not only have their advantages but also come in general with risks and/or other costs. However, it is safe to say that with Python you can, whenever the need arises, follow the same strict implementation and coding practices that other languages might require from the outset. In that sense, Python can provide the best of both worlds: *high-level abstraction* and *rigorous implementation*.

Efficiency and Productivity Through Python

At a high level, benefits from using Python can be measured in three dimensions:

Efficiency
    How can Python help in getting results faster, in saving costs, and in saving time?

Productivity
    How can Python help in getting more done with the same resources (people, assets, etc.)?

Quality
    What does Python allow one to do that alternative technologies do not allow for?

A discussion of these aspects can by nature not be exhaustive. However, it can highlight some arguments as a starting point.

Shorter time-to-results

A field where the efficiency of Python becomes quite obvious is interactive data analytics. This is a field that benefits tremendously from such powerful tools as IPython, Jupyter Notebook, and packages like `pandas`.

Consider a finance student who is writing their master's thesis and is interested in S&P 500 index values. They want to analyze historical index levels for, say, a few years to see how the volatility of the index has fluctuated over time and hope to find evidence that volatility, in contrast to some typical model assumptions, fluctuates over time and is far from being constant. The results should also be visualized. The student mainly has to do the following:

- Retrieve index level data from the web
- Calculate the annualized rolling standard deviation of the log returns (volatility)
- Plot the index level data and the volatility results

These tasks are complex enough that not too long ago one would have considered them to be something for professional financial analysts only. Today, even the finance student can easily cope with such problems. The following code shows how exactly this works—without worrying about syntax details at this stage (everything is explained in detail in subsequent chapters):

```
In [16]: import numpy as np     ❶
         import pandas as pd     ❶
         from pylab import plt, mpl     ❷

In [17]: plt.style.use('seaborn')     ❷
         mpl.rcParams['font.family'] = 'serif'     ❷
         %matplotlib inline

In [18]: data = pd.read_csv('../../source/tr_eikon_eod_data.csv',
                            index_col=0, parse_dates=True)     ❸
         data = pd.DataFrame(data['.SPX'])     ❹
         data.dropna(inplace=True)     ❹
         data.info()     ❺
         <class 'pandas.core.frame.DataFrame'>
         DatetimeIndex: 2138 entries, 2010-01-04 to 2018-06-29
         Data columns (total 1 columns):
         .SPX     2138 non-null float64
         dtypes: float64(1)
         memory usage: 33.4 KB

In [19]: data['rets'] = np.log(data / data.shift(1))     ❻
         data['vola'] = data['rets'].rolling(252).std() * np.sqrt(252)     ❼
```

```
In [20]: data[['.SPX', 'vola']].plot(subplots=True, figsize=(10, 6));   ❽
```

❶ This imports NumPy and pandas.

❷ This imports matplotlib and configures the plotting style and approach for Jupyter.

❸ pd.read_csv() allows the retrieval of remotely or locally stored data sets in comma-separated values (CSV) form.

❹ A subset of the data is picked and NaN ("not a number") values eliminated.

❺ This shows some metainformation about the data set.

❻ The log returns are calculated in vectorized fashion ("no looping" on the Python level).

❼ The rolling, annualized volatility is derived.

❽ This finally plots the two time series.

Figure 1-1 shows the graphical result of this brief interactive session. It can be considered almost amazing that a few lines of code suffice to implement three rather complex tasks typically encountered in financial analytics: data gathering, complex and repeated mathematical calculations, as well as visualization of the results. The example illustrates that pandas makes working with whole time series almost as simple as doing mathematical operations on floating-point numbers.

Translated to a professional finance context, the example implies that financial analysts can—when applying the right Python tools and packages that provide high-level abstractions—focus on their domain and not on the technical intrinsicalities. Analysts can also react faster, providing valuable insights almost in real time and making sure they are one step ahead of the competition. This example of *increased efficiency* can easily translate into measurable bottom-line effects.

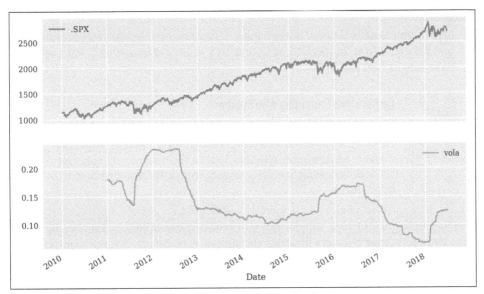

Figure 1-1. S&P 500 closing values and annualized volatility

Ensuring high performance

In general, it is accepted that Python has a rather concise syntax and that it is relatively efficient to code with. However, due to the very nature of Python being an interpreted language, the prejudice persists that Python often is too slow for compute-intensive tasks in finance. Indeed, depending on the specific implementation approach, Python can be really slow. But it *does not have to be slow*—it can be highly performing in almost any application area. In principle, one can distinguish at least three different strategies for better performance:

Idioms and paradigms
> In general, many different ways can lead to the same result in Python, but sometimes with rather different performance characteristics; "simply" choosing the right way (e.g., a specific implementation approach, such as the judicious use of data structures, avoiding loops through vectorization, or the use of a specific package such as pandas) can improve results significantly.

Compiling
> Nowadays, there are several performance packages available that provide compiled versions of important functions or that compile Python code statically or dynamically (at runtime or call time) to machine code, which can make such functions orders of magnitude faster than pure Python code; popular ones are Cython and Numba.

Parallelization

Many computational tasks, in particular in finance, can significantly benefit from parallel execution; this is nothing special to Python but something that can easily be accomplished with it.

Performance Computing with Python

Python per se is not a high-performance computing technology. However, Python has developed into an ideal platform to access current performance technologies. In that sense, Python has become something like a *glue language* for performance computing technologies.

This subsection sticks to a simple, but still realistic, example that touches upon all three strategies (later chapters illustrate the strategies in detail). A quite common task in financial analytics is to evaluate complex mathematical expressions on large arrays of numbers. To this end, Python itself provides everything needed:

```
In [21]: import math
         loops = 2500000
         a = range(1, loops)
         def f(x):
             return 3 * math.log(x) + math.cos(x) ** 2
         %timeit r = [f(x) for x in a]
         1.59 s ± 41.2 ms per loop (mean ± std. dev. of 7 runs, 1 loop each)
```

The Python interpreter needs about 1.6 seconds in this case to evaluate the function f() 2,500,000 times. The same task can be implemented using NumPy, which provides optimized (i.e., *precompiled*) functions to handle such array-based operations:

```
In [22]: import numpy as np
         a = np.arange(1, loops)
         %timeit r = 3 * np.log(a) + np.cos(a) ** 2
         87.9 ms ± 1.73 ms per loop (mean ± std. dev. of 7 runs, 10 loops each)
```

Using NumPy considerably reduces the execution time to about 88 milliseconds. However, there is even a package specifically dedicated to this kind of task. It is called numexpr, for "numerical expressions." It *compiles* the expression to improve upon the performance of the general NumPy functionality by, for example, avoiding in-memory copies of ndarray objects along the way:

```
In [23]: import numexpr as ne
         ne.set_num_threads(1)
         f = '3 * log(a) + cos(a) ** 2'
         %timeit r = ne.evaluate(f)
         50.6 ms ± 4.2 ms per loop (mean ± std. dev. of 7 runs, 10 loops each)
```

Using this more specialized approach further reduces execution time to about 50 milliseconds. However, numexpr also has built-in capabilities to parallelize the execution of the respective operation. This allows us to use multiple threads of a CPU:

```
In [24]: ne.set_num_threads(4)
         %timeit r = ne.evaluate(f)
         22.8 ms ± 1.76 ms per loop (mean ± std. dev. of 7 runs, 10 loops each)
```

Parallelization brings execution time further down to below 23 milliseconds in this case, with four threads utilized. Overall, this is a performance improvement of more than 90 times. Note, in particular, that this kind of improvement is possible without altering the basic problem/algorithm and without knowing any detail about compiling or parallelization approaches. The capabilities are accessible from a high level even by non-experts. However, one has to be aware, of course, of which capabilities and options exist.

This example shows that Python provides a number of options to make more out of existing resources—i.e., to *increase productivity*. With the parallel approach, three times as many calculations can be accomplished in the same amount of time as compared to the sequential approach—in this case simply by telling Python to use multiple available CPU threads instead of just one.

From Prototyping to Production

Efficiency in interactive analytics and performance when it comes to execution speed are certainly two benefits of Python to consider. Yet another major benefit of using Python for finance might at first sight seem a bit subtler; at second sight, it might present itself as an important strategic factor for financial institutions. It is the possibility to use Python end-to-end, from *prototyping to production*.

Today's practice in financial institutions around the globe, when it comes to financial development processes, is still often characterized by a separated, two-step process. On the one hand, there are the *quantitative analysts* ("quants") responsible for model development and technical prototyping. They like to use tools and environments like Matlab (*http://mathworks.com*) and R (*https://www.r-project.org*) that allow for rapid, interactive application development. At this stage of the development efforts, issues like performance, stability, deployment, access management, and version control, among others, are not that important. One is mainly looking for a proof of concept and/or a prototype that exhibits the main desired features of an algorithm or a whole application.

Once the prototype is finished, IT departments with their *developers* take over and are responsible for translating the existing *prototype code* into reliable, maintainable, and performant *production code*. Typically, at this stage there is a paradigm shift in that compiled languages, such as C++ or Java, are used to fulfill the requirements for deployment and production. Also, a formal development process with professional tools, version control, etc., is generally applied.

This two-step approach has a number of generally unintended consequences:

Inefficiencies
Prototype code is not reusable; algorithms have to be implemented twice; redundant efforts take time and resources; risks arise during translation

Diverse skill sets
Different departments show different skill sets and use different languages to implement "the same things"; people not only program but also speak different languages

Legacy code
Code is available and has to be maintained in different languages, often using different styles of implementation

Using Python, on the other hand, enables a *streamlined* end-to-end process from the first interactive prototyping steps to highly reliable and efficiently maintainable production code. The communication between different departments becomes easier. The training of the workforce is also more streamlined in that there is only one major language covering all areas of financial application building. It also avoids the inherent inefficiencies and redundancies when using different technologies in different steps of the development process. All in all, Python can provide a *consistent technological framework* for almost all tasks in financial analytics, financial application development, and algorithm implementation.

Data-Driven and AI-First Finance

Basically all the observations regarding the relationship of technology and the financial industry first formulated in 2014 for the first edition of this book still seem pretty current and important in August 2018, at the time of updating this chapter for the second edition of the book. However, this section comments on two major trends in the financial industry that are about to reshape it in a fundamental way. These two trends have mainly crystallized themselves over the last few years.

Data-Driven Finance

Some of the most important financial theories, such as MPT and CAPM, date as far back as to the 1950s and 1960s. However, they still represent a cornerstone in the education of students in such fields as economics, finance, financial engineering, and business administration. This might be surprising since the empirical support for most of these theories is meager at best, and the evidence is often in complete contrast to what the theories suggest and imply. On the other hand, their popularity is understandable since they are close to humans' expectations of how financial markets might behave and since they are elegant mathematical theories resting on a number of appealing, if in general too simplistic, assumptions.

The *scientific method*, say in physics, starts with *data*, for example from experiments or observations, and moves on to *hypotheses and theories* that are then *tested* against the data. If the tests are positive, the hypotheses and theories might be refined and properly written down, for instance, in the form of a research paper for publication. If the tests are negative, the hypotheses and theories are rejected and the search begins anew for ones that conform with the data. Since physical laws are stable over time, once such a law is discovered and well tested it is generally there to stay, in the best case, forever.

The history of (quantitative) finance in large parts contradicts the scientific method. In many cases, theories and models have been developed "from scratch" on the basis of simplifying mathematical assumptions with the goal of discovering elegant answers to central problems in finance. Among others, popular assumptions in finance are normally distributed returns for financial instruments and linear relationships between quantities of interest. Since these phenomena are hardly ever found in financial markets, it should not come as a surprise that empirical evidence for the elegant theories is often lacking. Many financial theories and models have been formulated, proven, and published first and have only later been tested empirically. To some extent, this is of course due to the fact that financial data back in the 1950s to the 1970s or even later was not available in the form that it is today even to students getting started with a bachelor's in finance.

The availability of such data to financial institutions has drastically increased since the early to mid-1990s, and nowadays even individuals doing financial research or getting involved in algorithmic trading have access to huge amounts of historical data down to the tick level as well as real-time tick data via streaming services. This allows us to return to the scientific method, which starts in general with the data before ideas, hypotheses, models, and strategies are devised.

A brief example shall illustrate how straightforward it has become today to retrieve professional data on a large scale even on a local machine, making use of Python and a professional data subscription to the Eikon Data APIs (*http://bit.ly/eikon_data_api*). The following example retrieves tick data for the Apple Inc. stock for one hour during a regular trading day. About 15,000 tick quotes, including volume information, are retrieved. While the symbol for the stock is AAPL, the Reuters Instrument Code (RIC) is AAPL.O:

```
In [26]: import eikon as ek    ❶

In [27]: data = ek.get_timeseries('AAPL.O', fields='*',
                                  start_date='2018-10-18 16:00:00',
                                  end_date='2018-10-18 17:00:00',
```

```
                                        interval='tick')  ❷

In [28]: data.info()  ❷
         <class 'pandas.core.frame.DataFrame'>
         DatetimeIndex: 35350 entries, 2018-10-18 16:00:00.002000 to 2018-10-18
          16:59:59.888000
         Data columns (total 2 columns):
         VALUE     35285 non-null float64
         VOLUME    35350 non-null float64
         dtypes: float64(2)
         memory usage: 828.5 KB

In [29]: data.tail()  ❸
Out[29]: AAPL.O                         VALUE  VOLUME
         Date
         2018-10-18 16:59:59.433  217.13    10.0
         2018-10-18 16:59:59.433  217.13    12.0
         2018-10-18 16:59:59.439  217.13   231.0
         2018-10-18 16:59:59.754  217.14   100.0
         2018-10-18 16:59:59.888  217.13   100.0
```

❶ Eikon Data API usage requires a subscription and an API connection.

❷ Retrieves the tick data for the Apple Inc. (AAPL.O) stock.

❸ Shows the last five rows of tick data.

The Eikon Data APIs give access not only to structured financial data, such as historical price data, but also to unstructured data such as *news articles*. The next example retrieves metadata for a small selection of news articles and shows the beginning of one of the articles as full text:

```
In [30]: news = ek.get_news_headlines('R:AAPL.O Language:LEN',
                                       date_from='2018-05-01',
                                       date_to='2018-06-29',
                                       count=7)  ❶

In [31]: news  ❶
Out[31]:
                                              versionCreated  \
         2018-06-28 23:00:00.000 2018-06-28 23:00:00.000
         2018-06-28 21:23:26.526 2018-06-28 21:23:26.526
         2018-06-28 19:48:32.627 2018-06-28 19:48:32.627
         2018-06-28 17:33:10.306 2018-06-28 17:33:10.306
         2018-06-28 17:33:07.033 2018-06-28 17:33:07.033
         2018-06-28 17:31:44.960 2018-06-28 17:31:44.960
         2018-06-28 17:00:00.000 2018-06-28 17:00:00.000


                                                        text  \
         2018-06-28 23:00:00.000  RPT-FOCUS-AI ambulances and robot doctors: Chi...
         2018-06-28 21:23:26.526  Why Investors Should Love Apple's (AAPL) TV En...
```

```
2018-06-28 19:48:32.627    Reuters Insider - Trump: We're reclaiming our ...
2018-06-28 17:33:10.306    Apple v. Samsung ends not with a whimper but a...
2018-06-28 17:33:07.033    Apple's trade-war discount extended for anothe...
2018-06-28 17:31:44.960    Other Products: Apple's fast-growing island of...
2018-06-28 17:00:00.000    Pokemon Go creator plans to sell the tech behi...

                                                           storyId  \
2018-06-28 23:00:00.000    urn:newsml:reuters.com:20180628:nL4N1TU4F8:6
2018-06-28 21:23:26.526    urn:newsml:reuters.com:20180628:nNRA6e2vft:1
2018-06-28 19:48:32.627    urn:newsml:reuters.com:20180628:nRTV1vNw1p:1
2018-06-28 17:33:10.306    urn:newsml:reuters.com:20180628:nNRA6e1oza:1
2018-06-28 17:33:07.033    urn:newsml:reuters.com:20180628:nNRA6e1pmv:1
2018-06-28 17:31:44.960    urn:newsml:reuters.com:20180628:nNRA6e1m3n:1
2018-06-28 17:00:00.000    urn:newsml:reuters.com:20180628:nL1N1TU0PC:3


                              sourceCode
2018-06-28 23:00:00.000         NS:RTRS
2018-06-28 21:23:26.526       NS:ZACKSC
2018-06-28 19:48:32.627         NS:CNBC
2018-06-28 17:33:10.306       NS:WALLST
2018-06-28 17:33:07.033       NS:WALLST
2018-06-28 17:31:44.960       NS:WALLST
2018-06-28 17:00:00.000         NS:RTRS
```

In [32]: story_html = ek.get_news_story(news.iloc[1, 2]) ❷

In [33]: from bs4 import BeautifulSoup ❸

In [34]: story = BeautifulSoup(story_html, 'html5lib').get_text() ❹

In [35]: print(story[83:958]) ❺
         Jun 28, 2018 For years, investors and Apple AAPL have been beholden to
         the iPhone, which is hardly a negative since its flagship product is
         largely responsible for turning Apple into one of the world's biggest
         companies. But Apple has slowly pushed into new growth areas, with
         streaming television its newest frontier. So let's take a look at what
         Apple has planned as it readies itself to compete against the likes of
         Netflix NFLX and Amazon AMZN in the battle for the new age of
         entertainment.Apple's second-quarter revenues jumped by 16% to reach
         $61.14 billion, with iPhone revenues up 14%. However, iPhone unit sales
         climbed only 3% and iPhone revenues accounted for over 62% of total Q2
         sales. Apple knows this is not a sustainable business model, because
         rare is the consumer product that can remain in vogue for decades. This
         is why Apple has made a big push into news,

❶ Retrieves metadata for a small selection of news articles.

❷ Retrieves the full text of a single article, delivered as an HTML document.

❸ Imports the BeautifulSoup HTML parsing package and ...

❹   … extracts the contents as plain text (a `str` object).

❺   Prints the beginning of the news article.

Although just scratching the surface, these two examples illustrate that structured and unstructured historical financial data is available in a standardized, efficient way via Python wrapper packages and data subscription services. In many circumstances, similar data sets can be accessed for free even by individuals who make use of, for instance, trading platforms such as the one by FXCM Group, LLC, that is introduced in Chapter 14 and also used in Chapter 16. Once the data is on the Python level—independent from the original source—the full power of the Python data analytics ecosystem can be harnessed.

Data-Driven Finance

Data is what drives finance these days. Even some of the largest and often most successful hedge funds call themselves "data-driven" instead of "finance-driven." More and more offerings are making huge amounts of data available to large and small institutions and individuals. Python is generally the programming language of choice to interact with the APIs and to process and analyze the data.

AI-First Finance

With the availability of large amounts of financial data via programmatic APIs, it has become much easier and more fruitful to apply methods from *artificial intelligence* (AI) in general and from *machine and deep learning* (ML, DL) in particular to financial problems, such as in algorithmic trading.

Python can be considered a first-class citizen in the AI world as well. It is often the programming language of choice for AI researchers and practitioners alike. In that sense, the financial domain benefits from developments in diverse fields, sometimes not even remotely connected to finance. As one example consider the `TensorFlow` open source package (*http://tensorflow.org*) for deep learning, which is developed and maintained by Google Inc. and used by (among others) its parent company Alphabet Inc. in its efforts to build, produce, and sell self-driving cars.

Although for sure not even remotely related to the problem of automatically, algorithmically trading stock, `TensorFlow` can, for example, be used to predict movements in financial markets. Chapter 15 provides a number of examples in this regard.

One of the most widely used Python packages for ML is `scikit-learn`. The code that follows shows how, in a highly simplified manner, classification algorithms from ML can be used to predict the direction of future market price movements and to base an algorithmic trading strategy on those predictions. All the details are explained in Chapter 15, so the example is therefore rather concise. First, the data import and the preparation of the features data (directional lagged log return data):

```
In [36]: import numpy as np
         import pandas as pd

In [37]: data = pd.read_csv('../../source/tr_eikon_eod_data.csv',
                            index_col=0, parse_dates=True)
         data = pd.DataFrame(data['AAPL.O'])   ❶
         data['Returns'] = np.log(data / data.shift())   ❷
         data.dropna(inplace=True)

In [38]: lags = 6

In [39]: cols = []
         for lag in range(1, lags + 1):
             col = 'lag_{}'.format(lag)
             data[col] = np.sign(data['Returns'].shift(lag))   ❸
             cols.append(col)
         data.dropna(inplace=True)
```

❶ Selects historical end-of-day data for the Apple Inc. stock (AAPL.O).

❷ Calculates the log returns over the complete history.

❸ Generates DataFrame columns with directional lagged log return data (+1 or -1).

Next, the instantiation of a model object for a *support vector machine* (SVM) algorithm, the fitting of the model, and the prediction step. Figure 1-2 shows that the prediction-based trading strategy, going long or short on Apple Inc. stock depending on the prediction, outperforms the passive benchmark investment in the stock itself:

```
In [40]: from sklearn.svm import SVC

In [41]: model = SVC(gamma='auto')   ❶

In [42]: model.fit(data[cols], np.sign(data['Returns']))   ❷
Out[42]: SVC(C=1.0, cache_size=200, class_weight=None, coef0=0.0,
             decision_function_shape='ovr', degree=3, gamma='auto', kernel='rbf',
             max_iter=-1, probability=False, random_state=None, shrinking=True,
             tol=0.001, verbose=False)

In [43]: data['Prediction'] = model.predict(data[cols])   ❸

In [44]: data['Strategy'] = data['Prediction'] * data['Returns']   ❹

In [45]: data[['Returns', 'Strategy']].cumsum().apply(np.exp).plot(
             figsize=(10, 6));   ❺
```

❶ Instantiates the model object.

❷ Fits the model, given the features and the label data (all directional).

❸ Uses the fitted model to create the predictions (in-sample), which are the positions of the trading strategy at the same time (long or short).

❹ Calculates the log returns of the trading strategy given the prediction values and the benchmark log returns.

❺ Plots the performance of the ML-based trading strategy compared to the performance of the passive benchmark investment.

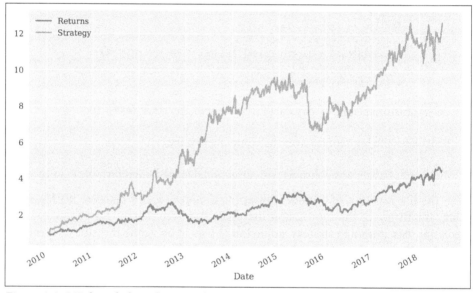

Figure 1-2. ML-based algorithmic trading strategy vs. passive benchmark investment in Apple Inc. stock

The simplified approach taken here does not account for transaction costs, nor does it separate the data set into training and testing subsets. However, it shows how straightforward the application of ML algorithms to financial data is, at least in a technical sense; practically, a number of important topics need to be considered (see López de Prado (2018)).

AI-First Finance

AI will reshape finance in a way that other fields have been reshaped already. The availability of large amounts of financial data via programmatic APIs functions as an enabler in this context. Basic methods from AI, ML, and DL are introduced in Chapter 13 and applied to algorithmic trading in Chapters 15 and 16. A proper treatment of *AI-first finance*, however, would require a book fully dedicated to the topic.

AI in finance, as a natural extension of data-driven finance, is for sure a fascinating and exciting field, both from a research and a practitioner's point of view. Although this book uses several methods from AI, ML, and DL in different contexts, overall the focus lies—in line with the subtitle of the book—on the fundamental Python techniques and approaches needed for *data-driven finance*. These are, however, equally important for AI-first finance.

Conclusion

Python as a language—and even more so as an ecosystem—is an ideal technological framework for the financial industry as whole and the individual working in finance alike. It is characterized by a number of benefits, like an elegant syntax, efficient development approaches, and usability for prototyping as well as production. With its huge amount of available packages, libraries, and tools, Python seems to have answers to most questions raised by recent developments in the financial industry in terms of analytics, data volumes and frequency, compliance and regulation, as well as technology itself. It has the potential to provide a single, powerful, consistent framework with which to streamline end-to-end development and production efforts even across larger financial institutions.

In addition, Python has become the programming language of choice for artificial intelligence in general and machine and deep learning in particular. Python is therefore the right language for data-driven finance as well as for AI-first finance, two recent trends that are about to reshape finance and the financial industry in fundamental ways.

Further Resources

The following books cover several aspects only touched upon in this chapter in more detail (e.g., Python tools, derivatives analytics, machine learning in general, and machine learning in finance):

- Hilpisch, Yves (2015). *Derivatives Analytics with Python* (*http://dawp.tpq.io*). Chichester, England: Wiley Finance.

- López de Prado, Marcos (2018). *Advances in Financial Machine Learning.* Hoboken, NJ: John Wiley & Sons.
- VanderPlas, Jake (2016). *Python Data Science Handbook.* Sebastopol, CA: O'Reilly.

When it comes to algorithmic trading, the author's company offers a range of online training programs that focus on Python and other tools and techniques required in this rapidly growing field:

- *http://pyalgo.tpq.io*
- *http://certificate.tpq.io*

Sources referenced in this chapter are, among others, the following:

- Ding, Cubillas (2010). "Optimizing the OTC Pricing and Valuation Infrastructure." Celent.
- Lewis, Michael (2014). *Flash Boys.* New York: W. W. Norton & Company.
- Patterson, Scott (2010). *The Quants.* New York: Crown Business.

## CHAPTER 2

Python Infrastructure

> In building a house, there is the problem of the selection of wood.
>
> It is essential that the carpenter's aim be to carry equipment that will cut well and, when he has time, to sharpen that equipment.
>
> —Miyamoto Musashi (*The Book of Five Rings*)

For someone new to Python, Python deployment might seem all but straightforward. The same holds true for the wealth of libraries and packages that can be installed optionally. First of all, there is not only *one* Python. Python comes in many different flavors, like CPython, Jython, IronPython, and PyPy. Then there is the divide between Python 2.7 and the 3.x world.[1]

Even after you've decided on a version, deployment is difficult for a number of additional reasons:

- The interpreter (a standard CPython installation) only comes with the so-called *standard library* (e.g., covering typical mathematical functions)
- Optional Python packages need to be installed separately—and there are hundreds of them
- Compiling/building such nonstandard packages on your own can be tricky due to dependencies and operating system–specific requirements
- Taking care of these dependencies and of version consistency over time (i.e., maintenance) is often tedious and time consuming

---

1 This edition is based on version 3.7 (the latest major release at the time of writing) of CPython, the original and most popular version of the Python programming language.

- Updates and upgrades for certain packages might necessitate recompiling a multitude of other packages
- Changing or replacing one package might cause trouble in (many) other places

Fortunately, there are tools and strategies available that can help. This chapter covers the following types of technologies that help with Python deployment:

Package managers
> Package managers like `pip` (*https://pypi.python.org/pypi/pip*) and `conda` (*http:// conda.pydata.org/docs/intro.html*) help with the installing, updating, and removing of Python packages; they also help with version consistency of different packages.

Virtual environment managers
> A virtual environment manager like `virtualenv` (*https://pypi.python.org/pypi/ virtualenv*) or `conda` allows you to manage multiple Python installations in parallel (e.g., to have both a Python 2.7 and 3.7 install on a single machine or to test the most recent development version of a fancy Python package without risk).[2]

Containers
> Docker (*http://docker.com*) containers represent complete filesystems containing all the pieces of a system needed to run certain software, like code, runtime, or system tools. For example, you can run an Ubuntu 18.04 operating system with a Python 3.7 install and the respective Python code in a Docker container hosted on a machine running macOS or Windows 10.

Cloud instances
> Deploying Python code for financial applications generally requires high availability, security, and also performance; these requirements can typically only be met by the use of professional compute and storage infrastructure that is nowadays available at attractive conditions in the form of fairly small to really large and powerful cloud instances. One benefit of a cloud instance (i.e., a virtual server) compared to a dedicated server rented longer-term is that users generally get charged only for the hours of actual usage; another advantage is that such cloud instances are available literally in a minute or two if needed, which helps with agile development and also with scalability.

The structure of this chapter is as follows:

"conda as a Package Manager" on page 35
> This section introduces `conda` as a package manager for Python.

---

2 A recent project called `pipenv` (*https://github.com/pypa/pipenv*) combines the capabilities of the package manager `pip` with those of the virtual environment manager `virtualenv`.

"conda as a Virtual Environment Manager" on page 41

This section focuses on conda's capabilities as a virtual environment manager.

"Using Docker Containers" on page 45

This section gives a brief overview of Docker as a containerization technology and focuses on the building of an Ubuntu-based container with a Python 3.7 installation.

"Using Cloud Instances" on page 50

The section shows how to deploy Python and Jupyter Notebook—a powerful, browser-based tool suite for Python development—in the cloud.

The goal of this chapter is to set up a proper Python installation with the most important tools as well as numerical, data analysis, and visualization packages on a professional infrastructure. This combination then serves as the backbone for implementing and deploying the Python code in later chapters, be it interactive financial analytics code or code in the form of scripts and modules.

conda as a Package Manager

Although conda can be installed standalone, an efficient way of doing it is via Miniconda, a minimal Python distribution including conda as a package and virtual environment manager.

Installing Miniconda

Miniconda is available for Windows, macOS, and Linux. You can download the different versions from the Miniconda webpage (*https://conda.io/miniconda.html*). In what follows, the Python 3.7 64-bit version is assumed. The main example in this section is a session in an Ubuntu-based Docker container which downloads the Linux 64-bit installer via wget and then installs Miniconda. The code as shown should work —perhaps with minor modifications—on any other Linux- or macOS-based machine as well:

```
$ docker run -ti -h py4fi -p 11111:11111 ubuntu:latest /bin/bash

root@py4fi:/# apt-get update; apt-get upgrade -y
...
root@py4fi:/# apt-get install -y bzip2 gcc wget
...
root@py4fi:/# cd root
root@py4fi:~# wget \
> https://repo.continuum.io/miniconda/Miniconda3-latest-Linux-x86_64.sh \
> -O miniconda.sh
...
HTTP request sent, awaiting response... 200 OK
Length: 62574861 (60M) [application/x-sh]
```

```
Saving to: 'miniconda.sh'

miniconda.sh          100%[====================>]  59.68M  5.97MB/s    in 11s

2018-09-15 09:44:28 (5.42 MB/s) - 'miniconda.sh' saved [62574861/62574861]

root@py4fi:~# bash miniconda.sh

Welcome to Miniconda3 4.5.11

In order to continue the installation process, please review the license
agreement.
Please, press ENTER to continue
>>>
```

Simply pressing the Enter key starts the installation process. After reviewing the
license agreement, approve the terms by answering yes:

```
...
Do you accept the license terms? [yes|no]
[no] >>> yes

Miniconda3 will now be installed into this location:
/root/miniconda3

  - Press ENTER to confirm the location
  - Press CTRL-C to abort the installation
  - Or specify a different location below

[/root/miniconda3] >>>
PREFIX=/root/miniconda3
installing: python-3.7. ...
...
installing: requests-2.19.1-py37_0 ...
installing: conda-4.5.11-py37_0 ...
installation finished.
```

After you have agreed to the licensing terms and have confirmed the install location
you should allow Miniconda to prepend the new Miniconda install location to the
PATH environment variable by answering yes once again:

```
Do you wish the installer to prepend the Miniconda3 install location
to PATH in your /root/.bashrc ? [yes|no]
[no] >>> yes

Appending source /root/miniconda3/bin/activate to /root/.bashrc
A backup will be made to: /root/.bashrc-miniconda3.bak


For this change to become active, you have to open a new terminal.

Thank you for installing Miniconda3!
root@py4fi:~#
```

After that, you might want to upgrade conda as well as Python:[3]

```
root@py4fi:~# export PATH="/root/miniconda3/bin/:$PATH"
root@py4fi:~# conda update -y conda python
...
root@py4fi:~# echo ". /root/miniconda3/etc/profile.d/conda.sh" >> ~/.bashrc
root@py4fi:~# bash
```

After this rather simple installation procedure, you'll have a basic Python install as well as conda available. The basic Python install comes with some nice batteries included, like the SQLite3 database engine (*https://sqlite.org*). You might try out whether you can start Python in a new shell instance after appending the relevant path to the respective environment variable (as done previously):

```
root@py4fi:~# python
Python 3.7.0 (default, Jun 28 2018, 13:15:42)
[GCC 7.2.0] :: Anaconda, Inc. on linux
Type "help", "copyright", "credits" or "license" for more information.
>>> print('Hello Python for Finance World.')
Hello Python for Finance World.
>>> exit()
root@py4fi:~#
```

Basic Operations with conda

conda can be used to efficiently handle, among other things, the installing, updating, and removing of Python packages. The following list provides an overview of the major functions:

Installing Python x.x
  `conda install python=x.x`

Updating Python
  `conda update python`

Installing a package
  `conda install $PACKAGE_NAME`

Updating a package
  `conda update $PACKAGE_NAME`

Removing a package
  `conda remove $PACKAGE_NAME`

Updating conda itself
  `conda update conda`

---

3 The Miniconda installer is in general not as regularly updated as conda and Python themselves.

Searching for packages
```
conda search $SEARCH_TERM
```

Listing installed packages
```
conda list
```

Given these capabilities, installing, for example, NumPy—one of the most important libraries of the so-called scientific stack—requires a single command only. When the installation takes place on a machine with an Intel processor, the procedure automatically installs the Intel Math Kernel Library (mkl) (*https://docs.continuum.io/mkl-optimizations/*), which speeds up numerical operations not only for NumPy but also for a few other scientific Python packages:[4]

```
root@py4fi:~# conda install numpy
Solving environment: done

## Package Plan ##

  environment location: /root/miniconda3

  added / updated specs:
    - numpy


The following packages will be downloaded:

    package                    |           build
    ---------------------------|-----------------
    mkl-2019.0                 |              117       204.4 MB
    intel-openmp-2019.0        |              117       721 KB
    mkl_random-1.0.1           |   py37h4414c95_1       372 KB
    libgfortran-ng-7.3.0       |       hdf63c60_0       1.3 MB
    numpy-1.15.1               |   py37h1d66e8a_0        37 KB
    numpy-base-1.15.1          |   py37h81de0dd_0       4.2 MB
    blas-1.0                   |              mkl         6 KB
    mkl_fft-1.0.4              |   py37h4414c95_1       149 KB
    ------------------------------------------------------------
                                           Total:       211.1 MB

The following NEW packages will be INSTALLED:

    blas:           1.0-mkl
    intel-openmp:   2019.0-117
    libgfortran-ng: 7.3.0-hdf63c60_0
    mkl:            2019.0-117
    mkl_fft:        1.0.4-py37h4414c95_1
```

---

4 Installing the metapackage nomkl, e.g. with `conda install numpy nomkl`, avoids the automatic installation and usage of mkl and related other packages.

```
    mkl_random:        1.0.1-py37h4414c95_1
    numpy:             1.15.1-py37h1d66e8a_0
    numpy-base:        1.15.1-py37h81de0dd_0

Proceed ([y]/n)? y


Downloading and Extracting Packages
mkl-2019.0            | 204.4 MB  | #################################### | 100%
...
numpy-1.15.1          | 37 KB     | #################################### | 100%
numpy-base-1.15.1     | 4.2 MB    | #################################### | 100%
...
root@py4fi:~#
```

Multiple packages can also be installed at once. The -y flag indicates that all (potential) questions shall be answered with yes:

```
root@py4fi:/# conda install -y ipython matplotlib pandas pytables scikit-learn \
> scipy
...
pytables-3.4.4        | 1.5 MB    | #################################### | 100%
kiwisolver-1.0.1      | 83 KB     | #################################### | 100%
icu-58.2              | 22.5 MB   | #################################### | 100%
Preparing transaction: done
Verifying transaction: done
Executing transaction: done
root@py4fi:~#
```

After the resulting installation procedure, some of the most important libraries for financial analytics are available in addition to the standard ones. These include:

IPython *(http://ipython.org)*
    An improved interactive Python shell

matplotlib *(http://matplotlib.org)*
    The standard plotting library in Python

NumPy *(http://numpy.org)*
    For efficient handling of numerical arrays

pandas *(http://pandas.pydata.org)*
    For management of tabular data, like financial time series data

PyTables *(http://pytables.org)*
    A Python wrapper for the HDF5 library *(http://hdfgroup.org)*

scikit-learn *(http://scikit-learn.org)*
    A package for machine learning and related tasks

SciPy *(http://scipy.org)*

A collection of scientific classes and functions (installed as a dependency)

This provides a basic tool set for data analysis in general and financial analytics in particular. The next example uses IPython and draws a set of pseudo-random numbers with NumPy:

```
root@py4fi:~# ipython
Python 3.7.0 (default, Jun 28 2018, 13:15:42)
Type 'copyright', 'credits' or 'license' for more information
IPython 6.5.0 -- An enhanced Interactive Python. Type '?' for help.

In [1]: import numpy as np

In [2]: np.random.seed(100)

In [3]: np.random.standard_normal((5, 4))
Out[3]:
array([[-1.74976547,  0.3426804 ,  1.1530358 , -0.25243604],
       [ 0.98132079,  0.51421884,  0.22117967, -1.07004333],
       [-0.18949583,  0.25500144, -0.45802699,  0.43516349],
       [-0.58359505,  0.81684707,  0.67272081, -0.10441114],
       [-0.53128038,  1.02973269, -0.43813562, -1.11831825]])

In [4]: exit
root@py4fi:~#
```

Executing `conda list` shows which packages are installed:

```
root@py4fi:~# conda list
# packages in environment at /root/miniconda3:
#
# Name                    Version                   Build  Channel
asn1crypto                0.24.0                   py37_0
backcall                  0.1.0                    py37_0
blas                      1.0                         mkl
blosc                     1.14.4               hdbcaa40_0
bzip2                     1.0.6                h14c3975_5
...
python                    3.7.0                hc3d631a_0
...
wheel                     0.31.1                   py37_0
xz                        5.2.4                h14c3975_4
yaml                      0.1.7                had09818_2
zlib                      1.2.11               ha838bed_2
root@py4fi:~#
```

If a package is not needed anymore, it is efficiently removed with `conda remove`:

```
root@py4fi:~# conda remove scikit-learn
Solving environment: done

## Package Plan ##
```

```
environment location: /root/miniconda3

removed specs:
  - scikit-learn


The following packages will be REMOVED:

  scikit-learn: 0.19.1-py37hedc7406_0

Proceed ([y]/n)? y

Preparing transaction: done
Verifying transaction: done
Executing transaction: done
root@py4fi:~#
```

conda as a package manager is already quite useful. However, its full power only becomes evident when adding virtual environment management to the mix.

Easy Package Management

Using conda as a package manager makes installing, updating, and removing Python packages a pleasant experience. There is no need to take care of building and compiling packages on your own—which can be tricky sometimes, given the list of dependencies a package specifies and the specifics to be considered on different operating systems.

conda as a Virtual Environment Manager

Depending on the version of the installer you choose, Miniconda provides a default Python 2.7 or 3.7 installation. The virtual environment management capabilities of conda allow one, for example, to add to a Python 3.7 default installation a completely separate installation of Python 2.7.x. To this end, conda offers the following functionality:

Creating a virtual environment
    conda create --name $ENVIRONMENT_NAME

Activating an environment
    conda activate $ENVIRONMENT_NAME

Deactivating an environment
    conda deactivate $ENVIRONMENT_NAME

Removing an environment

```
conda env remove --name $ENVIRONMENT_NAME
```

Exporting to an environment file

```
conda env export > $FILE_NAME
```

Creating an environment from a file

```
conda env create -f $FILE_NAME
```

Listing all environments

```
conda info --envs
```

As a simple illustration, the example code that follows creates an environment called
py27, installs IPython, and executes a line of Python 2.7.x code:

```
root@py4fi:~# conda create --name py27 python=2.7
Solving environment: done

## Package Plan ##

  environment location: /root/miniconda3/envs/py27

  added / updated specs:
    - python=2.7


The following NEW packages will be INSTALLED:

    ca-certificates: 2018.03.07-0
...
    python:          2.7.15-h1571d57_0
...
    zlib:            1.2.11-ha838bed_2

Proceed ([y]/n)? y

Preparing transaction: done
Verifying transaction: done
Executing transaction: done
#
# To activate this environment, use:
# > conda activate py27
#
# To deactivate an active environment, use:
# > conda deactivate
#

root@py4fi:~#
```

Notice how the prompt changes to include (py27) after the activation of the
environment:

```
root@py4fi:~# conda activate py27
(py27) root@py4fi:~# conda install ipython
Solving environment: done
...
Executing transaction: done
(py27) root@py4fi:~#
```

Finally, this allows you to use IPython with Python 2.7 syntax:

```
(py27) root@py4fi:~# ipython
Python 2.7.15 |Anaconda, Inc.| (default, May  1 2018, 23:32:55)
Type "copyright", "credits" or "license" for more information.

IPython 5.8.0 -- An enhanced Interactive Python.
?          -> Introduction and overview of IPython's features.
%quickref -> Quick reference.
help       -> Python's own help system.
object?    -> Details about 'object', use 'object??' for extra details.

In [1]: print "Hello Python for Finance World!"
Hello Python for Finance World!

In [2]: exit
(py27) root@py4fi:~#
```

As this example demonstrates, using conda as a virtual environment manager allows you to install different Python versions alongside each other. It also allows you to install different versions of certain packages. The default Python install is not influenced by such a procedure, nor are other environments which might exist on the same machine. All available environments can be shown via conda env list:

```
(py27) root@py4fi:~# conda env list
# conda environments:
#
base                     /root/miniconda3
py27                  *  /root/miniconda3/envs/py27

(py27) root@py4fi:~#
```

Sometimes it is necessary to share environment information with others or to use environment information on multiple machines. To this end, one can export the installed packages list to a file with conda env export. This only works properly by default if the machines use the same operating system, since the build versions are specified in the resulting YAML file, but they can be deleted to only specify the package version:

```
(py27) root@py4fi:~# conda env export --no-builds > py27env.yml
(py27) root@py4fi:~# cat py27env.yml
name: py27
channels:
  - defaults
dependencies:
```

```
    - backports=1.0
...
    - python=2.7.15
...
    - zlib=1.2.11
prefix: /root/miniconda3/envs/py27
```

```
(py27) root@py4fi:~#
```

Often a virtual environment, which is technically not that much more than a certain (sub)folder structure, is created to do some quick tests.[5] In such a case, the environment is easily removed after deactivation via conda env remove:

```
(py27) root@py4fi:/# conda deactivate
root@py4fi:~# conda env remove -y --name py27

Remove all packages in environment /root/miniconda3/envs/py27:


## Package Plan ##

  environment location: /root/miniconda3/envs/py27


The following packages will be REMOVED:

    backports:                          1.0-py27_1
...
    zlib:                               1.2.11-ha838bed_2

root@py4fi:~#
```

This concludes the overview of conda as a virtual environment manager.

Easy Environment Management

conda does not only help with managing packages; it is also a virtual environment manager for Python. It simplifies the creation of different Python environments, allowing you to have multiple versions of Python and optional packages available on the same machine without them influencing each other in any way. conda also allows you to export environment information so you can easily replicate it on multiple machines or share it with others.

---

5 In the official documentation (*https://packaging.python.org/installing/#creating-virtual-environments*) you find the following explanation: "Python 'Virtual Environments' allow Python packages to be installed in an isolated location for a particular application, rather than being installed globally."

Using Docker Containers

Docker containers (*http://docker.com*) have taken the IT world by storm. Although the technology is still relatively young, it has established itself as one of the benchmarks for the efficient development and deployment of almost any kind of software application.

For the purposes of this book it suffices to think of a Docker container as a separate ("containerized") filesystem that includes an operating system (e.g., Ubuntu Server 18.04), a (Python) runtime, additional system and development tools, as well as further (Python) libraries and packages as needed. Such a Docker container might run on a local machine with Windows 10 or on a cloud instance with a Linux operating system, for instance.

This section does not go into all the exciting details of Docker containers. It is rather a concise illustration of what the Docker technology can do in the context of Python deployment.[6]

Docker Images and Containers

However, before moving on to the illustration, two fundamental concepts need to be distinguished when talking about Docker. The first is a *Docker image*, which can be compared to a Python class. The second is a *Docker container*, which can be compared to an instance of the respective Python class.[7]

On a more technical level, you find the following definition for an *image* in the Docker glossary (*https://docs.docker.com/engine/reference/glossary/*):

> Docker images are the basis of containers. An Image is an ordered collection of root filesystem changes and the corresponding execution parameters for use within a container runtime. An image typically contains a union of layered filesystems stacked on top of each other. An image does not have state and it never changes.

Similarly, you find the following definition for a *container* in the Docker glossary, which makes the analogy to Python classes and instances of such classes transparent:

> A container is a runtime instance of a Docker image. A Docker container consists of: a Docker image, an execution environment, and a standard set of instructions.

Depending on the operating system, the installation of Docker is somewhat different. That is why this section does not go into the details. More information and further links are found on the About Docker CE page (*https://docs.docker.com/install/*).

---

6 See Matthias and Kane (2015) for a comprehensive introduction to the Docker technology.

7 If the terms are not yet clear, they will become so in Chapter 6.

Building an Ubuntu and Python Docker Image

This section illustrates the building of a Docker image based on the latest version of Ubuntu, which includes Miniconda as well as a few important Python packages. In addition, it does some Linux housekeeping by updating the Linux packages index, upgrading packages if required, and installing certain additional system tools. To this end, two scripts are needed. One is a bash script that does all the work on the Linux level.[8] The other is a so-called *Dockerfile*, which controls the building procedure for the image itself.

The bash script in Example 2-1 that does the installing consists of three major parts. The first part handles the Linux housekeeping. The second part installs Miniconda, while the third part installs optional Python packages. There are also more detailed comments inline.

Example 2-1. Script installing Python and optional packages

```
#!/bin/bash
#
# Script to Install
# Linux System Tools and
# Basic Python Components
#
# Python for Finance, 2nd ed.
# (c) Dr. Yves J. Hilpisch
#
# GENERAL LINUX
apt-get update  # updates the package index cache
apt-get upgrade -y  # updates packages
# installs system tools
apt-get install -y bzip2 gcc git htop screen vim wget
apt-get upgrade -y bash  # upgrades bash if necessary
apt-get clean  # cleans up the package index cache

# INSTALL MINICONDA
# downloads Miniconda
wget https://repo.continuum.io/miniconda/Miniconda3-latest-Linux-x86_64.sh -O \
  Miniconda.sh
bash Miniconda.sh -b  # installs it
rm -rf Miniconda.sh  # removes the installer
export PATH="/root/miniconda3/bin:$PATH"  # prepends the new path

# INSTALL PYTHON LIBRARIES
conda update -y conda python # updates conda & Python (if required)
```

---

8 Consult Robbins (2016) for a concise introduction to and quick overview of bash scripting. Also see *https:// www.gnu.org/software/bash*.

```
conda install -y pandas  # installs pandas
conda install -y ipython  # installs IPython shell
```

The *Dockerfile* in Example 2-2 uses the bash script in Example 2-1 to build a new Docker image. It also has its major parts commented inline.

Example 2-2. Dockerfile to build the image

```
#
# Building a Docker Image with
# the Latest Ubuntu Version and
# Basic Python Install
#
# Python for Finance, 2nd ed.
# (c) Dr. Yves J. Hilpisch
#

# latest Ubuntu version
FROM ubuntu:latest

# information about maintainer
MAINTAINER yves

# add the bash script
ADD install.sh /

# change rights for the script
RUN chmod u+x /install.sh

# run the bash script
RUN /install.sh

# prepend the new path
ENV PATH /root/miniconda3/bin:$PATH

# execute IPython when container is run
CMD ["ipython"]
```

If these two files are in a single folder and Docker is installed, then the building of the new Docker image is straightforward. Here, the tag `py4fi:basic` is used for the image. This tag is needed to reference the image, for example when running a container based on it:

```
~/Docker$ docker build -t py4fi:basic .

...

Removing intermediate container 5fec0c9b2239
  ---> accee128d9e9
Step 6/7 : ENV PATH /root/miniconda3/bin:$PATH
  ---> Running in a2bb97686255
```

```
Removing intermediate container a2bb97686255
 ---> 73b00c215351
Step 7/7 : CMD ["ipython"]
 ---> Running in ec7acd90c991
Removing intermediate container ec7acd90c991
 ---> 6c36b9117cd2
Successfully built 6c36b9117cd2
Successfully tagged py4fi:basic
~/Docker$
```

Existing Docker images can be listed via docker images. The new image should be at the top of the list:

```
(py4fi) ~/Docker$ docker images
REPOSITORY      TAG         IMAGE ID        CREATED             SIZE
py4fi           basic       6c36b9117cd2    About a minute ago  1.79GB
ubuntu          latest      cd6d8154f1e1    9 days ago          84.1MB
(py4fi) ~/Docker$
```

Successfully building the py4fi:basic allows you to run the respective Docker container with docker run. The parameter combination -ti is needed for interactive processes running within a Docker container, like a shell process (see the docker run reference page (*https://docs.docker.com/engine/reference/run/*)):

```
~/Docker$ docker run -ti py4fi:basic
Python 3.7.0 (default, Jun 28 2018, 13:15:42)
Type 'copyright', 'credits' or 'license' for more information
IPython 6.5.0 -- An enhanced Interactive Python. Type '?' for help.

In [1]: import numpy as np

In [2]: a = np.random.standard_normal((5, 3))

In [3]: import pandas as pd

In [4]: df = pd.DataFrame(a, columns=['a', 'b', 'c'])

In [5]: df
Out[5]:
          a         b         c
0 -1.412661 -0.881592  1.704623
1 -1.294977  0.546676  1.027046
2  1.156361  1.979057  0.989772
3  0.546736 -0.479821  0.693907
4 -1.972943 -0.193964  0.769500

In [6]:
```

Exiting IPython will exit the container as well since it is the only application running within the container. However, you can *detach* from a container by typing Ctrl-P +Ctrl-Q.

The docker ps command will still show the running container (and any other currently running containers) after you've detached from it:

```
~/Docker$ docker ps
CONTAINER ID   IMAGE          COMMAND      CREATED             STATUS
e815df8f0f4d   py4fi:basic    "ipython"    About a minute ago  Up About a minute
4518917de7dc   ubuntu:latest  "/bin/bash"  About an hour ago   Up About an hour
d081b5c7add0   ubuntu:latest  "/bin/bash"  21 hours ago        Up 21 hours
~/Docker$
```

Attaching to a Docker container is accomplished with the command docker attach $CONTAINER_ID (notice that a few letters of the $CONTAINER_ID are enough):

```
~/Docker$ docker attach e815d

In [6]: df.info()
<class 'pandas.core.frame.DataFrame'>
RangeIndex: 5 entries, 0 to 4
Data columns (total 3 columns):
a    5 non-null float64
b    5 non-null float64
c    5 non-null float64
dtypes: float64(3)
memory usage: 200.0 bytes

In [7]: exit
~/Docker$
```

The exit command terminates IPython and stops the Docker container. It can be removed with docker rm:

```
~/Docker$ docker rm e815d
e815d
~/Docker$
```

Similarly, the Docker image py4fi:basic can be removed via docker rmi if not needed any longer. While containers are relatively lightweight, single images might consume quite a bit of storage. In the case of the py4fi:basic image, the size is close to 2 GB. That is why you might want to regularly clean up the list of Docker images:

```
~/Docker$ docker rmi 6c36b9117cd2
```

Of course, there is much more to say about Docker containers and their benefits in certain application scenarios. But for the purposes of this book, it's enough to know that they provide a modern approach to deploy Python, to do Python development in a completely separate (containerized) environment, and to ship codes for algorithmic trading.

Benefits of Docker Containers

If you are not yet using Docker containers, you should consider doing so. They provide a number of benefits when it comes to Python deployment and development efforts, not only when working locally but in particular when working with remote cloud instances and servers deploying code for algorithmic trading.

Using Cloud Instances

This section shows how to set up a full-fledged Python infrastructure on a DigitalOcean (*http://digitalocean.com*) cloud instance. There are many other cloud providers out there, among them the leading provider, Amazon Web Services (AWS) (*http://aws.amazon.com*). However, DigitalOcean is well known for its simplicity and also its relatively low rates for its smaller cloud instances, called *Droplets*. The smallest Droplet, which is generally sufficient for exploration and development purposes, only costs 5 USD per month or 0.007 USD per hour. Usage is charged by the hour so that one can easily spin up a Droplet for 2 hours, say, destroy it afterward, and get charged just 0.014 USD.[9]

The goal of this section is to set up a Droplet on DigitalOcean that has a Python 3.7 installation plus typically needed packages (e.g., NumPy, pandas) in combination with a password-protected and Secure Sockets Layer (SSL)–encrypted Jupyter Notebook (*http://jupyter.org*) server installation. This server installation will provide three major tools that can be used via a regular browser:

Jupyter Notebook
    A popular interactive development environment that features a selection of different language kernels (e.g., for Python, R, and Julia).

Terminal
    A system shell implementation accessible via the browser that allows for all typical system administration tasks and for usage of helpful tools like Vim (*http://www.vim.org/download.php*) and git (*https://git-scm.com/*).

Editor
    A browser-based file editor with syntax highlighting for many different programming languages and file types as well as typical text/code editing capabilities.

Having Jupyter Notebook installed on a Droplet allows you to do Python development and deployment via the browser, circumventing the need to log in to the cloud instance via Secure Shell (SSH) access.

---

9 New users who sign up via this referral link (*http://bit.ly/do_sign_up*) get a starting credit of 10 USD for DigitalOcean.

To accomplish the goal of this section, a number of files are needed:

Server setup script
> This script orchestrates all the steps necessary, like, for instance, copying other files to the Droplet and running them on the Droplet.

Python and Jupyter installation script
> This installs Python, additional packages, and Jupyter Notebook, and starts the Jupyter Notebook server.

Jupyter Notebook configuration file
> This file is for the configuration of the Jupyter Notebook server, e.g., with respect to password protection.

RSA public and private key files
> These two files are needed for the SSL encryption of the Jupyter Notebook server.

The following subsections work backward through this list of files.

RSA Public and Private Keys

In order to create a secure connection to the Jupyter Notebook server via an arbitrary browser, an SSL certificate consisting of RSA public and private keys (*http://bit.ly/2ONvjvw*) is needed. In general, one would expect such a certificate to come from a so-called Certificate Authority (CA). For the purposes of this book, however, a self-generated certificate is "good enough."[10] A popular tool to generate RSA key pairs is OpenSSL (*http://openssl.org*). The brief interactive session that follows shows how to generate a certificate appropriate for use with a Jupyter Notebook server (insert your own values for the country name and other fields after the prompts):

```
~/cloud$ openssl req -x509 -nodes -days 365 -newkey \
> rsa:1024 -out cert.pem -keyout cert.key
Generating a 1024 bit RSA private key
..++++++
.......++++++
writing new private key to 'cert.key'
```

You are about to be asked to enter information that will be incorporated into your certificate request. What you are about to enter is what is called a Distinguished Name or a DN. There are quite a few fields, but you can leave some blank and others will have a default value. If you enter ., the field will be left blank.

```
Country Name (2 letter code) [AU]:DE
State or Province Name (full name) [Some-State]:Saarland
Locality Name (eg, city) []:Voelklingen
```

---

10 With a self-generated certificate you might need to add a security exception when prompted by the browser.

```
Organization Name (eg, company) [Internet Widgits Pty Ltd]:TPQ GmbH
Organizational Unit Name (eg, section) []:Python for Finance
Common Name (e.g. server FQDN or YOUR name) []:Jupyter
Email Address []:team@tpq.io
~/cloud$ ls
cert.key    cert.pem
~/cloud$
```

The two files *cert.key* and *cert.pem* need to be copied to the Droplet and need to be referenced by the Jupyter Notebook configuration file. This file is presented next.

Jupyter Notebook Configuration File

A public Jupyter Notebook server can be deployed securely as explained in the documentation (*http://bit.ly/2Ka0tfI*). Among other features, Jupyter Notebook can be password protected. To this end, there is a password hash code–generating function called passwd() available in the notebook.auth subpackage. The following code generates a password hash code with jupyter being the password itself:

```
~/cloud$ ipython
Python 3.7.0 (default, Jun 28 2018, 13:15:42)
Type 'copyright', 'credits' or 'license' for more information
IPython 6.5.0 -- An enhanced Interactive Python. Type '?' for help.

In [1]: from notebook.auth import passwd

In [2]: passwd('jupyter')
Out[2]: 'sha1:d4d34232ac3a:55ea0ffd78cc3299e3e5e6ecc0d36be0935d424b'

In [3]: exit
```

This hash code needs to be placed in the Jupyter Notebook configuration file as presented in Example 2-3. The configuration file assumes that the RSA key files have been copied on the Droplet to the */root/.jupyter/* folder.

Example 2-3. Jupyter Notebook configuration file

```
#
# Jupyter Notebook Configuration File
#
# Python for Finance, 2nd ed.
# (c) Dr. Yves J. Hilpisch
#
# SSL ENCRYPTION
# replace the following filenames (and files used) with your choice/files
c.NotebookApp.certfile = u'/root/.jupyter/cert.pem'
c.NotebookApp.keyfile = u'/root/.jupyter/cert.key'

# IP ADDRESS AND PORT
# set ip to '*' to bind on all IP addresses of the cloud instance
```

```
c.NotebookApp.ip = '*'
# it is a good idea to set a known, fixed default port for server access
c.NotebookApp.port = 8888

# PASSWORD PROTECTION
# here: 'jupyter' as password
# replace the hash code with the one for your strong password
c.NotebookApp.password = 'sha1:d4d34232ac3a:55ea0ffd78cc3299e3e5e6ecc0d36be0935d424b'

# NO BROWSER OPTION
# prevent Jupyter from trying to open a browser
c.NotebookApp.open_browser = False
```

Jupyter and Security

Deploying Jupyter Notebook in the cloud principally leads to a number of security issues since it is a full-fledged development environment accessible via a web browser. It is therefore of paramount importance to use the security measures that a Jupyter Notebook server provides by default, like password protection and SSL encryption. But this is just the beginning; further security measures might be advisable depending on what exactly is done on the cloud instance.

The next step is to make sure that Python and Jupyter Notebook get installed on the Droplet.

Installation Script for Python and Jupyter Notebook

The bash script to install Python and Jupyter Notebook is similar to the one presented in "Using Docker Containers" on page 45 to install Python via Miniconda in a Docker container. However, the script in Example 2-4 needs to start the Jupyter Notebook server as well. All major parts and lines of code are commented inline.

Example 2-4. Bash script to install Python and to run the Jupyter Notebook server

```
#!/bin/bash
#
# Script to Install
# Linux System Tools,
# Basic Python Packages and
# Jupyter Notebook Server
#
# Python for Finance, 2nd ed.
# (c) Dr. Yves J. Hilpisch
#
# GENERAL LINUX
apt-get update  # updates the package index cache
```

```
apt-get upgrade -y  # updates packages
apt-get install -y bzip2 gcc git htop screen vim wget  # installs system tools
apt-get upgrade -y bash  # upgrades bash if necessary
apt-get clean  # cleans up the package index cache

# INSTALLING MINICONDA
wget https://repo.continuum.io/miniconda/Miniconda3-latest-Linux-x86_64.sh -O \
  Miniconda.sh
bash Miniconda.sh -b  # installs Miniconda
rm Miniconda.sh  # removes the installer
# prepends the new path for current session
export PATH="/root/miniconda3/bin:$PATH"
# prepends the new path in the shell configuration
echo ". /root/miniconda3/etc/profile.d/conda.sh" >> ~/.bashrc
echo "conda activate" >> ~/.bashrc

# INSTALLING PYTHON LIBRARIES
# More packages can/must be added
# depending on the use case.
conda update -y conda # updates conda if required
conda create -y -n py4fi python=3.7  # creates an environment
source activate py4fi  # activates the new environment
conda install -y jupyter  # interactive data analytics in the browser
conda install -y pytables  # wrapper for HDF5 binary storage
conda install -y pandas  #  data analysis package
conda install -y matplotlib # standard plotting library
conda install -y scikit-learn  # machine learning library
conda install -y openpyxl  # library for Excel interaction
conda install -y pyyaml  # library to manage YAML files

pip install --upgrade pip  # upgrades the package manager
pip install cufflinks  # combining plotly with pandas

# COPYING FILES AND CREATING DIRECTORIES
mkdir /root/.jupyter
mv /root/jupyter_notebook_config.py /root/.jupyter/
mv /root/cert.* /root/.jupyter
mkdir /root/notebook
cd /root/notebook

# STARTING JUPYTER NOTEBOOK
jupyter notebook --allow-root

# STARTING JUPYTER NOTEBOOK
# as background process:
# jupyter notebook --allow-root &
```

This script needs to be copied to the Droplet and needs to be started by the orchestration script as described in the next subsection.

Script to Orchestrate the Droplet Setup

The second bash script, which sets up the Droplet, is the shortest one (Example 2-5). It mainly copies all the other files to the Droplet, whose IP address is expected as a parameter. In the final line it starts the *install.sh* bash script, which in turn does the installation itself and starts the Jupyter Notebook server.

Example 2-5. Bash script to set up the Droplet

```
#!/bin/bash
#
# Setting up a DigitalOcean Droplet
# with Basic Python Stack
# and Jupyter Notebook
#
# Python for Finance, 2nd ed.
# (c) Dr Yves J Hilpisch
#

# IP ADDRESS FROM PARAMETER
MASTER_IP=$1

# COPYING THE FILES
scp install.sh root@${MASTER_IP}:
scp cert.* jupyter_notebook_config.py root@${MASTER_IP}:

# EXECUTING THE INSTALLATION SCRIPT
ssh root@${MASTER_IP} bash /root/install.sh
```

Everything is now in place to give the setup code a try. On DigitalOcean, create a new Droplet with options similar to these:

Operating system
> Ubuntu 18.10 x64 (the newest version available at the time of this writing)

Size
> 1 core, 1 GB, 25 GB SSD (the smallest Droplet)

Data center region
> Frankfurt (since your author lives in Germany)

SSH key
> Add a (new) SSH key for password-less login [11]

---

[11] If you need assistance, visit either "How to Add SSH Keys to Droplets" (*https://do.co/2DIqnH9*) or "How to Create SSH Keys with PuTTY on Windows" (*https://do.co/2A0EAL0*).

Droplet name

You can go with the prespecified name or can choose something like `py4fi`

Clicking the Create button initiates the Droplet creation process, which generally takes about one minute. The major outcome of the setup procedure is the IP address, which might be, for instance, 46.101.156.199 if you chose Frankfurt as your data center location. Setting up the Droplet now is as easy as follows:

```
(py3) ~/cloud$ bash setup.sh 46.101.156.199
```

The resulting process might take a couple of minutes. It is finished when there is a message from the Jupyter Notebook server saying something like:

```
The Jupyter Notebook is running at: https://[all ip addresses on your
system]:8888/
```

In any current browser, visiting the following address accesses the running Jupyter Notebook server (note the `https` protocol):

```
https://46.101.156.199:8888
```

After perhaps requesting that you add a security exception, the Jupyter Notebook login screen prompting for a password (in our case, `jupyter`) should appear. You are now ready to start Python development in the browser via Jupyter Notebook, IPython via a terminal window, or the text file editor. Other file management capabilities, such as file upload, deletion of files, and creation of folders, are also available.

Benefits of the Cloud

Cloud instances like those from DigitalOcean and Jupyter Notebook are a powerful combination, allowing the Python developer and quant to work on and make use of professional compute and storage infrastructure. Professional cloud and data center providers make sure that your (virtual) machines are physically secure and highly available. Using cloud instances also keeps the cost of the exploration and development phase rather low, since usage generally gets charged by the hour without the need to enter into a long-term agreement.

Conclusion

Python is the programming language and technology platform of choice, not only for this book but for almost every leading financial institution. However, Python deployment can be tricky at best and sometimes even tedious and nerve-wracking. Fortunately, several technologies that help with the deployment issue have become available in recent years. The open source `conda` helps with both Python package and virtual environment management. Docker containers go even further, in that complete filesystems and runtime environments can be easily created in a technically shielded "sandbox" (i.e., the container). Going even one step further, cloud providers like DigitalOcean offer compute and storage capacity in professionally managed and secured data centers within minutes, billed by the hour. This in combination with a Python 3.7 installation and a secure Jupyter Notebook server installation provides a professional environment for Python development and deployment in the context of Python-for-finance projects.

Further Resources

For *Python package management*, consult the following resources:

- `pip` package manager page (*https://pypi.python.org/pypi/pip*)
- `conda` package manager page (*http://conda.pydata.org*)
- Installing Packages page (*https://packaging.python.org/installing/*)

For *virtual environment management*, consult these resources:

- `virtualenv` environment manager page (*https://pypi.python.org/pypi/virtualenv*)
- `conda` Managing Environments page (*http://bit.ly/2KDObMM*)
- `pipenv` package and environment manager (*https://github.com/pypa/pipenv*)

The following resources (among others) provide information about *Docker containers*:

- Docker home page (*http://docker.com*)
- Matthias, Karl, and Sean Kane (2015). *Docker: Up and Running*. Sebastopol, CA: O'Reilly.

For a concise introduction to and overview of the bash *scripting language*, see:

- Robbins, Arnold (2016). *Bash Pocket Reference*. Sebastopol, CA: O'Reilly.

How to *run a public Jupyter Notebook server securely* is explained in the Jupyter Notebook documentation (*http://bit.ly/2Ka0tfI*). There is also a hub available that allows the management of multiple users for a Jupyter Notebook server, called JupyterHub (*https://jupyterhub.readthedocs.io/en/stable/*).

To sign up on DigitalOcean with a 10 USD starting balance in your new account, visit the page *http://bit.ly/do_sign_up*. This pays for two months of usage of the smallest Droplet.

PART II

Mastering the Basics

This part of the book is concerned with the basics of Python programming. The topics covered in this part are fundamental for all other chapters to follow in subsequent parts and for Python usage in general.

The chapters are organized according to certain topics such that they can be used as a reference to which the reader can come to look up examples and details related to the topic of interest:

- Chapter 3 focuses on Python data types and structures.
- Chapter 4 is about NumPy and its ndarray class.
- Chapter 5 is about pandas and its DataFrame class.
- Chapter 6 discusses object-oriented programming (OOP) with Python.

Data Types and Structures

Bad programmers worry about the code. Good programmers worry about data structures and their relationships.

—Linus Torvalds

This chapter introduces the basic data types and data structures of Python, and is organized as follows:

"Basic Data Types" on page 62
    The first section introduces basic data types such as `int`, `float`, `bool`, and `str`.

"Basic Data Structures" on page 75
    The second section introduces the fundamental data structures of Python (e.g., `list` objects) and illustrates, among other things, control structures, functional programming approaches, and anonymous functions.

The aim of this chapter is to provide a general introduction to Python specifics when it comes to data types and structures. The reader equipped with a background from another programing language, say C or Matlab, should be able to easily grasp the differences that Python usage might bring along. The topics and idioms introduced here are important and fundamental for the chapters to come.

The chapter covers the following data types and structures:

Object type	Meaning	Used for
`int`	Integer value	Natural numbers
`float`	Floating-point number	Real numbers
`bool`	Boolean value	Something true or false
`str`	String object	Character, word, text
`tuple`	Immutable container	Fixed set of objects, record

Object type	Meaning	Used for
list	Mutable container	Changing set of objects
dict	Mutable container	Key-value store
set	Mutable container	Collection of unique objects

Basic Data Types

Python is a *dynamically typed* language, which means that the Python interpreter infers the type of an object at runtime. In comparison, compiled languages like C are generally *statically typed*. In these cases, the type of an object has to be specified for the object before compile time.[1]

Integers

One of the most fundamental data types is the integer, or int:

```
In [1]: a = 10
        type(a)
Out[1]: int
```

The built-in function type provides type information for all objects with standard and built-in types as well as for newly created classes and objects. In the latter case, the information provided depends on the description the programmer has stored with the class. There is a saying that "everything in Python is an object." This means, for example, that even simple objects like the int object just defined have built-in methods. For example, one can get the number of bits needed to represent the int object in memory by calling the method bit_length():

```
In [2]: a.bit_length()
Out[2]: 4
```

The number of bits needed increases the higher the integer value is that one assigns to the object:

```
In [3]: a = 100000
        a.bit_length()
Out[3]: 17
```

In general, there are so many different methods that it is hard to memorize all methods of all classes and objects. Advanced Python environments like IPython provide tab completion capabilities that show all the methods attached to an object. You simply type the object name followed by a dot (e.g., a.) and then press the Tab key. This

---

1 The Cython package (*http://www.cython.org*) brings static typing and compiling features to Python that are comparable to those in C. In fact, Cython is not only a *package*, it is a full-fledged hybrid *programming language* combining Python and C.

then provides a collection of methods you can call on the object. Alternatively, the Python built-in function dir gives a complete list of the attributes and methods of any object.

A specialty of Python is that integers can be arbitrarily large. Consider, for example, the googol number 10^{100}. Python has no problem with such large numbers:

```
In [4]: googol = 10 ** 100
        googol
Out[4]: 1000000000000000000000000000000000000000000000000000000000000000000000000
        0000000000000000000000000000000
```

```
In [5]: googol.bit_length()
Out[5]: 333
```

Large Integers

Python integers can be arbitrarily large. The interpreter simply uses as many bits/bytes as needed to represent the numbers.

Arithmetic operations on integers are also easy to implement:

```
In [6]: 1 + 4
Out[6]: 5
```

```
In [7]: 1 / 4
Out[7]: 0.25
```

```
In [8]: type(1 / 4)
Out[8]: float
```

Floats

The last expression returns the mathematically correct result of 0.25,[2] which gives rise to the next basic data type, the float. Adding a dot to an integer value, like in 1. or 1.0, causes Python to interpret the object as a float. Expressions involving a float also return a float object in general:[3]

```
In [9]: 1.6 / 4
Out[9]: 0.4
```

---

2 This is different in Python 2.x, where floor division is the default. Floor division in Python 3.x is accomplished by 3 // 4, which gives 0 as the result.

3 Here and in the following discussion, terms like float, float object, etc. are used interchangeably, acknowledging that every float is also an *object*. The same holds true for other object types.

```
In [10]: type (1.6 / 4)
Out[10]: float
```

A `float` is a bit more involved in that the computerized representation of rational or real numbers is in general not exact and depends on the specific technical approach taken. To illustrate what this implies, let us define another `float` object, b. `float` objects like this one are always represented internally up to a certain degree of accuracy only. This becomes evident when adding `0.1` to b:

```
In [11]: b = 0.35
         type(b)
Out[11]: float

In [12]: b + 0.1
Out[12]: 0.44999999999999996
```

The reason for this is that `float` objects are internally represented in binary format; that is, a decimal number $0 < n < 1$ is represented by a series of the form $n = \frac{x}{2} + \frac{y}{4} + \frac{z}{8} + ...$ For certain floating-point numbers the binary representation might involve a large number of elements or might even be an infinite series. However, given a fixed number of bits used to represent such a number—i.e., a fixed number of terms in the representation series—inaccuracies are the consequence. Other numbers can be represented *perfectly* and are therefore stored exactly even with a finite number of bits available. Consider the following example:

```
In [13]: c = 0.5
         c.as_integer_ratio()
Out[13]: (1, 2)
```

One-half, i.e., 0.5, is stored exactly because it has an exact (finite) binary representation as $0.5 = \frac{1}{2}$. However, for b = `0.35` one gets something different than the expected rational number $0.35 = \frac{7}{20}$:

```
In [14]: b.as_integer_ratio()
Out[14]: (3152519739159347, 9007199254740992)
```

The precision is dependent on the number of bits used to represent the number. In general, all platforms that Python runs on use the IEEE 754 double-precision standard (*http://bit.ly/2S0un95*)—i.e., 64 bits—for internal representation. This translates into a 15-digit relative accuracy.

Since this topic is of high importance for several application areas in finance, it is sometimes necessary to ensure the exact, or at least best possible, representation of numbers. For example, the issue can be of importance when summing over a large set of numbers. In such a situation, a certain kind and/or magnitude of representation error might, in aggregate, lead to significant deviations from a benchmark value.

The module `decimal` provides an arbitrary-precision object for floating-point numbers and several options to address precision issues when working with such numbers:

```
In [15]: import decimal
         from decimal import Decimal

In [16]: decimal.getcontext()
Out[16]: Context(prec=28, rounding=ROUND_HALF_EVEN, Emin=-999999, Emax=999999,
         capitals=1, clamp=0, flags=[], traps=[InvalidOperation, DivisionByZero,
         Overflow])

In [17]: d = Decimal(1) / Decimal (11)
         d
Out[17]: Decimal('0.09090909090909090909090909091')
```

One can change the precision of the representation by changing the respective attribute value of the Context object:

```
In [18]: decimal.getcontext().prec = 4    ❶

In [19]: e = Decimal(1) / Decimal (11)
         e
Out[19]: Decimal('0.09091')

In [20]: decimal.getcontext().prec = 50    ❷

In [21]: f = Decimal(1) / Decimal (11)
         f
Out[21]: Decimal('0.090909090909090909090909090909090909090909090909091')
```

❶ Lower precision than default.

❷ Higher precision than default.

If needed, the precision can in this way be adjusted to the exact problem at hand and one can operate with floating-point objects that exhibit different degrees of accuracy:

```
In [22]: g = d + e + f
         g
Out[22]: Decimal('0.27272818181818181818181818181909090909090909090909')
```

Arbitrary-Precision Floats

The module `decimal` provides an arbitrary-precision floating-point number object. In finance, it might sometimes be necessary to ensure high precision and to go beyond the 64-bit double-precision standard.

Booleans

In programming, evaluating a comparison or logical expression (such as 4 > 3, 4.5 <= 3.25 or (4 > 3) and (3 > 2)) yields one of True or False as output, two important Python keywords. Others are, for example, def, for, and if. A complete list of Python keywords is available in the keyword module:

```
In [23]: import keyword

In [24]: keyword.kwlist
Out[24]: ['False',
          'None',
          'True',
          'and',
          'as',
          'assert',
          'async',
          'await',
          'break',
          'class',
          'continue',
          'def',
          'del',
          'elif',
          'else',
          'except',
          'finally',
          'for',
          'from',
          'global',
          'if',
          'import',
          'in',
          'is',
          'lambda',
          'nonlocal',
          'not',
          'or',
          'pass',
          'raise',
          'return',
          'try',
          'while',
          'with',
          'yield']
```

True and False are of data type bool, standing for *Boolean value*. The following code shows Python's *comparison* operators applied to the same operands with the resulting bool objects:

```
In [25]: 4 > 3        ❶
Out[25]: True

In [26]: type(4 > 3)
Out[26]: bool

In [27]: type(False)
Out[27]: bool

In [28]: 4 >= 3       ❷
Out[28]: True

In [29]: 4 < 3        ❸
Out[29]: False

In [30]: 4 <= 3       ❹
Out[30]: False

In [31]: 4 == 3       ❺
Out[31]: False

In [32]: 4 != 3       ❻
Out[32]: True
```

❶ Is greater.

❷ Is greater or equal.

❸ Is smaller.

❹ Is smaller or equal.

❺ Is equal.

❻ Is not equal.

Often, *logical* operators are applied on bool objects, which in turn yields another bool object:

```
In [33]: True and True
Out[33]: True

In [34]: True and False
Out[34]: False

In [35]: False and False
Out[35]: False

In [36]: True or True
Out[36]: True
```

```
In [37]: True or False
Out[37]: True

In [38]: False or False
Out[38]: False

In [39]: not True
Out[39]: False

In [40]: not False
Out[40]: True
```

Of course, both types of operators are often combined:

```
In [41]: (4 > 3) and (2 > 3)
Out[41]: False

In [42]: (4 == 3) or (2 != 3)
Out[42]: True

In [43]: not (4 != 4)
Out[43]: True

In [44]: (not (4 != 4)) and (2 == 3)
Out[44]: False
```

One major application area is to control the code flow via other Python keywords, such as if or while (more examples later in the chapter):

```
In [45]: if 4 > 3:      ❶
             print('condition true')   ❷
         condition true

In [46]: i = 0    ❸
         while i < 4:    ❹
             print('condition true, i = ', i)   ❺
             i += 1   ❻
         condition true, i =  0
         condition true, i =  1
         condition true, i =  2
         condition true, i =  3
```

❶ If condition holds true, execute code to follow.

❷ The code to be executed if condition holds true.

❸ Initializes the parameter i with 0.

❹ As long as the condition holds true, execute and repeat the code to follow.

❺ Prints a text and the value of parameter i.

❻ Increases the parameter value by 1; i += 1 is the same as i = i + 1.

Numerically, Python attaches a value of 0 to False and a value of 1 to True. When transforming numbers to bool objects via the bool() function, a 0 gives False while all other numbers give True:

```
In [47]: int(True)
Out[47]: 1

In [48]: int(False)
Out[48]: 0

In [49]: float(True)
Out[49]: 1.0

In [50]: float(False)
Out[50]: 0.0

In [51]: bool(0)
Out[51]: False

In [52]: bool(0.0)
Out[52]: False

In [53]: bool(1)
Out[53]: True

In [54]: bool(10.5)
Out[54]: True

In [55]: bool(-2)
Out[55]: True
```

Strings

Now that natural and floating-point numbers can be represented, this subsection turns to text. The basic data type to represent text in Python is str. The str object has a number of helpful built-in methods. In fact, Python is generally considered to be a good choice when it comes to working with texts and text files of any kind and any size. A str object is generally defined by single or double quotation marks or by converting another object using the str() function (i.e., using the object's standard or user-defined str representation):

```
In [56]: t = 'this is a string object'
```

With regard to the built-in methods, you can, for example, capitalize the first word in this object:

```
In [57]: t.capitalize()
Out[57]: 'This is a string object'
```

Or you can split it into its single-word components to get a `list` object of all the words (more on `list` objects later):

```
In [58]: t.split()
Out[58]: ['this', 'is', 'a', 'string', 'object']
```

You can also search for a word and get the position (i.e., index value) of the first letter of the word back in a successful case:

```
In [59]: t.find('string')
Out[59]: 10
```

If the word is not in the `str` object, the method returns `-1`:

```
In [60]: t.find('Python')
Out[60]: -1
```

Replacing characters in a string is a typical task that is easily accomplished with the `replace()` method:

```
In [61]: t.replace(' ', '|')
Out[61]: 'this|is|a|string|object'
```

The stripping of strings—i.e., deletion of certain leading/lagging characters—is also often necessary:

```
In [62]: 'http://www.python.org'.strip('htp:/')
Out[62]: 'www.python.org'
```

Table 3-1 lists a number of helpful methods of the `str` object.

Table 3-1. Selected string methods

Method	Arguments	Returns/result
capitalize	()	Copy of the string with first letter capitalized
count	(*sub*[, *start*[, *end*]])	Count of the number of occurrences of substring
encode	([*encoding*[, *errors*]])	Encoded version of the string
find	(*sub*[, *start*[, *end*]])	(Lowest) index where substring is found
join	(*seq*)	Concatenation of strings in sequence *seq*
replace	(*old*, *new*[, *count*])	Replaces *old* by *new* the first *count* times
split	([*sep*[, *maxsplit*]])	List of words in string with *sep* as separator
splitlines	([*keepends*])	Separated lines with line ends/breaks if *keepends* is True
strip	(*chars*)	Copy of string with leading/lagging characters in *chars* removed
upper	()	Copy with all letters capitalized

Unicode Strings

A fundamental change from Python 2.7 (used for the first edition of the book) to Python 3.7 (used for this second edition) is the encoding and decoding of string objects and the introduction of Unicode (*http://bit.ly/1x41ytu*). This chapter does not go into the many details important in this context; for the purposes of this book, which mainly deals with numerical data and standard strings containing English words, this omission seems justified.

Excursion: Printing and String Replacements

Printing `str` objects or string representations of other Python objects is usually accomplished by the `print()` function:

```
In [63]: print('Python for Finance')  ❶
         Python for Finance

In [64]: print(t)  ❷
         this is a string object

In [65]: i = 0
         while i < 4:
             print(i)  ❸
             i += 1
         0
         1
         2
         3

In [66]: i = 0
         while i < 4:
             print(i, end='|')  ❹
             i += 1
         0|1|2|3|
```

❶   Prints a `str` object.

❷   Prints a `str` object referenced by a variable name.

❸   Prints the string representation of an `int` object.

❹   Specifies the final character(s) when printing; default is a line break (\n) as seen before.

Python offers powerful string replacement operations. There is the old way, via the % character, and the new way, via curly braces ({}) and `format()`. Both are still applied in practice. This section cannot provide an exhaustive illustration of all options, but the following code snippets show some important ones. First, the *old* way of doing it:

```
In [67]: 'this is an integer %d' % 15      ❶
Out[67]: 'this is an integer 15'

In [68]: 'this is an integer %4d' % 15      ❷
Out[68]: 'this is an integer   15'

In [69]: 'this is an integer %04d' % 15     ❸
Out[69]: 'this is an integer 0015'

In [70]: 'this is a float %f' % 15.3456     ❹
Out[70]: 'this is a float 15.345600'

In [71]: 'this is a float %.2f' % 15.3456   ❺
Out[71]: 'this is a float 15.35'

In [72]: 'this is a float %8f' % 15.3456    ❻
Out[72]: 'this is a float 15.345600'

In [73]: 'this is a float %8.2f' % 15.3456  ❼
Out[73]: 'this is a float     15.35'

In [74]: 'this is a float %08.2f' % 15.3456 ❽
Out[74]: 'this is a float 00015.35'

In [75]: 'this is a string %s' % 'Python'   ❾
Out[75]: 'this is a string Python'

In [76]: 'this is a string %10s' % 'Python' ❿
Out[76]: 'this is a string     Python'
```

❶   `int` object replacement.

❷   With fixed number of characters.

❸   With leading zeros if necessary.

❹   `float` object replacement.

❺   With fixed number of decimals.

❻   With fixed number of characters (and filled-up decimals).

❼   With fixed number of characters and decimals …

❽   … and leading zeros if necessary.

❾   `str` object replacement.

❿   With fixed number of characters.

Now, here are the same examples implemented in the *new* way. Notice the slight differences in the output in some places:

```
In [77]: 'this is an integer {:d}'.format(15)
Out[77]: 'this is an integer 15'

In [78]: 'this is an integer {:4d}'.format(15)
Out[78]: 'this is an integer   15'

In [79]: 'this is an integer {:04d}'.format(15)
Out[79]: 'this is an integer 0015'

In [80]: 'this is a float {:f}'.format(15.3456)
Out[80]: 'this is a float 15.345600'

In [81]: 'this is a float {:.2f}'.format(15.3456)
Out[81]: 'this is a float 15.35'

In [82]: 'this is a float {:8f}'.format(15.3456)
Out[82]: 'this is a float 15.345600'

In [83]: 'this is a float {:8.2f}'.format(15.3456)
Out[83]: 'this is a float     15.35'

In [84]: 'this is a float {:08.2f}'.format(15.3456)
Out[84]: 'this is a float 00015.35'

In [85]: 'this is a string {:s}'.format('Python')
Out[85]: 'this is a string Python'

In [86]: 'this is a string {:10s}'.format('Python')
Out[86]: 'this is a string Python    '
```

String replacements are particularly useful in the context of multiple printing operations where the printed data is updated, for instance, during a while loop:

```
In [87]: i = 0
         while i < 4:
             print('the number is %d' % i)
             i += 1
         the number is 0
         the number is 1
         the number is 2
         the number is 3

In [88]: i = 0
         while i < 4:
             print('the number is {:d}'.format(i))
             i += 1
         the number is 0
         the number is 1
         the number is 2
         the number is 3
```

Excursion: Regular Expressions

A powerful tool when working with `str` objects is *regular expressions*. Python provides such functionality in the module `re`:

```
In [89]: import re
```

Suppose a financial analyst is faced with a large text file, such as a CSV file, which contains certain time series and respective date-time information. More often than not, this information is delivered in a format that Python cannot interpret directly. However, the date-time information can generally be described by a regular expression. Consider the following `str` object, containing three date-time elements, three integers, and three strings. Note that triple quotation marks allow the definition of `str` objects over multiple rows:

```
In [90]: series = """
         '01/18/2014 13:00:00', 100, '1st';
         '01/18/2014 13:30:00', 110, '2nd';
         '01/18/2014 14:00:00', 120, '3rd'
         """
```

The following regular expression describes the format of the date-time information provided in the `str` object:[4]

```
In [91]: dt = re.compile("'[0-9/:\s]+'")  # datetime
```

Equipped with this regular expression, one can go on and find all the date-time elements. In general, applying regular expressions to `str` objects also leads to performance improvements for typical parsing tasks:

```
In [92]: result = dt.findall(series)
         result
Out[92]: ["'01/18/2014 13:00:00'", "'01/18/2014 13:30:00'", "'01/18/2014
         14:00:00'"]
```

Regular Expressions

When parsing `str` objects, consider using regular expressions, which can bring both convenience and performance to such operations.

The resulting `str` objects can then be parsed to generate Python `datetime` objects (see Appendix A for an overview of handling date and time data with Python). To

---

4 It is not possible to go into detail here, but there is a wealth of information available on the internet about regular expressions in general and for Python in particular. For an introduction to this topic, refer to Fitzgerald (2012).

parse the `str` objects containing the date-time information, one needs to provide information of how to parse them—again as a `str` object:

```
In [93]: from datetime import datetime
         pydt = datetime.strptime(result[0].replace("'", ""),
                                  '%m/%d/%Y %H:%M:%S')
         pydt
Out[93]: datetime.datetime(2014, 1, 18, 13, 0)

In [94]: print(pydt)
         2014-01-18 13:00:00

In [95]: print(type(pydt))
         <class 'datetime.datetime'>
```

Later chapters provide more information on date-time data, the handling of such data, and `datetime` objects and their methods. This is just meant to be a teaser for this important topic in finance.

Basic Data Structures

As a general rule, data structures are objects that contain a possibly large number of other objects. Among those that Python provides as built-in structures are:

`tuple`
An immutable collection of arbitrary objects; only a few methods available

`list`
A mutable collection of arbitrary objects; many methods available

`dict`
A key-value store object

`set`
An unordered collection object for other *unique* objects

Tuples

A `tuple` is an advanced data structure, yet it's still quite simple and limited in its applications. It is defined by providing objects in parentheses:

```
In [96]: t = (1, 2.5, 'data')
         type(t)
Out[96]: tuple
```

You can even drop the parentheses and provide multiple objects, just separated by commas:

```
In [97]: t = 1, 2.5, 'data'
         type(t)
Out[97]: tuple
```

Like almost all data structures in Python the tuple has a built-in index, with the help of which you can retrieve single or multiple elements of the tuple. It is important to remember that Python uses *zero-based numbering*, such that the third element of a tuple is at index position 2:

```
In [98]: t[2]
Out[98]: 'data'

In [99]: type(t[2])
Out[99]: str
```

 Zero-Based Numbering

In contrast to some other programming languages like Matlab, Python uses zero-based numbering schemes. For example, the first element of a tuple object has index value 0.

There are only two special methods that this object type provides: count() and index(). The first counts the number of occurrences of a certain object and the second gives the index value of the first appearance of it:

```
In [100]: t.count('data')
Out[100]: 1

In [101]: t.index(1)
Out[101]: 0
```

tuple objects are *immutable* objects. This means that they, once defined, cannot be changed easily.

Lists

Objects of type list are much more flexible and powerful in comparison to tuple objects. From a finance point of view, you can achieve a lot working only with list objects, such as storing stock price quotes and appending new data. A list object is defined through brackets and the basic capabilities and behaviors are similar to those of tuple objects:

```
In [102]: l = [1, 2.5, 'data']
          l[2]
Out[102]: 'data'
```

list objects can also be defined or converted by using the function list(). The following code generates a new list object by converting the tuple object from the previous example:

```
In [103]: l = list(t)
          l
Out[103]: [1, 2.5, 'data']

In [104]: type(l)
Out[104]: list
```

In addition to the characteristics of tuple objects, list objects are also expandable and reducible via different methods. In other words, whereas str and tuple objects are *immutable* sequence objects (with indexes) that cannot be changed once created, list objects are *mutable* and can be changed via different operations. You can append list objects to an existing list object, and more:

```
In [105]: l.append([4, 3])   ❶
          l
Out[105]: [1, 2.5, 'data', [4, 3]]

In [106]: l.extend([1.0, 1.5, 2.0])   ❷
          l
Out[106]: [1, 2.5, 'data', [4, 3], 1.0, 1.5, 2.0]

In [107]: l.insert(1, 'insert')   ❸
          l
Out[107]: [1, 'insert', 2.5, 'data', [4, 3], 1.0, 1.5, 2.0]

In [108]: l.remove('data')   ❹
          l
Out[108]: [1, 'insert', 2.5, [4, 3], 1.0, 1.5, 2.0]

In [109]: p = l.pop(3)   ❺
          print(l, p)
          [1, 'insert', 2.5, 1.0, 1.5, 2.0] [4, 3]
```

❶ Append list object at the end.

❷ Append elements of the list object.

❸ Insert object before index position.

❹ Remove first occurrence of object.

❺ Remove and return object at index position.

Slicing is also easily accomplished. Here, *slicing* refers to an operation that breaks down a data set into smaller parts (of interest):

```
In [110]: l[2:5]   ❶
Out[110]: [2.5, 1.0, 1.5]
```

❶ Return the third through fifth elements.

Table 3-2 provides a summary of selected operations and methods of the list object.

Table 3-2. Selected operations and methods of list objects

Method	Arguments	Returns/result
l[i] = x	[i]	Replaces i-th element by x
l[i:j:k] = s	[i:j:k]	Replaces every k-th element from i to $j-1$ by s
append	(x)	Appends x to object
count	(x)	Number of occurrences of object x
del l[i:j:k]	[i:j:k]	Deletes elements with index values i to $j-1$ and step size k
extend	(s)	Appends all elements of s to object
index	(x[, i[, j]])	First index of x between elements i and $j-1$
insert	(i, x)	Inserts x at/before index i
remove	(x)	Removes element x at first match
pop	(i)	Removes element with index i and returns it
reverse	()	Reverses all items in place
sort	([cmp[, key[, reverse]]])	Sorts all items in place

Excursion: Control Structures

Although a topic in themselves, *control structures* like for loops are maybe best introduced in Python based on list objects. This is due to the fact that looping in general takes place over list objects, which is quite different to what is often the standard in other languages. Take the following example. The for loop loops over the elements of the list object l with index values 2 to 4 and prints the square of the respective elements. Note the importance of the indentation (whitespace) in the second line:

```
In [111]: for element in l[2:5]:
              print(element ** 2)
          6.25
          1.0
          2.25
```

This provides a really high degree of flexibility in comparison to the typical counter-based looping. Counter-based looping is also an option with Python, but is accomplished using the range object:

```
In [112]: r = range(0, 8, 1)   ❶
          r
Out[112]: range(0, 8)

In [113]: type(r)
Out[113]: range
```

❶ Parameters are start, end, and step-size.

For comparison, the same loop is implemented using `range()` as follows:

```
In [114]: for i in range(2, 5):
              print(l[i] ** 2)
          6.25
          1.0
          2.25
```

Looping over Lists

In Python you can loop over arbitrary `list` objects, no matter what the content of the object is. This often avoids the introduction of a counter.

Python also provides the typical (conditional) control elements `if`, `elif`, and `else`. Their use is comparable in other languages:

```
In [115]: for i in range(1, 10):
              if i % 2 == 0:    ❶
                  print("%d is even" % i)
              elif i % 3 == 0:
                  print("%d is multiple of 3" % i)
              else:
                  print("%d is odd" % i)
          1 is odd
          2 is even
          3 is multiple of 3
          4 is even
          5 is odd
          6 is even
          7 is odd
          8 is even
          9 is multiple of 3
```

❶ % stands for modulo.

Similarly, `while` provides another means to control the flow:

```
In [116]: total = 0
          while total < 100:
              total += 1
          print(total)
          100
```

A specialty of Python is so-called *list comprehensions*. Instead of looping over existing `list` objects, this approach generates `list` objects via loops in a rather compact fashion:

```
In [117]: m = [i ** 2 for i in range(5)]
          m
Out[117]: [0, 1, 4, 9, 16]
```

In a certain sense, this already provides a first means to generate "something like" vectorized code in that loops are implicit rather than explicit (vectorization of code is discussed in more detail in Chapters 4 and 5).

Excursion: Functional Programming

Python provides a number of tools for functional programming support as well—i.e., the application of a function to a whole set of inputs (in our case list objects). Among these tools are filter(), map(), and reduce(). However, one needs a function definition first. To start with something really simple, consider a function f() that returns the square of the input x:

```
In [118]: def f(x):
              return x ** 2
          f(2)
Out[118]: 4
```

Of course, functions can be arbitrarily complex, with multiple input/parameter objects and even multiple outputs (return objects). However, consider the following function:

```
In [119]: def even(x):
              return x % 2 == 0
          even(3)
Out[119]: False
```

The return object is a Boolean. Such a function can be applied to a whole list object by using map():

```
In [120]: list(map(even, range(10)))
Out[120]: [True, False, True, False, True, False, True, False, True, False]
```

To this end, one can also provide a function definition directly as an argument to map(), making use of lambda or *anonymous* functions:

```
In [121]: list(map(lambda x: x ** 2, range(10)))
Out[121]: [0, 1, 4, 9, 16, 25, 36, 49, 64, 81]
```

Functions can also be used to filter a list object. In the following example, the filter returns elements of a list object that match the Boolean condition as defined by the even function:

```
In [122]: list(filter(even, range(15)))
Out[122]: [0, 2, 4, 6, 8, 10, 12, 14]
```

List Comprehensions, Functional Programming, Anonymous Functions

It can be considered good practice to avoid loops on the Python level as far as possible. List comprehensions and functional programming tools like `filter()`, `map()`, and `reduce()` provide means to write code without (explicit) loops that is both compact and in general more readable. `lambda` or anonymous functions are also powerful tools in this context.

Dicts

`dict` objects are dictionaries, and also mutable sequences, that allow data retrieval by keys (which can, for example, be `str` objects). They are so-called *key-value stores*. While `list` objects are ordered and sortable, `dict` objects are unordered and not sortable, in general.[5] An example best illustrates further differences to `list` objects. Curly braces are what define `dict` objects:

```
In [123]: d = {
                'Name' : 'Angela Merkel',
                'Country' : 'Germany',
                'Profession' : 'Chancelor',
                'Age' : 64
                }
          type(d)
Out[123]: dict

In [124]: print(d['Name'], d['Age'])
          Angela Merkel 64
```

Again, this class of objects has a number of built-in methods:

```
In [125]: d.keys()
Out[125]: dict_keys(['Name', 'Country', 'Profession', 'Age'])

In [126]: d.values()
Out[126]: dict_values(['Angela Merkel', 'Germany', 'Chancelor', 64])

In [127]: d.items()
Out[127]: dict_items([('Name', 'Angela Merkel'), ('Country', 'Germany'),
          ('Profession', 'Chancelor'), ('Age', 64)])

In [128]: birthday = True
          if birthday:
              d['Age'] += 1
          print(d['Age'])
          65
```

---

5 There are variants to the standard `dict` object, including among others an `OrderedDict` subclass, which remembers the order in which entries are added. See *https://docs.python.org/3/library/collections.html*.

There are several methods to get `iterator` objects from a `dict` object. The `iterator` objects behave like `list` objects when iterated over:

```
In [129]: for item in d.items():
              print(item)
          ('Name', 'Angela Merkel')
          ('Country', 'Germany')
          ('Profession', 'Chancelor')
          ('Age', 65)

In [130]: for value in d.values():
              print(type(value))
          <class 'str'>
          <class 'str'>
          <class 'str'>
          <class 'int'>
```

Table 3-3 provides a summary of selected operations and methods of the `dict` object.

Table 3-3. Selected operations and methods of dict objects

Method	Arguments	Returns/result
`d[k]`	`[k]`	Item of d with key *k*
`d[k] = x`	`[k]`	Sets item key *k* to *x*
`del d[k]`	`[k]`	Deletes item with key *k*
`clear`	`()`	Removes all items
`copy`	`()`	Makes a copy
`items`	`()`	Iterator over all items
`keys`	`()`	Iterator over all keys
`values`	`()`	Iterator over all values
`popitem`	`(k)`	Returns and removes item with key *k*
`update`	`([e])`	Updates items with items from *e*

Sets

The final data structure this section covers is the `set` object. Although set theory is a cornerstone of mathematics and also of financial theory, there are not too many practical applications for `set` objects. The objects are unordered collections of other objects, containing every element only once:

```
In [131]: s = set(['u', 'd', 'ud', 'du', 'd', 'du'])
          s
Out[131]: {'d', 'du', 'u', 'ud'}

In [132]: t = set(['d', 'dd', 'uu', 'u'])
```

With set objects, one can implement basic operations on sets as in mathematical set theory. For example, one can generate unions, intersections, and differences:

```
In [133]: s.union(t)  ❶
Out[133]: {'d', 'dd', 'du', 'u', 'ud', 'uu'}

In [134]: s.intersection(t)  ❷
Out[134]: {'d', 'u'}

In [135]: s.difference(t)  ❸
Out[135]: {'du', 'ud'}

In [136]: t.difference(s)  ❹
Out[136]: {'dd', 'uu'}

In [137]: s.symmetric_difference(t)  ❺
Out[137]: {'dd', 'du', 'ud', 'uu'}
```

❶ All of s and t.

❷ Items in both s and t.

❸ Items in s but not in t.

❹ Items in t but not in s.

❺ Items in either s or t but not both.

One application of set objects is to get rid of duplicates in a list object:

```
In [138]: from random import randint
          l = [randint(0, 10) for i in range(1000)]  ❶
          len(l)  ❷
Out[138]: 1000

In [139]: l[:20]
Out[139]: [4, 2, 10, 2, 1, 10, 0, 6, 0, 8, 10, 9, 2, 4, 7, 8, 10, 8, 8, 2]

In [140]: s = set(l)
          s
Out[140]: {0, 1, 2, 3, 4, 5, 6, 7, 8, 9, 10}
```

❶ 1,000 random integers between 0 and 10.

❷ Number of elements in l.

Conclusion

The basic Python interpreter provides a rich set of flexible data structures. From a finance point of view, the following can be considered the most important ones:

Basic data types

In Python in general and finance in particular, the classes `int`, `float`, `bool`, and `str` provide the atomic data types.

Standard data structures

The classes `tuple`, `list`, `dict`, and `set` have many application areas in finance, with `list` being a flexible all-rounder for a number use cases.

Further Resources

With regard to data types and structures, this chapter focuses on those topics that might be of particular importance for financial algorithms and applications. However, it can only represent a starting point for the exploration of data structures and data modeling in Python.

There are a number of valuable resources available to go deeper from here. The official documentation for Python data structures is found at *https://docs.python.org/3/tutorial/datastructures.html*.

Good references in book form are:

- Goodrich, Michael, et al. (2013). *Data Structures and Algorithms in Python.* Hoboken, NJ: John Wiley & Sons.
- Harrison, Matt (2017). *Illustrated Guide to Python 3.* CreateSpace Treading on Python Series.
- Ramalho, Luciano (2016). *Fluent Python.* Sebastopol, CA: O'Reilly.

For an introduction to regular expressions, see:

- Fitzgerald, Michael (2012). *Introducing Regular Expressions.* Sebastopol, CA: O'Reilly.

## CHAPTER 4

Numerical Computing with NumPy

Computers are useless. They can only give answers.

—Pablo Picasso

Although the Python interpreter itself already brings a rich variety of data structures with it, NumPy and other libraries add to these in a valuable fashion. This chapter focuses on NumPy, which provides a multidimensional array object to store homogeneous or heterogeneous data arrays and supports vectorization of code.

The chapter covers the following data structures:

Object type	Meaning	Used for
ndarray (regular)	*n*-dimensional array object	Large arrays of numerical data
ndarray (record)	2-dimensional array object	Tabular data organized in columns

This chapter is organized as follows:

"Arrays of Data" on page 86
    This section is about the handling of arrays of data with pure Python code.

"Regular NumPy Arrays" on page 90
    This is the core section about the regular NumPy ndarray class, the workhorse in almost all data-intensive Python use cases involving numerical data.

"Structured NumPy Arrays" on page 105
    This brief section introduces structured (or *record*) ndarray objects for the handling of tabular data with columns.

"Vectorization of Code" on page 106
 In this section, vectorization of code is discussed along with its benefits; the section also discusses the importance of memory layout in certain scenarios.

Arrays of Data

The previous chapter showed that Python provides some quite useful and flexible general data structures. In particular, list objects can be considered a real workhorse with many convenient characteristics and application areas. Using such a flexible (mutable) data structure has a cost, in the form of relatively high memory usage, slower performance, or both. However, scientific and financial applications generally have a need for high-performing operations on special data structures. One of the most important data structures in this regard is the *array*. Arrays generally structure other (fundamental) objects of the *same data type* in rows and columns.

Assume for the moment that only numbers are relevant, although the concept generalizes to other types of data as well. In the simplest case, a one-dimensional array then represents, mathematically speaking, a *vector* of, in general, real numbers, internally represented by float objects. It then consists of a *single* row or column of elements only. In the more common case, an array represents an $i \times j$ *matrix* of elements. This concept generalizes to $i \times j \times k$ *cubes* of elements in three dimensions as well as to general n-dimensional arrays of shape $i \times j \times k \times l \times \dots$.

Mathematical disciplines like linear algebra and vector space theory illustrate that such mathematical structures are of high importance in a number of scientific disciplines and fields. It can therefore prove fruitful to have available a specialized class of data structures explicitly designed to handle arrays conveniently and efficiently. This is where the Python library NumPy comes into play, with its powerful ndarray class. Before introducing this class in the next section, this section illustrates two alternatives for the handling of arrays.

Arrays with Python Lists

Arrays can be constructed with the built-in data structures presented in the previous chapter. list objects are particularly suited to accomplishing this task. A simple list can already be considered a one-dimensional array:

```
In [1]: v = [0.5, 0.75, 1.0, 1.5, 2.0]   ❶
```

❶ list object with numbers.

Since list objects can contain arbitrary other objects, they can also contain other list objects. In that way, two- and higher-dimensional arrays are easily constructed by nested list objects:

```
In [2]: m = [v, v, v]  ❶
        m  ❷
Out[2]: [[0.5, 0.75, 1.0, 1.5, 2.0],
         [0.5, 0.75, 1.0, 1.5, 2.0],
         [0.5, 0.75, 1.0, 1.5, 2.0]]
```

❶ list object with list objects ...

❷ ... resulting in a matrix of numbers.

One can also easily select rows via simple indexing or single elements via double indexing (whole columns, however, are not so easy to select):

```
In [3]: m[1]
Out[3]: [0.5, 0.75, 1.0, 1.5, 2.0]

In [4]: m[1][0]
Out[4]: 0.5
```

Nesting can be pushed further for even more general structures:

```
In [5]: v1 = [0.5, 1.5]
        v2 = [1, 2]
        m = [v1, v2]
        c = [m, m]  ❶
        c
Out[5]: [[[0.5, 1.5], [1, 2]], [[0.5, 1.5], [1, 2]]]

In [6]: c[1][1][0]
Out[6]: 1
```

❶ Cube of numbers.

Note that combining objects in the way just presented generally works with reference pointers to the original objects. What does that mean in practice? Have a look at the following operations:

```
In [7]: v = [0.5, 0.75, 1.0, 1.5, 2.0]
        m = [v, v, v]
        m
Out[7]: [[0.5, 0.75, 1.0, 1.5, 2.0],
         [0.5, 0.75, 1.0, 1.5, 2.0],
         [0.5, 0.75, 1.0, 1.5, 2.0]]
```

Now change the value of the first element of the v object and see what happens to the m object:

```
In [8]: v[0] = 'Python'
        m
Out[8]: [['Python', 0.75, 1.0, 1.5, 2.0],
         ['Python', 0.75, 1.0, 1.5, 2.0],
         ['Python', 0.75, 1.0, 1.5, 2.0]]
```

This can be avoided by using the deepcopy() function of the copy module:

```
In [9]: from copy import deepcopy
        v = [0.5, 0.75, 1.0, 1.5, 2.0]
        m = 3 * [deepcopy(v), ]   ❶
        m
Out[9]: [[0.5, 0.75, 1.0, 1.5, 2.0],
         [0.5, 0.75, 1.0, 1.5, 2.0],
         [0.5, 0.75, 1.0, 1.5, 2.0]]

In [10]: v[0] = 'Python'   ❷
         m   ❸
Out[10]: [[0.5, 0.75, 1.0, 1.5, 2.0],
          [0.5, 0.75, 1.0, 1.5, 2.0],
          [0.5, 0.75, 1.0, 1.5, 2.0]]
```

❶ Instead of reference pointer, physical copies are used.

❷ As a consequence, a change in the original object …

❸ … does not have any impact anymore.

The Python array Class

There is a dedicated array module available in Python. According to the documentation (*https://docs.python.org/3/library/array.html*):

> This module defines an object type which can compactly represent an array of basic values: characters, integers, floating point numbers. Arrays are sequence types and behave very much like lists, except that the type of objects stored in them is constrained. The type is specified at object creation time by using a type code, which is a single character.

Consider the following code, which instantiates an array object out of a list object:

```
In [11]: v = [0.5, 0.75, 1.0, 1.5, 2.0]

In [12]: import array

In [13]: a = array.array('f', v)   ❶
         a
Out[13]: array('f', [0.5, 0.75, 1.0, 1.5, 2.0])

In [14]: a.append(0.5)   ❷
         a
Out[14]: array('f', [0.5, 0.75, 1.0, 1.5, 2.0, 0.5])

In [15]: a.extend([5.0, 6.75])   ❷
         a
Out[15]: array('f', [0.5, 0.75, 1.0, 1.5, 2.0, 0.5, 5.0, 6.75])
```

```
In [16]: 2 * a  ❸
Out[16]: array('f', [0.5, 0.75, 1.0, 1.5, 2.0, 0.5, 5.0, 6.75, 0.5, 0.75, 1.0,
                     1.5, 2.0, 0.5, 5.0, 6.75])
```

❶ The instantiation of the `array` object with `float` as the type code.

❷ Major methods work similar to those of the `list` object.

❸ Although "scalar multiplication" works in principle, the result is not the mathematically expected one; rather, the elements are repeated.

Trying to append an object of a different data type than the one specified raises a `TypeError`:

```
In [17]: a.append('string')  ❶

         --------------------------------------
         TypeErrorTraceback (most recent call last)
         <ipython-input-17-14cd6281866b> in <module>()
         ----> 1 a.append('string')  ❶

         TypeError: must be real number, not str

In [18]: a.tolist()  ❷
Out[18]: [0.5, 0.75, 1.0, 1.5, 2.0, 0.5, 5.0, 6.75]
```

❶ Only `float` objects can be appended; other data types/type codes raise errors.

❷ However, the `array` object can easily be converted back to a `list` object if such flexibility is required.

An advantage of the `array` class is that it has built-in storage and retrieval functionality:

```
In [19]: f = open('array.apy', 'wb')  ❶
         a.tofile(f)  ❷
         f.close()  ❸

In [20]: with open('array.apy', 'wb') as f:  ❹
             a.tofile(f)  ❹

In [21]: !ls -n arr*  ❺
         -rw-r--r--@ 1 503  20  32 Nov  7 11:46 array.apy
```

❶ Opens a file on disk for writing binary data.

❷ Writes the `array` data to the file.

❸ Closes the file.

❹ Alternative: uses a `with` context for the same operation.

❺ Shows the file as written on disk.

As before, the data type of the `array` object is of importance when reading the data from disk:

```
In [22]: b = array.array('f')   ❶

In [23]: with open('array.apy', 'rb') as f:   ❷
             b.fromfile(f, 5)   ❸

In [24]: b   ❹
Out[24]: array('f', [0.5, 0.75, 1.0, 1.5, 2.0])

In [25]: b = array.array('d')   ❹

In [26]: with open('array.apy', 'rb') as f:
             b.fromfile(f, 2)   ❺

In [27]: b   ❻
Out[27]: array('d', [0.0004882813645963324, 0.12500002956949174])
```

❶ Instantiates a new `array` object with type code `float`.

❷ Opens the file for reading binary data …

❸ … and reads five elements in the b object.

❹ Instantiates a new `array` object with type code `double`.

❺ Reads two elements from the file.

❻ The difference in type codes leads to "wrong" numbers.

Regular NumPy Arrays

Composing array structures with `list` objects works, somewhat. But it is not really convenient, and the `list` class has not been built with this specific goal in mind. It has rather a much broader and more general scope. The `array` class is a bit more specialized, providing some useful features for working with arrays of data. However, a truly specialized class could be really beneficial to handle array-type structures.

The Basics

`numpy.ndarray` is just such a class, built with the specific goal of handling *n*-dimensional arrays both conveniently and efficiently—i.e., in a highly performant manner. The basic handling of instances of this class is again best illustrated by examples:

```
In [28]: import numpy as np  ❶

In [29]: a = np.array([0, 0.5, 1.0, 1.5, 2.0])  ❷
         a
Out[29]: array([0. , 0.5, 1. , 1.5, 2. ])

In [30]: type(a)  ❷
Out[30]: numpy.ndarray

In [31]: a = np.array(['a', 'b', 'c'])  ❸
         a
Out[31]: array(['a', 'b', 'c'], dtype='<U1')

In [32]: a = np.arange(2, 20, 2)  ❹
         a
Out[32]: array([ 2,  4,  6,  8, 10, 12, 14, 16, 18])

In [33]: a = np.arange(8, dtype=np.float)  ❺
         a
Out[33]: array([0., 1., 2., 3., 4., 5., 6., 7.])

In [34]: a[5:]  ❻
Out[34]: array([5., 6., 7.])

In [35]: a[:2]  ❻
Out[35]: array([0., 1.])
```

❶ Imports the numpy package.

❷ Creates an ndarray object out of a list object with floats.

❸ Creates an ndarray object out of a list object with strs.

❹ np.arange() works similar to range() …

❺ … but takes as additional input the dtype parameter.

❻ With one-dimensional ndarray objects, indexing works as usual.

A major feature of the ndarray class is the *multitude of built-in methods*. For instance:

```
In [36]: a.sum()  ❶
Out[36]: 28.0

In [37]: a.std()  ❷
Out[37]: 2.29128784747792
```

```
In [38]: a.cumsum()  ❸
Out[38]: array([ 0.,  1.,  3.,  6., 10., 15., 21., 28.])
```

❶ The sum of all elements.

❷ The standard deviation of the elements.

❸ The cumulative sum of all elements (starting at index position 0).

Another major feature is the (vectorized) *mathematical operations* defined on ndarray objects:

```
In [39]: l = [0., 0.5, 1.5, 3., 5.]
         2 * l  ❶
Out[39]: [0.0, 0.5, 1.5, 3.0, 5.0, 0.0, 0.5, 1.5, 3.0, 5.0]

In [40]: a
Out[40]: array([0., 1., 2., 3., 4., 5., 6., 7.])

In [41]: 2 * a  ❷
Out[41]: array([ 0.,  2.,  4.,  6.,  8., 10., 12., 14.])

In [42]: a ** 2  ❸
Out[42]: array([ 0.,  1.,  4.,  9., 16., 25., 36., 49.])

In [43]: 2 ** a  ❹
Out[43]: array([  1.,   2.,   4.,   8.,  16.,  32.,  64., 128.])

In [44]: a ** a  ❺
Out[44]: array([1.00000e+00, 1.00000e+00, 4.00000e+00, 2.70000e+01, 2.56000e+02,
                3.12500e+03, 4.66560e+04, 8.23543e+05])
```

❶ Scalar multiplication with list objects leads to a repetition of elements.

❷ By contrast, working with ndarray objects implements a proper scalar multiplication.

❸ This calculates element-wise the square values.

❹ This interprets the elements of the ndarray as the powers.

❺ This calculates the power of every element to itself.

Universal functions are another important feature of the NumPy package. They are "universal" in the sense that they in general operate on ndarray objects as well as on basic Python data types. However, when applying universal functions to, say, a Python float object, one needs to be aware of the reduced performance compared to the same functionality found in the math module:

```
In [45]: np.exp(a)  ❶
Out[45]: array([1.00000000e+00, 2.71828183e+00, 7.38905610e+00, 2.00855369e+01,
                5.45981500e+01, 1.48413159e+02, 4.03428793e+02, 1.09663316e+03])

In [46]: np.sqrt(a)  ❷
Out[46]: array([0.        , 1.        , 1.41421356, 1.73205081, 2.        ,
                2.23606798, 2.44948974, 2.64575131])

In [47]: np.sqrt(2.5)  ❸
Out[47]: 1.5811388300841898

In [48]: import math  ❹

In [49]: math.sqrt(2.5)  ❹
Out[49]: 1.5811388300841898

In [50]: math.sqrt(a)  ❺

         -------------------------------------
         TypeErrorTraceback (most recent call last)
         <ipython-input-50-b39de4150838> in <module>()
         ----> 1 math.sqrt(a)  ❺

         TypeError: only size-1 arrays can be converted to Python scalars

In [51]: %timeit np.sqrt(2.5)  ❻
         722 ns ± 13.7 ns per loop (mean ± std. dev. of 7 runs, 1000000 loops
         each)

In [52]: %timeit math.sqrt(2.5)  ❼
         91.8 ns ± 4.13 ns per loop (mean ± std. dev. of 7 runs, 10000000 loops
         each)
```

❶ Calculates the exponential values element-wise.

❷ Calculates the square root for every element.

❸ Calculates the square root for a Python float object.

❹ The same calculation, this time using the math module.

❺ The math.sqrt() function cannot be applied to the ndarray object directly.

❻ Applying the universal function np.sqrt() to a Python float object ...

❼ ... is much slower than the same operation with the math.sqrt() function.

Multiple Dimensions

The transition to more than one dimension is seamless, and all features presented so far carry over to the more general cases. In particular, the indexing system is made consistent across all dimensions:

```
In [53]: b = np.array([a, a * 2])   ❶
         b
Out[53]: array([[ 0.,  1.,  2.,  3.,  4.,  5.,  6.,  7.],
                [ 0.,  2.,  4.,  6.,  8., 10., 12., 14.]])

In [54]: b[0]   ❷
Out[54]: array([0., 1., 2., 3., 4., 5., 6., 7.])

In [55]: b[0, 2]   ❸
Out[55]: 2.0

In [56]: b[:, 1]   ❹
Out[56]: array([1., 2.])

In [57]: b.sum()   ❺
Out[57]: 84.0

In [58]: b.sum(axis=0)   ❻
Out[58]: array([ 0.,  3.,  6.,  9., 12., 15., 18., 21.])

In [59]: b.sum(axis=1)   ❼
Out[59]: array([28., 56.])
```

❶ Constructs a two-dimensional ndarray object out of the one-dimensional one.

❷ Selects the first row.

❸ Selects the third element in the first row; indices are separated, within the brackets, by a comma.

❹ Selects the second column.

❺ Calculates the sum of *all* values.

❻ Calculates the sum along the first axis; i.e., column-wise.

❼ Calculates the sum along the second axis; i.e., row-wise.

There are a number of ways to initialize (instantiate) ndarray objects. One is as presented before, via np.array. However, this assumes that all elements of the array are already available. In contrast, one might like to have the ndarray objects instantiated first to populate them later with results generated during the execution of code. To this end, one can use the following functions:

```
In [60]: c = np.zeros((2, 3), dtype='i', order='C')  ❶
         c
Out[60]: array([[0, 0, 0],
                [0, 0, 0]], dtype=int32)

In [61]: c = np.ones((2, 3, 4), dtype='i', order='C')  ❷
         c
Out[61]: array([[[1, 1, 1, 1],
                 [1, 1, 1, 1],
                 [1, 1, 1, 1]],

                [[1, 1, 1, 1],
                 [1, 1, 1, 1],
                 [1, 1, 1, 1]]], dtype=int32)

In [62]: d = np.zeros_like(c, dtype='f16', order='C')  ❸
         d
Out[62]: array([[[0., 0., 0., 0.],
                 [0., 0., 0., 0.],
                 [0., 0., 0., 0.]],

                [[0., 0., 0., 0.],
                 [0., 0., 0., 0.],
                 [0., 0., 0., 0.]]], dtype=float128)

In [63]: d = np.ones_like(c, dtype='f16', order='C')  ❸
         d
Out[63]: array([[[1., 1., 1., 1.],
                 [1., 1., 1., 1.],
                 [1., 1., 1., 1.]],

                [[1., 1., 1., 1.],
                 [1., 1., 1., 1.],
                 [1., 1., 1., 1.]]], dtype=float128)

In [64]: e = np.empty((2, 3, 2))  ❹
         e
Out[64]: array([[[0.00000000e+000, 0.00000000e+000],
                 [0.00000000e+000, 0.00000000e+000],
                 [0.00000000e+000, 0.00000000e+000]],

                [[0.00000000e+000, 0.00000000e+000],
                 [0.00000000e+000, 7.49874326e+247],
                 [1.28822975e-231, 4.33190018e-311]]])

In [65]: f = np.empty_like(c)  ❹
         f
Out[65]: array([[[            0,            0,            0,            0],
                 [            0,            0,            0,            0],
```

```
           [        0,          0,          0,          0]],

          [[        0,          0,          0,          0],
           [        0,          0,  740455269, 1936028450],
           [        0,  268435456, 1835316017,       2041]]], dtype=int32)

In [66]: np.eye(5)  ❺
Out[66]: array([[1., 0., 0., 0., 0.],
               [0., 1., 0., 0., 0.],
               [0., 0., 1., 0., 0.],
               [0., 0., 0., 1., 0.],
               [0., 0., 0., 0., 1.]])

In [67]: g = np.linspace(5, 15, 12)  ❻
         g
Out[67]: array([ 5.        ,  5.90909091,  6.81818182,  7.72727273,  8.63636364,
                9.54545455, 10.45454545, 11.36363636, 12.27272727, 13.18181818,
               14.09090909, 15.        ])
```

❶ Creates an ndarray object prepopulated with zeros.

❷ Creates an ndarray object prepopulated with ones.

❸ The same, but takes another ndarray object to infer the shape.

❹ Creates an ndarray object not prepopulated with anything (numbers depend on the bits present in the memory).

❺ Creates a square matrix as an ndarray object with the diagonal populated by ones.

❻ Creates a one-dimensional ndarray object with evenly spaced intervals between numbers; parameters used are start, end, and num (number of elements).

For all these functions, one can provide the following parameters:

shape
  Either an int, a sequence of int objects, or a reference to another ndarray

dtype (optional)
  A dtype—these are NumPy-specific data types for ndarray objects

order (optional)
  The order in which to store elements in memory: C for C-like (i.e., row-wise) or F for Fortran-like (i.e., column-wise)

Here, it becomes obvious how NumPy specializes the construction of arrays with the ndarray class, in comparison to the list -based approach:

- The ndarray object has built-in *dimensions* (axes).

- The ndarray object is *immutable*; its length (size) is fixed.

- It only allows for a *single data type* (np.dtype) for the whole array.

The array class by contrast shares only the characteristic of allowing for a single data type (type code, dtype).

The role of the order parameter is discussed later in the chapter. Table 4-1 provides an overview of selected np.dtype objects (i.e., the basic data types NumPy allows).

Table 4-1. NumPy dtype objects

dtype	Description	Example
?	Boolean	? (True or False)
i	Signed integer	i8 (64-bit)
u	Unsigned integer	u8 (64-bit)
f	Floating point	f8 (64-bit)
c	Complex floating point	c32 (256-bit)
m	timedelta	m (64-bit)
M	datetime	M (64-bit)
O	Object	O (pointer to object)
U	Unicode	U24 (24 Unicode characters)
V	Raw data (void)	V12 (12-byte data block)

Metainformation

Every ndarray object provides access to a number of useful attributes:

```
In [68]: g.size     ❶
Out[68]: 12

In [69]: g.itemsize    ❷
Out[69]: 8

In [70]: g.ndim    ❸
Out[70]: 1

In [71]: g.shape    ❹
Out[71]: (12,)

In [72]: g.dtype    ❺
Out[72]: dtype('float64')

In [73]: g.nbytes    ❻
Out[73]: 96
```

❶ The number of elements.

❷ The number of bytes used to represent one element.

❸ The number of dimensions.

❹ The shape of the ndarray object.

❺ The dtype of the elements.

❻ The total number of bytes used in memory.

Reshaping and Resizing

Although ndarray objects are immutable by default, there are multiple options to reshape and resize such an object. While *reshaping* in general just provides another *view* on the same data, *resizing* in general creates a *new* (temporary) object. First, some examples of reshaping:

```
In [74]: g = np.arange(15)

In [75]: g
Out[75]: array([ 0,  1,  2,  3,  4,  5,  6,  7,  8,  9, 10, 11, 12, 13, 14])

In [76]: g.shape   ❶
Out[76]: (15,)

In [77]: np.shape(g)   ❶
Out[77]: (15,)

In [78]: g.reshape((3, 5))   ❷
Out[78]: array([[ 0,  1,  2,  3,  4],
                [ 5,  6,  7,  8,  9],
                [10, 11, 12, 13, 14]])

In [79]: h = g.reshape((5, 3))   ❸
         h
Out[79]: array([[ 0,  1,  2],
                [ 3,  4,  5],
                [ 6,  7,  8],
                [ 9, 10, 11],
                [12, 13, 14]])

In [80]: h.T   ❹
Out[80]: array([[ 0,  3,  6,  9, 12],
                [ 1,  4,  7, 10, 13],
                [ 2,  5,  8, 11, 14]])

In [81]: h.transpose()   ❹
```

```
Out[81]: array([[ 0,  3,  6,  9, 12],
               [ 1,  4,  7, 10, 13],
               [ 2,  5,  8, 11, 14]])
```

❶ The shape of the original ndarray object.

❷ Reshaping to two dimensions (memory view).

❸ Creating a new object.

❹ The transpose of the new ndarray object.

During a reshaping operation, the total number of elements in the ndarray object is unchanged. During a resizing operation, this number changes—it either decreases ("down-sizing") or increases ("up-sizing"). Here some examples of resizing:

```
In [82]: g
Out[82]: array([ 0,  1,  2,  3,  4,  5,  6,  7,  8,  9, 10, 11, 12, 13, 14])

In [83]: np.resize(g, (3, 1))  ❶
Out[83]: array([[0],
               [1],
               [2]])

In [84]: np.resize(g, (1, 5))  ❶
Out[84]: array([[0, 1, 2, 3, 4]])

In [85]: np.resize(g, (2, 5))  ❶
Out[85]: array([[0, 1, 2, 3, 4],
               [5, 6, 7, 8, 9]])

In [86]: n = np.resize(g, (5, 4))  ❷
         n
Out[86]: array([[ 0,  1,  2,  3],
               [ 4,  5,  6,  7],
               [ 8,  9, 10, 11],
               [12, 13, 14,  0],
               [ 1,  2,  3,  4]])
```

❶ Two dimensions, down-sizing.

❷ Two dimensions, up-sizing.

Stacking is a special operation that allows the horizontal or vertical combination of two ndarray objects. However, the size of the "connecting" dimension must be the same:

```
In [87]: h
Out[87]: array([[ 0,  1,  2],
               [ 3,  4,  5],
```

```
              [ 6,  7,  8],
              [ 9, 10, 11],
              [12, 13, 14]])

In [88]: np.hstack((h, 2 * h))  ❶
Out[88]: array([[ 0,  1,  2,  0,  2,  4],
                [ 3,  4,  5,  6,  8, 10],
                [ 6,  7,  8, 12, 14, 16],
                [ 9, 10, 11, 18, 20, 22],
                [12, 13, 14, 24, 26, 28]])

In [89]: np.vstack((h, 0.5 * h))  ❷
Out[89]: array([[ 0. ,  1. ,  2. ],
                [ 3. ,  4. ,  5. ],
                [ 6. ,  7. ,  8. ],
                [ 9. , 10. , 11. ],
                [12. , 13. , 14. ],
                [ 0. ,  0.5,  1. ],
                [ 1.5,  2. ,  2.5],
                [ 3. ,  3.5,  4. ],
                [ 4.5,  5. ,  5.5],
                [ 6. ,  6.5,  7. ]])
```

❶ Horizontal stacking of two `ndarray` objects.

❷ Vertical stacking of two `ndarray` objects.

Another special operation is the *flattening* of a multidimensional `ndarray` object to a one-dimensional one. One can choose whether the flattening happens row-by-row (C order) or column-by-column (F order):

```
In [90]: h
Out[90]: array([[ 0,  1,  2],
                [ 3,  4,  5],
                [ 6,  7,  8],
                [ 9, 10, 11],
                [12, 13, 14]])

In [91]: h.flatten()  ❶
Out[91]: array([ 0,  1,  2,  3,  4,  5,  6,  7,  8,  9, 10, 11, 12, 13, 14])

In [92]: h.flatten(order='C')  ❶
Out[92]: array([ 0,  1,  2,  3,  4,  5,  6,  7,  8,  9, 10, 11, 12, 13, 14])

In [93]: h.flatten(order='F')  ❷
Out[93]: array([ 0,  3,  6,  9, 12,  1,  4,  7, 10, 13,  2,  5,  8, 11, 14])

In [94]: for i in h.flat:  ❸
             print(i, end=',')
         0,1,2,3,4,5,6,7,8,9,10,11,12,13,14,
In [95]: for i in h.ravel(order='C'):  ❹
```

```
           print(i, end=',')
      0,1,2,3,4,5,6,7,8,9,10,11,12,13,14,
In [96]: for i in h.ravel(order='F'):   ❹
           print(i, end=',')
      0,3,6,9,12,1,4,7,10,13,2,5,8,11,14,
```

❶ The default order for flattening is C.

❷ Flattening with F order.

❸ The flat attribute provides a flat iterator (C order).

❹ The ravel() method is an alternative to flatten().

Boolean Arrays

Comparison and logical operations in general work on ndarray objects the same way, element-wise, as on standard Python data types. Evaluating conditions yield by default a Boolean ndarray object (dtype is bool):

```
In [97]: h
Out[97]: array([[ 0,  1,  2],
                [ 3,  4,  5],
                [ 6,  7,  8],
                [ 9, 10, 11],
                [12, 13, 14]])

In [98]: h > 8   ❶
Out[98]: array([[False, False, False],
                [False, False, False],
                [False, False, False],
                [ True,  True,  True],
                [ True,  True,  True]])

In [99]: h <= 7   ❷
Out[99]: array([[ True,  True,  True],
                [ True,  True,  True],
                [ True,  True, False],
                [False, False, False],
                [False, False, False]])

In [100]: h == 5   ❸
Out[100]: array([[False, False, False],
                 [False, False,  True],
                 [False, False, False],
                 [False, False, False],
                 [False, False, False]])

In [101]: (h == 5).astype(int)   ❹
Out[101]: array([[0, 0, 0],
```

```
                    [0, 0, 1],
                    [0, 0, 0],
                    [0, 0, 0],
                    [0, 0, 0]])

In [102]: (h > 4) & (h <= 12)    ❺
Out[102]: array([[False, False, False],
                 [False, False,  True],
                 [ True,  True,  True],
                 [ True,  True,  True],
                 [ True, False, False]])
```

❶ Is value greater than …?

❷ Is value smaller or equal than …?

❸ Is value equal to …?

❹ Present `True` and `False` as integer values 0 and 1.

❺ Is value greater than … and smaller than or equal to …?

Such Boolean arrays can be used for indexing and data selection. Notice that the following operations flatten the data:

```
In [103]: h[h > 8]    ❶
Out[103]: array([ 9, 10, 11, 12, 13, 14])

In [104]: h[(h > 4) & (h <= 12)]    ❷
Out[104]: array([ 5,  6,  7,  8,  9, 10, 11, 12])

In [105]: h[(h < 4) | (h >= 12)]    ❸
Out[105]: array([ 0,  1,  2,  3, 12, 13, 14])
```

❶ Give me all values greater than …

❷ Give me all values greater than … *and* smaller than or equal to …

❸ Give me all values greater than … *or* smaller than or equal to …

A powerful tool in this regard is the `np.where()` function, which allows the definition of actions/operations depending on whether a condition is `True` or `False`. The result of applying `np.where()` is a new `ndarray` object of the same shape as the original one:

```
In [106]: np.where(h > 7, 1, 0)    ❶
Out[106]: array([[0, 0, 0],
                 [0, 0, 0],
                 [0, 0, 1],
                 [1, 1, 1],
                 [1, 1, 1]])
```

```
In [107]: np.where(h % 2 == 0, 'even', 'odd')  ❷
Out[107]: array([['even', 'odd', 'even'],
                 ['odd', 'even', 'odd'],
                 ['even', 'odd', 'even'],
                 ['odd', 'even', 'odd'],
                 ['even', 'odd', 'even']], dtype='<U4')

In [108]: np.where(h <= 7, h * 2, h / 2)  ❸
Out[108]: array([[ 0. ,  2. ,  4. ],
                 [ 6. ,  8. , 10. ],
                 [12. , 14. ,  4. ],
                 [ 4.5,  5. ,  5.5],
                 [ 6. ,  6.5,  7. ]])
```

❶   In the new object, set 1 if True and 0 otherwise.

❷   In the new object, set even if True and odd otherwise.

❸   In the new object, set two times the h element if True and half the h element otherwise.

Later chapters provide more examples of these important operations on ndarray objects.

Speed Comparison

We'll move on to structured arrays with NumPy shortly, but let us stick with regular arrays for a moment and see what the specialization brings in terms of performance.

As a simple example, consider the generation of a matrix/array of shape 5,000 × 5,000 elements, populated with pseudo-random, standard normally distributed numbers. The sum of all elements shall then be calculated. First, the pure Python approach, where list comprehensions are used:

```
In [109]: import random
          I = 5000

In [110]: %time mat = [[random.gauss(0, 1) for j in range(I)] \
                      for i in range(I)]  ❶
          CPU times: user 17.1 s, sys: 361 ms, total: 17.4 s
          Wall time: 17.4 s

In [111]: mat[0][:5]  ❷
Out[111]: [-0.40594967782329183,
           -1.357757478015285,
           0.05129566894355976,
           -0.8958429976582192,
           0.6234174778878331]
```

```
In [112]: %time sum([sum(l) for l in mat])  ❸
          CPU times: user 142 ms, sys: 1.69 ms, total: 144 ms
          Wall time: 143 ms

Out[112]: -3561.944965714259

In [113]: import sys
          sum([sys.getsizeof(l) for l in mat])  ❹
Out[113]: 215200000
```

❶ The creation of the matrix via a nested list comprehension.

❷ Some selected random numbers from those drawn.

❸ The sums of the single list objects are first calculated during a list comprehension; then the sum of the sums is taken.

❹ This adds up the memory usage of all list objects.

Let us now turn to NumPy and see how the same problem is solved there. For convenience, the NumPy subpackage random offers a multitude of functions to instantiate an ndarray object and populate it at the same time with pseudo-random numbers:

```
In [114]: %time mat = np.random.standard_normal((I, I))  ❶
          CPU times: user 1.01 s, sys: 200 ms, total: 1.21 s
          Wall time: 1.21 s

In [115]: %time mat.sum()  ❷
          CPU times: user 29.7 ms, sys: 1.15 ms, total: 30.8 ms
          Wall time: 29.4 ms

Out[115]: -186.12767026606448

In [116]: mat.nbytes  ❸
Out[116]: 200000000

In [117]: sys.getsizeof(mat)  ❸
Out[117]: 200000112
```

❶ Creates the ndarray object with standard normally distributed random numbers; it is faster by a factor of about 14.

❷ Calculates the sum of all values in the ndarray object; it is faster by a factor of 4.5.

❸ The NumPy approach also saves some memory since the memory overhead of the ndarray object is tiny compared to the size of the data itself.

Using NumPy Arrays

The use of NumPy for array-based operations and algorithms generally results in compact, easily readable code and significant performance improvements over pure Python code.

Structured NumPy Arrays

The specialization of the ndarray class obviously brings a number of valuable benefits
with it. However, a too narrow specialization might turn out to be too large a burden
to carry for the majority of array-based algorithms and applications. Therefore, NumPy
provides *structured* ndarray and *record* recarray objects (*http://bit.ly/2DHsXgn*) that
allow you to have a different dtype *per column*. What does "per column" mean? Consider the following initialization of a structured ndarray object:

```
In [118]: dt = np.dtype([('Name', 'S10'), ('Age', 'i4'),
                         ('Height', 'f'), ('Children/Pets', 'i4', 2)])   ❶

In [119]: dt   ❶
Out[119]: dtype([('Name', 'S10'), ('Age', '<i4'), ('Height', '<f4'),
          ('Children/Pets', '<i4', (2,))])

In [120]: dt = np.dtype({'names': ['Name', 'Age', 'Height', 'Children/Pets'],
                         'formats':'O int float int,int'.split()})   ❷

In [121]: dt   ❷
Out[121]: dtype([('Name', 'O'), ('Age', '<i8'), ('Height', '<f8'),
          ('Children/Pets', [('f0', '<i8'), ('f1', '<i8')])])

In [122]: s = np.array([('Smith', 45, 1.83, (0, 1)),
                       ('Jones', 53, 1.72, (2, 2))], dtype=dt)   ❸

In [123]: s   ❸
Out[123]: array([('Smith', 45, 1.83, (0, 1)), ('Jones', 53, 1.72, (2, 2))],
          dtype=[('Name', 'O'), ('Age', '<i8'), ('Height', '<f8'),
          ('Children/Pets', [('f0', '<i8'), ('f1', '<i8')])])

In [124]: type(s)   ❹
Out[124]: numpy.ndarray
```

❶ The complex dtype is composed.

❷ An alternative syntax to achieve the same result.

❸ The structured ndarray is instantiated with two records.

❹ The object type is still ndarray.

In a sense, this construction comes quite close to the operation for initializing tables in a SQL database: one has column names and column data types, with maybe some additional information (e.g., maximum number of characters per str object). The single columns can now be easily accessed by their names and the rows by their index values:

```
In [125]: s['Name']  ❶
Out[125]: array(['Smith', 'Jones'], dtype=object)

In [126]: s['Height'].mean()  ❷
Out[126]: 1.775

In [127]: s[0]  ❸
Out[127]: ('Smith', 45, 1.83, (0, 1))

In [128]: s[1]['Age']  ❹
Out[128]: 53
```

❶ Selecting a column by name.

❷ Calling a method on a selected column.

❸ Selecting a record.

❹ Selecting a field in a record.

In summary, structured arrays are a generalization of the regular ndarray object type in that the data type only has to be the same *per column*, like in tables in SQL databases. One advantage of structured arrays is that a single element of a column can be another multidimensional object and does not have to conform to the basic NumPy data types.

Structured Arrays

NumPy provides, in addition to regular arrays, structured (and record) arrays that allow the description and handling of table-like data structures with a variety of different data types per (named) column. They bring SQL table–like data structures to Python, with most of the benefits of regular ndarray objects (syntax, methods, performance).

Vectorization of Code

Vectorization is a strategy to get more compact code that is possibly executed faster. The fundamental idea is to conduct an operation on or to apply a function to a complex object "at once" and not by looping over the single elements of the object. In

Python, functional programming tools such as `map()` and `filter()` provide some basic means for vectorization. However, NumPy has vectorization built in deep down in its core.

Basic Vectorization

As demonstrated in the previous section, simple mathematical operations—such as calculating the sum of all elements—can be implemented on ndarray objects directly (via methods or universal functions). More general vectorized operations are also possible. For example, one can add two NumPy arrays element-wise as follows:

```
In [129]: np.random.seed(100)
          r = np.arange(12).reshape((4, 3))      ❶
          s = np.arange(12).reshape((4, 3)) * 0.5  ❷

In [130]: r  ❶
Out[130]: array([[ 0,  1,  2],
                 [ 3,  4,  5],
                 [ 6,  7,  8],
                 [ 9, 10, 11]])

In [131]: s  ❷
Out[131]: array([[0. , 0.5, 1. ],
                 [1.5, 2. , 2.5],
                 [3. , 3.5, 4. ],
                 [4.5, 5. , 5.5]])

In [132]: r + s  ❸
Out[132]: array([[ 0. ,  1.5,  3. ],
                 [ 4.5,  6. ,  7.5],
                 [ 9. , 10.5, 12. ],
                 [13.5, 15. , 16.5]])
```

❶ The first ndarray object with random numbers.

❷ The second ndarray object with random numbers.

❸ Element-wise addition as a vectorized operation (no looping).

NumPy also supports what is called *broadcasting*. This allows you to combine objects of different shape within a single operation. Previous examples have already made use of this. Consider the following examples:

```
In [133]: r + 3  ❶
Out[133]: array([[ 3,  4,  5],
                 [ 6,  7,  8],
                 [ 9, 10, 11],
                 [12, 13, 14]])

In [134]: 2 * r  ❷
```

```
Out[134]: array([[ 0,  2,  4],
                  [ 6,  8, 10],
                  [12, 14, 16],
                  [18, 20, 22]])

In [135]: 2 * r + 3   ❸
Out[135]: array([[ 3,  5,  7],
                  [ 9, 11, 13],
                  [15, 17, 19],
                  [21, 23, 25]])
```

❶ During scalar addition, the scalar is broadcast and added to every element.

❷ During scalar multiplication, the scalar is also broadcast to and multiplied with every element.

❸ This linear transformation combines both operations.

These operations work with differently shaped ndarray objects as well, up to a certain point:

```
In [136]: r
Out[136]: array([[ 0,  1,  2],
                  [ 3,  4,  5],
                  [ 6,  7,  8],
                  [ 9, 10, 11]])

In [137]: r.shape
Out[137]: (4, 3)

In [138]: s = np.arange(0, 12, 4)   ❶
          s   ❶
Out[138]: array([0, 4, 8])

In [139]: r + s   ❷
Out[139]: array([[ 0,  5, 10],
                  [ 3,  8, 13],
                  [ 6, 11, 16],
                  [ 9, 14, 19]])

In [140]: s = np.arange(0, 12, 3)   ❸
          s   ❸
Out[140]: array([0, 3, 6, 9])

In [141]: r + s   ❹

         ---------------------------------------------
         ValueErrorTraceback (most recent call last)
         <ipython-input-141-1890b26ec965> in <module>()
         ----> 1 r + s   ❹
```

```
ValueError: operands could not be broadcast together
              with shapes (4,3) (4,)

In [142]: r.transpose() + s   ❺
Out[142]: array([[ 0,  6, 12, 18],
                 [ 1,  7, 13, 19],
                 [ 2,  8, 14, 20]])

In [143]: sr = s.reshape(-1, 1)   ❻
          sr
Out[143]: array([[0],
                 [3],
                 [6],
                 [9]])

In [144]: sr.shape   ❻
Out[144]: (4, 1)

In [145]: r + s.reshape(-1, 1)   ❻
Out[145]: array([[ 0,  1,  2],
                 [ 6,  7,  8],
                 [12, 13, 14],
                 [18, 19, 20]])
```

❶ A new one-dimensional ndarray object of length 3.

❷ The r (matrix) and s (vector) objects can be added straightforwardly.

❸ Another one-dimensional ndarray object of length 4.

❹ The length of the new s (vector) object is now different from the length of the second dimension of the r object.

❺ Transposing the r object again allows for the vectorized addition.

❻ Alternatively, the shape of s can be changed to (4, 1) to make the addition work (the results are different, however).

Often, custom-defined Python functions work with ndarray objects as well. If the implementation allows, arrays can be used with functions just as int or float objects can. Consider the following function:

```
In [146]: def f(x):
              return 3 * x + 5   ❶

In [147]: f(0.5)   ❷
Out[147]: 6.5

In [148]: f(r)   ❸
```

```
Out[148]: array([[ 5,  8, 11],
                  [14, 17, 20],
                  [23, 26, 29],
                  [32, 35, 38]])
```

❶ A simple Python function implementing a linear transform on parameter x.

❷ The function f() applied to a Python float object.

❸ The same function applied to an ndarray object, resulting in a vectorized and element-wise evaluation of the function.

What NumPy does is to simply apply the function f to the object element-wise. In that sense, by using this kind of operation one does *not* avoid loops; one only avoids them on the Python level and delegates the looping to NumPy. On the NumPy level, looping over the ndarray object is taken care of by optimized code, most of it written in C and therefore generally faster than pure Python. This explains the "secret" behind the performance benefits of using NumPy for array-based use cases.

Memory Layout

When ndarray objects are initialized by using np.zeros(), as in "Multiple Dimensions" on page 94, an optional argument for the memory layout is provided. This argument specifies, roughly speaking, which elements of an array get stored in memory next to each other (contiguously). When working with small arrays, this has hardly any measurable impact on the performance of array operations. However, when arrays get large, and depending on the (financial) algorithm to be implemented on them, the story might be different. This is when *memory layout* comes into play (see, for instance, Eli Bendersky's article "Memory Layout of Multi-Dimensional Arrays" (*http://bit.ly/2K8rujN*)).

To illustrate the potential importance of the memory layout of arrays in science and finance, consider the following construction of multidimensional ndarray objects:

```
In [149]: x = np.random.standard_normal((1000000, 5))  ❶

In [150]: y = 2 * x + 3  ❷

In [151]: C = np.array((x, y), order='C')  ❸

In [152]: F = np.array((x, y), order='F')  ❹

In [153]: x = 0.0; y = 0.0  ❺

In [154]: C[:2].round(2)  ❻
Out[154]: array([[[-1.75,  0.34,  1.15, -0.25,  0.98],
                  [ 0.51,  0.22, -1.07, -0.19,  0.26],
```

```
                [-0.46,   0.44,  -0.58,   0.82,   0.67],
                ...,
                [-0.05,   0.14,   0.17,   0.33,   1.39],
                [ 1.02,   0.3 ,  -1.23,  -0.68,  -0.87],
                [ 0.83,  -0.73,   1.03,   0.34,  -0.46]],

               [[-0.5 ,   3.69,   5.31,   2.5 ,   4.96],
                [ 4.03,   3.44,   0.86,   2.62,   3.51],
                [ 2.08,   3.87,   1.83,   4.63,   4.35],
                ...,
                [ 2.9 ,   3.28,   3.33,   3.67,   5.78],
                [ 5.04,   3.6 ,   0.54,   1.65,   1.26],
                [ 4.67,   1.54,   5.06,   3.69,   2.07]]])
```

❶   An ndarray object with large asymmetry in the two dimensions.

❷   A linear transform of the original object data.

❸   This creates a two-dimensional ndarray object with C order (row-major).

❹   This creates a two-dimensional ndarray object with F order (column-major).

❺   Memory is freed up (contingent on garbage collection).

❻   Some numbers from the C object.

Let's look at some fundamental examples and use cases for both types of ndarray
objects and consider the speed with which they are executed given the different memory layouts:

```
In [155]: %timeit C.sum()   ❶
          4.36 ms ± 89.3 µs per loop (mean ± std. dev. of 7 runs, 100 loops each)

In [156]: %timeit F.sum()   ❶
          4.21 ms ± 71.4 µs per loop (mean ± std. dev. of 7 runs, 100 loops each)

In [157]: %timeit C.sum(axis=0)   ❷
          17.9 ms ± 776 µs per loop (mean ± std. dev. of 7 runs, 100 loops each)

In [158]: %timeit C.sum(axis=1)   ❸
          35.1 ms ± 999 µs per loop (mean ± std. dev. of 7 runs, 10 loops each)

In [159]: %timeit F.sum(axis=0)   ❷
          83.8 ms ± 2.63 ms per loop (mean ± std. dev. of 7 runs, 10 loops each)

In [160]: %timeit F.sum(axis=1)   ❸
          67.9 ms ± 5.16 ms per loop (mean ± std. dev. of 7 runs, 10 loops each)

In [161]: F = 0.0; C = 0.0
```

❶ Calculates the sum of all elements.

❷ Calculates the sums per row ("many").

❸ Calculates the sums per columns ("few").

We can summarize the performance results as follows:

- When calculating the sum of *all elements*, the memory layout does not really matter.
- The summing up over the C-ordered ndarray objects is faster both over rows and over columns (an *absolute* speed advantage).
- With the C-ordered (row-major) ndarray object, summing up over rows is *relatively* faster compared to summing up over columns.
- With the F-ordered (column-major) ndarray object, summing up over columns is *relatively* faster compared to summing up over rows.

Conclusion

NumPy is the package of choice for numerical computing in Python. The ndarray class is specifically designed to be convenient and efficient in the handling of (large) numerical data. Powerful methods and NumPy universal functions allow for vectorized code that mostly avoids slow loops on the Python level. Many approaches introduced in this chapter carry over to pandas and its DataFrame class as well (see Chapter 5).

Further Resources

Many helpful resources are provided at the NumPy website:

- *http://www.numpy.org/*

Good introductions to NumPy in book form are:

- McKinney, Wes (2017). *Python for Data Analysis*. Sebastopol, CA: O'Reilly.
- VanderPlas, Jake (2016). *Python Data Science Handbook*. Sebastopol, CA: O'Reilly.

## CHAPTER 5

Data Analysis with pandas

Data! Data! Data! I can't make bricks without clay!

—Sherlock Holmes

This chapter is about pandas, a library for data analysis with a focus on tabular data. pandas is a powerful tool that not only provides many useful classes and functions but also does a great job of wrapping functionality from other packages. The result is a user interface that makes data analysis, and in particular financial analysis, a convenient and efficient task.

This chapter covers the following fundamental data structures:

Object type	Meaning	Used for
DataFrame	2-dimensional data object with index	Tabular data organized in columns
Series	1-dimensional data object with index	Single (time) series of data

The chapter is organized as follows:

"The DataFrame Class" on page 114
> This section starts by exploring the basic characteristics and capabilities of the DataFrame class of pandas by using simple and small data sets; it then shows how to transform a NumPy ndarray object into a DataFrame object.

"Basic Analytics" on page 123 and "Basic Visualization" on page 126
> Basic analytics and visualization capabilities are introduced in these sections (later chapters go deeper into these topics).

"The Series Class" on page 128
> This rather brief section covers the Series class of pandas, which in a sense represents a special case of the DataFrame class with a single column of data only.

"GroupBy Operations" on page 130
> One of the strengths of the `DataFrame` class lies in grouping data according to a single or multiple columns. This section explores the grouping capabilities of pandas.

"Complex Selection" on page 132
> This section illustrates how the use of (complex) conditions allows for the easy selection of data from a `DataFrame` object.

"Concatenation, Joining, and Merging" on page 135
> The combining of different data sets into one is an important operation in data analysis. pandas provides different options to accomplish this task, as described in this section.

"Performance Aspects" on page 141
> Like Python in general, pandas often provides multiple options to accomplish the same goal. This section takes a brief look at potential performance differences.

The DataFrame Class

At the core of pandas (and this chapter) is the `DataFrame`, a class designed to efficiently handle data in tabular form—i.e., data characterized by a columnar organization. To this end, the `DataFrame` class provides, for instance, column labeling as well as flexible indexing capabilities for the rows (records) of the data set, similar to a table in a relational database or an Excel spreadsheet.

This section covers some fundamental aspects of the pandas `DataFrame` class. The class is so complex and powerful that only a fraction of its capabilities can be presented here. Subsequent chapters provide more examples and shed light on different aspects.

First Steps with the DataFrame Class

On a fundamental level, the `DataFrame` class is designed to manage indexed and labeled data, not too different from a SQL database table or a worksheet in a spreadsheet application. Consider the following creation of a `DataFrame` object:

```
In [1]: import pandas as pd   ❶

In [2]: df = pd.DataFrame([10, 20, 30, 40],   ❷
                          columns=['numbers'],   ❸
                          index=['a', 'b', 'c', 'd'])   ❹

In [3]: df   ❺
Out[3]:    numbers
        a       10
```

```
       b      20
       c      30
       d      40
```

❶ Imports `pandas`.

❷ Defines the data as a `list` object.

❸ Specifies the column label.

❹ Specifies the index values/labels.

❺ Shows the data as well as column and index labels of the `DataFrame` object.

This simple example already shows some major features of the `DataFrame` class when it comes to storing data:

- Data itself can be provided in different shapes and types (`list`, `tuple`, `ndarray`, and `dict` objects are candidates).
- Data is organized in columns, which can have custom names (labels).
- There is an index that can take on different formats (e.g., numbers, strings, time information).

Working with a `DataFrame` object is in general pretty convenient and efficient with regard to the handling of the object, e.g., compared to regular `ndarray` objects, which are more specialized and more restricted when one wants to (say) enlarge an existing object. At the same time, `DataFrame` objects are often as computationally efficient as `ndarray` objects. The following are simple examples showing how typical operations on a `DataFrame` object work:

```
In [4]: df.index    ❶
Out[4]: Index(['a', 'b', 'c', 'd'], dtype='object')

In [5]: df.columns    ❷
Out[5]: Index(['numbers'], dtype='object')

In [6]: df.loc['c']    ❸
Out[6]: numbers    30
        Name: c, dtype: int64

In [7]: df.loc[['a', 'd']]    ❹
Out[7]:    numbers
        a       10
        d       40

In [8]: df.iloc[1:3]    ❺
Out[8]:    numbers
```

```
            b       20
            c       30

In [9]: df.sum()   ❻
Out[9]: numbers    100
        dtype: int64

In [10]: df.apply(lambda x: x ** 2)   ❼
Out[10]:    numbers
         a      100
         b      400
         c      900
         d     1600

In [11]: df ** 2   ❽
Out[11]:    numbers
         a      100
         b      400
         c      900
         d     1600
```

❶ The index attribute and Index object.

❷ The columns attribute and Index object.

❸ Selects the value corresponding to index c.

❹ Selects the two values corresponding to indices a and d.

❺ Selects the second and third rows via the index positions.

❻ Calculates the sum of the single column.

❼ Uses the apply() method to calculate squares in vectorized fashion.

❽ Applies vectorization directly as with ndarray objects.

Contrary to NumPy ndarray objects, enlarging the DataFrame object in both dimensions is possible:

```
In [12]: df['floats'] = (1.5, 2.5, 3.5, 4.5)   ❶

In [13]: df
Out[13]:    numbers  floats
         a       10     1.5
         b       20     2.5
         c       30     3.5
         d       40     4.5

In [14]: df['floats']   ❷
```

```
Out[14]: a    1.5
         b    2.5
         c    3.5
         d    4.5
         Name: floats, dtype: float64
```

❶ Adds a new column with `float` objects provided as a `tuple` object.

❷ Selects this column and shows its data and index labels.

A whole `DataFrame` object can also be taken to define a new column. In such a case, indices are aligned automatically:

```
In [15]: df['names'] = pd.DataFrame(['Yves', 'Sandra', 'Lilli', 'Henry'],
                                     index=['d', 'a', 'b', 'c'])  ❶

In [16]: df
Out[16]:    numbers  floats   names
         a        10     1.5  Sandra
         b        20     2.5   Lilli
         c        30     3.5   Henry
         d        40     4.5    Yves
```

❶ Another new column is created based on a `DataFrame` object.

Appending data works similarly. However, in the following example a side effect is seen that is usually to be avoided—namely, the index gets replaced by a simple range index:

```
In [17]: df.append({'numbers': 100, 'floats': 5.75, 'names': 'Jil'},
                    ignore_index=True)  ❶
Out[17]:    numbers  floats   names
         0        10    1.50  Sandra
         1        20    2.50   Lilli
         2        30    3.50   Henry
         3        40    4.50    Yves
         4       100    5.75     Jil

In [18]: df = df.append(pd.DataFrame({'numbers': 100, 'floats': 5.75,
                                       'names': 'Jil'}, index=['y',]))  ❷

In [19]: df
Out[19]:    numbers  floats   names
         a        10    1.50  Sandra
         b        20    2.50   Lilli
         c        30    3.50   Henry
         d        40    4.50    Yves
         y       100    5.75     Jil

In [20]: df = df.append(pd.DataFrame({'names': 'Liz'}, index=['z',]),
                        sort=False)  ❸
```

```
In [21]: df
Out[21]:      numbers  floats   names
         a        10.0    1.50  Sandra
         b        20.0    2.50   Lilli
         c        30.0    3.50   Henry
         d        40.0    4.50    Yves
         y       100.0    5.75     Jil
         z         NaN     NaN     Liz

In [22]: df.dtypes  ❹
Out[22]: numbers     float64
         floats      float64
         names        object
         dtype: object
```

❶ Appends a new row via a dict object; this is a temporary operation during which index information gets lost.

❷ Appends the row based on a DataFrame object with index information; the original index information is preserved.

❸ Appends an incomplete data row to the DataFrame object, resulting in NaN values.

❹ Returns the different dtypes of the single columns; this is similar to what's possible with structured ndarray objects.

Although there are now missing values, the majority of method calls will still work:

```
In [23]: df[['numbers', 'floats']].mean()  ❶
Out[23]: numbers    40.00
         floats      3.55
         dtype: float64

In [24]: df[['numbers', 'floats']].std()  ❷
Out[24]: numbers    35.355339
         floats      1.662077
         dtype: float64
```

❶ Calculates the mean over the two columns specified (ignoring rows with NaN values).

❷ Calculates the standard deviation over the two columns specified (ignoring rows with NaN values).

Second Steps with the DataFrame Class

The example in this subsection is based on an `ndarray` object with standard normally distributed random numbers. It explores further features such as a `DatetimeIndex` to manage time series data:

```
In [25]: import numpy as np

In [26]: np.random.seed(100)

In [27]: a = np.random.standard_normal((9, 4))

In [28]: a
Out[28]: array([[-1.74976547,  0.3426804 ,  1.1530358 , -0.25243604],
                [ 0.98132079,  0.51421884,  0.22117967, -1.07004333],
                [-0.18949583,  0.25500144, -0.45802699,  0.43516349],
                [-0.58359505,  0.81684707,  0.67272081, -0.10441114],
                [-0.53128038,  1.02973269, -0.43813562, -1.11831825],
                [ 1.61898166,  1.54160517, -0.25187914, -0.84243574],
                [ 0.18451869,  0.9370822 ,  0.73100034,  1.36155613],
                [-0.32623806,  0.05567601,  0.22239961, -1.443217  ],
                [-0.75635231,  0.81645401,  0.75044476, -0.45594693]])
```

Although one can construct `DataFrame` objects more directly (as seen before), using an `ndarray` object is generally a good choice since `pandas` will retain the basic structure and will "only" add metainformation (e.g., index values). It also represents a typical use case for financial applications and scientific research in general. For example:

```
In [29]: df = pd.DataFrame(a)  ❶

In [30]: df
Out[30]:           0         1         2         3
         0 -1.749765  0.342680  1.153036 -0.252436
         1  0.981321  0.514219  0.221180 -1.070043
         2 -0.189496  0.255001 -0.458027  0.435163
         3 -0.583595  0.816847  0.672721 -0.104411
         4 -0.531280  1.029733 -0.438136 -1.118318
         5  1.618982  1.541605 -0.251879 -0.842436
         6  0.184519  0.937082  0.731000  1.361556
         7 -0.326238  0.055676  0.222400 -1.443217
         8 -0.756352  0.816454  0.750445 -0.455947
```

❶ Creates a `DataFrame` object from the `ndarray` object.

Table 5-1 lists the parameters that the `DataFrame()` function takes. In the table, "array-like" means a data structure similar to an `ndarray` object—a `list`, for example. `Index` is an instance of the pandas `Index` class.

Table 5-1. Parameters of DataFrame() function

Parameter	Format	Description
`data`	`ndarray/dict/DataFrame`	Data for `DataFrame`; `dict` can contain `Series`, `ndarray`, `list`
`index`	Index/array-like	Index to use; defaults to `range(n)`
`columns`	Index/array-like	Column headers to use; defaults to `range(n)`
`dtype`	dtype, default None	Data type to use/force; otherwise, it is inferred
`copy`	bool, default None	Copy data from inputs

As with structured arrays, and as seen before, `DataFrame` objects have column names that can be defined directly by assigning a `list` object with the right number of elements. This illustrates that one can define/change the attributes of the `DataFrame` object easily:

```
In [31]: df.columns = ['No1', 'No2', 'No3', 'No4']   ❶
```

```
In [32]: df
Out[32]:         No1       No2       No3       No4
         0 -1.749765  0.342680  1.153036 -0.252436
         1  0.981321  0.514219  0.221180 -1.070043
         2 -0.189496  0.255001 -0.458027  0.435163
         3 -0.583595  0.816847  0.672721 -0.104411
         4 -0.531280  1.029733 -0.438136 -1.118318
         5  1.618982  1.541605 -0.251879 -0.842436
         6  0.184519  0.937082  0.731000  1.361556
         7 -0.326238  0.055676  0.222400 -1.443217
         8 -0.756352  0.816454  0.750445 -0.455947
```

```
In [33]: df['No2'].mean()   ❷
Out[33]: 0.7010330941456459
```

❶ Specifies the column labels via a `list` object.

❷ Picking a column is now made easy.

To work with financial time series data efficiently, one must be able to handle time indices well. This can also be considered a major strength of `pandas`. For example, assume that our nine data entries in the four columns correspond to month-end data, beginning in January 2019. A `DatetimeIndex` object is then generated with the `date_range()` function as follows:

```
In [34]: dates = pd.date_range('2019-1-1', periods=9, freq='M')   ❶
```

```
In [35]: dates
Out[35]: DatetimeIndex(['2019-01-31', '2019-02-28', '2019-03-31', '2019-04-30',
                        '2019-05-31', '2019-06-30', '2019-07-31', '2019-08-31',
                        '2019-09-30'],
                       dtype='datetime64[ns]', freq='M')
```

❶ Creates a `DatetimeIndex` object.

Table 5-2 lists the parameters that the `date_range()` function takes.

Table 5-2. Parameters of date_range() function

Parameter	Format	Description
start	string/datetime	Left bound for generating dates
end	string/datetime	Right bound for generating dates
periods	integer/None	Number of periods (if start or end is None)
freq	string/DateOffset	Frequency string, e.g., 5D for 5 days
tz	string/None	Time zone name for localized index
normalize	bool, default None	Normalizes start and end to midnight
name	string, default None	Name of resulting index

The following code defines the just-created `DatetimeIndex` object as the relevant index object, making a time series of the original data set:

```
In [36]: df.index = dates

In [37]: df
Out[37]:                   No1       No2       No3       No4
         2019-01-31 -1.749765  0.342680  1.153036 -0.252436
         2019-02-28  0.981321  0.514219  0.221180 -1.070043
         2019-03-31 -0.189496  0.255001 -0.458027  0.435163
         2019-04-30 -0.583595  0.816847  0.672721 -0.104411
         2019-05-31 -0.531280  1.029733 -0.438136 -1.118318
         2019-06-30  1.618982  1.541605 -0.251879 -0.842436
         2019-07-31  0.184519  0.937082  0.731000  1.361556
         2019-08-31 -0.326238  0.055676  0.222400 -1.443217
         2019-09-30 -0.756352  0.816454  0.750445 -0.455947
```

When it comes to the generation of `DatetimeIndex` objects with the help of the `date_range()` function, there are a number of choices for the frequency parameter `freq`. Table 5-3 lists all the options.

Table 5-3. Frequency parameter values for date_range() function

Alias	Description
B	Business day frequency
C	Custom business day frequency (experimental)
D	Calendar day frequency
W	Weekly frequency
M	Month end frequency
BM	Business month end frequency

Alias	Description
MS	Month start frequency
BMS	Business month start frequency
Q	Quarter end frequency
BQ	Business quarter end frequency
QS	Quarter start frequency
BQS	Business quarter start frequency
A	Year end frequency
BA	Business year end frequency
AS	Year start frequency
BAS	Business year start frequency
H	Hourly frequency
T	Minutely frequency
S	Secondly frequency
L	Milliseconds
U	Microseconds

In some circumstances, it pays off to have access to the original data set in the form of the ndarray object. The values attribute provides direct access to it:

```
In [38]: df.values
Out[38]: array([[-1.74976547,  0.3426804 ,  1.1530358 , -0.25243604],
                [ 0.98132079,  0.51421884,  0.22117967, -1.07004333],
                [-0.18949583,  0.25500144, -0.45802699,  0.43516349],
                [-0.58359505,  0.81684707,  0.67272081, -0.10441114],
                [-0.53128038,  1.02973269, -0.43813562, -1.11831825],
                [ 1.61898166,  1.54160517, -0.25187914, -0.84243574],
                [ 0.18451869,  0.9370822 ,  0.73100034,  1.36155613],
                [-0.32623806,  0.05567601,  0.22239961, -1.443217  ],
                [-0.75635231,  0.81645401,  0.75044476, -0.45594693]])

In [39]: np.array(df)
Out[39]: array([[-1.74976547,  0.3426804 ,  1.1530358 , -0.25243604],
                [ 0.98132079,  0.51421884,  0.22117967, -1.07004333],
                [-0.18949583,  0.25500144, -0.45802699,  0.43516349],
                [-0.58359505,  0.81684707,  0.67272081, -0.10441114],
                [-0.53128038,  1.02973269, -0.43813562, -1.11831825],
                [ 1.61898166,  1.54160517, -0.25187914, -0.84243574],
                [ 0.18451869,  0.9370822 ,  0.73100034,  1.36155613],
                [-0.32623806,  0.05567601,  0.22239961, -1.443217  ],
                [-0.75635231,  0.81645401,  0.75044476, -0.45594693]])
```

Arrays and DataFrames

One can generate a `DataFrame` object from an `ndarray` object, but one can also easily generate an `ndarray` object out of a `DataFrame` by using the `values` attribute of the `DataFrame` class or the function `np.array()` of NumPy.

Basic Analytics

Like the `NumPy` `ndarray` class, the pandas `DataFrame` class has a multitude of convenience methods built in. As a starter, consider the methods `info()` and `describe()`:

```
In [40]: df.info()  ❶
         <class 'pandas.core.frame.DataFrame'>
         DatetimeIndex: 9 entries, 2019-01-31 to 2019-09-30
         Freq: M
         Data columns (total 4 columns):
         No1    9 non-null float64
         No2    9 non-null float64
         No3    9 non-null float64
         No4    9 non-null float64
         dtypes: float64(4)
         memory usage: 360.0 bytes

In [41]: df.describe()  ❷
Out[41]:            No1       No2       No3       No4
         count  9.000000  9.000000  9.000000  9.000000
         mean  -0.150212  0.701033  0.289193 -0.387788
         std    0.988306  0.457685  0.579920  0.877532
         min   -1.749765  0.055676 -0.458027 -1.443217
         25%   -0.583595  0.342680 -0.251879 -1.070043
         50%   -0.326238  0.816454  0.222400 -0.455947
         75%    0.184519  0.937082  0.731000 -0.104411
         max    1.618982  1.541605  1.153036  1.361556
```

❶ Provides metainformation regarding the data, columns, and index.

❷ Provides helpful summary statistics per column (for numerical data).

In addition, one can easily get the column-wise or row-wise sums, means, and cumulative sums:

```
In [43]: df.sum()  ❶
Out[43]: No1   -1.351906
         No2    6.309298
         No3    2.602739
         No4   -3.490089
         dtype: float64

In [44]: df.mean()  ❷
```

```
Out[44]: No1   -0.150212
         No2    0.701033
         No3    0.289193
         No4   -0.387788
         dtype: float64

In [45]: df.mean(axis=0)    ❷
Out[45]: No1   -0.150212
         No2    0.701033
         No3    0.289193
         No4   -0.387788
         dtype: float64

In [46]: df.mean(axis=1)    ❸
Out[46]: 2019-01-31   -0.126621
         2019-02-28    0.161669
         2019-03-31    0.010661
         2019-04-30    0.200390
         2019-05-31   -0.264500
         2019-06-30    0.516568
         2019-07-31    0.803539
         2019-08-31   -0.372845
         2019-09-30    0.088650
         Freq: M, dtype: float64

In [47]: df.cumsum()    ❹
Out[47]:                   No1       No2       No3       No4
         2019-01-31 -1.749765  0.342680  1.153036 -0.252436
         2019-02-28 -0.768445  0.856899  1.374215 -1.322479
         2019-03-31 -0.957941  1.111901  0.916188 -0.887316
         2019-04-30 -1.541536  1.928748  1.588909 -0.991727
         2019-05-31 -2.072816  2.958480  1.150774 -2.110045
         2019-06-30 -0.453834  4.500086  0.898895 -2.952481
         2019-07-31 -0.269316  5.437168  1.629895 -1.590925
         2019-08-31 -0.595554  5.492844  1.852294 -3.034142
         2019-09-30 -1.351906  6.309298  2.602739 -3.490089
```

❶ Column-wise sum.

❷ Column-wise mean.

❸ Row-wise mean.

❹ Column-wise cumulative sum (starting at first index position).

DataFrame objects also understand NumPy universal functions, as expected:

```
In [48]: np.mean(df)    ❶
Out[48]: No1   -0.150212
         No2    0.701033
         No3    0.289193
         No4   -0.387788
```

```
          dtype: float64

In [49]: np.log(df)  ❷
Out[49]:                 No1       No2       No3       No4
         2019-01-31      NaN -1.070957  0.142398      NaN
         2019-02-28 -0.018856 -0.665106 -1.508780      NaN
         2019-03-31      NaN -1.366486      NaN -0.832033
         2019-04-30      NaN -0.202303 -0.396425      NaN
         2019-05-31      NaN  0.029299      NaN      NaN
         2019-06-30  0.481797  0.432824      NaN      NaN
         2019-07-31 -1.690005 -0.064984 -0.313341  0.308628
         2019-08-31      NaN -2.888206 -1.503279      NaN
         2019-09-30      NaN -0.202785 -0.287089      NaN

In [50]: np.sqrt(abs(df))  ❸
Out[50]:                 No1       No2       No3       No4
         2019-01-31  1.322787  0.585389  1.073795  0.502430
         2019-02-28  0.990616  0.717091  0.470297  1.034429
         2019-03-31  0.435311  0.504977  0.676777  0.659669
         2019-04-30  0.763934  0.903796  0.820196  0.323127
         2019-05-31  0.728890  1.014757  0.661918  1.057506
         2019-06-30  1.272392  1.241614  0.501876  0.917843
         2019-07-31  0.429556  0.968030  0.854986  1.166857
         2019-08-31  0.571173  0.235958  0.471593  1.201340
         2019-09-30  0.869685  0.903578  0.866282  0.675238

In [51]: np.sqrt(abs(df)).sum()  ❹
Out[51]: No1    7.384345
         No2    7.075190
         No3    6.397719
         No4    7.538440
         dtype: float64

In [52]: 100 * df + 100  ❺
Out[52]:                 No1       No2       No3       No4
         2019-01-31 -74.976547 134.268040 215.303580  74.756396
         2019-02-28 198.132079 151.421884 122.117967  -7.004333
         2019-03-31  81.050417 125.500144  54.197301 143.516349
         2019-04-30  41.640495 181.684707 167.272081  89.558886
         2019-05-31  46.871962 202.973269  56.186438 -11.831825
         2019-06-30 261.898166 254.160517  74.812086  15.756426
         2019-07-31 118.451869 193.708220 173.100034 236.155613
         2019-08-31  67.376194 105.567601 122.239961 -44.321700
         2019-09-30  24.364769 181.645401 175.044476  54.405307
```

❶ Column-wise mean.

❷ Element-wise natural logarithm; a warning is raised but the calculation runs
through, resulting in multiple NaN values.

❸ Element-wise square root for the absolute values …

❹ … and column-wise mean values for the results.

❺ A linear transform of the numerical data.

NumPy Universal Functions

In general, one can apply NumPy universal functions to pandas DataFrame objects whenever they could be applied to an ndarray object containing the same type of data.

pandas is quite error tolerant, in the sense that it captures errors and just puts a NaN value where the respective mathematical operation fails. Not only this, but as briefly shown before, one can also work with such incomplete data sets as if they were complete in a number of cases. This comes in handy, since reality is characterized by incomplete data sets more often than one might wish.

Basic Visualization

Plotting of data is only one line of code away in general, once the data is stored in a DataFrame object (see Figure 5-1):

```
In [53]: from pylab import plt, mpl    ❶
         plt.style.use('seaborn')    ❶
         mpl.rcParams['font.family'] = 'serif'    ❶
         %matplotlib inline

In [54]: df.cumsum().plot(lw=2.0, figsize=(10, 6));    ❷
```

❶ Customizing the plotting style.

❷ Plotting the cumulative sums of the four columns as a line plot.

Basically, pandas provides a wrapper around matplotlib (see Chapter 7), specifically designed for DataFrame objects. Table 5-4 lists the parameters that the plot() method takes.

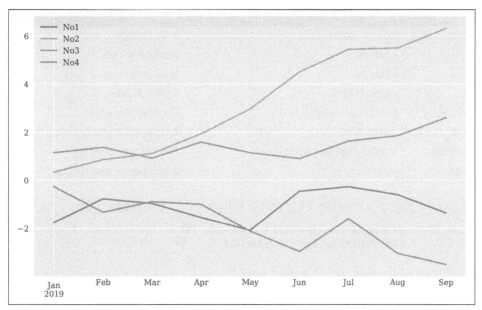

Figure 5-1. Line plot of a DataFrame object

Table 5-4. Parameters of plot() method

Parameter	Format	Description
x	label/position, default None	Only used when column values are x-ticks
y	label/position, default None	Only used when column values are y-ticks
subplots	boolean, default False	Plot columns in subplots
sharex	boolean, default True	Share the x-axis
sharey	boolean, default False	Share the y-axis
use_index	boolean, default True	Use DataFrame.index as x-ticks
stacked	boolean, default False	Stack (only for bar plots)
sort_columns	boolean, default False	Sort columns alphabetically before plotting
title	string, default None	Title for the plot
grid	boolean, default False	Show horizontal and vertical grid lines
legend	boolean, default True	Show legend of labels
ax	matplotlib axis object	matplotlib axis object to use for plotting
style	string or list/dictionary	Line plotting style (for each column)
kind	string (e.g., "line", "bar", "barh", "kde", "density")	Type of plot
logx	boolean, default False	Use logarithmic scaling of x-axis
logy	boolean, default False	Use logarithmic scaling of y-axis
xticks	sequence, default Index	X-ticks for the plot

Parameter	Format	Description
yticks	sequence, default Values	Y-ticks for the plot
xlim	2-tuple, list	Boundaries for x-axis
ylim	2-tuple, list	Boundaries for y-axis
rot	integer, default None	Rotation of x-ticks
secondary_y	boolean/sequence, default False	Plot on secondary y-axis
mark_right	boolean, default True	Automatic labeling of secondary axis
colormap	string/colormap object, default None	Color map to use for plotting
kwds	keywords	Options to pass to matplotlib

As another example, consider a bar plot of the same data (see Figure 5-2):

```
In [55]: df.plot.bar(figsize=(10, 6), rot=15);   ❶
         # df.plot(kind='bar', figsize=(10, 6))  ❷
```

❶ Plots the bar chart via .plot.bar().

❷ Alternative syntax: uses the kind parameter to change the plot type.

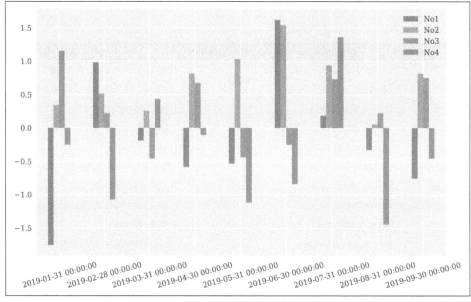

Figure 5-2. Bar plot of a DataFrame object

The Series Class

So far this chapter has worked mainly with the pandas DataFrame class. Series is another important class that comes with pandas. It is characterized by the fact that it has only a single column of data. In that sense, it is a specialization of the DataFrame class that shares many but not all of its characteristics and capabilities. A Series object is obtained when a single column is selected from a multicolumn DataFrame object:

```
In [56]: type(df)
Out[56]: pandas.core.frame.DataFrame

In [57]: S = pd.Series(np.linspace(0, 15, 7), name='series')

In [58]: S
Out[58]: 0     0.0
         1     2.5
         2     5.0
         3     7.5
         4    10.0
         5    12.5
         6    15.0
         Name: series, dtype: float64

In [59]: type(S)
Out[59]: pandas.core.series.Series

In [60]: s = df['No1']

In [61]: s
Out[61]: 2019-01-31   -1.749765
         2019-02-28    0.981321
         2019-03-31   -0.189496
         2019-04-30   -0.583595
         2019-05-31   -0.531280
         2019-06-30    1.618982
         2019-07-31    0.184519
         2019-08-31   -0.326238
         2019-09-30   -0.756352
         Freq: M, Name: No1, dtype: float64

In [62]: type(s)
Out[62]: pandas.core.series.Series
```

The main DataFrame methods are available for Series objects as well. For illustration, consider the mean() and plot() methods (see Figure 5-3):

```
In [63]: s.mean()
Out[63]: -0.15021177307319458

In [64]: s.plot(lw=2.0, figsize=(10, 6));
```

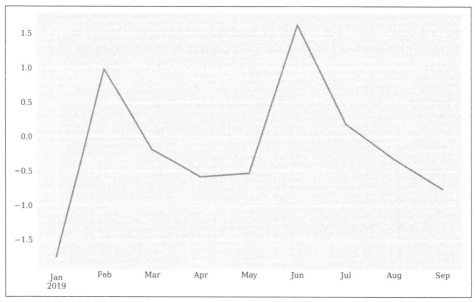

Figure 5-3. Line plot of a Series object

GroupBy Operations

pandas has powerful and flexible grouping capabilities. They work similarly to grouping in SQL as well as pivot tables in Microsoft Excel. To have something to group by
one can add, for instance, a column indicating the quarter the respective data of the
index belongs to:

```
In [65]: df['Quarter'] = ['Q1', 'Q1', 'Q1', 'Q2', 'Q2',
                          'Q2', 'Q3', 'Q3', 'Q3']
         df
Out[65]:                    No1       No2       No3       No4 Quarter
         2019-01-31 -1.749765  0.342680  1.153036 -0.252436      Q1
         2019-02-28  0.981321  0.514219  0.221180 -1.070043      Q1
         2019-03-31 -0.189496  0.255001 -0.458027  0.435163      Q1
         2019-04-30 -0.583595  0.816847  0.672721 -0.104411      Q2
         2019-05-31 -0.531280  1.029733 -0.438136 -1.118318      Q2
         2019-06-30  1.618982  1.541605 -0.251879 -0.842436      Q2
         2019-07-31  0.184519  0.937082  0.731000  1.361556      Q3
         2019-08-31 -0.326238  0.055676  0.222400 -1.443217      Q3
         2019-09-30 -0.756352  0.816454  0.750445 -0.455947      Q3
```

The following code groups by the Quarter column and outputs statistics for the single groups:

```
In [66]: groups = df.groupby('Quarter')  ❶
```

```
In [67]: groups.size()  ❷
```

```
Out[67]: Quarter
         Q1    3
         Q2    3
         Q3    3
         dtype: int64

In [68]: groups.mean()    ❸
Out[68]:                  No1        No2        No3        No4
         Quarter
         Q1         -0.319314   0.370634   0.305396  -0.295772
         Q2          0.168035   1.129395  -0.005765  -0.688388
         Q3         -0.299357   0.603071   0.567948  -0.179203

In [69]: groups.max()    ❹
Out[69]:                  No1        No2        No3        No4
         Quarter
         Q1          0.981321   0.514219   1.153036   0.435163
         Q2          1.618982   1.541605   0.672721  -0.104411
         Q3          0.184519   0.937082   0.750445   1.361556

In [70]: groups.aggregate([min, max]).round(2)    ❺
Out[70]:         No1          No2          No3          No4
                 min    max   min    max   min    max   min    max
         Quarter
         Q1     -1.75   0.98  0.26   0.51 -0.46   1.15 -1.07   0.44
         Q2     -0.58   1.62  0.82   1.54 -0.44   0.67 -1.12  -0.10
         Q3     -0.76   0.18  0.06   0.94  0.22   0.75 -1.44   1.36
```

❶ Groups according to the Quarter column.

❷ Gives the number of rows in each group.

❸ Gives the mean per column.

❹ Gives the maximum value per column.

❺ Gives both the minimum and maximum values per column.

Grouping can also be done with multiple columns. To this end, another column, indicating whether the month of the index date is odd or even, is introduced:

```
In [71]: df['Odd_Even'] = ['Odd', 'Even', 'Odd', 'Even', 'Odd', 'Even',
                           'Odd', 'Even', 'Odd']

In [72]: groups = df.groupby(['Quarter', 'Odd_Even'])

In [73]: groups.size()
Out[73]: Quarter  Odd_Even
         Q1       Even        1
                  Odd         2
         Q2       Even        2
```

```
                    Odd       1
         Q3         Even      1
                    Odd       2
         dtype: int64

In [74]: groups[['No1', 'No4']].aggregate([sum, np.mean])
Out[74]:                          No1                No4
                             sum      mean       sum      mean
         Quarter Odd_Even
         Q1      Even      0.981321  0.981321 -1.070043 -1.070043
                 Odd      -1.939261 -0.969631  0.182727  0.091364
         Q2      Even      1.035387  0.517693 -0.946847 -0.473423
                 Odd      -0.531280 -0.531280 -1.118318 -1.118318
         Q3      Even     -0.326238 -0.326238 -1.443217 -1.443217
                 Odd      -0.571834 -0.285917  0.905609  0.452805
```

Complex Selection

Often, data selection is accomplished by formulation of conditions on column values, and potentially combining multiple such conditions logically. Consider the following data set:

```
In [75]: data = np.random.standard_normal((10, 2))   ❶

In [76]: df = pd.DataFrame(data, columns=['x', 'y'])   ❷

In [77]: df.info()   ❷
         <class 'pandas.core.frame.DataFrame'>
         RangeIndex: 10 entries, 0 to 9
         Data columns (total 2 columns):
         x    10 non-null float64
         y    10 non-null float64
         dtypes: float64(2)
         memory usage: 240.0 bytes

In [78]: df.head()   ❸
Out[78]:          x         y
         0  1.189622 -1.690617
         1 -1.356399 -1.232435
         2 -0.544439 -0.668172
         3  0.007315 -0.612939
         4  1.299748 -1.733096

In [79]: df.tail()   ❹
Out[79]:          x         y
         5 -0.983310  0.357508
         6 -1.613579  1.470714
         7 -1.188018 -0.549746
         8 -0.940046 -0.827932
         9  0.108863  0.507810
```

❶   ndarray object with standard normally distributed random numbers.

❷   DataFrame object with the same random numbers.

❸   The first five rows via the head() method.

❹   The final five rows via the tail() method.

The following code illustrates the application of Python's comparison operators and logical operators on values in the two columns:

```
In [80]: df['x'] > 0.5   ❶
Out[80]: 0    True
         1    False
         2    False
         3    False
         4    True
         5    False
         6    False
         7    False
         8    False
         9    False
         Name: x, dtype: bool

In [81]: (df['x'] > 0) & (df['y'] < 0)   ❷
Out[81]: 0    True
         1    False
         2    False
         3    True
         4    True
         5    False
         6    False
         7    False
         8    False
         9    False
         dtype: bool

In [82]: (df['x'] > 0) | (df['y'] < 0)   ❸
Out[82]: 0    True
         1    True
         2    True
         3    True
         4    True
         5    False
         6    False
         7    True
         8    True
         9    True
         dtype: bool
```

❶ Check whether value in column x is greater than 0.5.

❷ Check whether value in column x is positive *and* value in column y is negative.

❸ Check whether value in column x is positive *or* value in column y is negative.

Using the resulting Boolean `Series` objects, complex data (row) selection is straightforward. Alternatively, one can use the `query()` method and pass the conditions as `str` objects:

```
In [83]: df[df['x'] > 0]    ❶
Out[83]:          x          y
         0  1.189622 -1.690617
         3  0.007315 -0.612939
         4  1.299748 -1.733096
         9  0.108863  0.507810

In [84]: df.query('x > 0')    ❶
Out[84]:          x          y
         0  1.189622 -1.690617
         3  0.007315 -0.612939
         4  1.299748 -1.733096
         9  0.108863  0.507810

In [85]: df[(df['x'] > 0) & (df['y'] < 0)]    ❷
Out[85]:          x          y
         0  1.189622 -1.690617
         3  0.007315 -0.612939
         4  1.299748 -1.733096

In [86]: df.query('x > 0 & y < 0')    ❷
Out[86]:          x          y
         0  1.189622 -1.690617
         3  0.007315 -0.612939
         4  1.299748 -1.733096

In [87]: df[(df.x > 0) | (df.y < 0)]    ❸
Out[87]:          x          y
         0  1.189622 -1.690617
         1 -1.356399 -1.232435
         2 -0.544439 -0.668172
         3  0.007315 -0.612939
         4  1.299748 -1.733096
         7 -1.188018 -0.549746
         8 -0.940046 -0.827932
         9  0.108863  0.507810
```

❶ All rows for which the value in column x is greater than 0.

❷ All rows for which the value in column x is positive *and* the value in column y is negative.

❸ All rows for which the value in column x is positive *or* the value in column y is negative (columns are accessed here via the respective attributes).

Comparison operators can also be applied to complete `DataFrame` objects at once:

```
In [88]: df > 0    ❶
Out[88]:       x      y
         0   True  False
         1  False  False
         2  False  False
         3   True  False
         4   True  False
         5  False   True
         6  False   True
         7  False  False
         8  False  False
         9   True   True

In [89]: df[df > 0]    ❷
Out[89]:          x         y
         0  1.189622       NaN
         1       NaN       NaN
         2       NaN       NaN
         3  0.007315       NaN
         4  1.299748       NaN
         5       NaN  0.357508
         6       NaN  1.470714
         7       NaN       NaN
         8       NaN       NaN
         9  0.108863  0.507810
```

❶ Which values in the `DataFrame` object are positive?

❷ Select all such values and put a NaN in all other places.

Concatenation, Joining, and Merging

This section walks through different approaches to combine two simple data sets in the form of `DataFrame` objects. The two simple data sets are:

```
In [90]: df1 = pd.DataFrame(['100', '200', '300', '400'],
                            index=['a', 'b', 'c', 'd'],
                            columns=['A',])

In [91]: df1
Out[91]:    A
         a  100
```

```
             b  200
             c  300
             d  400

In [92]: df2 = pd.DataFrame(['200', '150', '50'],
                            index=['f', 'b', 'd'],
                            columns=['B',])

In [93]: df2
Out[93]:      B
          f  200
          b  150
          d   50
```

Concatenation

Concatenation or *appending* basically means that rows are added from one `DataFrame` object to another one. This can be accomplished via the `append()` method or via the `pd.concat()` function. A major consideration is how the index values are handled:

```
In [94]: df1.append(df2, sort=False)    ❶
Out[94]:      A    B
          a  100  NaN
          b  200  NaN
          c  300  NaN
          d  400  NaN
          f  NaN  200
          b  NaN  150
          d  NaN   50

In [95]: df1.append(df2, ignore_index=True, sort=False)    ❷
Out[95]:      A    B
          0  100  NaN
          1  200  NaN
          2  300  NaN
          3  400  NaN
          4  NaN  200
          5  NaN  150
          6  NaN   50

In [96]: pd.concat((df1, df2), sort=False)    ❸
Out[96]:      A    B
          a  100  NaN
          b  200  NaN
          c  300  NaN
          d  400  NaN
          f  NaN  200
          b  NaN  150
          d  NaN   50

In [97]: pd.concat((df1, df2), ignore_index=True, sort=False)    ❹
Out[97]:      A    B
```

```
0   100   NaN
1   200   NaN
2   300   NaN
3   400   NaN
4   NaN   200
5   NaN   150
6   NaN    50
```

❶ Appends data from `df2` to `df1` as new rows.

❷ Does the same but ignores the indices.

❸ Has the same effect as the first append operation.

❹ Has the same effect as the second append operation.

Joining

When joining the two data sets, the sequence of the `DataFrame` objects also matters but in a different way. Only the index values from the first `DataFrame` object are used. This default behavior is called a *left join*:

```
In [98]: df1.join(df2)  ❶
Out[98]:        A    B
           a  100  NaN
           b  200  150
           c  300  NaN
           d  400   50

In [99]: df2.join(df1)  ❷
Out[99]:        B    A
           f  200  NaN
           b  150  200
           d   50  400
```

❶ Index values of `df1` are relevant.

❷ Index values of `df2` are relevant.

There are a total of four different join methods available, each leading to a different behavior with regard to how index values and the corresponding data rows are handled:

```
In [100]: df1.join(df2, how='left')  ❶
Out[100]:        A    B
            a  100  NaN
            b  200  150
            c  300  NaN
            d  400   50
```

```
In [101]: df1.join(df2, how='right')   ❷
Out[101]:      A    B
          f  NaN  200
          b  200  150
          d  400   50

In [102]: df1.join(df2, how='inner')   ❸
Out[102]:      A    B
          b  200  150
          d  400   50

In [103]: df1.join(df2, how='outer')   ❹
Out[103]:      A    B
          a  100  NaN
          b  200  150
          c  300  NaN
          d  400   50
          f  NaN  200
```

❶   Left join is the default operation.

❷   Right join is the same as reversing the sequence of the DataFrame objects.

❸   Inner join only preserves those index values found in both indices.

❹   Outer join preserves all index values from both indices.

A join can also happen based on an empty DataFrame object. In this case, the columns are created *sequentially*, leading to behavior similar to a left join:

```
In [104]: df = pd.DataFrame()

In [105]: df['A'] = df1['A']   ❶

In [106]: df
Out[106]:      A
          a  100
          b  200
          c  300
          d  400

In [107]: df['B'] = df2   ❷

In [108]: df
Out[108]:      A    B
          a  100  NaN
          b  200  150
          c  300  NaN
          d  400   50
```

❶   df1 as first column A.

❷ df2 as second column B.

Making use of a dictionary to combine the data sets yields a result similar to an outer join since the columns are created *simultaneously*:

```
In [109]: df = pd.DataFrame({'A': df1['A'], 'B': df2['B']})  ❶
```

```
In [110]: df
Out[110]:      A    B
          a  100  NaN
          b  200  150
          c  300  NaN
          d  400   50
          f  NaN  200
```

❶ The columns of the `DataFrame` objects are used as values in the `dict` object.

Merging

While a join operation takes place based on the indices of the `DataFrame` objects to be joined, a merge operation typically takes place on a column shared between the two data sets. To this end, a new column C is added to both original `DataFrame` objects:

```
In [111]: c = pd.Series([250, 150, 50], index=['b', 'd', 'c'])
          df1['C'] = c
          df2['C'] = c
```

```
In [112]: df1
Out[112]:      A      C
          a  100    NaN
          b  200  250.0
          c  300   50.0
          d  400  150.0
```

```
In [113]: df2
Out[113]:      B      C
          f  200    NaN
          b  150  250.0
          d   50  150.0
```

By default, the merge operation in this case takes place based on the single shared column C. Other options are available, however, such as an *outer* merge:

```
In [114]: pd.merge(df1, df2)  ❶
Out[114]:      A      C    B
          0  100    NaN  200
          1  200  250.0  150
          2  400  150.0   50
```

```
In [115]: pd.merge(df1, df2, on='C')  ❶
Out[115]:      A      C    B
```

```
                    0   100    NaN   200
                    1   200  250.0   150
                    2   400  150.0    50

In [116]: pd.merge(df1, df2, how='outer')  ❷
Out[116]:        A      C     B
              0  100    NaN   200
              1  200  250.0   150
              2  300   50.0   NaN
              3  400  150.0    50
```

❶ The default merge on column C.

❷ An outer merge is also possible, preserving all data rows.

Many more types of merge operations are available, a few of which are illustrated in the following code:

```
In [117]: pd.merge(df1, df2, left_on='A', right_on='B')
Out[117]:        A    C_x    B  C_y
              0  200  250.0  200  NaN

In [118]: pd.merge(df1, df2, left_on='A', right_on='B', how='outer')
Out[118]:        A    C_x    B    C_y
              0  100    NaN  NaN    NaN
              1  200  250.0  200    NaN
              2  300   50.0  NaN    NaN
              3  400  150.0  NaN    NaN
              4  NaN    NaN  150  250.0
              5  NaN    NaN   50  150.0

In [119]: pd.merge(df1, df2, left_index=True, right_index=True)
Out[119]:        A    C_x    B    C_y
              b  200  250.0  150  250.0
              d  400  150.0   50  150.0

In [120]: pd.merge(df1, df2, on='C', left_index=True)
Out[120]:        A      C    B
              f  100    NaN  200
              b  200  250.0  150
              d  400  150.0   50

In [121]: pd.merge(df1, df2, on='C', right_index=True)
Out[121]:        A      C    B
              a  100    NaN  200
              b  200  250.0  150
              d  400  150.0   50

In [122]: pd.merge(df1, df2, on='C', left_index=True, right_index=True)
Out[122]:        A      C    B
              b  200  250.0  150
              d  400  150.0   50
```

Performance Aspects

Many examples in this chapter illustrate that there are often multiple options to achieve the same goal with pandas. This section compares such options for adding up two columns element-wise. First, the data set, generated with NumPy:

```
In [123]: data = np.random.standard_normal((1000000, 2))    ❶

In [124]: data.nbytes    ❶
Out[124]: 16000000

In [125]: df = pd.DataFrame(data, columns=['x', 'y'])    ❷

In [126]: df.info()    ❷
          <class 'pandas.core.frame.DataFrame'>
          RangeIndex: 1000000 entries, 0 to 999999
          Data columns (total 2 columns):
          x    1000000 non-null float64
          y    1000000 non-null float64
          dtypes: float64(2)
          memory usage: 15.3 MB
```

❶ The ndarray object with random numbers.

❷ The DataFrame object with the random numbers.

Second, some options to accomplish the task at hand with performance values:

```
In [127]: %time res = df['x'] + df['y']    ❶
          CPU times: user 7.35 ms, sys: 7.43 ms, total: 14.8 ms
          Wall time: 7.48 ms

In [128]: res[:3]
Out[128]: 0    0.387242
          1   -0.969343
          2   -0.863159
          dtype: float64

In [129]: %time res = df.sum(axis=1)    ❷
          CPU times: user 130 ms, sys: 30.6 ms, total: 161 ms
          Wall time: 101 ms

In [130]: res[:3]
Out[130]: 0    0.387242
          1   -0.969343
          2   -0.863159
          dtype: float64

In [131]: %time res = df.values.sum(axis=1)    ❸
          CPU times: user 50.3 ms, sys: 2.75 ms, total: 53.1 ms
          Wall time: 27.9 ms
```

```
In [132]: res[:3]
Out[132]: array([ 0.3872424 , -0.96934273, -0.86315944])

In [133]: %time res = np.sum(df, axis=1)   ❹
          CPU times: user 127 ms, sys: 15.1 ms, total: 142 ms
          Wall time: 73.7 ms

In [134]: res[:3]
Out[134]: 0    0.387242
          1   -0.969343
          2   -0.863159
          dtype: float64

In [135]: %time res = np.sum(df.values, axis=1)   ❺
          CPU times: user 49.3 ms, sys: 2.36 ms, total: 51.7 ms
          Wall time: 26.9 ms

In [136]: res[:3]
Out[136]: array([ 0.3872424 , -0.96934273, -0.86315944])
```

❶ Working with the columns (Series objects) directly is the fastest approach.

❷ This calculates the sums by calling the sum() method on the DataFrame object.

❸ This calculates the sums by calling the sum() method on the ndarray object.

❹ This calculates the sums by using the function np.sum() on the DataFrame object.

❺ This calculates the sums by using the function np.sum() on the ndarray object.

Finally, two more options which are based on the methods eval() and apply(), respectively:[1]

```
In [137]: %time res = df.eval('x + y')   ❶
          CPU times: user 25.5 ms, sys: 17.7 ms, total: 43.2 ms
          Wall time: 22.5 ms

In [138]: res[:3]
Out[138]: 0    0.387242
          1   -0.969343
          2   -0.863159
          dtype: float64

In [139]: %time res = df.apply(lambda row: row['x'] + row['y'], axis=1)   ❷
          CPU times: user 19.6 s, sys: 83.3 ms, total: 19.7 s
```

---

1 The application of the eval() method requires the numexpr package (*http://bit.ly/2qNWFrH*) to be installed.

```
        Wall time: 19.9 s

In [140]: res[:3]
Out[140]: 0     0.387242
          1    -0.969343
          2    -0.863159
          dtype: float64
```

❶ eval() is a method dedicated to evaluation of (complex) numerical expressions;
   columns can be directly addressed.

❷ The slowest option is to use the apply() method row-by-row; this is like looping
   on the Python level over all rows.

> **Choose Wisely**
>
> pandas often provides multiple options to accomplish the same
> goal. If unsure of which to use, compare the options to verify that
> the best possible performance is achieved when time is critical. In
> this simple example, execution times differ by orders of magnitude.

Conclusion

pandas is a powerful tool for data analysis and has become the central package in the
so-called *PyData* stack. Its DataFrame class is particularly suited to working with tabular data of any kind. Most operations on such objects are vectorized, leading not
only—as in the NumPy case—to concise code but also to high performance in general.
In addition, pandas makes working with incomplete data sets convenient (which is
not the case with NumPy, for instance). pandas and the DataFrame class will be central
in many later chapters of the book, where additional features will be used and introduced when necessary.

Further Reading

pandas is an open source project with both online documentation and a PDF version
available for download.[2] The website provides links to both, and additional resources:

• *http://pandas.pydata.org/*

---

2 At the time of this writing, the PDF version has a total of more than 2,500 pages.

As for NumPy, recommended references for pandas in book form are:

- McKinney, Wes (2017). *Python for Data Analysis*. Sebastopol, CA: O'Reilly.
- VanderPlas, Jake (2016). *Python Data Science Handbook*. Sebastopol, CA: O'Reilly.

## CHAPTER 6

Object-Oriented Programming

> The purpose of software engineering is to control complexity, not to create it.
>
> —Pamela Zave

Object-oriented programming (OOP) is one of the most popular programming paradigms today. Used in the right way, it provides a number of advantages compared to, for example, procedural programming. In many cases, OOP seems to be particularly suited for financial modeling and implementing financial algorithms. However, there are also many critics, voicing their skepticism about single aspects of OOP or even the paradigm as a whole. This chapter takes a neutral stance, in that OOP is considered an important tool that might not be the best one for every single problem, but that should be at the disposal of programmers and quants working in finance.

With OOP, some new language comes along. The most important terms for the purposes of this book and chapter are (more follow later):

Class
    An abstract definition of a certain type of objects. For example, a human being.

Object
    An instance of a class. For example, Sandra.

Attribute
    A feature of the class (*class attribute*) or of an instance of the class (*instance attribute*). For example, being a mammal, being male or female, or color of the eyes.

Method
    An operation that the class or an instance of the class can implement. For example, walking.

Parameters
   Input taken by a method to influence its behavior. For example, three steps.

Instantiation
   The process of creating a specific object based on an abstract class.

Translated into Python code, a simple class implementing the example of a human being might look as follows:

```
In [1]: class HumanBeing(object):    ❶
            def __init__(self, first_name, eye_color):    ❷
                self.first_name = first_name    ❸
                self.eye_color = eye_color    ❹
                self.position = 0    ❺
            def walk_steps(self, steps):    ❻
                self.position += steps    ❼
```

❶   Class definition statement; `self` refers to the current instance of the class.

❷   Special method called during instantiation.

❸   First name attribute initialized with parameter value.

❹   Eye color attribute initialized with parameter value.

❺   Position attribute initialized with 0.

❻   Method definition for walking with `steps` as parameter.

❼   Code that changes the position given the `steps` value.

Based on the class definition, a new Python object can be instantiated and used:

```
In [2]: Sandra = HumanBeing('Sandra', 'blue')    ❶

In [3]: Sandra.first_name    ❷
Out[3]: 'Sandra'

In [4]: Sandra.position    ❷
Out[4]: 0

In [5]: Sandra.walk_steps(5)    ❸

In [6]: Sandra.position    ❹
Out[6]: 5
```

❶   The instantiation.

❷   Accessing attribute values.

❸ Calling the method.

❹ Accessing the updated `position` value.

There are several *human aspects* that might speak for the use of OOP:

Natural way of thinking
Human thinking typically evolves around real-world or abstract objects, like a car or a financial instrument. OOP is suited to modeling such objects with their characteristics.

Reducing complexity
Via different approaches, OOP helps to reduce the complexity of a problem or algorithm and to model it feature-by-feature.

Nicer user interfaces
OOP allows in many cases for nicer user interfaces and more compact code. This becomes evident, for example, when looking at the `NumPy ndarray` class or `pandas DataFrame` class.

Pythonic way of modeling
Independent of the pros and cons of OOP, it is simply the dominant paradigm in Python. This is where the saying "everything is an object in Python" comes from. OOP also allows the programmer to build custom classes whose instances behave like every other instance of a standard Python class.

There are also several *technical aspects* that might speak for OOP:

Abstraction
The use of attributes and methods allows building abstract, flexible models of objects, with a focus on what is relevant and neglecting what is not needed. In finance, this might mean having a general class that models a financial instrument in abstract fashion. Instances of such a class would then be concrete financial products, engineered and offered by an investment bank, for example.

Modularity
OOP simplifies breaking code down into multiple modules which are then linked to form the complete codebase. For example, modeling a European option on a stock could be achieved by a single class or by two classes, one for the underlying stock and one for the option itself.

Inheritance
Inheritance refers to the concept that one class can *inherit* attributes and methods from another class. In finance, starting with a general financial instrument, the next level could be a general derivative instrument, then a European option,

then a European call option. Every class might inherit attributes and methods from class(es) on a higher level.

Aggregation

Aggregation refers to the case in which an object is at least partly made up of multiple other objects that might exist independently. A class modeling a European call option might have as attributes other objects for the underlying stock and the relevant short rate for discounting. The objects representing the stock and the short rate can be used independently by other objects as well.

Composition

Composition is similar to aggregation, but here the single objects cannot exist independently of each other. Consider a custom-tailored interest rate swap with a fixed leg and a floating leg. The two legs do not exist independently of the swap itself.

Polymorphism

Polymorphism can take on multiple forms. Of particular importance in a Python context is what is called *duck typing*. This refers to the fact that standard operations can be implemented on many different classes and their instances without knowing exactly what object one is dealing with. For a class of financial instruments this might mean that one can call a method get_current_price() independent of the specific type of the object (stock, option, swap).

Encapsulation

This concept refers to the approach of making data within a class accessible only via public methods. A class modeling a stock might have an attribute cur rent_stock_price. Encapsulation would then give access to the attribute value via a method get_current_stock_price() and would hide the data from the user (i.e., make it private). This approach might avoid unintended effects by simply working with and possibly changing attribute values. However, there are limits as to how data can be made private in a Python class.

On a somewhat higher level, many of these aspects can be summarized by *two generals goals* in software engineering:

Reusability

Concepts like inheritance and polymorphism improve code reusability and increase the efficiency and productivity of the programmer. They also simplify code maintenance.

Nonredundancy

At the same time, these approaches allow one to build almost nonredundant code, avoiding double implementation effort and reducing debugging and testing effort as well as maintenance effort. They might also lead to a smaller overall codebase.

This chapter is organized as follows:

"A Look at Python Objects" on page 149
This section takes a look at some Python objects through the lens of OOP.

"Basics of Python Classes" on page 154
This section introduces central elements of OOP in Python and uses financial instruments and portfolio positions as major examples.

"Python Data Model" on page 159
This section discusses important elements of the Python data model and roles that certain special methods play.

A Look at Python Objects

Let's start by taking a brief look at some standard objects encountered in previous chapters through the eyes of an OOP programmer.

int

To start simple, consider an integer object. Even with such a simple Python object, the major OOP features are present:

```
In [7]: n = 5   ❶

In [8]: type(n)   ❷
Out[8]: int

In [9]: n.numerator   ❸
Out[9]: 5

In [10]: n.bit_length()   ❹
Out[10]: 3

In [11]: n + n   ❺
Out[11]: 10

In [12]: 2 * n   ❻
Out[12]: 10

In [13]: n.__sizeof__()   ❼
Out[13]: 28
```

❶ New instance n.

❷ Type of the object.

❸ An attribute.

❹ A method.

❺ Applying the + operator (addition).

❻ Applying the * operator (multiplication).

❼ Calling the special method __sizeof__() to get the memory usage in bytes.[1]

list

list objects have some more methods but basically behave the same way:

```
In [14]: l = [1, 2, 3, 4]   ❶

In [15]: type(l)   ❷
Out[15]: list

In [16]: l[0]   ❸
Out[16]: 1

In [17]: l.append(10)   ❹

In [18]: l + l   ❺
Out[18]: [1, 2, 3, 4, 10, 1, 2, 3, 4, 10]

In [19]: 2 * l   ❻
Out[19]: [1, 2, 3, 4, 10, 1, 2, 3, 4, 10]

In [20]: sum(l)   ❼
Out[20]: 20

In [21]: l.__sizeof__()   ❽
Out[21]: 104
```

❶ New instance l.

❷ Type of the object.

❸ Selecting an element via indexing.

❹ A method.

---

1 Special attributes and methods in Python are characterized by double leading and trailing underscores as in __XYZ__(). n.__sizeof__() returns the size of the Python object n in bytes.

❺ Applying the + operator (concatenation).

❻ Applying the * operator (concatenation).

❼ Applying the standard Python function sum().

❽ Calling the special method __sizeof__() to get the memory usage in bytes.

ndarray

int and list objects are standard Python objects. The NumPy ndarray object is a "custom-made" object from an open source package:

```
In [22]: import numpy as np   ❶

In [23]: a = np.arange(16).reshape((4, 4))   ❷

In [24]: a   ❷
Out[24]: array([[ 0,  1,  2,  3],
                [ 4,  5,  6,  7],
                [ 8,  9, 10, 11],
                [12, 13, 14, 15]])

In [25]: type(a)   ❸
Out[25]: numpy.ndarray
```

❶ Importing numpy.

❷ A new instance a.

❸ Type of the object.

Although the ndarray object is not a standard object, it behaves in many cases as if it were one—thanks to the Python data model, as explained later in this chapter:

```
In [26]: a.nbytes   ❶
Out[26]: 128

In [27]: a.sum()   ❷
Out[27]: 120

In [28]: a.cumsum(axis=0)   ❸
Out[28]: array([[ 0,  1,  2,  3],
                [ 4,  6,  8, 10],
                [12, 15, 18, 21],
                [24, 28, 32, 36]])

In [29]: a + a   ❹
Out[29]: array([[ 0,  2,  4,  6],
```

```
                    [ 8, 10, 12, 14],
                    [16, 18, 20, 22],
                    [24, 26, 28, 30]])

In [30]: 2 * a  ❺
Out[30]: array([[ 0,  2,  4,  6],
                [ 8, 10, 12, 14],
                [16, 18, 20, 22],
                [24, 26, 28, 30]])

In [31]: sum(a)  ❻
Out[31]: array([24, 28, 32, 36])

In [32]: np.sum(a)  ❼
Out[32]: 120

In [33]: a.__sizeof__()  ❽
Out[33]: 112
```

❶ An attribute.

❷ A method (aggregation).

❸ A method (no aggregation).

❹ Applying the + operator (addition).

❺ Applying the * operator (multiplication).

❻ Applying the standard Python function sum().

❼ Applying the NumPy universal function np.sum().

❽ Calling the special method __sizeof__() to get the memory usage in bytes.

DataFrame

Finally, a quick look at the pandas DataFrame object, which behaves similarly to the ndarray object. First, the instantiation of the DataFrame object based on the ndarray object:

```
In [34]: import pandas as pd  ❶

In [35]: df = pd.DataFrame(a, columns=list('abcd'))  ❷

In [36]: type(df)  ❸
Out[36]: pandas.core.frame.DataFrame
```

❶ Importing pandas.

❷ A new instance df.

❸ Type of the object.

Second, a look at attributes, methods, and operations:

```
In [37]: df.columns   ❶
Out[37]: Index(['a', 'b', 'c', 'd'], dtype='object')

In [38]: df.sum()   ❷
Out[38]: a    24
         b    28
         c    32
         d    36
         dtype: int64

In [39]: df.cumsum()   ❸
Out[39]:     a   b   c   d
         0   0   1   2   3
         1   4   6   8  10
         2  12  15  18  21
         3  24  28  32  36

In [40]: df + df   ❹
Out[40]:     a   b   c   d
         0   0   2   4   6
         1   8  10  12  14
         2  16  18  20  22
         3  24  26  28  30

In [41]: 2 * df   ❺
Out[41]:     a   b   c   d
         0   0   2   4   6
         1   8  10  12  14
         2  16  18  20  22
         3  24  26  28  30

In [42]: np.sum(df)   ❻
Out[42]: a    24
         b    28
         c    32
         d    36
         dtype: int64

In [43]: df.__sizeof__()   ❼
Out[43]: 208
```

❶ An attribute.

❷ A method (aggregation).

❸ A method (no aggregation).

❹ Applying the + operator (addition).

❺ Applying the * operator (multiplication).

❻ Applying the NumPy universal function np.sum().

❼ Calling the special method __sizeof__() to get the memory usage in bytes.

Basics of Python Classes

This section covers major concepts and the concrete syntax to make use of OOP in Python. The context now is about building custom classes to model types of objects that cannot be easily, efficiently, or properly modeled by existing Python object types. Throughout, the example of a *financial instrument* is used.

Two lines of code suffice to create a new Python class:

```
In [44]: class FinancialInstrument(object):  ❶
              pass  ❷

In [45]: fi = FinancialInstrument()  ❸

In [46]: type(fi)  ❹
Out[46]: __main__.FinancialInstrument

In [47]: fi  ❺
Out[47]: <__main__.FinancialInstrument at 0x116767278>

In [48]: fi.__str__()  ❺
Out[48]: '<__main__.FinancialInstrument object at 0x116767278>'

In [49]: fi.price = 100  ❻

In [50]: fi.price  ❻
Out[50]: 100
```

❶ Class definition statement.[2]

❷ Some code; here simply the pass keyword.

---

[2] Camel-case naming for classes is recommended. However, if there is no ambiguity, lowercase or snake case (as in financial_instrument) can also be used.

❸ A new instance of the class named `aapl`.

❹ The type of the object.

❺ Every Python object comes with certain "special" attributes and methods (from `object`); here, the special method to retrieve the string representation is called.

❻ So-called data attributes—in contrast to regular attributes—can be defined on the fly for every object.

An important special method is `__init__`, which gets called during every instantiation of an object. It takes as parameters the object itself (`self`, by convention) and potentially multiple others:

```
In [51]: class FinancialInstrument(object):
             author = 'Yves Hilpisch'  ❶
             def __init__(self, symbol, price):  ❷
                 self.symbol = symbol  ❸
                 self.price = price  ❸

In [52]: FinancialInstrument.author  ❶
Out[52]: 'Yves Hilpisch'

In [53]: aapl = FinancialInstrument('AAPL', 100)  ❹

In [54]: aapl.symbol  ❺
Out[54]: 'AAPL'

In [55]: aapl.author  ❻
Out[55]: 'Yves Hilpisch'

In [56]: aapl.price = 105  ❼

In [57]: aapl.price  ❼
Out[57]: 105
```

❶ Definition of a class attribute (inherited by every instance).

❷ The special method `__init__` called during initialization.

❸ Definition of the instance attributes (individual to every instance).

❹ A new instance of the class named `fi`.

❺ Accessing an instance attribute.

❻ Accessing a class attribute.

❼ Changing the value of an instance attribute.

Prices of financial instruments change regularly, but the symbol of a financial instrument probably does not change. To introduce encapsulation to the class definition, two methods, `get_price()` and `set_price()`, might be defined. The code that follows additionally inherits from the previous class definition (and not from `object` anymore):

```
In [58]: class FinancialInstrument(FinancialInstrument):  ❶
             def get_price(self):  ❷
                 return self.price  ❷
             def set_price(self, price):  ❸
                 self.price = price  ❹

In [59]: fi = FinancialInstrument('AAPL', 100)  ❺

In [60]: fi.get_price()  ❻
Out[60]: 100

In [61]: fi.set_price(105)  ❼

In [62]: fi.get_price()  ❻
Out[62]: 105

In [63]: fi.price  ❽
Out[63]: 105
```

❶ Class definition via inheritance from previous version.

❷ Defines the `get_price()` method.

❸ Defines the `set_price()` method …

❹ … and updates the instance attribute value given the parameter value.

❺ A new instance based on the new class definition named `fi`.

❻ Calls the `get_price()` method to read the instance attribute value.

❼ Updates the instance attribute value via `set_price()`.

❽ Direct access to the instance attribute.

Encapsulation generally has the goal of hiding data from the user working with a class. Adding *getter* and *setter* methods is one part of achieving this goal. However, this does not prevent the user from directly accessing and manipulating instance attributes. This is where *private* instance attributes come into play. They are defined by two leading underscores:

```
In [64]: class FinancialInstrument(object):
             def __init__(self, symbol, price):
                 self.symbol = symbol
                 self.__price = price    ❶
             def get_price(self):
                 return self.__price
             def set_price(self, price):
                 self.__price = price

In [65]: fi = FinancialInstrument('AAPL', 100)

In [66]: fi.get_price()    ❷
Out[66]: 100

In [67]: fi.__price    ❸

---------------------------------------------------------------
AttributeError                         Traceback (most recent call last)
<ipython-input-67-bd62f6cadb79> in <module>
----> 1 fi.__price    ❸

AttributeError: 'FinancialInstrument' object has no attribute '__price'

In [68]: fi._FinancialInstrument__price    ❹
Out[68]: 100

In [69]: fi._FinancialInstrument__price = 105    ❹

In [70]: fi.set_price(100)    ❺
```

❶ Price is defined as a private instance attribute.

❷ The method get_price() returns its value.

❸ Trying to access the attribute directly raises an error.

❹ If the class name is prepended with a single leading underscore, direct access and manipulation are still possible.

❺ Sets the price back to its original value.

Encapsulation in Python

Although encapsulation can basically be implemented for Python classes via private instance attributes and respective methods dealing with them, the hiding of data from the user cannot be fully enforced. In that sense, it is more an engineering principle in Python than a technical feature of Python classes.

Consider another class that models a portfolio position of a financial instrument. With the two classes *aggregation* as a concept is easily illustrated. An instance of the PortfolioPosition class takes an instance of the FinancialInstrument class as an attribute value. Adding an instance attribute, such as position_size, one can then calculate, for instance, the position value:

```
In [71]: class PortfolioPosition(object):
             def __init__(self, financial_instrument, position_size):
                 self.position = financial_instrument    ❶
                 self.__position_size = position_size    ❷
             def get_position_size(self):
                 return self.__position_size
             def update_position_size(self, position_size):
                 self.__position_size = position_size
             def get_position_value(self):
                 return self.__position_size * \
                         self.position.get_price()       ❸

In [72]: pp = PortfolioPosition(fi, 10)

In [73]: pp.get_position_size()
Out[73]: 10

In [74]: pp.get_position_value()    ❸
Out[74]: 1000

In [75]: pp.position.get_price()    ❹
Out[75]: 100

In [76]: pp.position.set_price(105)    ❺

In [77]: pp.get_position_value()    ❻
Out[77]: 1050
```

❶   An instance attribute based on an instance of the FinancialInstrument class.

❷   A private instance attribute of the PortfolioPosition class.

❸   Calculates the position value based on the attributes.

❹ Methods attached to the instance attribute object can be accessed directly (could be hidden as well).

❺ Updates the price of the financial instrument.

❻ Calculates the new position value based on the updated price.

Python Data Model

The examples in the previous section highlighted some aspects of the so-called Python *data* or *object model* (*https://docs.python.org/3/reference/datamodel.html*). The Python data model allows you to design classes that consistently interact with basic language constructs of Python. Among others, it supports (see Ramalho (2015), p. 4) the following tasks and constructs:

- Iteration
- Collection handling
- Attribute access
- Operator overloading
- Function and method invocation
- Object creation and destruction
- String representation (e.g., for printing)
- Managed contexts (i.e., with blocks)

Since the Python data model is so important, this section is dedicated to an example (from Ramalho (2015), with slight adjustments) that explores several aspects of it. It implements a class for one-dimensional, three-element vectors (think of vectors in Euclidean space). First, the special method __init__:

```
In [78]: class Vector(object):
             def __init__(self, x=0, y=0, z=0):   ❶
                 self.x = x   ❶
                 self.y = y   ❶
                 self.z = z   ❶

In [79]: v = Vector(1, 2, 3)   ❷

In [80]: v   ❸
Out[80]: <__main__.Vector at 0x1167789e8>
```

❶ Three preinitialized instance attributes (think three-dimensional space).

❷ A new instance of the class named v.

❸ The default string representation.

The special method __repr__ allows the definition of custom string representations:

```
In [81]: class Vector(Vector):
             def __repr__(self):
                 return 'Vector(%r, %r, %r)' % (self.x, self.y, self.z)

In [82]: v = Vector(1, 2, 3)

In [83]: v  ❶
Out[83]: Vector(1, 2, 3)

In [84]: print(v)  ❶
         Vector(1, 2, 3)
```

❶ The new string representation.

`abs()` and `bool()` are two standard Python functions whose behavior on the `Vector` class can be defined via the special methods __abs__ and __bool__:

```
In [85]: class Vector(Vector):
             def __abs__(self):
                 return (self.x ** 2 +  self.y ** 2 +
                         self.z ** 2) ** 0.5  ❶

             def __bool__(self):
                 return bool(abs(self))

In [86]: v = Vector(1, 2, -1)  ❷

In [87]: abs(v)
Out[87]: 2.449489742783178

In [88]: bool(v)
Out[88]: True

In [89]: v = Vector()  ❸

In [90]: v  ❸
Out[90]: Vector(0, 0, 0)

In [91]: abs(v)
Out[91]: 0.0

In [92]: bool(v)
Out[92]: False
```

❶ Returns the Euclidean norm given the three attribute values.

❷ A new `Vector` object with nonzero attribute values.

❸ A new `Vector` object with zero attribute values only.

As shown multiple times, the + and * operators can be applied to almost any Python object. The behavior is defined through the special methods __add__ and __mul__:

```
In [93]: class Vector(Vector):
             def __add__(self, other):
                 x = self.x + other.x
                 y = self.y + other.y
                 z = self.z + other.z
                 return Vector(x, y, z)  ❶

             def __mul__(self, scalar):
                 return Vector(self.x * scalar,
                               self.y * scalar,
                               self.z * scalar)  ❶

In [94]: v = Vector(1, 2, 3)

In [95]: v + Vector(2, 3, 4)
Out[95]: Vector(3, 5, 7)

In [96]: v * 2
Out[96]: Vector(2, 4, 6)
```

❶ In this case, each special method returns an object of its own kind.

Another standard Python function is `len()`, which gives the length of an object in number of elements. This function accesses the special method __len__ when called on an object. On the other hand, the special method __getitem__ makes indexing via the square bracket notation possible:

```
In [97]: class Vector(Vector):
             def __len__(self):
                 return 3  ❶

             def __getitem__(self, i):
                 if i in [0, -3]: return self.x
                 elif i in [1, -2]: return self.y
                 elif i in [2, -1]: return self.z
                 else: raise IndexError('Index out of range.')

In [98]: v = Vector(1, 2, 3)

In [99]: len(v)
Out[99]: 3

In [100]: v[0]
Out[100]: 1

In [101]: v[-2]
```

```
Out[101]: 2

In [102]: v[3]
```

```
---------------------------------------------------------------
IndexError                              Traceback (most recent call last)
<ipython-input-102-f998c57dcc1e> in <module>
----> 1 v[3]

<ipython-input-97-b0ca25eef7b3> in __getitem__(self, i)
      7         elif i in [1, -2]: return self.y
      8         elif i in [2, -1]: return self.z
----> 9         else: raise IndexError('Index out of range.')

IndexError: Index out of range.
```

❶ All instances of the Vector class have a length of three.

Finally, the special method __iter__ defines the behavior during iterations over elements of an object. An object for which this operation is defined is called *iterable*. For instance, all collections and containers are iterable:

```
In [103]: class Vector(Vector):
              def __iter__(self):
                  for i in range(len(self)):
                      yield self[i]

In [104]: v = Vector(1, 2, 3)

In [105]: for i in range(3):    ❶
              print(v[i])    ❶
          1
          2
          3

In [106]: for coordinate in v:    ❷
              print(coordinate)    ❷
          1
          2
          3
```

❶ Indirect iteration using index values (via __getitem__).

❷ Direct iteration over the class instance (using __iter__).

Enhancing Python

The Python data model allows the definition of Python classes that interact with standard Python operators, functions, etc., seamlessly. This makes Python a rather flexible programming language that can easily be enhanced by new classes and types of objects.

As a summary, the following section provides the Vector class definition in a single code block.

The Vector Class

```
In [107]: class Vector(object):
              def __init__(self, x=0, y=0, z=0):
                  self.x = x
                  self.y = y
                  self.z = z

              def __repr__(self):
                  return 'Vector(%r, %r, %r)' % (self.x, self.y, self.z)

              def __abs__(self):
                  return (self.x ** 2 +  self.y ** 2 + self.z ** 2) ** 0.5

              def __bool__(self):
                  return bool(abs(self))

              def __add__(self, other):
                  x = self.x + other.x
                  y = self.y + other.y
                  z = self.z + other.z
                  return Vector(x, y, z)

              def __mul__(self, scalar):
                  return Vector(self.x * scalar,
                                self.y * scalar,
                                self.z * scalar)

              def __len__(self):
                  return 3

              def __getitem__(self, i):
                  if i in [0, -3]: return self.x
                  elif i in [1, -2]: return self.y
                  elif i in [2, -1]: return self.z
                  else: raise IndexError('Index out of range.')

              def __iter__(self):
                  for i in range(len(self)):
                      yield self[i]
```

Conclusion

This chapter introduces notions and approaches from object-oriented programming, both theoretically and through Python examples. OOP is one of the main programming paradigms used in Python. It not only allows for the modeling and implementation of rather complex applications, but also allows one to create custom objects that behave like standard Python objects due to the flexible Python data model. Although there are many critics who argue against OOP, it is safe to say that it provides the Python programmer and quant with powerful tools that are helpful when a certain degree of complexity is reached. The derivatives pricing package developed and discussed in Part V presents such a case where OOP seems the only sensible programming paradigm to deal with the inherent complexities and requirements for abstraction.

Further Resources

The following are valuable online resources about OOP in general and Python programming and OOP in particular:

- Lecture Notes on Object-Oriented Programming (*http://bit.ly/2qLJU0S*)
- Object-Oriented Programming in Python (*http://bit.ly/2DKGZhB*)

A great resource in book form about Python object orientation and the Python data model is:

- Ramalho, Luciano (2016). *Fluent Python*. Sebastopol, CA: O'Reilly.

## PART III

Financial Data Science

This part of the book is about basic techniques, approaches, and packages for financial data science. Many topics (such as visualization) and many packages (such as `scikit-learn` (*http://scikit-learn.org/stable/*)) are fundamental for data science with Python. In that sense, this part equips the quants and financial analysts with the Python tools they need to become *financial data scientists*.

Like in Part II, the chapters are organized according to topics such that they can each be used as a reference for the topic of interest:

- Chapter 7 discusses static and interactive visualization with `matplotlib` and `plotly`.
- Chapter 8 is about handling financial time series data with `pandas`.
- Chapter 9 focuses on getting input/output (I/O) operations right and fast.
- Chapter 10 is all about making Python code fast.
- Chapter 11 focuses on frequently required mathematical tools in finance.
- Chapter 12 looks at using Python to implement methods from stochastics.
- Chapter 13 is about statistical and machine learning approaches.

## CHAPTER 7

Data Visualization

Use a picture. It's worth a thousand words.

—Arthur Brisbane (1911)

This chapter is about the basic visualization capabilities of the `matplotlib` (*http://www.matplotlib.org*) and `plotly` (*http://plot.ly*) packages.

Although there are more visualization packages available, `matplotlib` has established itself as the benchmark and, in many situations, a robust and reliable visualization tool. It is both easy to use for standard plots and flexible when it comes to more complex plots and customizations. In addition, it is tightly integrated with `NumPy` and `pandas` and the data structures they provide.

`matplotlib` only allows for the generation of plots in the form of bitmaps (for example, in PNG or JPG format). On the other hand, modern web technologies—based, for example, on the Data-Driven Documents (D3.js) standard (*https://d3js.org/*)—allow for nice interactive and also embeddable plots (interactive, for example, in that one can zoom in to inspect certain areas in greater detail). A package that makes it convenient to create such D3.js plots with Python is `plotly`. A smaller additional library, called `Cufflinks`, tightly integrates `plotly` with `pandas DataFrame` objects and allows for the creation of popular financial plots (such as candlestick charts).

This chapter mainly covers the following topics:

"Static 2D Plotting" on page 168
This section introduces `matplotlib` and presents a selection of typical 2D plots, from the most simple to some more advanced ones with two scales or different subplots.

Based on `matplotlib`, a selection of 3D plots useful for certain financial applications are presented in this section.

This section introduces `plotly` and `Cufflinks` to create interactive 2D plots. Making use of the `QuantFigure` feature of `Cufflinks`, this section is also about typical financial plots used, for example, in technical stock analysis.

This chapter cannot be comprehensive with regard to data visualization with Python, `matplotlib`, or `plotly`, but it provides a number of examples for the basic and important capabilities of these packages for finance. Other examples are also found in later chapters. For instance, Chapter 8 shows in more depth how to visualize financial time series data with the `pandas` library.

Static 2D Plotting

Before creating the sample data and starting to plot, some imports and customizations:

```
In [1]: import matplotlib as mpl      ❶

In [2]: mpl.__version__      ❷
Out[2]: '3.0.0'

In [3]: import matplotlib.pyplot as plt      ❸

In [4]: plt.style.use('seaborn')      ❹

In [5]: mpl.rcParams['font.family'] = 'serif'      ❺

In [6]: %matplotlib inline
```

❶ Imports `matplotlib` with the usual abbreviation `mpl`.

❷ The version of `matplotlib` used.

❸ Imports the main plotting (sub)package with the usual abbreviation `plt`.

❹ Sets the plotting style (*http://bit.ly/2KaPFhs*) to `seaborn`.

❺ Sets the font to be `serif` in all plots.

One-Dimensional Data Sets

The most fundamental, but nevertheless quite powerful, plotting function is `plt.plot()`. In principle, it needs two sets of numbers:

x values
> A `list` or an array containing the *x* coordinates (values of the abscissa)

y values
> A `list` or an array containing the *y* coordinates (values of the ordinate)

The number of *x* and *y* values provided must match, of course. Consider the following code, whose output is presented in Figure 7-1:

```
In [7]: import numpy as np

In [8]: np.random.seed(1000)   ❶

In [9]: y = np.random.standard_normal(20)   ❷

In [10]: x = np.arange(len(y))   ❸
         plt.plot(x, y);   ❹
```

❶ Fixes the seed for the random number generator for reproducibility.

❷ Draws the random numbers (*y* values).

❸ Fixes the integers (*x* values).

❹ Calls the `plt.plot()` function with the x and y objects.

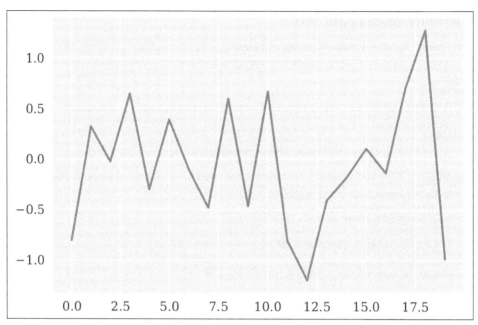

Figure 7-1. Plot given x and y values

plt.plot() notices when an ndarray object is passed. In this case, there is no need to provide the "extra" information of the *x* values. If one only provides the *y* values, plt.plot() takes the index values as the respective *x* values. Therefore, the following single line of code generates exactly the same output (see Figure 7-2):

```
In [11]: plt.plot(y);
```

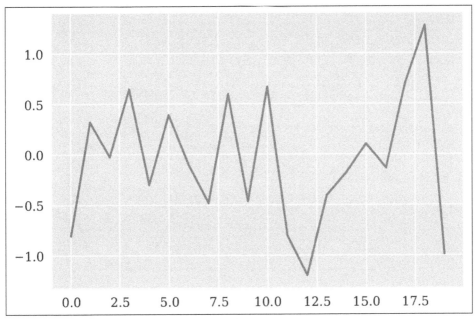

Figure 7-2. Plot given data as an ndarray object

NumPy Arrays and matplotlib

You can simply pass NumPy ndarray objects to matplotlib functions. matplotlib is able to interpret the data structures for simplified plotting. However, be careful to not pass a too large and/or complex array.

Since the majority of the ndarray methods return an ndarray object, one can also pass the object with a method (or even multiple methods, in some cases) attached. By calling the cumsum() method on the ndarray object with the sample data, one gets the cumulative sum of this data and, as to be expected, a different output (see Figure 7-3):

```
In [12]: plt.plot(y.cumsum());
```

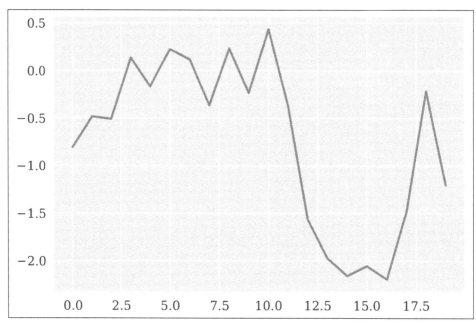

Figure 7-3. Plot given an ndarray object with a method attached

In general, the default plotting style does not satisfy typical requirements for reports, publications, etc. For example, one might want to customize the font used (e.g., for compatibility with LaTeX fonts), to have labels at the axes, or to plot a grid for better readability. This is where plotting styles come into play. In addition, `matplotlib` offers a large number of functions to customize the plotting style. Some are easily accessible; for others one has to dig a bit deeper. Easily accessible, for example, are those functions that manipulate the axes and those that relate to grids and labels (see Figure 7-4):

```
In [13]: plt.plot(y.cumsum())
         plt.grid(False)    ❶
         plt.axis('equal');  ❷
```

❶ Turns off the grid.

❷ Leads to equal scaling for the two axes.

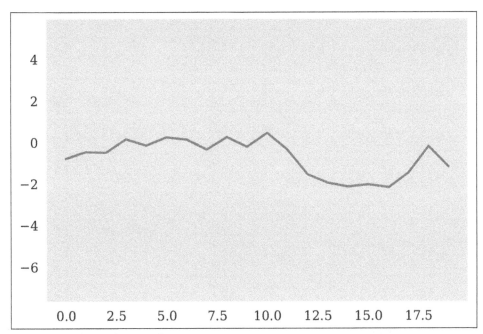

Figure 7-4. Plot without grid

Other options for `plt.axis()` are given in Table 7-1, the majority of which have to be passed as a `str` object.

Table 7-1. Options for plt.axis()

Parameter	Description
Empty	Returns current axis limits
off	Turns axis lines and labels off
equal	Leads to equal scaling
scaled	Produces equal scaling via dimension changes
tight	Makes all data visible (tightens limits)
image	Makes all data visible (with data limits)
[xmin, xmax, ymin, ymax]	Sets limits to given (`list` of) values

In addition, one can directly set the minimum and maximum values of each axis by using `plt.xlim()` and `plt.ylim()`. The following code provides an example whose output is shown in Figure 7-5:

```
In [14]: plt.plot(y.cumsum())
         plt.xlim(-1, 20)
         plt.ylim(np.min(y.cumsum()) - 1,
                 np.max(y.cumsum()) + 1);
```

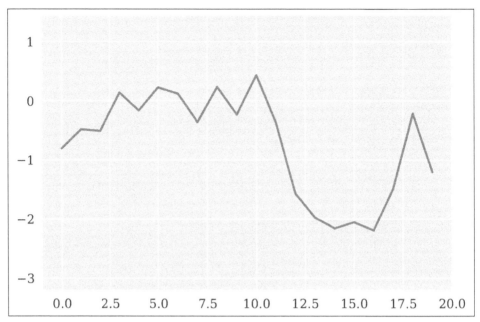

Figure 7-5. Plot with custom axis limits

For the sake of better readability, a plot usually contains a number of labels—e.g., a title and labels describing the nature of the x and y values. These are added by the functions plt.title(), plt.xlabel(), and plt.ylabel(), respectively. By default, plot() plots continuous lines, even if discrete data points are provided. The plotting of discrete points is accomplished by choosing a different style option. Figure 7-6 overlays (red) points and a (blue) line with line width of 1.5 points:

```
In [15]: plt.figure(figsize=(10, 6))    ❶
         plt.plot(y.cumsum(), 'b', lw=1.5)    ❷
         plt.plot(y.cumsum(), 'ro')    ❸
         plt.xlabel('index')    ❹
         plt.ylabel('value')    ❺
         plt.title('A Simple Plot');    ❻
```

❶ Increases the size of the figure.

❷ Plots the data as a line in blue with line width of 1.5 points.

❸ Plots the data as red (thick) dots.

❹ Places a label on the x-axis.

❺ Places a label on the y-axis.

6 Places a title.

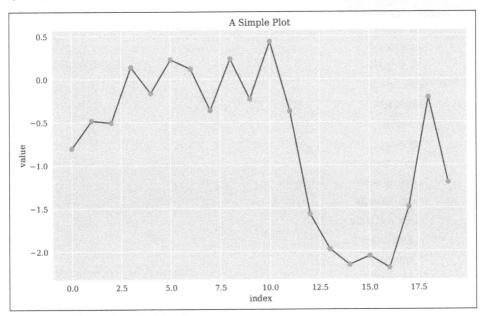

Figure 7-6. Plot with typical labels

By default, `plt.plot()` supports the color abbreviations in Table 7-2.

Table 7-2. Standard color abbreviations

Character	Color
b	Blue
g	Green
r	Red
c	Cyan
m	Magenta
y	Yellow
k	Black
w	White

In terms of line and/or point styles, `plt.plot()` supports the characters listed in Table 7-3.

Table 7-3. Standard style characters

Character	Symbol
-	Solid line style
- -	Dashed line style
-.	Dash-dot line style
:	Dotted line style
.	Point marker
,	Pixel marker
o	Circle marker
v	Triangle_down marker
^	Triangle_up marker
<	Triangle_left marker
>	Triangle_right marker
1	Tri_down marker
2	Tri_up marker
3	Tri_left marker
4	Tri_right marker
s	Square marker
p	Pentagon marker
*	Star marker
h	Hexagon1 marker
H	Hexagon2 marker
+	Plus marker
x	X marker
D	Diamond marker
d	Thin diamond marker
		Vline marker
_	Hline marker

Any color abbreviation can be combined with any style character. In this way, one can make sure that different data sets are easily distinguished. The plotting style is also reflected in the legend.

Two-Dimensional Data Sets

Plotting one-dimensional data can be considered a special case. In general, data sets will consist of multiple separate subsets of data. The handling of such data sets follows the same rules with `matplotlib` as with one-dimensional data. However, a number of additional issues might arise in such a context. For example, two data sets might have such a different scaling that they cannot be plotted using the same y- and/or x-axis scaling. Another issue might be that one might want to visualize two different data sets in different ways, e.g., one by a line plot and the other by a bar plot.

The following code generates a two-dimensional sample data set as a NumPy ndarray object of shape 20 × 2 with standard normally distributed pseudo-random numbers. On this array, the method cumsum() is called to calculate the cumulative sum of the sample data along axis 0 (i.e., the first dimension):

```
In [16]: y = np.random.standard_normal((20, 2)).cumsum(axis=0)
```

In general, one can also pass such two-dimensional arrays to plt.plot(). It will then automatically interpret the contained data as separate data sets (along axis 1, i.e., the second dimension). A respective plot is shown in Figure 7-7:

```
In [17]: plt.figure(figsize=(10, 6))
         plt.plot(y, lw=1.5)
         plt.plot(y, 'ro')
         plt.xlabel('index')
         plt.ylabel('value')
         plt.title('A Simple Plot');
```

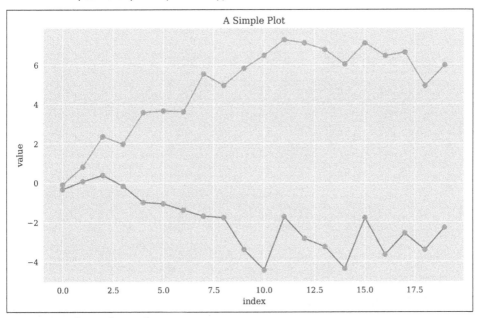

Figure 7-7. Plot with two data sets

In such a case, further annotations might be helpful to better read the plot. You can add individual labels to each data set and have them listed in the legend. The function `plt.legend()` accepts different locality parameters. 0 stands for *best location*, in the sense that as little data as possible is hidden by the legend.

Figure 7-8 shows the plot of the two data sets, this time with a legend. In the generating code, the `ndarray` object is not passed as a whole but the two data subsets (`y[:, 0]` and `y[:, 1]`) are accessed separately, which allows you to attach individual labels to them:

```
In [18]: plt.figure(figsize=(10, 6))
         plt.plot(y[:, 0], lw=1.5, label='1st')  ❶
         plt.plot(y[:, 1], lw=1.5, label='2nd')  ❶
         plt.plot(y, 'ro')
         plt.legend(loc=0)  ❷
         plt.xlabel('index')
         plt.ylabel('value')
         plt.title('A Simple Plot');
```

❶ Defines labels for the data subsets.

❷ Places a legend in the "best" location.

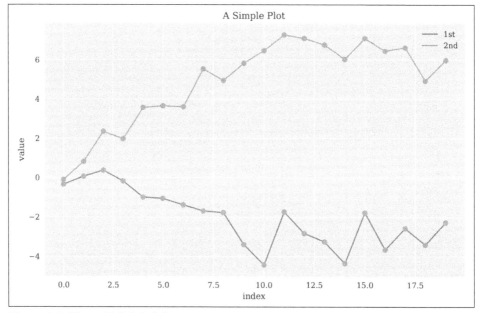

Figure 7-8. Plot with labeled data sets

Further location options for `plt.legend()` include those presented in Table 7-4.

Table 7-4. Options for plt.legend()

Loc	Description
Default	Upper right
0	Best possible
1	Upper right
2	Upper left
3	Lower left
4	Lower right
5	Right
6	Center left
7	Center right
8	Lower center
9	Upper center
10	Center

Multiple data sets with a similar scaling, like simulated paths for the same financial risk factor, can be plotted using a single y-axis. However, often data sets show rather different scalings and the plotting of such data with a single y-scale generally leads to a significant loss of visual information. To illustrate the effect, the following example scales the first of the two data subsets by a factor of 100 and plots the data again (see Figure 7-9):

```
In [19]: y[:, 0] = y[:, 0] * 100   ❶
```

```
In [20]: plt.figure(figsize=(10, 6))
         plt.plot(y[:, 0], lw=1.5, label='1st')
         plt.plot(y[:, 1], lw=1.5, label='2nd')
         plt.plot(y, 'ro')
         plt.legend(loc=0)
         plt.xlabel('index')
         plt.ylabel('value')
         plt.title('A Simple Plot');
```

❶ Rescales the first data subset.

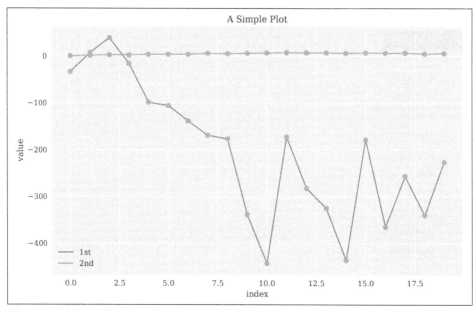

Figure 7-9. Plot with two differently scaled data sets

Inspection of Figure 7-9 reveals that the first data set is still "visually readable," while the second data set now looks like a straight line with the new scaling of the y-axis. In a sense, information about the second data set now gets "visually lost." There are two basic approaches to resolve this problem through means of plotting, as opposed to adjusting the data (e.g., through rescaling):

- Use of two y-axes (left/right)
- Use of two subplots (upper/lower, left/right)

The following example introduces a second y-axis to the plot. Figure 7-10 now has two different y-axes. The left y-axis is for the first data set while the right y-axis is for the second. Consequently, there are also two legends:

```
In [21]: fig, ax1 = plt.subplots()    ❶
         plt.plot(y[:, 0], 'b', lw=1.5, label='1st')
         plt.plot(y[:, 0], 'ro')
         plt.legend(loc=8)
         plt.xlabel('index')
         plt.ylabel('value 1st')
         plt.title('A Simple Plot')
         ax2 = ax1.twinx()    ❷
         plt.plot(y[:, 1], 'g', lw=1.5, label='2nd')
         plt.plot(y[:, 1], 'ro')
         plt.legend(loc=0)
         plt.ylabel('value 2nd');
```

❶ Defines the figure and axis objects.

❷ Creates a second axis object that shares the x-axis.

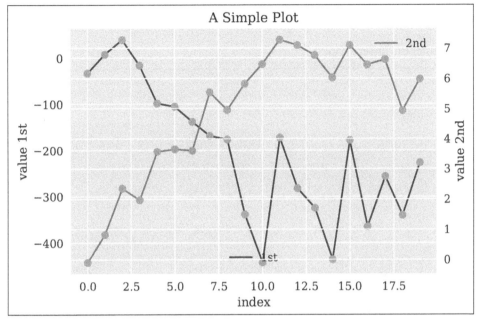

Figure 7-10. Plot with two data sets and two y-axes

The key lines of code are those that help manage the axes:

```
fig, ax1 = plt.subplots()
ax2 = ax1.twinx()
```

By using the `plt.subplots()` function, one gets direct access to the underlying plotting objects (the figure, subplots, etc.). It allows one, for example, to generate a second subplot that shares the x-axis with the first subplot. In Figure 7-10, then, the two subplots actually *overlay* each other.

Next, consider the case of two *separate* subplots. This option gives even more freedom to handle the two data sets, as Figure 7-11 illustrates:

```
In [22]: plt.figure(figsize=(10, 6))
         plt.subplot(211)  ❶
         plt.plot(y[:, 0], lw=1.5, label='1st')
         plt.plot(y[:, 0], 'ro')
         plt.legend(loc=0)
         plt.ylabel('value')
         plt.title('A Simple Plot')
         plt.subplot(212)  ❷
         plt.plot(y[:, 1], 'g', lw=1.5, label='2nd')
```

```
plt.plot(y[:, 1], 'ro')
plt.legend(loc=0)
plt.xlabel('index')
plt.ylabel('value');
```

❶ Defines the upper subplot 1.

❷ Defines the lower subplot 2.

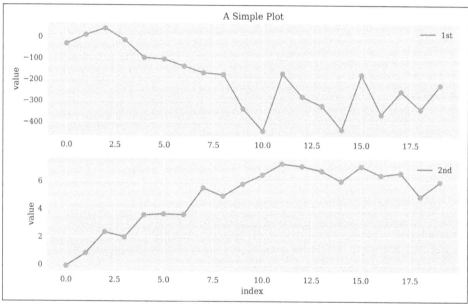

Figure 7-11. Plot with two subplots

The placing of subplots in a matplotlib figure object is accomplished by the use of a special coordinate system. plt.subplot() takes as arguments three integers for numrows, numcols, and fignum (either separated by commas or not). numrows specifies the number of *rows*, numcols the number of *columns*, and fignum the number of the *subplot*, starting with 1 and ending with numrows * numcols. For example, a figure with nine equally sized subplots would have numrows=3, numcols=3, and fig num=1,2,...,9. The lower-right subplot would have the following "coordinates": plt.subplot(3, 3, 9).

Sometimes, it might be necessary or desired to choose two different plot types to visualize such data. With the subplot approach one has the freedom to combine arbitrary kinds of plots that matplotlib offers.[1]

---

1 For an overview of which plot types are available, visit the matplotlib gallery (*http://bit.ly/2RYvMwS*).

Figure 7-12 combines a line/point plot with a bar chart:

```
In [23]: plt.figure(figsize=(10, 6))
         plt.subplot(121)
         plt.plot(y[:, 0], lw=1.5, label='1st')
         plt.plot(y[:, 0], 'ro')
         plt.legend(loc=0)
         plt.xlabel('index')
         plt.ylabel('value')
         plt.title('1st Data Set')
         plt.subplot(122)
         plt.bar(np.arange(len(y)), y[:, 1], width=0.5,
                 color='g', label='2nd')  ❶
         plt.legend(loc=0)
         plt.xlabel('index')
         plt.title('2nd Data Set');
```

❶   Creates a bar subplot.

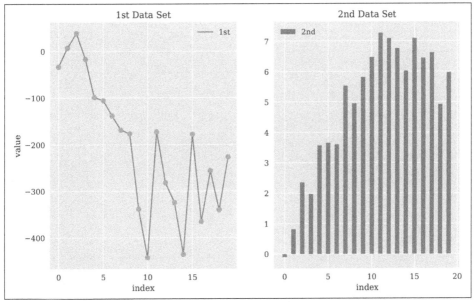

Figure 7-12. Plot combining line/point subplot with bar subplot

Other Plot Styles

When it comes to two-dimensional plotting, line and point plots are probably the most important ones in finance; this is because many data sets embody time series data, which generally is visualized by such plots. Chapter 8 addresses financial time series data in detail. However, this section sticks with a two-dimensional data set of random numbers and illustrates some alternative, and for financial applications useful, visualization approaches.

The first is the *scatter plot*, where the values of one data set serve as the *x* values for the other data set. Figure 7-13 shows such a plot. This plot type might be used, for example, for plotting the returns of one financial time series against those of another one. This example uses a new two-dimensional data set with some more data:

```
In [24]: y = np.random.standard_normal((1000, 2))  ❶
```

```
In [25]: plt.figure(figsize=(10, 6))
         plt.plot(y[:, 0], y[:, 1], 'ro')  ❷
         plt.xlabel('1st')
         plt.ylabel('2nd')
         plt.title('Scatter Plot');
```

❶ Creates a larger data set with random numbers.

❷ Scatter plot produced via the `plt.plot()` function.

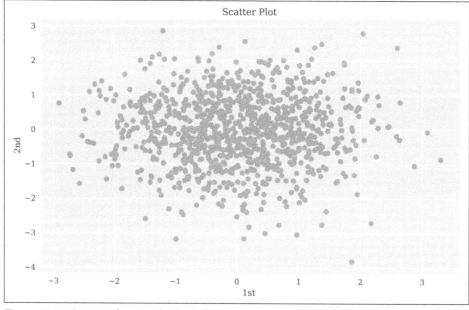

Figure 7-13. Scatter plot via plt.plot() function

`matplotlib` also provides a specific function to generate scatter plots. It basically works in the same way, but provides some additional features. Figure 7-14 shows the corresponding scatter plot to Figure 7-13, this time generated using the `plt.scat ter()` function:

```
In [26]: plt.figure(figsize=(10, 6))
         plt.scatter(y[:, 0], y[:, 1], marker='o')  ❶
         plt.xlabel('1st')
```

```
        plt.ylabel('2nd')
        plt.title('Scatter Plot');
```

❶ Scatter plot produced via the `plt.scatter()` function.

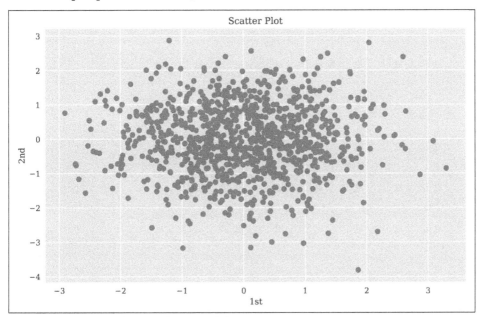

Figure 7-14. Scatter plot via plt.scatter() function

Among other things, the `plt.scatter()` plotting function allows the addition of a third dimension, which can be visualized through different colors and be described by the use of a color bar. Figure 7-15 shows a scatter plot where there is a third dimension illustrated by different colors of the single dots and with a color bar as a legend for the colors. To this end, the following code generates a third data set with random data, this time consisting of integers between 0 and 10:

```
In [27]: c = np.random.randint(0, 10, len(y))

In [28]: plt.figure(figsize=(10, 6))
         plt.scatter(y[:, 0], y[:, 1],
                     c=c,      ❶
                     cmap='coolwarm',   ❷
                     marker='o')   ❸
         plt.colorbar()
         plt.xlabel('1st')
         plt.ylabel('2nd')
         plt.title('Scatter Plot');
```

❶ Includes the third data set.

❷ Chooses the color map.

❸ Defines the marker to be a thick dot.

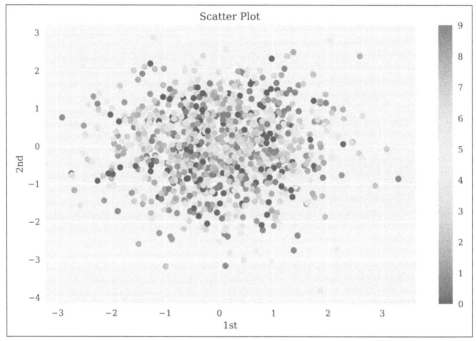

Figure 7-15. Scatter plot with third dimension

Another type of plot, the *histogram*, is also often used in the context of financial returns. Figure 7-16 puts the frequency values of the two data sets next to each other in the same plot:

```
In [29]: plt.figure(figsize=(10, 6))
         plt.hist(y, label=['1st', '2nd'], bins=25)  ❶
         plt.legend(loc=0)
         plt.xlabel('value')
         plt.ylabel('frequency')
         plt.title('Histogram');
```

❶ Histogram plot produced via the `plt.hist()` function.

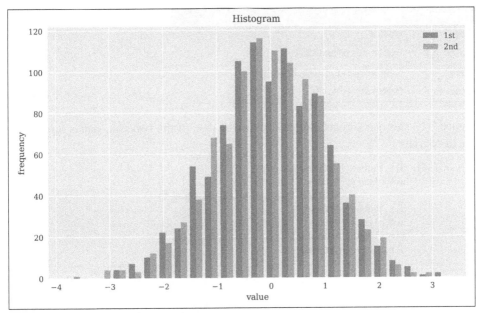

Figure 7-16. Histogram for two data sets

Since the histogram is such an important plot type for financial applications, let's take a closer look at the use of `plt.hist()`. The following example illustrates the parameters that are supported:

```
plt.hist(x, bins=10, range=None, normed=False, weights=None, cumulative=False,
bottom=None, histtype='bar', align='mid', orientation='vertical', rwidth=None,
log=False, color=None, label=None, stacked=False, hold=None, **kwargs)
```

Table 7-5 provides a description of the main parameters of the `plt.hist()` function.

Table 7-5. Parameters for plt.hist()

Parameter	Description
x	`list` object(s), `ndarray` object
bins	Number of bins
range	Lower and upper range of bins
normed	Norming such that integral value is 1
weights	Weights for every value in x
cumulative	Every bin contains the counts of the lower bins
histtype	Options (strings): `bar`, `barstacked`, `step`, `stepfilled`
align	Options (strings): `left`, `mid`, `right`
orientation	Options (strings): `horizontal`, `vertical`
rwidth	Relative width of the bars

Parameter	Description
log	Log scale
color	Color per data set (array-like)
label	String or sequence of strings for labels
stacked	Stacks multiple data sets

Figure 7-17 shows a similar plot; this time, the data of the two data sets is stacked in the histogram:

```
In [30]: plt.figure(figsize=(10, 6))
         plt.hist(y, label=['1st', '2nd'], color=['b', 'g'],
                  stacked=True, bins=20, alpha=0.5)
         plt.legend(loc=0)
         plt.xlabel('value')
         plt.ylabel('frequency')
         plt.title('Histogram');
```

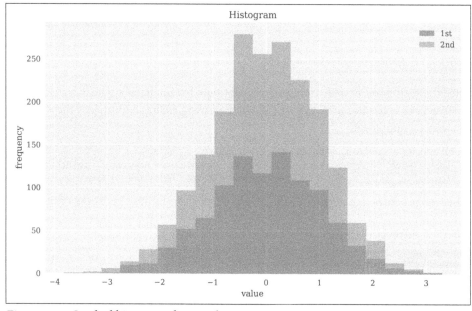

Figure 7-17. Stacked histogram for two data sets

Another useful plot type is the *boxplot*. Similar to the histogram, the boxplot allows both a concise overview of the characteristics of a data set and easy comparison of multiple data sets. Figure 7-18 shows such a plot for our data sets:

```
In [31]: fig, ax = plt.subplots(figsize=(10, 6))
         plt.boxplot(y)    ❶
         plt.setp(ax, xticklabels=['1st', '2nd'])    ❷
         plt.xlabel('data set')
```

```
plt.ylabel('value')
plt.title('Boxplot');
```

❶ Boxplot produced via the `plt.boxplot()` function.

❷ Sets individual *x* labels.

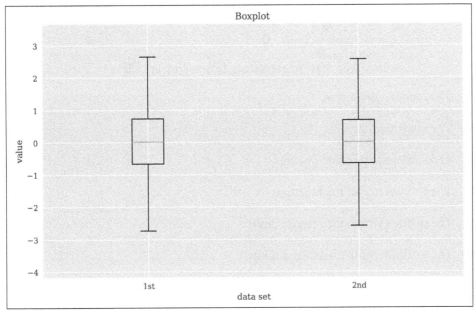

Figure 7-18. Boxplot for two data sets

This last example uses the function `plt.setp()`, which sets properties for a (set of) plotting instance(s). For example, consider a line plot generated by:

```
line = plt.plot(data, 'r')
```

The following code changes the style of the line to "dashed":

```
plt.setp(line, linestyle='--')
```

This way, one can easily change parameters after the plotting instance ("artist object") has been generated.

As a final illustration in this section, consider a mathematically inspired plot that can also be found as an example in the `matplotlib` gallery (*http://www.matplotlib.org/ gallery.html*). It plots a function and highlights graphically the area below the function from a lower and to an upper limit—in other words, the integral value of the function between the lower and upper limits. The integral (value) to be illustrated is $\int_a^b f(x)dx$ with $f(x) = \frac{1}{2} \cdot e^x + 1$, $a = \frac{1}{2}$, and $b = \frac{3}{2}$. Figure 7-19 shows the resulting plot and demonstrates that `matplotlib` seamlessly handles LaTeX typesetting for the inclusion of mathematical formulae into plots. First, the function definition, with integral limits as variables and data sets for the *x* and *y* values:

```
In [32]: def func(x):
             return 0.5 * np.exp(x) + 1    ❶
         a, b = 0.5, 1.5    ❷
         x = np.linspace(0, 2)    ❸
         y = func(x)    ❹
         Ix = np.linspace(a, b)    ❺
         Iy = func(Ix)    ❻
         verts = [(a, 0)] + list(zip(Ix, Iy)) + [(b, 0)]    ❼
```

❶ The function definition.

❷ The integral limits.

❸ The *x* values to plot the function.

❹ The *y* values to plot the function.

❺ The *x* values within the integral limits.

❻ The *y* values within the integral limits.

❼ The `list` object with multiple `tuple` objects representing coordinates for the polygon to be plotted.

Second, the plotting itself, which is a bit involved due to the many single objects to be placed explicitly:

```
In [33]: from matplotlib.patches import Polygon
         fig, ax = plt.subplots(figsize=(10, 6))
         plt.plot(x, y, 'b', linewidth=2)    ❶
         plt.ylim(bottom=0)    ❷
         poly = Polygon(verts, facecolor='0.7', edgecolor='0.5')    ❸
         ax.add_patch(poly)    ❸
         plt.text(0.5 * (a + b), 1, r'$\int_a^b f(x)\mathrm{d}x$',
                  horizontalalignment='center', fontsize=20)    ❹
         plt.figtext(0.9, 0.075, '$x$')    ❺
         plt.figtext(0.075, 0.9, '$f(x)$')    ❺
         ax.set_xticks((a, b))    ❻
         ax.set_xticklabels(('$a$', '$b$'))    ❻
         ax.set_yticks([func(a), func(b)])    ❼
         ax.set_yticklabels(('$f(a)$', '$f(b)$'));    ❼
```

❶ Plots the function values as a blue line.

❷ Defines the minimum *y* value for the ordinate axis.

❸   Plots the polygon (integral area) in gray.

❹   Places the integral formula in the plot.

❺   Places the axis labels.

❻   Places the *x* labels.

❼   Places the *y* labels.

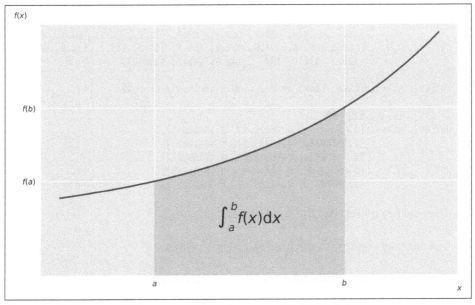

Figure 7-19. Exponential function, integral area, and LaTeX labels

Static 3D Plotting

There are not too many fields in finance that really benefit from visualization in three dimensions. However, one application area is volatility surfaces showing implied volatilities simultaneously for a number of times-to-maturity and strikes of the traded options used. See also Appendix B for an example of value and vega surfaces being visualized for a European call option. In what follows, the code artificially generates a plot that resembles a volatility surface. To this end, consider the parameters:

- *Strike values* between 50 and 150
- *Times-to-maturity* between 0.5 and 2.5 years

This provides a two-dimensional coordinate system. The NumPy np.meshgrid() function can generate such a system out of two one-dimensional ndarray objects:

```
In [34]: strike = np.linspace(50, 150, 24)  ❶

In [35]: ttm = np.linspace(0.5, 2.5, 24)  ❷

In [36]: strike, ttm = np.meshgrid(strike, ttm)  ❸

In [37]: strike[:2].round(1)  ❸
Out[37]: array([[ 50. ,  54.3,  58.7,  63. ,  67.4,  71.7,  76.1,  80.4,  84.8,
                  89.1,  93.5,  97.8, 102.2, 106.5, 110.9, 115.2, 119.6, 123.9,
                 128.3, 132.6, 137. , 141.3, 145.7, 150. ],
                [ 50. ,  54.3,  58.7,  63. ,  67.4,  71.7,  76.1,  80.4,  84.8,
                  89.1,  93.5,  97.8, 102.2, 106.5, 110.9, 115.2, 119.6, 123.9,
                 128.3, 132.6, 137. , 141.3, 145.7, 150. ]])

In [38]: iv = (strike - 100) ** 2 / (100 * strike) / ttm  ❹

In [39]: iv[:5, :3]  ❹
Out[39]: array([[1.        , 0.76695652, 0.58132045],
                [0.85185185, 0.65333333, 0.4951989 ],
                [0.74193548, 0.56903226, 0.43130227],
                [0.65714286, 0.504     , 0.38201058],
                [0.58974359, 0.45230769, 0.34283001]])
```

❶ The ndarray object with the strike values.

❷ The ndarray object with the time-to-maturity values.

❸ The two two-dimensional ndarray objects (grids) created.

❹ The dummy implied volatility values.

The plot resulting from the following code is shown in Figure 7-20:

```
In [40]: from mpl_toolkits.mplot3d import Axes3D  ❶
         fig = plt.figure(figsize=(10, 6))
         ax = fig.gca(projection='3d')  ❷
         surf = ax.plot_surface(strike, ttm, iv, rstride=2, cstride=2,
                                cmap=plt.cm.coolwarm, linewidth=0.5,
                                antialiased=True)  ❸
         ax.set_xlabel('strike')  ❹
         ax.set_ylabel('time-to-maturity')  ❺
         ax.set_zlabel('implied volatility')  ❻
         fig.colorbar(surf, shrink=0.5, aspect=5);  ❼
```

❶ Imports the relevant 3D plotting features, which is required although Axes3D is not directly used.

❷ Sets up a canvas for 3D plotting.

❸ Creates the 3D plot.

❹ Sets the x-axis label.

❺ Sets the y-axis label.

❻ Sets the z-axis label.

❼ Creates a color bar.

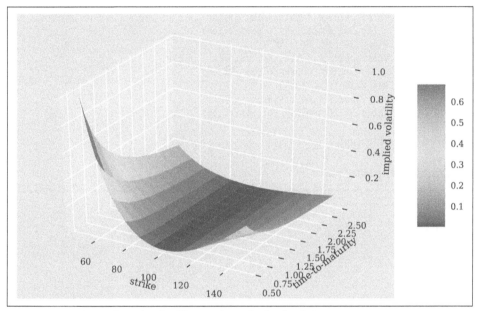

Figure 7-20. 3D surface plot for (dummy) implied volatilities

Table 7-6 provides a description of the different parameters the `plt.plot_surface()` function can take.

Table 7-6. Parameters for plot_surface()

Parameter	Description
X, Y, Z	Data values as 2D arrays
rstride	Array row stride (step size)
cstride	Array column stride (step size)
color	Color of the surface patches
cmap	Color map for the surface patches

Parameter	Description
facecolors	Face colors for the individual patches
norm	Instance of Normalize to map values to colors
vmin	Minimum value to map
vmax	Maximum value to map
shade	Whether to shade the face colors

As with two-dimensional plots, the line style can be replaced by single points or, as in what follows, single triangles. Figure 7-21 plots the same data as a 3D scatter plot but now also with a different viewing angle, using the view_init() method to set it:

```
In [41]: fig = plt.figure(figsize=(10, 6))
         ax = fig.add_subplot(111, projection='3d')
         ax.view_init(30, 60)  ❶
         ax.scatter(strike, ttm, iv, zdir='z', s=25,
                    c='b', marker='^')  ❷
         ax.set_xlabel('strike')
         ax.set_ylabel('time-to-maturity')
         ax.set_zlabel('implied volatility');
```

❶ Sets the viewing angle.

❷ Creates a 3D scatter plot.

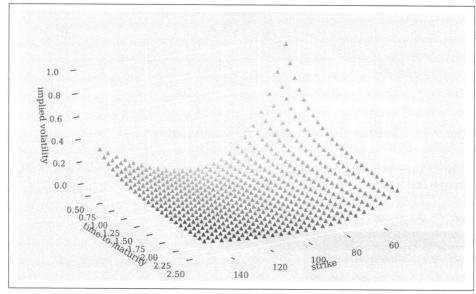

Figure 7-21. 3D scatter plot for (dummy) implied volatilities

Interactive 2D Plotting

matplotlib allows you to create plots that are static bitmap objects or of PDF format. Nowadays, there are many libraries available to create interactive plots based on the D3.js standard. Such plots enable zooming in and out, hover effects for data inspection, and more. They can in general also be easily embedded in web pages.

A popular platform and plotting library is plotly (*http://plot.ly*). It is dedicated to visualization for data science and is in widespread use in the data science community. Major benefits of plotly are its tight integration with the Python ecosystem and the ease of use—in particular when combined with pandas DataFrame objects and the wrapper package Cufflinks (*http://github.com/santosjorge/cufflinks*).

For some functionality, a free account (*https://plot.ly/accounts/login/?action=login#/*) is required. Once the credentials are granted they should be stored locally for permanent use. For details, see the "Getting Started with Plotly for Python" guide (*https://plot.ly/python/getting-started/*).

This section focuses on selected aspects only, in that Cufflinks is used exclusively to create interactive plots from data stored in DataFrame objects.

Basic Plots

To get started from within a Jupyter Notebook context, some imports are required and the *notebook mode* should be turned on:

```
In [42]: import pandas as pd

In [43]: import cufflinks as cf       ❶
In [44]: import plotly.offline as plyo   ❷

In [45]: plyo.init_notebook_mode(connected=True)   ❸
```

❶ Imports Cufflinks.

❷ Imports the offline plotting capabilities of plotly.

❸ Turns on the notebook plotting mode.

> ### Remote or Local Rendering
>
> With plotly, there is also the option to get the plots rendered on the plotly servers. However, the notebook mode is generally much faster, in particular when dealing with larger data sets. That said, some functionality, like the streaming plot service of plotly, is only available via communication with the server.

The examples that follow rely again on pseudo-random numbers, this time stored in a DataFrame object with DatetimeIndex (i.e., as time series data):

```
In [46]: a = np.random.standard_normal((250, 5)).cumsum(axis=0)  ❶

In [47]: index = pd.date_range('2019-1-1',  ❷
                               freq='B',  ❸
                               periods=len(a))  ❹

In [48]: df = pd.DataFrame(100 + 5 * a,  ❺
                           columns=list('abcde'),  ❻
                           index=index)  ❼

In [49]: df.head()  ❽
Out[49]:                      a           b           c          d           e
         2019-01-01  109.037535   98.693865  104.474094  96.878857  100.621936
         2019-01-02  107.598242   97.005738  106.789189  97.966552  100.175313
         2019-01-03  101.639668  100.332253  103.183500  99.747869  107.902901
         2019-01-04   98.500363  101.208283  100.966242  94.023898  104.387256
         2019-01-07   93.941632  103.319168  105.674012  95.891062   86.547934
```

❶ The standard normally distributed pseudo-random numbers.

❷ The start date for the DatetimeIndex object.

❸ The frequency ("business daily").

❹ The number of periods needed.

❺ A linear transform of the raw data.

❻ The column headers as single characters.

❼ The DatetimeIndex object.

❽ The first five rows of data.

Cufflinks adds a new method to the DataFrame class: df.iplot(). This method uses plotly in the backend to create interactive plots. The code examples in this section all make use of the option to download the interactive plot as a static bitmap, which in turn is embedded in the text. In the Jupyter Notebook environment, the created plots are all interactive. The result of the following code is shown in Figure 7-22:

```
In [50]: plyo.iplot(  ❶
             df.iplot(asFigure=True),  ❷
             image='png',  ❸
             filename='ply_01'  ❹
         )
```

❶ This makes use of the offline (notebook mode) capabilities of plotly.

❷ The df.iplot() method is called with parameter asFigure=True to allow for local plotting and embedding.

❸ The image option provides in addition a static bitmap version of the plot.

❹ The filename for the bitmap to be saved is specified (the file type extension is added automatically).

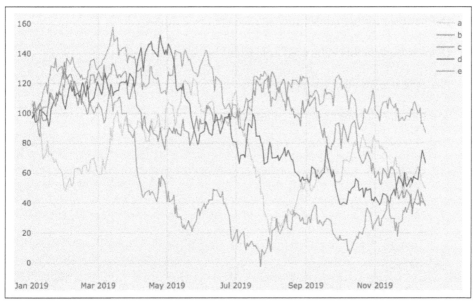

Figure 7-22. Line plot for time series data with plotly, pandas, and Cufflinks

As with matplotlib in general and with the pandas plotting functionality, there are multiple parameters available to customize such plots (see Figure 7-23):

```
In [51]: plyo.iplot(
             df[['a', 'b']].iplot(asFigure=True,
                 theme='polar',   ❶
                 title='A Time Series Plot',   ❷
                 xTitle='date',   ❸
                 yTitle='value',   ❹
                 mode={'a': 'markers', 'b': 'lines+markers'},   ❺
                 symbol={'a': 'circle', 'b': 'diamond'},   ❻
                 size=3.5,   ❼
                 colors={'a': 'blue', 'b': 'magenta'},   ❽
                     ),
             image='png',
```

```
            filename='ply_02'
    )
```

❶ Selects a theme (plotting style) for the plot.

❷ Adds a title.

❸ Adds an x-axis label.

❹ Adds a y-axis label.

❺ Defines the plotting *mode* (line, marker, etc.) by column.

❻ Defines the symbols to be used as markers by column.

❼ Fixes the size for all markers.

❽ Specifies the plotting color by column.

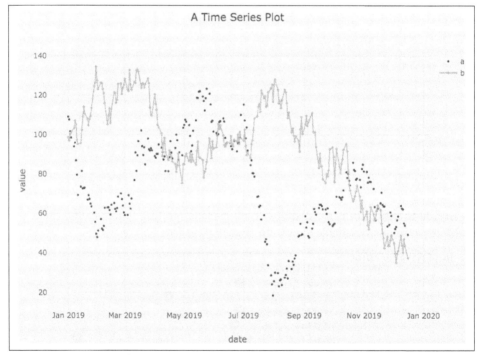

Figure 7-23. Line plot for two columns of the DataFrame object with customizations

Similar to matplotlib, plotly allows for a number of different plotting types. Plotting types available via Cufflinks are chart, scatter, bar, box, spread, ratio, heat map, surface, histogram, bubble, bubble3d, scatter3d, scattergeo, ohlc, candle, pie, and choropleth. As an example of a plotting type different from a line plot, consider the histogram (see Figure 7-24):

```
In [52]: plyo.iplot(
             df.iplot(kind='hist',     ❶
                      subplots=True,    ❷
                      bins=15,          ❸
                      asFigure=True),
             image='png',
             filename='ply_03'
         )
```

❶ Specifies the plotting type.

❷ Requires separate subplots for every column.

❸ Sets the bins parameter (buckets to be used = bars to be plotted).

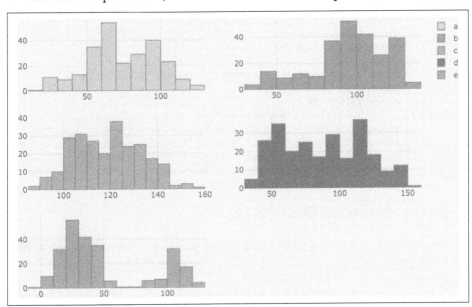

Figure 7-24. Histograms per column of the DataFrame object

Financial Plots

The combination of plotly, Cufflinks, and pandas proves particularly powerful when working with financial time series data. Cufflinks provides specialized functionality to create typical financial plots and to add typical financial charting elements, such as the Relative Strength Index (RSI), to name but one example. To this end, a persistent `QuantFig` object is created that can be plotted the same way as a `DataFrame` object with `Cufflinks`.

This subsection uses a real financial data set, time series data for the EUR/USD exchange rate (source: FXCM Forex Capital Markets Ltd.):

```
In [54]: raw = pd.read_csv('../../source/fxcm_eur_usd_eod_data.csv',
                           index_col=0, parse_dates=True)  ❶

In [55]: raw.info()  ❷
         <class 'pandas.core.frame.DataFrame'>
         DatetimeIndex: 1547 entries, 2013-01-01 22:00:00 to 2017-12-31 22:00:00
         Data columns (total 8 columns):
         BidOpen     1547 non-null float64
         BidHigh     1547 non-null float64
         BidLow      1547 non-null float64
         BidClose    1547 non-null float64
         AskOpen     1547 non-null float64
         AskHigh     1547 non-null float64
         AskLow      1547 non-null float64
         AskClose    1547 non-null float64
         dtypes: float64(8)
         memory usage: 108.8 KB

In [56]: quotes = raw[['AskOpen', 'AskHigh', 'AskLow', 'AskClose']]  ❸
         quotes = quotes.iloc[-60:]  ❹
         quotes.tail()  ❺
Out[56]:                      AskOpen  AskHigh   AskLow  AskClose
         2017-12-25 22:00:00  1.18667  1.18791  1.18467   1.18587
         2017-12-26 22:00:00  1.18587  1.19104  1.18552   1.18885
         2017-12-27 22:00:00  1.18885  1.19592  1.18885   1.19426
         2017-12-28 22:00:00  1.19426  1.20256  1.19369   1.20092
         2017-12-31 22:00:00  1.20092  1.20144  1.19994   1.20144
```

❶ Reads the financial data from a CSV file.

❷ The resulting `DataFrame` object consists of multiple columns and more than 1,500 data rows.

❸ Selects four columns from the `DataFrame` object (Open-High-Low-Close, or OHLC).

❹ Only a few data rows are used for the visualization.

❺ Returns the final five rows of the resulting data set `quotes`.

During instantiation, the `QuantFig` object takes the `DataFrame` object as input and allows for some basic customization. Plotting the data stored in the `QuantFig` object `qf` then happens with the `qf.iplot()` method (see Figure 7-25):

```
In [57]: qf = cf.QuantFig(
                quotes,              ❶
                title='EUR/USD Exchange Rate',    ❷
                legend='top',        ❸
                name='EUR/USD'       ❹
          )

In [58]: plyo.iplot(
                qf.iplot(asFigure=True),
                image='png',
                filename='qf_01'
          )
```

❶ The DataFrame object is passed to the QuantFig constructor.

❷ This adds a figure title.

❸ The legend is placed at the top of the plot.

❹ This gives the data set a name.

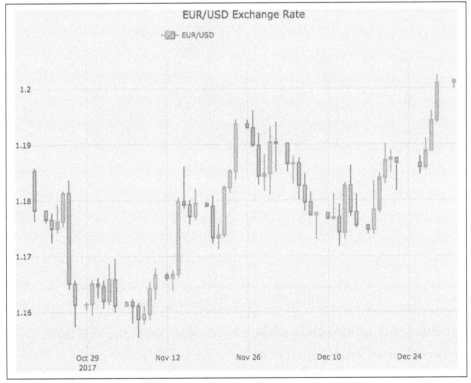

Figure 7-25. OHLC plot of EUR/USD data

Adding typical financial charting elements, such as Bollinger bands, is possible via different methods available for the `QuantFig` object (see Figure 7-26):

```
In [59]: qf.add_bollinger_bands(periods=15,    ❶
                                 boll_std=2)     ❷

In [60]: plyo.iplot(qf.iplot(asFigure=True),
                    image='png',
                    filename='qf_02'
        )
```

❶ The number of periods for the Bollinger band.

❷ The number of standard deviations to be used for the band width.

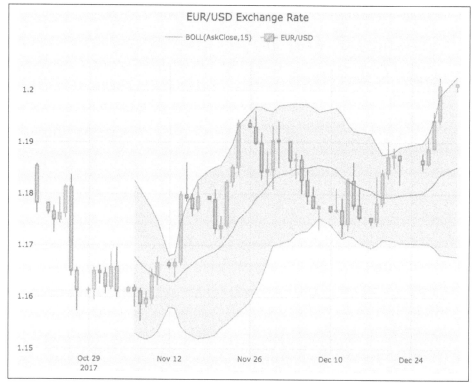

Figure 7-26. OHLC plot of EUR/USD data with Bollinger band

Certain financial indicators, such as RSI, may be added as a subplot (see Figure 7-27):

```
In [61]: qf.add_rsi(periods=14,    ❶
                    showbands=False)  ❷

In [62]: plyo.iplot(
                qf.iplot(asFigure=True),
```

```
              image='png',
              filename='qf_03'
    )
```

❶ Fixes the RSI period.

❷ Does not show an upper or lower band.

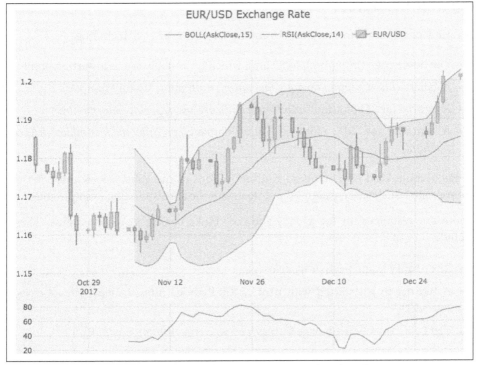

Figure 7-27. OHLC plot of EUR/USD data with Bollinger band and RSI

Conclusion

`matplotlib` can be considered both the benchmark and an all-rounder when it comes to data visualization in Python. It is tightly integrated with `NumPy` and `pandas`, and the basic functionality is easily and conveniently accessed. However, `matplotlib` is a mighty library with a somewhat complex API. This makes it impossible to give a broad overview of all the capabilities of `matplotlib` in this chapter.

This chapter introduces the basic functions of `matplotlib` for 2D and 3D plotting useful in many financial contexts. Other chapters provide further examples of how to use the package for visualization.

In addition, this chapter covers `plotly` in combination with `Cufflinks`. This combination makes the creation of interactive `D3.js` plots a convenient affair since only a single method call on a `DataFrame` object is necessary in general. All technicalities are taken care of in the backend. Furthermore, `Cufflinks` provides with the `QuantFig` object an easy way to create typical financial plots with popular financial indicators.

Further Resources

A variety of resources for `matplotlib` can be found on the web, including:

- The home page (*http://matplotlib.org*), which is probably the best starting point
- A gallery (*http://matplotlib.org/gallery.html*) with many useful examples
- A tutorial for 2D plotting (*http://matplotlib.org/users/pyplot_tutorial.html*)
- A tutorial for 3D plotting (*http://matplotlib.org/mpl_toolkits/mplot3d/tutorial.html*)

It has become kind of a standard routine to consult the gallery, look there for an appropriate visualization example, and start with the corresponding example code.

The major resources for the `plotly` and `Cufflinks` packages are also online. These include:

- The `plotly` home page (*http://plot.ly*)
- A tutorial to get started with `plotly` for Python (*https://plot.ly/python/getting-started/*)
- The `Cufflinks` GitHub page (*https://github.com/santosjorge/cufflinks*)

## CHAPTER 8

Financial Time Series

[T]ime is what keeps everything from happening at once.

—Ray Cummings

Financial time series data is one of the most important types of data in finance. This is data indexed by date and/or time. For example, prices of stocks over time represent financial time series data. Similarly, the EUR/USD exchange rate over time represents a financial time series; the exchange rate is quoted in brief intervals of time, and a collection of such quotes then is a time series of exchange rates.

There is no financial discipline that gets by without considering time an important factor. This mainly is the same as with physics and other sciences. The major tool to cope with time series data in Python is pandas. Wes McKinney, the original and main author of pandas, started developing the library when working as an analyst at AQR Capital Management, a large hedge fund. It is safe to say that pandas has been designed from the ground up to work with financial time series data.

The chapter is mainly based on two financial time series data sets in the form of comma-separated values (CSV) files. It proceeds along the following lines:

"Correlation Analysis" on page 222

This section presents a case study based on financial time series data for the S&P 500 stock index and the VIX volatility index. It provides some support for the stylized (empirical) fact that both indices are negatively correlated.

"High-Frequency Data" on page 228

This section works with high-frequency data, or *tick data*, which has become commonplace in finance. pandas again proves powerful in handling such data sets.

Financial Data

This section works with a locally stored financial data set in the form of a CSV file. Technically, such files are simply text files with a data row structure characterized by commas that separate single values. Before importing the data, some package imports and customizations:

```
In [1]: import numpy as np
        import pandas as pd
        from pylab import mpl, plt
        plt.style.use('seaborn')
        mpl.rcParams['font.family'] = 'serif'
        %matplotlib inline
```

Data Import

pandas provides a number of different functions and DataFrame methods to import data stored in different formats (CSV, SQL, Excel, etc.) and to export data to different formats (see Chapter 9 for more details). The following code uses the pd.read_csv() function to import the time series data set from the CSV file:[1]

```
In [2]: filename = '../../source/tr_eikon_eod_data.csv'  ❶

In [3]: f = open(filename, 'r')  ❷
        f.readlines()[:5]  ❸
Out[3]: ['Date,AAPL.O,MSFT.O,INTC.O,AMZN.O,GS.N,SPY,.SPX,.VIX,EUR=,XAU=,GDX,
        ,GLD\n',
         '2010-01-01,,,,,,,,,1.4323,1096.35,,\n',
         '2010-01-04,30.57282657,30.95,20.88,133.9,173.08,113.33,1132.99,20.04,
        ,1.4411,1120.0,47.71,109.8\n',
         '2010-01-05,30.625683660000004,30.96,20.87,134.69,176.14,113.63,1136.52,
        ,19.35,1.4368,1118.65,48.17,109.7\n',
         '2010-01-06,30.138541290000003,30.77,20.8,132.25,174.26,113.71,1137.14,
        ,19.16,1.4412,1138.5,49.34,111.51\n']
```

---

1 The file contains end-of-day (EOD) data for different financial instruments as retrieved from the Thomson Reuters Eikon Data API.

```
In [4]: data = pd.read_csv(filename,  ❸
                           index_col=0,  ❹
                           parse_dates=True)  ❺

In [5]: data.info()  ❻
        <class 'pandas.core.frame.DataFrame'>
        DatetimeIndex: 2216 entries, 2010-01-01 to 2018-06-29
        Data columns (total 12 columns):
        AAPL.O    2138 non-null float64
        MSFT.O    2138 non-null float64
        INTC.O    2138 non-null float64
        AMZN.O    2138 non-null float64
        GS.N      2138 non-null float64
        SPY       2138 non-null float64
        .SPX      2138 non-null float64
        .VIX      2138 non-null float64
        EUR=      2216 non-null float64
        XAU=      2211 non-null float64
        GDX       2138 non-null float64
        GLD       2138 non-null float64
        dtypes: float64(12)
        memory usage: 225.1 KB
```

❶ Specifies the path and filename.

❷ Shows the first five rows of the raw data (Linux/Mac).

❸ The filename passed to the `pd.read_csv()` function.

❹ Specifies that the first column shall be handled as an index.

❺ Specifies that the index values are of type `datetime`.

❻ The resulting `DataFrame` object.

At this stage, a financial analyst probably takes a first look at the data, either by inspecting or visualizing it (see Figure 8-1):

```
In [6]: data.head()  ❶
Out[6]:
                     AAPL.O  MSFT.O  INTC.O  AMZN.O    GS.N     SPY     .SPX   .VIX  \
        Date
        2010-01-01      NaN     NaN     NaN     NaN     NaN     NaN      NaN    NaN
        2010-01-04  30.572827  30.950   20.88  133.90  173.08  113.33  1132.99  20.04
        2010-01-05  30.625684  30.960   20.87  134.69  176.14  113.63  1136.52  19.35
        2010-01-06  30.138541  30.770   20.80  132.25  174.26  113.71  1137.14  19.16
        2010-01-07  30.082827  30.452   20.60  130.00  177.67  114.19  1141.69  19.06

                     EUR=    XAU=    GDX    GLD
```

```
         Date
         2010-01-01  1.4323  1096.35   NaN    NaN
         2010-01-04  1.4411  1120.00  47.71  109.80
         2010-01-05  1.4368  1118.65  48.17  109.70
         2010-01-06  1.4412  1138.50  49.34  111.51
         2010-01-07  1.4318  1131.90  49.10  110.82

In [7]: data.tail()  ❷
Out[7]:
                  AAPL.O  MSFT.O  INTC.O   AMZN.O    GS.N     SPY     .SPX    .VIX  \
         Date
         2018-06-25  182.17   98.39   50.71  1663.15  221.54  271.00  2717.07  17.33
         2018-06-26  184.43   99.08   49.67  1691.09  221.58  271.60  2723.06  15.92
         2018-06-27  184.16   97.54   48.76  1660.51  220.18  269.35  2699.63  17.91
         2018-06-28  185.50   98.63   49.25  1701.45  223.42  270.89  2716.31  16.85
         2018-06-29  185.11   98.61   49.71  1699.80  220.57  271.28  2718.37  16.09

                    EUR=     XAU=    GDX     GLD
         Date
         2018-06-25  1.1702  1265.00  22.01  119.89
         2018-06-26  1.1645  1258.64  21.95  119.26
         2018-06-27  1.1552  1251.62  21.81  118.58
         2018-06-28  1.1567  1247.88  21.93  118.22
         2018-06-29  1.1683  1252.25  22.31  118.65

In [8]: data.plot(figsize=(10, 12), subplots=True);  ❸
```

❶ The first five rows …

❷ … and the final five rows are shown.

❸ This visualizes the complete data set via multiple subplots.

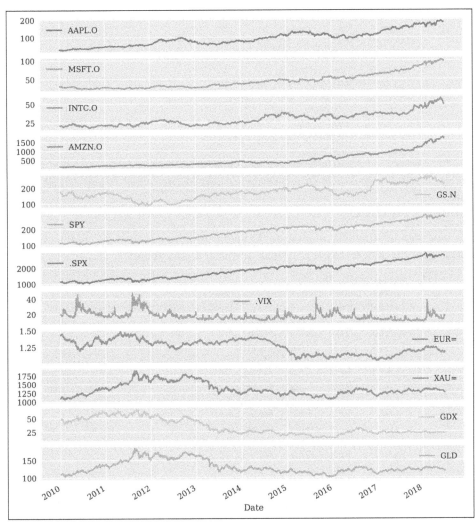

Figure 8-1. Financial time series data as line plots

The data used is from the Thomson Reuters (TR) Eikon Data API. In the TR world symbols for financial instruments are called *Reuters Instrument Codes* (RICs). The financial instruments that the single RICs represent are:

```
In [9]: instruments = ['Apple Stock', 'Microsoft Stock',
                       'Intel Stock', 'Amazon Stock', 'Goldman Sachs Stock',
                       'SPDR S&P 500 ETF Trust', 'S&P 500 Index',
                       'VIX Volatility Index', 'EUR/USD Exchange Rate',
                       'Gold Price', 'VanEck Vectors Gold Miners ETF',
                       'SPDR Gold Trust']

In [10]: for ric, name in zip(data.columns, instruments):
```

```
            print('{:8s} | {}'.format(ric, name))
AAPL.O  | Apple Stock
MSFT.O  | Microsoft Stock
INTC.O  | Intel Stock
AMZN.O  | Amazon Stock
GS.N    | Goldman Sachs Stock
SPY     | SPDR S&P 500 ETF Trust
.SPX    | S&P 500 Index
.VIX    | VIX Volatility Index
EUR=    | EUR/USD Exchange Rate
XAU=    | Gold Price
GDX     | VanEck Vectors Gold Miners ETF
GLD     | SPDR Gold Trust
```

Summary Statistics

The next step the financial analyst might take is to have a look at different summary statistics for the data set to get a "feeling" for what it is all about:

```
In [11]: data.info()  ❶
         <class 'pandas.core.frame.DataFrame'>
         DatetimeIndex: 2216 entries, 2010-01-01 to 2018-06-29
         Data columns (total 12 columns):
         AAPL.O    2138 non-null float64
         MSFT.O    2138 non-null float64
         INTC.O    2138 non-null float64
         AMZN.O    2138 non-null float64
         GS.N      2138 non-null float64
         SPY       2138 non-null float64
         .SPX      2138 non-null float64
         .VIX      2138 non-null float64
         EUR=      2216 non-null float64
         XAU=      2211 non-null float64
         GDX       2138 non-null float64
         GLD       2138 non-null float64
         dtypes: float64(12)
         memory usage: 225.1 KB

In [12]: data.describe().round(2)  ❷
Out[12]:
            AAPL.O   MSFT.O   INTC.O   AMZN.O      GS.N      SPY     .SPX     .VIX \
count      2138.00  2138.00  2138.00  2138.00   2138.00  2138.00  2138.00  2138.00
mean         93.46    44.56    29.36   480.46    170.22   180.32  1802.71    17.03
std          40.55    19.53     8.17   372.31     42.48    48.19   483.34     5.88
min          27.44    23.01    17.66   108.61     87.70   102.20  1022.58     9.14
25%          60.29    28.57    22.51   213.60    146.61   133.99  1338.57    13.07
50%          90.55    39.66    27.33   322.06    164.43   186.32  1863.08    15.58
75%         117.24    54.37    34.71   698.85    192.13   210.99  2108.94    19.07
max         193.98   102.49    57.08  1750.08    273.38   286.58  2872.87    48.00

              EUR=     XAU=      GDX      GLD
count      2216.00  2211.00  2138.00  2138.00
```

```
mean        1.25    1349.01     33.57    130.09
std         0.11     188.75     15.17     18.78
min         1.04    1051.36     12.47    100.50
25%         1.13    1221.53     22.14    117.40
50%         1.27    1292.61     25.62    124.00
75%         1.35    1428.24     48.34    139.00
max         1.48    1898.99     66.63    184.59
```

❶ info() gives some metainformation about the DataFrame object.

❷ describe() provides useful standard statistics per column.

Quick Insights

pandas provides a number of methods to gain a quick overview over newly imported financial time series data sets, such as info() and describe(). They also allow for quick checks of whether the importing procedure worked as desired (e.g., whether the Data Frame object indeed has an index of type DatetimeIndex).

There are also options, of course, to customize what types of statistic to derive and display:

```
In [13]: data.mean()    ❶
Out[13]: AAPL.O        93.455973
         MSFT.O        44.561115
         INTC.O        29.364192
         AMZN.O       480.461251
         GS.N         170.216221
         SPY          180.323029
         .SPX        1802.713106
         .VIX          17.027133
         EUR=           1.248587
         XAU=        1349.014130
         GDX           33.566525
         GLD          130.086590
         dtype: float64

In [14]: data.aggregate([min,      ❷
                         np.mean,   ❸
                         np.std,    ❹
                         np.median, ❺
                         max]       ❻
                ).round(2)
Out[14]:
              AAPL.O  MSFT.O  INTC.O  AMZN.O    GS.N     SPY     .SPX   .VIX  EUR= \
         min    27.44   23.01   17.66  108.61   87.70  102.20  1022.58   9.14  1.04
         mean   93.46   44.56   29.36  480.46  170.22  180.32  1802.71  17.03  1.25
         std    40.55   19.53    8.17  372.31   42.48   48.19   483.34   5.88  0.11
         median 90.55   39.66   27.33  322.06  164.43  186.32  1863.08  15.58  1.27
```

```
max      193.98  102.49    57.08  1750.08  273.38  286.58  2872.87  48.00  1.48

                XAU=     GDX     GLD
min          1051.36   12.47  100.50
mean         1349.01   33.57  130.09
std           188.75   15.17   18.78
median       1292.61   25.62  124.00
max          1898.99   66.63  184.59
```

❶ The mean value per column.

❷ The minimum value per column.

❸ The mean value per column.

❹ The standard deviation per column.

❺ The median per column.

❻ The maximum value per column.

Using the `aggregate()` method also allows one to pass custom functions.

Changes over Time

Statistical analysis methods are often based on changes over time and not the absolute values themselves. There are multiple options to calculate the changes in a time series over time, including absolute differences, percentage changes, and logarithmic (log) returns.

First, the absolute differences, for which `pandas` provides a special method:

```
In [15]: data.diff().head()  ❶
Out[15]:
                 AAPL.O   MSFT.O  INTC.O  AMZN.O   GS.N   SPY   .SPX   .VIX    EUR=  \
Date
2010-01-01          NaN      NaN     NaN     NaN    NaN   NaN    NaN    NaN     NaN
2010-01-04          NaN      NaN     NaN     NaN    NaN   NaN    NaN    NaN  0.0088
2010-01-05     0.052857    0.010   -0.01    0.79   3.06  0.30   3.53  -0.69 -0.0043
2010-01-06    -0.487142   -0.190   -0.07   -2.44  -1.88  0.08   0.62  -0.19  0.0044
2010-01-07    -0.055714   -0.318   -0.20   -2.25   3.41  0.48   4.55  -0.10 -0.0094

                XAU=    GDX    GLD
Date
2010-01-01       NaN    NaN    NaN
2010-01-04     23.65    NaN    NaN
2010-01-05     -1.35   0.46  -0.10
2010-01-06     19.85   1.17   1.81
2010-01-07     -6.60  -0.24  -0.69
```

```
In [16]: data.diff().mean()  ❷
Out[16]: AAPL.O    0.064737
         MSFT.O    0.031246
         INTC.O    0.013540
         AMZN.O    0.706608
         GS.N      0.028224
         SPY       0.072103
         .SPX      0.732659
         .VIX     -0.019583
         EUR=     -0.000119
         XAU=      0.041887
         GDX      -0.015071
         GLD      -0.003455
         dtype: float64
```

❶   diff() provides the absolute changes between two index values.

❷   Of course, aggregation operations can be applied in addition.

From a statistics point of view, absolute changes are not optimal because they are dependent on the scale of the time series data itself. Therefore, percentage changes are usually preferred. The following code derives the percentage changes or percentage returns (also: simple returns) in a financial context and visualizes their mean values per column (see Figure 8-2):

```
In [17]: data.pct_change().round(3).head()  ❶
Out[17]:
               AAPL.O  MSFT.O  INTC.O  AMZN.O    GS.N    SPY    .SPX    .VIX    EUR=  \
Date
2010-01-01      NaN     NaN     NaN     NaN     NaN     NaN     NaN     NaN     NaN
2010-01-04      NaN     NaN     NaN     NaN     NaN     NaN     NaN     NaN   0.006
2010-01-05    0.002   0.000  -0.000   0.006   0.018   0.003   0.003  -0.034  -0.003
2010-01-06   -0.016  -0.006  -0.003  -0.018  -0.011   0.001   0.001  -0.010   0.003
2010-01-07   -0.002  -0.010  -0.010  -0.017   0.020   0.004   0.004  -0.005  -0.007

               XAU=     GDX     GLD
Date
2010-01-01      NaN     NaN     NaN
2010-01-04    0.022     NaN     NaN
2010-01-05   -0.001   0.010  -0.001
2010-01-06    0.018   0.024   0.016
2010-01-07   -0.006  -0.005  -0.006

In [18]: data.pct_change().mean().plot(kind='bar', figsize=(10, 6));  ❷
```

❶   pct_change() calculates the percentage change between two index values.

❷   The mean values of the results are visualized as a bar plot.

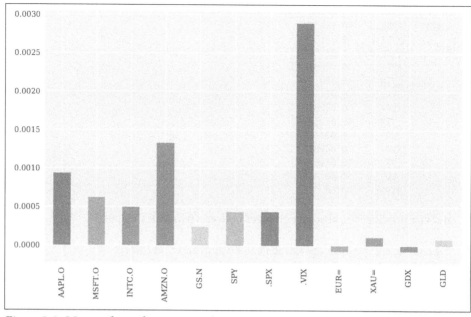

Figure 8-2. Mean values of percentage changes as bar plot

As an alternative to percentage returns, log returns can be used. In some scenarios, they are easier to handle and therefore often preferred in a financial context.[2] Figure 8-3 shows the cumulative log returns for the single financial time series. This type of plot leads to some form of *normalization*:

```
In [19]: rets = np.log(data / data.shift(1))    ❶

In [20]: rets.head().round(3)    ❷
Out[20]:
                 AAPL.O  MSFT.O  INTC.O  AMZN.O    GS.N    SPY   .SPX    .VIX    EUR=  \
Date
2010-01-01       NaN     NaN     NaN     NaN     NaN     NaN    NaN     NaN     NaN
2010-01-04       NaN     NaN     NaN     NaN     NaN     NaN    NaN     NaN   0.006
2010-01-05     0.002   0.000  -0.000   0.006   0.018   0.003  0.003  -0.035  -0.003
2010-01-06    -0.016  -0.006  -0.003  -0.018  -0.011   0.001  0.001  -0.010   0.003
2010-01-07    -0.002  -0.010  -0.010  -0.017   0.019   0.004  0.004  -0.005  -0.007

                 XAU=     GDX     GLD
Date
2010-01-01       NaN     NaN     NaN
2010-01-04     0.021     NaN     NaN
2010-01-05    -0.001   0.010  -0.001
```

---

2 One of the advantages is additivity over time, which does not hold true for simple percentage changes/ returns.

```
2010-01-06  0.018  0.024  0.016
2010-01-07 -0.006 -0.005 -0.006
```

```
In [21]: rets.cumsum().apply(np.exp).plot(figsize=(10, 6));  ❸
```

❶ Calculates the log returns in vectorized fashion.

❷ A subset of the results.

❸ Plots the cumulative log returns over time; first the cumsum() method is called, then np.exp() is applied to the results.

Figure 8-3. Cumulative log returns over time

Resampling

Resampling is an important operation on financial time series data. Usually this takes the form of *downsampling*, meaning that, for example, a tick data series is resampled to one-minute intervals or a time series with daily observations is resampled to one with weekly or monthly observations (as shown in Figure 8-4):

```
In [22]: data.resample('1w', label='right').last().head()  ❶
Out[22]:
                 AAPL.O MSFT.O INTC.O AMZN.O    GS.N     SPY    .SPX   .VIX \
Date
2010-01-03         NaN    NaN    NaN    NaN     NaN     NaN     NaN    NaN
2010-01-10   30.282827  30.66  20.83 133.52  174.31  114.57 1144.98  18.13
2010-01-17   29.418542  30.86  20.80 127.14  165.21  113.64 1136.03  17.91
```

```
2010-01-24  28.249972   28.96   19.91  121.43  154.12  109.21  1091.76  27.31
2010-01-31  27.437544   28.18   19.40  125.41  148.72  107.39  1073.87  24.62

              EUR=     XAU=     GDX     GLD
Date
2010-01-03  1.4323  1096.35     NaN     NaN
2010-01-10  1.4412  1136.10   49.84  111.37
2010-01-17  1.4382  1129.90   47.42  110.86
2010-01-24  1.4137  1092.60   43.79  107.17
2010-01-31  1.3862  1081.05   40.72  105.96

In [23]: data.resample('1m', label='right').last().head()   ❷
Out[23]:
              AAPL.O   MSFT.O  INTC.O  AMZN.O    GS.N       SPY     .SPX  \
Date
2010-01-31  27.437544  28.1800   19.40  125.41  148.72  107.3900  1073.87
2010-02-28  29.231399  28.6700   20.53  118.40  156.35  110.7400  1104.49
2010-03-31  33.571395  29.2875   22.29  135.77  170.63  117.0000  1169.43
2010-04-30  37.298534  30.5350   22.84  137.10  145.20  118.8125  1186.69
2010-05-31  36.697106  25.8000   21.42  125.46  144.26  109.3690  1089.41

              .VIX     EUR=     XAU=    GDX      GLD
Date
2010-01-31  24.62  1.3862  1081.05  40.72  105.960
2010-02-28  19.50  1.3625  1116.10  43.89  109.430
2010-03-31  17.59  1.3510  1112.80  44.41  108.950
2010-04-30  22.05  1.3295  1178.25  50.51  115.360
2010-05-31  32.07  1.2305  1215.71  49.86  118.881

In [24]: rets.cumsum().apply(np.exp). resample('1m', label='right').last(
                            ).plot(figsize=(10, 6));   ❸
```

❶ EOD data gets resampled to *weekly* time intervals …

❷ … and *monthly* time intervals.

❸ This plots the cumulative log returns over time: first, the cumsum() method is
called, then np.exp() is applied to the results; finally, the resampling takes place.

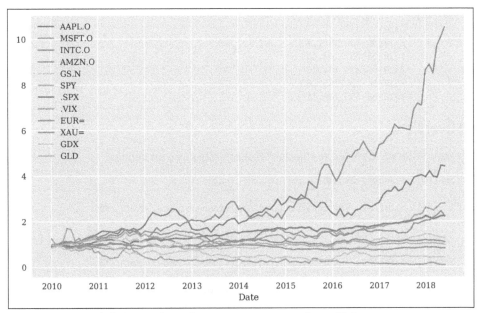

Figure 8-4. Resampled cumulative log returns over time (monthly)

Avoiding Foresight Bias

When resampling, `pandas` takes by default in many cases the left label (or index value) of the interval. To be financially consistent, make sure to use the right label (index value) and in general the last available data point in the interval. Otherwise, a foresight bias might sneak into the financial analysis.[3]

Rolling Statistics

It is financial tradition to work with *rolling statistics*, often also called *financial indicators* or *financial studies*. Such rolling statistics are basic tools for financial chartists and technical traders, for example. This section works with a single financial time series only:

```
In [25]: sym = 'AAPL.O'

In [26]: data = pd.DataFrame(data[sym]).dropna()

In [27]: data.tail()
```

---

3 *Foresight bias*—or, in its strongest form, *perfect foresight*—means that at some point in the financial analysis, data is used that only becomes available at a later point. The result might be "too good" results, for example, when backtesting a trading strategy.

```
Out[27]:                   AAPL.O
            Date
            2018-06-25   182.17
            2018-06-26   184.43
            2018-06-27   184.16
            2018-06-28   185.50
            2018-06-29   185.11
```

An Overview

It is straightforward to derive standard rolling statistics with pandas:

```
In [28]: window = 20  ❶

In [29]: data['min'] = data[sym].rolling(window=window).min()  ❷

In [30]: data['mean'] = data[sym].rolling(window=window).mean()  ❸

In [31]: data['std'] = data[sym].rolling(window=window).std()  ❹

In [32]: data['median'] = data[sym].rolling(window=window).median()  ❺

In [33]: data['max'] = data[sym].rolling(window=window).max()  ❻

In [34]: data['ewma'] = data[sym].ewm(halflife=0.5, min_periods=window).mean()  ❼
```

❶ Defines the window; i.e., the number of index values to include.

❷ Calculates the rolling minimum value.

❸ Calculates the rolling mean value.

❹ Calculates the rolling standard deviation.

❺ Calculates the rolling median value.

❻ Calculates the rolling maximum value.

❼ Calculates the exponentially weighted moving average, with decay in terms of a half life of 0.5.

To derive more specialized financial indicators, additional packages are generally needed (see, for instance, the financial plots with Cufflinks in "Interactive 2D Plotting" on page 195). Custom ones can also easily be applied via the apply() method.

The following code shows a subset of the results and visualizes a selection of the calculated rolling statistics (see Figure 8-5):

```
In [35]: data.dropna().head()
Out[35]:
```

```
                 AAPL.O          min         mean          std       median          max  \
Date
2010-02-01   27.818544   27.437544   29.580892   0.933650   29.821542   30.719969
2010-02-02   27.979972   27.437544   29.451249   0.968048   29.711113   30.719969
2010-02-03   28.461400   27.437544   29.343035   0.950665   29.685970   30.719969
2010-02-04   27.435687   27.435687   29.207892   1.021129   29.547113   30.719969
2010-02-05   27.922829   27.435687   29.099892   1.037811   29.419256   30.719969


                 ewma
Date
2010-02-01   27.805432
2010-02-02   27.936337
2010-02-03   28.330134
2010-02-04   27.659299
2010-02-05   27.856947
```

```
In [36]: ax = data[['min', 'mean', 'max']].iloc[-200:].plot(
              figsize=(10, 6), style=['g--', 'r--', 'g--'], lw=0.8)   ❶
         data[sym].iloc[-200:].plot(ax=ax, lw=2.0);   ❷
```

❶ Plots three rolling statistics for the final 200 data rows.

❷ Adds the original time series data to the plot.

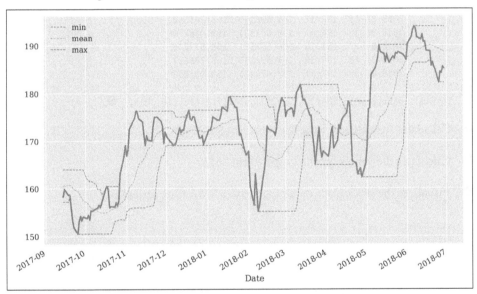

Figure 8-5. Rolling statistics for minimum, mean, maximum values

A Technical Analysis Example

Rolling statistics are a major tool in the so-called *technical analysis* of stocks, as compared to the fundamental analysis which focuses, for instance, on financial reports and the strategic positions of the company whose stock is being analyzed.

A decades-old trading strategy based on technical analysis is using two *simple moving averages* (SMAs). The idea is that the trader should go long on a stock (or financial instrument in general) when the shorter-term SMA is above the longer-term SMA and should go short when the opposite holds true. The concepts can be made precise with pandas and the capabilities of the DataFrame object.

Rolling statistics are generally only calculated when there is enough data given the window parameter specification. As Figure 8-6 shows, the SMA time series only start at the day for which there is enough data given the specific parameterization:

```
In [37]: data['SMA1'] = data[sym].rolling(window=42).mean()    ❶

In [38]: data['SMA2'] = data[sym].rolling(window=252).mean()   ❷

In [39]: data[[sym, 'SMA1', 'SMA2']].tail()
Out[39]:                 AAPL.O        SMA1        SMA2
         Date
         2018-06-25      182.17    185.606190    168.265556
         2018-06-26      184.43    186.087381    168.418770
         2018-06-27      184.16    186.607381    168.579206
         2018-06-28      185.50    187.089286    168.736627
         2018-06-29      185.11    187.470476    168.901032

In [40]: data[[sym, 'SMA1', 'SMA2']].plot(figsize=(10, 6));    ❸
```

❶ Calculates the values for the shorter-term SMA.

❷ Calculates the values for the longer-term SMA.

❸ Visualizes the stock price data plus the two SMA time series.

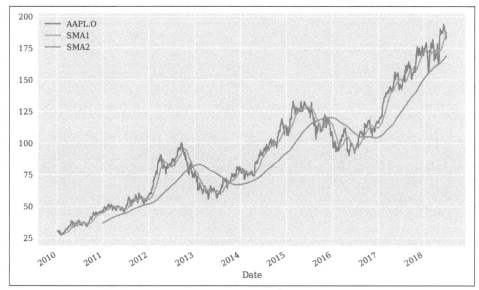

Figure 8-6. Apple stock price and two simple moving averages

In this context, the SMAs are only a means to an end. They are used to derive positions to implement a trading strategy. Figure 8-7 visualizes a long position by a value of 1 and a short position by a value of -1. The change in the position is triggered (visually) by a crossover of the two lines representing the SMA time series:

```
In [41]: data.dropna(inplace=True)  ❶

In [42]: data['positions'] = np.where(data['SMA1'] > data['SMA2'],  ❷
                               1,  ❸
                               -1)  ❹

In [43]: ax = data[[sym, 'SMA1', 'SMA2', 'positions']].plot(figsize=(10, 6),
                                                 secondary_y='positions')
         ax.get_legend().set_bbox_to_anchor((0.25, 0.85));
```

❶ Only complete data rows are kept.

❷ If the shorter-term SMA value is greater than the longer-term one …

❸ … go long on the stock (put a 1).

❹ Otherwise, go short on the stock (put a -1).

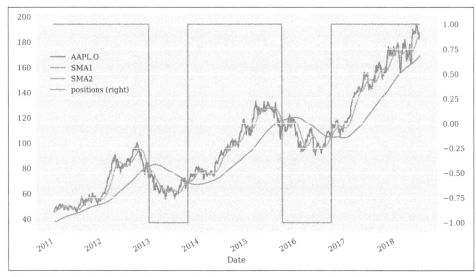

Figure 8-7. Apple stock price, two simple moving averages and positions

The trading strategy implicitly derived here only leads to a few trades per se: only when the position value changes (i.e., a crossover happens) does a trade take place. Including opening and closing trades, this would add up to just six trades in total.

Correlation Analysis

As a further illustration of how to work with pandas and financial time series data, consider the case of the S&P 500 stock index and the VIX volatility index. It is a stylized fact that when the S&P 500 rises, the VIX falls in general, and vice versa. This is about *correlation* and not *causation*. This section shows how to come up with some supporting statistical evidence for the stylized fact that the S&P 500 and the VIX are (highly) negatively correlated.[4]

The Data

The data set now consists of two financial times series, both visualized in Figure 8-8:

```
In [44]: raw = pd.read_csv('../../source/tr_eikon_eod_data.csv',
                    index_col=0, parse_dates=True)    ❶

In [45]: data = raw[['.SPX', '.VIX']].dropna()
```

---

4 One reason behind this is that when the stock index comes down—during a crisis, for instance—trading volume goes up, and therewith also the volatility. When the stock index is on the rise, investors generally are calm and do not see much incentive to engage in heavy trading. In particular, long-only investors then try to ride the trend even further.

```
In [46]: data.tail()
Out[46]:              .SPX    .VIX
         Date
         2018-06-25  2717.07  17.33
         2018-06-26  2723.06  15.92
         2018-06-27  2699.63  17.91
         2018-06-28  2716.31  16.85
         2018-06-29  2718.37  16.09

In [47]: data.plot(subplots=True, figsize=(10, 6));
```

❶ Reads the EOD data (originally from the Thomson Reuters Eikon Data API) from a CSV file.

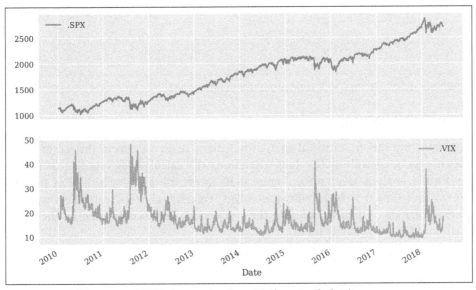

Figure 8-8. S&P 500 and VIX time series data (different subplots)

When plotting (parts of) the two time series in a single plot and with adjusted scalings, the stylized fact of negative correlation between the two indices becomes evident through simple visual inspection (Figure 8-9):

```
In [48]: data.loc[:'2012-12-31'].plot(secondary_y='.VIX', figsize=(10, 6));  ❶
```

❶ `.loc[:DATE]` selects the data until the given value DATE.

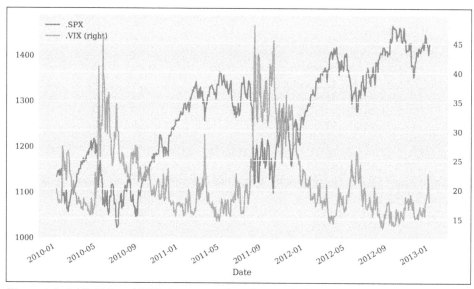

Figure 8-9. S&P 500 and VIX time series data (same plot)

Logarithmic Returns

As pointed out earlier, statistical analysis in general relies on returns instead of absolute changes or even absolute values. Therefore, we'll calculate log returns first before any further analysis takes place. Figure 8-10 shows the high variability of the log returns over time. For both indices so-called "volatility clusters" can be spotted. In general, periods of high volatility in the stock index are accompanied by the same phenomena in the volatility index:

```
In [49]: rets = np.log(data / data.shift(1))

In [50]: rets.head()
Out[50]:                  .SPX       .VIX
         Date
         2010-01-04        NaN        NaN
         2010-01-05   0.003111  -0.035038
         2010-01-06   0.000545  -0.009868
         2010-01-07   0.003993  -0.005233
         2010-01-08   0.002878  -0.050024

In [51]: rets.dropna(inplace=True)

In [52]: rets.plot(subplots=True, figsize=(10, 6));
```

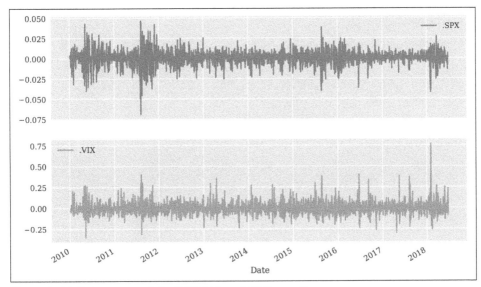

Figure 8-10. Log returns of the S&P 500 and VIX over time

In such a context, the pandas `scatter_matrix()` plotting function comes in handy for visualizations. It plots the log returns of the two series against each other, and one can add either a histogram or a kernel density estimator (KDE) on the diagonal (see Figure 8-11):

```
In [53]: pd.plotting.scatter_matrix(rets,    ❶
                                     alpha=0.2,    ❷
                                     diagonal='hist',    ❸
                                     hist_kwds={'bins': 35},    ❹
                                     figsize=(10, 6));
```

❶ The data set to be plotted.

❷ The `alpha` parameter for the opacity of the dots.

❸ What to place on the diagonal; here: a histogram of the column data.

❹ Keywords to be passed to the histogram plotting function.

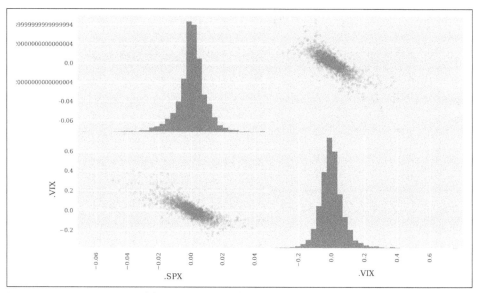

Figure 8-11. Log returns of the S&P 500 and VIX as a scatter matrix

OLS Regression

With all these preparations, an ordinary least-squares (OLS) regression analysis is convenient to implement. Figure 8-12 shows a scatter plot of the log returns and the linear regression line through the cloud of dots. The slope is obviously negative, providing support for the stylized fact about the negative correlation between the two indices:

```
In [54]: reg = np.polyfit(rets['.SPX'], rets['.VIX'], deg=1)    ❶

In [55]: ax = rets.plot(kind='scatter', x='.SPX', y='.VIX', figsize=(10, 6))    ❷
             ax.plot(rets['.SPX'], np.polyval(reg, rets['.SPX']), 'r', lw=2);    ❸
```

❶   This implements a linear OLS regression.

❷   This plots the log returns as a scatter plot …

❸   … to which the linear regression line is added.

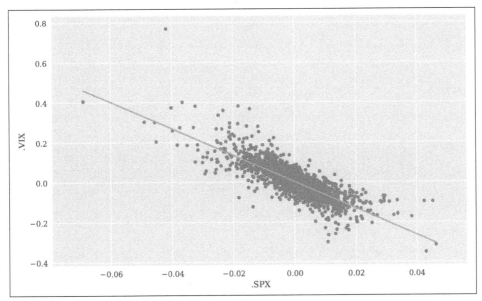

Figure 8-12. Log returns of the S&P 500 and VIX as a scatter matrix

Correlation

Finally, we consider correlation measures directly. Two such measures are considered: a static one taking into account the complete data set and a rolling one showing the correlation for a fixed window over time. Figure 8-13 illustrates that the correlation indeed varies over time but that it is always, given the parameterization, negative. This provides strong support for the stylized fact that the S&P 500 and the VIX indices are (strongly) negatively correlated:

```
In [56]: rets.corr()   ❶
Out[56]:           .SPX       .VIX
         .SPX  1.000000 -0.804382
         .VIX -0.804382  1.000000

In [57]: ax = rets['.SPX'].rolling(window=252).corr(
                       rets['.VIX']).plot(figsize=(10, 6))   ❷
         ax.axhline(rets.corr().iloc[0, 1], c='r');   ❸
```

❶ The correlation matrix for the whole `DataFrame`.

❷ This plots the rolling correlation over time ...

❸ ... and adds the static value to the plot as horizontal line.

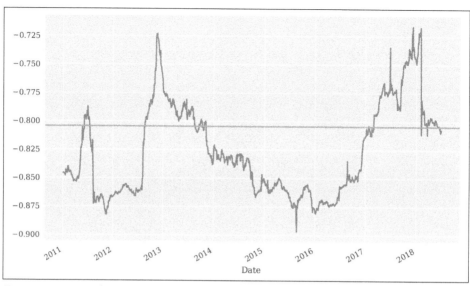

Figure 8-13. Correlation between S&P 500 and VIX (static and rolling)

High-Frequency Data

This chapter is about financial time series analysis with pandas. Tick data sets are a special case of financial time series. Frankly, they can be handled more or less in the same ways as, for instance, the EOD data set used throughout this chapter so far. Importing such data sets also is quite fast in general with pandas. The data set used comprises 17,352 data rows (see also Figure 8-14):

```
In [59]: %%time
         # data from FXCM Forex Capital Markets Ltd.
         tick = pd.read_csv('../../source/fxcm_eur_usd_tick_data.csv',
                            index_col=0, parse_dates=True)
         CPU times: user 1.07 s, sys: 149 ms, total: 1.22 s
         Wall time: 1.16 s

In [60]: tick.info()
         <class 'pandas.core.frame.DataFrame'>
         DatetimeIndex: 461357 entries, 2018-06-29 00:00:00.082000 to 2018-06-29
          20:59:00.607000
         Data columns (total 2 columns):
         Bid     461357 non-null float64
         Ask     461357 non-null float64
         dtypes: float64(2)
         memory usage: 10.6 MB

In [61]: tick['Mid'] = tick.mean(axis=1)   ❶

In [62]: tick['Mid'].plot(figsize=(10, 6));
```

● Calculates the `Mid` price for every data row.

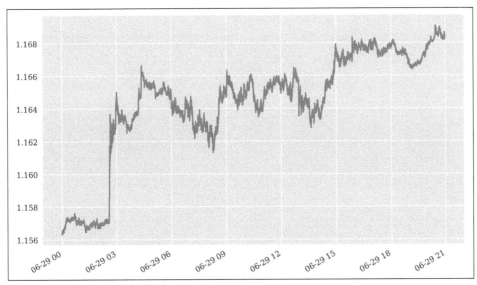

Figure 8-14. Tick data for EUR/USD exchange rate

Working with tick data is generally a scenario where resampling of financial time series data is needed. The code that follows resamples the tick data to five-minute bar data (see Figure 8-15), which can then be used, for example, to backtest algorithmic trading strategies or to implement a technical analysis:

```
In [63]: tick_resam = tick.resample(rule='5min', label='right').last()

In [64]: tick_resam.head()
Out[64]:                          Bid      Ask       Mid
         2018-06-29 00:05:00  1.15649  1.15651  1.156500
         2018-06-29 00:10:00  1.15671  1.15672  1.156715
         2018-06-29 00:15:00  1.15725  1.15727  1.157260
         2018-06-29 00:20:00  1.15720  1.15722  1.157210
         2018-06-29 00:25:00  1.15711  1.15712  1.157115

In [65]: tick_resam['Mid'].plot(figsize=(10, 6));
```

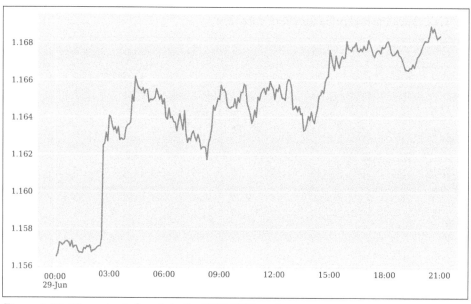

Figure 8-15. Five-minute bar data for EUR/USD exchange rate

Conclusion

This chapter deals with financial time series, probably the most important data type in the financial field. pandas is a powerful package to deal with such data sets, allowing not only for efficient data analyses but also easy visualizations, for instance. pandas is also helpful in reading such data sets from different sources as well as in exporting the data sets to different technical file formats. This is illustrated in the subsequent chapter.

Further Resources

Good references in book form for the topics covered in this chapter are:

- McKinney, Wes (2017). *Python for Data Analysis*. Sebastopol, CA: O'Reilly.
- VanderPlas, Jake (2016). *Python Data Science Handbook*. Sebastopol, CA: O'Reilly.

## CHAPTER 9

Input/Output Operations

It is a capital mistake to theorize before one has data.

—Sherlock Holmes

As a general rule, the majority of data, be it in a finance context or any other application area, is stored on hard disk drives (HDDs) or some other form of permanent storage device, like solid state disks (SSDs) or hybrid disk drives. Storage capacities have been steadily increasing over the years, while costs per storage unit (e.g., per megabyte) have been steadily falling.

At the same time, stored data volumes have been increasing at a much faster pace than the typical random access memory (RAM) available even in the largest machines. This makes it necessary not only to store data to disk for permanent storage, but also to compensate for lack of sufficient RAM by swapping data from RAM to disk and back.

Input/output (I/O) operations are therefore important tasks when it comes to finance applications and data-intensive applications in general. Often they represent the bottleneck for performance-critical computations, since I/O operations cannot typically shuffle data fast enough to the RAM[1] and from the RAM to the disk. In a sense, CPUs are often "starving" due to slow I/O operations.

Although the majority of today's financial and corporate analytics efforts are confronted with big data (e.g., of petascale size), single analytics tasks generally use data subsets that fall in the "mid" data category. A study by Microsoft Research concludes:

---

[1] Here, no distinction is made between different levels of RAM and processor caches. The optimal use of current memory architectures is a topic in itself.

Our measurements as well as other recent work shows that the majority of real-world analytic jobs process less than 100 GB of input, but popular infrastructures such as Hadoop/MapReduce were originally designed for petascale processing.

—Appuswamy et al. (2013)

In terms of frequency, single financial analytics tasks generally process data of not more than a couple of gigabytes (GB) in size—and this is a sweet spot for Python and the libraries of its scientific stack, such as NumPy, pandas, and PyTables. Data sets of such a size can also be analyzed in-memory, leading to generally high speeds with today's CPUs and GPUs. However, the data has to be read into RAM and the results have to be written to disk, meanwhile ensuring that today's performance requirements are met.

This chapter addresses the following topics:

"Basic I/O with Python" on page 232
> Python has built-in functions to serialize and store any object on disk and to read it from disk into RAM; apart from that, Python is strong when it comes to working with text files and SQL databases. NumPy also provides dedicated functions for fast binary storage and retrieval of ndarray objects.

"I/O with pandas" on page 245
> The pandas library provides a plenitude of convenience functions and methods to read data stored in different formats (e.g., CSV, JSON) and to write data to files in diverse formats.

"I/O with PyTables" on page 253
> PyTables uses the HDF5 standard (*http://www.hdfgroup.org*) with hierarchical database structure and binary storage to accomplish fast I/O operations for large data sets; speed often is only bound by the hardware used.

"I/O with TsTables" on page 268
> TsTables is a package that builds on top of PyTables and allows for fast storage and retrieval of time series data.

Basic I/O with Python

Python itself comes with a multitude of I/O capabilities, some optimized for performance, others more for flexibility. In general, however, they are easily used in interactive as well as in production settings.

Writing Objects to Disk

For later use, for documentation, or for sharing with others, one might want to store Python objects on disk. One option is to use the pickle module. This module can serialize the majority of Python objects. *Serialization* refers to the conversion of an object (hierarchy) to a byte stream; *deserialization* is the opposite operation.

As usual, some imports and customizations with regard to plotting first:

```
In [1]: from pylab import plt, mpl
        plt.style.use('seaborn')
        mpl.rcParams['font.family'] = 'serif'
        %matplotlib inline
```

The example that follows works with (pseudo-)random data, this time stored in a list object:

```
In [2]: import pickle    ❶
        import numpy as np
        from random import gauss    ❷
```

```
In [3]: a = [gauss(1.5, 2) for i in range(1000000)]    ❸
```

```
In [4]: path = '/Users/yves/Temp/data/'    ❹
```

```
In [5]: pkl_file = open(path + 'data.pkl', 'wb')    ❺
```

❶ Imports the `pickle` module from the standard library.

❷ Import `gauss` to generate normally distributed random numbers.

❸ Creates a larger `list` object with random numbers.

❹ Specifies the path where to store the data files.

❺ Opens a file for writing in binary mode (`wb`).

The two major functions to serialize and deserialize Python objects are `pickle.dump()`, for writing objects, and `pickle.load()`, for loading them into memory:

```
In [6]: %time pickle.dump(a, pkl_file)    ❶
        CPU times: user 37.2 ms, sys: 15.3 ms, total: 52.5 ms
        Wall time: 50.8 ms
```

```
In [7]: pkl_file.close()    ❷
```

```
In [8]: ll $path*    ❸
        -rw-r--r--  1 yves  staff  9002006 Oct 19 12:11
        /Users/yves/Temp/data/data.pkl
```

```
In [9]: pkl_file = open(path + 'data.pkl', 'rb')    ❹
```

```
In [10]: %time b = pickle.load(pkl_file)    ❺
         CPU times: user 34.1 ms, sys: 16.7 ms, total: 50.8 ms
```

```
                    Wall time: 48.7 ms

    In [11]: a[:3]
    Out[11]: [6.517874180585469, -0.5552400459507827, 2.8488946310833096]

    In [12]: b[:3]
    Out[12]: [6.517874180585469, -0.5552400459507827, 2.8488946310833096]

    In [13]: np.allclose(np.array(a), np.array(b))   ❻
    Out[13]: True
```

❶ Serializes the object a and saves it to the file.

❷ Closes the file.

❸ Shows the file on disk and its size (Mac/Linux).

❹ Opens the file for reading in binary mode (rb).

❺ Reads the object from disk and deserializes it.

❻ Converting a and b to ndarrary objects, np.allclose() verifies that both contain the same data (numbers).

Storing and retrieving a single object with pickle obviously is quite simple. What about two objects?

```
    In [14]: pkl_file = open(path + 'data.pkl', 'wb')

    In [15]: %time pickle.dump(np.array(a), pkl_file)   ❶
             CPU times: user 58.1 ms, sys: 6.09 ms, total: 64.2 ms
             Wall time: 32.5 ms

    In [16]: %time pickle.dump(np.array(a) ** 2, pkl_file)   ❷
             CPU times: user 66.7 ms, sys: 7.22 ms, total: 73.9 ms
             Wall time: 39.3 ms

    In [17]: pkl_file.close()

    In [18]: ll $path*   ❸
             -rw-r--r--  1 yves   staff  16000322 Oct 19 12:11
             /Users/yves/Temp/data/data.pkl
```

❶ Serializes the ndarray version of a and saves it.

❷ Serializes the squared ndarray version of a and saves it.

❸ The file now has roughly double the size from before.

What about reading the two ndarray objects back into memory?

```
In [19]: pkl_file = open(path + 'data.pkl', 'rb')

In [20]: x = pickle.load(pkl_file)   ❶
         x[:4]
Out[20]: array([ 6.51787418, -0.55524005,  2.84889463,  5.94489175])

In [21]: y = pickle.load(pkl_file)   ❷
         y[:4]
Out[21]: array([42.48268383,  0.30829151,  8.11620062, 35.34173791])

In [22]: pkl_file.close()
```

❶ This retrieves the object that was stored *first*.

❷ This retrieves the object that was stored *second*.

Obviously, pickle stores objects according to the *first in, first out* (FIFO) principle. There is one major problem with this: there is no metainformation available to the user to know beforehand what is stored in a pickle file.

A sometimes helpful workaround is to not store single objects, but a dict object containing all the other objects:

```
In [23]: pkl_file = open(path + 'data.pkl', 'wb')
         pickle.dump({'x': x, 'y': y}, pkl_file)   ❶
         pkl_file.close()

In [24]: pkl_file = open(path + 'data.pkl', 'rb')
         data = pickle.load(pkl_file)   ❷
         pkl_file.close()
         for key in data.keys():
             print(key, data[key][:4])
         x [ 6.51787418 -0.55524005  2.84889463  5.94489175]
         y [42.48268383  0.30829151  8.11620062 35.34173791]

In [25]: !rm -f $path*
```

❶ Stores a dict object containing the two ndarray objects.

❷ Retrieves the dict object.

This approach requires writing and reading all the objects at once, but this is a compromise one can probably live with in many circumstances given the higher convenience it brings along.

Compatibility Issues

The use of `pickle` for the serialization of objects is generally straightforward. However, it might lead to problems when, e.g., a Python package is upgraded and the new version of the package cannot work anymore with the serialized object from the older version. It might also lead to problems when sharing such an object across platforms and operating systems. It is therefore in general advisable to work with the built-in reading and writing capabilities of the packages such as `NumPy` and `pandas` that are discussed in the following sections.

Reading and Writing Text Files

Text processing can be considered a strength of Python. In fact, many corporate and scientific users use Python for exactly this task. With Python one has multiple options to work with `str` objects, as well as with text files in general.

Assume the case of quite a large set of data that shall be shared as a CSV file. Although such files have a special internal structure, they are basically plain text files. The following code creates a dummy data set as an `ndarray` object, creates a `DatetimeIndex` object, combines the two, and stores the data as a CSV text file:

```
In [26]: import pandas as pd

In [27]: rows = 5000        ❶
         a = np.random.standard_normal((rows, 5)).round(4)        ❷

In [28]: a        ❷
Out[28]: array([[-0.0892, -1.0508, -0.5942,  0.3367,  1.508 ],
                [ 2.1046,  3.2623,  0.704 , -0.2651,  0.4461],
                [-0.0482, -0.9221,  0.1332,  0.1192,  0.7782],
                ...,
                [ 0.3026, -0.2005, -0.9947,  1.0203, -0.6578],
                [-0.7031, -0.6989, -0.8031, -0.4271,  1.9963],
                [ 2.4573,  2.2151,  0.158 , -0.7039, -1.0337]])

In [29]: t = pd.date_range(start='2019/1/1', periods=rows, freq='H')        ❸

In [30]: t        ❸
Out[30]: DatetimeIndex(['2019-01-01 00:00:00', '2019-01-01 01:00:00',
                        '2019-01-01 02:00:00', '2019-01-01 03:00:00',
                        '2019-01-01 04:00:00', '2019-01-01 05:00:00',
                        '2019-01-01 06:00:00', '2019-01-01 07:00:00',
                        '2019-01-01 08:00:00', '2019-01-01 09:00:00',
                        ...
                        '2019-07-27 22:00:00', '2019-07-27 23:00:00',
                        '2019-07-28 00:00:00', '2019-07-28 01:00:00',
                        '2019-07-28 02:00:00', '2019-07-28 03:00:00',
                        '2019-07-28 04:00:00', '2019-07-28 05:00:00',
```

```
                        '2019-07-28 06:00:00', '2019-07-28 07:00:00'],
                        dtype='datetime64[ns]', length=5000, freq='H')

In [31]: csv_file = open(path + 'data.csv', 'w')    ❹

In [32]: header = 'date,no1,no2,no3,no4,no5\n'    ❺

In [33]: csv_file.write(header)    ❺
Out[33]: 25

In [34]: for t_, (no1, no2, no3, no4, no5) in zip(t, a):    ❻
             s = '{},{},{},{},{},{}\n'.format(t_, no1, no2, no3, no4, no5)    ❼
             csv_file.write(s)    ❽

In [35]: csv_file.close()

In [36]: ll $path*
             -rw-r--r--  1 yves  staff  284757 Oct 19 12:11
             /Users/yves/Temp/data/data.csv
```

❶ Defines the number of rows for the data set.

❷ Creates the ndarray object with the random numbers.

❸ Creates a DatetimeIndex object of appropriate length (hourly intervals).

❹ Opens a file for writing (w).

❺ Defines the header row (column labels) and writes it as the first line.

❻ Combines the data row-wise …

❼ … into str objects …

❽ … and writes it line-by-line (appending to the CSV text file).

The other way around works quite similarly. First, open the now-existing CSV file. Second, read its content line-by-line using the .readline() or .readlines() methods of the file object:

```
In [37]: csv_file = open(path + 'data.csv', 'r')    ❶

In [38]: for i in range(5):
             print(csv_file.readline(), end='')    ❷
         date,no1,no2,no3,no4,no5
         2019-01-01 00:00:00,-0.0892,-1.0508,-0.5942,0.3367,1.508
         2019-01-01 01:00:00,2.1046,3.2623,0.704,-0.2651,0.4461
         2019-01-01 02:00:00,-0.0482,-0.9221,0.1332,0.1192,0.7782
         2019-01-01 03:00:00,-0.359,-2.4955,0.6164,0.712,-1.4328
```

```
In [39]: csv_file.close()

In [40]: csv_file = open(path + 'data.csv', 'r')   ❶

In [41]: content = csv_file.readlines()   ❸

In [42]: content[:5]   ❹
Out[42]: ['date,no1,no2,no3,no4,no5\n',
          '2019-01-01 00:00:00,-0.0892,-1.0508,-0.5942,0.3367,1.508\n',
          '2019-01-01 01:00:00,2.1046,3.2623,0.704,-0.2651,0.4461\n',
          '2019-01-01 02:00:00,-0.0482,-0.9221,0.1332,0.1192,0.7782\n',
          '2019-01-01 03:00:00,-0.359,-2.4955,0.6164,0.712,-1.4328\n']

In [43]: csv_file.close()
```

❶ Opens the file for reading (r).

❷ Reads the file contents line-by-line and prints them.

❸ Reads the file contents in a single step …

❹ … the result of which is a list object with all lines as separate str objects.

CSV files are so important and commonplace that there is a csv module in the Python standard library that simplifies the processing of these files. Two helpful reader (iterator) objects of the csv module return either a list of list objects or a list of dict objects:

```
In [44]: import csv

In [45]: with open(path + 'data.csv', 'r') as f:
             csv_reader = csv.reader(f)   ❶
             lines = [line for line in csv_reader]

In [46]: lines[:5]   ❶
Out[46]: [['date', 'no1', 'no2', 'no3', 'no4', 'no5'],
          ['2019-01-01 00:00:00', '-0.0892', '-1.0508', '-0.5942', '0.3367',
           '1.508'],
          ['2019-01-01 01:00:00', '2.1046', '3.2623', '0.704', '-0.2651',
           '0.4461'],
          ['2019-01-01 02:00:00', '-0.0482', '-0.9221', '0.1332', '0.1192',
           '0.7782'],
          ['2019-01-01 03:00:00', '-0.359', '-2.4955', '0.6164', '0.712',
           '-1.4328']]

In [47]: with open(path + 'data.csv', 'r') as f:
             csv_reader = csv.DictReader(f)   ❷
             lines = [line for line in csv_reader]

In [48]: lines[:3]   ❷
```

```
Out[48]: [OrderedDict([('date', '2019-01-01 00:00:00'),
                       ('no1', '-0.0892'),
                       ('no2', '-1.0508'),
                       ('no3', '-0.5942'),
                       ('no4', '0.3367'),
                       ('no5', '1.508')]),
          OrderedDict([('date', '2019-01-01 01:00:00'),
                       ('no1', '2.1046'),
                       ('no2', '3.2623'),
                       ('no3', '0.704'),
                       ('no4', '-0.2651'),
                       ('no5', '0.4461')]),
          OrderedDict([('date', '2019-01-01 02:00:00'),
                       ('no1', '-0.0482'),
                       ('no2', '-0.9221'),
                       ('no3', '0.1332'),
                       ('no4', '0.1192'),
                       ('no5', '0.7782')])]

In [49]: !rm -f $path*
```

❶ csv.reader() returns every single line as a list object.

❷ csv.DictReader() returns every single line as an OrderedDict, which is a special case of a dict object.

Working with SQL Databases

Python can work with any kind of Structured Query Language (SQL) database, and in general also with any kind of NoSQL database. One SQL or *relational* database that is delivered with Python by default is SQLite3 (*http://www.sqlite.org*). With it, the basic Python approach to SQL databases can be easily illustrated:[2]

```
In [50]: import sqlite3 as sq3

In [51]: con = sq3.connect(path + 'numbs.db')   ❶

In [52]: query = 'CREATE TABLE numbs (Date date, No1 real, No2 real)'   ❷

In [53]: con.execute(query)   ❸
Out[53]: <sqlite3.Cursor at 0x102655f10>

In [54]: con.commit()   ❹
```

---

[2] For an overview of available database connectors for Python, visit *https://wiki.python.org/moin/DatabaseInterfaces*. Instead of working directly with relational databases, object relational mappers such as SQLAlchemy (*https://www.sqlalchemy.org/*) often prove useful. They introduce an abstraction layer that allows for more Pythonic, object-oriented code. They also allow you to more easily exchange one relational database for another in the backend.

```
In [55]: q = con.execute   ❺

In [56]: q('SELECT * FROM sqlite_master').fetchall()   ❻
Out[56]: [('table',
           'numbs',
           'numbs',
           2,
           'CREATE TABLE numbs (Date date, No1 real, No2 real)')]
```

❶ Opens a database connection; a file is created if it does not exist.

❷ A SQL query that creates a table with three columns.[3]

❸ Executes the query ...

❹ ... and commits the changes.

❺ Defines a short alias for the `con.execute()` method.

❻ Fetches metainformation about the database, showing the just-created table as the single object.

Now that there is a database file with a table, this table can be populated with data. Each row consists of a `datetime` object and two `float` objects:

```
In [57]: import datetime

In [58]: now = datetime.datetime.now()
         q('INSERT INTO numbs VALUES(?, ?, ?)', (now, 0.12, 7.3))   ❶
Out[58]: <sqlite3.Cursor at 0x102655f80>

In [59]: np.random.seed(100)

In [60]: data = np.random.standard_normal((10000, 2)).round(4)   ❷

In [61]: %%time
         for row in data:   ❸
             now = datetime.datetime.now()
             q('INSERT INTO numbs VALUES(?, ?, ?)', (now, row[0], row[1]))
         con.commit()
         CPU times: user 115 ms, sys: 6.69 ms, total: 121 ms
         Wall time: 124 ms

In [62]: q('SELECT * FROM numbs').fetchmany(4)   ❹
Out[62]: [('2018-10-19 12:11:15.564019', 0.12, 7.3),
          ('2018-10-19 12:11:15.592956', -1.7498, 0.3427),
```

---

3 See *https://www.sqlite.org/lang.html* for an overview of the SQLite3 language dialect.

```
              ('2018-10-19 12:11:15.593033', 1.153, -0.2524),
              ('2018-10-19 12:11:15.593051', 0.9813, 0.5142)]

In [63]: q('SELECT * FROM numbs WHERE no1 > 0.5').fetchmany(4)   ❺
Out[63]: [('2018-10-19 12:11:15.593033', 1.153, -0.2524),
          ('2018-10-19 12:11:15.593051', 0.9813, 0.5142),
          ('2018-10-19 12:11:15.593104', 0.6727, -0.1044),
          ('2018-10-19 12:11:15.593134', 1.619, 1.5416)]

In [64]: pointer = q('SELECT * FROM numbs')   ❻

In [65]: for i in range(3):
             print(pointer.fetchone())   ❼
         ('2018-10-19 12:11:15.564019', 0.12, 7.3)
         ('2018-10-19 12:11:15.592956', -1.7498, 0.3427)
         ('2018-10-19 12:11:15.593033', 1.153, -0.2524)

In [66]: rows = pointer.fetchall()   ❽
         rows[:3]
Out[66]: [('2018-10-19 12:11:15.593051', 0.9813, 0.5142),
          ('2018-10-19 12:11:15.593063', 0.2212, -1.07),
          ('2018-10-19 12:11:15.593073', -0.1895, 0.255)]
```

❶ Writes a single row (or record) to the numbs table.

❷ Creates a larger dummy data set as an ndarray object.

❸ Iterates over the rows of the ndarray object.

❹ Retrieves a number of rows from the table.

❺ The same, but with a condition on the values in the No1 column.

❻ Defines a pointer object …

❼ … that behaves like a generator object.

❽ Retrieves all the remaining rows.

Finally, one might want to delete the table object in the database if it's not required anymore:

```
In [67]: q('DROP TABLE IF EXISTS numbs')   ❶
Out[67]: <sqlite3.Cursor at 0x1187a7420>

In [68]: q('SELECT * FROM sqlite_master').fetchall()   ❷
Out[68]: []

In [69]: con.close()   ❸
```

```
In [70]: !rm -f $path*    ❹
```

❶ Removes the table from the database.

❷ There are no table objects left after this operation.

❸ Closes the database connection.

❹ Removes the database file from disk.

SQL databases are a rather broad topic; indeed, too broad and complex to be covered in any significant way in this chapter. The basic messages are:

- Python integrates well with almost any database technology.
- The basic SQL syntax is mainly determined by the database in use; the rest is what is called "Pythonic."

A few more examples based on SQLite3 are included later in this chapter.

Writing and Reading NumPy Arrays

NumPy itself has functions to write and read ndarray objects in a convenient and performant fashion. This saves effort in some circumstances, such as when converting NumPy dtype objects into specific database data types (e.g., for SQLite3). To illustrate that NumPy can be an efficient replacement for a SQL-based approach, the following code replicates the example from the previous section with NumPy.

Instead of pandas, the code uses the np.arange() function of NumPy to generate an ndarray object with datetime objects (*http://bit.ly/2DnwAqZ*) stored:

```
In [71]: dtimes = np.arange('2019-01-01 10:00:00', '2025-12-31 22:00:00',
                            dtype='datetime64[m]')    ❶

In [72]: len(dtimes)
Out[72]: 3681360

In [73]: dty = np.dtype([('Date', 'datetime64[m]'),
                        ('No1', 'f'), ('No2', 'f')])    ❷

In [74]: data = np.zeros(len(dtimes), dtype=dty)    ❸

In [75]: data['Date'] = dtimes    ❹

In [76]: a = np.random.standard_normal((len(dtimes), 2)).round(4)    ❺

In [77]: data['No1'] = a[:, 0]    ❻
         data['No2'] = a[:, 1]    ❻
```

```
In [78]: data.nbytes    ❼
Out[78]: 58901760
```

❶ Creates an ndarray object with datetime as the dtype.

❷ Defines the special dtype object for the structured array.

❸ Instantiates an ndarray object with the special dtype.

❹ Populates the Date column.

❺ The dummy data sets ...

❻ ... which populate the No1 and No2 columns.

❼ The size of the structured array in bytes.

Saving of ndarray objects is highly optimized and therefore quite fast. Almost 60 MB of data takes a fraction of a second to save on disk (here using an SSD). A larger ndarray object with 480 MB of data takes about half a second to save on disk:[4]

```
In [79]: %time np.save(path + 'array', data)    ❶
         CPU times: user 37.4 ms, sys: 58.9 ms, total: 96.4 ms
         Wall time: 77.9 ms

In [80]: ll $path*    ❷
         -rw-r--r--  1 yves   staff   58901888 Oct 19 12:11
         /Users/yves/Temp/data/array.npy

In [81]: %time np.load(path + 'array.npy')    ❸
         CPU times: user 1.67 ms, sys: 44.8 ms, total: 46.5 ms
         Wall time: 44.6 ms

Out[81]: array([('2019-01-01T10:00',  1.5131,  0.6973),
                ('2019-01-01T10:01', -1.722 , -0.4815),
                ('2019-01-01T10:02',  0.8251,  0.3019), ...,
                ('2025-12-31T21:57',  1.372 ,  0.6446),
                ('2025-12-31T21:58', -1.2542,  0.1612),
                ('2025-12-31T21:59', -1.1997, -1.097 )],
              dtype=[('Date', '<M8[m]'), ('No1', '<f4'), ('No2', '<f4')])

In [82]: %time data = np.random.standard_normal((10000, 6000)).round(4)    ❹
         CPU times: user 2.69 s, sys: 391 ms, total: 3.08 s
```

---

4 Note that such times might vary significantly even on the same machine when repeated multiple times, because they depend, among other factors, on what the machine is doing CPU-wise and I/O-wise at the same time.

```
            Wall time: 2.78 s

In [83]: data.nbytes   ❷
Out[83]: 480000000

In [84]: %time np.save(path + 'array', data)   ❹
            CPU times: user 42.9 ms, sys: 300 ms, total: 343 ms
            Wall time: 481 ms

In [85]: ll $path*   ❹
            -rw-r--r--  1 yves   staff  480000128 Oct 19 12:11
            /Users/yves/Temp/data/array.npy

In [86]: %time np.load(path + 'array.npy')   ❹
            CPU times: user 2.32 ms, sys: 363 ms, total: 365 ms
            Wall time: 363 ms

Out[86]: array([[ 0.3066,  0.5951,  0.5826, ...,  1.6773,  0.4294, -0.2216],
               [ 0.8769,  0.7292, -0.9557, ...,  0.5084,  0.9635, -0.4443],
               [-1.2202, -2.5509, -0.0575, ..., -1.6128,  0.4662, -1.3645],
               ...,
               [-0.5598,  0.2393, -2.3716, ...,  1.7669,  0.2462,  1.035 ],
               [ 0.273 ,  0.8216, -0.0749, ..., -0.0552, -0.8396,  0.3077],
               [-0.6305,  0.8331,  1.3702, ...,  0.3493,  0.1981,  0.2037]])

In [87]: !rm -f $path*
```

❶ This saves the structured ndarray object on disk.

❷ The size on disk is hardly larger than in memory (due to binary storage).

❸ This loads the structured ndarray object from disk.

❹ A larger regular ndarray object.

These examples illustrate that writing to disk in this case is mainly hardware-bound, since the speeds observed represent roughly the advertised writing speed of standard SSDs at the time of this writing (about 500 MB/s).

In any case, one can expect that this form of data storage and retrieval is faster when compared to SQL databases or using the pickle module for serialization. There are two reasons: first, the data is mainly numeric; second, NumPy uses binary storage, which reduces the overhead almost to zero. Of course, one does not have the functionality of a SQL database available with this approach, but PyTables will help in this regard, as subsequent sections show.

I/O with pandas

One of the major strengths of pandas is that it can read and write different data formats natively, including:

- CSV (comma-separated values)
- SQL (Structured Query Language)
- XLS/XSLX (Microsoft Excel files)
- JSON (JavaScript Object Notation)
- HTML (HyperText Markup Language)

Table 9-1 lists the supported formats and the corresponding import and export functions/methods of pandas and the DataFrame class, respectively. The parameters that, for example, the pd.read_csv() import function takes are described in the documentation for pandas.read_csv (*http://bit.ly/2DaB9C7*).

Table 9-1. Import-export functions and methods

Format	Input	Output	Remark
CSV	pd.read_csv()	.to_csv()	Text file
XLS/XLSX	pd.read_excel()	.to_excel()	Spreadsheet
HDF	pd.read_hdf()	.to_hdf()	HDF5 database
SQL	pd.read_sql()	.to_sql()	SQL table
JSON	pd.read_json()	.to_json()	JavaScript Object Notation
MSGPACK	pd.read_msgpack()	.to_msgpack()	Portable binary format
HTML	pd.read_html()	.to_html()	HTML code
GBQ	pd.read_gbq()	.to_gbq()	Google Big Query format
DTA	pd.read_stata()	.to_stata()	Formats 104, 105, 108, 113-115, 117
Any	pd.read_clipboard()	.to_clipboard()	E.g., from HTML page
Any	pd.read_pickle()	.to_pickle()	(Structured) Python object

The test case is again a larger set of float objects:

```
In [88]: data = np.random.standard_normal((1000000, 5)).round(4)

In [89]: data[:3]
Out[89]: array([[ 0.4918,  1.3707,  0.137 ,  0.3981, -1.0059],
                [ 0.4516,  1.4445,  0.0555, -0.0397,  0.44  ],
                [ 0.1629, -0.8473, -0.8223, -0.4621, -0.5137]])
```

To this end, this section also revisits SQLite3 and compares the performance to alternative formats using pandas.

Working with SQL Databases

All that follows with regard to SQLite3 should be familiar by now:

```
In [90]: filename = path + 'numbers'

In [91]: con = sq3.Connection(filename + '.db')

In [92]: query = 'CREATE TABLE numbers (No1 real, No2 real,\
                  No3 real, No4 real, No5 real)'   ❶

In [93]: q = con.execute
         qm = con.executemany

In [94]: q(query)
Out[94]: <sqlite3.Cursor at 0x1187a76c0>
```

❶ Creates a table with five columns for real numbers (`float` objects).

This time, the `.executemany()` method can be applied since the data is available in a single `ndarray` object. Reading and working with the data works as before. Query results can also be visualized easily (see Figure 9-1):

```
In [95]: %%time
         qm('INSERT INTO numbers VALUES (?, ?, ?, ?, ?)', data)   ❶
         con.commit()
         CPU times: user 7.3 s, sys: 195 ms, total: 7.49 s
         Wall time: 7.71 s

In [96]: ll $path*
         -rw-r--r--  1 yves  staff  52633600 Oct 19 12:11
          /Users/yves/Temp/data/numbers.db

In [97]: %%time
         temp = q('SELECT * FROM numbers').fetchall()   ❷
         print(temp[:3])
         [(0.4918, 1.3707, 0.137, 0.3981, -1.0059), (0.4516, 1.4445, 0.0555,
          -0.0397, 0.44), (0.1629, -0.8473, -0.8223, -0.4621, -0.5137)]
         CPU times: user 1.7 s, sys: 124 ms, total: 1.82 s
         Wall time: 1.9 s

In [98]: %%time
         query = 'SELECT * FROM numbers WHERE No1 > 0 AND No2 < 0'
         res = np.array(q(query).fetchall()).round(3)   ❸
         CPU times: user 639 ms, sys: 64.7 ms, total: 704 ms
         Wall time: 702 ms

In [99]: res = res[::100]   ❹
         plt.figure(figsize=(10, 6))
         plt.plot(res[:, 0], res[:, 1], 'ro')   ❹
```

❶ Inserts the whole data set into the table in a single step.

---

❷   Retrieves all the rows from the table in a single step.

❸   Retrieves a selection of the rows and transforms it to an ndarray object.

❹   Plots a subset of the query result.

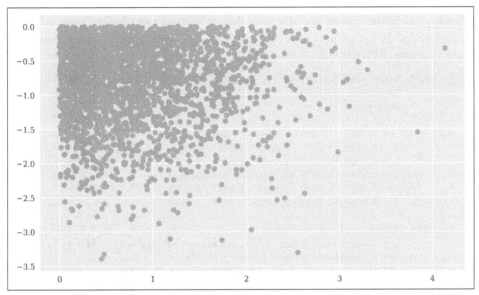

Figure 9-1. Scatter plot of the query result (selection)

From SQL to pandas

A generally more efficient approach, however, is the reading of either whole tables or query results with pandas. When one can read a whole table into memory, analytical queries can generally be executed much faster than when using the SQL disk-based approach (out-of-memory).

Reading the whole table with pandas takes roughly the same amount of time as reading it into a NumPy ndarray object. There as here, the bottleneck performance-wise is the SQL database:

```
In [100]: %time data = pd.read_sql('SELECT * FROM numbers', con)   ❶
          CPU times: user 2.17 s, sys: 180 ms, total: 2.35 s
          Wall time: 2.32 s

In [101]: data.head()
Out[101]:        No1      No2      No3      No4      No5
          0   0.4918   1.3707   0.1370   0.3981  -1.0059
          1   0.4516   1.4445   0.0555  -0.0397   0.4400
          2   0.1629  -0.8473  -0.8223  -0.4621  -0.5137
```

```
3  1.3064  0.9125  0.5142 -0.7868 -0.3398
4 -0.1148 -1.5215 -0.7045 -1.0042 -0.0600
```

❶ Reads all rows of the table into the `DataFrame` object named `data`.

The data is now in-memory, which allows for much faster analytics. The speedup is often an order of magnitude or more. `pandas` can also master more complex queries, although it is neither meant nor able to replace SQL databases when it comes to complex relational data structures. The result of the query with multiple conditions combined is shown in Figure 9-2:

```
In [102]: %time data[(data['No1'] > 0) & (data['No2'] < 0)].head()   ❶
          CPU times: user 47.1 ms, sys: 12.3 ms, total: 59.4 ms
          Wall time: 33.4 ms

Out[102]:        No1     No2     No3     No4     No5
          2    0.1629 -0.8473 -0.8223 -0.4621 -0.5137
          5    0.1893 -0.0207 -0.2104  0.9419  0.2551
          8    1.4784 -0.3333 -0.7050  0.3586 -0.3937
          10   0.8092 -0.9899  1.0364 -1.0453  0.0579
          11   0.9065 -0.7757 -0.9267  0.7797  0.0863

In [103]: %%time
          q = '(No1 < -0.5 | No1 > 0.5) & (No2 < -1 | No2 > 1)'   ❷
          res = data[['No1', 'No2']].query(q)   ❷
          CPU times: user 95.4 ms, sys: 22.4 ms, total: 118 ms
          Wall time: 56.4 ms

In [104]: plt.figure(figsize=(10, 6))
          plt.plot(res['No1'], res['No2'], 'ro');
```

❶ Two conditions combined logically.

❷ Four conditions combined logically.

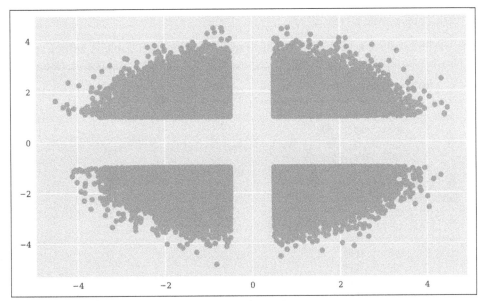

Figure 9-2. Scatter plot of the query result (selection)

As expected, using the in-memory analytics capabilities of pandas leads to a signifi-cant speedup, provided pandas is able to replicate the respective SQL statement.

This is not the only advantage of using pandas, since pandas is tightly integrated with a number of other packages (including PyTables, the topic of the subsequent sec-tion). Here, it suffices to know that the combination of both can speed up I/O opera-tions considerably. This is shown in the following:

```
In [105]: h5s = pd.HDFStore(filename + '.h5s', 'w')  ❶

In [106]: %time h5s['data'] = data  ❷
          CPU times: user 46.7 ms, sys: 47.1 ms, total: 93.8 ms
          Wall time: 99.7 ms

In [107]: h5s  ❸
Out[107]: <class 'pandas.io.pytables.HDFStore'>
          File path: /Users/yves/Temp/data/numbers.h5s

In [108]: h5s.close()  ❹
```

❶ This opens an HDF5 database file for writing; in pandas an HDFStore object is created.

❷ The complete DataFrame object is stored in the database file via binary storage.

❸ The HDFStore object information.

❹ The database file is closed.

The whole `DataFrame` with all the data from the original SQL table is written much faster when compared to the same procedure with SQLite3. Reading is even faster:

```
In [109]: %%time
          h5s = pd.HDFStore(filename + '.h5s', 'r')  ❶
          data_ = h5s['data']  ❷
          h5s.close()  ❸
          CPU times: user 11 ms, sys: 18.3 ms, total: 29.3 ms
          Wall time: 29.4 ms

In [110]: data_ is data  ❹
Out[110]: False

In [111]: (data_ == data).all()  ❺
Out[111]: No1    True
          No2    True
          No3    True
          No4    True
          No5    True
          dtype: bool

In [112]: np.allclose(data_, data)  ❺
Out[112]: True

In [113]: ll $path*  ❻
          -rw-r--r--  1 yves  staff  52633600 Oct 19 12:11
          /Users/yves/Temp/data/numbers.db
          -rw-r--r--  1 yves  staff  48007240 Oct 19 12:11
          /Users/yves/Temp/data/numbers.h5s
```

❶ This opens the HDF5 database file for reading.

❷ The `DataFrame` is read and stored in-memory as `data_`.

❸ The database file is closed.

❹ The two `DataFrame` objects are not the same …

❺ … but they now contain the same data.

❻ Binary storage generally comes with less size overhead compared to SQL tables, for instance.

Working with CSV Files

One of the most widely used formats to exchange financial data is the CSV format. Although it is not really standardized, it can be processed by any platform and the

---

vast majority of applications concerned with data and financial analytics. Earlier, we saw how to write and read data to and from CSV files with standard Python functionality (see "Reading and Writing Text Files" on page 236). pandas makes this whole procedure a bit more convenient, the code more concise, and the execution in general faster (see also Figure 9-3):

```
In [114]: %time data.to_csv(filename + '.csv')   ❶
          CPU times: user 6.44 s, sys: 139 ms, total: 6.58 s
          Wall time: 6.71 s

In [115]: ll $path
          total 283672
          -rw-r--r--  1 yves  staff  43834157 Oct 19 12:11 numbers.csv
          -rw-r--r--  1 yves  staff  52633600 Oct 19 12:11 numbers.db
          -rw-r--r--  1 yves  staff  48007240 Oct 19 12:11 numbers.h5s

In [116]: %time df = pd.read_csv(filename + '.csv')   ❷
          CPU times: user 1.12 s, sys: 111 ms, total: 1.23 s
          Wall time: 1.23 s

In [117]: df[['No1', 'No2', 'No3', 'No4']].hist(bins=20, figsize=(10, 6));
```

❶ The .to_csv() method writes the DataFrame data to disk in CSV format.

❷ The pd.read_csv() method then reads it back into memory as a new DataFrame object.

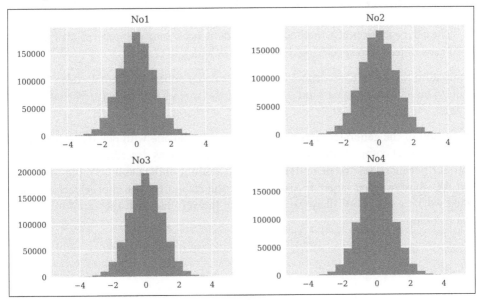

Figure 9-3. Histograms for selected columns

Working with Excel Files

The following code briefly demonstrates how pandas can write data in Excel format and read data from Excel spreadsheets. In this case, the data set is restricted to 100,000 rows (see also Figure 9-4):

```
In [118]: %time data[:100000].to_excel(filename + '.xlsx')   ❶
          CPU times: user 25.9 s, sys: 520 ms, total: 26.4 s
          Wall time: 27.3 s

In [119]: %time df = pd.read_excel(filename + '.xlsx', 'Sheet1')   ❷
          CPU times: user 5.78 s, sys: 70.1 ms, total: 5.85 s
          Wall time: 5.91 s

In [120]: df.cumsum().plot(figsize=(10, 6));
In [121]: ll $path*
          -rw-r--r--  1 yves  staff  43834157 Oct 19 12:11
          /Users/yves/Temp/data/numbers.csv
          -rw-r--r--  1 yves  staff  52633600 Oct 19 12:11
          /Users/yves/Temp/data/numbers.db
          -rw-r--r--  1 yves  staff  48007240 Oct 19 12:11
          /Users/yves/Temp/data/numbers.h5s
          -rw-r--r--  1 yves  staff   4032725 Oct 19 12:12
          /Users/yves/Temp/data/numbers.xlsx

In [122]: rm -f $path*
```

❶ The .to_excel() method writes the DataFrame data to disk in XLSX format.

❷ The pd.read_excel() method then reads it back into memory as a new Data Frame object, also specifying the sheet from which to read.

Generating the Excel spreadsheet file with a smaller subset of the data takes quite a while. This illustrates what kind of overhead the spreadsheet structure brings along with it.

Inspection of the generated files reveals that the DataFrame with HDFStore combination is the most compact alternative (using compression, as described in the next section, further increases the benefits). The same amount of data as a CSV file—i.e., as a text file—is somewhat larger in size. This is one reason for the slower performance when working with CSV files, the other being the very fact that they are "only" general text files.

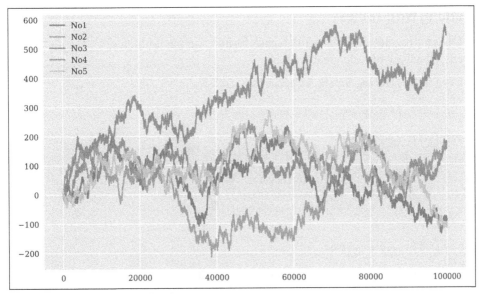

Figure 9-4. Line plots for all columns

I/O with PyTables

PyTables is a Python binding for the HDF5 database standard. It is specifically designed to optimize the performance of I/O operations and make best use of the available hardware. The library's import name is `tables`. Similar to `pandas`, when it comes to in-memory analytics PyTables is neither able nor meant to be a full replacement for SQL databases. However, it brings along some features that further close the gap. For example, a PyTables database can have many tables, and it supports compression and indexing and also nontrivial queries on tables. In addition, it can store NumPy arrays efficiently and has its own flavor of array-like data structures.

To begin with, some imports:

```
In [123]: import tables as tb  ❶
          import datetime as dt
```

❶ The package name is PyTables, the import name is `tables`.

Working with Tables

PyTables provides a file-based database format, similar to SQLite3.[5] The following opens a database file and creates a table:

```
In [124]: filename = path + 'pytab.h5'

In [125]: h5 = tb.open_file(filename, 'w')    ❶

In [126]: row_des = {
                     'Date': tb.StringCol(26, pos=1),    ❷
                     'No1': tb.IntCol(pos=2),    ❸
                     'No2': tb.IntCol(pos=3),    ❸
                     'No3': tb.Float64Col(pos=4),    ❹
                     'No4': tb.Float64Col(pos=5)    ❹
                     }

In [127]: rows = 2000000

In [128]: filters = tb.Filters(complevel=0)    ❺

In [129]: tab = h5.create_table('/', 'ints_floats',    ❻
                                row_des,    ❼
                                title='Integers and Floats',    ❽
                                expectedrows=rows,    ❾
                                filters=filters)    ❿

In [130]: type(tab)
Out[130]: tables.table.Table

In [131]: tab
Out[131]: /ints_floats (Table(0,)) 'Integers and Floats'
            description := {
            "Date": StringCol(itemsize=26, shape=(), dflt=b'', pos=0),
            "No1": Int32Col(shape=(), dflt=0, pos=1),
            "No2": Int32Col(shape=(), dflt=0, pos=2),
            "No3": Float64Col(shape=(), dflt=0.0, pos=3),
            "No4": Float64Col(shape=(), dflt=0.0, pos=4)}
            byteorder := 'little'
            chunkshape := (2621,)
```

❶ Opens the database file in HDF5 binary storage format.

❷ The Date column for date-time information (as a str object).

❸ The two columns to store int objects.

---

[5] Many other databases require a server/client architecture. For interactive data and financial analytics, file-based databases prove a bit more convenient and also sufficient for most purposes.

❹ The two columns to store `float` objects.

❺ Via `Filters` objects, compression levels can be specified, among other things.

❻ The node (path) and technical name of the table.

❼ The description of the row data structure.

❽ The name (title) of the table.

❾ The expected number of rows; allows for optimizations.

❿ The `Filters` object to be used for the table.

To populate the table with numerical data, two `ndarray` objects with random numbers are generated: one with random integers, the other with random floating-point numbers. The population of the table happens via a simple Python loop:

```
In [132]: pointer = tab.row  ❶

In [133]: ran_int = np.random.randint(0, 10000, size=(rows, 2))  ❷

In [134]: ran_flo = np.random.standard_normal((rows, 2)).round(4)  ❸

In [135]: %%time
          for i in range(rows):
              pointer['Date'] = dt.datetime.now()  ❹
              pointer['No1'] = ran_int[i, 0]  ❹
              pointer['No2'] = ran_int[i, 1]  ❹
              pointer['No3'] = ran_flo[i, 0]  ❹
              pointer['No4'] = ran_flo[i, 1]  ❹
              pointer.append()  ❺
          tab.flush()  ❻
          CPU times: user 8.16 s, sys: 78.7 ms, total: 8.24 s
          Wall time: 8.25 s

In [136]: tab  ❼
Out[136]: /ints_floats (Table(2000000,)) 'Integers and Floats'
            description := {
            "Date": StringCol(itemsize=26, shape=(), dflt=b'', pos=0),
            "No1": Int32Col(shape=(), dflt=0, pos=1),
            "No2": Int32Col(shape=(), dflt=0, pos=2),
            "No3": Float64Col(shape=(), dflt=0.0, pos=3),
            "No4": Float64Col(shape=(), dflt=0.0, pos=4)}
            byteorder := 'little'
            chunkshape := (2621,)

In [137]: ll $path*
```

```
-rw-r--r--  1 yves  staff  100156248 Oct 19 12:12
/Users/yves/Temp/data/pytab.h5
```

❶ A pointer object is created.

❷ The `ndarray` object with the random `int` objects is created.

❸ The `ndarray` object with the random `float` objects is created.

❹ The `datetime` object and the two `int` and two `float` objects are written row-by-row.

❺ The new row is appended.

❻ All written rows are flushed; i.e., committed as permanent changes.

❼ The changes are reflected in the `Table` object description.

The Python loop is quite slow in this case. There is a more performant and Pythonic way to accomplish the same result, by the use of `NumPy` structured arrays. Equipped with the complete data set stored in a structured array, the creation of the table boils down to a single line of code. Note that the row description is not needed anymore; `PyTables` uses the dtype object of the structured array to infer the data types instead:

```
In [138]: dty = np.dtype([('Date', 'S26'), ('No1', '<i4'), ('No2', '<i4'),
                          ('No3', '<f8'), ('No4', '<f8')])   ❶

In [139]: sarray = np.zeros(len(ran_int), dtype=dty)   ❷

In [140]: sarray[:4]   ❸
Out[140]: array([(b'', 0, 0, 0., 0.), (b'', 0, 0, 0., 0.), (b'', 0, 0, 0., 0.),
                (b'', 0, 0, 0., 0.)],
               dtype=[('Date', 'S26'), ('No1', '<i4'), ('No2', '<i4'), ('No3', '<f8'),
                ('No4', '<f8')])

In [141]: %%time
          sarray['Date'] = dt.datetime.now()    ❹
          sarray['No1'] = ran_int[:, 0]   ❹
          sarray['No2'] = ran_int[:, 1]   ❹
          sarray['No3'] = ran_flo[:, 0]   ❹
          sarray['No4'] = ran_flo[:, 1]   ❹
          CPU times: user 161 ms, sys: 42.7 ms, total: 204 ms
          Wall time: 207 ms

In [142]: %%time
          h5.create_table('/', 'ints_floats_from_array', sarray,
                          title='Integers and Floats',
                          expectedrows=rows, filters=filters)   ❺
          CPU times: user 42.9 ms, sys: 51.4 ms, total: 94.3 ms
```

```
        Wall time: 96.6 ms

Out[142]: /ints_floats_from_array (Table(2000000,)) 'Integers and Floats'
            description := {
            "Date": StringCol(itemsize=26, shape=(), dflt=b'', pos=0),
            "No1": Int32Col(shape=(), dflt=0, pos=1),
            "No2": Int32Col(shape=(), dflt=0, pos=2),
            "No3": Float64Col(shape=(), dflt=0.0, pos=3),
            "No4": Float64Col(shape=(), dflt=0.0, pos=4)}
            byteorder := 'little'
            chunkshape := (2621,)
```

❶ This defines the special dtype object.

❷ This creates the structured array with zeros (and empty strings).

❸ A few records from the ndarray object.

❹ The columns of the ndarray object are populated at once.

❺ This creates the Table object *and* populates it with the data.

This approach is an order of magnitude faster, has more concise code, and achieves the same result:

```
In [143]: type(h5)
Out[143]: tables.file.File

In [144]: h5  ❶
Out[144]: File(filename=/Users/yves/Temp/data/pytab.h5, title='', mode='w',
            root_uep='/', filters=Filters(complevel=0, shuffle=False,
            bitshuffle=False, fletcher32=False, least_significant_digit=None))
            / (RootGroup) ''
            /ints_floats (Table(2000000,)) 'Integers and Floats'
              description := {
              "Date": StringCol(itemsize=26, shape=(), dflt=b'', pos=0),
              "No1": Int32Col(shape=(), dflt=0, pos=1),
              "No2": Int32Col(shape=(), dflt=0, pos=2),
              "No3": Float64Col(shape=(), dflt=0.0, pos=3),
              "No4": Float64Col(shape=(), dflt=0.0, pos=4)}
              byteorder := 'little'
              chunkshape := (2621,)
            /ints_floats_from_array (Table(2000000,)) 'Integers and Floats'
              description := {
              "Date": StringCol(itemsize=26, shape=(), dflt=b'', pos=0),
              "No1": Int32Col(shape=(), dflt=0, pos=1),
              "No2": Int32Col(shape=(), dflt=0, pos=2),
              "No3": Float64Col(shape=(), dflt=0.0, pos=3),
              "No4": Float64Col(shape=(), dflt=0.0, pos=4)}
              byteorder := 'little'
              chunkshape := (2621,)
```

```
In [145]: h5.remove_node('/', 'ints_floats_from_array')  ❷
```

❶ The description of the File object with the two Table objects.

❷ This removes the second Table object with the redundant data.

The Table object behaves pretty similar to NumPy structured ndarray objects in most cases (see also Figure 9-5):

```
In [146]: tab[:3]  ❶
Out[146]: array([(b'2018-10-19 12:12:28.227771', 8576, 5991, -0.0528, 0.2468),
                 (b'2018-10-19 12:12:28.227858', 2990, 9310, -0.0261, 0.3932),
                 (b'2018-10-19 12:12:28.227868', 4400, 4823,  0.9133, 0.2579)],
          dtype=[('Date', 'S26'), ('No1', '<i4'), ('No2', '<i4'), ('No3', '<f8'),
          ('No4', '<f8')])

In [147]: tab[:4]['No4']  ❷
Out[147]: array([ 0.2468,  0.3932,  0.2579, -0.5582])

In [148]: %time np.sum(tab[:]['No3'])  ❸
          CPU times: user 76.7 ms, sys: 74.8 ms, total: 151 ms
          Wall time: 152 ms

Out[148]: 88.8542999999997

In [149]: %time np.sum(np.sqrt(tab[:]['No1']))  ❸
          CPU times: user 91 ms, sys: 57.9 ms, total: 149 ms
          Wall time: 164 ms

Out[149]: 133349920.3689251

In [150]: %%time
          plt.figure(figsize=(10, 6))
          plt.hist(tab[:]['No3'], bins=30);  ❹
          CPU times: user 328 ms, sys: 72.1 ms, total: 400 ms
          Wall time: 456 ms
```

❶ Selecting rows via indexing.

❷ Selecting column values only via indexing.

❸ Applying NumPy universal functions.

❹ Plotting a column from the Table object.

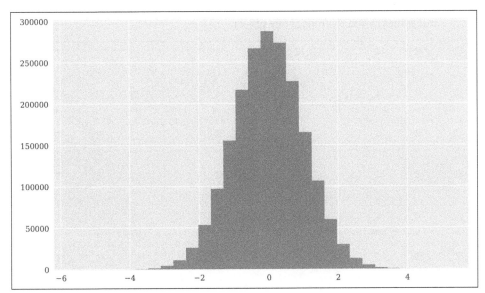

Figure 9-5. Histogram of column data

PyTables also provides flexible tools to query data via typical SQL-like statements, as in the following example (the result of which is illustrated in Figure 9-6; compare it with Figure 9-2, based on a pandas query):

```
In [151]: query = '((No3 < -0.5) | (No3 > 0.5)) & ((No4 < -1) | (No4 > 1))'   ❶

In [152]: iterator = tab.where(query)   ❷

In [153]: %time res = [(row['No3'], row['No4']) for row in iterator]   ❸
          CPU times: user 269 ms, sys: 64.4 ms, total: 333 ms
          Wall time: 294 ms

In [154]: res = np.array(res)   ❹
          res[:3]
Out[154]: array([[0.7694, 1.4866],
                 [0.9201, 1.3346],
                 [1.4701, 1.8776]])

In [155]: plt.figure(figsize=(10, 6))
          plt.plot(res.T[0], res.T[1], 'ro');
```

❶ The query as a str object, four conditions combined by logical operators.

❷ The iterator object based on the query.

❸ The rows resulting from the query are collected via a list comprehension …

❹ … and transformed to an ndarray object.

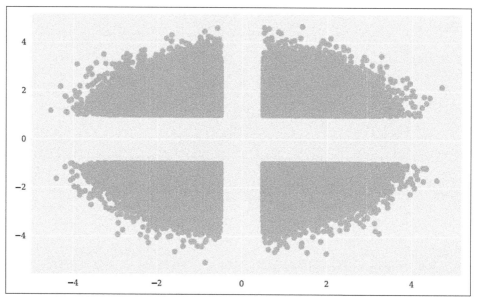

Figure 9-6. Scatter plot of column data

Fast Queries

Both pandas and PyTables are able to process relatively complex, SQL-like queries and selections. They are both optimized for speed when it comes to such operations. Although there are limits to these approaches compared to relational databases, for most numerical and financial applications these are often not relevant.

As the following examples show, working with data stored in PyTables as Table objects gives the impression of working with NumPy or pandas objects in-memory, both from a *syntax* and a *performance* point of view:

```
In [156]: %%time
          values = tab[:]['No3']
          print('Max %18.3f' % values.max())
          print('Ave %18.3f' % values.mean())
          print('Min %18.3f' % values.min())
          print('Std %18.3f' % values.std())
          Max             5.224
          Ave             0.000
          Min            -5.649
          Std             1.000
          CPU times: user 163 ms, sys: 70.4 ms, total: 233 ms
          Wall time: 234 ms
```

```
In [157]: %%time
          res = [(row['No1'], row['No2']) for row in
                  tab.where('((No1 > 9800) | (No1 < 200)) \
                      & ((No2 > 4500) & (No2 < 5500))')]
          CPU times: user 165 ms, sys: 52.5 ms, total: 218 ms
          Wall time: 155 ms

In [158]: for r in res[:4]:
              print(r)
          (91, 4870)
          (9803, 5026)
          (9846, 4859)
          (9823, 5069)

In [159]: %%time
          res = [(row['No1'], row['No2']) for row in
                  tab.where('(No1 == 1234) & (No2 > 9776)')]
          CPU times: user 58.9 ms, sys: 40.5 ms, total: 99.4 ms
          Wall time: 81 ms

In [160]: for r in res:
              print(r)
          (1234, 9841)
          (1234, 9821)
          (1234, 9867)
          (1234, 9987)
          (1234, 9849)
          (1234, 9800)
```

Working with Compressed Tables

A major advantage of working with PyTables is the approach it takes to compression.
It uses compression not only to save space on disk, but also to improve the performance of I/O operations in certain hardware scenarios. How does this work? When
I/O is the bottleneck and the CPU is able to (de)compress data fast, the net effect of
compression in terms of speed might be positive. Since the following examples are
based on the I/O of a standard SSD, there is no speed advantage of compression to be
observed. However, there is also almost no *disadvantage* to using compression:

```
In [161]: filename = path + 'pytabc.h5'

In [162]: h5c = tb.open_file(filename, 'w')

In [163]: filters = tb.Filters(complevel=5,        ❶
                               complib='blosc')    ❷

In [164]: tabc = h5c.create_table('/', 'ints_floats', sarray,
                                  title='Integers and Floats',
                                  expectedrows=rows, filters=filters)

In [165]: query = '((No3 < -0.5) | (No3 > 0.5)) & ((No4 < -1) | (No4 > 1))'
```

```
In [166]: iteratorc = tabc.where(query)   ❸

In [167]: %time res = [(row['No3'], row['No4']) for row in iteratorc]   ❹
          CPU times: user 300 ms, sys: 50.8 ms, total: 351 ms
          Wall time: 311 ms

In [168]: res = np.array(res)
          res[:3]
Out[168]: array([[0.7694, 1.4866],
                 [0.9201, 1.3346],
                 [1.4701, 1.8776]])
```

❶ The complevel (compression level) parameter can take values between 0 (no compression) and 9 (highest compression).

❷ The Blosc compression engine (*http://blosc.org*) is used, which is optimized for performance.

❸ This creates the iterator object, based on the query from before.

❹ The rows resulting from the query are collected via a list comprehension.

Generating the compressed Table object with the original data and doing analytics on it is slightly slower compared to the uncompressed Table object. What about reading the data into an ndarray object? Let's check:

```
In [169]: %time arr_non = tab.read()   ❶
          CPU times: user 63 ms, sys: 78.5 ms, total: 142 ms
          Wall time: 149 ms

In [170]: tab.size_on_disk
Out[170]: 100122200

In [171]: arr_non.nbytes
Out[171]: 100000000

In [172]: %time arr_com = tabc.read()   ❷
          CPU times: user 106 ms, sys: 55.5 ms, total: 161 ms
          Wall time: 173 ms

In [173]: tabc.size_on_disk
Out[173]: 41306140

In [174]: arr_com.nbytes
Out[174]: 100000000

In [175]: ll $path*   ❸
          -rw-r--r--  1 yves  staff  200312336 Oct 19 12:12
          /Users/yves/Temp/data/pytab.h5
```

```
         -rw-r--r--  1 yves  staff   41341436 Oct 19 12:12
         /Users/yves/Temp/data/pytabc.h5

In [176]: h5c.close()  ❹
```

❶ Reading from the uncompressed `Table` object `tab`.

❷ Reading from the compressed `Table` object `tabc`.

❸ Comparing the sizes—the size of the compressed table is significantly reduced.

❹ Closing the database file.

The examples show that there is hardly any speed difference when working with compressed `Table` objects as compared to uncompressed ones. However, file sizes on disk might—depending on the quality of the data—be significantly reduced, which has a number of benefits:

- Storage costs are reduced.
- Backup costs are reduced.
- Network traffic is reduced.
- Network speed is improved (storage on and retrieval from remote servers is faster).
- CPU utilization is increased to overcome I/O bottlenecks.

Working with Arrays

"Basic I/O with Python" on page 232 showed that `NumPy` has built-in fast writing and reading capabilities for `ndarray` objects. `PyTables` is also quite fast and efficient when it comes to storing and retrieving `ndarray` objects, and since it is based on a hierarchical database structure, many convenience features come on top:

```
In [177]: %%time
          arr_int = h5.create_array('/', 'integers', ran_int)  ❶
          arr_flo = h5.create_array('/', 'floats', ran_flo)    ❷
          CPU times: user 4.26 ms, sys: 37.2 ms, total: 41.5 ms
          Wall time: 46.2 ms

In [178]: h5  ❸
Out[178]: File(filename=/Users/yves/Temp/data/pytab.h5, title='', mode='w',
          root_uep='/', filters=Filters(complevel=0, shuffle=False,
          bitshuffle=False, fletcher32=False, least_significant_digit=None))
          / (RootGroup) ''
          /floats (Array(2000000, 2)) ''
            atom := Float64Atom(shape=(), dflt=0.0)
```

```
            maindim := 0
            flavor := 'numpy'
            byteorder := 'little'
            chunkshape := None
        /integers (Array(2000000, 2)) ''
            atom := Int64Atom(shape=(), dflt=0)
            maindim := 0
            flavor := 'numpy'
            byteorder := 'little'
            chunkshape := None
        /ints_floats (Table(2000000,)) 'Integers and Floats'
            description := {
            "Date": StringCol(itemsize=26, shape=(), dflt=b'', pos=0),
            "No1": Int32Col(shape=(), dflt=0, pos=1),
            "No2": Int32Col(shape=(), dflt=0, pos=2),
            "No3": Float64Col(shape=(), dflt=0.0, pos=3),
            "No4": Float64Col(shape=(), dflt=0.0, pos=4)}
            byteorder := 'little'
            chunkshape := (2621,)

In [179]: ll $path*
          -rw-r--r--  1 yves   staff  262344490 Oct 19 12:12
          /Users/yves/Temp/data/pytab.h5
          -rw-r--r--  1 yves   staff   41341436 Oct 19 12:12
          /Users/yves/Temp/data/pytabc.h5

In [180]: h5.close()

In [181]: !rm -f $path*
```

❶ Stores the `ran_int` ndarray object.

❷ Stores the `ran_flo` ndarray object.

❸ The changes are reflected in the object description.

Writing these objects directly to an HDF5 database is faster than looping over the objects and writing the data row-by-row to a `Table` object or using the approach via structured `ndarray` objects.

HDF5-Based Data Storage

The HDF5 hierarchical database (file) format is a powerful alternative to, for example, relational databases when it comes to structured numerical and financial data. Both on a standalone basis when using `PyTables` directly and when combining it with the capabilities of `pandas`, one can expect to get almost the maximum I/O performance that the available hardware allows.

Out-of-Memory Computations

PyTables supports out-of-memory operations, which makes it possible to implement array-based computations that do not fit in memory. To this end, consider the following code based on the EArray class. This type of object can be expanded in one dimension (row-wise), while the number of columns (elements per row) needs to be fixed:

```
In [182]: filename = path + 'earray.h5'

In [183]: h5 = tb.open_file(filename, 'w')

In [184]: n = 500   ❶

In [185]: ear = h5.create_earray('/', 'ear',   ❷
                                 atom=tb.Float64Atom(),   ❸
                                 shape=(0, n))   ❹

In [186]: type(ear)
Out[186]: tables.earray.EArray

In [187]: rand = np.random.standard_normal((n, n))   ❺
          rand[:4, :4]
Out[187]: array([[-1.25983231,  1.11420699,  0.1667485 ,  0.7345676 ],
                 [-0.13785424,  1.22232417,  1.36303097,  0.13521042],
                 [ 1.45487119, -1.47784078,  0.15027672,  0.86755989],
                 [-0.63519366,  0.1516327 , -0.64939447, -0.45010975]])

In [188]: %%time
          for _ in range(750):
              ear.append(rand)   ❻
          ear.flush()
CPU times: user 814 ms, sys: 1.18 s, total: 1.99 s
Wall time: 2.53 s

In [189]: ear
Out[189]: /ear (EArray(375000, 500)) ''
            atom := Float64Atom(shape=(), dflt=0.0)
            maindim := 0
            flavor := 'numpy'
            byteorder := 'little'
            chunkshape := (16, 500)

In [190]: ear.size_on_disk
Out[190]: 1500032000
```

❶ The fixed number of columns.

❷ The path and technical name of the EArray object.

❸ The atomic `dtype` object of the single values.

❹ The shape for instantiation (no rows, n columns).

❺ The `ndarray` object with the random numbers ...

❻ ... that gets appended many times.

For out-of-memory computations that do not lead to aggregations, another `EArray` object of the same shape (size) is needed. `PyTables` has a special module to cope with numerical expressions efficiently. It is called `Expr` and is based on the numerical expression library `numexpr` (*https://numexpr.readthedocs.io*). The code that follows uses `Expr` to calculate the mathematical expression in Equation 9-1 on the whole `EArray` object from before.

Equation 9-1. Example mathematical expression

$$y = 3 \sin(x) + \sqrt{|x|}$$

The results are stored in the `out` `EArray` object, and the expression evaluation happens chunk-wise:

```
In [191]: out = h5.create_earray('/', 'out',
                                   atom=tb.Float64Atom(),
                                   shape=(0, n))

In [192]: out.size_on_disk
Out[192]: 0

In [193]: expr = tb.Expr('3 * sin(ear) + sqrt(abs(ear))')   ❶

In [194]: expr.set_output(out, append_mode=True)   ❷

In [195]: %time expr.eval()   ❸
          CPU times: user 3.08 s, sys: 1.7 s, total: 4.78 s
          Wall time: 4.03 s

Out[195]: /out (EArray(375000, 500)) ''
            atom := Float64Atom(shape=(), dflt=0.0)
            maindim := 0
            flavor := 'numpy'
            byteorder := 'little'
            chunkshape := (16, 500)

In [196]: out.size_on_disk
Out[196]: 1500032000

In [197]: out[0, :10]
```

```
Out[197]: array([-1.73369462,  3.74824436,  0.90627898,  2.86786818,
                  1.75424957,
                 -0.91108973, -1.68313885,  1.29073295, -1.68665599, -1.71345309])
```

```
In [198]: %time out_ = out.read()    ❹
          CPU times: user 1.03 s, sys: 1.1 s, total: 2.13 s
          Wall time: 2.22 s
```

```
In [199]: out_[0, :10]
Out[199]: array([-1.73369462,  3.74824436,  0.90627898,  2.86786818,
                  1.75424957,
                 -0.91108973, -1.68313885,  1.29073295, -1.68665599, -1.71345309])
```

❶ Transforms a `str` object–based expression to an `Expr` object.

❷ Defines the output to be the `out` `EArray` object.

❸ Initiates the evaluation of the expression.

❹ Reads the whole `EArray` into memory.

Given that the whole operation takes place out-of-memory, it can be considered quite fast, in particular as it is executed on standard hardware. As a benchmark, the in-memory performance of the `numexpr` module (see also Chapter 10) can be considered. It is faster, but not by a huge margin:

```
In [200]: import numexpr as ne    ❶
```

```
In [201]: expr = '3 * sin(out_) + sqrt(abs(out_))'    ❷
```

```
In [202]: ne.set_num_threads(1)    ❸
Out[202]: 4
```

```
In [203]: %time ne.evaluate(expr)[0, :10]    ❹
          CPU times: user 2.51 s, sys: 1.54 s, total: 4.05 s
          Wall time: 4.94 s
```

```
Out[203]: array([-1.64358578,  0.22567882,  3.31363043,  2.50443549,
                  4.27413965,
                 -1.41600606, -1.68373023,  4.01921805, -1.68117412, -1.66053597])
```

```
In [204]: ne.set_num_threads(4)    ❺
Out[204]: 1
```

```
In [205]: %time ne.evaluate(expr)[0, :10]    ❻
          CPU times: user 3.39 s, sys: 1.94 s, total: 5.32 s
          Wall time: 2.96 s
```

```
Out[205]: array([-1.64358578,  0.22567882,  3.31363043,  2.50443549,
                  4.27413965,
                 -1.41600606, -1.68373023,  4.01921805, -1.68117412, -1.66053597])
```

```
In [206]: h5.close()

In [207]: !rm -f $path*
```

❶ Imports the module for *in-memory* evaluations of numerical expressions.

❷ The numerical expression as a `str` object.

❸ Sets the number of threads to one.

❹ Evaluates the numerical expression in-memory with one thread.

❺ Sets the number of threads to four.

❻ Evaluates the numerical expression in-memory with four threads.

I/O with TsTables

The package `TsTables` uses `PyTables` to build a high-performance storage for time series data. The major usage scenario is "write once, retrieve multiple times." This is a typical scenario in financial analytics, where data is created in the markets, retrieved in real-time or asynchronously, and stored on disk for later usage. That usage might be in a larger trading strategy backtesting program that requires different subsets of a historical financial time series over and over again. It is then important that data retrieval happens fast.

Sample Data

As usual, the first task is the generation of a sample data set that is large enough to illustrate the benefits of `TsTables`. The following code generates three rather long financial time series based on the simulation of a geometric Brownian motion (see Chapter 12):

```
In [208]: no = 5000000    ❶
          co = 3    ❷
          interval = 1. / (12 * 30 * 24 * 60)    ❸
          vol = 0.2    ❹

In [209]: %%time
          rn = np.random.standard_normal((no, co))    ❺
          rn[0] = 0.0    ❻
          paths = 100 * np.exp(np.cumsum(-0.5 * vol ** 2 * interval +
                  vol * np.sqrt(interval) * rn, axis=0))    ❼
          paths[0] = 100    ❽
          CPU times: user 869 ms, sys: 175 ms, total: 1.04 s
          Wall time: 812 ms
```

❶ The number of time steps.

❷ The number of time series.

❸ The time interval as a year fraction.

❹ The volatility.

❺ Standard normally distributed random numbers.

❻ Sets the initial random numbers to zero.

❼ The simulation based on an Euler discretization.

❽ Sets the initial values of the paths to 100.

Since TsTables works pretty well with pandas DataFrame objects, the data is transformed to such an object (see also Figure 9-7):

```
In [210]: dr = pd.date_range('2019-1-1', periods=no, freq='1s')

In [211]: dr[-6:]
Out[211]: DatetimeIndex(['2019-02-27 20:53:14', '2019-02-27 20:53:15',
                          '2019-02-27 20:53:16', '2019-02-27 20:53:17',
                          '2019-02-27 20:53:18', '2019-02-27 20:53:19'],
                         dtype='datetime64[ns]', freq='S')

In [212]: df = pd.DataFrame(paths, index=dr, columns=['ts1', 'ts2', 'ts3'])

In [213]: df.info()
          <class 'pandas.core.frame.DataFrame'>
          DatetimeIndex: 5000000 entries, 2019-01-01 00:00:00 to 2019-02-27
           20:53:19
          Freq: S
          Data columns (total 3 columns):
          ts1      float64
          ts2      float64
          ts3      float64
          dtypes: float64(3)
          memory usage: 152.6 MB

In [214]: df.head()
Out[214]:                           ts1         ts2         ts3
          2019-01-01 00:00:00  100.000000  100.000000  100.000000
          2019-01-01 00:00:01  100.018443   99.966644   99.998255
          2019-01-01 00:00:02  100.069023  100.004420   99.986646
          2019-01-01 00:00:03  100.086757  100.000246   99.992042
          2019-01-01 00:00:04  100.105448  100.036033   99.950618

In [215]: df[::100000].plot(figsize=(10, 6));
```

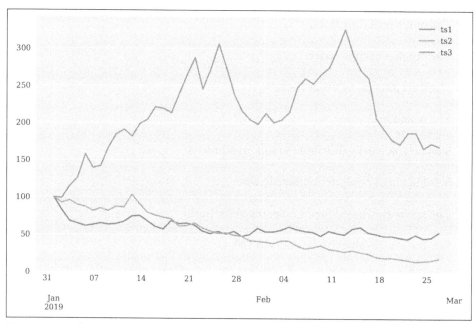

Figure 9-7. Selected data points of the financial time series

Data Storage

TsTables stores financial time series data based on a specific chunk-based structure that allows for fast retrieval of arbitrary data subsets defined by some time interval. To this end, the package adds the function `create_ts()` to PyTables. To provide the data types for the table columns, the following uses a method based on the `tb.Is Description` class from PyTables:

```
In [216]: import tstables as tstab

In [217]: class ts_desc(tb.IsDescription):
              timestamp = tb.Int64Col(pos=0)    ❶
              ts1 = tb.Float64Col(pos=1)    ❷
              ts2 = tb.Float64Col(pos=2)    ❷
              ts3 = tb.Float64Col(pos=3)    ❷

In [218]: h5 = tb.open_file(path + 'tstab.h5', 'w')    ❸

In [219]: ts = h5.create_ts('/', 'ts', ts_desc)    ❹

In [220]: %time ts.append(df)    ❺
          CPU times: user 1.36 s, sys: 497 ms, total: 1.86 s
          Wall time: 1.29 s

In [221]: type(ts)
Out[221]: tstables.tstable.TsTable
```

```
In [222]: ls -n $path
          total 328472
          -rw-r--r--  1 501  20  157037368 Oct 19 12:13 tstab.h5
```

❶ The column for the timestamps.

❷ The columns to store the numerical data.

❸ Opens an HDF5 database file for writing (w).

❹ Creates the TsTable object based on the ts_desc object.

❺ Appends the data from the DataFrame object to the TsTable object.

Data Retrieval

Writing data with TsTables obviously is quite fast, even if hardware-dependent. The same holds true for reading chunks of the data back into memory. Conveniently, TsTables returns a DataFrame object (see also Figure 9-8):

```
In [223]: read_start_dt = dt.datetime(2019, 2, 1, 0, 0)   ❶
          read_end_dt = dt.datetime(2019, 2, 5, 23, 59)   ❷

In [224]: %time rows = ts.read_range(read_start_dt, read_end_dt)   ❸
          CPU times: user 182 ms, sys: 73.5 ms, total: 255 ms
          Wall time: 163 ms

In [225]: rows.info()   ❹
          <class 'pandas.core.frame.DataFrame'>
          DatetimeIndex: 431941 entries, 2019-02-01 00:00:00 to 2019-02-05
            23:59:00
          Data columns (total 3 columns):
          ts1    431941 non-null float64
          ts2    431941 non-null float64
          ts3    431941 non-null float64
          dtypes: float64(3)
          memory usage: 13.2 MB

In [226]: rows.head()   ❹
Out[226]:                            ts1        ts2        ts3
          2019-02-01 00:00:00  52.063640  40.474580  217.324713
          2019-02-01 00:00:01  52.087455  40.471911  217.250070
          2019-02-01 00:00:02  52.084808  40.458013  217.228712
          2019-02-01 00:00:03  52.073536  40.451408  217.302912
          2019-02-01 00:00:04  52.056133  40.450951  217.207481

In [227]: h5.close()

In [228]: (rows[::500] / rows.iloc[0]).plot(figsize=(10, 6));
```

❶ The start time of the interval.

❷ The end time of the interval.

❸ The function `ts.read_range()` returns a `DataFrame` object for the interval.

❹ The `DataFrame` object has a few hundred thousand data rows.

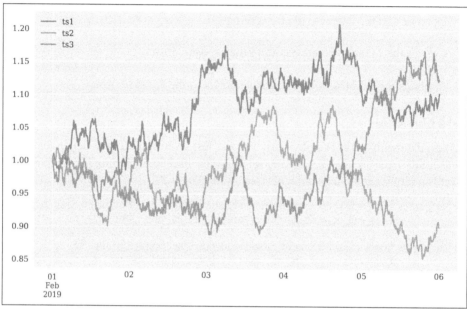

Figure 9-8. A specific time interval of the financial time series (normalized)

To better illustrate the performance of the `TsTables`-based data retrieval, consider the following benchmark, which retrieves 100 chunks of data consisting of 3 days' worth of 1-second bars. The retrieval of a `DataFrame` with 345,600 rows of data takes less than one-tenth of a second:

```
In [229]: import random

In [230]: h5 = tb.open_file(path + 'tstab.h5', 'r')

In [231]: ts = h5.root.ts._f_get_timeseries()   ❶

In [232]: %%time
          for _ in range(100):   ❷
              d = random.randint(1, 24)   ❸
              read_start_dt = dt.datetime(2019, 2, d, 0, 0, 0)
              read_end_dt = dt.datetime(2019, 2, d + 3, 23, 59, 59)
              rows = ts.read_range(read_start_dt, read_end_dt)
```

```
            CPU times: user 7.17 s, sys: 1.65 s, total: 8.81 s
            Wall time: 4.78 s

In [233]: rows.info()      ❹
            <class 'pandas.core.frame.DataFrame'>
            DatetimeIndex: 345600 entries, 2019-02-04 00:00:00 to 2019-02-07
              23:59:59
            Data columns (total 3 columns):
            ts1    345600 non-null float64
            ts2    345600 non-null float64
            ts3    345600 non-null float64
            dtypes: float64(3)
            memory usage: 10.5 MB

In [234]: !rm $path/tstab.h5
```

❶   This connects to the TsTable object.

❷   The data retrieval is repeated many times.

❸   The starting day value is randomized.

❹   The last DataFrame object is retrieved.

Conclusion

SQL-based or relational databases have advantages when it comes to complex data structures that exhibit lots of relations between single objects/tables. This might justify in some circumstances their performance disadvantage over pure NumPy ndarray-based or pandas DataFrame–based approaches.

Many application areas in finance or science in general can succeed with a mainly array-based data modeling approach. In these cases, huge performance improvements can be realized by making use of native NumPy I/O capabilities, a combination of NumPy and PyTables capabilities, or the pandas approach via HDF5-based stores. TsTables is particularly useful when working with large (financial) time series data sets, especially in "write once, retrieve multiple times" scenarios.

While a recent trend has been to use cloud-based solutions—where the cloud is made up of a large number of computing nodes based on commodity hardware—one should carefully consider, especially in a financial context, which hardware architecture best serves the analytics requirements. A study by Microsoft sheds some light on this topic:

> We claim that a single "scale-up" server can process each of these jobs and do as well or better than a cluster in terms of performance, cost, power, and server density.
>
> —Appuswamy et al. (2013)

Companies, research institutions, and others involved in data analytics should therefore analyze first what specific tasks have to be accomplished in general and then decide on the hardware/software architecture, in terms of:

Scaling out
Using a cluster with many commodity nodes with standard CPUs and relatively low memory

Scaling up
Using one or a few powerful servers with many-core CPUs, possibly also GPUs or even TPUs when machine and deep learning play a role, and large amounts of memory

Scaling up hardware and applying appropriate implementation approaches might significantly influence performance, which is the focus of the next chapter.

Further Resources

The paper cited at the beginning and end of the chapter is a good read, and a good starting point to think about hardware architecture for financial analytics:

- Appuswamy, Raja, et al. (2013). "Nobody Ever Got Fired for Buying a Cluster" (*http://bit.ly/2RZOpR8*). Microsoft Technical Report.

As usual, the web provides many valuable resources with regard to the topics and Python packages covered in this chapter:

- For serialization of Python objects with `pickle`, refer to the documentation (*http://docs.python.org/3/library/pickle.html*).

- An overview of the I/O capabilities of `NumPy` is provided on the website (*http://docs.scipy.org/doc/numpy/reference/routines.io.html*).

- For I/O with `pandas`, see the respective section in the online documentation (*http://pandas.pydata.org/pandas-docs/stable/io.html*).

- The `PyTables` home page (*http://www.pytables.org*) provides both tutorials and detailed documentation.

- More information on `TsTables` can be found on its GitHub page (*http://github.com/afiedler/tstables/*).

A friendly fork for `TsTables` is found at *http://github.com/yhilpisch/tstables*. Use `pip install git+git://github.com/yhilpisch/tstables` to install the package from this fork, which is maintained for compatibility with newer versions of `pandas` and other Python packages.

## CHAPTER 10

Performance Python

Don't lower your expectations to meet your performance. Raise your level of performance to meet your expectations.

—Ralph Marston

It is a long-lived prejudice that Python per se is a relatively slow programming language and not appropriate to implement computationally demanding tasks in finance. Beyond the fact that Python is an interpreted language, the reasoning is usually along the following lines: Python is slow when it comes to loops; loops are often required to implement financial algorithms; therefore Python is too slow for financial algorithm implementation. Another line of reasoning is: other (compiled) programming languages are fast at executing loops (such as C or C++); loops are often required for financial algorithms; therefore these (compiled) programming languages are well suited for finance and financial algorithm implementation.

Admittedly, it is possible to write proper Python code that executes rather slowly—perhaps too slowly for many application areas. This chapter is about approaches to speed up typical tasks and algorithms often encountered in a financial context. It shows that with a judicious use of data structures, choosing the right implementation idioms and paradigms, as well as using the right performance packages, Python is able to compete even with compiled programming languages. This is due to, among other factors, getting compiled itself.

To this end, this chapter introduces different approaches to speed up code:

Vectorization
> Making use of Python's vectorization capabilities is one approach already used extensively in previous chapters.

Dynamic compiling

Using the `Numba` package allows one to dynamically compile pure Python code using LLVM technology (*https://llvm.org/*).

Static compiling

`Cython` is not only a Python package but a hybrid language that combines Python and C; it allows one, for instance, to use static type declarations and to statically compile such adjusted code.

Multiprocessing

The `multiprocessing` module of Python allows for easy and simple parallelization of code execution.

This chapter addresses the following topics:

"Loops" on page 276

This section addresses Python loops and how to speed them up.

"Algorithms" on page 282

This section is concerned with standard mathematical algorithms that are often used for performance benchmarks, such as Fibonacci number generation.

"Binomial Trees" on page 294

The binomial option pricing model is a widely used financial model that allows for an interesting case study about a more involved financial algorithm.

"Monte Carlo Simulation" on page 299

Similarly, Monte Carlo simulation is widely used in financial practice for pricing and risk management. It is computationally demanding and has long been considered the domain of such languages as C or C++.

"Recursive pandas Algorithm" on page 305

This section addresses the speedup of a recursive algorithm based on financial time series data. In particular, it presents different implementations for an algorithm calculating an exponentially weighted moving average (EWMA).

Loops

This section tackles the Python loop issue. The task is rather simple: a function shall be written that draws a certain "large" number of random numbers and returns the average of the values. The execution time is of interest, which can be estimated by the magic functions `%time` and `%timeit`.

Python

Let's get started "slowly"—forgive the pun. In pure Python, such a function might look like `average_py()`:

```
In [1]: import random

In [2]: def average_py(n):
            s = 0          ❶
            for i in range(n):
                s += random.random()    ❷
            return s / n    ❸

In [3]: n = 10000000    ❹

In [4]: %time average_py(n)    ❺
        CPU times: user 1.82 s, sys: 10.4 ms, total: 1.83 s
        Wall time: 1.93 s

Out[4]: 0.5000590124747943

In [5]: %timeit average_py(n)    ❻
        1.31 s ± 159 ms per loop (mean ± std. dev. of 7 runs, 1 loop each)

In [6]: %time sum([random.random() for _ in range(n)]) / n    ❼
        CPU times: user 1.55 s, sys: 188 ms, total: 1.74 s
        Wall time: 1.74 s

Out[6]: 0.49987031710661173
```

❶ Initializes the variable value for s.

❷ Adds the uniformly distributed random values from the interval (0, 1) to s.

❸ Returns the average value (mean).

❹ Defines the number of iterations for the loop.

❺ Times the function once.

❻ Times the function multiple times for a more reliable estimate.

❼ Uses a `list` comprehension instead of the function.

This sets the benchmark for the other approaches to follow.

NumPy

The strength of NumPy lies in its vectorization capabilities. Formally, loops vanish on the Python level; the looping takes place one level deeper based on optimized and compiled routines provided by NumPy.[1] The function `average_np()` makes use of this approach:

```
In [7]: import numpy as np

In [8]: def average_np(n):
            s = np.random.random(n)   ❶
            return s.mean()   ❷

In [9]: %time average_np(n)
        CPU times: user 180 ms, sys: 43.2 ms, total: 223 ms
        Wall time: 224 ms

Out[9]: 0.49988861556468317

In [10]: %timeit average_np(n)
         128 ms ± 2.01 ms per loop (mean ± std. dev. of 7 runs, 10 loops each)

In [11]: s = np.random.random(n)
         s.nbytes   ❸
Out[11]: 80000000
```

❶ Draws the random numbers "all at once" (no Python loop).

❷ Returns the average value (mean).

❸ Number of bytes used for the created `ndarray` object.

The speedup is considerable, reaching almost a factor of 10 or an order of magnitude. However, the price that must be paid is significantly higher memory usage. This is due to the fact that NumPy attains speed by preallocating data that can be processed in the compiled layer. As a consquence, there is no way, given this approach, to work with "streamed" data. This increased memory usage might even be prohibitively large depending on the algorithm or problem at hand.

---

1 NumPy can also make use of dedicated mathematics libraries, such as the Intel Math Kernel Library (MKL) (*https://software.intel.com/en-us/mkl*).

Vectorization and Memory

It is tempting to write vectorized code with NumPy whenever possible due to the concise syntax and speed improvements typically observed. However, these benefits often come at the price of a much higher memory footprint.

Numba

Numba (*https://numba.pydata.org/*) is a package that allows the *dynamic compiling* of pure Python code by the use of LLVM. The application in a simple case, like the one at hand, is surprisingly straightforward and the dynamically compiled function aver age_nb() can be called directly from Python:

```
In [12]: import numba

In [13]: average_nb = numba.jit(average_py)    ❶

In [14]: %time average_nb(n)    ❷
         CPU times: user 204 ms, sys: 34.3 ms, total: 239 ms
         Wall time: 278 ms

Out[14]: 0.4998865391283664

In [15]: %time average_nb(n)    ❸
         CPU times: user 80.9 ms, sys: 457 µs, total: 81.3 ms
         Wall time: 81.7 ms

Out[15]: 0.5001357454250273

In [16]: %timeit average_nb(n)    ❸
         75.5 ms ± 1.95 ms per loop (mean ± std. dev. of 7 runs, 10 loops each)
```

❶ This creates the Numba function.

❷ The compiling happens during runtime, leading to some overhead.

❸ From the second execution (with the same input data types), the execution is faster.

The combination of pure Python with Numba beats the NumPy version *and* preserves the memory efficiency of the original loop-based implementation. It is also obvious that the application of Numba in such simple cases comes with hardly any programming overhead.

No Free Lunch

The application of Numba sometimes seems like magic when one compares the performance of the Python code to the compiled version, especially given its ease of use. However, there are many use cases for which Numba is not suited and for which performance gains are hardly observed or even impossible to achieve.

Cython

Cython (*http://cython.org*) allows one to *statically compile* Python code. However, the application is not as simple as with Numba since the code generally needs to be changed to see significant speed improvements. To begin with, consider the Cython function `average_cy1()`, which introduces static type declarations for the used variables:

```
In [17]: %load_ext Cython
```

```
In [18]: %%cython -a
         import random   ❶
         def average_cy1(int n):   ❷
             cdef int i   ❷
             cdef float s = 0   ❷
             for i in range(n):
                 s += random.random()
             return s / n
Out[18]: <IPython.core.display.HTML object>
```

```
In [19]: %time average_cy1(n)
         CPU times: user 695 ms, sys: 4.31 ms, total: 699 ms
         Wall time: 711 ms
```

```
Out[19]: 0.49997106194496155
```

```
In [20]: %timeit average_cy1(n)
         752 ms ± 91.1 ms per loop (mean ± std. dev. of 7 runs, 1 loop each)
```

❶   Imports the `random` module within the Cython context.

❷   Adds static type declarations for the variables n, i, and s.

Some speedup is observed, but not even close to that achieved by, for example, the NumPy version. A bit more Cython optimization is necessary to beat even the Numba version:

```
In [21]: %%cython
         from libc.stdlib cimport rand   ❶
         cdef extern from 'limits.h':   ❷
             int INT_MAX   ❷
```

```
        cdef int i
        cdef float rn
        for i in range(5):
            rn = rand() / INT_MAX    ❸
            print(rn)
        0.6792964339256287
        0.934692919254303
        0.3835020661354065
        0.5194163918495178
        0.8309653401374817


In [22]: %%cython -a
        from libc.stdlib cimport rand    ❶
        cdef extern from 'limits.h':     ❷
            int INT_MAX    ❷
        def average_cy2(int n):
            cdef int i
            cdef float s = 0
            for i in range(n):
                s += rand() / INT_MAX    ❸
            return s / n
Out[22]: <IPython.core.display.HTML object>


In [23]: %time average_cy2(n)
        CPU times: user 78.5 ms, sys: 422 µs, total: 79 ms
        Wall time: 79.1 ms


Out[23]: 0.500017523765564


In [24]: %timeit average_cy2(n)
        65.4 ms ± 706 µs per loop (mean ± std. dev. of 7 runs, 10 loops each)
```

❶ Imports a random number generator from C.

❷ Imports a constant value for the scaling of the random numbers.

❸ Adds uniformly distributed random numbers from the interval (0, 1), after scaling.

This further optimized Cython version, average_cy2(), is now a bit faster than the Numba version. However, the effort has also been a bit larger. Compared to the NumPy version, Cython also preserves the memory efficiency of the original loop-based implementation.

Cython = Python + C

Cython allows developers to tweak code for performance as much as possible or as little as sensible—starting with a pure Python version, for instance, and adding more and more elements from C to the code. The compilation step itself can also be parameterized to further optimize the compiled version.

Algorithms

This section applies the performance-enhancing techniques from the previous section to some well-known problems and algorithms from mathematics. These algorithms are regularly used for performance benchmarks.

Prime Numbers

Prime numbers play an important role not only in theoretical mathematics but also in many applied computer science disciplines, such as encryption. A *prime number* is a positive natural number greater than 1 that is only divisible without remainder by 1 and itself. There are no other factors. While it is difficult to find larger prime numbers due to their rarity, it is easy to prove that a number is not prime. The only thing that is needed is a factor other than 1 that divides the number without a remainder.

Python

There are a number of algorithmic implementations available to test if numbers are prime. The following is a Python version that is not yet optimal from an algorithmic point of view but is already quite efficient. The execution time for the larger prime p2, however, is long:

```
In [25]: def is_prime(I):
             if I % 2 == 0: return False   ❶
             for i in range(3, int(I ** 0.5) + 1, 2):   ❷
                 if I % i == 0: return False   ❸
             return True   ❹

In [26]: n = int(1e8 + 3)   ❺
         n
Out[26]: 100000003

In [27]: %time is_prime(n)
         CPU times: user 35 µs, sys: 0 ns, total: 35 µs
         Wall time: 39.1 µs

Out[27]: False

In [28]: p1 = int(1e8 + 7)   ❺
         p1
```

```
Out[28]: 100000007

In [29]: %time is_prime(p1)
         CPU times: user 776 µs, sys: 1 µs, total: 777 µs
         Wall time: 787 µs

Out[29]: True

In [30]: p2 = 100109100129162907    ❻

In [31]: p2.bit_length()    ❻
Out[31]: 57

In [32]: %time is_prime(p2)
         CPU times: user 22.6 s, sys: 44.7 ms, total: 22.6 s
         Wall time: 22.7 s

Out[32]: True
```

❶ If the number is even, `False` is returned immediately.

❷ The loop starts at 3 and goes until the square root of I plus 1 with step size 2.

❸ As soon as a factor is identified the function returns `False`.

❹ If no factor is found, `True` is returned.

❺ Relatively small non-prime and prime numbers.

❻ A larger prime number which requires longer execution times.

Numba

The loop structure of the algorithm in the function `is_prime()` lends itself well to being dynamically compiled with `Numba`. The overhead again is minimal but the speedup considerable:

```
In [33]: is_prime_nb = numba.jit(is_prime)

In [34]: %time is_prime_nb(n)    ❶
         CPU times: user 87.5 ms, sys: 7.91 ms, total: 95.4 ms
         Wall time: 93.7 ms

Out[34]: False

In [35]: %time is_prime_nb(n)    ❷
         CPU times: user 9 µs, sys: 1e+03 ns, total: 10 µs
         Wall time: 13.6 µs

Out[35]: False
```

```
In [36]: %time is_prime_nb(p1)
         CPU times: user 26 µs, sys: 0 ns, total: 26 µs
         Wall time: 31 µs

Out[36]: True

In [37]: %time is_prime_nb(p2)  ❸
         CPU times: user 1.72 s, sys: 9.7 ms, total: 1.73 s
         Wall time: 1.74 s

Out[37]: True
```

❶ The first call of is_prime_nb() involves the compiling overhead.

❷ From the second call, the speedup becomes fully visible.

❸ The speedup for the larger prime is about an order of magnitude.

Cython

The application of Cython is straightforward as well. A plain Cython version without type declarations already speeds up the code significantly:

```
In [38]: %%cython
         def is_prime_cy1(I):
             if I % 2 == 0: return False
             for i in range(3, int(I ** 0.5) + 1, 2):
                 if I % i == 0: return False
             return True

In [39]: %timeit is_prime(p1)
         394 µs ± 14.7 µs per loop (mean ± std. dev. of 7 runs, 1000 loops each)

In [40]: %timeit is_prime_cy1(p1)
         243 µs ± 6.58 µs per loop (mean ± std. dev. of 7 runs, 1000 loops each)
```

However, real improvements only materialize with the static type declarations. The Cython version then even is slightly faster than the Numba one:

```
In [41]: %%cython
         def is_prime_cy2(long I):  ❶
             cdef long i  ❶
             if I % 2 == 0: return False
             for i in range(3, int(I ** 0.5) + 1, 2):
                 if I % i == 0: return False
             return True

In [42]: %timeit is_prime_cy2(p1)
         87.6 µs ± 27.7 µs per loop (mean ± std. dev. of 7 runs, 10000 loops each)

In [43]: %time is_prime_nb(p2)
```

```
        CPU times: user 1.68 s, sys: 9.73 ms, total: 1.69 s
        Wall time: 1.7 s

Out[43]: True

In [44]: %time is_prime_cy2(p2)
        CPU times: user 1.66 s, sys: 9.47 ms, total: 1.67 s
        Wall time: 1.68 s

Out[44]: True
```

❶ Static type declarations for the two variables I and i.

Multiprocessing

So far, all the optimization efforts have focused on the sequential code execution. In particular with prime numbers, there might be a need to check multiple numbers at the same time. To this end, the multiprocessing module (*https://docs.python.org/3/library/multiprocessing.html*) can help speed up the code execution further. It allows one to spawn multiple Python processes that run in parallel. The application is straightforward in the simple case at hand. First, an mp.Pool object is set up with multiple processes. Second, the function to be executed is *mapped* to the prime numbers to be checked:

```
In [45]: import multiprocessing as mp

In [46]: pool = mp.Pool(processes=4)   ❶

In [47]: %time pool.map(is_prime, 10 * [p1])   ❷
        CPU times: user 1.52 ms, sys: 2.09 ms, total: 3.61 ms
        Wall time: 9.73 ms

Out[47]: [True, True, True, True, True, True, True, True, True, True]

In [48]: %time pool.map(is_prime_nb, 10 * [p2])   ❷
        CPU times: user 13.9 ms, sys: 4.8 ms, total: 18.7 ms
        Wall time: 10.4 s

Out[48]: [True, True, True, True, True, True, True, True, True, True]

In [49]: %time pool.map(is_prime_cy2, 10 * [p2])   ❷
        CPU times: user 9.8 ms, sys: 3.22 ms, total: 13 ms
        Wall time: 9.51 s

Out[49]: [True, True, True, True, True, True, True, True, True, True]
```

❶ The mp.Pool object is instantiated with multiple processes.

❷ Then the respective function is mapped to a list object with prime numbers.

The observed speedup is significant. The Python function `is_prime()` takes more than 20 seconds for the larger prime number p2. Both the `is_prime_nb()` and the `is_prime_cy2()` functions take less than 10 seconds for 10 times the prime number p2 when executed in parallel with four processes.

Parallel Processing

Parallel processing should be considered whenever different problems of the same type need to be solved. The effect can be huge when powerful hardware is available with many cores and sufficient working memory. `multiprocessing` is one easy-to-use module from the standard library.

Fibonacci Numbers

Fibonacci numbers and sequences can be derived based on a simple algorithm. Start with two ones: 1, 1. From the third number, the next Fibonacci number is derived as the sum of the two preceding ones: 1, 1, 2, 3, 5, 8, 13, 21, ... This section analyzes two different implementations, a recursive one and an iterative one.

Recursive algorithm

Similar to regular Python loops, it is known that regular recursive function implementations are relatively slow with Python. Such functions call themselves potentially a large number of times to come up with the final result. The function `fib_rec_py1()` presents such an implementation. In this case, Numba does not help at all with speeding up the execution. However, Cython shows significant speedups based on static type declarations only:

```
In [50]: def fib_rec_py1(n):
             if n < 2:
                 return n
             else:
                 return fib_rec_py1(n - 1) + fib_rec_py1(n - 2)

In [51]: %time fib_rec_py1(35)
         CPU times: user 6.55 s, sys: 29 ms, total: 6.58 s
         Wall time: 6.6 s

Out[51]: 9227465

In [52]: fib_rec_nb = numba.jit(fib_rec_py1)

In [53]: %time fib_rec_nb(35)
         CPU times: user 3.87 s, sys: 24.2 ms, total: 3.9 s
         Wall time: 3.91 s

Out[53]: 9227465
```

```
In [54]: %%cython
         def fib_rec_cy(int n):
             if n < 2:
                 return n
             else:
                 return fib_rec_cy(n - 1) + fib_rec_cy(n - 2)

In [55]: %time fib_rec_cy(35)
         CPU times: user 751 ms, sys: 4.37 ms, total: 756 ms
         Wall time: 755 ms

Out[55]: 9227465
```

The major problem with the recursive algorithm is that intermediate results are not cached but rather recalculated. To avoid this particular problem, a decorator can be used that takes care of the caching of intermediate results. This speeds up the execution by multiple orders of magnitude:

```
In [56]: from functools import lru_cache as cache

In [57]: @cache(maxsize=None)    ❶
         def fib_rec_py2(n):
             if n < 2:
                 return n
             else:
                 return fib_rec_py2(n - 1) + fib_rec_py2(n - 2)

In [58]: %time fib_rec_py2(35)    ❷
         CPU times: user 64 µs, sys: 28 µs, total: 92 µs
         Wall time: 98 µs

Out[58]: 9227465

In [59]: %time fib_rec_py2(80)    ❷
         CPU times: user 38 µs, sys: 8 µs, total: 46 µs
         Wall time: 51 µs

Out[59]: 23416728348467685
```

❶ Caching intermediate results ...

❷ ... leads to tremendous speedups in this case.

Iterative algorithm

Although the algorithm to calculate the *n*th Fibonacci number *can* be implemented recursively, it doesn't *have* to be. The following presents an iterative implementation which is even in pure Python faster than the cached variant of the recursive implementation. This is also the terrain where Numba leads to further improvements. However, the Cython version comes out as the winner:

```
In [60]: def fib_it_py(n):
             x, y = 0, 1
             for i in range(1, n + 1):
                 x, y = y, x + y
             return x

In [61]: %time fib_it_py(80)
         CPU times: user 19 µs, sys: 1e+03 ns, total: 20 µs
         Wall time: 26 µs

Out[61]: 23416728348467685

In [62]: fib_it_nb = numba.jit(fib_it_py)

In [63]: %time fib_it_nb(80)
         CPU times: user 57 ms, sys: 6.9 ms, total: 63.9 ms
         Wall time: 62 ms

Out[63]: 23416728348467685

In [64]: %time fib_it_nb(80)
         CPU times: user 7 µs, sys: 1 µs, total: 8 µs
         Wall time: 12.2 µs

Out[64]: 23416728348467685

In [65]: %%cython
         def fib_it_cy1(int n):
             cdef long i
             cdef long x = 0, y = 1
             for i in range(1, n + 1):
                 x, y = y, x + y
             return x

In [66]: %time fib_it_cy1(80)
         CPU times: user 4 µs, sys: 1e+03 ns, total: 5 µs
         Wall time: 11 µs

Out[66]: 23416728348467685
```

Now that everything is so fast, one might wonder why we're just calculating the 80th Fibonacci number and not the 150th, for instance. The problem is with the available data types. While Python can basically handle arbitrarily large numbers (see "Basic Data Types" on page 62), this is not true in general for the compiled languages. With Cython one can, however, rely on a special data type to allow for numbers larger than the double float object with 64 bits allows for:

```
In [67]: %%time
         fn = fib_rec_py2(150)  ❶
         print(fn)  ❶
         9969216677189303386214405760200
         CPU times: user 361 µs, sys: 115 µs, total: 476 µs
         Wall time: 430 µs

In [68]: fn.bit_length()  ❷
Out[68]: 103

In [69]: %%time
         fn = fib_it_nb(150)  ❸
         print(fn)  ❸
         6792540214324356296
         CPU times: user 270 µs, sys: 78 µs, total: 348 µs
         Wall time: 297 µs

In [70]: fn.bit_length()  ❹
Out[70]: 63

In [71]: %%time
         fn = fib_it_cy1(150)  ❸
         print(fn)  ❸
         6792540214324356296
         CPU times: user 255 µs, sys: 71 µs, total: 326 µs
         Wall time: 279 µs

In [72]: fn.bit_length()  ❹
Out[72]: 63

In [73]: %%cython
         cdef extern from *:
             ctypedef int int128 '__int128_t'  ❺
         def fib_it_cy2(int n):
             cdef int128 i  ❺
             cdef int128 x = 0, y = 1  ❺
             for i in range(1, n + 1):
                 x, y = y, x + y
             return x

In [74]: %%time
         fn = fib_it_cy2(150)  ❻
         print(fn)  ❻
         9969216677189303386214405760200
         CPU times: user 280 µs, sys: 115 µs, total: 395 µs
         Wall time: 328 µs

In [75]: fn.bit_length()  ❻
Out[75]: 103
```

❶ The Python version is fast and correct.

---

❷ The resulting integer has a bit length of 103 (> 64).

❸ The Numba and Cython versions are faster but incorrect.

❹ They suffer from an overflow issue due to the restriction to 64-bit int objects.

❺ Imports the special 128-bit int object type and uses it.

❻ The Cython version fib_it_cy2() now is faster *and* correct.

The Number Pi

The final algorithm analyzed in this section is a Monte Carlo simulation–based algorithm to derive digits for the number pi (π).[2] The basic idea relies on the fact that the area A of a circle is given by $A = \pi r^2$. Therefore, $\pi = \frac{A}{r^2}$. For a unit circle with radius r = 1, it holds that $\pi = A$. The idea of the algorithm is to simulate random points with coordinate values (x, y), with $x, y \in [-1, 1]$. The area of an origin-centered square with side length of 2 is exactly 4. The area of the origin-centered unit circle is a fraction of the area of such a square. This fraction can be estimated by Monte Carlo simulation: count all the points in the square, then count all the points in the circle, and divide the number of points in the circle by the number of points in the square. The following example demonstrates (see Figure 10-1):

```
In [76]: import random
         import numpy as np
         from pylab import mpl, plt
         plt.style.use('seaborn')
         mpl.rcParams['font.family'] = 'serif'
         %matplotlib inline

In [77]: rn = [(random.random() * 2 - 1, random.random() * 2 - 1)
               for _ in range(500)]

In [78]: rn = np.array(rn)
         rn[:5]
Out[78]: array([[ 0.45583018, -0.27676067],
                [-0.70120038,  0.15196888],
                [ 0.07224045,  0.90147321],
                [-0.17450337, -0.47660912],
                [ 0.94896746, -0.31511879]])

In [79]: fig = plt.figure(figsize=(7, 7))
         ax = fig.add_subplot(1, 1, 1)
```

---

2 The examples are inspired by a post on Code Review Stack Exchange (*http://bit.ly/2DnzGeq*).

```
circ = plt.Circle((0, 0), radius=1, edgecolor='g', lw=2.0,
                   facecolor='None')    ❶
box = plt.Rectangle((-1, -1), 2, 2, edgecolor='b', alpha=0.3)    ❷
ax.add_patch(circ)    ❶
ax.add_patch(box)    ❷
plt.plot(rn[:, 0], rn[:, 1], 'r.')    ❸
plt.ylim(-1.1, 1.1)
plt.xlim(-1.1, 1.1)
```

❶ Draws the unit circle.

❷ Draws the square with side length of 2.

❸ Draws the uniformly distributed random dots.

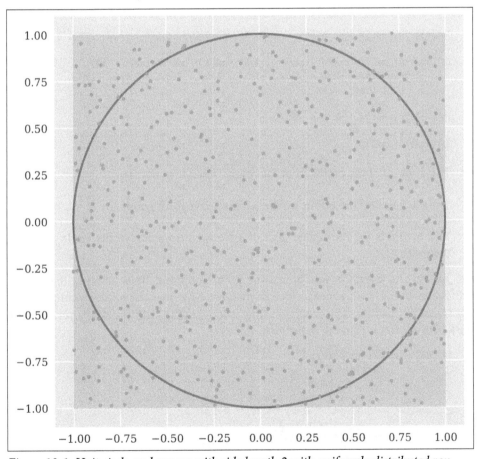

Figure 10-1. Unit circle and square with side length 2 with uniformly distributed random points

A NumPy implementation of this algorithm is rather concise but also memory-intensive. Total execution time given the parameterization is about one second:

```
In [80]: n = int(1e7)

In [81]: %time rn = np.random.random((n, 2)) * 2 - 1
         CPU times: user 450 ms, sys: 87.9 ms, total: 538 ms
         Wall time: 573 ms

In [82]: rn.nbytes
Out[82]: 160000000

In [83]: %time distance = np.sqrt((rn ** 2).sum(axis=1))    ❶
         distance[:8].round(3)
         CPU times: user 537 ms, sys: 198 ms, total: 736 ms
         Wall time: 651 ms

Out[83]: array([1.181, 1.061, 0.669, 1.206, 0.799, 0.579, 0.694, 0.941])

In [84]: %time frac = (distance <= 1.0).sum() / len(distance)    ❷
         CPU times: user 47.9 ms, sys: 6.77 ms, total: 54.7 ms
         Wall time: 28 ms

In [85]: pi_mcs = frac * 4    ❸
         pi_mcs    ❸
Out[85]: 3.1413396
```

❶   The distance of the points from the origin (Euclidean norm).

❷   The fraction of those points on the circle relative to all points.

❸   This accounts for the square area of 4 for the estimation of the circle area and therewith of π.

mcs_pi_py() is a Python function using a for loop and implementing the Monte Carlo simulation in a memory-efficient manner. Note that the random numbers are not scaled in this case. The execution time is longer than with the NumPy version, but the Numba version is faster than NumPy in this case:

```
In [86]: def mcs_pi_py(n):
             circle = 0
             for _ in range(n):
                 x, y = random.random(), random.random()
                 if (x ** 2 + y ** 2) ** 0.5 <= 1:
                     circle += 1
             return (4 * circle) / n

In [87]: %time mcs_pi_py(n)
         CPU times: user 5.47 s, sys: 23 ms, total: 5.49 s
         Wall time: 5.43 s
```

```
Out[87]: 3.1418964

In [88]: mcs_pi_nb = numba.jit(mcs_pi_py)

In [89]: %time mcs_pi_nb(n)
         CPU times: user 319 ms, sys: 6.36 ms, total: 326 ms
         Wall time: 326 ms

Out[89]: 3.1422012

In [90]: %time mcs_pi_nb(n)
         CPU times: user 284 ms, sys: 3.92 ms, total: 288 ms
         Wall time: 291 ms

Out[90]: 3.142066
```

A plain Cython version with static type declarations only does not perform that much faster than the Python version. However, relying again on the random number generation capabilities of C further speeds up the calculation considerably:

```
In [91]: %%cython -a
         import random
         def mcs_pi_cy1(int n):
             cdef int i, circle = 0
             cdef float x, y
             for i in range(n):
                 x, y = random.random(), random.random()
                 if (x ** 2 + y ** 2) ** 0.5 <= 1:
                     circle += 1
             return (4 * circle) / n
Out[91]: <IPython.core.display.HTML object>

In [92]: %time mcs_pi_cy1(n)
         CPU times: user 1.15 s, sys: 8.24 ms, total: 1.16 s
         Wall time: 1.16 s

Out[92]: 3.1417132

In [93]: %%cython -a
         from libc.stdlib cimport rand
         cdef extern from 'limits.h':
             int INT_MAX
         def mcs_pi_cy2(int n):
             cdef int i, circle = 0
             cdef float x, y
             for i in range(n):
                 x, y = rand() / INT_MAX, rand() / INT_MAX
                 if (x ** 2 + y ** 2) ** 0.5 <= 1:
                     circle += 1
             return (4 * circle) / n
Out[93]: <IPython.core.display.HTML object>
```

```
In [94]: %time mcs_pi_cy2(n)
         CPU times: user 170 ms, sys: 1.45 ms, total: 172 ms
         Wall time: 172 ms

Out[94]: 3.1419388
```

Algorithm Types

The algorithms analyzed in this section might not be directly
related to financial algorithms. However, the advantage is that they
are simple and easy to understand. In addition, typical algorithmic
problems encountered in a financial context can be discussed
within this simplified context.

Binomial Trees

A popular numerical method to value options is the binomial option pricing model
pioneered by Cox, Ross, and Rubinstein (1979). This method relies on representing
the possible future evolution of an asset by a (recombining) tree. In this model, as in
the Black-Scholes-Merton (1973) setup, there is a *risky asset*, an index or stock, and a
riskless asset, a bond. The relevant time interval from today until the maturity of the
option is divided in general into equidistant subintervals of length Δt. Given an index
level at time s of S_s, the index level at $t = s + \Delta t$ is given by $S_t = S_s \cdot m$, where m is
chosen randomly from $\{u, d\}$ with $0 < d < e^{r\Delta t} < u = e^{\sigma\sqrt{\Delta t}}$ as well as $u = \frac{1}{d}$. r is the
constant, riskless short rate.

Python

The code that follows presents a Python implementation that creates a recombining
tree based on some fixed numerical parameters for the model:

```
In [95]: import math

In [96]: S0 = 36.      ❶
         T = 1.0       ❷
         r = 0.06      ❸
         sigma = 0.2   ❹

In [97]: def simulate_tree(M):
             dt = T / M    ❺
             u = math.exp(sigma * math.sqrt(dt))   ❻
             d = 1 / u     ❻
             S = np.zeros((M + 1, M + 1))
             S[0, 0] = S0
             z = 1
             for t in range(1, M + 1):
                 for i in range(z):
```

```
                S[i, t] = S[i, t-1] * u
                S[i+1, t] = S[i, t-1] * d
            z += 1
        return S
```

❶ Initial value of the risky asset.

❷ Time horizon for the binomial tree simulation.

❸ Constant short rate.

❹ Constant volatility factor.

❺ Length of the time intervals.

❻ Factors for the upward and downward movements.

Contrary to what happens in typical tree plots, an upward movement is represented in the ndarray object as a sideways movement, which decreases the ndarray size considerably:

```
In [98]: np.set_printoptions(formatter={'float':
                                    lambda x: '%6.2f' % x})

In [99]: simulate_tree(4)  ❶
Out[99]: array([[ 36.00,  39.79,  43.97,  48.59,  53.71],
               [  0.00,  32.57,  36.00,  39.79,  43.97],
               [  0.00,   0.00,  29.47,  32.57,  36.00],
               [  0.00,   0.00,   0.00,  26.67,  29.47],
               [  0.00,   0.00,   0.00,   0.00,  24.13]])

In [100]: %time simulate_tree(500)  ❷
          CPU times: user 148 ms, sys: 4.49 ms, total: 152 ms
          Wall time: 154 ms

Out[100]: array([[ 36.00,  36.32,  36.65,  ..., 3095.69, 3123.50, 3151.57],
                [  0.00,  35.68,  36.00,  ..., 3040.81, 3068.13, 3095.69],
                [  0.00,   0.00,  35.36,  ..., 2986.89, 3013.73, 3040.81],
                ...,
                [  0.00,   0.00,   0.00,  ...,    0.42,    0.42,    0.43],
                [  0.00,   0.00,   0.00,  ...,    0.00,    0.41,    0.42],
                [  0.00,   0.00,   0.00,  ...,    0.00,    0.00,    0.41]])
```

❶ Tree with 4 time intervals.

❷ Tree with 500 time intervals.

NumPy

With some trickery, such a binomial tree can be created with NumPy based on fully vectorized code:

```
In [101]: M = 4

In [102]: up = np.arange(M + 1)
          up = np.resize(up, (M + 1, M + 1))  ❶
          up
Out[102]: array([[0, 1, 2, 3, 4],
                 [0, 1, 2, 3, 4],
                 [0, 1, 2, 3, 4],
                 [0, 1, 2, 3, 4],
                 [0, 1, 2, 3, 4]])

In [103]: down = up.T * 2  ❷
          down
Out[103]: array([[0, 0, 0, 0, 0],
                 [2, 2, 2, 2, 2],
                 [4, 4, 4, 4, 4],
                 [6, 6, 6, 6, 6],
                 [8, 8, 8, 8, 8]])

In [104]: up - down  ❸
Out[104]: array([[ 0,  1,  2,  3,  4],
                 [-2, -1,  0,  1,  2],
                 [-4, -3, -2, -1,  0],
                 [-6, -5, -4, -3, -2],
                 [-8, -7, -6, -5, -4]])

In [105]: dt = T / M

In [106]: S0 * np.exp(sigma * math.sqrt(dt) * (up - down))  ❹
Out[106]: array([[ 36.00,  39.79,  43.97,  48.59,  53.71],
                 [ 29.47,  32.57,  36.00,  39.79,  43.97],
                 [ 24.13,  26.67,  29.47,  32.57,  36.00],
                 [ 19.76,  21.84,  24.13,  26.67,  29.47],
                 [ 16.18,  17.88,  19.76,  21.84,  24.13]])
```

❶ ndarray object with gross *upward* movements.

❷ ndarray object with gross *downward* movements.

❸ ndarray object with *net* upward (positive) and downward (negative) movements.

❹ Tree for four time intervals (upper-right triangle of values).

In the NumPy case, the code is a bit more compact. However, more importantly, NumPy vectorization achieves a speedup of an order of magnitude while not using more memory:

```
In [107]: def simulate_tree_np(M):
              dt = T / M
              up = np.arange(M + 1)
              up = np.resize(up, (M + 1, M + 1))
              down = up.transpose() * 2
              S = S0 * np.exp(sigma * math.sqrt(dt) * (up - down))
              return S

In [108]: simulate_tree_np(4)
Out[108]: array([[ 36.00,  39.79,  43.97,  48.59,  53.71],
                 [ 29.47,  32.57,  36.00,  39.79,  43.97],
                 [ 24.13,  26.67,  29.47,  32.57,  36.00],
                 [ 19.76,  21.84,  24.13,  26.67,  29.47],
                 [ 16.18,  17.88,  19.76,  21.84,  24.13]])

In [109]: %time simulate_tree_np(500)
          CPU times: user 8.72 ms, sys: 7.07 ms, total: 15.8 ms
          Wall time: 12.9 ms

Out[109]: array([[ 36.00,  36.32,  36.65,  ..., 3095.69, 3123.50, 3151.57],
                 [ 35.36,  35.68,  36.00,  ..., 3040.81, 3068.13, 3095.69],
                 [ 34.73,  35.05,  35.36,  ..., 2986.89, 3013.73, 3040.81],
                 ...,
                 [  0.00,   0.00,   0.00,  ...,    0.42,    0.42,    0.43],
                 [  0.00,   0.00,   0.00,  ...,    0.41,    0.41,    0.42],
                 [  0.00,   0.00,   0.00,  ...,    0.40,    0.41,    0.41]])
```

Numba

This financial algorithm should be well suited to optimization through Numba dynamic compilation. And indeed, another speedup compared to the NumPy version of an order of magnitude is observed. This makes the Numba version orders of magnitude faster than the Python (or rather hybrid) version:

```
In [110]: simulate_tree_nb = numba.jit(simulate_tree)

In [111]: simulate_tree_nb(4)
Out[111]: array([[ 36.00,  39.79,  43.97,  48.59,  53.71],
                 [  0.00,  32.57,  36.00,  39.79,  43.97],
                 [  0.00,   0.00,  29.47,  32.57,  36.00],
                 [  0.00,   0.00,   0.00,  26.67,  29.47],
                 [  0.00,   0.00,   0.00,   0.00,  24.13]])

In [112]: %time simulate_tree_nb(500)
          CPU times: user 425 µs, sys: 193 µs, total: 618 µs
          Wall time: 625 µs
```

```
Out[112]: array([[ 36.00,   36.32,   36.65, ...,  3095.69, 3123.50, 3151.57],
                 [  0.00,   35.68,   36.00, ...,  3040.81, 3068.13, 3095.69],
                 [  0.00,    0.00,   35.36, ...,  2986.89, 3013.73, 3040.81],
                 ...,
                 [  0.00,    0.00,    0.00, ...,     0.42,    0.42,    0.43],
                 [  0.00,    0.00,    0.00, ...,     0.00,    0.41,    0.42],
                 [  0.00,    0.00,    0.00, ...,     0.00,    0.00,    0.41]])

In [113]: %timeit simulate_tree_nb(500)
          559 µs ± 46.1 µs per loop (mean ± std. dev. of 7 runs, 1000 loops each)
```

Cython

As before, Cython requires more adjustments to the code to see significant improvements. The following version uses mainly static type declarations and certain imports that improve the performance compared to the regular Python imports and functions, respectively:

```
In [114]: %%cython -a
          import numpy as np
          cimport cython
          from libc.math cimport exp, sqrt
          cdef float S0 = 36.
          cdef float T = 1.0
          cdef float r = 0.06
          cdef float sigma = 0.2
          def simulate_tree_cy(int M):
              cdef int z, t, i
              cdef float dt, u, d
              cdef float[:, :] S = np.zeros((M + 1, M + 1),
                                            dtype=np.float32)     ❶
              dt = T / M
              u = exp(sigma * sqrt(dt))
              d = 1 / u
              S[0, 0] = S0
              z = 1
              for t in range(1, M + 1):
                  for i in range(z):
                      S[i, t] = S[i, t-1] * u
                      S[i+1, t] = S[i, t-1] * d
                  z += 1
              return np.array(S)
Out[114]: <IPython.core.display.HTML object>
```

❶ Declaring the ndarray object to be a C array is critical for performance.

The Cython version shaves off another 30% of the execution time compared to the Numba version:

```
In [115]: simulate_tree_cy(4)
Out[115]: array([[ 36.00,  39.79,  43.97,  48.59,  53.71],
```

```
                  [  0.00,  32.57,  36.00,  39.79,  43.97],
                  [  0.00,   0.00,  29.47,  32.57,  36.00],
                  [  0.00,   0.00,   0.00,  26.67,  29.47],
                  [  0.00,   0.00,   0.00,   0.00,  24.13]], dtype=float32)

In [116]: %time simulate_tree_cy(500)
          CPU times: user 2.21 ms, sys: 1.89 ms, total: 4.1 ms
          Wall time: 2.45 ms

Out[116]: array([[  36.00,   36.32,   36.65, ...,  3095.77,  3123.59,  3151.65],
                 [   0.00,   35.68,   36.00, ...,  3040.89,  3068.21,  3095.77],
                 [   0.00,    0.00,   35.36, ...,  2986.97,  3013.81,  3040.89],
                 ...,
                 [   0.00,    0.00,    0.00, ...,     0.42,     0.42,     0.43],
                 [   0.00,    0.00,    0.00, ...,     0.00,     0.41,     0.42],
                 [   0.00,    0.00,    0.00, ...,     0.00,     0.00,     0.41]],
                 dtype=float32)

In [117]: %timeit S = simulate_tree_cy(500)
          363 µs ± 29.5 µs per loop (mean ± std. dev. of 7 runs, 1000 loops each)
```

Monte Carlo Simulation

Monte Carlo simulation is an indispensable numerical tool in computational finance. It has been in use since long before the advent of modern computers. Banks and other financial institutions use it, among others, for pricing and risk management purposes. As a numerical method it is perhaps the most flexible and powerful one in finance. However, it often also is the most computationally demanding one. That is why Python was long dismissed as a proper programming language to implement algorithms based on Monte Carlo simulation—at least for real-world application scenarios.

This section analyzes the Monte Carlo simulation of the geometric Brownian motion, a simple yet still widely used stochastic process to model the evolution of stock prices or index levels. Among others, the Black-Scholes-Merton (1973) theory of option pricing draws on this process. In their setup the underlying of the option to be valued follows the stochastic differential equation (SDE), as seen in Equation 10-1. S_t is the value of the underlying at time t; r is the constant, riskless short rate; σ is the constant instantaneous volatility; and Z_t is a Brownian motion.

Equation 10-1. Black-Scholes-Merton SDE (geometric Brownian motion)

$$dS_t = rS_t dt + \sigma S_t dZ_t$$

This SDE can be discretized over equidistant time intervals and simulated according to Equation 10-2, which represents an Euler scheme. In this case, z is a standard normally distributed random number. For M time intervals, the length of the time interval is given as $\Delta t \equiv \frac{T}{M}$ where T is the time horizon for the simulation (for example, the maturity date of an option to be valued).

Equation 10-2. Black-Scholes-Merton difference equation (Euler scheme)

$$S_t = S_{t-\Delta t} \exp\left(\left(r - \frac{\sigma^2}{2}\right)\Delta t + \sigma\sqrt{\Delta t}z\right)$$

The Monte Carlo estimator for a European call option is then given by Equation 10-3, where $S_T(i)$ is the ith simulated value of the underlying at maturity T for a total number of simulated paths I with $i = 1, 2, ..., I$.

Equation 10-3. Monte Carlo estimator for European call option

$$C_0 = e^{-rT}\frac{1}{I}\sum_I \max\left(S_T(i) - K, 0\right)$$

Python

First, a Python—or rather a hybrid—version, `mcs_simulation_py()`, that implements the Monte Carlo simulation according to Equation 10-2. It is hybrid since it implements Python loops on `ndarray` objects. As seen previously, this might make for a good basis to dynamically compile the code with `Numba`. As before, the execution time sets the benchmark. Based on the simulation, a European put option is valued:

```
In [118]: M = 100      ❶
          I = 50000     ❷

In [119]: def mcs_simulation_py(p):
              M, I = p
              dt = T / M
              S = np.zeros((M + 1, I))
              S[0] = S0
              rn = np.random.standard_normal(S.shape)     ❸
              for t in range(1, M + 1):     ❹
                  for i in range(I):     ❹
                      S[t, i] = S[t-1, i] * math.exp((r - sigma ** 2 / 2) * dt +
                                   sigma * math.sqrt(dt) * rn[t, i])     ❹
              return S

In [120]: %time S = mcs_simulation_py((M, I))
          CPU times: user 5.55 s, sys: 52.9 ms, total: 5.6 s
          Wall time: 5.62 s

In [121]: S[-1].mean()      ❺
Out[121]: 38.22291254503985
```

```
In [122]: S0 * math.exp(r * T)   ❻
Out[122]: 38.22611567563295

In [123]: K = 40.   ❼

In [124]: C0 = math.exp(-r * T) * np.maximum(K - S[-1], 0).mean()   ❽

In [125]: C0  #   ❽
Out[125]: 3.860545188088036
```

❶ The number of time intervals for discretization.

❷ The number of paths to be simulated.

❸ The random numbers, drawn in a single vectorized step.

❹ The nested loop implementing the simulation based on the Euler scheme.

❺ The mean end-of-period value based on the simulation.

❻ The theoretically expected end-of-period value.

❼ The strike price of the European put option.

❽ The Monte Carlo estimator for the option.

Figure 10-2 shows a histogram of the simulated values at the end of the simulation period (maturity of the European put option).

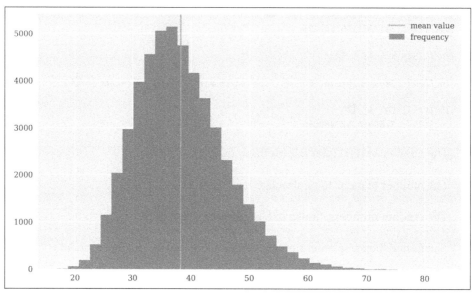

Figure 10-2. Frequency distribution of the simulated end-of-period values

NumPy

The NumPy version, mcs_simulation_np(), is not too different. It still has one Python loop, namely over the time intervals. The other dimension is handled by vectorized code over all paths. It is about 20 times faster than the first version:

```
In [127]: def mcs_simulation_np(p):
              M, I = p
              dt = T / M
              S = np.zeros((M + 1, I))
              S[0] = S0
              rn = np.random.standard_normal(S.shape)
              for t in range(1, M + 1):    ❶
                  S[t] = S[t-1] * np.exp((r - sigma ** 2 / 2) * dt +
                                  sigma * math.sqrt(dt) * rn[t])  ❷
              return S

In [128]: %time S = mcs_simulation_np((M, I))
          CPU times: user 252 ms, sys: 32.9 ms, total: 285 ms
          Wall time: 252 ms

In [129]: S[-1].mean()
Out[129]: 38.235136032258595

In [130]: %timeit S = mcs_simulation_np((M, I))
          202 ms ± 27.7 ms per loop (mean ± std. dev. of 7 runs, 1 loop each)
```

❶ The loop over the time intervals.

❷   The Euler scheme with vectorized NumPy code handling all paths at once.

Numba

It should not come as a surprise anymore that Numba is applied to such an algorithm type easily, and with significant performance improvements. The Numba version, mcs_simulation_nb(), is slightly faster than the NumPy version:

```
In [131]: mcs_simulation_nb = numba.jit(mcs_simulation_py)

In [132]: %time S = mcs_simulation_nb((M, I))    ❶
          CPU times: user 673 ms, sys: 36.7 ms, total: 709 ms
          Wall time: 764 ms

In [133]: %time S = mcs_simulation_nb((M, I))    ❷
          CPU times: user 239 ms, sys: 20.8 ms, total: 259 ms
          Wall time: 265 ms

In [134]: S[-1].mean()
Out[134]: 38.22350694016539

In [135]: C0 = math.exp(-r * T) * np.maximum(K - S[-1], 0).mean()

In [136]: C0
Out[136]: 3.8303077438193833

In [137]: %timeit S = mcs_simulation_nb((M, I))    ❷
          248 ms ± 20.6 ms per loop (mean ± std. dev. of 7 runs, 1 loop each)
```

❶   First call with compile-time overhead.

❷   Second call without that overhead.

Cython

With Cython, again not surprisingly, the effort required to speed up the code is higher. However, the speedup itself is not greater. The Cython version, mcs_simula tion_cy(), seems to be even a bit slower compared to the NumPy and Numba versions. Among other factors, some time is needed to transform the simulation results to an ndarray object:

```
In [138]: %%cython
          import numpy as np
          cimport numpy as np
          cimport cython
          from libc.math cimport exp, sqrt
          cdef float S0 = 36.
          cdef float T = 1.0
          cdef float r = 0.06
```

```
cdef float sigma = 0.2
@cython.boundscheck(False)
@cython.wraparound(False)
def mcs_simulation_cy(p):
    cdef int M, I
    M, I = p
    cdef int t, i
    cdef float dt = T / M
    cdef double[:, :] S = np.zeros((M + 1, I))
    cdef double[:, :] rn = np.random.standard_normal((M + 1, I))
    S[0] = S0
    for t in range(1, M + 1):
        for i in range(I):
            S[t, i] = S[t-1, i] * exp((r - sigma ** 2 / 2) * dt +
                              sigma * sqrt(dt) * rn[t, i])
    return np.array(S)

In [139]: %time S = mcs_simulation_cy((M, I))
          CPU times: user 237 ms, sys: 65.2 ms, total: 302 ms
          Wall time: 271 ms

In [140]: S[-1].mean()
Out[140]: 38.241735841791574

In [141]: %timeit S = mcs_simulation_cy((M, I))
          221 ms ± 9.26 ms per loop (mean ± std. dev. of 7 runs, 1 loop each)
```

Multiprocessing

Monte Carlo simulation is a task that lends itself well to parallelization. One approach would be to parallelize the simulation of 100,000 paths, say, into 10 processes simulating 10,000 paths each. Another would be to parallelize the simulation of the 100,000 paths into multiple processes, each simulating a different financial instrument, for example. The former case—namely, the parallel simulation of a larger number of paths based on a fixed number of separate processes—is illustrated in what follows.

The following code again makes use of the multiprocessing module. It divides the total number of paths to be simulated I into smaller chunks of size $\frac{I}{p}$ with $p > 0$. After all the single tasks are finished, the results are put together in a single ndarray object via np.hstack(). This approach can be applied to any of the versions presented previously. For the particular parameterization chosen here, there is no speedup to be observed through this parallelization approach:

```
In [142]: import multiprocessing as mp

In [143]: pool = mp.Pool(processes=4)  ❶

In [144]: p = 20  ❷
```

```
In [145]: %timeit S = np.hstack(pool.map(mcs_simulation_np,
                                 p * [(M, int(I / p))]))
          288 ms ± 10.2 ms per loop (mean ± std. dev. of 7 runs, 1 loop each)

In [146]: %timeit S = np.hstack(pool.map(mcs_simulation_nb,
                                 p * [(M, int(I / p))]))
          258 ms ± 8.69 ms per loop (mean ± std. dev. of 7 runs, 1 loop each)

In [147]: %timeit S = np.hstack(pool.map(mcs_simulation_cy,
                                 p * [(M, int(I / p))]))
          274 ms ± 11.9 ms per loop (mean ± std. dev. of 7 runs, 1 loop each)
```

❶ The `Pool` object for parallelization.

❷ The number of chunks into which the simulation is divided.

> **Multiprocessing Strategies**
>
> In finance, there are many algorithms that are useful for paralleli-
> zation. Some of these even allow the application of different strate-
> gies to parallelize the code. Monte Carlo simulation is a good
> example in that multiple simulations can easily be executed in par-
> allel, either on a single machine or on multiple machines, and that
> the algorithm itself allows a single simulation to be distributed over
> multiple processes.

Recursive pandas Algorithm

This section addresses a somewhat special topic which is, however, an important one
in financial analytics: the implementation of recursive functions on financial time
series data stored in a pandas `DataFrame` object. While pandas allows for sophisticated vectorized operations on `DataFrame` objects, certain recursive algorithms are hard
or impossible to vectorize, leaving the financial analyst with slowly executed Python
loops on `DataFrame` objects. The examples that follow implement what is called the
exponentially weighted moving average (EWMA) in a simple form.

The EWMA for a financial time series $S_t, t \in \{0, \cdots, T\}$, is given by Equation 10-4.

Equation 10-4. Exponentially weighted moving average (EWMA)

$$EWMA_0 = S_0$$
$$EWMA_t = \alpha \cdot S_t + (1 - \alpha) \cdot EWMA_{t-1}, t \in \{1, \cdots, T\}$$

Although simple in nature and straightforward to implement, such an algorithm
might lead to rather slow code.

Python

Consider first the Python version that iterates over the `DatetimeIndex` of a `Data Frame` object containing financial time series data for a single financial instrument (see Chapter 8). Figure 10-3 visualizes the financial time series and the EWMA time series:

```
In [148]: import pandas as pd

In [149]: sym = 'SPY'

In [150]: data = pd.DataFrame(pd.read_csv('../../source/tr_eikon_eod_data.csv',
                              index_col=0, parse_dates=True)[sym]).dropna()

In [151]: alpha = 0.25

In [152]: data['EWMA'] = data[sym]    ❶

In [153]: %%time
          for t in zip(data.index, data.index[1:]):
              data.loc[t[1], 'EWMA'] = (alpha * data.loc[t[1], sym] +
                                        (1 - alpha) * data.loc[t[0], 'EWMA'])    ❷
          CPU times: user 588 ms, sys: 16.4 ms, total: 605 ms
          Wall time: 591 ms

In [154]: data.head()
Out[154]:                    SPY         EWMA
          Date
          2010-01-04    113.33    113.330000
          2010-01-05    113.63    113.405000
          2010-01-06    113.71    113.481250
          2010-01-07    114.19    113.658438
          2010-01-08    114.57    113.886328

In [155]: data[data.index > '2017-1-1'].plot(figsize=(10, 6));
```

❶ Initializes the EWMA column.

❷ Implements the algorithm based on a Python loop.

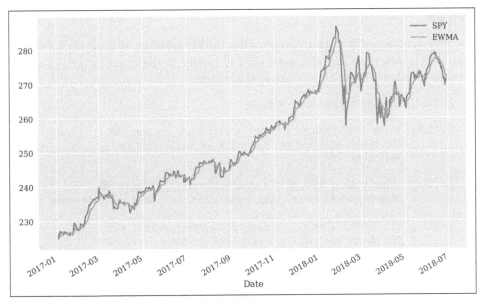

Figure 10-3. Financial time series with EWMA

Now consider more general Python function `ewma_py()`. It can be applied directly on the column or the raw financial times series data in the form of an `ndarray` object:

```
In [156]: def ewma_py(x, alpha):
              y = np.zeros_like(x)
              y[0] = x[0]
              for i in range(1, len(x)):
                  y[i] = alpha * x[i] + (1-alpha) * y[i-1]
              return y

In [157]: %time data['EWMA_PY'] = ewma_py(data[sym], alpha)        ❶
          CPU times: user 33.1 ms, sys: 1.22 ms, total: 34.3 ms
          Wall time: 33.9 ms

In [158]: %time data['EWMA_PY'] = ewma_py(data[sym].values, alpha) ❷
          CPU times: user 1.61 ms, sys: 44 µs, total: 1.65 ms
          Wall time: 1.62 ms
```

❶ Applies the function to the `Series` object directly (i.e., the column).

❷ Applies the function to the `ndarray` object containing the raw data.

This approach already speeds up the code execution considerably—by a factor of from about 20 to more than 100.

Numba

The very structure of this algorithm promises further speedups when applying Numba. And indeed, when the function ewma_nb() is applied to the ndarray version of the data, the speedup is again by an order of magnitude:

```
In [159]: ewma_nb = numba.jit(ewma_py)

In [160]: %time data['EWMA_NB'] = ewma_nb(data[sym], alpha)    ❶
          CPU times: user 269 ms, sys: 11.4 ms, total: 280 ms
          Wall time: 294 ms

In [161]: %timeit data['EWMA_NB'] = ewma_nb(data[sym], alpha)    ❶
          30.9 ms ± 1.21 ms per loop (mean ± std. dev. of 7 runs, 10 loops each)

In [162]: %time data['EWMA_NB'] = ewma_nb(data[sym].values, alpha)    ❷
          CPU times: user 94.1 ms, sys: 3.78 ms, total: 97.9 ms
          Wall time: 97.6 ms

In [163]: %timeit data['EWMA_NB'] = ewma_nb(data[sym].values, alpha)    ❷
          134 µs ± 12.5 µs per loop (mean ± std. dev. of 7 runs, 10000 loops each)
```

❶ Applies the function to the Series object directly (i.e., the column).

❷ Applies the function to the ndarray object containing the raw data.

Cython

The Cython version, ewma_cy(), also achieves considerable speed improvements but it is not as fast as the Numba version in this case:

```
In [164]: %%cython
          import numpy as np
          cimport cython
          @cython.boundscheck(False)
          @cython.wraparound(False)
          def ewma_cy(double[:] x, float alpha):
              cdef int i
              cdef double[:] y = np.empty_like(x)
              y[0] = x[0]
              for i in range(1, len(x)):
                  y[i] = alpha * x[i] + (1 - alpha) * y[i - 1]
              return y

In [165]: %time data['EWMA_CY'] = ewma_cy(data[sym].values, alpha)
          CPU times: user 2.98 ms, sys: 1.41 ms, total: 4.4 ms
          Wall time: 5.96 ms

In [166]: %timeit data['EWMA_CY'] = ewma_cy(data[sym].values, alpha)
          1.29 ms ± 194 µs per loop (mean ± std. dev. of 7 runs, 1000 loops each)
```

This final example illustrates again that there are in general multiple options to implement (nonstandard) algorithms. All options might lead to exactly the same results, while also showing considerably different performance characteristics. The execution times in this example range from 0.1 ms to 500 ms—a factor of 5,000 times.

Best Versus First-Best

It is easy in general to translate algorithms to the Python programming language. However, it is equally easy to implement algorithms in a way that is unnecessarily slow given the menu of performance options available. For interactive financial analytics, a *first-best* solution—i.e., one that does the trick but which might not be the fastest possible nor the most memory-efficient one—might be perfectly fine. For financial applications in production, one should strive to implement the *best* solution, even though this might involve a bit more research and some formal benchmarking.

Conclusion

The Python ecosystem provides a number of ways to improve the performance of code:

Idioms and paradigms
Some Python paradigms and idioms might be more performant than others, given a specific problem; in many cases, for instance, vectorization is a paradigm that not only leads to more concise code but also to higher speeds (sometimes at the cost of a larger memory footprint).

Packages
There are a wealth of packages available for different types of problems, and using a package adapted to the problem can often lead to much higher performance; good examples are NumPy with the ndarray class and pandas with the DataFrame class.

Compiling
Powerful packages for speeding up financial algorithms are Numba and Cython for the dynamic and static compilation of Python code.

Parallelization
Some Python packages, such as multiprocessing, allow for the easy parallelization of Python code; the examples in this chapter only use parallelization on a single machine but the Python ecosystem also offers technologies for multi-machine (cluster) parallelization.

A major benefit of the performance approaches presented in this chapter is that they are in general easily implementable, meaning that the additional effort required is regularly low. In other words, performance improvements often are low-hanging fruit given the performance packages available as of today.

Further Resources

For all the performance packages introduced in this chapter, there are helpful web resources available:

- *http://cython.org* is the home of the Cython package and compiler project.
- The documentation for the multiprocessing module is found at *https://docs.python.org/3/library/multiprocessing.html*.
- Information on Numba can be found at *http://github.com/numba/numba* and *https://numba.pydata.org*.

For references in book form, see the following:

- Gorelick, Misha, and Ian Ozsvald (2014). *High Performance Python*. Sebastopol, CA: O'Reilly.
- Smith, Kurt (2015). *Cython*. Sebastopol, CA: O'Reilly.

Original papers cited in this chapter:

- Black, Fischer, and Myron Scholes (1973). "The Pricing of Options and Corporate Liabilities." *Journal of Political Economy*, Vol. 81, No. 3, pp. 638–659.
- Cox, John, Stephen Ross, and Mark Rubinstein (1979). "Option Pricing: A Simplified Approach." *Journal of Financial Economics*, Vol. 7, No. 3, pp. 229–263.
- Merton, Robert (1973). "Theory of Rational Option Pricing." *Bell Journal of Economics and Management Science*, Vol. 4, pp. 141–183.

## CHAPTER 11

Mathematical Tools

The mathematicians are the priests of the modern world.

—Bill Gaede

Since the arrival of the so-called Rocket Scientists on Wall Street in the 1980s and 1990s, finance has evolved into a discipline of applied mathematics. While early research papers in finance came with lots of text and few mathematical expressions and equations, current ones are mainly comprised of mathematical expressions and equations with some explanatory text around.

This chapter introduces some useful mathematical tools for finance, without providing a detailed background for each of them. There are many useful books available on this topic, so this chapter focuses on how to use the tools and techniques with Python. In particular, it covers:

"Approximation" on page 312
  Regression and interpolation are among the most often used numerical techniques in finance.

"Convex Optimization" on page 328
  A number of financial disciplines need tools for convex optimization (for instance, derivatives analytics when it comes to model calibration).

"Integration" on page 334
  In particular, the valuation of financial (derivative) assets often boils down to the evaluation of integrals.

"Symbolic Computation" on page 337
  Python provides with SymPy a powerful package for symbolic mathematics, for example, to solve (systems of) equations.

Approximation

To begin with, the usual imports:

```
In [1]: import numpy as np
        from pylab import plt, mpl
```

```
In [2]: plt.style.use('seaborn')
        mpl.rcParams['font.family'] = 'serif'
        %matplotlib inline
```

Throughout this section, the main example function is the following, which is comprised of a trigonometric term and a linear term:

```
In [3]: def f(x):
            return np.sin(x) + 0.5 * x
```

The main focus is the approximation of this function over a given interval by *regression* and *interpolation* techniques. First, a plot of the function to get a better view of what exactly the approximation shall achieve. The interval of interest shall be $[-2\pi, 2\pi]$. Figure 11-1 displays the function over the fixed interval defined via the np.lin space() function. The function create_plot() is a helper function to create the same type of plot required multiple times in this chapter:

```
In [4]: def create_plot(x, y, styles, labels, axlabels):
            plt.figure(figsize=(10, 6))
            for i in range(len(x)):
                plt.plot(x[i], y[i], styles[i], label=labels[i])
                plt.xlabel(axlabels[0])
                plt.ylabel(axlabels[1])
            plt.legend(loc=0)
```

```
In [5]: x = np.linspace(-2 * np.pi, 2 * np.pi, 50)   ❶
```

```
In [6]: create_plot([x], [f(x)], ['b'], ['f(x)'], ['x', 'f(x)'])
```

❶   The *x* values used for the plotting and the calculations.

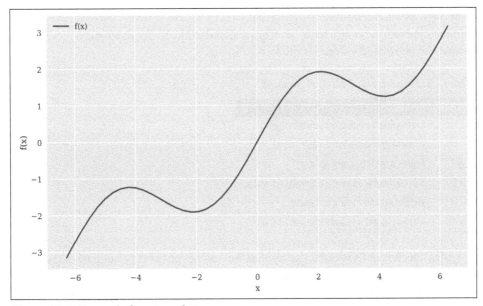

Figure 11-1. Example function plot

Regression

Regression is a rather efficient tool when it comes to function approximation. It is not only suited to approximating one-dimensional functions but also works well in higher dimensions. The numerical techniques needed to come up with regression results are easily implemented and quickly executed. Basically, the task of regression, given a set of so-called basis functions b_d, $d \in \{1, \cdots, D\}$, is to find optimal parameters $\alpha_1^*, \cdots, \alpha_D^*$ according to Equation 11-1, where $y_i \equiv f(x_i)$ for $i \in \{1, \cdots, I\}$ observation points. The x_i are considered *independent* observations and the y_i *dependent* observations (in a functional or statistical sense).

Equation 11-1. Minimization problem of regression

$$\min_{\alpha_1, \cdots, \alpha_D} \frac{1}{I} \sum_{i=1}^{I} \left(y_i - \sum_{d=1}^{D} \alpha_d \cdot b_d(x_i) \right)^2$$

Monomials as basis functions

One of the simplest cases is to take monomials as basis functions—i.e., $b_1 = 1, b_2 = x, b_3 = x^2, b_4 = x^3, \cdots$. In such a case, NumPy has built-in functions for both the determination of the optimal parameters (namely, `np.polyfit()`) and the evaluation of the approximation given a set of input values (namely, `np.polyval()`).

Table 11-1 lists the parameters the `np.polyfit()` function takes. Given the returned optimal regression coefficients p from `np.polyfit()`, `np.polyval(p, x)` then returns the regression values for the *x* coordinates.

Table 11-1. Parameters of polyfit() function

Parameter	Description
x	*x* coordinates (independent variable values)
y	*y* coordinates (dependent variable values)
deg	Degree of the fitting polynomial
full	If True, returns diagnostic information in addition
w	Weights to apply to the *y* coordinates
cov	If True, returns covariance matrix in addition

In typical vectorized fashion, the application of `np.polyfit()` and `np.polyval()` takes on the following form for a linear regression (i.e., for deg=1). Given the regression estimates stored in the `ry` array, we can compare the regression result with the original function as presented in Figure 11-2. Of course, a linear regression cannot account for the `sin` part of the example function:

```
In [7]: res = np.polyfit(x, f(x), deg=1, full=True)   ❶

In [8]: res   ❷
Out[8]: (array([ 4.28841952e-01, -1.31499950e-16]),
         array([21.03238686]),
         2,
         array([1., 1.]),
         1.1102230246251565e-14)

In [9]: ry = np.polyval(res[0], x)   ❸

In [10]: create_plot([x, x], [f(x), ry], ['b', 'r.'],
                     ['f(x)', 'regression'], ['x', 'f(x)'])
```

❶ Linear regression step.

❷ Full results: regression parameters, residuals, effective rank, singular values, and relative condition number.

❸ Evaluation using the regression parameters.

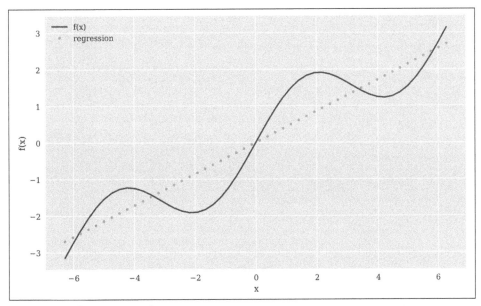

Figure 11-2. Linear regression

To account for the sin part of the example function, higher-order monomials are necessary. The next regression attempt takes monomials up to the order of 5 as basis functions. It should not be too surprising that the regression result, as seen in Figure 11-3, now looks much closer to the original function. However, it is still far from being perfect:

```
In [11]: reg = np.polyfit(x, f(x), deg=5)
         ry = np.polyval(reg, x)

In [12]: create_plot([x, x], [f(x), ry], ['b', 'r.'],
                      ['f(x)', 'regression'], ['x', 'f(x)'])
```

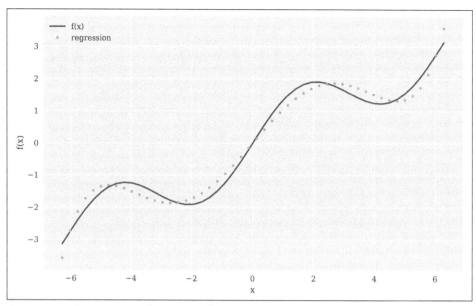

Figure 11-3. Regression with monomials up to order 5

The last attempt takes monomials up to order 7 to approximate the example function. In this case the result, as presented in Figure 11-4, is quite convincing:

```
In [13]: reg = np.polyfit(x, f(x), 7)
         ry = np.polyval(reg, x)

In [14]: np.allclose(f(x), ry)   ❶
Out[14]: False

In [15]: np.mean((f(x) - ry) ** 2)   ❷
Out[15]: 0.0017769134759517689

In [16]: create_plot([x, x], [f(x), ry], ['b', 'r.'],
                      ['f(x)', 'regression'], ['x', 'f(x)'])
```

❶ Checks whether the function and regression values are the same (or at least close).

❷ Calculates the *Mean Squared Error* (MSE) for the regression values given the function values.

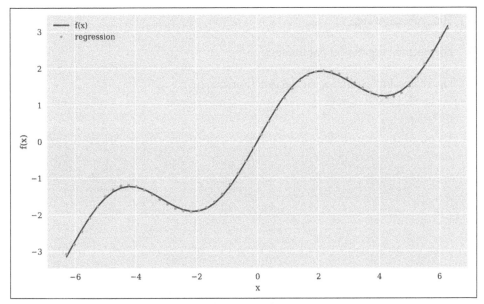

Figure 11-4. Regression with monomials up to order 7

Individual basis functions

In general, one can reach better regression results by choosing better sets of basis functions, e.g., by exploiting knowledge about the function to approximate. In this case, the individual basis functions have to be defined via a matrix approach (i.e., using a NumPy ndarray object). First, the case with monomials up to order 3 (Figure 11-5). The central function here is np.linalg.lstsq():

```
In [17]: matrix = np.zeros((3 + 1, len(x)))   ❶
            matrix[3, :] = x ** 3   ❷
            matrix[2, :] = x ** 2   ❷
            matrix[1, :] = x   ❷
            matrix[0, :] = 1   ❷

In [18]: reg = np.linalg.lstsq(matrix.T, f(x), rcond=None)[0]   ❸

In [19]: reg.round(4)   ❹
Out[19]: array([ 0.    ,  0.5628, -0.    , -0.0054])

In [20]: ry = np.dot(reg, matrix)   ❺

In [21]: create_plot([x, x], [f(x), ry], ['b', 'r.'],
                      ['f(x)', 'regression'], ['x', 'f(x)'])
```

❶ The ndarray object for the basis function values (matrix).

❷ The basis function values from constant to cubic.

---

❸ The regression step.

❹ The optimal regression parameters.

❺ The regression estimates for the function values.

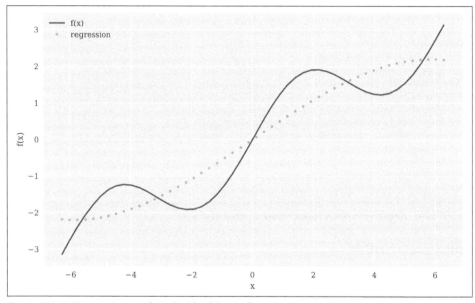

Figure 11-5. Regression with individual basis functions

The result in Figure 11-5 is not as good as expected based on our previous experience with monomials. Using the more general approach allows us to exploit knowledge about the example function—namely that there is a `sin` part in the function. Therefore, it makes sense to include a sine function in the set of basis functions. For simplicity, the highest-order monomial is replaced. The fit now is perfect, as the numbers and Figure 11-6 illustrate:

```
In [22]: matrix[3, :] = np.sin(x)  ❶

In [23]: reg = np.linalg.lstsq(matrix.T, f(x), rcond=None)[0]

In [24]: reg.round(4)  ❷
Out[24]: array([0. , 0.5, 0. , 1. ])

In [25]: ry = np.dot(reg, matrix)

In [26]: np.allclose(f(x), ry)  ❸
Out[26]: True

In [27]: np.mean((f(x) - ry) ** 2)  ❸
```

```
Out[27]: 3.404735992885531e-31

In [28]: create_plot([x, x], [f(x), ry], ['b', 'r.'],
                     ['f(x)', 'regression'], ['x', 'f(x)'])
```

❶ The new basis function exploiting knowledge about the example function.

❷ The optimal regression parameters recover the original parameters.

❸ The regression now leads to a perfect fit.

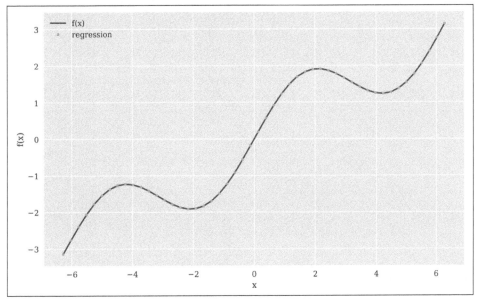

Figure 11-6. Regression with the sine basis function

Noisy data

Regression can cope equally well with *noisy* data, be it data from simulation or from
(nonperfect) measurements. To illustrate this point, independent observations with
noise and dependent observations with noise are generated. Figure 11-7 reveals that
the regression results are closer to the original function than the noisy data points. In
a sense, the regression averages out the noise to some extent:

```
In [29]: xn = np.linspace(-2 * np.pi, 2 * np.pi, 50)   ❶
         xn = xn + 0.15 * np.random.standard_normal(len(xn))   ❷
         yn = f(xn) + 0.25 * np.random.standard_normal(len(xn))   ❸

In [30]: reg = np.polyfit(xn, yn, 7)
         ry = np.polyval(reg, xn)
```

```
In [31]: create_plot([x, x], [f(x), ry], ['b', 'r.'],
                      ['f(x)', 'regression'], ['x', 'f(x)'])
```

❶ The new deterministic *x* values.

❷ Introducing noise to the *x* values.

❸ Introducing noise to the *y* values.

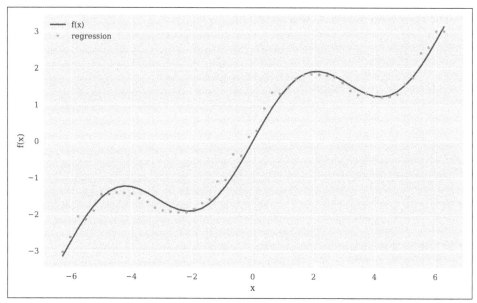

Figure 11-7. Regression for noisy data

Unsorted data

Another important aspect of regression is that the approach also works seamlessly with unsorted data. The previous examples all rely on sorted *x* data. This does not have to be the case. To make the point, let's look at yet another randomization approach for the *x* values. In this case, one can hardly identify any structure by just visually inspecting the raw data:

```
In [32]: xu = np.random.rand(50) * 4 * np.pi - 2 * np.pi  ❶
         yu = f(xu)
```

```
In [33]: print(xu[:10].round(2))  ❶
         print(yu[:10].round(2))  ❶
         [-4.17 -0.11 -1.91  2.33  3.34 -0.96  5.81  4.92 -4.56 -5.42]
         [-1.23 -0.17 -1.9   1.89  1.47 -1.29  2.45  1.48 -1.29 -1.95]
```

```
In [34]: reg = np.polyfit(xu, yu, 5)
         ry = np.polyval(reg, xu)
```

```
In [35]: create_plot([xu, xu], [yu, ry], ['b.', 'ro'],
                      ['f(x)', 'regression'], ['x', 'f(x)'])
```

❶ Randomizes the *x* values.

As with the noisy data, the regression approach does not care for the order of the observation points. This becomes obvious upon inspecting the structure of the minimization problem in Equation 11-1. It is also obvious by the results, presented in Figure 11-8.

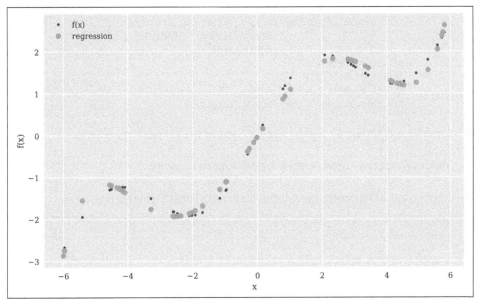

Figure 11-8. Regression for unsorted data

Multiple dimensions

Another convenient characteristic of the least-squares regression approach is that it carries over to multiple dimensions without too many modifications. As an example function take fm(), as presented next:

```
In [36]: def fm(p):
             x, y = p
             return np.sin(x) + 0.25 * x + np.sqrt(y) + 0.05 * y ** 2
```

To properly visualize this function, *grids* (in two dimensions) of independent data points are needed. Based on such two-dimensional grids of independent and resulting dependent data points, embodied in the following by X, Y, and Z, Figure 11-9 presents the shape of the function fm():

```
In [37]: x = np.linspace(0, 10, 20)
         y = np.linspace(0, 10, 20)
         X, Y = np.meshgrid(x, y)  ❶

In [38]: Z = fm((X, Y))
         x = X.flatten()  ❷
         y = Y.flatten()  ❷

In [39]: from mpl_toolkits.mplot3d import Axes3D  ❸

In [40]: fig = plt.figure(figsize=(10, 6))
         ax = fig.gca(projection='3d')
         surf = ax.plot_surface(X, Y, Z, rstride=2, cstride=2,
                                cmap='coolwarm', linewidth=0.5,
                                antialiased=True)
         ax.set_xlabel('x')
         ax.set_ylabel('y')
         ax.set_zlabel('f(x, y)')
         fig.colorbar(surf, shrink=0.5, aspect=5)
```

❶ Generates 2D ndarray objects ("grids") out of the 1D ndarray objects.

❷ Yields 1D ndarray objects from the 2D ndarray objects.

❸ Imports the 3D plotting capabilities from matplotlib as required.

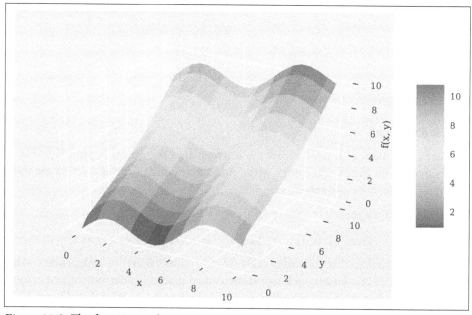

Figure 11-9. The function with two parameters

To get good regression results, the set of basis functions is essential. Therefore, factoring in knowledge about the function `fm()` itself, both an `np.sin()` and an `np.sqrt()` function are included. Figure 11-10 shows the perfect regression results visually:

```
In [41]: matrix = np.zeros((len(x), 6 + 1))
         matrix[:, 6] = np.sqrt(y)   ❶
         matrix[:, 5] = np.sin(x)    ❷
         matrix[:, 4] = y ** 2
         matrix[:, 3] = x ** 2
         matrix[:, 2] = y
         matrix[:, 1] = x
         matrix[:, 0] = 1

In [42]: reg = np.linalg.lstsq(matrix, fm((x, y)), rcond=None)[0]

In [43]: RZ = np.dot(matrix, reg).reshape((20, 20))   ❸

In [44]: fig = plt.figure(figsize=(10, 6))
         ax = fig.gca(projection='3d')
         surf1 = ax.plot_surface(X, Y, Z, rstride=2, cstride=2,
                     cmap=mpl.cm.coolwarm, linewidth=0.5,
                     antialiased=True)   ❹
         surf2 = ax.plot_wireframe(X, Y, RZ, rstride=2, cstride=2,
                              label='regression')   ❺
         ax.set_xlabel('x')
         ax.set_ylabel('y')
         ax.set_zlabel('f(x, y)')
         ax.legend()
         fig.colorbar(surf, shrink=0.5, aspect=5)
```

❶ The `np.sqrt()` function for the y parameter.

❷ The `np.sin()` function for the x parameter.

❸ Transforms the regression results to the grid structure.

❹ Plots the original function surface.

❺ Plots the regression surface.

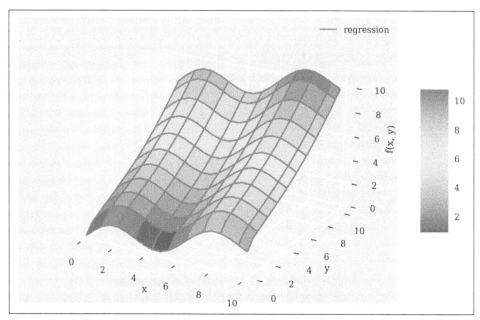

Figure 11-10. Regression surface for function with two parameters

Regression

Least-squares regression approaches have multiple areas of application, including simple function approximation and function approximation based on noisy or unsorted data. These approaches can be applied to one-dimensional as well as multidimensional problems. Due to the underlying mathematics, the application is "almost always the same."

Interpolation

Compared to regression, *interpolation* (e.g., with cubic splines) is more involved mathematically. It is also limited to low-dimensional problems. Given an ordered set of observation points (ordered in the *x* dimension), the basic idea is to do a regression between two neighboring data points in such a way that not only are the data points perfectly matched by the resulting piecewise-defined interpolation function, but also the function is continuously differentiable at the data points. Continuous differentiability requires at least interpolation of degree 3—i.e., with cubic splines. However, the approach also works in general with quadratic and even linear splines.

The following code implements a linear splines interpolation, the result of which is shown in Figure 11-11:

```
In [45]: import scipy.interpolate as spi ❶

In [46]: x = np.linspace(-2 * np.pi, 2 * np.pi, 25)

In [47]: def f(x):
             return np.sin(x) + 0.5 * x

In [48]: ipo = spi.splrep(x, f(x), k=1) ❷

In [49]: iy = spi.splev(x, ipo) ❸

In [50]: np.allclose(f(x), iy) ❹
Out[50]: True

In [51]: create_plot([x, x], [f(x), iy], ['b', 'ro'],
                      ['f(x)', 'interpolation'], ['x', 'f(x)'])
```

❶ Imports the required subpackage from SciPy.

❷ Implements a linear spline interpolation.

❸ Derives the interpolated values.

❹ Checks whether the interpolated values are close (enough) to the function values.

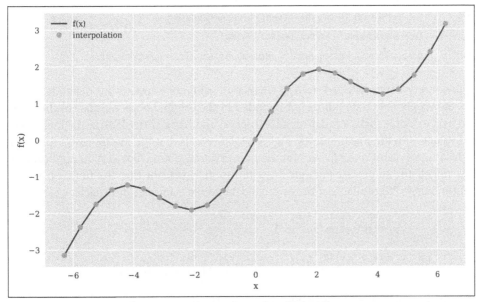

Figure 11-11. Linear splines interpolation (complete data set)

The application itself, given an *x*-ordered set of data points, is as simple as the application of np.polyfit() and np.polyval(). Here, the respective functions are `sci.splrep()` and `sci.splev()`. Table 11-2 lists the major parameters that the `sci.splrep()` function takes.

Table 11-2. Parameters of splrep() function

Parameter	Description
x	(Ordered) *x* coordinates (independent variable values)
y	(*x*-ordered) *y* coordinates (dependent variable values)
w	Weights to apply to the *y* coordinates
xb, xe	Interval to fit; if None then `[x[0], x[-1]]`
k	Order of the spline fit ($1 \leq k \leq 5$)
s	Smoothing factor (the larger, the more smoothing)
full_output	If True, returns additional output
quiet	If True, suppresses messages

Table 11-3 lists the parameters that the `sci.splev()` function takes.

Table 11-3. Parameters of splev() function

Parameter	Description
x	(Ordered) *x* coordinates (independent variable values)
tck	Sequence of length 3 returned by `splrep()` (knots, coefficients, degree)
der	Order of derivative (0 for function, 1 for first derivative)
ext	Behavior if x not in knot sequence (0 = extrapolate, 1 = return 0, 2 = raise `ValueError`)

Spline interpolation is often used in finance to generate estimates for dependent values of independent data points not included in the original observations. To this end, the next example picks a much smaller interval and has a closer look at the interpolated values with the linear splines. Figure 11-12 reveals that the interpolation function indeed interpolates *linearly* between two observation points. For certain applications this might not be precise enough. In addition, it is evident that the function is not continuously differentiable at the original data points—another drawback:

```
In [52]: xd = np.linspace(1.0, 3.0, 50)   ❶
         iyd = spi.splev(xd, ipo)

In [53]: create_plot([xd, xd], [f(xd), iyd], ['b', 'ro'],
                      ['f(x)', 'interpolation'], ['x', 'f(x)'])
```

❶ Smaller interval with more points.

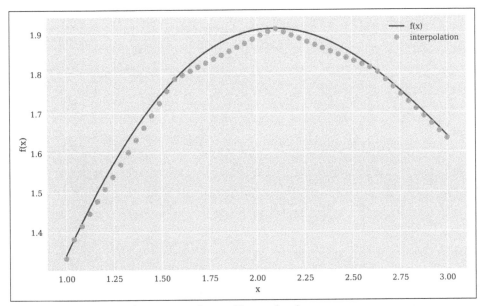

Figure 11-12. Linear splines interpolation (data subset)

A repetition of the complete exercise, this time using cubic splines, improves the results considerably (see Figure 11-13):

```
In [54]: ipo = spi.splrep(x, f(x), k=3)  ❶
         iyd = spi.splev(xd, ipo)  ❷

In [55]: np.allclose(f(xd), iyd)  ❸
Out[55]: False

In [56]: np.mean((f(xd) - iyd) ** 2)  ❹
Out[56]: 1.1349319851436892e-08

In [57]: create_plot([xd, xd], [f(xd), iyd], ['b', 'ro'],
                      ['f(x)', 'interpolation'], ['x', 'f(x)'])
```

❶ Cubic splines interpolation on complete data sets.

❷ Results applied to the smaller interval.

❸ The interpolation is still not perfect …

❹ … but better than before.

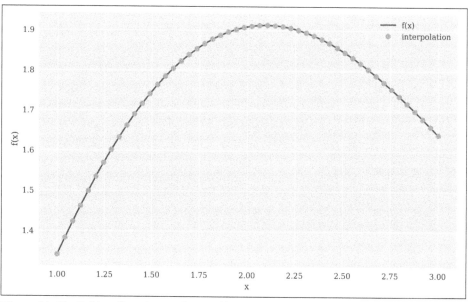

Figure 11-13. Cubic splines interpolation (data subset)

Interpolation

In those cases where spline interpolation can be applied, one can expect better approximation results compared to a least-squares regression approach. However, remember that sorted (and "non-noisy") data is required and that the approach is limited to low-dimensional problems. It is also computationally more demanding and might therefore take (much) longer than regression in certain use cases.

Convex Optimization

In finance and economics, *convex optimization* plays an important role. Examples are the calibration of option pricing models to market data or the optimization of an agent's utility function. As an example, take the function fm():

```
In [58]: def fm(p):
             x, y = p
             return (np.sin(x) + 0.05 * x ** 2
                 + np.sin(y) + 0.05 * y ** 2)
```

Figure 11-14 shows the function graphically for the defined intervals for x and y. Visual inspection already reveals that this function has multiple local minima. The existence of a global minimum cannot really be confirmed by this particular graphical representation, but it seems to exist:

```
In [59]: x = np.linspace(-10, 10, 50)
         y = np.linspace(-10, 10, 50)
         X, Y = np.meshgrid(x, y)
         Z = fm((X, Y))

In [60]: fig = plt.figure(figsize=(10, 6))
         ax = fig.gca(projection='3d')
         surf = ax.plot_surface(X, Y, Z, rstride=2, cstride=2,
                                cmap='coolwarm', linewidth=0.5,
                                antialiased=True)
         ax.set_xlabel('x')
         ax.set_ylabel('y')
         ax.set_zlabel('f(x, y)')
         fig.colorbar(surf, shrink=0.5, aspect=5)
```

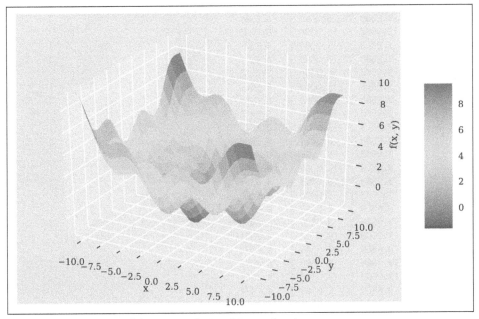

Figure 11-14. Linear splines interpolation (data subset)

Global Optimization

In what follows, both a *global* minimization approach and a *local* one are implemented. The functions `sco.brute()` and `sco.fmin()` that are applied are from `scipy.optimize`.

To have a closer look behind the scenes during minimization procedures, the following code amends the original function by an option to output current parameter values as well as the function value. This allows us to keep track of all relevant information for the procedure:

```
In [61]: import scipy.optimize as sco   ❶

In [62]: def fo(p):
             x, y = p
             z = np.sin(x) + 0.05 * x ** 2 + np.sin(y) + 0.05 * y ** 2
             if output == True:
                 print('%8.4f | %8.4f | %8.4f' % (x, y, z))   ❷
             return z

In [63]: output = True
         sco.brute(fo, ((-10, 10.1, 5), (-10, 10.1, 5)), finish=None)   ❸
         -10.0000 | -10.0000 |  11.0880
         -10.0000 | -10.0000 |  11.0880
         -10.0000 |  -5.0000 |   7.7529
         -10.0000 |   0.0000 |   5.5440
         -10.0000 |   5.0000 |   5.8351
         -10.0000 |  10.0000 |  10.0000
          -5.0000 | -10.0000 |   7.7529
          -5.0000 |  -5.0000 |   4.4178
          -5.0000 |   0.0000 |   2.2089
          -5.0000 |   5.0000 |   2.5000
          -5.0000 |  10.0000 |   6.6649
           0.0000 | -10.0000 |   5.5440
           0.0000 |  -5.0000 |   2.2089
           0.0000 |   0.0000 |   0.0000
           0.0000 |   5.0000 |   0.2911
           0.0000 |  10.0000 |   4.4560
           5.0000 | -10.0000 |   5.8351
           5.0000 |  -5.0000 |   2.5000
           5.0000 |   0.0000 |   0.2911
           5.0000 |   5.0000 |   0.5822
           5.0000 |  10.0000 |   4.7471
          10.0000 | -10.0000 |  10.0000
          10.0000 |  -5.0000 |   6.6649
          10.0000 |   0.0000 |   4.4560
          10.0000 |   5.0000 |   4.7471
          10.0000 |  10.0000 |   8.9120

Out[63]: array([0., 0.])
```

❶ Imports the required subpackage from SciPy.

❷ The information to print out if output = True.

❸ The brute force optimization.

The optimal parameter values, given the initial parameterization of the function, are x = y = 0. The resulting function value is also 0, as a quick review of the preceding output reveals. One might be inclined to accept this as the global minimum. However, the first parameterization here is quite rough, in that step sizes of 5 for both input parameters are used. This can of course be refined considerably, leading to better results in this case—and showing that the previous solution is not the optimal one:

```
In [64]: output = False
         opt1 = sco.brute(fo, ((-10, 10.1, 0.1), (-10, 10.1, 0.1)), finish=None)

In [65]: opt1
Out[65]: array([-1.4, -1.4])

In [66]: fm(opt1)
Out[66]: -1.7748994599769203
```

The optimal parameter values are now x = y = -1.4 and the minimal function value for the global minimization is about −1.7749.

Local Optimization

The local convex optimization that follows draws on the results from the global optimization. The function sco.fmin() takes as input the function to minimize and the starting parameter values. Optional parameter values are the input parameter tolerance and function value tolerance, as well as the maximum number of iterations and function calls. The local optimization further improves the result:

```
In [67]: output = True
         opt2 = sco.fmin(fo, opt1, xtol=0.001, ftol=0.001,
                         maxiter=15, maxfun=20)   ❶
         -1.4000 |   -1.4000 |   -1.7749
         -1.4700 |   -1.4000 |   -1.7743
         -1.4000 |   -1.4700 |   -1.7743
         -1.3300 |   -1.4700 |   -1.7696
         -1.4350 |   -1.4175 |   -1.7756
         -1.4350 |   -1.3475 |   -1.7722
         -1.4088 |   -1.4394 |   -1.7755
         -1.4438 |   -1.4569 |   -1.7751
         -1.4328 |   -1.4427 |   -1.7756
         -1.4591 |   -1.4208 |   -1.7752
         -1.4213 |   -1.4347 |   -1.7757
         -1.4235 |   -1.4096 |   -1.7755
         -1.4305 |   -1.4344 |   -1.7757
         -1.4168 |   -1.4516 |   -1.7753
         -1.4305 |   -1.4260 |   -1.7757
         -1.4396 |   -1.4257 |   -1.7756
         -1.4259 |   -1.4325 |   -1.7757
         -1.4259 |   -1.4241 |   -1.7757
         -1.4304 |   -1.4177 |   -1.7757
         -1.4270 |   -1.4288 |   -1.7757
         Warning: Maximum number of function evaluations has been exceeded.

In [68]: opt2
Out[68]: array([-1.42702972, -1.42876755])
```

```
In [69]: fm(opt2)
Out[69]: -1.7757246992239009
```

❶ The local convex optimization.

For many convex optimization problems it is advisable to have a global minimization before the local one. The major reason for this is that local convex optimization algorithms can easily be trapped in a local minimum (or do "basin hopping"), ignoring completely better local minima and/or a global minimum. The following shows that setting the starting parameterization to x = y = 2 gives, for example, a "minimum" value of above zero:

```
In [70]: output = False
         sco.fmin(fo, (2.0, 2.0), maxiter=250)
         Optimization terminated successfully.
                  Current function value: 0.015826
                  Iterations: 46
                  Function evaluations: 86

Out[70]: array([4.2710728 , 4.27106945])
```

Constrained Optimization

So far, this section only considers unconstrained optimization problems. However, large classes of economic or financial optimization problems are constrained by one or multiple constraints. Such constraints can formally take on the form of equalities or inequalities.

As a simple example, consider the utility maximization problem of an (expected utility maximizing) investor who can invest in two risky securities. Both securities cost $q_a = q_b = 10$ USD today. After one year, they have a payoff of 15 USD and 5 USD, respectively, in state u, and of 5 USD and 12 USD, respectively, in state d. Both states are equally likely. Denote the vector payoffs for the two securities by r_a and r_b, respectively.

The investor has a budget of $w_0 = 100$ USD to invest and derives utility from future wealth according to the utility function $u(w) = \sqrt{w}$, where w is the wealth (USD amount) available. Equation 11-2 is a formulation of the maximization problem where a, b are the numbers of securities bought by the investor.

Equation 11-2. Expected utility maximization problem (1)

$$\max_{a,b} E\big(u\big(w_1\big)\big) = p\sqrt{w_{1u}} + (1-p)\sqrt{w_{1d}}$$
$$w_1 = a \cdot r_a + b \cdot r_b$$
$$w_0 \geq a \cdot q_a + b \cdot q_b$$
$$a, b \geq 0$$

Putting in all numerical assumptions, one gets the problem in Equation 11-3. Note the change to the minimization of the negative expected utility.

Equation 11-3. Expected utility maximization problem (2)

$$\min_{a,b} - E\big(u\big(w_1\big)\big) = -\big(0.5 \cdot \sqrt{w_{1u}} + 0.5 \cdot \sqrt{w_{1d}}\big)$$
$$w_{1u} = a \cdot 15 + b \cdot 5$$
$$w_{1d} = a \cdot 5 + b \cdot 12$$
$$100 \geq a \cdot 10 + b \cdot 10$$
$$a, b \geq 0$$

To solve this problem, the `scipy.optimize.minimize()` function is appropriate. This function takes as input—in addition to the function to be minimized—conditions in the form of equalities and inequalities (as a `list` of `dict` objects) as well as boundaries for the parameters (as a `tuple` of `tuple` objects).[1] The following translates the problem from Equation 11-3 into Python code:

```
In [71]: import math

In [72]: def Eu(p):      ❶
             s, b = p
             return -(0.5 * math.sqrt(s * 15 + b * 5) +
                      0.5 * math.sqrt(s * 5 + b * 12))

In [73]: cons = ({'type': 'ineq',
                  'fun': lambda p: 100 - p[0] * 10 - p[1] * 10})      ❷

In [74]: bnds = ((0, 1000), (0, 1000))      ❸

In [75]: result = sco.minimize(Eu, [5, 5], method='SLSQP',
                               bounds=bnds, constraints=cons)      ❹
```

---

1 For details and examples of how to use the `minimize` function, refer to the documentation (*http://bit.ly/ using_minimize*).

❶ The function to be *minimized*, in order to maximize the expected utility.

❷ The inequality constraint as a `dict` object.

❸ The boundary values for the parameters (chosen to be wide enough).

❹ The constrained optimization.

The `result` object contains all the relevant information. With regard to the minimal function value, one needs to recall to shift the sign back:

```
In [76]: result
Out[76]:      fun: -9.700883611487832
              jac: array([-0.48508096, -0.48489535])
          message: 'Optimization terminated successfully.'
             nfev: 21
              nit: 5
             njev: 5
           status: 0
          success: True
                x: array([8.02547122, 1.97452878])

In [77]: result['x']   ❶
Out[77]: array([8.02547122, 1.97452878])

In [78]: -result['fun']   ❷
Out[78]: 9.700883611487832

In [79]: np.dot(result['x'], [10, 10])   ❸
Out[79]: 99.99999999999999
```

❶ The optimal parameter values (i.e., the optimal portfolio).

❷ The negative minimum function value as the optimal solution value.

❸ The budget constraint is binding; all wealth is invested.

Integration

Especially when it comes to valuation and option pricing, integration is an important mathematical tool. This stems from the fact that risk-neutral values of derivatives can be expressed in general as the discounted *expectation* of their payoff under the risk-neutral or martingale measure. The expectation in turn is a sum in the discrete case and an integral in the continuous case. The subpackage `scipy.integrate` provides different functions for numerical integration. The example function is known from "Approximation" on page 312:

```
In [80]: import scipy.integrate as sci

In [81]: def f(x):
             return np.sin(x) + 0.5 * x
```

The integration interval shall be [0.5, 9.5], leading to the definite integral as in Equation 11-4.

Equation 11-4. Integral of example function

$$\int_{0.5}^{9.5} f(x)dx = \int_{0.5}^{9.5} \sin(x) + \frac{x}{2}dx$$

The following code defines the major Python objects to evaluate the integral:

```
In [82]: x = np.linspace(0, 10)
         y = f(x)
         a = 0.5    ❶
         b = 9.5    ❷
         Ix = np.linspace(a, b)    ❸
         Iy = f(Ix)    ❹
```

❶ Left integration limit.

❷ Right integration limit.

❸ Integration interval values.

❹ Integration function values.

Figure 11-15 visualizes the integral value as the gray-shaded area under the function:[2]

```
In [83]: from matplotlib.patches import Polygon

In [84]: fig, ax = plt.subplots(figsize=(10, 6))
         plt.plot(x, y, 'b', linewidth=2)
         plt.ylim(bottom=0)
         Ix = np.linspace(a, b)
         Iy = f(Ix)
         verts = [(a, 0)] + list(zip(Ix, Iy)) + [(b, 0)]
         poly = Polygon(verts, facecolor='0.7', edgecolor='0.5')
         ax.add_patch(poly)
         plt.text(0.75 * (a + b), 1.5, r"$\int_a^b f(x)dx$",
                 horizontalalignment='center', fontsize=20)
         plt.figtext(0.9, 0.075, '$x$')
         plt.figtext(0.075, 0.9, '$f(x)$')
         ax.set_xticks((a, b))
```

---

2 See Chapter 7 for a more detailed discussion of this type of plot.

```
ax.set_xticklabels(('$a$', '$b$'))
ax.set_yticks([f(a), f(b)]);
```

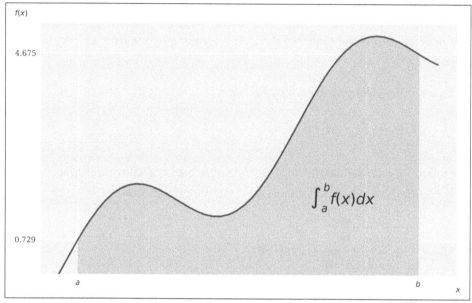

Figure 11-15. Integral value as shaded area

Numerical Integration

The scipy.integrate subpackage contains a selection of functions to numerically integrate a given mathematical function for upper and lower integration limits. Examples are sci.fixed_quad() for *fixed Gaussian quadrature*, sci.quad() for *adaptive quadrature*, and sci.romberg() for *Romberg integration*:

```
In [85]: sci.fixed_quad(f, a, b)[0]
Out[85]: 24.366995967084602

In [86]: sci.quad(f, a, b)[0]
Out[86]: 24.374754718086752

In [87]: sci.romberg(f, a, b)
Out[87]: 24.374754718086713
```

There are also a number of integration functions that take as input list or ndarray objects with function values and input values, respectively. Examples in this regard are sci.trapz(), using the *trapezoidal* rule, and sci.simps(), implementing *Simpson's* rule:

```
In [88]: xi = np.linspace(0.5, 9.5, 25)

In [89]: sci.trapz(f(xi), xi)
```

```
Out[89]: 24.352733271544516

In [90]: sci.simps(f(xi), xi)
Out[90]: 24.37496418455075
```

Integration by Simulation

The valuation of options and derivatives by Monte Carlo simulation (see Chapter 12) rests on the insight that one can evaluate an integral by simulation. To this end, draw *I* random values of x between the integral limits and evaluate the integration function at every random value for x. Sum up all the function values and take the average to arrive at an average function value over the integration interval. Multiply this value by the length of the integration interval to derive an estimate for the integral value.

The following code shows how the Monte Carlo estimated integral value converges—although not monotonically—to the real one when one increases the number of random draws. The estimator is already quite close for relatively small numbers of random draws:

```
In [91]: for i in range(1, 20):
             np.random.seed(1000)
             x = np.random.random(i * 10) * (b - a) + a    ❶
             print(np.mean(f(x)) * (b - a))
         24.804762279331463
         26.522918898332378
         26.265547519223976
         26.02770339943824
         24.99954181440844
         23.881810141621663
         23.527912274843253
         23.507857658961207
         23.67236746066989
         23.679410416062886
         24.424401707879305
         24.239005346819056
         24.115396924962802
         24.424191987566726
         23.924933080533783
         24.19484212027875
         24.117348378249833
         24.100690929662274
         23.76905109847816
```

❶ Number of random x values is increased with every iteration.

Symbolic Computation

The previous sections are mainly concerned with numerical computation. This section now introduces *symbolic* computation, which can be applied beneficially in many areas of finance. To this end, SymPy, a library specifically dedicated to symbolic computation, is generally used.

Basics

SymPy introduces new classes of objects. A fundamental class is the Symbol class:

```
In [92]: import sympy as sy

In [93]: x = sy.Symbol('x')    ❶
         y = sy.Symbol('y')    ❶

In [94]: type(x)
Out[94]: sympy.core.symbol.Symbol

In [95]: sy.sqrt(x)    ❷
Out[95]: sqrt(x)

In [96]: 3 + sy.sqrt(x) - 4 ** 2    ❸
Out[96]: sqrt(x) - 13

In [97]: f = x ** 2 + 3 + 0.5 * x ** 2 + 3 / 2    ❹

In [98]: sy.simplify(f)    ❺
Out[98]: 1.5*x**2 + 4.5
```

❶ Defines symbols to work with.

❷ Applies a function on a symbol.

❸ A numerical expression defined on symbol.

❹ A function defined symbolically.

❺ The function expression simplified.

This already illustrates a major difference to regular Python code. Although x has no numerical value, the square root of x is nevertheless defined with SymPy since x is a Symbol object. In that sense, sy.sqrt(x) can be part of arbitrary mathematical expressions. Notice that SymPy in general automatically simplifies a given mathematical expression. Similarly, one can define arbitrary functions using Symbol objects. They are not to be confused with Python functions.

SymPy provides three basic renderers for mathematical expressions:

- LaTeX-based
- Unicode-based

- ASCII-based

When working, for example, solely in a Jupyter Notebook environment (HTML-based), LaTeX rendering is generally a good (i.e., visually appealing) choice. The code that follows sticks to the simplest option, ASCII, to illustrate that there is no manual typesetting involved:

```
In [99]: sy.init_printing(pretty_print=False, use_unicode=False)

In [100]: print(sy.pretty(f))
               2
          1.5*x  + 4.5

In [101]: print(sy.pretty(sy.sqrt(x) + 0.5))
          ___
          \/ x  + 0.5
```

This section cannot go into details, but SymPy also provides many other useful mathematical functions—for example, when it comes to numerically evaluating π. The following example shows the first and final 40 characters of the string representation of π up to the 400,000th digit. It also searches for a six-digit, day-first birthday—a popular task in certain mathematics and IT circles:

```
In [102]: %time pi_str = str(sy.N(sy.pi, 400000))   ❶
          CPU times: user 400 ms, sys: 10.9 ms, total: 411 ms
          Wall time: 501 ms

In [103]: pi_str[:42]   ❷
Out[103]: '3.141592653589793238462643383279502884197l'

In [104]: pi_str[-40:]   ❸
Out[104]: '8245672736856312185020980470362464176198'

In [105]: %time pi_str.find('061072')   ❹
          CPU times: user 115 µs, sys: 1e+03 ns, total: 116 µs
          Wall time: 120 µs

Out[105]: 80847
```

❶ Returns the string representation of the first 400,000 digits of π.

❷ Shows the first 40 digits ...

❸ ... and the final 40 digits.

❹ Searches for a birthday date in the string.

Equations

A strength of SymPy is solving equations, e.g., of the form $x^2 - 1 = 0$. In general, SymPy presumes that one is looking for a solution to the equation obtained by equating the given expression to zero. Therefore, equations like $x^2 - 1 = 3$ might have to be reformulated to get the desired result. Of course, SymPy can cope with more complex expressions, like $x^3 + 0.5x^2 - 1 = 0$. Finally, it can also deal with problems involving imaginary numbers, such as $x^2 + y^2 = 0$:

```
In [106]: sy.solve(x ** 2 - 1)
Out[106]: [-1, 1]

In [107]: sy.solve(x ** 2 - 1 - 3)
Out[107]: [-2, 2]

In [108]: sy.solve(x ** 3 + 0.5 * x ** 2 - 1)
Out[108]: [0.858094329496553, -0.679047164748276 - 0.839206763026694*I,
           -0.679047164748276 + 0.839206763026694*I]

In [109]: sy.solve(x ** 2 + y ** 2)
Out[109]: [{x: -I*y}, {x: I*y}]
```

Integration and Differentiation

Another strength of SymPy is integration and differentiation. The example that follows revisits the example function used for numerical- and simulation-based integration and derives both a *symbolically* and a *numerically* exact solution. Symbol objects for the integration limits objects are required to get started:

```
In [110]: a, b = sy.symbols('a b')     ❶

In [111]: I = sy.Integral(sy.sin(x) + 0.5 * x, (x, a, b))     ❷

In [112]: print(sy.pretty(I))     ❷
              b
              /
             |
             |   (0.5*x + sin(x)) dx
             |
             /
             a

In [113]: int_func = sy.integrate(sy.sin(x) + 0.5 * x, x)     ❸

In [114]: print(sy.pretty(int_func))     ❸
                 2
          0.25*x   - cos(x)

In [115]: Fb = int_func.subs(x, 9.5).evalf()     ❹
          Fa = int_func.subs(x, 0.5).evalf()     ❹
```

```
In [116]: Fb - Fa  ❺
Out[116]: 24.3747547180867
```

❶ The Symbol objects for the integral limits.

❷ The Integral object defined and pretty-printed.

❸ The antiderivative derived and pretty-printed.

❹ The values of the antiderivative at the limits, obtained via the .subs() and .evalf() methods.

❺ The exact numerical value of the integral.

The integral can also be solved symbolically with the symbolic integration limits:

```
In [117]: int_func_limits = sy.integrate(sy.sin(x) + 0.5 * x, (x, a, b))  ❶

In [118]: print(sy.pretty(int_func_limits))  ❶
                 2          2
        - 0.25*a  + 0.25*b  + cos(a) - cos(b)

In [119]: int_func_limits.subs({a : 0.5, b : 9.5}).evalf()  ❷
Out[119]: 24.3747547180868

In [120]: sy.integrate(sy.sin(x) + 0.5 * x, (x, 0.5, 9.5))  ❸
Out[120]: 24.3747547180867
```

❶ Solving the integral symbolically.

❷ Solving the integral numerically, using a dict object during substitution.

❸ Solving the integral numerically in a single step.

Differentiation

The derivative of the antiderivative yields in general the original function. Applying the sy.diff() function to the symbolic antiderivative illustrates this:

```
In [121]: int_func.diff()
Out[121]: 0.5*x + sin(x)
```

As with the integration example, differentiation shall now be used to derive the exact solution of the convex minimization problem this chapter looked at earlier. To this end, the respective function is defined symbolically, partial derivatives are derived, and the roots are identified.

A necessary but not sufficient condition for a global minimum is that both partial derivatives are zero. However, there is no guarantee of a symbolic solution. Both algorithmic and (multiple) existence issues come into play here. However, one can solve the two first-order conditions numerically, providing "educated" guesses based on the global and local minimization efforts from before:

```
In [122]: f = (sy.sin(x) + 0.05 * x ** 2
              + sy.sin(y) + 0.05 * y ** 2)  ❶

In [123]: del_x = sy.diff(f, x)  ❷
          del_x  ❷
Out[123]: 0.1*x + cos(x)

In [124]: del_y = sy.diff(f, y)  ❷
          del_y  ❷
Out[124]: 0.1*y + cos(y)

In [125]: xo = sy.nsolve(del_x, -1.5)  ❸
          xo  ❸
Out[125]: -1.42755177876459

In [126]: yo = sy.nsolve(del_y, -1.5)  ❸
          yo  ❸
Out[126]: -1.42755177876459

In [127]: f.subs({x : xo, y : yo}).evalf()  ❹
Out[127]: -1.77572565314742
```

❶ The symbolic version of the function.

❷ The two partial derivatives derived and printed.

❸ Educated guesses for the roots and resulting optimal values.

❹ The global minimum function value.

Again, providing uneducated/arbitrary guesses might trap the algorithm in a local minimum instead of the global one:

```
In [128]: xo = sy.nsolve(del_x, 1.5)  ❶
          xo
Out[128]: 1.74632928225285

In [129]: yo = sy.nsolve(del_y, 1.5)  ❶
          yo
Out[129]: 1.74632928225285

In [130]: f.subs({x : xo, y : yo}).evalf()  ❷
Out[130]: 2.27423381055640
```

❶ Uneducated guesses for the roots.

❷ The local minimum function value.

This numerically illustrates that the first-order conditions are necessary but not sufficient.

Symbolic Computations

When doing (financial) mathematics with Python, SymPy and symbolic computations prove to be a valuable tool. Especially for interactive financial analytics, this can be a more efficient approach compared to nonsymbolic approaches.

Conclusion

This chapter covers selected mathematical topics and tools important to finance. For example, the approximation of functions is important in many financial areas, like factor-based models, yield curve interpolation, and regression-based Monte Carlo valuation approaches for American options. Convex optimization techniques are also regularly needed in finance; for example, when calibrating parametric option pricing models to market quotes or implied volatilities of options.

Numerical integration is central to, for example, the pricing of options and derivatives. Having derived the risk-neutral probability measure for a (set of) stochastic process(es), option pricing boils down to taking the expectation of the option's payoff under the risk-neutral measure and discounting this value back to the present date. Chapter 12 covers the simulation of several types of stochastic processes under the risk-neutral measure.

Finally, this chapter introduces symbolic computation with SymPy. For a number of mathematical operations, like integration, differentiation, or the solving of equations, symbolic computation can prove a useful and efficient tool.

Further Resources

For further information on the Python libraries used in this chapter, consult the following web resources:

- See the NumPy Reference (*http://docs.scipy.org/doc/numpy/reference/*) for details on the NumPy functions used in this chapter.
- Visit the SciPy documentation on optimization and root finding for details on scipy.optimize (*http://docs.scipy.org/doc/scipy/reference/optimize.html*).

- Integration with `scipy.integrate` is explained in "Integration and ODEs" (*http://docs.scipy.org/doc/scipy/reference/integrate.html*).

- The `SymPy` website (*http://sympy.org*) provides a wealth of examples and detailed documentation.

For a mathematical reference for the topics covered in this chapter, see:

- Brandimarte, Paolo (2006). *Numerical Methods in Finance and Economics: A MATLAB-Based Introduction*. 2nd ed., Hoboken, NJ: John Wiley & Sons.

## CHAPTER 12

Stochastics

Predictability is not how things will go, but how they can go.

—Raheel Farooq

Nowadays, stochastics is one of the most important mathematical and numerical disciplines in finance. In the beginning of the modern era of finance, mainly in the 1970s and 1980s, the major goal of financial research was to come up with closed-form solutions for, e.g., option prices given a specific financial model. The requirements have drastically changed in recent years in that not only is the correct valuation of single financial instruments important to participants in the financial markets, but also the consistent valuation of whole derivatives books, for example. Similarly, to come up with consistent risk measures across a whole financial institution, like value-at-risk and credit valuation adjustments, one needs to take into account the whole book of the institution and all its counterparties. Such daunting tasks can only be tackled by flexible and efficient numerical methods. Therefore, stochastics in general and Monte Carlo simulation in particular have risen to prominence in the financial field.

This chapter introduces the following topics from a Python perspective:

"Random Numbers" on page 346
> It all starts with pseudo-random numbers, which build the basis for all simulation efforts; although quasi-random numbers (e.g., based on Sobol sequences) have gained some popularity in finance, pseudo-random numbers still seem to be the benchmark.

"Simulation" on page 352
> In finance, two simulation tasks are of particular importance: simulation of *random variables* and of *stochastic processes*.

"Valuation" on page 375

The two main disciplines when it comes to valuation are the valuation of derivatives with *European exercise* (at a specific date) and *American exercise* (over a specific time interval); there are also instruments with *Bermudan exercise*, or exercise at a finite set of specific dates.

"Risk Measures" on page 383

Simulation lends itself pretty well to the calculation of risk measures like value-at-risk, credit value-at-risk, and credit valuation adjustments.

Random Numbers

Throughout this chapter, to generate random numbers,[1] the functions provided by the `numpy.random` subpackage are used:

```
In [1]: import math
        import numpy as np
        import numpy.random as npr   ❶
        from pylab import plt, mpl

In [2]: plt.style.use('seaborn')
        mpl.rcParams['font.family'] = 'serif'
        %matplotlib inline
```

❶ Imports the random number generation subpackage from NumPy.

For example, the `rand()` function returns random numbers from the open interval $[0,1)$ in the shape provided as a parameter to the function. The return object is an `ndarray` object. Such numbers can be easily transformed to cover other intervals of the real line. For instance, if one wants to generate random numbers from the interval $[a, b) = [5, 10)$, one can transform the returned numbers from `npr.rand()` as in the next example—this also works in multiple dimensions due to NumPy broadcasting:

```
In [3]: npr.seed(100)   ❶
        np.set_printoptions(precision=4)   ❶

In [4]: npr.rand(10)   ❷
Out[4]: array([0.5434, 0.2784, 0.4245, 0.8448, 0.0047, 0.1216, 0.6707, 0.8259,
               0.1367, 0.5751])

In [5]: npr.rand(5, 5)   ❸
Out[5]: array([[0.8913, 0.2092, 0.1853, 0.1084, 0.2197],
               [0.9786, 0.8117, 0.1719, 0.8162, 0.2741],
               [0.4317, 0.94  , 0.8176, 0.3361, 0.1754],
               [0.3728, 0.0057, 0.2524, 0.7957, 0.0153],
```

---

1 For simplicity, we will speak of *random numbers* knowing that all numbers used will be *pseudo-random*.

```
                [0.5988, 0.6038, 0.1051, 0.3819, 0.0365]])

In [6]: a = 5.    ❹
        b = 10.   ❺
        npr.rand(10) * (b - a) + a   ❻
Out[6]: array([9.4521, 9.9046, 5.2997, 9.4527, 7.8845, 8.7124, 8.1509, 7.9092,
               5.1022, 6.0501])

In [7]: npr.rand(5, 5) * (b - a) + a   ❼
Out[7]: array([[7.7234, 8.8456, 6.2535, 6.4295, 9.262 ],
               [9.875 , 9.4243, 6.7975, 7.9943, 6.774 ],
               [6.701 , 5.8904, 6.1885, 5.2243, 7.5272],
               [6.8813, 7.964 , 8.1497, 5.713 , 9.6692],
               [9.7319, 8.0115, 6.9388, 6.8159, 6.0217]])
```

❶ Fixes the seed value for reproducibility and fixes the number of digits for print-outs.

❷ Uniformly distributed random numbers as *one-dimensional* ndarray object.

❸ Uniformly distributed random numbers as *two-dimensional* ndarray object.

❹ Lower limit …

❺ … and upper limit …

❻ … for the transformation to another interval.

❼ The same transformation for two dimensions.

Table 12-1 lists functions to generate simple random numbers (*http://bit.ly/2Fo39Yh*).

Table 12-1. Functions for simple random number generation

Function	Parameters	Returns/result
rand	d0, d1, ..., dn	Random values in the given shape
randn	d0, d1, ..., dn	A sample (or samples) from the standard normal distribution
randint	low[, high, size]	Random integers from low (inclusive) to high (exclusive)
random_integers	low[, high, size]	Random integers between low and high, inclusive
random_sample	[size]	Random floats in the half-open interval [0.0, 1.0)
random	[size]	Random floats in the half-open interval [0.0, 1.0)
ranf	[size]	Random floats in the half-open interval [0.0, 1.0)
sample	[size]	Random floats in the half-open interval [0.0, 1.0)
choice	a[, size, replace, p]	Random sample from a given 1D array
bytes	length	Random bytes

It is straightforward to visualize some random draws generated by selected functions from Table 12-1. Figure 12-1 shows the results graphically for two continuous distributions and two discrete ones:

```
In [8]: sample_size = 500
        rn1 = npr.rand(sample_size, 3)        ❶
        rn2 = npr.randint(0, 10, sample_size)    ❷
        rn3 = npr.sample(size=sample_size)    ❶
        a = [0, 25, 50, 75, 100]    ❸
        rn4 = npr.choice(a, size=sample_size)    ❸

In [9]: fig, ((ax1, ax2), (ax3, ax4)) = plt.subplots(nrows=2, ncols=2,
                                                       figsize=(10, 8))
        ax1.hist(rn1, bins=25, stacked=True)
        ax1.set_title('rand')
        ax1.set_ylabel('frequency')
        ax2.hist(rn2, bins=25)
        ax2.set_title('randint')
        ax3.hist(rn3, bins=25)
        ax3.set_title('sample')
        ax3.set_ylabel('frequency')
        ax4.hist(rn4, bins=25)
        ax4.set_title('choice');
```

❶ Uniformly distributed random numbers.

❷ Random integers for a given interval.

❸ Randomly sampled values from a finite list object.

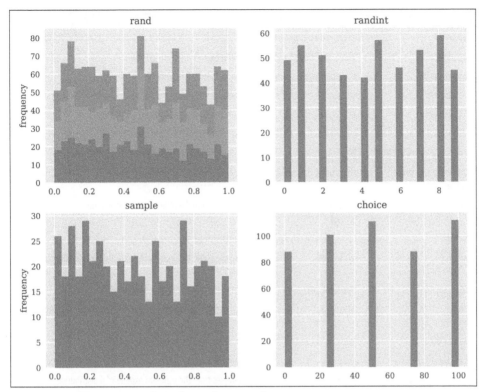

Figure 12-1. Histograms of simple random numbers

Table 12-2 lists functions for generating random numbers according to different distributions (*http://bit.ly/2A02jv5*).

Table 12-2. Functions to generate random numbers according to different distribution laws

Function	Parameters	Returns/result
beta	a, b[, size]	Samples for a beta distribution over [0, 1]
binomial	n, p[, size]	Samples from a binomial distribution
chisquare	df[, size]	Samples from a chi-square distribution
dirichlet	alpha[, size]	Samples from the Dirichlet distribution
exponential	[scale, size]	Samples from the exponential distribution
f	dfnum, dfden[, size]	Samples from an F distribution
gamma	shape[, scale, size]	Samples from a gamma distribution
geometric	p[, size]	Samples from the geometric distribution
gumbel	[loc, scale, size]	Samples from a Gumbel distribution
hypergeometric	ngood, nbad, nsample[, size]	Samples from a hypergeometric distribution

Function	Parameters	Returns/result
laplace	[loc, scale, size]	Samples from the Laplace or double exponential distribution
logistic	[loc, scale, size]	Samples from a logistic distribution
lognormal	[mean, sigma, size]	Samples from a log-normal distribution
logseries	p[, size]	Samples from a logarithmic series distribution
multinomial	n, pvals[, size]	Samples from a multinomial distribution
multivariate_normal	mean, cov[, size]	Samples from a multivariate normal distribution
negative_binomial	n, p[, size]	Samples from a negative binomial distribution
noncentral_chisquare	df, nonc[, size]	Samples from a noncentral chi-square distribution
noncentral_f	dfnum, dfden, nonc[, size]	Samples from the noncentral F distribution
normal	[loc, scale, size]	Samples from a normal (Gaussian) distribution
pareto	a[, size]	Samples from a Pareto II or Lomax distribution with the specified shape
poisson	[lam, size]	Samples from a Poisson distribution
power	a[, size]	Samples in [0, 1] from a power distribution with positive exponent a − 1
rayleigh	[scale, size]	Samples from a Rayleigh distribution
standard_cauchy	[size]	Samples from standard Cauchy distribution with mode = 0
standard_exponential	[size]	Samples from the standard exponential distribution
standard_gamma	shape[, size]	Samples from a standard gamma distribution
standard_normal	[size]	Samples from a standard normal distribution (mean=0, stdev=1)
standard_t	df[, size]	Samples from a Student's t distribution with df degrees of freedom
triangular	left, mode, right[, size]	Samples from the triangular distribution over the interval [left, right]
uniform	[low, high, size]	Samples from a uniform distribution
vonmises	mu, kappa[, size]	Samples from a von Mises distribution
wald	mean, scale[, size]	Samples from a Wald, or inverse Gaussian, distribution
weibull	a[, size]	Samples from a Weibull distribution
zipf	a[, size]	Samples from a Zipf distribution

Although there is much criticism around the use of (standard) normal distributions in finance, they are an indispensable tool and still the most widely used type of distribution, in analytical as well as numerical applications. One reason is that many financial models directly rest in one way or another on a normal distribution or a lognormal distribution. Another reason is that many financial models that do not rest directly on a (log-)normal assumption can be discretized, and therewith approximated for simulation purposes, by the use of the normal distribution.

As an illustration, Figure 12-2 visualizes random draws from the following distributions:

- *Standard normal* with mean of 0 and standard deviation of 1
- *Normal* with mean of 100 and standard deviation of 20
- *Chi square* with 0.5 degrees of freedom
- *Poisson* with lambda of 1

Figure 12-2 shows the results for the three continuous distributions and the discrete one (Poisson). The Poisson distribution is used, for example, to simulate the arrival of (rare) external events, like a jump in the price of an instrument or an exogenic shock. Here is the code that generates it:

```
In [10]: sample_size = 500
         rn1 = npr.standard_normal(sample_size)      ❶
         rn2 = npr.normal(100, 20, sample_size)      ❷
         rn3 = npr.chisquare(df=0.5, size=sample_size)   ❸
         rn4 = npr.poisson(lam=1.0, size=sample_size)    ❹

In [11]: fig, ((ax1, ax2), (ax3, ax4)) = plt.subplots(nrows=2, ncols=2,
                                                       figsize=(10, 8))
         ax1.hist(rn1, bins=25)
         ax1.set_title('standard normal')
         ax1.set_ylabel('frequency')
         ax2.hist(rn2, bins=25)
         ax2.set_title('normal(100, 20)')
         ax3.hist(rn3, bins=25)
         ax3.set_title('chi square')
         ax3.set_ylabel('frequency')
         ax4.hist(rn4, bins=25)
         ax4.set_title('Poisson');
```

❶ Standard normally distributed random numbers.

❷ Normally distributed random numbers.

❸ Chi-square distributed random numbers.

❹ Poisson distributed numbers.

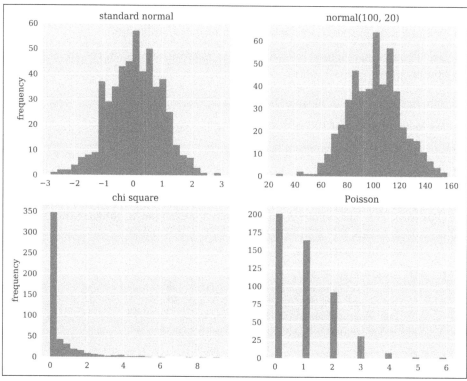

Figure 12-2. Histograms of random samples for different distributions

NumPy and Random Numbers

This section shows that NumPy is a powerful (even indispensable) tool when generating pseudo-random numbers in Python. The creation of small or large ndarray objects with such numbers is not only convenient but also performant.

Simulation

Monte Carlo simulation (MCS) is among the most important numerical techniques in finance, if not *the* most important and widely used. This mainly stems from the fact that it is the most flexible numerical method when it comes to the evaluation of mathematical expressions (e.g., integrals), and specifically the valuation of financial derivatives. The flexibility comes at the cost of a relatively high computational burden, though, since often hundreds of thousands or even millions of complex computations have to be carried out to come up with a single value estimate.

Random Variables

Consider, for example, the Black-Scholes-Merton setup for option pricing. In their setup, the level of a stock index S_T at a future date T given a level S_0 as of today is given according to Equation 12-1.

Equation 12-1. Simulating future index level in Black-Scholes-Merton setup

$$S_T = S_0 \exp\left(\left(r - \frac{1}{2}\sigma^2\right)T + \sigma\sqrt{T}z\right)$$

The variables and parameters have the following meaning:

S_T
> Index level at date T

r
> Constant riskless short rate

σ
> Constant volatility (= standard deviation of returns) of S

z
> Standard normally distributed random variable

This financial model is parameterized and simulated as follows. The output of this simulation code is shown in Figure 12-3:

```
In [12]: S0 = 100      ❶
         r = 0.05       ❷
         sigma = 0.25   ❸
         T = 2.0        ❹
         I = 10000      ❺
         ST1 = S0 * np.exp((r - 0.5 * sigma ** 2) * T +
                 sigma * math.sqrt(T) * npr.standard_normal(I))   ❻

In [13]: plt.figure(figsize=(10, 6))
         plt.hist(ST1, bins=50)
         plt.xlabel('index level')
         plt.ylabel('frequency');
```

❶ The initial index level.

❷ The constant riskless short rate.

❸ The constant volatility factor.

❹ The horizon in year fractions.

❺   The number of simulations.

❻   The simulation itself via a vectorized expression; the discretization scheme makes use of the `npr.standard_normal()` function.

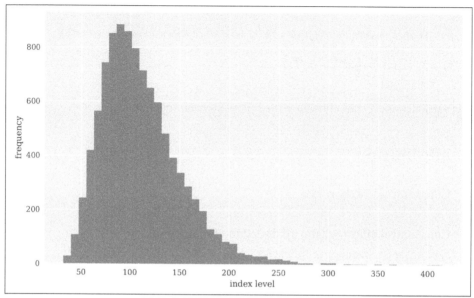

Figure 12-3. Statically simulated geometric Brownian motion (via npr.standard_normal())

Figure 12-3 suggests that the distribution of the random variable as defined in Equation 12-1 is *log-normal*. One could therefore also try to use the `npr.lognormal()` function to directly derive the values for the random variable. In that case, one has to provide the mean and the standard deviation to the function:

```
In [14]: ST2 = S0 * npr.lognormal((r - 0.5 * sigma ** 2) * T,
                                   sigma * math.sqrt(T), size=I)   ❶
```

```
In [15]: plt.figure(figsize=(10, 6))
         plt.hist(ST2, bins=50)
         plt.xlabel('index level')
         plt.ylabel('frequency');
```

❶   The simulation via a vectorized expression; the discretization scheme makes use of the `npr.lognormal()` function.

The result is shown in Figure 12-4.

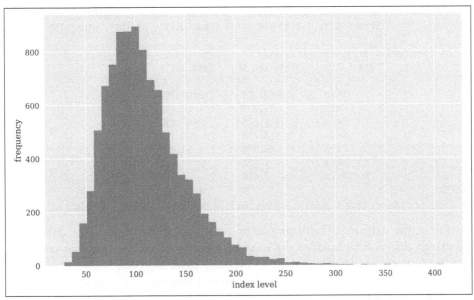

Figure 12-4. Statically simulated geometric Brownian motion (via npr.lognormal())

By visual inspection, Figures 12-3 and 12-4 indeed look pretty similar. This can be verified a bit more rigorously by comparing statistical moments of the resulting distributions. To compare the distributional characteristics of simulation results, the `scipy.stats` subpackage and the helper function `print_statistics()`, as defined here, prove useful:

```
In [16]: import scipy.stats as scs

In [17]: def print_statistics(a1, a2):
             ''' Prints selected statistics.

             Parameters
             ==========
             a1, a2: ndarray objects
                 results objects from simulation
             '''
             sta1 = scs.describe(a1)  ❶
             sta2 = scs.describe(a2)  ❶
             print('%14s %14s %14s' %
                 ('statistic', 'data set 1', 'data set 2'))
             print(45 * "-")
             print('%14s %14.3f %14.3f' % ('size', sta1[0], sta2[0]))
             print('%14s %14.3f %14.3f' % ('min', sta1[1][0], sta2[1][0]))
             print('%14s %14.3f %14.3f' % ('max', sta1[1][1], sta2[1][1]))
             print('%14s %14.3f %14.3f' % ('mean', sta1[2], sta2[2]))
             print('%14s %14.3f %14.3f' % ('std', np.sqrt(sta1[3]),
                                                   np.sqrt(sta2[3])))
```

```
        print('%14s %14.3f %14.3f' % ('skew', sta1[4], sta2[4]))
        print('%14s %14.3f %14.3f' % ('kurtosis', sta1[5], sta2[5]))

In [18]: print_statistics(ST1, ST2)
            statistic     data set 1     data set 2
        --------------------------------------------
                 size      10000.000      10000.000
                  min         32.327         28.230
                  max        414.825        409.110
                 mean        110.730        110.431
                  std         40.300         39.878
                 skew          1.122          1.115
             kurtosis          2.438          2.217
```

❶ The `scs.describe()` function gives back important statistics for a data set.

Obviously, the statistics of both simulation results are quite similar. The differences are mainly due to what is called the *sampling error* in simulation. Another error can also be introduced when *discretely* simulating *continuous* stochastic processes— namely the *discretization error*, which plays no role here due to the static nature of the simulation approach.

Stochastic Processes

Roughly speaking, a *stochastic process* is a sequence of random variables. In that sense, one should expect something similar to a sequence of repeated simulations of a random variable when simulating a process. This is mainly true, apart from the fact that the draws are typically not independent but rather depend on the result(s) of the previous draw(s). In general, however, stochastic processes used in finance exhibit the *Markov property*, which mainly says that tomorrow's value of the process only depends on today's state of the process, and not any other more "historic" state or even the whole path history. The process then is also called *memoryless*.

Geometric Brownian motion

Consider now the Black-Scholes-Merton model in its dynamic form, as described by the stochastic differential equation (SDE) in Equation 12-2. Here, Z_t is a standard Brownian motion. The SDE is called a *geometric Brownian motion*. The values of S_t are log-normally distributed and the (marginal) returns $\frac{dS_t}{S_t}$ normally.

Equation 12-2. Stochastic differential equation in Black-Scholes-Merton setup

$$dS_t = rS_t dt + \sigma S_t dZ_t$$

The SDE in Equation 12-2 can be discretized exactly by an Euler scheme. Such a scheme is presented in Equation 12-3, with Δt being the fixed discretization interval and z_t being a standard normally distributed random variable.

Equation 12-3. Simulating index levels dynamically in Black-Scholes-Merton setup

$$S_t = S_{t-\Delta t} \exp\left(\left(r - \frac{1}{2}\sigma^2\right)\Delta t + \sigma\sqrt{\Delta t}z_t\right)$$

As before, translation into Python and NumPy code is straightforward. The resulting end values for the index level are log-normally distributed again, as Figure 12-5 illustrates. The first four moments are also quite close to those resulting from the static simulation approach:

```
In [19]: I = 10000   ❶
         M = 50   ❷
         dt = T / M   ❸
         S = np.zeros((M + 1, I))   ❹
         S[0] = S0   ❺
         for t in range(1, M + 1):
             S[t] = S[t - 1] * np.exp((r - 0.5 * sigma ** 2) * dt +
                    sigma * math.sqrt(dt) * npr.standard_normal(I))   ❻

In [20]: plt.figure(figsize=(10, 6))
         plt.hist(S[-1], bins=50)
         plt.xlabel('index level')
         plt.ylabel('frequency');
```

❶ The number of paths to be simulated.

❷ The number of time intervals for the discretization.

❸ The length of the time interval in year fractions.

❹ The two-dimensional `ndarray` object for the index levels.

❺ The initial values for the initial point in time $t = 0$.

❻ The simulation via semivectorized expression; the loop is over the points in time starting at $t = 1$ and ending at $t = T$.

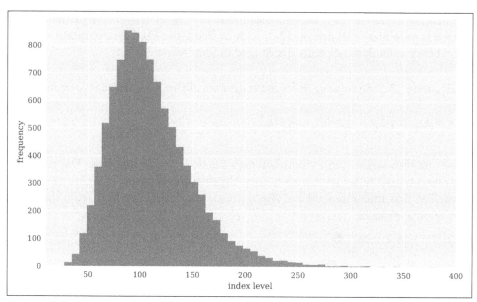

Figure 12-5. Dynamically simulated geometric Brownian motion at maturity

Following is a comparison of the statistics resulting from the dynamic simulation as well as from the static simulation. Figure 12-6 shows the first 10 simulated paths:

```
In [21]: print_statistics(S[-1], ST2)
            statistic      data set 1     data set 2
         -------------------------------------------
                 size     10000.000      10000.000
                  min        27.746         28.230
                  max       382.096        409.110
                 mean       110.423        110.431
                  std        39.179         39.878
                 skew         1.069          1.115
             kurtosis         2.028          2.217

In [22]: plt.figure(figsize=(10, 6))
         plt.plot(S[:, :10], lw=1.5)
         plt.xlabel('time')
         plt.ylabel('index level');
```

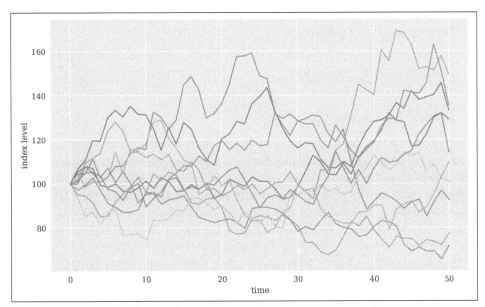

Figure 12-6. Dynamically simulated geometric Brownian motion paths

Using the dynamic simulation approach not only allows us to visualize paths as displayed in Figure 12-6, but also to value options with American/Bermudan exercise or options whose payoff is path-dependent. One gets the full dynamic picture over time, so to say.

Square-root diffusion

Another important class of financial processes is *mean-reverting processes*, which are used to model short rates or volatility processes, for example. A popular and widely used model is the *square-root diffusion*, as proposed by Cox, Ingersoll, and Ross (1985). Equation 12-4 provides the respective SDE.

Equation 12-4. Stochastic differential equation for square-root diffusion

$$dx_t = \kappa(\theta - x_t)dt + \sigma\sqrt{x_t}dZ_t$$

The variables and parameters have the following meaning:

x_t

Process level at date t

κ

Mean-reversion factor

θ

Long-term mean of the process

σ

Constant volatility parameter

Z_t

Standard Brownian motion

It is well known that the values of x_t are chi-squared distributed. However, as stated before, many financial models can be discretized and approximated by using the normal distribution (i.e., a so-called Euler discretization scheme). While the Euler scheme is exact for the geometric Brownian motion, it is biased for the majority of other stochastic processes. Even if there is an exact scheme available—one for the square-root diffusion will be presented later—the use of an Euler scheme might be desirable for numerical and/or computational reasons. Defining $s = t - \Delta t$ and $x^+ \equiv \max(x, 0)$, Equation 12-5 presents such an Euler scheme. This particular one is generally called *full truncation* in the literature (see Hilpisch (2015) for more details and other schemes).

Equation 12-5. Euler discretization for square-root diffusion

$$\tilde{x}_t = \tilde{x}_s + \kappa\left(\theta - \tilde{x}_s^+\right)\Delta t + \sigma\sqrt{\tilde{x}_s^+}\sqrt{\Delta t}z_t$$
$$x_t = \tilde{x}_t^+$$

The square-root diffusion has the convenient and realistic characteristic that the values of x_t remain strictly positive. When discretizing it by an Euler scheme, negative values cannot be excluded. That is the reason why one works always with the positive version of the originally simulated process. In the simulation code, one therefore needs two ndarray objects instead of only one. Figure 12-7 shows the result of the simulation graphically as a histogram:

```
In [23]: x0 = 0.05        ❶
         kappa = 3.0       ❷
         theta = 0.02      ❸
         sigma = 0.1       ❹
         I = 10000
         M = 50
         dt = T / M

In [24]: def srd_euler():
             xh = np.zeros((M + 1, I))
             x = np.zeros_like(xh)
             xh[0] = x0
             x[0] = x0
             for t in range(1, M + 1):
```

```
            xh[t] = (xh[t - 1] +
                     kappa * (theta - np.maximum(xh[t - 1], 0)) * dt +
                     sigma * np.sqrt(np.maximum(xh[t - 1], 0)) *
                     math.sqrt(dt) * npr.standard_normal(I))  ❺
            x = np.maximum(xh, 0)
            return x
        x1 = srd_euler()

In [25]: plt.figure(figsize=(10, 6))
         plt.hist(x1[-1], bins=50)
         plt.xlabel('value')
         plt.ylabel('frequency');
```

❶ The initial value (e.g., for a short rate).

❷ The mean reversion factor.

❸ The long-term mean value.

❹ The volatility factor.

❺ The simulation based on an Euler scheme.

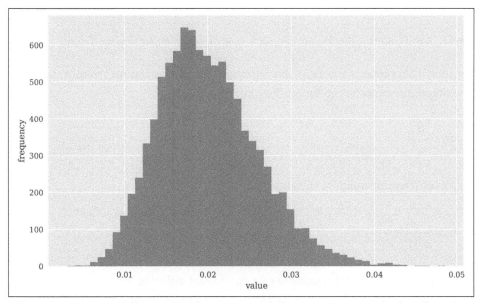

Figure 12-7. Dynamically simulated square-root diffusion at maturity (Euler scheme)

Figure 12-8 then shows the first 10 simulated paths, illustrating the resulting negative average drift (due to $x_0 > \theta$) and the convergence to $\theta = 0.02$:

```
In [26]: plt.figure(figsize=(10, 6))
         plt.plot(x1[:, :10], lw=1.5)
         plt.xlabel('time')
         plt.ylabel('index level');
```

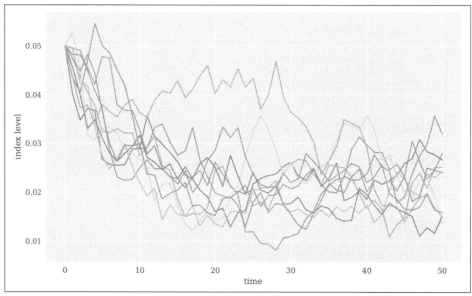

Figure 12-8. Dynamically simulated square-root diffusion paths (Euler scheme)

Equation 12-6 presents the exact discretization scheme for the square-root diffusion based on the noncentral chi-square distribution $\chi_d'^2$ with

$$df = \frac{4\theta\kappa}{\sigma^2}$$

degrees of freedom and noncentrality parameter

$$nc = \frac{4\kappa e^{-\kappa\Delta t}}{\sigma^2\left(1 - e^{-\kappa\Delta t}\right)}x_s$$

Equation 12-6. Exact discretization for square-root diffusion

$$x_t = \frac{\sigma^2\left(1 - e^{-\kappa\Delta t}\right)}{4\kappa}\chi_d'^2\left(\frac{4\kappa e^{-\kappa\Delta t}}{\sigma^2\left(1 - e^{-\kappa\Delta t}\right)}x_s\right)$$

The Python implementation of this discretization scheme is a bit more involved but still quite concise. Figure 12-9 shows the output at maturity of the simulation with the exact scheme as a histogram:

```
In [27]: def srd_exact():
             x = np.zeros((M + 1, I))
             x[0] = x0
             for t in range(1, M + 1):
                 df = 4 * theta * kappa / sigma ** 2      ❶
                 c = (sigma ** 2 * (1 - np.exp(-kappa * dt))) / (4 * kappa)      ❶
                 nc = np.exp(-kappa * dt) / c * x[t - 1]      ❶
                 x[t] = c * npr.noncentral_chisquare(df, nc, size=I)      ❶
             return x
         x2 = srd_exact()
```

```
In [28]: plt.figure(figsize=(10, 6))
         plt.hist(x2[-1], bins=50)
         plt.xlabel('value')
         plt.ylabel('frequency');
```

❶ Exact discretization scheme, making use of npr.noncentral_chisquare().

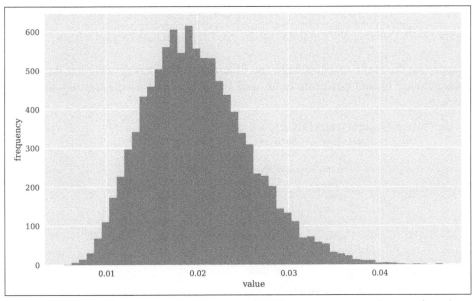

Figure 12-9. Dynamically simulated square-root diffusion at maturity (exact scheme)

Figure 12-10 presents as before the first 10 simulated paths, again displaying the negative average drift and the convergence to θ:

```
In [29]: plt.figure(figsize=(10, 6))
         plt.plot(x2[:, :10], lw=1.5)
```

```
plt.xlabel('time')
plt.ylabel('index level');
```

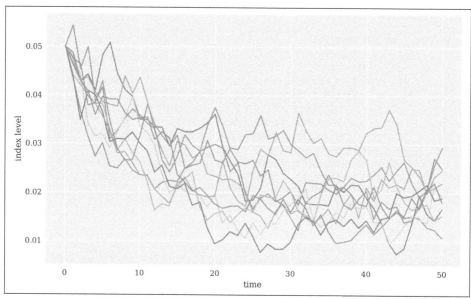

Figure 12-10. Dynamically simulated square-root diffusion paths (exact scheme)

Comparing the main statistics from the different approaches reveals that the biased Euler scheme indeed performs quite well when it comes to the desired statistical properties:

```
In [30]: print_statistics(x1[-1], x2[-1])
            statistic      data set 1      data set 2
         ---------------------------------------------
                 size     10000.000       10000.000
                  min         0.003           0.005
                  max         0.049           0.047
                 mean         0.020           0.020
                  std         0.006           0.006
                 skew         0.529           0.532
             kurtosis         0.289           0.273

In [31]: I = 250000
         %time x1 = srd_euler()
         CPU times: user 1.62 s, sys: 184 ms, total: 1.81 s
         Wall time: 1.08 s

In [32]: %time x2 = srd_exact()
         CPU times: user 3.29 s, sys: 39.8 ms, total: 3.33 s
         Wall time: 1.98 s

In [33]: print_statistics(x1[-1], x2[-1])
         x1 = 0.0; x2 = 0.0
```

statistic	data set 1	data set 2
size	250000.000	250000.000
min	0.002	0.003
max	0.071	0.055
mean	0.020	0.020
std	0.006	0.006
skew	0.563	0.579
kurtosis	0.492	0.520

However, a major difference can be observed in terms of execution speed, since sampling from the noncentral chi-square distribution is more computationally demanding than from the standard normal distribution. The exact scheme takes roughly twice as much time for virtually the same results as with the Euler scheme.

Stochastic volatility

One of the major simplifying assumptions of the Black-Scholes-Merton model is the *constant* volatility. However, volatility in general is neither constant nor deterministic —it is *stochastic*. Therefore, a major advancement with regard to financial modeling was achieved in the early 1990s with the introduction of so-called *stochastic volatility models*. One of the most popular models that fall into that category is that of Heston (1993), which is presented in Equation 12-7.

Equation 12-7. Stochastic differential equations for Heston stochastic volatility model

$$dS_t = rS_t dt + \sqrt{v_t} S_t dZ_t^1$$
$$dv_t = \kappa_v(\theta_v - v_t)dt + \sigma_v \sqrt{v_t} dZ_t^2$$
$$dZ_t^1 dZ_t^2 = \rho$$

The meaning of the variables and parameters can now be inferred easily from the discussion of the geometric Brownian motion and the square-root diffusion. The parameter ρ represents the instantaneous correlation between the two standard Brownian motions Z_t^1, Z_t^2. This allows us to account for a stylized fact called the *leverage effect*, which in essence states that volatility goes up in times of stress (declining markets) and goes down in times of a bull market (rising markets).

Consider the following parameterization of the model. To account for the correlation between the two stochastic processes, one needs to determine the Cholesky decomposition of the correlation matrix:

```
In [34]: S0 = 100.
         r = 0.05
         v0 = 0.1    ❶
         kappa = 3.0
         theta = 0.25
```

```
            sigma = 0.1
            rho = 0.6    ❷
            T = 1.0

In [35]: corr_mat = np.zeros((2, 2))
            corr_mat[0, :] = [1.0, rho]
            corr_mat[1, :] = [rho, 1.0]
            cho_mat = np.linalg.cholesky(corr_mat)   ❸

In [36]: cho_mat    ❸
Out[36]: array([[1. , 0. ],
                [0.6, 0.8]])
```

❶ Initial (instantaneous) volatility value.

❷ Fixed correlation between the two Brownian motions.

❸ Cholesky decomposition and resulting matrix.

Before the start of the simulation of the stochastic processes the whole set of random numbers for both processes is generated, looking to use set 0 for the index process and set 1 for the volatility process. For the volatility process modeled by a square-root diffusion, the Euler scheme is chosen, taking into account the correlation via the Cholesky matrix:

```
In [37]: M = 50
            I = 10000
            dt = T / M

In [38]: ran_num = npr.standard_normal((2, M + 1, I))   ❶

In [39]: v = np.zeros_like(ran_num[0])
            vh = np.zeros_like(v)

In [40]: v[0] = v0
            vh[0] = v0

In [41]: for t in range(1, M + 1):
                ran = np.dot(cho_mat, ran_num[:, t, :])   ❷
                vh[t] = (vh[t - 1] +
                        kappa * (theta - np.maximum(vh[t - 1], 0)) * dt +
                        sigma * np.sqrt(np.maximum(vh[t - 1], 0)) *
                        math.sqrt(dt) * ran[1])   ❸

In [42]: v = np.maximum(vh, 0)
```

❶ Generates the three-dimensional random number data set.

❷ Picks out the relevant random number subset and transforms it via the Cholesky matrix.

❸ Simulates the paths based on an Euler scheme.

The simulation of the index level process also takes into account the correlation and uses the (in this case) exact Euler scheme for the geometric Brownian motion. Figure 12-11 shows the simulation results at maturity as a histogram for both the index level process and the volatility process:

```
In [43]: S = np.zeros_like(ran_num[0])
         S[0] = S0
         for t in range(1, M + 1):
             ran = np.dot(cho_mat, ran_num[:, t, :])
             S[t] = S[t - 1] * np.exp((r - 0.5 * v[t]) * dt +
                             np.sqrt(v[t]) * ran[0] * np.sqrt(dt))

In [44]: fig, (ax1, ax2) = plt.subplots(1, 2, figsize=(10, 6))
         ax1.hist(S[-1], bins=50)
         ax1.set_xlabel('index level')
         ax1.set_ylabel('frequency')
         ax2.hist(v[-1], bins=50)
         ax2.set_xlabel('volatility');
```

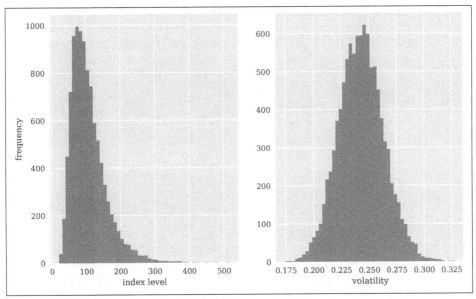

Figure 12-11. Dynamically simulated stochastic volatility process at maturity

This illustrates another advantage of working with the Euler scheme for the square-root diffusion: *correlation is easily and consistently accounted for* since one only draws standard normally distributed random numbers. There is no simple way of achieving the same with a mixed approach (i.e., using Euler for the index and the noncentral chi-square-based exact approach for the volatility process).

An inspection of the first 10 simulated paths of each process (see Figure 12-12) shows that the volatility process is drifting positively on average and that it, as expected, converges to θ = 0.25:

```
In [45]: print_statistics(S[-1], v[-1])
               statistic     data set 1     data set 2
         --------------------------------------------
                    size     10000.000      10000.000
                     min        20.556          0.174
                     max       517.798          0.328
                    mean       107.843          0.243
                     std        51.341          0.020
                    skew         1.577          0.124
                kurtosis         4.306          0.048

In [46]: fig, (ax1, ax2) = plt.subplots(2, 1, sharex=True,
                                         figsize=(10, 6))
         ax1.plot(S[:, :10], lw=1.5)
         ax1.set_ylabel('index level')
         ax2.plot(v[:, :10], lw=1.5)
         ax2.set_xlabel('time')
         ax2.set_ylabel('volatility');
```

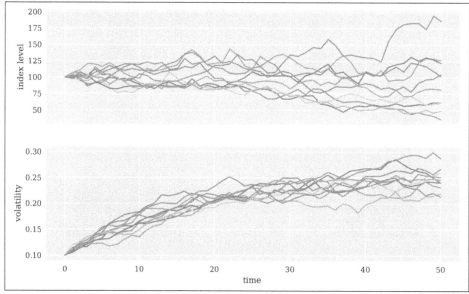

Figure 12-12. Dynamically simulated stochastic volatility process paths

Having a brief look at the statistics for the maturity date for both data sets reveals a pretty high maximum value for the index level process. In fact, this is much higher than a geometric Brownian motion with constant volatility could ever climb, *ceteris paribus*.

Jump diffusion

Stochastic volatility and the leverage effect are stylized (empirical) facts found in a number of markets. Another important stylized fact is the existence of *jumps* in asset prices and, for example, volatility. In 1976, Merton published his jump diffusion model, enhancing the Black-Scholes-Merton setup through a model component generating jumps with log-normal distribution. The risk-neutral SDE is presented in Equation 12-8.

Equation 12-8. Stochastic differential equation for Merton jump diffusion model

$$dS_t = (r - r_j)S_t dt + \sigma S_t dZ_t + J_t S_t dN_t$$

For completeness, here is an overview of the variables' and parameters' meaning:

S_t

    Index level at date t

r

    Constant riskless short rate

$r_j \equiv \lambda \cdot \left(e^{\mu_j + \delta^2/2} - 1 \right)$

    Drift correction for jump to maintain risk neutrality

σ

    Constant volatility of S

Z_t

    Standard Brownian motion

J_t

    Jump at date t with distribution …

-   … $\log (1 + J_t) \approx \mathbf{N}\left(\log (1 + \mu_j) - \frac{\delta^2}{2}, \delta^2 \right)$ with …
-   … $\mathbf{N}$ as the cumulative distribution function of a standard normal random variable

N_t

    Poisson process with intensity λ

Equation 12-9 presents an Euler discretization for the jump diffusion where the z_t^n are standard normally distributed and the y_t are Poisson distributed with intensity λ.

Equation 12-9. Euler discretization for Merton jump diffusion model

$$S_t = S_{t-\Delta t} \left(e^{\left(r - r_j - \sigma^2/2\right)\Delta t + \sigma \sqrt{\Delta t} z_t^1} + \left(e^{\mu_j + \delta z_t^2} - 1 \right) y_t \right)$$

Given the discretization scheme, consider the following numerical parameterization:

```
In [47]: S0 = 100.
         r = 0.05
         sigma = 0.2
         lamb = 0.75    ❶
         mu = -0.6       ❷
         delta = 0.25   ❸
         rj = lamb * (math.exp(mu + 0.5 * delta ** 2) - 1)    ❹

In [48]: T = 1.0
         M = 50
         I = 10000
         dt = T / M
```

❶ The jump intensity.

❷ The mean jump size.

❸ The jump volatility.

❹ The drift correction.

This time, three sets of random numbers are needed. Notice in Figure 12-13 the second peak (bimodal frequency distribution), which is due to the jumps:

```
In [49]: S = np.zeros((M + 1, I))
         S[0] = S0
         sn1 = npr.standard_normal((M + 1, I))    ❶
         sn2 = npr.standard_normal((M + 1, I))    ❶
         poi = npr.poisson(lamb * dt, (M + 1, I))    ❷
         for t in range(1, M + 1, 1):
             S[t] = S[t - 1] * (np.exp((r - rj - 0.5 * sigma ** 2) * dt +
                                sigma * math.sqrt(dt) * sn1[t]) +
                                (np.exp(mu + delta * sn2[t]) - 1) *
                                poi[t])    ❸
             S[t] = np.maximum(S[t], 0)

In [50]: plt.figure(figsize=(10, 6))
         plt.hist(S[-1], bins=50)
         plt.xlabel('value')
         plt.ylabel('frequency');
```

❶ Standard normally distributed random numbers.

❷ Poisson distributed random numbers.

❸ Simulation based on the exact Euler scheme.

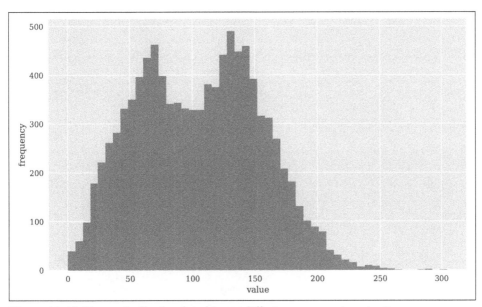

Figure 12-13. Dynamically simulated jump diffusion process at maturity

The negative jumps can also be spotted in the first 10 simulated index level paths, as presented in Figure 12-14:

```
In [51]: plt.figure(figsize=(10, 6))
         plt.plot(S[:, :10], lw=1.5)
         plt.xlabel('time')
         plt.ylabel('index level');
```

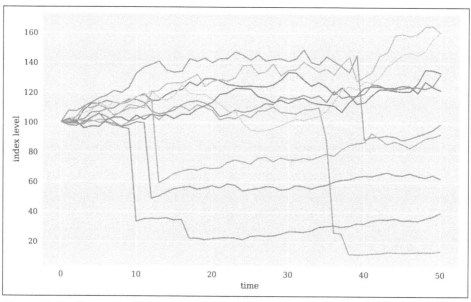

Figure 12-14. Dynamically simulated jump diffusion process paths

Variance Reduction

Because the Python functions used so far generate *pseudo-random* numbers and due to the varying sizes of the samples drawn, the resulting sets of numbers might not exhibit statistics close enough to the expected or desired ones. For example, one would expect a set of standard normally distributed random numbers to show a mean of 0 and a standard deviation of 1. Let us check what statistics different sets of random numbers exhibit. To achieve a realistic comparison, the seed value for the random number generator is fixed:

```
In [52]: print('%15s %15s' % ('Mean', 'Std. Deviation'))
         print(31 * '-')
         for i in range(1, 31, 2):
             npr.seed(100)
             sn = npr.standard_normal(i ** 2 * 10000)
             print('%15.12f %15.12f' % (sn.mean(), sn.std()))
                    Mean   Std. Deviation
         -------------------------------
          0.001150944833  1.006296354600
          0.002841204001  0.995987967146
          0.001998082016  0.997701714233
          0.001322322067  0.997771186968
          0.000592711311  0.998388962646
         -0.000339730751  0.998399891450
         -0.000228109010  0.998657429396
          0.000295768719  0.998877333340
          0.000257107789  0.999284894532
```

```
    -0.000357870642  0.999456401088
    -0.000528443742  0.999617831131
    -0.000300171536  0.999445228838
    -0.000162924037  0.999516059328
     0.000135778889  0.999611052522
     0.000182006048  0.999619405229

In [53]: i ** 2 * 10000
Out[53]: 8410000
```

The results show that the statistics "somehow" get better the larger the number of draws becomes.[2] But they still do not match the desired ones, even in our largest sample with more than 8,000,000 random numbers.

Fortunately, there are easy-to-implement, generic variance reduction techniques available to improve the matching of the first two moments of the (standard) normal distribution. The first technique is to use *antithetic variates*. This approach simply draws only half the desired number of random draws, and adds the same set of random numbers with the opposite sign afterward.[3] For example, if the random number generator (i.e., the respective Python function) draws 0.5, then another number with value –0.5 is added to the set. By construction, the mean value of such a data set must equal zero.

With NumPy this is concisely implemented by using the function np.concatenate(). The following repeats the exercise from before, this time using antithetic variates:

```
In [54]: sn = npr.standard_normal(int(10000 / 2))
         sn = np.concatenate((sn, -sn))  ❶

In [55]: np.shape(sn)  ❷
Out[55]: (10000,)

In [56]: sn.mean()  ❸
Out[56]: 2.842170943040401e-18

In [57]: print('%15s %15s' % ('Mean', 'Std. Deviation'))
         print(31 * "-")
         for i in range(1, 31, 2):
             npr.seed(1000)
             sn = npr.standard_normal(i ** 2 * int(10000 / 2))
             sn = np.concatenate((sn, -sn))
             print("%15.12f %15.12f" % (sn.mean(), sn.std()))
                    Mean   Std. Deviation
         -------------------------------
          0.000000000000  1.009653753942
```

---

2 The approach here is inspired by the Law of Large Numbers.

3 The described method works for symmetric median 0 random variables only, like standard normally distributed random variables, which are almost exclusively used throughout.

```
-0.000000000000   1.000413716783
 0.000000000000   1.002925061201
-0.000000000000   1.000755212673
 0.000000000000   1.001636910076
-0.000000000000   1.000726758438
-0.000000000000   1.001621265149
 0.000000000000   1.001203722778
-0.000000000000   1.000556669784
-0.000000000000   1.000113464185
-0.000000000000   0.999435175324
-0.000000000000   0.999356961431
-0.000000000000   0.999641436845
-0.000000000000   0.999642768905
-0.000000000000   0.999638303451
```

❶ This concatenates the two `ndarray` objects …

❷ … to arrive at the desired number of random numbers.

❸ The resulting mean value is zero (within standard floating-point arithmetic errors).

As immediately noticed, this approach corrects the first moment perfectly—which should not come as a surprise due to the very construction of the data set. However, this approach does not have any influence on the second moment, the standard deviation. Using another variance reduction technique, called *moment matching*, helps correct in one step both the first and second moments:

```
In [58]: sn = npr.standard_normal(10000)

In [59]: sn.mean()
Out[59]: -0.001165998295162494

In [60]: sn.std()
Out[60]: 0.991255920204605

In [61]: sn_new = (sn - sn.mean()) / sn.std()   ❶

In [62]: sn_new.mean()
Out[62]: -2.3803181647963357e-17

In [63]: sn_new.std()
Out[63]: 0.9999999999999999
```

❶ Corrects both the first and second moment in a single step.

By subtracting the mean from every single random number and dividing every single number by the standard deviation, this technique ensures that the set of random numbers matches the desired first and second moments of the standard normal distribution (almost) perfectly.

The following function utilizes the insight with regard to variance reduction techniques and generates standard normal random numbers for process simulation using either two, one, or no variance reduction technique(s):

```
In [64]: def gen_sn(M, I, anti_paths=True, mo_match=True):
             ''' Function to generate random numbers for simulation.

             Parameters
             ==========
             M: int
                 number of time intervals for discretization
             I: int
                 number of paths to be simulated
             anti_paths: boolean
                 use of antithetic variates
             mo_math: boolean
                 use of moment matching
             '''
             if anti_paths is True:
                 sn = npr.standard_normal((M + 1, int(I / 2)))
                 sn = np.concatenate((sn, -sn), axis=1)
             else:
                 sn = npr.standard_normal((M + 1, I))
             if mo_match is True:
                 sn = (sn - sn.mean()) / sn.std()
             return sn
```

Vectorization and Simulation

Vectorization with NumPy is a natural, concise, and efficient approach to implementing Monte Carlo simulation algorithms in Python. However, using NumPy vectorization comes with a larger memory footprint in general. For alternatives that might be equally fast, see Chapter 10.

Valuation

One of the most important applications of Monte Carlo simulation is the *valuation of contingent claims* (options, derivatives, hybrid instruments, etc.). Simply stated, in a risk-neutral world, the value of a contingent claim is the discounted expected payoff under the risk-neutral (martingale) measure. This is the probability measure that makes all risk factors (stocks, indices, etc.) drift at the riskless short rate, making the discounted processes martingales. According to the Fundamental Theorem of Asset Pricing, the existence of such a probability measure is equivalent to the absence of arbitrage.

A financial option embodies the right to buy (*call option*) or sell (*put option*) a specified financial instrument at a given maturity date (*European option*), or over a specified period of time (*American option*), at a given price (*strike price*). Let us first consider the simpler case of European options in terms of valuation.

European Options

The payoff of a European call option on an index at maturity is given by $h(S_T) \equiv \max(S_T - K, 0)$, where S_T is the index level at maturity date T and K is the strike price. Given a, or in complete markets *the*, risk-neutral measure for the relevant stochastic process (e.g., geometric Brownian motion), the price of such an option is given by the formula in Equation 12-10.

Equation 12-10. Pricing by risk-neutral expectation

$$C_0 = e^{-rT} E_0^Q(h(S_T)) = e^{-rT} \int_0^\infty h(s) q(s) ds$$

Chapter 11 sketches how to numerically evaluate an integral by Monte Carlo simulation. This approach is used in the following and applied to Equation 12-10. Equation 12-11 provides the respective Monte Carlo estimator for the European option, where $\tilde{S}_T^i$ is the Tth simulated index level at maturity.

Equation 12-11. Risk-neutral Monte Carlo estimator

$$\widetilde{C_0} = e^{-rT} \frac{1}{I} \sum_{i=1}^I h\left(\tilde{S}_T^i\right)$$

Consider now the following parameterization for the geometric Brownian motion and the valuation function gbm_mcs_stat(), taking as a parameter only the strike price. Here, only the index level at maturity is simulated. As a reference, consider the case with a strike price of $K = 105$:

```
In [65]: S0 = 100.
         r = 0.05
         sigma = 0.25
         T = 1.0
         I = 50000

In [66]: def gbm_mcs_stat(K):
             ''' Valuation of European call option in Black-Scholes-Merton
             by Monte Carlo simulation (of index level at maturity)

             Parameters
             ==========
             K: float
                 (positive) strike price of the option
```

```
Returns
=======
C0: float
    estimated present value of European call option
'''
sn = gen_sn(1, I)
# simulate index level at maturity
ST = S0 * np.exp((r - 0.5 * sigma ** 2) * T
                + sigma * math.sqrt(T) * sn[1])
# calculate payoff at maturity
hT = np.maximum(ST - K, 0)
# calculate MCS estimator
C0 = math.exp(-r * T) * np.mean(hT)
return C0
```

```
In [67]: gbm_mcs_stat(K=105.)   ❶
Out[67]: 10.044221852841922
```

❶ The Monte Carlo estimator value for the European call option.

Next, consider the dynamic simulation approach and allow for European put options in addition to the call option. The function gbm_mcs_dyna() implements the algorithm. The code also compares option price estimates for a call and a put stroke at the same level:

```
In [68]: M = 50   ❶
```

```
In [69]: def gbm_mcs_dyna(K, option='call'):
             ''' Valuation of European options in Black-Scholes-Merton
             by Monte Carlo simulation (of index level paths)

             Parameters
             ==========
             K: float
                 (positive) strike price of the option
             option : string
                 type of the option to be valued ('call', 'put')

             Returns
             =======
             C0: float
                 estimated present value of European call option
             '''
             dt = T / M
             # simulation of index level paths
             S = np.zeros((M + 1, I))
             S[0] = S0
             sn = gen_sn(M, I)
             for t in range(1, M + 1):
                 S[t] = S[t - 1] * np.exp((r - 0.5 * sigma ** 2) * dt
                         + sigma * math.sqrt(dt) * sn[t])
             # case-based calculation of payoff
```

```
            if option == 'call':
                hT = np.maximum(S[-1] - K, 0)
            else:
                hT = np.maximum(K - S[-1], 0)
            # calculation of MCS estimator
            C0 = math.exp(-r * T) * np.mean(hT)
            return C0

In [70]: gbm_mcs_dyna(K=110., option='call')  ❷
Out[70]: 7.950008525028434

In [71]: gbm_mcs_dyna(K=110., option='put')  ❸
Out[71]: 12.629934942682004
```

❶ The number of time intervals for the discretization.

❷ The Monte Carlo estimator value for the European *call* option.

❸ The Monte Carlo estimator value for the European *put* option.

The question is how well these simulation-based valuation approaches perform relative to the benchmark value from the Black-Scholes-Merton valuation formula. To find out, the following code generates respective option values/estimates for a range of strike prices, using the analytical option pricing formula for European calls found in the module bsm_functions.py (see "Python Script" on page 392).

First, we compare the results from the static simulation approach with precise analytical values:

```
In [72]: from bsm_functions import bsm_call_value

In [73]: stat_res = []  ❶
         dyna_res = []  ❶
         anal_res = []  ❶
         k_list = np.arange(80., 120.1, 5.)  ❷
         np.random.seed(100)

In [74]: for K in k_list:
             stat_res.append(gbm_mcs_stat(K))  ❸
             dyna_res.append(gbm_mcs_dyna(K))  ❸
             anal_res.append(bsm_call_value(S0, K, T, r, sigma))  ❸

In [75]: stat_res = np.array(stat_res)  ❹
         dyna_res = np.array(dyna_res)  ❹
         anal_res = np.array(anal_res)  ❹
```

❶ Instantiates empty list objects to collect the results.

❷ Creates an ndarray object containing the range of strike prices.

❸ Simulates/calculates and collects the option values for all strike prices.

❹ Transforms the list objects to ndarray objects.

Figure 12-15 shows the results. All valuation differences are smaller than 1% absolutely. There are both negative and positive value differences:

```
In [76]: plt.figure(figsize=(10, 6))
         fig, (ax1, ax2) = plt.subplots(2, 1, sharex=True, figsize=(10, 6))
         ax1.plot(k_list, anal_res, 'b', label='analytical')
         ax1.plot(k_list, stat_res, 'ro', label='static')
         ax1.set_ylabel('European call option value')
         ax1.legend(loc=0)
         ax1.set_ylim(bottom=0)
         wi = 1.0
         ax2.bar(k_list - wi / 2, (anal_res - stat_res) / anal_res * 100, wi)
         ax2.set_xlabel('strike')
         ax2.set_ylabel('difference in %')
         ax2.set_xlim(left=75, right=125);
Out[76]: <Figure size 720x432 with 0 Axes>
```

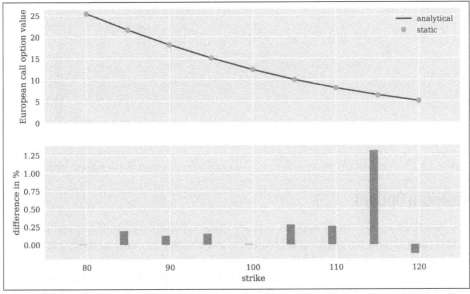

Figure 12-15. Analytical option values vs. Monte Carlo estimators (static simulation)

A similar picture emerges for the dynamic simulation and valuation approach, whose results are reported in Figure 12-16. Again, all valuation differences are smaller than 1% absolutely, with both positive and negative deviations. As a general rule, the quality of the Monte Carlo estimator can be controlled for by adjusting the number of time intervals M used and/or the number of paths I simulated:

```
In [77]: fig, (ax1, ax2) = plt.subplots(2, 1, sharex=True, figsize=(10, 6))
         ax1.plot(k_list, anal_res, 'b', label='analytical')
         ax1.plot(k_list, dyna_res, 'ro', label='dynamic')
         ax1.set_ylabel('European call option value')
         ax1.legend(loc=0)
         ax1.set_ylim(bottom=0)
         wi = 1.0
         ax2.bar(k_list - wi / 2, (anal_res - dyna_res) / anal_res * 100, wi)
         ax2.set_xlabel('strike')
         ax2.set_ylabel('difference in %')
         ax2.set_xlim(left=75, right=125);
```

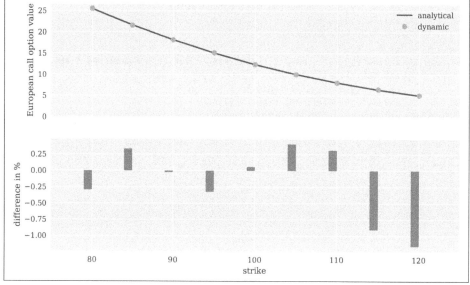

Figure 12-16. Analytical option values vs. Monte Carlo estimators (dynamic simulation)

American Options

The valuation of American options is more involved compared to European options. In this case, an *optimal stopping* problem has to be solved to come up with a fair value of the option. Equation 12-12 formulates the valuation of an American option as such a problem. The problem formulation is already based on a discrete time grid for use with numerical simulation. In a sense, it is therefore more correct to speak of an option value given *Bermudan* exercise. For the time interval converging to zero length, the value of the Bermudan option converges to the one of the American option.

Equation 12-12. American option prices as optimal stopping problem

$$V_0 = \sup_{\tau \in \{0, \Delta t, 2\Delta t, \ldots, T\}} e^{-rT} E_0^Q(h_\tau(S_\tau))$$

The algorithm described in the following is called *Least-Squares Monte Carlo* (LSM) and is from the paper by Longstaff and Schwartz (2001). It can be shown that the value of an American (Bermudan) option at any given date t is given as $V_t(s) = \max(h_t(s), C_t(s))$, where $C_t(s) = \mathbf{E}_t^Q\left(e^{-r\Delta t}V_{t+\Delta t}(S_{t+\Delta t}) \mid S_t = s\right)$ is the so-called *continuation value* of the option given an index level of $S_t = s$.

Consider now that we have simulated I paths of the index level over M time intervals of equal size Δt. Define $Y_{t,i} \equiv e^{-r\Delta t}V_{t+\Delta t,i}$ to be the simulated continuation value for path i at time t. We cannot use this number directly because it would imply perfect foresight. However, we can use the cross section of all such simulated continuation values to estimate the (expected) continuation value by least-squares regression.

Given a set of basis functions b_d, $d = 1, \cdots, D$, the continuation value is then given by the regression estimate $\hat{C}_{t,i} = \sum_{d=1}^{D} \alpha_{d,t}^* \cdot b_d(S_{t,i})$, where the optimal regression parameters α^* are the solution of the least-squares problem stated in Equation 12-13.

Equation 12-13. Least-squares regression for American option valuation

$$\min_{\alpha_{1,t},\dots,\alpha_{D,t}} \frac{1}{I}\sum_{i=1}^{I}\left(Y_{t,i} - \sum_{d=1}^{D} \alpha_{d,t} \cdot b_d(S_{t,i})\right)^2$$

The function `gbm_mcs_amer()` implements the LSM algorithm for both American call and put options:[4]

```
In [78]: def gbm_mcs_amer(K, option='call'):
             ''' Valuation of American option in Black-Scholes-Merton
             by Monte Carlo simulation by LSM algorithm

             Parameters
             ==========
             K: float
                 (positive) strike price of the option
             option: string
                 type of the option to be valued ('call', 'put')

             Returns
             =======
             C0: float
                 estimated present value of American call option
             '''
             dt = T / M
             df = math.exp(-r * dt)
             # simulation of index levels
             S = np.zeros((M + 1, I))
             S[0] = S0
```

---

4 For algorithmic details, refer to Hilpisch (2015).

```
sn = gen_sn(M, I)
for t in range(1, M + 1):
    S[t] = S[t - 1] * np.exp((r - 0.5 * sigma ** 2) * dt
                + sigma * math.sqrt(dt) * sn[t])
# case based calculation of payoff
if option == 'call':
    h = np.maximum(S - K, 0)
else:
    h = np.maximum(K - S, 0)
# LSM algorithm
V = np.copy(h)
for t in range(M - 1, 0, -1):
    reg = np.polyfit(S[t], V[t + 1] * df, 7)
    C = np.polyval(reg, S[t])
    V[t] = np.where(C > h[t], V[t + 1] * df, h[t])
# MCS estimator
C0 = df * np.mean(V[1])
return C0
```

```
In [79]: gbm_mcs_amer(110., option='call')
Out[79]: 7.721705606305352
```

```
In [80]: gbm_mcs_amer(110., option='put')
Out[80]: 13.609997625418051
```

The European value of an option represents a lower bound to the American option's value. The difference is generally called the *early exercise premium*. What follows compares European and American option values for the same range of strikes as before to estimate the early exercise premium, this time with puts:[5]

```
In [81]: euro_res = []
         amer_res = []
```

```
In [82]: k_list = np.arange(80., 120.1, 5.)
```

```
In [83]: for K in k_list:
             euro_res.append(gbm_mcs_dyna(K, 'put'))
             amer_res.append(gbm_mcs_amer(K, 'put'))
```

```
In [84]: euro_res = np.array(euro_res)
         amer_res = np.array(amer_res)
```

Figure 12-17 shows that for the range of strikes chosen the early exercise premium can rise to up to 10%:

```
In [85]: fig, (ax1, ax2) = plt.subplots(2, 1, sharex=True, figsize=(10, 6))
         ax1.plot(k_list, euro_res, 'b', label='European put')
         ax1.plot(k_list, amer_res, 'ro', label='American put')
```

---

5 Since no dividend payments are assumed (having an index in mind), there generally is no early exercise premium for call options (i.e., no incentive to exercise the option early).

```
ax1.set_ylabel('call option value')
ax1.legend(loc=0)
wi = 1.0
ax2.bar(k_list - wi / 2, (amer_res - euro_res) / euro_res * 100, wi)
ax2.set_xlabel('strike')
ax2.set_ylabel('early exercise premium in %')
ax2.set_xlim(left=75, right=125);
```

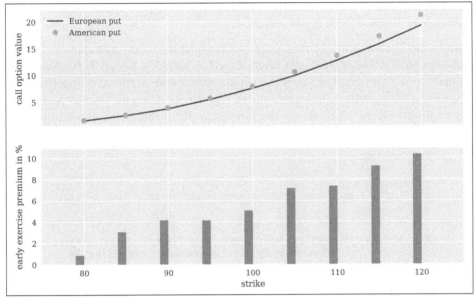

Figure 12-17. European vs. American Monte Carlo estimators

Risk Measures

In addition to valuation, *risk management* is another important application area of stochastic methods and simulation. This section illustrates the calculation/estimation of two of the most common risk measures applied today in the finance industry.

Value-at-Risk

Value-at-risk (VaR) is one of the most widely used risk measures, and a much debated one. Loved by practitioners for its intuitive appeal, it is widely discussed and criticized by many—mainly on theoretical grounds, with regard to its limited ability to capture what is called *tail risk* (more on this shortly). In words, VaR is a number denoted in currency units (e.g., USD, EUR, JPY) indicating a loss (of a portfolio, a single position, etc.) that is not exceeded with some confidence level (probability) over a given period of time.

Consider a stock position, worth 1 million USD today, that has a VaR of 50,000 USD at a confidence level of 99% over a time period of 30 days (one month). This VaR figure says that with a probability of 99% (i.e., in 99 out of 100 cases), the loss to be expected over a period of 30 days will *not exceed* 50,000 USD. However, it does not say anything about the size of the loss once a loss beyond 50,000 USD occurs—i.e., if the maximum loss is 100,000 or 500,000 USD what the probability of such a specific "higher than VaR loss" is. All it says is that there is a 1% probability that a loss of a *minimum of 50,000 USD or higher* will occur.

Assume the Black-Scholes-Merton setup and consider the following parameterization and simulation of index levels at a future date $T = 30/365$ (a period of 30 days). The estimation of VaR figures requires the simulated absolute profits and losses relative to the value of the position today in a sorted manner, i.e., from the severest loss to the largest profit. Figure 12-18 shows the histogram of the simulated absolute performance values:

```
In [86]: S0 = 100
         r = 0.05
         sigma = 0.25
         T = 30 / 365.
         I = 10000

In [87]: ST = S0 * np.exp((r - 0.5 * sigma ** 2) * T +
                 sigma * np.sqrt(T) * npr.standard_normal(I))  ❶

In [88]: R_gbm = np.sort(ST - S0)  ❷

In [89]: plt.figure(figsize=(10, 6))
         plt.hist(R_gbm, bins=50)
         plt.xlabel('absolute return')
         plt.ylabel('frequency');
```

❶ Simulates end-of-period values for the geometric Brownian motion.

❷ Calculates the absolute profits and losses per simulation run and sorts the values.

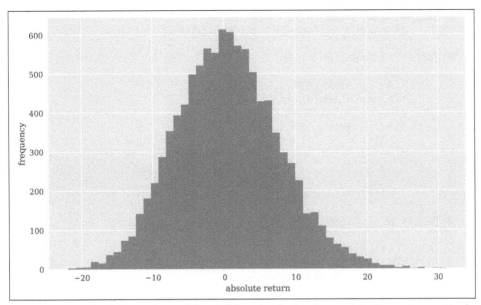

Figure 12-18. Absolute profits and losses from simulation (geometric Brownian motion)

Having the `ndarray` object with the sorted results, the `scs.scoreatpercentile()` function already does the trick. All one has to do is to define the percentiles of interest (in percent values). In the `list` object `percs`, `0.1` translates into a confidence level of 100% – 0.1% = 99.9%. The 30-day VaR given a confidence level of 99.9% in this case is 18.8 currency units, while it is 8.5 at the 90% confidence level:

```
In [91]: percs = [0.01, 0.1, 1., 2.5, 5.0, 10.0]
         var = scs.scoreatpercentile(R_gbm, percs)
         print('%16s %16s' % ('Confidence Level', 'Value-at-Risk'))
         print(33 * '-')
         for pair in zip(percs, var):
             print('%16.2f %16.3f' % (100 - pair[0], -pair[1]))
         Confidence Level     Value-at-Risk
         ---------------------------------
                    99.99            21.814
                    99.90            18.837
                    99.00            15.230
                    97.50            12.816
                    95.00            10.824
                    90.00             8.504
```

As a second example, recall the jump diffusion setup from Merton, which is simulated dynamically. In this case, with the jump component having a negative mean, one sees something like a bimodal distribution for the simulated profits/losses in Figure 12-19. From a normal distribution point of view, one sees a pronounced left *fat tail*:

```
In [92]: dt = 30. / 365 / M
         rj = lamb * (math.exp(mu + 0.5 * delta ** 2) - 1)

In [93]: S = np.zeros((M + 1, I))
         S[0] = S0
         sn1 = npr.standard_normal((M + 1, I))
         sn2 = npr.standard_normal((M + 1, I))
         poi = npr.poisson(lamb * dt, (M + 1, I))
         for t in range(1, M + 1, 1):
             S[t] = S[t - 1] * (np.exp((r - rj - 0.5 * sigma ** 2) * dt
                                + sigma * math.sqrt(dt) * sn1[t])
                                + (np.exp(mu + delta * sn2[t]) - 1)
                                * poi[t])
             S[t] = np.maximum(S[t], 0)

In [94]: R_jd = np.sort(S[-1] - S0)

In [95]: plt.figure(figsize=(10, 6))
         plt.hist(R_jd, bins=50)
         plt.xlabel('absolute return')
         plt.ylabel('frequency');
```

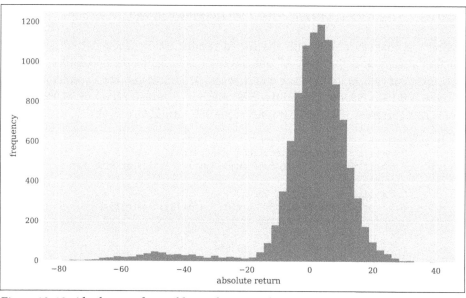

Figure 12-19. Absolute profits and losses from simulation (jump diffusion)

For this process and parameterization, the VaR over 30 days at the 90% level is almost identical as with the geometric Brownian motion, while it is more than *three times* as high at the 99.9% level (70 vs. 18.8 currency units):

```
In [96]: percs = [0.01, 0.1, 1., 2.5, 5.0, 10.0]
         var = scs.scoreatpercentile(R_jd, percs)
         print('%16s %16s' % ('Confidence Level', 'Value-at-Risk'))
         print(33 * '-')
         for pair in zip(percs, var):
             print('%16.2f %16.3f' % (100 - pair[0], -pair[1]))
         Confidence Level    Value-at-Risk
         ---------------------------------
                    99.99           76.520
                    99.90           69.396
                    99.00           55.974
                    97.50           46.405
                    95.00           24.198
                    90.00            8.836
```

This illustrates the problem of capturing the tail risk so often encountered in financial markets by the standard VaR measure.

To further illustrate the point, Figure 12-20 lastly shows the VaR measures for both cases in direct comparison graphically. As the plot reveals, the VaR measures behave completely differently given a range of typical confidence levels:

```
In [97]: percs = list(np.arange(0.0, 10.1, 0.1))
         gbm_var = scs.scoreatpercentile(R_gbm, percs)
         jd_var = scs.scoreatpercentile(R_jd, percs)

In [98]: plt.figure(figsize=(10, 6))
         plt.plot(percs, gbm_var, 'b', lw=1.5, label='GBM')
         plt.plot(percs, jd_var, 'r', lw=1.5, label='JD')
         plt.legend(loc=4)
         plt.xlabel('100 - confidence level [%]')
         plt.ylabel('value-at-risk')
         plt.ylim(ymax=0.0);
```

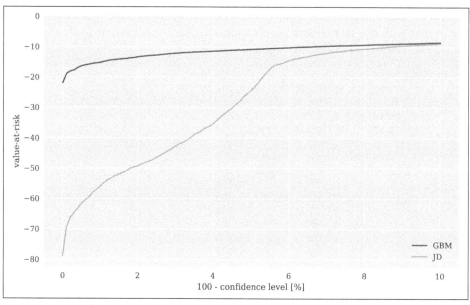

Figure 12-20. Value-at-risk for geometric Brownian motion and jump diffusion

Credit Valuation Adjustments

Other important risk measures are the credit value-at-risk (CVaR) and the credit valuation adjustment (CVA), which is derived from the CVaR. Roughly speaking, CVaR is a measure for the risk resulting from the possibility that a counterparty might not be able to honor its obligations—for example, if the counterparty goes bankrupt. In such a case there are two main assumptions to be made: the *probability of default* and the (average) *loss level*.

To make it specific, consider again the benchmark setup of Black-Scholes-Merton with the parameterization in the following code. In the simplest case, one considers a fixed (average) loss level L and a fixed probability p of default (per year) of a counterparty. Using the Poisson distribution, default scenarios are generated as follows, taking into account that a default can only occur once:

```
In [99]: S0 = 100.
         r = 0.05
         sigma = 0.2
         T = 1.
         I = 100000

In [100]: ST = S0 * np.exp((r - 0.5 * sigma ** 2) * T
                   + sigma * np.sqrt(T) * npr.standard_normal(I))

In [101]: L = 0.5    ❶
```

```
In [102]: p = 0.01   ❷

In [103]: D = npr.poisson(p * T, I)   ❸

In [104]: D = np.where(D > 1, 1, D)   ❹
```

❶ Defines the loss level.

❷ Defines the probability of default.

❸ Simulates default events.

❹ Limits defaults to one such event.

Without default, the risk-neutral value of the future index level should be equal to the current value of the asset today (up to differences resulting from numerical errors). The CVaR and the present value of the asset, adjusted for the credit risk, are given as follows:

```
In [105]: math.exp(-r * T) * np.mean(ST)   ❶
Out[105]: 99.94767178982691

In [106]: CVaR = math.exp(-r * T) * np.mean(L * D * ST)   ❷
          CVaR   ❷
Out[106]: 0.4883560258963962

In [107]: S0_CVA = math.exp(-r * T) * np.mean((1 - L * D) * ST)   ❸
          S0_CVA   ❸
Out[107]: 99.45931576393053

In [108]: S0_adj = S0 - CVaR   ❹
          S0_adj   ❹
Out[108]: 99.5116439741036
```

❶ Discounted average simulated value of the asset at T.

❷ CVaR as the discounted average of the future losses in the case of a default.

❸ Discounted average simulated value of the asset at T, adjusted for the simulated losses from default.

❹ Current price of the asset adjusted by the simulated CVaR.

In this particular simulation example, one observes roughly 1,000 losses due to credit risk, which is to be expected given the assumed default probability of 1% and 100,000 simulated paths. Figure 12-21 shows the complete frequency distribution of the losses due to a default. Of course, in the large majority of cases (i.e., in about 99,000 of the 100,000 cases) there is no loss to observe:

```
In [109]: np.count_nonzero(L * D * ST)  ❶
Out[109]: 978
```

```
In [110]: plt.figure(figsize=(10, 6))
          plt.hist(L * D * ST, bins=50)
          plt.xlabel('loss')
          plt.ylabel('frequency')
          plt.ylim(ymax=175);
```

❶   Number of default events and therewith loss events.

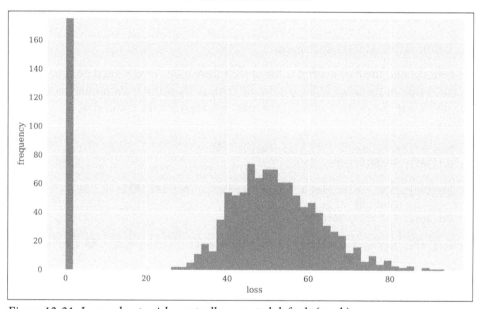

Figure 12-21. Losses due to risk-neutrally expected default (stock)

Consider now the case of a European call option. Its value is about 10.4 currency units at a strike of 100. The CVaR is about 5 cents given the same assumptions with regard to probability of default and loss level:

```
In [111]: K = 100.
          hT = np.maximum(ST - K, 0)
```

```
In [112]: C0 = math.exp(-r * T) * np.mean(hT)  ❶
          C0  ❶
Out[112]: 10.396916492839354
```

```
In [113]: CVaR = math.exp(-r * T) * np.mean(L * D * hT)  ❷
          CVaR  ❷
Out[113]: 0.05159099858923533
```

```
In [114]: C0_CVA = math.exp(-r * T) * np.mean((1 - L * D) * hT)  ❸
```

```
        C0_CVA  ❸
Out[114]: 10.34532549425012
```

❶ The Monte Carlo estimator value for the European call option.

❷ The CVaR as the discounted average of the future losses in the case of a default.

❸ The Monte Carlo estimator value for the European call option, adjusted for the simulated losses from default.

Compared to the case of a regular asset, the option case has somewhat different characteristics. One only sees a little more than 500 losses due to a default, although there are again 1,000 defaults in total. This results from the fact that the payoff of the option at maturity has a high probability of being zero. Figure 12-22 shows that the CVaR for the option has quite a different frequency distribution compared to the regular asset case:

```
In [115]: np.count_nonzero(L * D * hT)  ❶
Out[115]: 538

In [116]: np.count_nonzero(D)  ❷
Out[116]: 978

In [117]: I - np.count_nonzero(hT)  ❸
Out[117]: 44123

In [118]: plt.figure(figsize=(10, 6))
          plt.hist(L * D * hT, bins=50)
          plt.xlabel('loss')
          plt.ylabel('frequency')
          plt.ylim(ymax=350);
```

❶ The number of losses due to default.

❷ The number of defaults.

❸ The number of cases for which the option expires worthless.

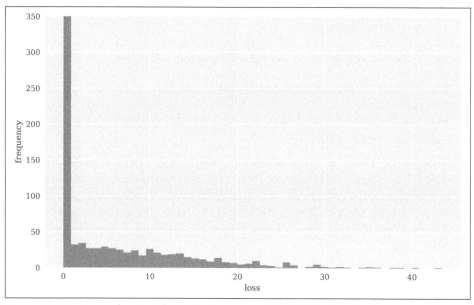

Figure 12-22. Losses due to risk-neutrally expected default (call option)

Python Script

The following presents an implementation of central functions related to the Black-Scholes-Merton model for the analytical pricing of European (call) options. For details of the model, see Black and Scholes (1973) as well as Merton (1973). See Appendix B for an alternative implementation based on a Python class.

```
#
# Valuation of European call options
# in Black-Scholes-Merton model
# incl. vega function and implied volatility estimation
# bsm_functions.py
#
# (c) Dr. Yves J. Hilpisch
# Python for Finance, 2nd ed.
#


def bsm_call_value(S0, K, T, r, sigma):
    ''' Valuation of European call option in BSM model.
    Analytical formula.

    Parameters
    ==========
    S0: float
        initial stock/index level
    K: float
```

```
        strike price
    T: float
        maturity date (in year fractions)
    r: float
        constant risk-free short rate
    sigma: float
        volatility factor in diffusion term

    Returns
    =======
    value: float
        present value of the European call option
    '''
    from math import log, sqrt, exp
    from scipy import stats

    S0 = float(S0)
    d1 = (log(S0 / K) + (r + 0.5 * sigma ** 2) * T) / (sigma * sqrt(T))
    d2 = (log(S0 / K) + (r - 0.5 * sigma ** 2) * T) / (sigma * sqrt(T))
    # stats.norm.cdf --> cumulative distribution function
    #                         for normal distribution
    value = (S0 * stats.norm.cdf(d1, 0.0, 1.0) -
            K * exp(-r * T) * stats.norm.cdf(d2, 0.0, 1.0))
    return value


def bsm_vega(S0, K, T, r, sigma):
    ''' Vega of European option in BSM model.

    Parameters
    ==========
    S0: float
        initial stock/index level
    K: float
        strike price
    T: float
        maturity date (in year fractions)
    r: float
        constant risk-free short rate
    sigma: float
        volatility factor in diffusion term

    Returns
    =======
    vega: float
        partial derivative of BSM formula with respect
        to sigma, i.e. vega

    '''
    from math import log, sqrt
    from scipy import stats
```

```
        S0 = float(S0)
        d1 = (log(S0 / K) + (r + 0.5 * sigma ** 2) * T) / (sigma * sqrt(T))
        vega = S0 * stats.norm.pdf(d1, 0.0, 1.0) * sqrt(T)
        return vega

    # Implied volatility function


    def bsm_call_imp_vol(S0, K, T, r, C0, sigma_est, it=100):
        ''' Implied volatility of European call option in BSM model.

        Parameters
        ==========
        S0: float
            initial stock/index level
        K: float
            strike price
        T: float
            maturity date (in year fractions)
        r: float
            constant risk-free short rate
        sigma_est: float
            estimate of impl. volatility
        it: integer
            number of iterations

        Returns
        =======
        simga_est: float
            numerically estimated implied volatility
        '''
        for i in range(it):
            sigma_est -= ((bsm_call_value(S0, K, T, r, sigma_est) - C0) /
                          bsm_vega(S0, K, T, r, sigma_est))
        return sigma_est
```

Conclusion

This chapter deals with methods and techniques important to the application of
Monte Carlo simulation in finance. In particular, it first shows how to generate
pseudo-random numbers based on different distribution laws. It proceeds with the
simulation of random variables and stochastic processes, which is important in many
financial areas. Two application areas are discussed in some depth in this chapter:
valuation of options with European and American exercise and the estimation of risk
measures like value-at-risk and credit valuation adjustments.

The chapter illustrates that Python in combination with NumPy is well suited to implementing even such computationally demanding tasks as the valuation of American
options by Monte Carlo simulation. This is mainly due to the fact that the majority of

functions and classes of `NumPy` are implemented in C, which leads to considerable speed advantages in general over pure Python code. A further benefit is the compactness and readability of the resulting code due to vectorized operations.

Further Resources

The original article introducing Monte Carlo simulation to finance is:

- Boyle, Phelim (1977). "Options: A Monte Carlo Approach." *Journal of Financial Economics*, Vol. 4, No. 4, pp. 322–338.

Other original papers cited in this chapter are (see also Chapter 18):

- Black, Fischer, and Myron Scholes (1973). "The Pricing of Options and Corporate Liabilities." *Journal of Political Economy*, Vol. 81, No. 3, pp. 638–659.
- Cox, John, Jonathan Ingersoll, and Stephen Ross (1985). "A Theory of the Term Structure of Interest Rates." *Econometrica*, Vol. 53, No. 2, pp. 385–407.
- Heston, Steven (1993). "A Closed-Form Solution for Options with Stochastic Volatility with Applications to Bond and Currency Options." *The Review of Financial Studies*, Vol. 6, No. 2, 327–343.
- Merton, Robert (1973). "Theory of Rational Option Pricing." *Bell Journal of Economics and Management Science*, Vol. 4, pp. 141–183.
- Merton, Robert (1976). "Option Pricing When the Underlying Stock Returns Are Discontinuous." *Journal of Financial Economics*, Vol. 3, No. 3, pp. 125–144.

The following books cover the topics of this chapter in more depth (however, the first one does not cover technical implementation details):

- Glasserman, Paul (2004). *Monte Carlo Methods in Financial Engineering*. New York: Springer.
- Hilpisch, Yves (2015). *Derivatives Analytics with Python* (*http://dawp.tpq.io*). Chichester, England: Wiley Finance.

It took until the turn of the century for an efficient method to value American options by Monte Carlo simulation to finally be published:

- Longstaff, Francis, and Eduardo Schwartz (2001). "Valuing American Options by Simulation: A Simple Least Squares Approach." *Review of Financial Studies*, Vol. 14, No. 1, pp. 113–147.

A broad and in-depth treatment of credit risk is provided in:

- Duffie, Darrell, and Kenneth Singleton (2003). *Credit Risk—Pricing, Measurement, and Management*. Princeton, NJ: Princeton University Press.

I can prove anything by statistics except the truth.

—George Canning

Statistics is a vast field, but the tools and results it provides have become indispensable for finance. This explains the popularity of domain-specific languages like R (*https://www.r-project.org/*) in the finance industry. The more elaborate and complex statistical models become, the more important it is to have available easy-to-use and high-performing computational solutions.

A single chapter in a book like this one cannot do justice to the richness and depth of the field of statistics. Therefore, the approach—as in many other chapters—is to focus on selected topics that seem of importance or that provide a good starting point when it comes to the use of Python for the particular tasks at hand. The chapter has four focal points:

"Normality Tests" on page 398
A large number of important financial models, like modern or mean-variance portfolio theory (MPT) and the capital asset pricing model (CAPM), rest on the assumption that returns of securities are normally distributed. Therefore, this chapter presents approaches to test a given time series for normality of returns.

"Portfolio Optimization" on page 415
MPT can be considered one of the biggest successes of statistics in finance. Starting in the early 1950s with the work of pioneer Harry Markowitz, this theory began to replace people's reliance on judgment and experience with rigorous mathematical and statistical methods when it comes to the investment of money in financial markets. In that sense, it is maybe the first real quantitative model and approach in finance.

"Bayesian Statistics" on page 429

On a conceptual level, Bayesian statistics introduces the notion of *beliefs* of agents and the *updating of beliefs* to statistics. When it comes to linear regression, for example, this might take the form of having a statistical distribution for regression parameters instead of single point estimates (e.g., for the intercept and slope of the regression line). Nowadays, Bayesian methods are widely used in finance, which is why this section illustrates Bayesian methods based on some examples.

"Machine Learning" on page 444

Machine learning (or statistical learning) is based on advanced statistical methods and is considered a subdiscipline of artificial intelligence (AI). Like statistics itself, machine learning offers a rich set of approaches and models to learn from data sets and create predictions based on what is learned. Different algorithms of learning are distinguished, such as those for *supervised learning* or *unsupervised learning*. The types of problems solved by the algorithms differ as well, such as *estimation* or *classification*. The examples presented in this chapter fall in the category of *supervised learning for classification*.

Many aspects in this chapter relate to date and/or time information. Refer to Appendix A for an overview of handling such data with Python, NumPy, and pandas.

Normality Tests

The *normal distribution* can be considered the most important distribution in finance and one of the major statistical building blocks of financial theory. Among others, the following cornerstones of financial theory rest to a large extent on the assumption that returns of a financial instrument are normally distributed:[1]

Portfolio theory

When stock returns are normally distributed, optimal portfolio choice can be cast into a setting where only the (expected) *mean return* and the *variance of the returns* (or the volatility) as well as the *covariances* between different stocks are relevant for an investment decision (i.e., an optimal portfolio composition).

Capital asset pricing model

Again, when stock returns are normally distributed, prices of single stocks can be elegantly expressed in linear relationship to a broad market index; the relationship is generally expressed by a measure for the co-movement of a single stock with the market index called beta or β.

---

[1] Another central assumption is the one of *linearity*. For example, financial markets are assumed, in general, to exhibit a linear relationship between demand, say for shares of a stock, and the price to be paid for the shares. In other words, markets are assumed, in general, to be perfectly liquid in the sense that varying demand does not have any influence on the unit price for a financial instrument.

Efficient markets hypothesis

An *efficient* market is a market where prices reflect all available information, where "all" can be defined more narrowly or more widely (e.g., as in "all publicly available" information vs. including also "only privately available" information). If this hypothesis holds true, then stock prices fluctuate randomly and returns are normally distributed.

Option pricing theory

Brownian motion is *the* benchmark model for the modeling of random price movements of financial instruments; the famous Black-Scholes-Merton option pricing formula uses a geometric Brownian motion as the model for a stock's random price fluctuations over time, leading to log-normally distributed prices and normally distributed returns.

This by far nonexhaustive list underpins the importance of the normality assumption in finance.

Benchmark Case

To set the stage for further analyses, the analysis starts with the geometric Brownian motion as one of the canonical stochastic processes used in financial modeling. The following can be said about the characteristics of paths from a geometric Brownian motion S:

Normal log returns

Log returns $\log \frac{S_t}{S_s} = \log S_t - \log S_s$ between two times $0 < s < t$ are *normally* distributed.

Log-normal values

At any time $t > 0$, the values S_t are *log-normally* distributed.

For what follows, the plotting setup is taken care of first. Then a number of Python packages, including `scipy.stats` (*http://docs.scipy.org/doc/scipy/reference/stats.html*) and `statsmodels.api` (*http://statsmodels.sourceforge.net/stable/*), are imported:

```
In [1]: import math
        import numpy as np
        import scipy.stats as scs
        import statsmodels.api as sm
        from pylab import mpl, plt

In [2]: plt.style.use('seaborn')
        mpl.rcParams['font.family'] = 'serif'
        %matplotlib inline
```

The following uses the function gen_paths() to generate sample Monte Carlo paths for the geometric Brownian motion (see also Chapter 12):

```
In [3]: def gen_paths(S0, r, sigma, T, M, I):
            ''' Generate Monte Carlo paths for geometric Brownian motion.

            Parameters
            ==========
            S0: float
                initial stock/index value
            r: float
                constant short rate
            sigma: float
                constant volatility
            T: float
                final time horizon
            M: int
                number of time steps/intervals
            I: int
                number of paths to be simulated

            Returns
            =======
            paths: ndarray, shape (M + 1, I)
                simulated paths given the parameters
            '''
            dt = T / M
            paths = np.zeros((M + 1, I))
            paths[0] = S0
            for t in range(1, M + 1):
                rand = np.random.standard_normal(I)
                rand = (rand - rand.mean()) / rand.std()        ❶
                paths[t] = paths[t - 1] * np.exp((r - 0.5 * sigma ** 2) * dt +
                                        sigma * math.sqrt(dt) * rand)   ❷
            return paths
```

❶ Matching first and second moment.

❷ Vectorized Euler discretization of geometric Brownian motion.

The simulation is based on the parameterization for the Monte Carlo simulation as shown here, generating, in combination with the function gen_paths(), 250,000 paths with 50 time steps each. Figure 13-1 shows the first 10 simulated paths:

```
In [4]: S0 = 100.         ❶
        r = 0.05          ❷
        sigma = 0.2       ❸
        T = 1.0           ❹
        M = 50            ❺
        I = 250000        ❻
        np.random.seed(1000)
```

```
In [5]: paths = gen_paths(S0, r, sigma, T, M, I)

In [6]: S0 * math.exp(r * T)   ❼
Out[6]: 105.12710963760242

In [7]: paths[-1].mean()   ❼
Out[7]: 105.12645392478755

In [8]: plt.figure(figsize=(10, 6))
        plt.plot(paths[:, :10])
        plt.xlabel('time steps')
        plt.ylabel('index level');
```

❶ Initial value for simulated processes.

❷ Constant short rate.

❸ Constant volatility factor.

❹ Time horizon in year fractions.

❺ Number of time intervals.

❻ Number of simulated processes.

❼ Expected value and average simulated value.

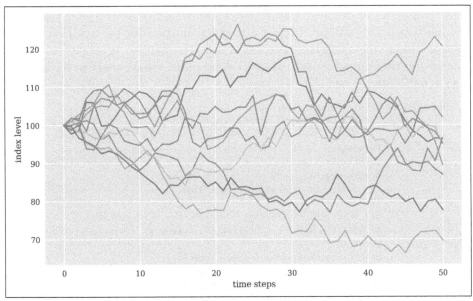

Figure 13-1. Ten simulated paths of geometric Brownian motion

The main interest is in the distribution of the log returns. To this end, an ndarray object with all the log returns is created based on the simulated paths. Here, a single simulated path and the resulting log returns are shown:

```
In [9]: paths[:, 0].round(4)
Out[9]: array([100.    ,  97.821 ,  98.5573, 106.1546, 105.899 ,  99.8363,
               100.0145, 102.6589, 105.6643, 107.1107, 108.7943, 108.2449,
               106.4105, 101.0575, 102.0197, 102.6052, 109.6419, 109.5725,
               112.9766, 113.0225, 112.5476, 114.5585, 109.942 , 112.6271,
               112.7502, 116.3453, 115.0443, 113.9586, 115.8831, 117.3705,
               117.9185, 110.5539, 109.9687, 104.9957, 108.0679, 105.7822,
               105.1585, 104.3304, 108.4387, 105.5963, 108.866 , 108.3284,
               107.0077, 106.0034, 104.3964, 101.0637,  98.3776,  97.135 ,
                95.4254,  96.4271,  96.3386])

In [10]: log_returns = np.log(paths[1:] / paths[:-1])

In [11]: log_returns[:, 0].round(4)
Out[11]: array([-0.022 ,  0.0075,  0.0743, -0.0024, -0.059 ,  0.0018,  0.0261,
                 0.0289,  0.0136,  0.0156, -0.0051, -0.0171, -0.0516,  0.0095,
                 0.0057,  0.0663, -0.0006,  0.0306,  0.0004, -0.0042,  0.0177,
                -0.0411,  0.0241,  0.0011,  0.0314, -0.0112, -0.0095,  0.0167,
                 0.0128,  0.0047, -0.0645, -0.0053, -0.0463,  0.0288, -0.0214,
                -0.0059, -0.0079,  0.0386, -0.0266,  0.0305, -0.0049, -0.0123,
                -0.0094, -0.0153, -0.0324, -0.0269, -0.0127, -0.0178,  0.0104,
                -0.0009])
```

This is something one might experience in financial markets as well: days when one makes a *positive return* on an investment and other days when one is *losing money* relative to the most recent wealth position.

The function print_statistics() is a wrapper function for the scs.describe() function from the scipy.stats subpackage. It mainly generates a better (human-)readable output for such statistics as the mean, the skewness, or the kurtosis of a given (historical or simulated) data set:

```
In [13]: def print_statistics(array):
             ''' Prints selected statistics.

             Parameters
             ==========
             array: ndarray
                 object to generate statistics on
             '''
             sta = scs.describe(array)
             print('%14s %15s' % ('statistic', 'value'))
             print(30 * '-')
             print('%14s %15.5f' % ('size', sta[0]))
             print('%14s %15.5f' % ('min', sta[1][0]))
             print('%14s %15.5f' % ('max', sta[1][1]))
             print('%14s %15.5f' % ('mean', sta[2]))
```

```
                print('%14s %15.5f' % ('std', np.sqrt(sta[3])))
                print('%14s %15.5f' % ('skew', sta[4]))
                print('%14s %15.5f' % ('kurtosis', sta[5]))

In [14]: print_statistics(log_returns.flatten())
              statistic              value
         ---------------------------------
                   size  12500000.00000
                    min        -0.15664
                    max         0.15371
                   mean         0.00060
                    std         0.02828
                   skew         0.00055
               kurtosis         0.00085

In [15]: log_returns.mean() * M + 0.5 * sigma ** 2   ❶
Out[15]: 0.05000000000000005

In [16]: log_returns.std() * math.sqrt(M)   ❷
Out[16]: 0.20000000000000015
```

❶ Annualized mean log return after correction for the Itô term.[2]

❷ Annualized volatility; i.e., annualized standard deviation of log returns.

The data set in this case consists of 12,500,000 data points with the values mainly lying between +/− 0.15. One would expect annualized values of 0.05 for the mean return (after correcting for the Itô term) and 0.2 for the standard deviation (volatility). The annualized values almost match these values perfectly (multiply the mean value by 50 and correct it for the Itô term; multiply the standard deviation by $\sqrt{50}$). One reason for the good match is the use of moment matching for variance reduction when drawing the random numbers (see "Variance Reduction" on page 372).

Figure 13-2 compares the frequency distribution of the simulated log returns with the probability density function (PDF) of the normal distribution given the parameterizations for r and sigma. The function used is norm.pdf() from the scipy.stats subpackage. There is obviously quite a good fit:

```
In [17]: plt.figure(figsize=(10, 6))
         plt.hist(log_returns.flatten(), bins=70, density=True,
                  label='frequency', color='b')
         plt.xlabel('log return')
         plt.ylabel('frequency')
         x = np.linspace(plt.axis()[0], plt.axis()[1])
         plt.plot(x, scs.norm.pdf(x, loc=r / M, scale=sigma / np.sqrt(M)),
```

---

2 For the fundamentals of stochastic and Itô calculus needed in this context, refer to Glasserman (2004).

```
               'r', lw=2.0, label='pdf')  ❶
         plt.legend();
```

❶   Plots the PDF for the assumed parameters scaled to the interval length.

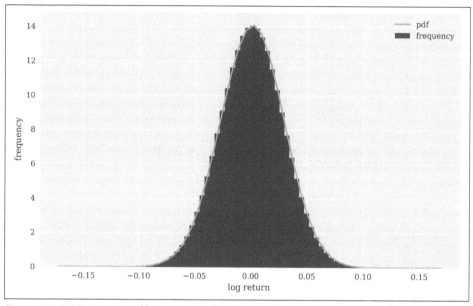

Figure 13-2. Histogram of log returns of geometric Brownian motion and normal density function

Comparing a frequency distribution (histogram) with a theoretical PDF is not the only way to graphically "test" for normality. So-called *quantile-quantile (QQ) plots* are also well suited for this task. Here, sample quantile values are compared to theoretical quantile values. For normally distributed sample data sets, such a plot might look like Figure 13-3, with the absolute majority of the quantile values (dots) lying on a straight line:

```
In [18]: sm.qqplot(log_returns.flatten()[::500], line='s')
         plt.xlabel('theoretical quantiles')
         plt.ylabel('sample quantiles');
```

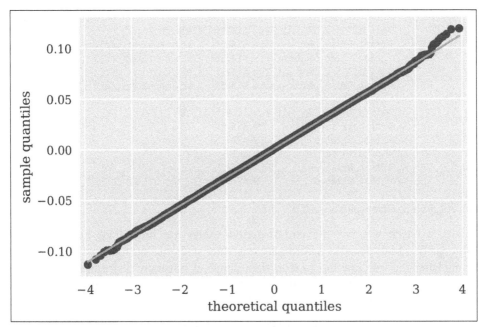

Figure 13-3. Quantile-quantile plot for log returns of geometric Brownian motion

However appealing the graphical approaches might be, they generally cannot replace more rigorous testing procedures. The function `normality_tests()` used in the next example combines three different statistical tests:

Skewness test (`skewtest()`)
  This tests whether the skew of the sample data is "normal" (i.e., has a value close enough to zero).

Kurtosis test (`kurtosistest()`)
  Similarly, this tests whether the kurtosis of the sample data is "normal" (again, close enough to zero).

Normality test (`normaltest()`)
  This combines the other two test approaches to test for normality.

The test values indicate that the log returns of the geometric Brownian motion are indeed normally distributed—i.e., they show p-values of 0.05 or above:

```
In [19]: def normality_tests(arr):
             ''' Tests for normality distribution of given data set.

             Parameters
             ==========
             array: ndarray
                 object to generate statistics on
```

```
'''
print('Skew of data set   %14.3f' % scs.skew(arr))
print('Skew test p-value %14.3f' % scs.skewtest(arr)[1])
print('Kurt of data set   %14.3f' % scs.kurtosis(arr))
print('Kurt test p-value %14.3f' % scs.kurtosistest(arr)[1])
print('Norm test p-value %14.3f' % scs.normaltest(arr)[1])

In [20]: normality_tests(log_returns.flatten())  ❶
         Skew of data set            0.001
         Skew test p-value           0.430
         Kurt of data set            0.001
         Kurt test p-value           0.541
         Norm test p-value           0.607
```

❶ All *p*-values are well above 0.05.

Finally, a check whether the end-of-period values are indeed log-normally distributed. This boils down to a normality test, since one only has to transform the data
by applying the log function to it to then arrive at normally distributed values (or
maybe not). Figure 13-4 plots both the log-normally distributed end-of-period values
and the transformed ones ("log index level"):

```
In [21]: f, (ax1, ax2) = plt.subplots(1, 2, figsize=(10, 6))
         ax1.hist(paths[-1], bins=30)
         ax1.set_xlabel('index level')
         ax1.set_ylabel('frequency')
         ax1.set_title('regular data')
         ax2.hist(np.log(paths[-1]), bins=30)
         ax2.set_xlabel('log index level')
         ax2.set_title('log data')
```

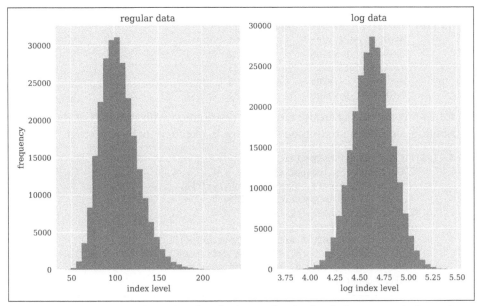

Figure 13-4. Histogram of simulated end-of-period index levels for geometric Brownian motion

The statistics for the data set show expected behavior—for example, a mean value close to 105. The log index level values have skew and kurtosis values close to zero and they show high *p*-values, providing strong support for the normal distribution hypothesis:

```
In [22]: print_statistics(paths[-1])
              statistic            value
         ---------------------------------
                   size    250000.00000
                    min        42.74870
                    max       233.58435
                   mean       105.12645
                    std        21.23174
                   skew         0.61116
               kurtosis         0.65182

In [23]: print_statistics(np.log(paths[-1]))
              statistic            value
         ---------------------------------
                   size    250000.00000
                    min         3.75534
                    max         5.45354
                   mean         4.63517
                    std         0.19998
                   skew        -0.00092
               kurtosis        -0.00327
```

```
In [24]: normality_tests(np.log(paths[-1]))
         Skew of data set           -0.001
         Skew test p-value           0.851
         Kurt of data set           -0.003
         Kurt test p-value           0.744
         Norm test p-value           0.931
```

Figure 13-5 compares again the frequency distribution with the PDF of the normal distribution, showing a pretty good fit (as now is, of course, to be expected):

```
In [25]: plt.figure(figsize=(10, 6))
         log_data = np.log(paths[-1])
         plt.hist(log_data, bins=70, density=True,
                  label='observed', color='b')
         plt.xlabel('index levels')
         plt.ylabel('frequency')
         x = np.linspace(plt.axis()[0], plt.axis()[1])
         plt.plot(x, scs.norm.pdf(x, log_data.mean(), log_data.std()),
                  'r', lw=2.0, label='pdf')
         plt.legend();
```

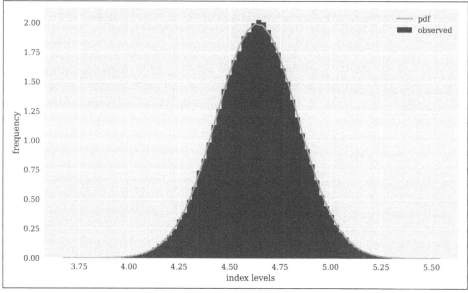

Figure 13-5. Histogram of log index levels of geometric Brownian motion and normal density function

Figure 13-6 also supports the hypothesis that the log index levels are normally distributed:

```
In [26]: sm.qqplot(log_data, line='s')
         plt.xlabel('theoretical quantiles')
         plt.ylabel('sample quantiles');
```

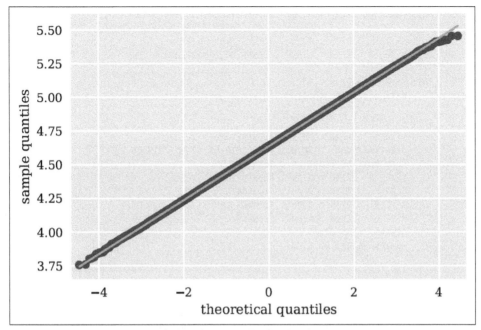

Figure 13-6. Quantile-quantile plot for log index levels of geometric Brownian motion

Normality

The normality assumption with regard to the uncertain returns of financial instruments is central to a number of financial theories. Python provides efficient statistical and graphical means to test whether time series data is normally distributed or not.

Real-World Data

This section analyzes four historical financial time series, two for technology stocks and two for exchange traded funds (ETFs):

- `APPL.O`: Apple Inc. stock price
- `MSFT.O`: Microsoft Inc. stock price
- `SPY`: SPDR S&P 500 ETF Trust
- `GLD`: SPDR Gold Trust

The data management tool of choice is `pandas` (see Chapter 8). Figure 13-7 shows the normalized prices over time:

```
In [27]: import pandas as pd
```

```
In [28]: raw = pd.read_csv('../../source/tr_eikon_eod_data.csv',
                           index_col=0, parse_dates=True).dropna()

In [29]: symbols = ['SPY', 'GLD', 'AAPL.O', 'MSFT.O']

In [30]: data = raw[symbols]
         data = data.dropna()

In [31]: data.info()
         <class 'pandas.core.frame.DataFrame'>
         DatetimeIndex: 2138 entries, 2010-01-04 to 2018-06-29
         Data columns (total 4 columns):
         SPY        2138 non-null float64
         GLD        2138 non-null float64
         AAPL.O     2138 non-null float64
         MSFT.O     2138 non-null float64
         dtypes: float64(4)
         memory usage: 83.5 KB

In [32]: data.head()
Out[32]:              SPY     GLD     AAPL.O  MSFT.O
         Date
         2010-01-04  113.33  109.80  30.572827  30.950
         2010-01-05  113.63  109.70  30.625684  30.960
         2010-01-06  113.71  111.51  30.138541  30.770
         2010-01-07  114.19  110.82  30.082827  30.452
         2010-01-08  114.57  111.37  30.282827  30.660

In [33]: (data / data.iloc[0] * 100).plot(figsize=(10, 6))
```

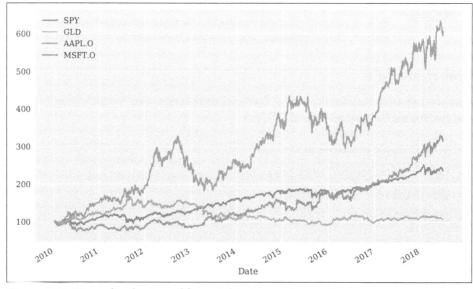

Figure 13-7. Normalized prices of financial instruments over time

Figure 13-8 shows the log returns of the financial instruments as histograms:

```
In [34]: log_returns = np.log(data / data.shift(1))
         log_returns.head()
Out[34]:                    SPY        GLD      AAPL.O      MSFT.O
         Date
         2010-01-04        NaN        NaN        NaN        NaN
         2010-01-05  0.002644  -0.000911   0.001727   0.000323
         2010-01-06  0.000704   0.016365  -0.016034  -0.006156
         2010-01-07  0.004212  -0.006207  -0.001850  -0.010389
         2010-01-08  0.003322   0.004951   0.006626   0.006807

In [35]: log_returns.hist(bins=50, figsize=(10, 8));
```

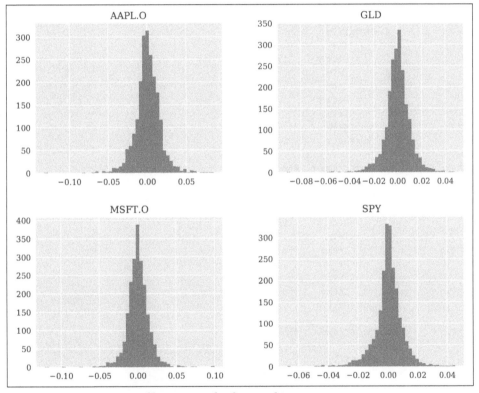

Figure 13-8. Histograms of log returns for financial instruments

As a next step, consider the different statistics for the time series data sets. The kurtosis values seem to be especially far from normal for all four data sets:

```
In [36]: for sym in symbols:
             print('\nResults for symbol {}'.format(sym))
             print(30 * '-')
             log_data = np.array(log_returns[sym].dropna())
             print_statistics(log_data)   ❶
```

```
Results for symbol SPY
-----------------------------
     statistic        value
-----------------------------
          size     2137.00000
           min       -0.06734
           max        0.04545
          mean        0.00041
           std        0.00933
          skew       -0.52189
      kurtosis        4.52432

Results for symbol GLD
-----------------------------
     statistic        value
-----------------------------
          size     2137.00000
           min       -0.09191
           max        0.04795
          mean        0.00004
           std        0.01020
          skew       -0.59934
      kurtosis        5.68423

Results for symbol AAPL.O
-----------------------------
     statistic        value
-----------------------------
          size     2137.00000
           min       -0.13187
           max        0.08502
          mean        0.00084
           std        0.01591
          skew       -0.23510
      kurtosis        4.78964

Results for symbol MSFT.O
-----------------------------
     statistic        value
-----------------------------
          size     2137.00000
           min       -0.12103
           max        0.09941
          mean        0.00054
           std        0.01421
          skew       -0.09117
      kurtosis        7.29106
```

❶ Statistics for time series of financial instruments.

Figure 13-9 shows the QQ plot for the SPY ETF. Obviously, the sample quantile values do not lie on a straight line, indicating "non-normality." On the left and right sides there are many values that lie well below the line and well above the line, respectively. In other words, the time series data exhibits *fat tails*. This term refers to a (frequency) distribution where large negative and positive values are observed more often than a normal distribution would imply. The same conclusions can be drawn from Figure 13-10, which presents the data for the Microsoft stock. There also seems to be evidence for a fat-tailed distribution:

```
In [37]: sm.qqplot(log_returns['SPY'].dropna(), line='s')
         plt.title('SPY')
         plt.xlabel('theoretical quantiles')
         plt.ylabel('sample quantiles');
In [38]: sm.qqplot(log_returns['MSFT.O'].dropna(), line='s')
         plt.title('MSFT.O')
         plt.xlabel('theoretical quantiles')
         plt.ylabel('sample quantiles');
```

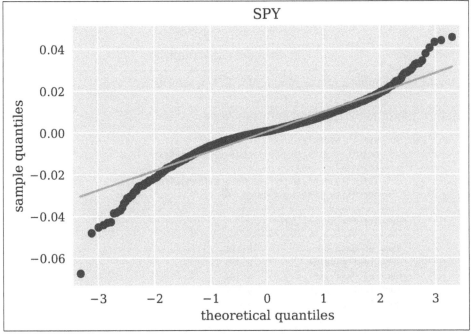

Figure 13-9. Quantile-quantile plot for SPY log returns

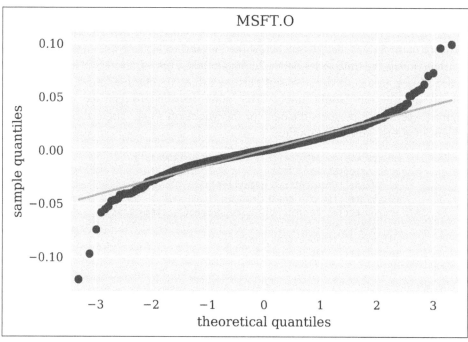

Figure 13-10. Quantile-quantile plot for MSFT.O log returns

This finally leads to the statistical normality tests:

```
In [39]: for sym in symbols:
             print('\nResults for symbol {}'.format(sym))
             print(32 * '-')
             log_data = np.array(log_returns[sym].dropna())
             normality_tests(log_data)  ❶

         Results for symbol SPY
         -------------------------------
         Skew of data set           -0.522
         Skew test p-value           0.000
         Kurt of data set            4.524
         Kurt test p-value           0.000
         Norm test p-value           0.000

         Results for symbol GLD
         -------------------------------
         Skew of data set           -0.599
         Skew test p-value           0.000
         Kurt of data set            5.684
         Kurt test p-value           0.000
         Norm test p-value           0.000

         Results for symbol AAPL.O
         -------------------------------
```

```
Skew of data set          -0.235
Skew test p-value          0.000
Kurt of data set           4.790
Kurt test p-value          0.000
Norm test p-value          0.000

Results for symbol MSFT.O
-------------------------------
Skew of data set          -0.091
Skew test p-value          0.085
Kurt of data set           7.291
Kurt test p-value          0.000
Norm test p-value          0.000
```

❶ Normality test results for the times series of the financial instruments.

The *p*-values of the different tests are all zero, *strongly rejecting the test hypothesis* that the different sample data sets are normally distributed. This shows that the normal assumption for stock market returns and other asset classes—as, for example, embodied in the geometric Brownian motion model—cannot be justified in general and that one might have to use richer models that are able to generate fat tails (e.g., jump diffusion models or models with stochastic volatility).

Portfolio Optimization

Modern or mean-variance portfolio theory is a major cornerstone of financial theory. Based on this theoretical breakthrough the Nobel Prize in Economics was awarded to its inventor, Harry Markowitz, in 1990. Although formulated in the 1950s, it is still a theory taught to finance students and applied in practice today (often with some minor or major modifications).[3] This section illustrates the fundamental principles of the theory.

Chapter 5 in the book by Copeland, Weston, and Shastri (2005) provides an introduction to the formal topics associated with MPT. As pointed out previously, the assumption of normally distributed returns is fundamental to the theory:

> By looking only at mean and variance, we are necessarily assuming that no other statistics are necessary to describe the distribution of end-of-period wealth. Unless investors have a special type of utility function (quadratic utility function), it is necessary to assume that returns have a normal distribution, which can be completely described by mean and variance.

---

3 See Markowitz (1952).

The Data

The analysis and examples that follow use the same financial instruments as before. The basic idea of MPT is to make use of *diversification* to achieve a minimal portfolio risk given a target return level or a maximum portfolio return given a certain level of risk. One would expect such diversification effects for the right combination of a larger number of assets and a certain diversity in the assets. However, to convey the basic ideas and to show typical effects, four financial instruments shall suffice. Figure 13-11 shows the frequency distribution of the log returns for the financial instruments:

```
In [40]: symbols = ['AAPL.O', 'MSFT.O', 'SPY', 'GLD']  ❶

In [41]: noa = len(symbols)  ❷

In [42]: data = raw[symbols]

In [43]: rets = np.log(data / data.shift(1))

In [44]: rets.hist(bins=40, figsize=(10, 8));
```

❶ Four financial instruments for portfolio composition.

❷ Number of financial instruments defined.

The *covariance matrix* for the financial instruments to be invested in is the central piece of the portfolio selection process. pandas has a built-in method to generate the covariance matrix on which the same scaling factor is applied:

```
In [45]: rets.mean() * 252  ❶
Out[45]: AAPL.O    0.212359
         MSFT.O    0.136648
         SPY       0.102928
         GLD       0.009141
         dtype: float64

In [46]: rets.cov() * 252  ❷
Out[46]:             AAPL.O    MSFT.O       SPY       GLD
         AAPL.O    0.063773  0.023427  0.021039  0.001513
         MSFT.O    0.023427  0.050917  0.022244 -0.000347
         SPY       0.021039  0.022244  0.021939  0.000062
         GLD       0.001513 -0.000347  0.000062  0.026209
```

❶ Annualized mean returns.

❷ Annualized covariance matrix.

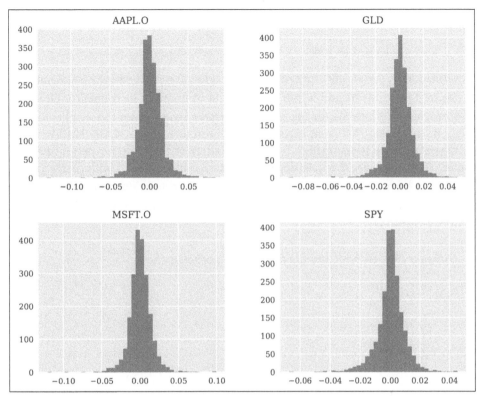

Figure 13-11. Histograms of log returns of financial instruments

The Basic Theory

In what follows, it is assumed that an investor is not allowed to set up short positions in a financial instrument. Only long positions are allowed, which implies that 100% of the investor's wealth has to be divided among the available instruments in such a way that all positions are long (positive) *and* that the positions add up to 100%. Given the four instruments, one could, for example, invest equal amounts into every such instrument—i.e., 25% of the available wealth in each. The following code generates four uniformly distributed random numbers between 0 and 1 and then normalizes the values such that the sum of all values equals 1:

```
In [47]: weights = np.random.random(noa)      ❶
         weights /= np.sum(weights)            ❷

In [48]: weights
Out[48]: array([0.07650728, 0.06021919, 0.63364218, 0.22963135])

In [49]: weights.sum()
Out[49]: 1.0
```

❶ Random portfolio weights …

❷ … normalized to 1 or 100%.

As verified here, the weights indeed add up to 1; i.e., $\sum_I w_i = 1$, where I is the number of financial instruments and $w_i > 0$ is the weight of financial instrument i. Equation 13-1 provides the formula for the *expected portfolio return* given the weights for the single instruments. This is an *expected* portfolio return in the sense that historical mean performance is assumed to be the best estimator for future (expected) performance. Here, the r_i are the state-dependent future returns (vector with return values assumed to be normally distributed) and μ_i is the expected return for instrument i. Finally, w^T is the transpose of the weights vector and μ is the vector of the expected security returns.

Equation 13-1. General formula for expected portfolio return

$$
\begin{aligned}
\mu_p &= \mathrm{E}\!\left(\sum_I w_i r_i\right) \\
&= \sum_I w_i \mathrm{E}(r_i) \\
&= \sum_I w_i \mu_i \\
&= w^T \mu
\end{aligned}
$$

Translated into Python this boils down to a single line of code including annualization:

```
In [50]: np.sum(rets.mean() * weights) * 252   ❶
Out[50]: 0.09179459482057793
```

❶ Annualized portfolio return given the portfolio weights.

The second object of importance in MPT is the *expected portfolio variance*. The covariance between two securities is defined by $\sigma_{ij} = \sigma_{ji} = \mathrm{E}(r_i - \mu_i)(r_j - \mu_j)$. The variance of a security is the special case of the covariance with itself: $\sigma_i^2 = \mathrm{E}((r_i - \mu_i)^2)$. Equation 13-2 provides the covariance matrix for a portfolio of securities (assuming an equal weight of 1 for every security).

$$\Sigma = \begin{bmatrix} \sigma_1^2 & \sigma_{12} & \cdots & \sigma_{1I} \\ \sigma_{21} & \sigma_2^2 & \cdots & \sigma_{2I} \\ \vdots & \vdots & \ddots & \vdots \\ \sigma_{I1} & \sigma_{I2} & \cdots & \sigma_I^2 \end{bmatrix}$$

Figure 13-12. Portfolio covariance matrix

Equipped with the portfolio covariance matrix, Equation 13-2 then provides the formula for the expected portfolio variance.

Equation 13-2. General formula for expected portfolio variance

$$\sigma_p^2 = \mathrm{E}((r - \mu)^2)$$
$$= \sum_{i \in I} \sum_{j \in I} w_i w_j \sigma_{ij}$$
$$= w^T \Sigma w$$

In Python, this all again boils down to a single line of code, making heavy use of NumPy vectorization capabilities. The `np.dot()` function gives the dot product of two vectors/matrices. The `T` attribute or `transpose()` method gives the transpose of a vector or matrix. Given the portfolio variance, the (expected) portfolio standard deviation or volatility $\sigma_p = \sqrt{\sigma_p^2}$ is then only one square root away:

```
In [51]: np.dot(weights.T, np.dot(rets.cov() * 252, weights))  ❶
Out[51]: 0.014763288666485574

In [52]: math.sqrt(np.dot(weights.T, np.dot(rets.cov() * 252, weights)))  ❷
Out[52]: 0.12150427427249452
```

❶ Annualized *portfolio variance* given the portfolio weights.

❷ Annualized *portfolio volatility* given the portfolio weights.

Python and Vectorization

The MPT example shows how efficient it is with Python to translate mathematical concepts, like portfolio return or portfolio variance, into executable, vectorized code (an argument made in Chapter 1).

This mainly completes the tool set for mean-variance portfolio selection. Of paramount interest to investors is what risk-return profiles are possible for a given set of financial instruments, and their statistical characteristics. To this end, the following implements a Monte Carlo simulation (see Chapter 12) to generate random portfolio weight vectors on a larger scale. For every simulated allocation, the code records the resulting expected portfolio return and variance. To simplify the code, two functions, port_ret() and port_vol(), are defined:

```
In [53]: def port_ret(weights):
             return np.sum(rets.mean() * weights) * 252
```

```
In [54]: def port_vol(weights):
             return np.sqrt(np.dot(weights.T, np.dot(rets.cov() * 252, weights)))
```

```
In [55]: prets = []
         pvols = []
         for p in range (2500):    ❶
             weights = np.random.random(noa)    ❶
             weights /= np.sum(weights)    ❶
             prets.append(port_ret(weights))    ❷
             pvols.append(port_vol(weights))    ❷
         prets = np.array(prets)
         pvols = np.array(pvols)
```

❶ Monte Carlo simulation of portfolio weights.

❷ Collects the resulting statistics in list objects.

Figure 13-13 illustrates the results of the Monte Carlo simulation. In addition, it provides results for the Sharpe ratio, defined as $SR \equiv \frac{\mu_p - r_f}{\sigma_p}$—i.e., the expected excess return of the portfolio over the risk-free short rate r_f divided by the expected standard deviation of the portfolio. For simplicity, $r_f \equiv 0$ is assumed:

```
In [56]: plt.figure(figsize=(10, 6))
         plt.scatter(pvols, prets, c=prets / pvols,
                     marker='o', cmap='coolwarm')
         plt.xlabel('expected volatility')
         plt.ylabel('expected return')
         plt.colorbar(label='Sharpe ratio');
```

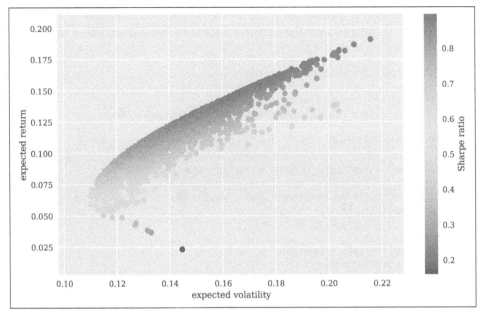

Figure 13-13. Expected return and volatility for random portfolio weights

It is clear by inspection of Figure 13-13 that not all weight distributions perform well when measured in terms of mean and volatility. For example, for a fixed risk level of, say, 15%, there are multiple portfolios that all show different returns. As an investor, one is generally interested in the maximum return given a fixed risk level or the minimum risk given a fixed return expectation. This set of portfolios then makes up the so-called *efficient frontier*. This is derived later in this section.

Optimal Portfolios

This *minimization* function is quite general and allows for equality constraints, inequality constraints, and numerical bounds for the parameters.

First, the *maximization of the Sharpe ratio*. Formally, the negative value of the Sharpe ratio is minimized to derive at the maximum value and the optimal portfolio composition. The constraint is that all parameters (weights) add up to 1. This can be formulated as follows using the conventions of the minimize() function (*http://bit.ly/using_minimize*).[4] The parameter values (weights) are also bound to be between 0 and 1. These values are provided to the minimization function as a tuple of tuples.

---

4 An alternative to np.sum(x) - 1 would be to write np.sum(x) == 1, taking into account that with Python the Boolean True value equals 1 and the False value equals 0.

The only input that is missing for a call of the optimization function is a starting parameter list (initial guess for the weights vector). An equal distribution of weights will do:

```
In [57]: import scipy.optimize as sco

In [58]: def min_func_sharpe(weights):   ❶
             return -port_ret(weights) / port_vol(weights)   ❶

In [59]: cons = ({'type': 'eq', 'fun': lambda x:  np.sum(x) - 1})   ❷

In [60]: bnds = tuple((0, 1) for x in range(noa))   ❸

In [61]: eweights = np.array(noa * [1. / noa,])   ❹
         eweights   ❹
Out[61]: array([0.25, 0.25, 0.25, 0.25])

In [62]: min_func_sharpe(eweights)
Out[62]: -0.8436203363155397
```

❶ Function to be minimized.

❷ Equality constraint.

❸ Bounds for the parameters.

❹ Equal weights vector.

Calling the function returns more than just the optimal parameter values. The results are stored in an object called opts. The main interest lies in getting the optimal portfolio composition. To this end, one can access the results object by providing the key of interest; i.e., x in this case:

```
In [63]: %%time
         opts = sco.minimize(min_func_sharpe, eweights,
                             method='SLSQP', bounds=bnds,
                             constraints=cons)   ❶
         CPU times: user 67.6 ms, sys: 1.94 ms, total: 69.6 ms
         Wall time: 75.2 ms

In [64]: opts   ❷
Out[64]:      fun: -0.8976673894052725
         jac: array([ 8.96826386e-05,  8.30739737e-05, -2.45958567e-04,
         1.92895532e-05])
         message: 'Optimization terminated successfully.'
            nfev: 36
             nit: 6
            njev: 6
          status: 0
         success: True
```

```
        x: array([0.51191354, 0.19126414, 0.25454109, 0.04228123])

In [65]: opts['x'].round(3)    ❸
Out[65]: array([0.512, 0.191, 0.255, 0.042])

In [66]: port_ret(opts['x']).round(3)    ❹
Out[66]: 0.161

In [67]: port_vol(opts['x']).round(3)    ❺
Out[67]: 0.18

In [68]: port_ret(opts['x']) / port_vol(opts['x'])    ❻
Out[68]: 0.8976673894052725
```

❶ The optimization (i.e., minimization of function min_func_sharpe()).

❷ The results from the optimization.

❸ The optimal portfolio weights.

❹ The resulting portfolio return.

❺ The resulting portfolio volatility.

❻ The maximum Sharpe ratio.

Next, the *minimization of the variance* of the portfolio. This is the same as minimizing
the volatility:

```
In [69]: optv = sco.minimize(port_vol, eweights,
                             method='SLSQP', bounds=bnds,
                             constraints=cons)    ❶

In [70]: optv
Out[70]:       fun: 0.1094215526341138
               jac: array([0.11098004, 0.10948556, 0.10939826, 0.10944918])
           message: 'Optimization terminated successfully.'
              nfev: 54
               nit: 9
              njev: 9
            status: 0
           success: True
                 x: array([1.62630326e-18, 1.06170720e-03, 5.43263079e-01,
            4.55675214e-01])

In [71]: optv['x'].round(3)
Out[71]: array([0.   , 0.001, 0.543, 0.456])

In [72]: port_vol(optv['x']).round(3)
Out[72]: 0.109
```

```
In [73]: port_ret(optv['x']).round(3)
Out[73]: 0.06

In [74]: port_ret(optv['x']) / port_vol(optv['x'])
Out[74]: 0.5504173653075624
```

❶ The minimization of the portfolio volatility.

This time, the portfolio is made up of only three financial instruments. This portfolio mix leads to the so-called *minimum volatility* or *minimum variance portfolio*.

Efficient Frontier

The derivation of all optimal portfolios—i.e., all portfolios with minimum volatility for a given target return level (or all portfolios with maximum return for a given risk level)—is similar to the previous optimizations. The only difference is that one has to iterate over multiple starting conditions.

The approach taken is to fix a target return level and to derive for each such level those portfolio weights that lead to the minimum volatility value. For the optimization, this leads to two conditions: one for the target return level, `tret`, and one for the sum of the portfolio weights as before. The boundary values for each parameter stay the same. When iterating over different target return levels (`trets`), one condition for the minimization changes. That is why the constraints dictionary is updated during every loop:

```
In [75]: cons = ({'type': 'eq', 'fun': lambda x:  port_ret(x) - tret},
                  {'type': 'eq', 'fun': lambda x:  np.sum(x) - 1})  ❶

In [76]: bnds = tuple((0, 1) for x in weights)

In [77]: %%time
         trets = np.linspace(0.05, 0.2, 50)
         tvols = []
         for tret in trets:
             res = sco.minimize(port_vol, eweights, method='SLSQP',
                                bounds=bnds, constraints=cons)  ❷
             tvols.append(res['fun'])
         tvols = np.array(tvols)
         CPU times: user 2.6 s, sys: 13.1 ms, total: 2.61 s
         Wall time: 2.66 s
```

❶ The two binding constraints for the efficient frontier.

❷ The minimization of portfolio volatility for different target returns.

Figure 13-14 shows the optimization results. The thick line indicates the optimal portfolios given a certain target return; the dots are, as before, the random portfolios. In addition, the figure shows two larger stars, one for the minimum volatility/

variance portfolio (the leftmost portfolio) and one for the portfolio with the maximum Sharpe ratio:

```
In [78]: plt.figure(figsize=(10, 6))
         plt.scatter(pvols, prets, c=prets / pvols,
                     marker='.', alpha=0.8, cmap='coolwarm')
         plt.plot(tvols, trets, 'b', lw=4.0)
         plt.plot(port_vol(opts['x']), port_ret(opts['x']),
                  'y*', markersize=15.0)
         plt.plot(port_vol(optv['x']), port_ret(optv['x']),
                  'r*', markersize=15.0)
         plt.xlabel('expected volatility')
         plt.ylabel('expected return')
         plt.colorbar(label='Sharpe ratio')
```

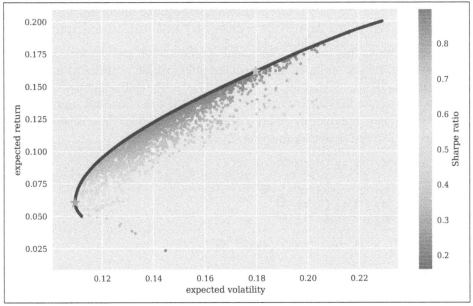

Figure 13-14. Minimum risk portfolios for given return levels (efficient frontier)

The *efficient frontier* is comprised of all optimal portfolios with a higher return than the absolute minimum variance portfolio. These portfolios dominate all other portfolios in terms of expected returns given a certain risk level.

Capital Market Line

In addition to risky financial instruments like stocks or commodities (such as gold), there is in general one universal, riskless investment opportunity available: *cash* or *cash accounts*. In an idealized world, money held in a cash account with a large bank can be considered riskless (e.g., through public deposit insurance schemes). The downside is that such a riskless investment generally yields only a small return, some-times close to zero.

However, taking into account such a riskless asset enhances the efficient investment opportunity set for investors considerably. The basic idea is that investors first determine an efficient portfolio of risky assets and then add the riskless asset to the mix. By adjusting the proportion of the investor's wealth to be invested in the riskless asset it is possible to achieve any risk-return profile that lies on the straight line (in the risk-return space) between the riskless asset and the efficient portfolio.

Which efficient portfolio (out of the many options) is to be taken to invest in optimally? It is the one portfolio where the tangent line of the efficient frontier goes exactly through the risk-return point of the riskless portfolio. For example, consider a riskless interest rate of $r_f = 0.01$. The portfolio is to be found on the efficient frontier for which the tangent goes through the point $(\sigma_f, r_f) = (0, 0.01)$ in risk-return space.

For the calculations that follow, a functional approximation and the first derivative for the efficient frontier are used. Cubic splines interpolation provides such a differentiable functional approximation (see Chapter 11). For the spline interpolation, only those portfolios from the efficient frontier are used. Via this numerical approach it is possible to define a continuously differentiable function f(x) for the efficient frontier and the respective first derivative function df(x):

```
In [79]: import scipy.interpolate as sci

In [80]: ind = np.argmin(tvols)        ❶
         evols = tvols[ind:]           ❷
         erets = trets[ind:]           ❷

In [81]: tck = sci.splrep(evols, erets)     ❸

In [82]: def f(x):
             ''' Efficient frontier function (splines approximation). '''
             return sci.splev(x, tck, der=0)
         def df(x):
             ''' First derivative of efficient frontier function. '''
             return sci.splev(x, tck, der=1)
```

❶ Index position of minimum volatility portfolio.

❷ Relevant portfolio volatility and return values.

❸ Cubic splines interpolation on these values.

What is now to be derived is a linear function $t(x) = a + b \cdot x$ representing the line that passes through the riskless asset in risk-return space and that is tangent to the efficient frontier. Equation 13-3 describes all three conditions that the function $t(x)$ needs to satisfy.

Equation 13-3. Mathematical conditions for capital market line

$$t(x) = a + b \cdot x$$
$$t(0) = r_f \qquad \Leftrightarrow \qquad a = r_f$$
$$t(x) = f(x) \qquad \Leftrightarrow \qquad a + b \cdot x = f(x)$$
$$t'(x) = f'(x) \qquad \Leftrightarrow \qquad b = f'(x)$$

Since there is no closed formula for the efficient frontier or the first derivative of it, one has to solve the system of equations in Equation 13-3 numerically. To this end, define a Python function that returns the values of all three equations given the parameter set $p = (a, b, x)$.

The function sco.fsolve() from scipy.optimize is capable of solving such a system of equations. In addition to the function equations(), an initial parameterization is provided. Note that success or failure of the optimization might depend on the initial parameterization, which therefore has to be chosen carefully—generally by a combination of educated guesses with trial and error:

```
In [83]: def equations(p, rf=0.01):
             eq1 = rf - p[0]    ❶
             eq2 = rf + p[1] * p[2] - f(p[2])   ❶
             eq3 = p[1] - df(p[2])   ❶
             return eq1, eq2, eq3

In [84]: opt = sco.fsolve(equations, [0.01, 0.5, 0.15])   ❷

In [85]: opt   ❸
Out[85]: array([0.01     , 0.84470952, 0.19525391])

In [86]: np.round(equations(opt), 6)   ❹
Out[86]: array([ 0.,  0., -0.])
```

❶ The equations describing the capital market line (CML).

❷ Solving these equations for given initial values.

❸ The optimal parameter values.

❹ The equation values are all zero.

Figure 13-15 presents the results graphically; the star represents the optimal portfolio from the efficient frontier for which the tangent line passes through the riskless asset point $(0, r_f = 0.01)$:

```
In [87]: plt.figure(figsize=(10, 6))
         plt.scatter(pvols, prets, c=(prets - 0.01) / pvols,
                     marker='.', cmap='coolwarm')
         plt.plot(evols, erets, 'b', lw=4.0)
         cx = np.linspace(0.0, 0.3)
         plt.plot(cx, opt[0] + opt[1] * cx, 'r', lw=1.5)
         plt.plot(opt[2], f(opt[2]), 'y*', markersize=15.0)
         plt.grid(True)
         plt.axhline(0, color='k', ls='--', lw=2.0)
         plt.axvline(0, color='k', ls='--', lw=2.0)
         plt.xlabel('expected volatility')
         plt.ylabel('expected return')
         plt.colorbar(label='Sharpe ratio')
```

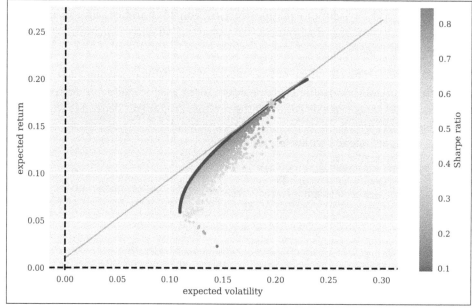

Figure 13-15. Capital market line and tangent portfolio (star) for risk-free rate of 1%

The portfolio weights of the optimal (tangent) portfolio are as follows. Only three of the four assets are in the mix:

```
In [88]: cons = ({'type': 'eq', 'fun': lambda x:  port_ret(x) - f(opt[2])},
                 {'type': 'eq', 'fun': lambda x:  np.sum(x) - 1})   ❶
         res = sco.minimize(port_vol, eweights, method='SLSQP',
                            bounds=bnds, constraints=cons)

In [89]: res['x'].round(3)   ❷
Out[89]: array([0.59 , 0.221, 0.189, 0.   ])

In [90]: port_ret(res['x'])
Out[90]: 0.1749328414905194
```

```
In [91]: port_vol(res['x'])
Out[91]: 0.19525371793918325

In [92]: port_ret(res['x']) / port_vol(res['x'])
Out[92]: 0.8959257899765407
```

❶ Binding constraints for the tangent portfolio (gold star in Figure 13-15).

❷ The portfolio weights for this particular portfolio.

Bayesian Statistics

Bayesian statistics nowadays is widely popular in empirical finance. This chapter can for sure not lay the foundations for all concepts of the field. The reader should therefore consult, if needed, a textbook like the one by Geweke (2005) for a general introduction or Rachev (2008) for one that is financially motivated.

Bayes' Formula

The most common interpretation of Bayes' formula in finance is the *diachronic interpretation*. This mainly states that over time one learns new information about certain variables or parameters of interest, like the mean return of a time series. Equation 13-4 states the theorem formally.

Equation 13-4. Bayes's formula

$$p(H \mid D) = \frac{p(H) \cdot p(D \mid H)}{p(D)}$$

Here, H stands for an event, the hypothesis, and D represents the data an experiment or the real world might present.[5] On the basis of these fundamental notions, one has:

p(H)
    The *prior* probability

p(D)
    The probability for the data under any hypothesis, called the *normalizing constant*

p(D | H)
    The *likelihood* (i.e., the probability) of the data under hypothesis H

---

5 For a Python-based introduction into these and other fundamental concepts of Bayesian statistics, refer to Downey (2013).

$p(H \mid D)$

The *posterior* probability; i.e., after one has seen the data

Consider a simple example. There two boxes, B_1 and B_2. Box B_1 contains 30 black balls and 60 red balls, while box B_2 contains 60 black balls and 30 red balls. A ball is randomly drawn from one of the two boxes. Assume the ball is *black*. What are the probabilities for the hypotheses "H_1: Ball is from box B_1"; and "H_2: Ball is from box B_2," respectively?

Before the random draw of the the ball, both hypotheses are equally likely. After it is clear that the ball is black, one has to update the probability for both hypotheses according to Bayes' formula. Consider hypothesis H_1:

- *Prior*: $p(H_1) = \frac{1}{2}$
- *Normalizing constant*: $p(D) = \frac{1}{2} \cdot \frac{1}{3} + \frac{1}{2} \cdot \frac{2}{3} = \frac{1}{2}$
- *Likelihood*: $p(D \mid H_1) = \frac{1}{3}$

This gives the updated probability for H_1 of $p(H_1 \mid D) = \frac{\frac{1}{2} \cdot \frac{1}{3}}{\frac{1}{2}} = \frac{1}{3}$.

This result also makes sense intuitively. The probability of drawing a black ball from box B_2 is twice as high as that of the same event happening with box B_1. Therefore, having drawn a black ball, the hypothesis H_2 has with $p(H_2 \mid D) = \frac{2}{3}$ an updated probability two times as high as the updated probability for hypothesis H_1.

Bayesian Regression

With PyMC3 the Python ecosystem provides a comprehensive package to technically implement Bayesian statistics and probabilistic programming.

Consider the following example based on noisy data around a straight line.[6] First, a linear ordinary least-squares regression (see Chapter 11) is implemented on the data set, the result of which is visualized in Figure 13-16:

```
In [1]: import numpy as np
        import pandas as pd
        import datetime as dt
        from pylab import mpl, plt

In [2]: plt.style.use('seaborn')
        mpl.rcParams['font.family'] = 'serif'
        np.random.seed(1000)
        %matplotlib inline
```

---

6 Examples originally provided by Thomas Wiecki, one of the main authors of the PyMC3 package.

```
In [3]: x = np.linspace(0, 10, 500)
        y = 4 + 2 * x + np.random.standard_normal(len(x)) * 2

In [4]: reg = np.polyfit(x, y, 1)

In [5]: reg
Out[5]: array([2.03384161, 3.77649234])

In [6]: plt.figure(figsize=(10, 6))
        plt.scatter(x, y, c=y, marker='v', cmap='coolwarm')
        plt.plot(x, reg[1] + reg[0] * x, lw=2.0)
        plt.colorbar()
        plt.xlabel('x')
        plt.ylabel('y')
```

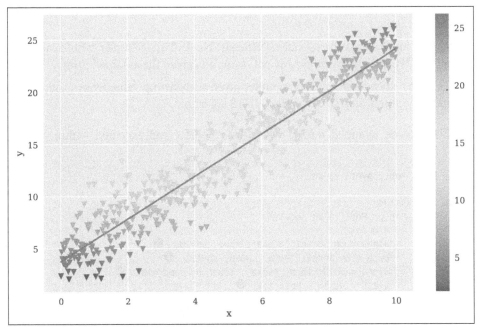

Figure 13-16. Sample data points and regression line

The results of the OLS regression approach are fixed values for the two parameters of the regression line (intercept and slope). Note that the highest-order monomial factor (in this case, the slope of the regression line) is at index level 0 and that the intercept is at index level 1. The original parameters 2 and 4 are not perfectly recovered, but this of course is due to the noise included in the data.

Second, a Bayesian regression making use of the PyMC3 package. Here, it is assumed that the parameters are distributed in a certain way. For example, consider the equation describing the regression line $\hat{y}(x) = \alpha + \beta \cdot x$. Assume now the following *priors*:

- α is normally distributed with mean 0 and a standard deviation of 20.
- β is normally distributed with mean 0 and a standard deviation of 10.

For the *likelihood*, assume a normal distribution with a mean of $\hat{y}(x)$ and a uniformly distributed standard deviation of between 0 and 10.

A major element of Bayesian regression is *Markov chain Monte Carlo (MCMC) sampling* (*https://en.wikipedia.org/wiki/Markov_chain_Monte_Carlo*).[7] In principle, this is the same as drawing balls multiple times from boxes, as in the simple example in the previous section—just in a more systematic, automated way.

For the technical sampling, there are three different functions to call:

- find_MAP() finds the starting point for the sampling algorithm by deriving the *local maximum a posteriori point.*

- NUTS() implements the so-called "efficient No-U-Turn Sampler with dual averaging" (NUTS) algorithm for MCMC sampling given the assumed priors.

- sample() draws a number of samples given the starting value from find_MAP() and the optimal step size from the NUTS algorithm.

All this is to be wrapped into a PyMC3 Model object and executed within a with statement:

```
In [8]: import pymc3 as pm

In [9]: %%time
        with pm.Model() as model:
            # model
            alpha = pm.Normal('alpha', mu=0, sd=20)    ❶
            beta = pm.Normal('beta', mu=0, sd=10)    ❶
            sigma = pm.Uniform('sigma', lower=0, upper=10)    ❶
            y_est = alpha + beta * x    ❷
            likelihood = pm.Normal('y', mu=y_est, sd=sigma,
                                   observed=y)    ❸

            # inference
            start = pm.find_MAP()    ❹
            step = pm.NUTS()    ❺
            trace = pm.sample(100, tune=1000, start=start,
                              progressbar=True)    ❻
        logp = -1,067.8, ||grad|| = 60.354: 100%|████████████| 28/28 [00:00<00:00,
        474.70it/s]
```

---

7 For example, the Monte Carlo algorithms used throughout the book and analyzed in detail in Chapter 12 all generate so-called *Markov chains*, since the immediate next step/value only depends on the current state of the process and not on any other historic state or value.

```
          Only 100 samples in chain.
          Auto-assigning NUTS sampler...
          Initializing NUTS using jitter+adapt_diag...
          Multiprocess sampling (2 chains in 2 jobs)
          NUTS: [sigma, beta, alpha]
          Sampling 2 chains: 100%|███████| 2200/2200 [00:03<00:00,
          690.96draws/s]

          CPU times: user 6.2 s, sys: 1.72 s, total: 7.92 s
          Wall time: 1min 28s

In [10]: pm.summary(trace)  ❼
Out[10]:
                 mean        sd  mc_error   hpd_2.5   hpd_97.5       n_eff      Rhat
         alpha  3.764027  0.174796  0.013177  3.431739  4.070091  152.446951  0.996281
         beta   2.036318  0.030519  0.002230  1.986874  2.094008  106.505590  0.999155
         sigma  2.010398  0.058663  0.004517  1.904395  2.138187  188.643293  0.998547

In [11]: trace[0]  ❽
Out[11]: {'alpha': 3.9303300798212444,
          'beta': 2.0020264758995463,
          'sigma_interval__': -1.3519315719461853,
          'sigma': 2.0555476283253156}
```

❶ Defines the priors.

❷ Specifies the linear regression.

❸ Defines the likelihood.

❹ Finds the starting value by optimization.

❺ Instantiates the MCMC algorithm.

❻ Draws posterior samples using NUTS.

❼ Shows summary statistics from samplings.

❽ Estimates from the first sample.

The three estimates shown are rather close to the original values (4, 2, 2). However, the whole procedure yields more estimates. They are best illustrated with the help of a *trace plot*, as in Figure 13-17—i.e., a plot showing the resulting posterior distribution for the different parameters as well as all single estimates per sample. The posterior distribution gives an intuitive sense about the uncertainty in the estimates:

```
In [12]: pm.traceplot(trace, lines={'alpha': 4, 'beta': 2, 'sigma': 2});
```

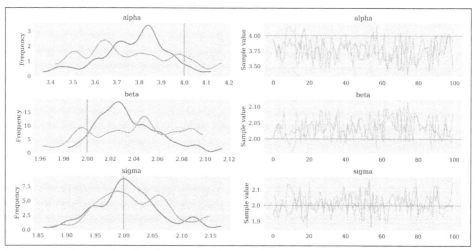

Figure 13-17. Posterior distributions and trace plots

Taking only the `alpha` and `beta` values from the regression, one can draw all resulting regression lines as shown in Figure 13-18:

```
In [13]: plt.figure(figsize=(10, 6))
         plt.scatter(x, y, c=y, marker='v', cmap='coolwarm')
         plt.colorbar()
         plt.xlabel('x')
         plt.ylabel('y')
         for i in range(len(trace)):
             plt.plot(x, trace['alpha'][i] + trace['beta'][i] * x)  ❶
```

❶ Plots single regression lines.

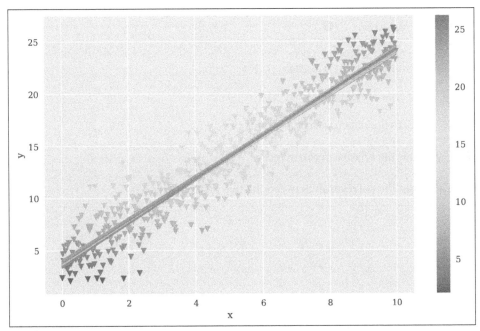

Figure 13-18. Regression lines based on the different estimates

Two Financial Instruments

Having introduced Bayesian regression with PyMC3 based on dummy data, the move
to real financial data is straightforward. The example uses financial time series data
for the two exchange traded funds (ETFs) GLD and GDX (see Figure 13-19):

```
In [14]: raw = pd.read_csv('../../source/tr_eikon_eod_data.csv',
                           index_col=0, parse_dates=True)

In [15]: data = raw[['GDX', 'GLD']].dropna()

In [16]: data = data / data.iloc[0]    ❶

In [17]: data.info()
         <class 'pandas.core.frame.DataFrame'>
         DatetimeIndex: 2138 entries, 2010-01-04 to 2018-06-29
         Data columns (total 2 columns):
         GDX    2138 non-null float64
         GLD    2138 non-null float64
         dtypes: float64(2)
         memory usage: 50.1 KB

In [18]: data.iloc[-1] / data.iloc[0] - 1    ❷
Out[18]: GDX   -0.532383
         GLD    0.080601
         dtype: float64
```

```
In [19]: data.corr()  ❸
Out[19]:            GDX       GLD
         GDX   1.00000   0.71539
         GLD   0.71539   1.00000

In [20]: data.plot(figsize=(10, 6));
```

❶ Normalizes the data to a starting value of 1.

❷ Calculates the relative performances.

❸ Calculates the correlation between the two instruments.

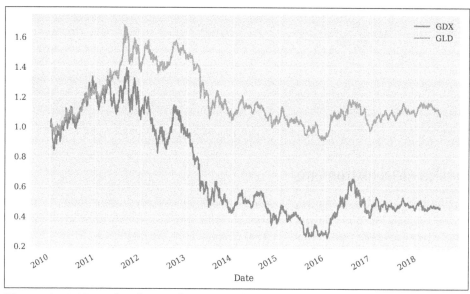

Figure 13-19. Normalized prices for GLD and GDX over time

In what follows, the dates of the single data points are visualized in scatter plots. To this end, the DatetimeIndex object of the DataFrame is transformed to matplotlib dates. Figure 13-20 shows a scatter plot of the time series data, plotting the GLD values against the GDX values and illustrating the dates of each data pair by different colorings:[8]

```
In [21]: data.index[:3]
Out[21]: DatetimeIndex(['2010-01-04', '2010-01-05', '2010-01-06'],
               dtype='datetime64[ns]', name='Date', freq=None)
```

---

8 Note all visualizations here are based on normalized price data and not, as might be better in real-world applications, on return data, for instance.

```
In [22]: mpl_dates = mpl.dates.date2num(data.index.to_pydatetime())   ❶
         mpl_dates[:3]
Out[22]: array([733776., 733777., 733778.])

In [23]: plt.figure(figsize=(10, 6))
         plt.scatter(data['GDX'], data['GLD'], c=mpl_dates,
                     marker='o', cmap='coolwarm')
         plt.xlabel('GDX')
         plt.ylabel('GLD')
         plt.colorbar(ticks=mpl.dates.DayLocator(interval=250),
                      format=mpl.dates.DateFormatter('%d %b %y'));   ❷
```

❶ Converts the DatetimeIndex object to matplotlib dates.

❷ Customizes the color bar for the dates.

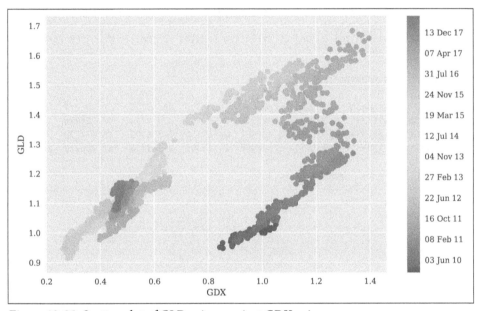

Figure 13-20. Scatter plot of GLD prices against GDX prices

The following code implements a Bayesian regression on the basis of these two time series. The parameterizations are essentially the same as in the previous example with dummy data. Figure 13-21 shows the results from the MCMC sampling procedure given the assumptions about the prior probability distributions for the three parameters:

```
In [24]: with pm.Model() as model:
             alpha = pm.Normal('alpha', mu=0, sd=20)
             beta = pm.Normal('beta', mu=0, sd=20)
             sigma = pm.Uniform('sigma', lower=0, upper=50)
```

```
y_est = alpha + beta * data['GDX'].values

likelihood = pm.Normal('GLD', mu=y_est, sd=sigma,
                        observed=data['GLD'].values)

start = pm.find_MAP()
step = pm.NUTS()
trace = pm.sample(250, tune=2000, start=start,
                  progressbar=True)
logp = 1,493.7, ||grad|| = 188.29: 100%|████████| 27/27 [00:00<00:00,
1609.34it/s]
Only 250 samples in chain.
Auto-assigning NUTS sampler...
Initializing NUTS using jitter+adapt_diag...
Multiprocess sampling (2 chains in 2 jobs)
NUTS: [sigma, beta, alpha]
Sampling 2 chains: 100%|████████| 4500/4500 [00:09<00:00,
465.07draws/s]
The estimated number of effective samples is smaller than 200 for some
parameters.
```

```
In [25]: pm.summary(trace)
Out[25]:
```

	mean	sd	mc_error	hpd_2.5	hpd_97.5	n_eff	Rhat
alpha	0.913335	0.005983	0.000356	0.901586	0.924714	184.264900	1.001855
beta	0.385394	0.007746	0.000461	0.369154	0.398291	215.477738	1.001570
sigma	0.119484	0.001964	0.000098	0.115305	0.123315	312.260213	1.005246

```
In [26]: fig = pm.traceplot(trace)
```

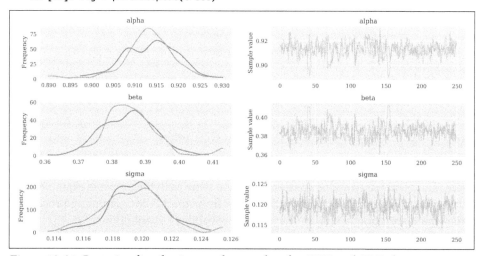

Figure 13-21. Posterior distributions and trace plots for GDX and GLD data

Figure 13-22 adds all the resulting regression lines to the scatter plot from before. However, all the regression lines are pretty close to each other:

```
In [27]: plt.figure(figsize=(10, 6))
         plt.scatter(data['GDX'], data['GLD'], c=mpl_dates,
                     marker='o', cmap='coolwarm')
         plt.xlabel('GDX')
         plt.ylabel('GLD')
         for i in range(len(trace)):
             plt.plot(data['GDX'],
                      trace['alpha'][i] + trace['beta'][i] * data['GDX'])
         plt.colorbar(ticks=mpl.dates.DayLocator(interval=250),
                      format=mpl.dates.DateFormatter('%d %b %y'));
```

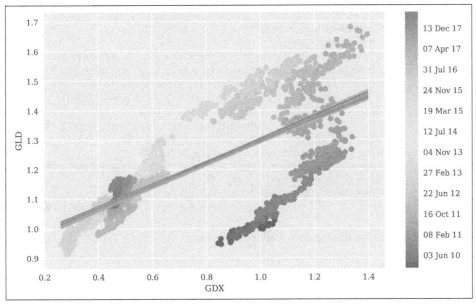

Figure 13-22. Multiple Bayesian regression lines through GDX and GLD data

The figure reveals a major drawback of the regression approach used: the approach does not take into account evolutions over time. That is, the most recent data is treated the same way as the oldest data.

Updating Estimates over Time

As pointed out before, the Bayesian approach in finance is generally most useful when seen as diachronic—i.e., in the sense that new data revealed over time allows for better regressions and estimates through updating or learning.

To incorporate this concept in the current example, assume that the regression parameters are not only random and distributed in some fashion, but that they follow some kind of *random walk* over time. It is the same generalization used when making the transition in financial theory from random variables to stochastic processes (which are essentially ordered sequences of random variables).

To this end, define a new PyMC3 model, this time specifying parameter values as random walks. After having specified the distributions of the random walk parameters, one proceeds with specifying the random walks for alpha and beta. To make the whole procedure more efficient, 50 data points at a time share common coefficients:

```
In [28]: from pymc3.distributions.timeseries import GaussianRandomWalk

In [29]: subsample_alpha = 50
         subsample_beta = 50

In [30]: model_randomwalk = pm.Model()
         with model_randomwalk:
             sigma_alpha = pm.Exponential('sig_alpha', 1. / .02, testval=.1)   ❶
             sigma_beta = pm.Exponential('sig_beta', 1. / .02, testval=.1)     ❶
             alpha = GaussianRandomWalk('alpha', sigma_alpha ** -2,
                             shape=int(len(data) / subsample_alpha))            ❷
             beta = GaussianRandomWalk('beta', sigma_beta ** -2,
                             shape=int(len(data) / subsample_beta))             ❷
             alpha_r = np.repeat(alpha, subsample_alpha)   ❸
             beta_r = np.repeat(beta, subsample_beta)   ❸
             regression = alpha_r + beta_r * data['GDX'].values[:2100]   ❹
             sd = pm.Uniform('sd', 0, 20)   ❺
             likelihood = pm.Normal('GLD', mu=regression, sd=sd,
                             observed=data['GLD'].values[:2100])   ❻
```

❶ Defines priors for the random walk parameters.

❷ Models for the random walks.

❸ Brings the parameter vectors to interval length.

❹ Defines the regression model.

❺ The prior for the standard deviation.

❻ Defines the likelihood with mu from regression results.

All these definitions are a bit more involved than before due to the use of random walks instead of a single random variable. However, the inference steps with the MCMC sampling remain essentially the same. Note, though, that the computational burden increases substantially since the algorithm has to estimate parameters per random walk sample—i.e., 1,950 / 50 = 39 parameter combinations in this case (instead of 1, as before):

```
In [31]: %%time
         import scipy.optimize as sco
         with model_randomwalk:
             start = pm.find_MAP(vars=[alpha, beta],
                                 fmin=sco.fmin_l_bfgs_b)
             step = pm.NUTS(scaling=start)
             trace_rw = pm.sample(250, tune=1000, start=start,
                                  progressbar=True)
         logp = -6,657:    2%||            | 82/5000 [00:00<00:08, 550.29it/s]
         Only 250 samples in chain.
         Auto-assigning NUTS sampler...
         Initializing NUTS using jitter+adapt_diag...
         Multiprocess sampling (2 chains in 2 jobs)
         NUTS: [sd, beta, alpha, sig_beta, sig_alpha]
         Sampling 2 chains: 100%|████████| 2500/2500 [02:48<00:00,  8.59draws/s]

         CPU times: user 27.5 s, sys: 3.68 s, total: 31.2 s
         Wall time: 5min 3s

In [32]: pm.summary(trace_rw).head()   ❶
Out[32]:
                   mean        sd  mc_error  hpd_2.5  hpd_97.5       n_eff  \
    alpha__0   0.673846  0.040224  0.001376  0.592655  0.753034  1004.616544
    alpha__1   0.424819  0.041257  0.001618  0.348102  0.509757   804.760648
    alpha__2   0.456817  0.057200  0.002011  0.321125  0.553173   800.225916
    alpha__3   0.268148  0.044879  0.001725  0.182744  0.352197   724.967532
    alpha__4   0.651465  0.057472  0.002197  0.544076  0.761216   978.073246

                   Rhat
    alpha__0   0.998637
    alpha__1   0.999540
    alpha__2   0.998075
    alpha__3   0.998995
    alpha__4   0.998060
```

❶ The summary statistics per interval (first five and `alpha` only).

Figure 13-23 illustrates the evolution of the regression parameters `alpha` and `beta` over time by plotting a subset of the estimates:

```
In [33]: sh = np.shape(trace_rw['alpha'])   ❶
         sh   ❶
Out[33]: (500, 42)

In [34]: part_dates = np.linspace(min(mpl_dates),
                                  max(mpl_dates), sh[1])   ❷

In [35]: index = [dt.datetime.fromordinal(int(date)) for
                  date in part_dates]   ❷

In [36]: alpha = {'alpha_%i' % i: v for i, v in
                  enumerate(trace_rw['alpha']) if i < 20}   ❸
```

```
In [37]: beta = {'beta_%i' % i: v for i, v in
                 enumerate(trace_rw['beta']) if i < 20} ❸

In [38]: df_alpha = pd.DataFrame(alpha, index=index)  ❸

In [39]: df_beta = pd.DataFrame(beta, index=index)  ❸

In [40]: ax = df_alpha.plot(color='b', style='-.', legend=False,
                            lw=0.7, figsize=(10, 6))
         df_beta.plot(color='r', style='-.', legend=False,
                      lw=0.7, ax=ax)
         plt.ylabel('alpha/beta');
```

❶   Shape of the object with parameter estimates.

❷   Creates a list of dates to match the number of intervals.

❸   Collects the relevant parameter time series in two DataFrame objects.

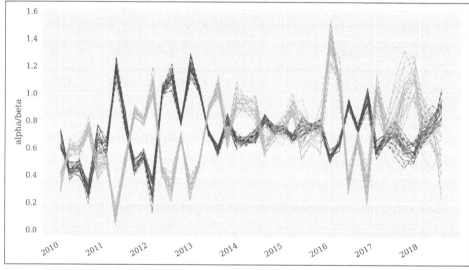

Figure 13-23. Selected parameter estimates over time

Absolute Price Data Versus Relative Return Data

The analyses in this section are based on normalized price data. This is for illustration purposes only, because the respective graphical results are easier to understand and interpret (they are visually "more appealing"). For real-world financial applications one would instead rely on return data, for instance, to ensure stationarity of the time series data.

Using the mean alpha and beta values, Figure 13-24 illustrates how the regression is updated over time. The 39 different regression lines resulting from the mean alpha and beta values are displayed. It is obvious that updating over time improves the regression fit (for the current/most recent data) significantly—in other words, "every time period needs its own regression":

```
In [41]: plt.figure(figsize=(10, 6))
         plt.scatter(data['GDX'], data['GLD'], c=mpl_dates,
                     marker='o', cmap='coolwarm')
         plt.colorbar(ticks=mpl.dates.DayLocator(interval=250),
                      format=mpl.dates.DateFormatter('%d %b %y'))
         plt.xlabel('GDX')
         plt.ylabel('GLD')
         x = np.linspace(min(data['GDX']), max(data['GDX']))
         for i in range(sh[1]):        ❶
             alpha_rw = np.mean(trace_rw['alpha'].T[i])
             beta_rw = np.mean(trace_rw['beta'].T[i])
             plt.plot(x, alpha_rw + beta_rw * x, '--', lw=0.7,
                      color=plt.cm.coolwarm(i / sh[1]))
```

❶ Plots the regression lines for all time intervals of length 50.

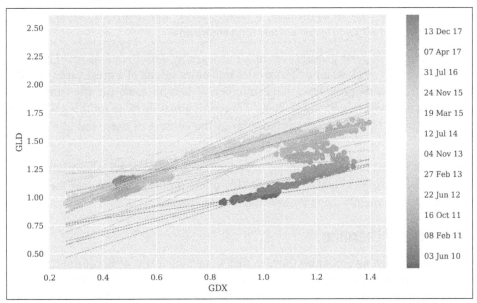

Figure 13-24. Scatter plot with time-dependent regression lines (updated estimates)

This concludes the section on Bayesian statistics. Python offers with PyMC3 a comprehensive package to implement different approaches from Bayesian statistics and probabilistic programming (*https://oreil.ly/2PApqqL*). Bayesian regression in particular is a tool that has become quite popular and important in quantitative finance.

Machine Learning

In finance and many other fields, the "name of the game" these days is *machine learning* (ML). As the following quote puts it:

> Econometrics might be good enough to succeed in financial academia (for now), but succeeding in practice requires ML.
>
> —Marcos López de Prado (2018)

Machine learning subsumes different types of algorithms that are basically able to learn *on their own* certain relationships, patterns, etc. from raw data. "Further Resources" on page 463 lists a number of books that can be consulted on the mathematical and statistical aspects of machine learning approaches and algorithms as well as on topics related to their implementation and practical use. For example, Alpaydin (2016) provides a gentle introduction to the field and gives a nontechnical overview of the types of algorithms that are typically used.

This section takes a rigorously practical approach and focuses on selected implementation aspects only—with a view on the techniques used in Chapter 15. However, the algorithms and techniques introduced can of course be used in many different financial areas and not only in algorithmic trading. The section covers two types of algorithms: *unsupervised* and *supervised* learning algorithms.

One of the most popular packages for machine learning with Python is `scikit-learn` (*http://scikit-learn.org*). It not only provides implementations of a great variety of ML algorithms, but also provides a large number of helpful tools for pre- and post-processing activities related to ML tasks. This section mainly relies on this package. It also uses `TensorFlow` (*http://tensorflow.org*) in the context of deep neural networks (DNNs).

VanderPlas (2016) provides a concise introduction to different ML algorithms based on Python and `scikit-learn`. Albon (2018) offers a number of recipes for typical tasks in ML, also mainly using Python and `scikit-learn`.

Unsupervised Learning

Unsupervised learning embodies the idea that a machine learning algorithm discovers insights from raw data without any further guidance. One such algorithm is the *k-means* clustering algorithm that clusters a raw data set into a number of subsets and assigns these subsets *labels* ("cluster 0," "cluster 1," etc.). Another one is *Gaussian mixture*.[9]

---

[9] For more unsupervised learning algorithms available in `scikit-learn`, see the documentation (*http://scikit-learn.org/stable/unsupervised_learning.html*).

The data

Among other things, scikit-learn allows the creation of sample data sets for different types of ML problems. The following creates a sample data set suited to illustrating *k*-means clustering.

First, some standard imports and configurations:

```
In [1]: import numpy as np
        import pandas as pd
        import datetime as dt
        from pylab import mpl, plt
```

```
In [2]: plt.style.use('seaborn')
        mpl.rcParams['font.family'] = 'serif'
        np.random.seed(1000)
        np.set_printoptions(suppress=True, precision=4)
        %matplotlib inline
```

Second, the creation of the sample data set. Figure 13-25 visualizes the sample data:

```
In [3]: from sklearn.datasets.samples_generator import make_blobs
```

```
In [4]: X, y = make_blobs(n_samples=250, centers=4,
                          random_state=500, cluster_std=1.25)  ❶
```

```
In [5]: plt.figure(figsize=(10, 6))
        plt.scatter(X[:, 0], X[:, 1], s=50);
```

❶ Creates the sample data set for clustering with 250 samples and 4 centers.

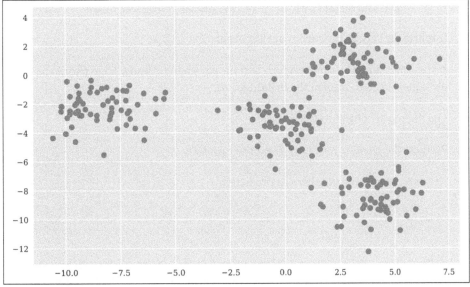

Figure 13-25. Sample data for the application of clustering algorithms

k-means clustering

One of the convenient features of scikit-learn is that it provides a standardized API to apply different kinds of algorithms. The following code shows the basic steps for *k*-means clustering that are repeated for other models afterwards:

- Importing the model class
- Instantiating a model object
- Fitting the model object to some data
- Predicting the outcome given the fitted model for some data

Figure 13-26 shows the results:

```
In [6]: from sklearn.cluster import KMeans    ❶

In [7]: model = KMeans(n_clusters=4, random_state=0)    ❷

In [8]: model.fit(X)    ❸
Out[8]: KMeans(algorithm='auto', copy_x=True, init='k-means++', max_iter=300,
               n_clusters=4, n_init=10, n_jobs=None, precompute_distances='auto',
               random_state=0, tol=0.0001, verbose=0)

In [9]: y_kmeans = model.predict(X)    ❹

In [10]: y_kmeans[:12]    ❺
Out[10]: array([1, 1, 0, 3, 0, 1, 3, 3, 3, 0, 2, 2], dtype=int32)

In [11]: plt.figure(figsize=(10, 6))
         plt.scatter(X[:, 0], X[:, 1], c=y_kmeans,  cmap='coolwarm');
```

❶ Imports the model class from scikit-learn.

❷ Instantiates a model object, given certain parameters; knowledge about the sample data is used to inform the instantiation.

❸ Fits the model object to the raw data.

❹ Predicts the cluster (number) given the raw data.

❺ Shows some cluster numbers as predicted.

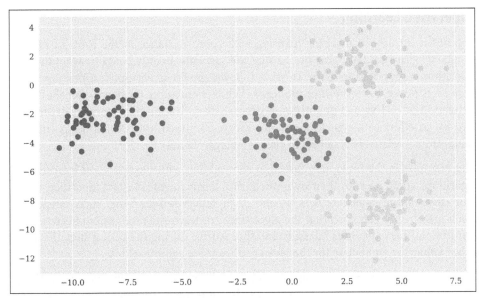

Figure 13-26. Sample data and identified clusters

Gaussian mixture

As an alternative clustering method, consider Gaussian mixture. The application is the same, and with the appropriate parameterization, the results are also the same:

```
In [12]: from sklearn.mixture import GaussianMixture

In [13]: model = GaussianMixture(n_components=4, random_state=0)

In [14]: model.fit(X)
Out[14]: GaussianMixture(covariance_type='full', init_params='kmeans',
             max_iter=100,
             means_init=None, n_components=4, n_init=1, precisions_init=None,
                 random_state=0, reg_covar=1e-06, tol=0.001, verbose=0,
                 verbose_interval=10, warm_start=False, weights_init=None)

In [15]: y_gm = model.predict(X)

In [16]: y_gm[:12]
Out[16]: array([1, 1, 0, 3, 0, 1, 3, 3, 3, 0, 2, 2])

In [17]: (y_gm == y_kmeans).all()  ❶
Out[17]: True
```

❶ The results from *k*-means clustering and Gaussian mixture are the same.

Supervised Learning

Supervised learning is machine learning with some guidance in the form of known results or observed data. This means that the raw data already contains what the ML algorithm is supposed to learn. In what follows, the focus lies on *classification problems* as opposed to *estimation problems*. While estimation problems are about the estimation of real-valued quantities in general, classification problems are characterized by an effort to assign to a certain feature combination a certain class (integer value) from a relatively small set of classes (integer values).

The examples in the previous subsection showed that with unsupervised learning the algorithms come up with their own categorical labels for the clusters identified. With four clusters, the labels are 0, 1, 2, and 3. In supervised learning, such categorical labels are already given, so that the algorithm can learn the *relationship* between the features and the categories (classes). In other words, during the fitting step, the algorithm *knows* the right class for the given feature value combinations.

This subsection illustrates the application of the following classification algorithms: Gaussian Naive Bayes, logistic regression, decision trees, deep neural networks, and support vector machines.[10]

The data

Again, `scikit-learn` allows the creation of an appropriate sample data set to apply classification algorithms. In order to be able to visualize the results, the sample data only contains two real-valued, informative features and a single binary label (a binary label is characterized by two different classes only, 0 and 1). The following code creates the sample data, shows some extracts of the data, and visualizes the data (see Figure 13-27):

```
In [18]: from sklearn.datasets import make_classification

In [19]: n_samples = 100

In [20]: X, y = make_classification(n_samples=n_samples, n_features=2,
                                    n_informative=2, n_redundant=0,
                                    n_repeated=0, random_state=250)

In [21]: X[:5]  ❶
Out[21]: array([[ 1.6876, -0.7976],
                [-0.4312, -0.7606],
                [-1.4393, -1.2363],
                [ 1.118 , -1.8682],
```

---

10 For an overview of the classification algorithms for supervised learning available in `scikit-learn`, refer to the documentation (*http://scikit-learn.org/stable/supervised_learning.html*). Note that many of these algorithms are also available for estimation instead of classification.

```
          [ 0.0502,  0.659 ]])

In [22]: X.shape  ❶
Out[22]: (100, 2)

In [23]: y[:5]  ❷
Out[23]: array([1, 0, 0, 1, 1])

In [24]: y.shape  ❷
Out[24]: (100,)

plt.figure(figsize=(10, 6))
plt.hist(X);
In [25]: plt.figure(figsize=(10, 6))
         plt.scatter(x=X[:, 0], y=X[:, 1], c=y, cmap='coolwarm');
```

❶ The two informative, real-valued features.

❷ The single binary label.

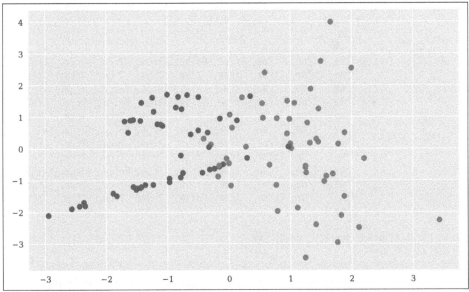

Figure 13-27. Sample data for the application of classification algorithms

Gaussian Naive Bayes

Gaussian Naive Bayes (GNB) is generally considered to be a good baseline algorithm
for a multitude of different classification problems. The application is in line with the
steps outlined in "k-means clustering" on page 446:

```
In [26]: from sklearn.naive_bayes import GaussianNB
         from sklearn.metrics import accuracy_score
```

```
In [27]: model = GaussianNB()

In [28]: model.fit(X, y)
Out[28]: GaussianNB(priors=None, var_smoothing=1e-09)

In [29]: model.predict_proba(X).round(4)[:5]  ❶
Out[29]: array([[0.0041, 0.9959],
                [0.8534, 0.1466],
                [0.9947, 0.0053],
                [0.0182, 0.9818],
                [0.5156, 0.4844]])

In [30]: pred = model.predict(X)  ❷

In [31]: pred  ❷
Out[31]: array([1, 0, 0, 1, 0, 0, 1, 1, 1, 0, 0, 0, 0, 0, 1, 1, 0, 1, 0, 1, 1,
         0,
         0, 0, 1, 0, 0, 0, 0, 0, 1, 0, 1, 1, 0, 0, 0, 1, 1, 0, 1, 0, 0, 0,
         0, 1, 1, 1, 0, 0, 1, 0, 0, 1, 1, 1, 1, 1, 0, 0, 0, 1, 1, 1, 1, 0,
         0, 0, 1, 0, 0, 1, 1, 1, 1, 1, 1, 0, 0, 1, 0, 0, 0, 1, 0, 0, 0, 1,
         0, 1, 1, 1, 1, 1, 0, 0, 0, 0, 0, 0])

In [32]: pred == y  ❸
Out[32]: array([ True,  True,  True,  True, False,  True,  True,  True,  True,
                 True, False,  True,  True,  True,  True,  True,  True,  True,
                 True,  True,  True,  True, False, False, False,  True,  True,
                 True,  True,  True,  True,  True,  True, False,  True,  True,
                 True,  True,  True,  True,  True,  True,  True,  True,  True,
                 True,  True,  True,  True,  True,  True, False,  True, False,
                 True,  True,  True,  True,  True,  True,  True,  True,  True,
                 True,  True, False,  True,  True,  True,  True,  True,  True,
                 True,  True,  True,  True,  True,  True, False,  True, False,
                 True,  True,  True,  True,  True,  True,  True,  True,  True,
                 True,  True, False,  True, False,  True,  True,  True,  True,
                 True])

In [33]: accuracy_score(y, pred)  ❹
Out[33]: 0.87
```

❶ Shows the probabilities that the algorithm assigns to each class after fitting.

❷ Based on the probabilities, predicts the binary classes for the data set.

❸ Compares the predicted classes with the real ones.

❹ Calculates the accuracy score given the predicted values.

Figure 13-28 visualizes the correct and false predictions from GNB:

```
In [34]: Xc = X[y == pred]  ❶
         Xf = X[y != pred]  ❷
```

```
In [35]: plt.figure(figsize=(10, 6))
         plt.scatter(x=Xc[:, 0], y=Xc[:, 1], c=y[y == pred],
                 marker='o', cmap='coolwarm')    ❶
         plt.scatter(x=Xf[:, 0], y=Xf[:, 1], c=y[y != pred],
                 marker='x', cmap='coolwarm')    ❷
```

❶ Selects the *correct* predictions and plots them.

❷ Selects the *false* predictions and plots them.

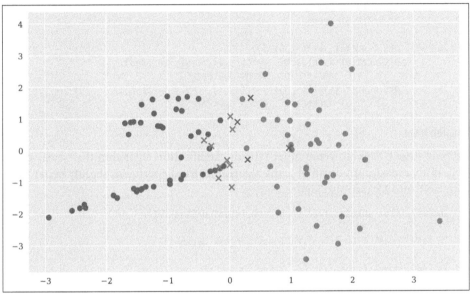

Figure 13-28. Correct (dots) and false predictions (crosses) from GNB

Logistic regression

Logistic regression (LR) is a fast and scalable classification algorithm. The accuracy in this particular case is slightly better than with GNB:

```
In [36]: from sklearn.linear_model import LogisticRegression

In [37]: model = LogisticRegression(C=1, solver='lbfgs')

In [38]: model.fit(X, y)
Out[38]: LogisticRegression(C=1, class_weight=None, dual=False,
             fit_intercept=True,
                 intercept_scaling=1, max_iter=100, multi_class='warn',
                 n_jobs=None, penalty='l2', random_state=None, solver='lbfgs',
                 tol=0.0001, verbose=0, warm_start=False)

In [39]: model.predict_proba(X).round(4)[:5]
```

```
Out[39]: array([[0.011 , 0.989 ],
                [0.7266, 0.2734],
                [0.971 , 0.029 ],
                [0.04  , 0.96  ],
                [0.4843, 0.5157]])

In [40]: pred = model.predict(X)

In [41]: accuracy_score(y, pred)
Out[41]: 0.9

In [42]: Xc = X[y == pred]
         Xf = X[y != pred]

In [43]: plt.figure(figsize=(10, 6))
         plt.scatter(x=Xc[:, 0], y=Xc[:, 1], c=y[y == pred],
                     marker='o', cmap='coolwarm')
         plt.scatter(x=Xf[:, 0], y=Xf[:, 1], c=y[y != pred],
                     marker='x', cmap='coolwarm');
```

Decision trees

Decision trees (DTs) are yet another type of classification algorithm that scales quite
well. With a maximum depth of 1, the algorithm already performs slightly better than
both GNB and LR (see also Figure 13-29):

```
In [44]: from sklearn.tree import DecisionTreeClassifier

In [45]: model = DecisionTreeClassifier(max_depth=1)

In [46]: model.fit(X, y)
Out[46]: DecisionTreeClassifier(class_weight=None, criterion='gini',
             max_depth=1,
                         max_features=None, max_leaf_nodes=None,
                         min_impurity_decrease=0.0, min_impurity_split=None,
                         min_samples_leaf=1, min_samples_split=2,
             min_weight_fraction_leaf=0.0, presort=False, random_state=None,
                         splitter='best')

In [47]: model.predict_proba(X).round(4)[:5]
Out[47]: array([[0.08, 0.92],
                [0.92, 0.08],
                [0.92, 0.08],
                [0.08, 0.92],
                [0.08, 0.92]])

In [48]: pred = model.predict(X)

In [49]: accuracy_score(y, pred)
Out[49]: 0.92

In [50]: Xc = X[y == pred]
```

```
        Xf = X[y != pred]

In [51]: plt.figure(figsize=(10, 6))
         plt.scatter(x=Xc[:, 0], y=Xc[:, 1], c=y[y == pred],
                 marker='o', cmap='coolwarm')
         plt.scatter(x=Xf[:, 0], y=Xf[:, 1], c=y[y != pred],
                 marker='x', cmap='coolwarm');
```

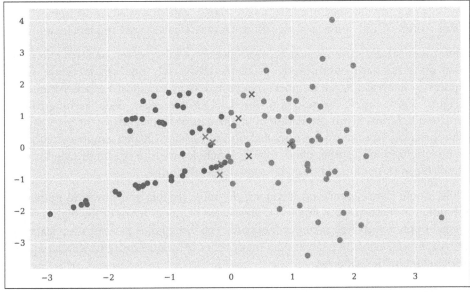

Figure 13-29. Correct (dots) and false predictions (crosses) from DT (max_depth=1)

However, increasing the maximum depth parameter for the decision tree allows one
to reach a perfect result:

```
In [52]: print('{:>8s} | {:8s}'.format('depth', 'accuracy'))
         print(20 * '-')
         for depth in range(1, 7):
             model = DecisionTreeClassifier(max_depth=depth)
             model.fit(X, y)
             acc = accuracy_score(y, model.predict(X))
             print('{:8d} | {:8.2f}'.format(depth, acc))
         depth | accuracy
         --------------------
                1 |    0.92
                2 |    0.92
                3 |    0.94
                4 |    0.97
                5 |    0.99
                6 |    1.00
```

Deep neural networks

Deep neural networks (DNNs) are considered to be among the most powerful—but also computationally demanding—algorithms for both estimation and classification. The open sourcing of the `TensorFlow` package by Google and related success stories are in part responsible for their popularity. DNNs are capable of learning and modeling complex nonlinear relationships. Although their origins date back to the 1970s, they only recently have become feasible on a large scale due to advances in hardware (CPUs, GPUs, TPUs), numerical algorithms, and related software implementations.

While other ML algorithms, such as linear models of LR type, can be fitted efficiently based on a standard optimization problem, DNNs rely on *deep learning*, which requires in general a large number of repeated steps to adjust certain parameters (weights) and compare the results to the data. In that sense, deep learning can be compared to Monte Carlo simulation in mathematical finance where the price of, say, a European call option can be estimated on the basis of 100,000 simulated paths for the underlying. On the other hand, the Black-Scholes-Merton option pricing formula is available in closed form and can be evaluated analytically.

While Monte Carlo simulation is among the most flexible and powerful numerical techniques in mathematical finance, there's a cost to pay in terms of the high computational burden and large memory footprint. The same holds true for deep learning, which is more flexible in general than many other ML algorithms but which requires greater computational power.

DNNs with scikit-learn. Although it is quite different in nature, `scikit-learn` provides the same API for its `MLPClassifier` algorithm class,[11] which is a DNN model, as for the other ML algorithms used before. With just two so-called *hidden layers* it reaches a perfect result on the test data (the hidden layers are what make deep learning out of simple learning—e.g., "learning" weights in the context of a linear regression instead of using OLS regression to derive them directly):

```
In [53]: from sklearn.neural_network import MLPClassifier

In [54]: model = MLPClassifier(solver='lbfgs', alpha=1e-5,
                               hidden_layer_sizes=2 * [75], random_state=10)

In [55]: %time model.fit(X, y)
         CPU times: user 537 ms, sys: 14.2 ms, total: 551 ms
         Wall time: 340 ms

Out[55]: MLPClassifier(activation='relu', alpha=1e-05, batch_size='auto',
              beta_1=0.9,
```

---

11 For more details and available parameters, refer to the documentation on the multi-layer perceptron classifier (*http://scikit-learn.org/stable/modules/generated/sklearn.neural_network.MLPClassifier.html*).

```
              beta_2=0.999, early_stopping=False, epsilon=1e-08,
              hidden_layer_sizes=[75, 75], learning_rate='constant',
              learning_rate_init=0.001, max_iter=200, momentum=0.9,
              n_iter_no_change=10, nesterovs_momentum=True, power_t=0.5,
              random_state=10, shuffle=True, solver='lbfgs', tol=0.0001,
              validation_fraction=0.1, verbose=False, warm_start=False)

In [56]: pred = model.predict(X)
         pred
Out[56]: array([1, 0, 0, 1, 1, 0, 1, 1, 1, 0, 1, 0, 0, 0, 1, 1, 0, 1, 0, 1, 1,
         0,
         1, 1, 0, 0, 0, 0, 0, 0, 1, 0, 1, 0, 0, 0, 0, 1, 1, 0, 1, 0, 0, 0,
         0, 1, 1, 1, 0, 0, 1, 1, 0, 0, 1, 1, 1, 1, 0, 0, 0, 1, 1, 1, 1, 1,
         0, 0, 1, 0, 0, 1, 1, 1, 1, 1, 1, 0, 1, 1, 1, 0, 0, 1, 0, 0, 0, 1,
             0, 1, 1, 1, 0, 1, 1, 0, 0, 0, 0, 0])

In [57]: accuracy_score(y, pred)
Out[57]: 1.0
```

DNNs with TensorFlow. The API of TensorFlow is different from the scikit-learn standard. However, the application of the DNNClassifier class is similarly straightforward:

```
In [58]: import tensorflow as tf
         tf.logging.set_verbosity(tf.logging.ERROR)   ❶

In [59]: fc = [tf.contrib.layers.real_valued_column('features')]   ❷

In [60]: model = tf.contrib.learn.DNNClassifier(hidden_units=5 * [250],
                                                 n_classes=2,
                                                 feature_columns=fc)   ❸

In [61]: def input_fn():   ❹
             fc = {'features': tf.constant(X)}
             la = tf.constant(y)
             return fc, la

In [62]: %time model.fit(input_fn=input_fn, steps=100)   ❺
         CPU times: user 7.1 s, sys: 1.35 s, total: 8.45 s
         Wall time: 4.71 s

Out[62]: DNNClassifier(params={'head':
         <tensorflow.contrib.learn.python.learn ... head._BinaryLogisticHead
         object at 0x1a3ee692b0>, 'hidden_units': [250, 250, 250, 250, 250],
         'feature_columns': (_RealValuedColumn(column_name='features',
         dimension=1, default_value=None, dtype=tf.float32, normalizer=None),),
         'optimizer': None, 'activation_fn': <function relu at 0x1a3aa75b70>,
         'dropout': None, 'gradient_clip_norm': None,
         'embedding_lr_multipliers': None, 'input_layer_min_slice_size': None})

In [63]: model.evaluate(input_fn=input_fn, steps=1)   ❻
Out[63]: {'loss': 0.18724777,
```

```
            'accuracy': 0.91,
            'labels/prediction_mean': 0.5003989,
            'labels/actual_label_mean': 0.5,
            'accuracy/baseline_label_mean': 0.5,
            'auc': 0.9782,
            'auc_precision_recall': 0.97817385,
            'accuracy/threshold_0.500000_mean': 0.91,
            'precision/positive_threshold_0.500000_mean': 0.9019608,
            'recall/positive_threshold_0.500000_mean': 0.92,
            'global_step': 100}

In [64]: pred = np.array(list(model.predict(input_fn=input_fn)))   ❻
         pred[:10]   ❻
Out[64]: array([1, 0, 0, 1, 1, 0, 1, 1, 1, 1])

In [65]: %time model.fit(input_fn=input_fn, steps=750)   ❼
         CPU times: user 29.8 s, sys: 7.51 s, total: 37.3 s
         Wall time: 13.6 s

Out[65]: DNNClassifier(params={'head':
            <tensorflow.contrib.learn.python.learn ... head._BinaryLogisticHead
            object at 0x1a3ee692b0>, 'hidden_units': [250, 250, 250, 250, 250],
            'feature_columns': (_RealValuedColumn(column_name='features',
            dimension=1, default_value=None, dtype=tf.float32, normalizer=None),),
            'optimizer': None, 'activation_fn': <function relu at 0x1a3aa75b70>,
            'dropout': None, 'gradient_clip_norm': None,
            'embedding_lr_multipliers': None, 'input_layer_min_slice_size': None})

In [66]: model.evaluate(input_fn=input_fn, steps=1)   ❽
Out[66]: {'loss': 0.09271307,
            'accuracy': 0.94,
            'labels/prediction_mean': 0.5274486,
            'labels/actual_label_mean': 0.5,
            'accuracy/baseline_label_mean': 0.5,
            'auc': 0.99759996,
            'auc_precision_recall': 0.9977609,
            'accuracy/threshold_0.500000_mean': 0.94,
            'precision/positive_threshold_0.500000_mean': 0.9074074,
            'recall/positive_threshold_0.500000_mean': 0.98,
            'global_step': 850}
```

❶ Sets the verbosity for TensorFlow logging.

❷ Defines the real-valued features abstractly.

❸ Instantiates the model object.

❹ Features and label data are to be delivered by a function.

❺ Fits the model through learning and evaluates it.

➏ Predicts the label values based on the feature values.

➐ Retrains the model based on more learning steps; the previous results are taken as a starting point.

➑ Accuracy increases after retraining.

This only scratches the surface of `TensorFlow`, which is used in a number of demanding use cases, such as Alphabet Inc.'s effort to build self-driving cars. In terms of speed, the training of `TensorFlow`'s models in general benefits significantly from the use of specialized hardware such as GPUs and TPUs instead of CPUs.

Feature transforms

For a number of reasons, it might be beneficial or even necessary to transform real-valued features. The following code shows some typical transformations and visualizes the results for comparison in Figure 13-30:

```
In [67]: from sklearn import preprocessing

In [68]: X[:5]
Out[68]: array([[ 1.6876, -0.7976],
                [-0.4312, -0.7606],
                [-1.4393, -1.2363],
                [ 1.118 , -1.8682],
                [ 0.0502,  0.659 ]])

In [69]: Xs = preprocessing.StandardScaler().fit_transform(X)   ➊
         Xs[:5]
Out[69]: array([[ 1.2881, -0.5489],
                [-0.3384, -0.5216],
                [-1.1122, -0.873 ],
                [ 0.8509, -1.3399],
                [ 0.0312,  0.5273]])

In [70]: Xm = preprocessing.MinMaxScaler().fit_transform(X)     ➋
         Xm[:5]
Out[70]: array([[0.7262, 0.3563],
                [0.3939, 0.3613],
                [0.2358, 0.2973],
                [0.6369, 0.2122],
                [0.4694, 0.5523]])

In [71]: Xn1 = preprocessing.Normalizer(norm='l1').transform(X)  ➌
         Xn1[:5]
Out[71]: array([[ 0.6791, -0.3209],
                [-0.3618, -0.6382],
                [-0.5379, -0.4621],
                [ 0.3744, -0.6256],
                [ 0.0708,  0.9292]])
```

```
In [72]: Xn2 = preprocessing.Normalizer(norm='l2').transform(X)  ❸
         Xn2[:5]
Out[72]: array([[ 0.9041, -0.4273],
                [-0.4932, -0.8699],
                [-0.7586, -0.6516],
                [ 0.5135, -0.8581],
                [ 0.076 ,  0.9971]])

In [73]: plt.figure(figsize=(10, 6))
         markers = ['o', '.', 'x', '^', 'v']
         data_sets = [X, Xs, Xm, Xn1, Xn2]
         labels = ['raw', 'standard', 'minmax', 'norm(1)', 'norm(2)']
         for x, m, l in zip(data_sets, markers, labels):
             plt.scatter(x=x[:, 0], y=x[:, 1], c=y,
                         marker=m, cmap='coolwarm', label=l)
         plt.legend();
```

❶ Transforms the features data to standard normally distributed data with zero mean and unit variance.

❷ Transforms the features data to a given range for every feature as defined by the minimum and maximum values per feature.

❸ Scales the features data individually to the unit norm (L1 or L2).

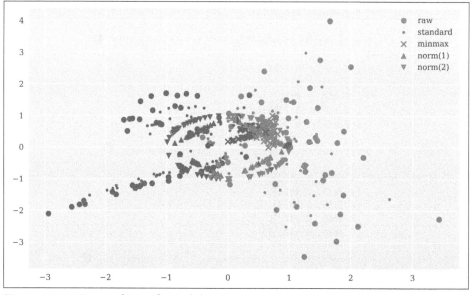

Figure 13-30. Raw and transformed data in comparison

In terms of pattern recognition tasks, a transformation to categorical features is often helpful or even required to achieve acceptable results. To this end, the real values of the features are mapped to a limited, fixed number of possible integer values (categories, classes):

```
In [74]: X[:5]
Out[74]: array([[ 1.6876, -0.7976],
                [-0.4312, -0.7606],
                [-1.4393, -1.2363],
                [ 1.118 , -1.8682],
                [ 0.0502,  0.659 ]])

In [75]: Xb = preprocessing.Binarizer().fit_transform(X)  ❶
         Xb[:5]
Out[75]: array([[1., 0.],
                [0., 0.],
                [0., 0.],
                [1., 0.],
                [1., 1.]])

In [76]: 2 ** 2  ❷
Out[76]: 4

In [77]: Xd = np.digitize(X, bins=[-1, 0, 1])  ❸
         Xd[:5]
Out[77]: array([[3, 1],
                [1, 1],
                [0, 0],
                [3, 0],
                [2, 2]])

In [78]: 4 ** 2  ❹
Out[78]: 16
```

❶ Transforms the features to binary features.

❷ The number of possible feature value combinations for two binary features.

❸ Transforms the features to categorical features based on a list of values used for binning.

❹ The number of possible feature value combinations, with three values used for binning for two features.

Train-test splits: Support vector machines

At this point, every seasoned ML researcher and practitioner reading this probably has concerns with regard to the implementations in this section: they all rely on the same data for training, learning, and prediction. The quality of an ML algorithm can of course be better judged when different data (sub)sets are used for training and learning on the one hand and testing on the other hand. This comes closer to a real-world application scenario.

Again, scikit-learn provides a function to accomplish such an approach efficiently. In particular, the train_test_split() function allows the splitting of data sets into training and test data in a randomized, but nevertheless repeatable, fashion.

The following code uses yet another classification algorithm, the *support vector machine* (SVM). It first fits the SVM model based on the training data:

```
In [79]: from sklearn.svm import SVC
         from sklearn.model_selection import train_test_split

In [80]: train_x, test_x, train_y, test_y = train_test_split(X, y, test_size=0.33,
                                                             random_state=0)

In [81]: model = SVC(C=1, kernel='linear')

In [82]: model.fit(train_x, train_y)  ❶
Out[82]: SVC(C=1, cache_size=200, class_weight=None, coef0=0.0,
             decision_function_shape='ovr', degree=3, gamma='auto_deprecated',
             kernel='linear', max_iter=-1, probability=False, random_state=None,
             shrinking=True, tol=0.001, verbose=False)

In [83]: pred_train = model.predict(train_x)  ❷

In [84]: accuracy_score(train_y, pred_train)  ❸
Out[84]: 0.9402985074626866
```

❶ Fits the model based on the training data.

❷ Predicts the training data label values.

❸ The accuracy of the training data prediction ("in-sample").

Next, the testing of the fitted model based on the test data. Figure 13-31 shows the correct and false predictions for the test data. The accuracy on the test data is—as one would naturally expect—lower than on the training data:

```
In [85]: pred_test = model.predict(test_x)  ❶

In [86]: test_y == pred_test  ❷
Out[86]: array([ True,  True,  True,  True,  True,  True,  True,  True,  True,
                 True, False, False, False,  True,  True,  True, False, False,
                False,  True,  True,  True,  True,  True,  True,  True,  True,
                 True,  True,  True,  True, False,  True])

In [87]: accuracy_score(test_y, pred_test)  ❷
Out[87]: 0.7878787878787878
```

```
In [88]: test_c = test_x[test_y == pred_test]
         test_f = test_x[test_y != pred_test]

In [89]: plt.figure(figsize=(10, 6))
         plt.scatter(x=test_c[:, 0], y=test_c[:, 1], c=test_y[test_y == pred_test],
                     marker='o', cmap='coolwarm')
         plt.scatter(x=test_f[:, 0], y=test_f[:, 1], c=test_y[test_y != pred_test],
                     marker='x', cmap='coolwarm');
```

❶ Predicts the testing data label values based on the test data.

❷ Evaluates the accuracy of the fitted model for the test data ("out-of-sample").

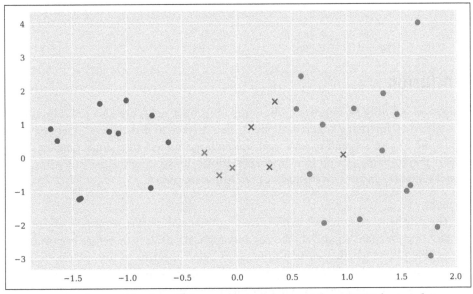

Figure 13-31. Correct (dots) and false predictions (crosses) from SVM for test data

The SVM classification algorithm provides a number of options for the kernel to be used. Depending on the problem at hand, different kernels might lead to quite different results (i.e., accuracy scores), as the following analysis shows. The code first transforms the real-valued features into categorical ones:

```
In [90]: bins = np.linspace(-4.5, 4.5, 50)

In [91]: Xd = np.digitize(X, bins=bins)

In [92]: Xd[:5]
Out[92]: array([[34, 21],
                [23, 21],
                [17, 18],
                [31, 15],
                [25, 29]])
```

```
In [93]: train_x, test_x, train_y, test_y = train_test_split(Xd, y, test_size=0.33,
                                                              random_state=0)

In [94]: print('{:>8s} | {:8s}'.format('kernel', 'accuracy'))
         print(20 * '-')
         for kernel in ['linear', 'poly', 'rbf', 'sigmoid']:
             model = SVC(C=1, kernel=kernel, gamma='auto')
             model.fit(train_x, train_y)
             acc = accuracy_score(test_y, model.predict(test_x))
             print('{:>8s} | {:8.3f}'.format(kernel, acc))
           kernel | accuracy
         --------------------
           linear |    0.848
             poly |    0.758
              rbf |    0.788
          sigmoid |    0.455
```

Conclusion

Statistics is not only an important discipline in its own right, but also provides indispensable tools for many other disciplines, like finance and the social sciences. It is impossible to give a broad overview of such a large subject in a single chapter. This chapter therefore focuses on four important topics, illustrating the use of Python and several statistics libraries on the basis of realistic examples:

Normality

The normality assumption with regard to financial market returns is an important one for many financial theories and applications; it is therefore important to be able to test whether certain time series data conforms to this assumption. As seen in "Normality Tests" on page 398—via graphical and statistical means—real-world return data generally is *not* normally distributed.

Portfolio optimization

MPT, with its focus on the mean and variance/volatility of returns, can be considered not only one of the first but also one of the major conceptual successes of statistics in finance; the important concept of investment *diversification* is beautifully illustrated in this context.

Bayesian statistics

Bayesian statistics in general (and Bayesian regression in particular) has become a popular tool in finance, since this approach overcomes some shortcomings of other approaches, as introduced, for instance, in Chapter 11; even if the mathematics and the formalism are more involved, the fundamental ideas—like the updating of probability/distribution beliefs over time—are easily grasped (at least intuitively).

Machine learning

Nowadays, machine learning has established itself in the financial domain alongside traditional statistical methods and techniques. The chapter introduces ML algorithms for unsupervised learning (such as *k*-means clustering) and supervised learning (such as DNN classifiers) and illustrates selected related topics, such as feature transforms and train-test splits.

Further Resources

For more information on the topics and packages covered in this chapter, consult the following online resources:

- The documentation on `SciPy`'s statistical functions (*http://docs.scipy.org/doc/scipy/reference/stats.html*)
- The documentation of the `statsmodels` library (*http://statsmodels.source forge.net/stable/*)
- Details on the optimization functions (*http://docs.scipy.org/doc/scipy/reference/optimize.html*) used in this chapter
- The documentation for `PyMC3` (*http://docs.pymc.io*)
- The documentation for `scikit-learn` (*http://scikit-learn.org*)

Useful references in book form for more background information are:

- Albon, Chris (2018). *Machine Learning with Python Cookbook*. Sebastopol, CA: O'Reilly.
- Alpaydin, Ethem (2016). *Machine Learning*. Cambridge, MA: MIT Press.
- Copeland, Thomas, Fred Weston, and Kuldeep Shastri (2005). *Financial Theory and Corporate Policy*. Boston, MA: Pearson.
- Downey, Allen (2013). *Think Bayes*. Sebastopol, CA: O'Reilly.
- Geweke, John (2005). *Contemporary Bayesian Econometrics and Statistics*. Hoboken, NJ: John Wiley & Sons.
- Hastie, Trevor, Robert Tibshirani, and Jerome Friedman (2009). *The Elements of Statistical Learning: Data Mining, Inference, and Prediction*. New York: Springer.
- James, Gareth, et al. (2013). *An Introduction to Statistical Learning—With Applications in R*. New York: Springer.
- López de Prado, Marcos (2018). *Advances in Financial Machine Learning*. Hoboken, NJ: John Wiley & Sons.
- Rachev, Svetlozar, et al. (2008). *Bayesian Methods in Finance*. Hoboken, NJ: John Wiley & Sons.

- VanderPlas, Jake (2016). *Python Data Science Handbook*. Sebastopol, CA: O'Reilly.

The paper introducing modern portfolio theory is:

Markowitz, Harry (1952). "Portfolio Selection." Journal of Finance, Vol. 7, pp. 77–91.

## PART IV

Algorithmic Trading

This part of the book is about the use of Python for algorithmic trading. More and more trading platforms and brokers allow their clients to use, for example, REST APIs to programmatically retrieve historical data or streaming data, or to place buy and sell orders. What has been the domain of large financial institutions for a long period now has become accessible even to retail algorithmic traders. In this space, Python has secured a top position as a programming language and technology platform. Among other factors, this is driven by the fact that many trading platforms, such as the one from FXCM Forex Capital Markets, provide easy-to-use Python wrapper packages for their REST APIs.

This part of the book comprises three chapters:

- Chapter 14 introduces the FXCM trading platform, its REST API, and the `fxcmpy` wrapper package.
- Chapter 15 focuses on the use of methods from statistics and machine learning to derive algorithmic trading strategies; the chapter also shows how to use vectorized backtesting.
- Chapter 16 looks at the deployment of automated algorithmic trading strategies; it addresses capital management, backtesting for performance and risk, online algorithms, and deployment.

CHAPTER 14
The FXCM Trading Platform

Financial institutions like to call what they do trading. Let's be honest. It's not trading; it's betting.

—Graydon Carter

This chapter introduces the trading platform from FXCM Group, LLC ("FXCM" hereafter), with its RESTful and streaming application programming interface (API), as well as the Python wrapper package fxcmpy. FXCM offers to retail and institutional traders a number of financial products that can be traded both via traditional trading applications and programmatically via the API. The focus of the products lies on currency pairs as well as contracts for difference (CFDs) on major stock indices and commodities, etc.

Risk Disclaimer

Trading forex/CFDs on margin carries a high level of risk and may not be suitable for all investors as you could sustain losses in excess of deposits. Leverage can work against you. The products are intended for retail and professional clients. Due to the certain restrictions imposed by the local law and regulation, German resident retail client(s) could sustain a total loss of deposited funds but are not subject to subsequent payment obligations beyond the deposited funds. Be aware and fully understand all risks associated with the market and trading. Prior to trading any products, carefully consider your financial situation and experience level. Any opinions, news, research, analyses, prices, or other information is provided as general market commentary, and does not constitute investment advice. The market commentary has not been prepared in accordance with legal requirements designed to promote the independence of investment research, and it is therefore not subject to any prohibition on dealing ahead of dissemination. FXCM and the author will not accept liability for any loss or damage, including without limitation to, any loss of profit, which may arise directly or indirectly from use of or reliance on such information.

The trading platform of FXCM allows even individual traders with smaller capital positions to implement and deploy algorithmic trading strategies.

This chapter covers the basic functionalities of the FXCM trading API and the fxcmpy Python package required to implement an automated algorithmic trading strategy programmatically. It is structured as follows:

"Getting Started" on page 469
    This section shows how to set up everything to work with the FXCM REST API for algorithmic trading.

"Retrieving Data" on page 469
    This section shows how to retrieve and work with financial data (down to the tick level).

"Working with the API" on page 474
    This section illustrates typical tasks implemented using the REST API, such as retrieving historical and streaming data, placing orders, and looking up account information.

Getting Started

Detailed documentation of the FXCM API is found at *https://fxcm.github.io/rest-api-docs*. To install the Python wrapper package `fxcmpy`, execute this command in the shell:

```
pip install fxcmpy
```

The documentation for the `fxcmpy` package is found at *http://fxcmpy.tpq.io*.

To get started with the FXCM trading API and the `fxcmpy` package, a free demo account (*https://www.fxcm.com/uk/forex-trading-demo/*) with FXCM is sufficient.[1] The next step is to create a unique API token—say, YOUR_FXCM_API_TOKEN—from within the demo account. A connection to the API is then opened, for example, via:

```
import fxcmpy
api = fxcmpy.fxcmpy(access_token=YOUR_FXCM_API_TOKEN, log_level='error')
```

Alternatively, a configuration file (say, *fxcm.cfg*) can be used to connect to the API. This file's contents should look as follows:

```
[FXCM]
log_level = error
log_file = PATH_TO_AND_NAME_OF_LOG_FILE
access_token = YOUR_FXCM_API_TOKEN
```

One can then connect to the API via:

```
import fxcmpy
api = fxcmpy.fxcmpy(config_file='fxcm.cfg')
```

By default, the `fxcmpy` class connects to the demo server. However, by the use of the server parameter, the connection can be made to the live trading server (if such an account exists):

```
api = fxcmpy.fxcmpy(config_file='fxcm.cfg', server='demo')   ❶
api = fxcmpy.fxcmpy(config_file='fxcm.cfg', server='real')   ❷
```

❶ Connects to the demo server.

❷ Connects to the live trading server.

Retrieving Data

FXCM provides access to historical market price data sets, such as tick data, in a prepackaged variant. This means that one can retrieve, for instance, compressed files from FXCM servers that contain tick data for the EUR/USD exchange rate for week

---

1 Note that FXCM demo accounts are only offered for certain countries.

26 of 2018, as described in the following subsection. The retrieval of historical candles data from the API is explained in the subsequent subsection.

Retrieving Tick Data

For a number of currency pairs, FXCM provides historical tick data. The fxcmpy package makes retrieval of such tick data and working with it convenient. First, some imports:

```
In [1]: import time
        import numpy as np
        import pandas as pd
        import datetime as dt
        from pylab import mpl, plt

In [2]: plt.style.use('seaborn')
        mpl.rcParams['font.family'] = 'serif'
        %matplotlib inline
```

Second, a look at the available symbols (currency pairs) for which tick data is available:

```
In [3]: from fxcmpy import fxcmpy_tick_data_reader as tdr

In [4]: print(tdr.get_available_symbols())
        ('AUDCAD', 'AUDCHF', 'AUDJPY', 'AUDNZD', 'CADCHF', 'EURAUD', 'EURCHF',
         'EURGBP', 'EURJPY', 'EURUSD', 'GBPCHF', 'GBPJPY', 'GBPNZD', 'GBPUSD',
         'GBPCHF', 'GBPJPY', 'GBPNZD', 'NZDCAD', 'NZDCHF', 'NZDJPY', 'NZDUSD',
         'USDCAD', 'USDCHF', 'USDJPY')
```

The following code retrieves one week's worth of tick data for a single symbol. The resulting pandas DataFrame object has more than 1.5 million data rows:

```
In [5]: start = dt.datetime(2018, 6, 25)   ❶
        stop = dt.datetime(2018, 6, 30)    ❶

In [6]: td = tdr('EURUSD', start, stop)    ❶

In [7]: td.get_raw_data().info()           ❷
        <class 'pandas.core.frame.DataFrame'>
        Index: 1963779 entries, 06/24/2018 21:00:12.290 to 06/29/2018
         20:59:00.607
        Data columns (total 2 columns):
        Bid     float64
        Ask     float64
        dtypes: float64(2)
        memory usage: 44.9+ MB

In [8]: td.get_data().info()               ❸
        <class 'pandas.core.frame.DataFrame'>
        DatetimeIndex: 1963779 entries, 2018-06-24 21:00:12.290000 to 2018-06-29
         20:59:00.607000
```

```
         Data columns (total 2 columns):
         Bid     float64
         Ask     float64
         dtypes: float64(2)
         memory usage: 44.9 MB

In [9]: td.get_data().head()
Out[9]:                                   Bid       Ask
        2018-06-24 21:00:12.290   1.1662   1.16660
        2018-06-24 21:00:16.046   1.1662   1.16650
        2018-06-24 21:00:22.846   1.1662   1.16658
        2018-06-24 21:00:22.907   1.1662   1.16660
        2018-06-24 21:00:23.441   1.1662   1.16663
```

❶ This retrieves the data file, unpacks it, and stores the raw data in a DataFrame object (as an attribute to the resulting object).

❷ The td.get_raw_data() method returns the DataFrame object with the raw data; i.e., with the index values still being str objects.

❸ The td.get_data() method returns a DataFrame object for which the index has been transformed to a DatetimeIndex.

Since the tick data is stored in a DataFrame object, it is straightforward to pick a subset of the data and to implement typical financial analytics tasks on it. Figure 14-1 shows a plot of the mid prices derived for the subset and a simple moving average (SMA):

```
In [10]: sub = td.get_data(start='2018-06-29 12:00:00',
                           end='2018-06-29 12:15:00')   ❶

In [11]: sub.head()
Out[11]:                                   Bid       Ask
         2018-06-29 12:00:00.011   1.16497   1.16498
         2018-06-29 12:00:00.071   1.16497   1.16497
         2018-06-29 12:00:00.079   1.16497   1.16498
         2018-06-29 12:00:00.091   1.16495   1.16498
         2018-06-29 12:00:00.205   1.16496   1.16498

In [12]: sub['Mid'] = sub.mean(axis=1)   ❷

In [13]: sub['SMA'] = sub['Mid'].rolling(1000).mean()   ❸

In [14]: sub[['Mid', 'SMA']].plot(figsize=(10, 6), lw=0.75);
```

❶ Picks a subset of the complete data set.

❷ Calculates the mid prices from the bid and ask prices.

❸ Derives SMA values over intervals of 1,000 ticks.

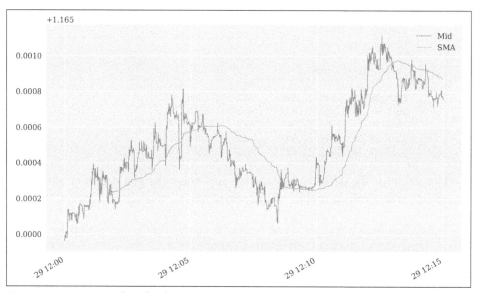

Figure 14-1. Historical mid tick prices for EUR/USD and SMA

Retrieving Candles Data

FXCM also provides access to historical candles data (beyond the API)—i.e., to data for certain homogeneous time intervals ("bars") with open, high, low, and close values for both bid and ask prices.

First, a look at the available symbols for which candles data is provided:

```
In [15]: from fxcmpy import fxcmpy_candles_data_reader as cdr

In [16]: print(cdr.get_available_symbols())
         ('AUDCAD', 'AUDCHF', 'AUDJPY', 'AUDNZD', 'CADCHF', 'EURAUD', 'EURCHF',
          'EURGBP', 'EURJPY', 'EURUSD', 'GBPCHF', 'GBPJPY', 'GBPNZD', 'GBPUSD',
          'GBPCHF', 'GBPJPY', 'GBPNZD', 'NZDCAD', 'NZDCHF', 'NZDJPY', 'NZDUSD',
          'USDCAD', 'USDCHF', 'USDJPY')
```

Second, the data retrieval itself. It is similar to the tick data retrieval. The only difference is that a `period` value—i.e., the bar length—needs to be specified (e.g., `m1` for one minute, `H1` for one hour, or `D1` for one day):

```
In [17]: start = dt.datetime(2018, 5, 1)
         stop = dt.datetime(2018, 6, 30)

In [18]: period = 'H1'  ❶

In [19]: candles = cdr('EURUSD', start, stop, period)
```

```
In [20]: data = candles.get_data()

In [21]: data.info()
         <class 'pandas.core.frame.DataFrame'>
         DatetimeIndex: 1080 entries, 2018-04-29 21:00:00 to 2018-06-29 20:00:00
         Data columns (total 8 columns):
         BidOpen     1080 non-null float64
         BidHigh     1080 non-null float64
         BidLow      1080 non-null float64
         BidClose    1080 non-null float64
         AskOpen     1080 non-null float64
         AskHigh     1080 non-null float64
         AskLow      1080 non-null float64
         AskClose    1080 non-null float64
         dtypes: float64(8)
         memory usage: 75.9 KB

In [22]: data[data.columns[:4]].tail()    ❷
Out[22]:                       BidOpen  BidHigh   BidLow  BidClose
         2018-06-29 16:00:00  1.16768  1.16820  1.16731   1.16769
         2018-06-29 17:00:00  1.16769  1.16826  1.16709   1.16781
         2018-06-29 18:00:00  1.16781  1.16816  1.16668   1.16684
         2018-06-29 19:00:00  1.16684  1.16792  1.16638   1.16774
         2018-06-29 20:00:00  1.16774  1.16904  1.16758   1.16816

In [23]: data[data.columns[4:]].tail()    ❸
Out[23]:                       AskOpen  AskHigh   AskLow  AskClose
         2018-06-29 16:00:00  1.16769  1.16820  1.16732   1.16771
         2018-06-29 17:00:00  1.16771  1.16827  1.16711   1.16782
         2018-06-29 18:00:00  1.16782  1.16817  1.16669   1.16686
         2018-06-29 19:00:00  1.16686  1.16794  1.16640   1.16775
         2018-06-29 20:00:00  1.16775  1.16907  1.16760   1.16861
```

❶ Specifies the period value.

❷ Open, high, low, close values for the *bid* prices.

❸ Open, high, low, close values for the *ask* prices.

To conclude this section, the following code calculates mid close prices and two SMAs, and plots the results (see Figure 14-2):

```
In [24]: data['MidClose'] = data[['BidClose', 'AskClose']].mean(axis=1)    ❶

In [25]: data['SMA1'] = data['MidClose'].rolling(30).mean()    ❷
         data['SMA2'] = data['MidClose'].rolling(100).mean()   ❷

In [26]: data[['MidClose', 'SMA1', 'SMA2']].plot(figsize=(10, 6));
```

❶ Calculates the mid close prices from the bid and ask close prices.

❷ Calculates two SMAs, one for a shorter time interval, one for a longer one.

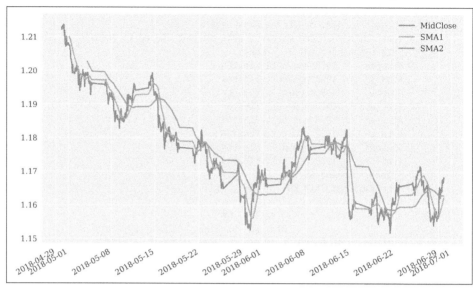

Figure 14-2. Historical hourly mid close prices for EUR/USD and two SMAs

Working with the API

While the previous sections demonstrate retrieving prepackaged historical tick data and candles data from FXCM servers, this section shows how to retrieve historical data via the API. For this, a connection object to the FXCM API is needed. Therefore, first the import of the fxcmpy package, the connection to the API (based on the unique API token), and a look at the available instruments:

```
In [27]: import fxcmpy

In [28]: fxcmpy.__version__
Out[28]: '1.1.33'

In [29]: api = fxcmpy.fxcmpy(config_file='../fxcm.cfg')  ❶

In [30]: instruments = api.get_instruments()

In [31]: print(instruments)
         ['EUR/USD', 'XAU/USD', 'GBP/USD', 'UK100', 'USDOLLAR', 'XAG/USD', 'GER30',
          'FRA40', 'USD/CNH', 'EUR/JPY', 'USD/JPY', 'CHN50', 'GBP/JPY', 'AUD/JPY',
          'CHF/JPY', 'USD/CHF', 'GBP/CHF', 'AUD/USD', 'EUR/AUD', 'EUR/CHF',
          'EUR/CAD', 'EUR/GBP', 'AUD/CAD', 'NZD/USD', 'USD/CAD', 'CAD/JPY',
          'GBP/AUD', 'NZD/JPY', 'US30', 'GBP/CAD', 'SOYF', 'GBP/NZD', 'AUD/NZD',
          'USD/SEK', 'EUR/SEK', 'EUR/NOK', 'USD/NOK', 'USD/MXN', 'AUD/CHF',
          'EUR/NZD', 'USD/ZAR', 'USD/HKD', 'ZAR/JPY', 'BTC/USD', 'USD/TRY',
          'EUR/TRY', 'NZD/CHF', 'CAD/CHF', 'NZD/CAD', 'TRY/JPY', 'AUS200',
```

```
               'ESP35', 'HKG33', 'JPN225', 'NAS100', 'SPX500', 'Copper', 'EUSTX50',
               'USOil', 'UKOil', 'NGAS', 'Bund']
```

❶ This connects to the API; adjust the path/filename.

Retrieving Historical Data

Once connected, data retrieval for specific time intervals is accomplished via a single
method call. When using the get_candles() method, the parameter period can be
one of m1, m5, m15, m30, H1, H2, H3, H4, H6, H8, D1, W1, or M1. The following code gives a
few examples. Figure 14-3 shows one-minute bar ask close prices for the EUR/USD
instrument (currency pair):

```
In [32]: candles = api.get_candles('USD/JPY', period='D1', number=10)  ❶

In [33]: candles[candles.columns[:4]]  ❶
Out[33]:                        bidopen  bidclose  bidhigh   bidlow
         date
         2018-10-08 21:00:00  113.760   113.219  113.937  112.816
         2018-10-09 21:00:00  113.219   112.946  113.386  112.863
         2018-10-10 21:00:00  112.946   112.267  113.281  112.239
         2018-10-11 21:00:00  112.267   112.155  112.528  111.825
         2018-10-12 21:00:00  112.155   112.200  112.491  111.873
         2018-10-14 21:00:00  112.163   112.130  112.270  112.109
         2018-10-15 21:00:00  112.130   111.758  112.230  111.619
         2018-10-16 21:00:00  112.151   112.238  112.333  111.727
         2018-10-17 21:00:00  112.238   112.636  112.670  112.009
         2018-10-18 21:00:00  112.636   112.168  112.725  111.942

In [34]: candles[candles.columns[4:]]  ❶
Out[34]:                        askopen  askclose  askhigh   asklow  tickqty
         date
         2018-10-08 21:00:00  113.840   113.244  113.950  112.827   184835
         2018-10-09 21:00:00  113.244   112.970  113.399  112.875   321755
         2018-10-10 21:00:00  112.970   112.287  113.294  112.265   329174
         2018-10-11 21:00:00  112.287   112.175  112.541  111.835   568231
         2018-10-12 21:00:00  112.175   112.243  112.504  111.885   363233
         2018-10-14 21:00:00  112.219   112.181  112.294  112.145      581
         2018-10-15 21:00:00  112.181   111.781  112.243  111.631   322304
         2018-10-16 21:00:00  112.163   112.271  112.345  111.740   253420
         2018-10-17 21:00:00  112.271   112.664  112.682  112.022   542166
         2018-10-18 21:00:00  112.664   112.237  112.738  111.955   369012

In [35]: start = dt.datetime(2017, 1, 1)  ❷
         end = dt.datetime(2018, 1, 1)  ❷

In [36]: candles = api.get_candles('EUR/GBP', period='D1',
                                   start=start, stop=end)  ❷

In [37]: candles.info()  ❷
         <class 'pandas.core.frame.DataFrame'>
```

```
DatetimeIndex: 309 entries, 2017-01-03 22:00:00 to 2018-01-01 22:00:00
Data columns (total 9 columns):
bidopen     309 non-null float64
bidclose    309 non-null float64
bidhigh     309 non-null float64
bidlow      309 non-null float64
askopen     309 non-null float64
askclose    309 non-null float64
askhigh     309 non-null float64
asklow      309 non-null float64
tickqty     309 non-null int64
dtypes: float64(8), int64(1)
memory usage: 24.1 KB
```

In [38]: candles = api.get_candles('EUR/USD', period='m1', number=250)   ❸

In [39]: candles['askclose'].plot(figsize=(10, 6))

❶   Retrieves the 10 most recent end-of-day prices.

❷   Retrieves end-of-day prices for a whole year.

❸   Retrieves the most recent one-minute bar prices available.

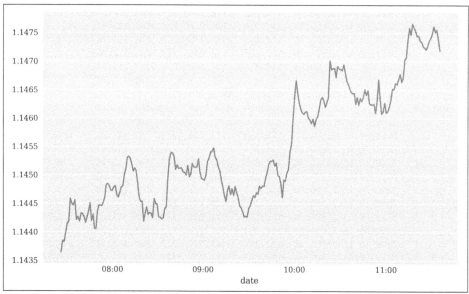

Figure 14-3. Historical ask close prices for EUR/USD (minute bars)

Retrieving Streaming Data

While *historical* data is important to, for example, backtest algorithmic trading strategies, continuous access to *real-time or streaming* data (during trading hours) is required to deploy and automate algorithmic trading strategies. The FXCM API allows for the subscription to real-time data streams for all instruments. The fxcmpy wrapper package supports this functionality, among others, in that it allows users to provide user-defined functions (so-called *callback functions*) to process the real-time data stream.

The following code presents a simple callback function—it only prints out selected elements of the data set retrieved—and uses it to process data retrieved in real time after subscribing to the desired instrument (here, EUR/USD):

```
In [40]: def output(data, dataframe):
             print('%3d | %s | %s | %6.5f, %6.5f'
                  % (len(dataframe), data['Symbol'],
                     pd.to_datetime(int(data['Updated']), unit='ms'),
                     data['Rates'][0], data['Rates'][1]))    ❶

In [41]: api.subscribe_market_data('EUR/USD', (output,))    ❷
             1 | EUR/USD | 2018-10-19 11:36:39.735000 | 1.14694, 1.14705
             2 | EUR/USD | 2018-10-19 11:36:39.776000 | 1.14694, 1.14706
             3 | EUR/USD | 2018-10-19 11:36:40.714000 | 1.14695, 1.14707
             4 | EUR/USD | 2018-10-19 11:36:41.646000 | 1.14696, 1.14708
             5 | EUR/USD | 2018-10-19 11:36:41.992000 | 1.14696, 1.14709
             6 | EUR/USD | 2018-10-19 11:36:45.131000 | 1.14696, 1.14708
             7 | EUR/USD | 2018-10-19 11:36:45.247000 | 1.14696, 1.14709

In [42]: api.get_last_price('EUR/USD')    ❸
Out[42]: Bid       1.14696
         Ask       1.14709
         High      1.14775
         Low       1.14323
         Name: 2018-10-19 11:36:45.247000, dtype: float64

In [43]: api.unsubscribe_market_data('EUR/USD')    ❹
             8 | EUR/USD | 2018-10-19 11:36:48.239000 | 1.14696, 1.14708
```

❶ The callback function that prints out certain elements of the retrieved data set.

❷ The subscription to a specific real-time data stream; data is processed asynchronously as long as there is no "unsubscribe" event.

❸ During the subscription, the .get_last_price() method returns the last available data set.

❹ This unsubscribes from the real-time data stream.

Callback Functions

Callback functions are a flexible means to process real-time streaming data based on a Python function or even multiple such functions. They can be used for simple tasks, such as the printing of incoming data, or complex tasks, such as generating trading signals based on online trading algorithms (see Chapter 16).

Placing Orders

The FXCM API allows the placement and management of all types of orders that are also available via the trading application of FXCM (such as entry orders or trailing stop loss orders).[2] However, the following code illustrates basic market buy and sell orders only since they are in general sufficient to at least get started with algorithmic trading. It first verifies that there are no open positions, then opens different positions (via the create_market_buy_order() method):

```
In [44]: api.get_open_positions()   ❶
Out[44]: Empty DataFrame
         Columns: []
         Index: []

In [45]: order = api.create_market_buy_order('EUR/USD', 10)   ❷

In [46]: sel = ['tradeId', 'amountK', 'currency',
                'grossPL', 'isBuy']   ❸

In [47]: api.get_open_positions()[sel]   ❸
Out[47]:      tradeId  amountK currency  grossPL  isBuy
         0  132607899       10  EUR/USD  0.17436   True

In [48]: order = api.create_market_buy_order('EUR/GBP', 5)   ❹

In [49]: api.get_open_positions()[sel]
Out[49]:      tradeId  amountK currency  grossPL  isBuy
         0  132607899       10  EUR/USD  0.17436   True
         1  132607928        5  EUR/GBP -1.53367   True
```

❶ Shows the open positions for the connected (default) account.

❷ Opens a position of 100,000 in the EUR/USD currency pair.[3]

---

2 See the documentation (*http://fxcmpy.tpq.io*) for details.

3 Quantities are in thousands of the instrument for currency pairs. Also note that different accounts might have different leverage ratios (*https://www.fxcm.com/uk/accounts/forex-cfd-leverage/*). This implies that the same position might require more or less equity (margin) depending on the relevant leverage ratio. Adjust the example quantities to lower values if necessary.

❸ Shows the open positions for selected elements only.

❹ Opens another position of 50,000 in the EUR/GBP currency pair.

While the create_market_buy_order() function opens or increases positions, the create_market_sell_order() function allows one to close or decrease positions. There are also more general methods that allow the closing out of positions, as the following code illustrates:

```
In [50]: order = api.create_market_sell_order('EUR/USD', 3)   ❶

In [51]: order = api.create_market_buy_order('EUR/GBP', 5)    ❷

In [52]: api.get_open_positions()[sel]   ❸
Out[52]:      tradeId  amountK currency  grossPL  isBuy
        0  132607899       10  EUR/USD  0.17436   True
        1  132607928        5  EUR/GBP -1.53367   True
        2  132607930        3  EUR/USD -1.33369  False
        3  132607932        5  EUR/GBP -1.64728   True

In [53]: api.close_all_for_symbol('EUR/GBP')   ❹

In [54]: api.get_open_positions()[sel]
Out[54]:      tradeId  amountK currency  grossPL  isBuy
        0  132607899       10  EUR/USD  0.17436   True
        1  132607930        3  EUR/USD -1.33369  False

In [55]: api.close_all()   ❺

In [56]: api.get_open_positions()
Out[56]: Empty DataFrame
         Columns: []
         Index: []
```

❶ This reduces the position in the EUR/USD currency pair.

❷ This increases the position in the EUR/GBP currency pair.

❸ For EUR/GBP there are now two open long positions; contrary to the EUR/USD position, they are not netted.

❹ The close_all_for_symbol() method closes all positions for the specified symbol.

❺ The close_all() method closes all open positions.

Account Information

Beyond, for example, open positions, the FXCM API allows retrieval of more general account information as well. For example, one can look up the default account (if there are multiple accounts) or get an overview of the equity and margin situation:

```
In [57]: api.get_default_account()  ❶
Out[57]: 1090495

In [58]: api.get_accounts().T  ❷
Out[58]:
                                    0
         accountId           1090495
         accountName        01090495
         balance              4915.2
         dayPL                -41.97
         equity               4915.2
         grossPL                   0
         hedging                   Y
         mc                        N
         mcDate
         ratePrecision             0
         t                         6
         usableMargin         4915.2
         usableMargin3        4915.2
         usableMargin3Perc       100
         usableMarginPerc        100
         usdMr                     0
         usdMr3                    0
```

❶ Shows the default accountId value.

❷ Shows for all accounts the financial situation and some parameters.

Conclusion

This chapter is about the REST API of FXCM for algorithmic trading and covers the following topics:

- Setting everything up for API usage
- Retrieving historical tick data
- Retrieving historical candles data
- Retrieving streaming data in real time
- Placing market buy and sell orders
- Looking up account information

The FXCM API and the `fxcmpy` wrapper package provide, of course, more functionality, but these are the basic building blocks needed to get started with algorithmic trading.

Further Resources

For further details on the FXCM trading API and the Python wrapper package, consult the documentation:

- Trading API (*https://fxcm.github.io/rest-api-docs*)
- `fxcmpy` package (*http://fxcmpy.tpq.io*)

For a comprehensive online training program covering Python for algorithmic trading, see *http://certificate.tpq.io*.

## CHAPTER 15

Trading Strategies

[T]hey were silly enough to think you can look at the past to predict the future.

—*The Economist*[1]

This chapter is about the vectorized backtesting of algorithmic trading strategies. The term *algorithmic trading strategy* is used to describe any type of financial trading strategy that is based on an algorithm designed to take long, short, or neutral positions in financial instruments on its own without human interference. A simple algorithm, such as "altering every five minutes between a long and a neutral position in the stock of Apple, Inc.," satisfies this definition. For the purposes of this chapter and a bit more technically, an algorithmic trading strategy is represented by some Python code that, given the availability of new data, decides whether to buy or sell a financial instrument in order to take long, short, or neutral positions in it.

The chapter does not provide an overview of algorithmic trading strategies (see "Further Resources" on page 519 for references that cover algorithmic trading strategies in more detail). It rather focuses on the technical aspects of the *vectorized backtesting* approach for a select few such strategies. With this approach the financial data on which the strategy is tested is manipulated in general as a whole, applying vectorized operations on `NumPy` `ndarray` and `pandas` `DataFrame` objects that store the financial data.[2]

Another focus of the chapter is the application of *machine and deep learning algorithms* to formulate algorithmic trading strategies. To this end, classification

---

1 Source: "Does the Past Predict the Future?" Economist.com, 23 September 2009, available at *https://www.economist.com/free-exchange/2009/09/23/does-the-past-predict-the-future*.

2 An alternative approach would be the *event-based backtesting* of trading strategies, during which the arrival of new data in markets is simulated by explicitly looping over every single new data point.

algorithms are trained on historical data in order to predict future directional market movements. This in general requires the transformation of the financial data from real values to a relatively small number of categorical values.[3] This allows us to harness the pattern recognition power of such algorithms.

The chapter is broken down into the following sections:

"Simple Moving Averages" on page 484
  This section focuses on an algorithmic trading strategy based on simple moving averages and how to backtest such a strategy.

"Random Walk Hypothesis" on page 491
  This section introduces the random walk hypothesis.

"Linear OLS Regression" on page 494
  This section looks at using OLS regression to derive an algorithmic trading strategy.

"Clustering" on page 499
  In this section, we explore using unsupervised learning algorithms to derive algorithmic trading strategies.

"Frequency Approach" on page 501
  This section introduces a simple frequentist approach for algorithmic trading.

"Classification" on page 504
  Here we look at classification algorithms from machine learning for algorithmic trading.

"Deep Neural Networks" on page 512
  This section focuses on deep neural networks and how to use them for algorithmic trading.

Simple Moving Averages

Trading based on simple moving averages (SMAs) is a decades-old trading approach (see, for example, the paper by Brock et al. (1992)). Although many traders use SMAs for their discretionary trading, they can also be used to formulate simple algorithmic trading strategies. This section uses SMAs to introduce vectorized backtesting of algorithmic trading strategies. It builds on the technical analysis example in Chapter 8.

---

3 Note that when working with real values, every pattern might be unique or at least rather rare, which makes it difficult to train an algorithm and to conclude anything from an observed pattern.

Data Import

First, some imports:

```
In [1]: import numpy as np
        import pandas as pd
        import datetime as dt
        from pylab import mpl, plt
```

```
In [2]: plt.style.use('seaborn')
        mpl.rcParams['font.family'] = 'serif'
        %matplotlib inline
```

Second, the reading of the raw data and the selection of the financial time series for a single symbol, the stock of Apple, Inc. (AAPL.O). The analysis in this section is based on end-of-day data; intraday data is used in subsequent sections:

```
In [3]: raw = pd.read_csv('../../source/tr_eikon_eod_data.csv',
                          index_col=0, parse_dates=True)
```

```
In [4]: raw.info()
        <class 'pandas.core.frame.DataFrame'>
        DatetimeIndex: 2216 entries, 2010-01-01 to 2018-06-29
        Data columns (total 12 columns):
        AAPL.O    2138 non-null float64
        MSFT.O    2138 non-null float64
        INTC.O    2138 non-null float64
        AMZN.O    2138 non-null float64
        GS.N      2138 non-null float64
        SPY       2138 non-null float64
        .SPX      2138 non-null float64
        .VIX      2138 non-null float64
        EUR=      2216 non-null float64
        XAU=      2211 non-null float64
        GDX       2138 non-null float64
        GLD       2138 non-null float64
        dtypes: float64(12)
        memory usage: 225.1 KB
```

```
In [5]: symbol = 'AAPL.O'
```

```
In [6]: data = (
            pd.DataFrame(raw[symbol])
            .dropna()
        )
```

Trading Strategy

Third, the calculation of the SMA values for two different rolling window sizes. Figure 15-1 shows the three time series visually:

```
In [7]: SMA1 = 42   ❶
        SMA2 = 252  ❷

In [8]: data['SMA1'] = data[symbol].rolling(SMA1).mean()  ❶
        data['SMA2'] = data[symbol].rolling(SMA2).mean()  ❷

In [9]: data.plot(figsize=(10, 6));
```

❶   Calculates the values for the *shorter* SMA.

❷   Calculates the values for the *longer* SMA.

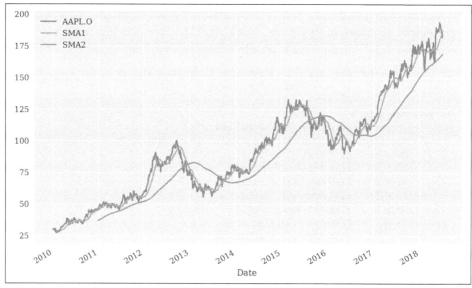

Figure 15-1. Apple stock price and two simple moving averages

Fourth, the derivation of the positions. The trading rules are:

- Go *long* (= +1) when the shorter SMA is above the longer SMA.
- Go *short* (= -1) when the shorter SMA is below the longer SMA.[4]

The positions are visualized in Figure 15-2:

```
In [10]: data.dropna(inplace=True)

In [11]: data['Position'] = np.where(data['SMA1'] > data['SMA2'], 1, -1)  ❶

In [12]: data.tail()
```

---

4 Similarly, for a *long only* strategy one would use +1 for a *long* position and 0 for a *neutral* position.

```
Out[12]:                AAPL.O        SMA1        SMA2  Position
         Date
         2018-06-25  182.17  185.606190  168.265556         1
         2018-06-26  184.43  186.087381  168.418770         1
         2018-06-27  184.16  186.607381  168.579206         1
         2018-06-28  185.50  187.089286  168.736627         1
         2018-06-29  185.11  187.470476  168.901032         1

In [13]: ax = data.plot(secondary_y='Position', figsize=(10, 6))
         ax.get_legend().set_bbox_to_anchor((0.25, 0.85));
```

❶ np.where(cond, a, b) evaluates the condition cond element-wise and places a
when True and b otherwise.

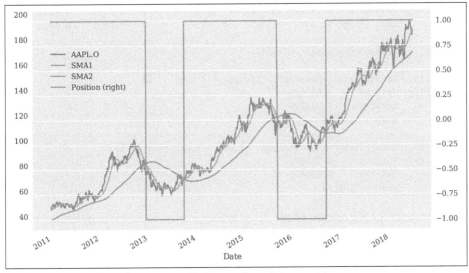

Figure 15-2. Apple stock price, two SMAs, and resulting positions

This replicates the results derived in Chapter 8. What is not addressed there is if following the trading rules—i.e., implementing the algorithmic trading strategy—is
superior compared to the benchmark case of simply going long on the Apple stock
over the whole period. Given that the strategy leads to two periods only during which
the Apple stock should be shorted, differences in the performance can only result
from these two periods.

Vectorized Backtesting

The vectorized backtesting can now be implemented as follows. First, the log returns
are calculated. Then the positionings, represented as +1 or -1, are multiplied by the
relevant log return. This simple calculation is possible since a long position earns the
return of the Apple stock and a short position earns the negative return of the Apple

stock. Finally, the log returns for the Apple stock and the algorithmic trading strategy based on SMAs need to be added up and the exponential function applied to arrive at the performance values:

```
In [14]: data['Returns'] = np.log(data[symbol] / data[symbol].shift(1))   ❶

In [15]: data['Strategy'] = data['Position'].shift(1) * data['Returns']   ❷

In [16]: data.round(4).head()
Out[16]:                      AAPL.O      SMA1      SMA2 Position  Returns Strategy
         Date
         2010-12-31  46.0800  45.2810  37.1207         1      NaN      NaN
         2011-01-03  47.0814  45.3497  37.1862         1   0.0215   0.0215
         2011-01-04  47.3271  45.4126  37.2525         1   0.0052   0.0052
         2011-01-05  47.7142  45.4661  37.3223         1   0.0081   0.0081
         2011-01-06  47.6757  45.5226  37.3921         1  -0.0008  -0.0008

In [17]: data.dropna(inplace=True)

In [18]: np.exp(data[['Returns', 'Strategy']].sum())   ❸
Out[18]: Returns     4.017148
         Strategy    5.811299
         dtype: float64

In [19]: data[['Returns', 'Strategy']].std() * 252 ** 0.5   ❹
Out[19]: Returns     0.250571
         Strategy    0.250407
         dtype: float64
```

❶ Calculates the log returns of the Apple stock (i.e., the benchmark investment).

❷ Multiplies the position values, shifted by one day, by the log returns of the Apple stock; the shift is required to avoid a foresight bias.[5]

❸ Sums up the log returns for the strategy and the benchmark investment and calculates the exponential value to arrive at the absolute performance.

❹ Calculates the annualized volatility for the strategy and the benchmark investment.

The numbers show that the algorithmic trading strategy indeed outperforms the benchmark investment of passively holding the Apple stock. Due to the type and characteristics of the strategy, the annualized volatility is the same, such that it also outperforms the benchmark investment on a risk-adjusted basis.

---

5 The basic idea is that the algorithm can only set up a position in the Apple stock given *today's market data* (e.g., just before the close). The position then earns *tomorrow's return*.

To gain a better picture of the overall performance, Figure 15-3 shows the performance of the Apple stock and the algorithmic trading strategy over time:

```
In [20]: ax = data[['Returns', 'Strategy']].cumsum(
             ).apply(np.exp).plot(figsize=(10, 6))
         data['Position'].plot(ax=ax, secondary_y='Position', style='--')
         ax.get_legend().set_bbox_to_anchor((0.25, 0.85));
```

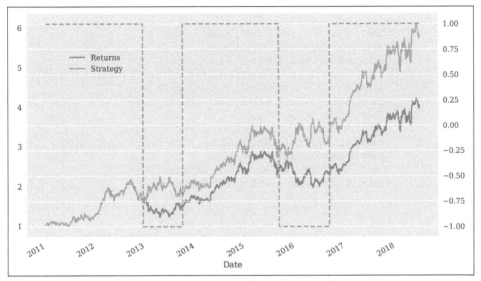

Figure 15-3. Performance of Apple stock and SMA-based trading strategy over time

Simplifications

The vectorized backtesting approach as introduced in this subsection is based on a number of simplifying assumptions. Among others, transactions costs (fixed fees, bid-ask spreads, lending costs,
etc.) are not included. This might be justifiable for a trading strategy that leads to a few trades only over multiple years. It is also
assumed that all trades take place at the end-of-day closing prices
for the Apple stock. A more realistic backtesting approach would
take these and other (market microstructure) elements into
account.

Optimization

A natural question that arises is if the chosen parameters SMA1=42 and SMA2=252 are
the "right" ones. In general, investors prefer higher returns to lower returns *ceteris
paribus*. Therefore, one might be inclined to search for those parameters that maximize the return over the relevant period. To this end, a brute force approach can be
used that simply repeats the whole vectorized backtesting procedure for different

parameter combinations, records the results, and does a ranking afterward. This is what the following code does:

```
In [21]: from itertools import product

In [22]: sma1 = range(20, 61, 4)    ❶
         sma2 = range(180, 281, 10)  ❷

In [23]: results = pd.DataFrame()
         for SMA1, SMA2 in product(sma1, sma2):  ❸
             data = pd.DataFrame(raw[symbol])
             data.dropna(inplace=True)
             data['Returns'] = np.log(data[symbol] / data[symbol].shift(1))
             data['SMA1'] = data[symbol].rolling(SMA1).mean()
             data['SMA2'] = data[symbol].rolling(SMA2).mean()
             data.dropna(inplace=True)
             data['Position'] = np.where(data['SMA1'] > data['SMA2'], 1, -1)
             data['Strategy'] = data['Position'].shift(1) * data['Returns']
             data.dropna(inplace=True)
             perf = np.exp(data[['Returns', 'Strategy']].sum())
             results = results.append(pd.DataFrame(
                         {'SMA1': SMA1, 'SMA2': SMA2,
                          'MARKET': perf['Returns'],
                          'STRATEGY': perf['Strategy'],
                          'OUT': perf['Strategy'] - perf['Returns']},
                         index=[0]), ignore_index=True)  ❹
```

❶ Specifies the parameter values for SMA1.

❷ Specifies the parameter values for SMA2.

❸ Combines all values for SMA1 with those for SMA2.

❹ Records the vectorized backtesting results in a DataFrame object.

The following code gives an overview of the results and shows the seven best-performing parameter combinations of all those backtested. The ranking is implemented according to the outperformance of the algorithmic trading strategy compared to the benchmark investment. The performance of the benchmark investment varies since the choice of the SMA2 parameter influences the length of the time interval and data set on which the vectorized backtest is implemented:

```
In [24]: results.info()
         <class 'pandas.core.frame.DataFrame'>
         RangeIndex: 121 entries, 0 to 120
         Data columns (total 5 columns):
         SMA1        121 non-null int64
         SMA2        121 non-null int64
         MARKET      121 non-null float64
         STRATEGY    121 non-null float64
```

```
OUT          121 non-null float64
dtypes: float64(3), int64(2)
memory usage: 4.8 KB

In [25]: results.sort_values('OUT', ascending=False).head(7)
Out[25]:      SMA1  SMA2   MARKET   STRATEGY        OUT
          56    40   190  4.650342  7.175173  2.524831
          39    32   240  4.045619  6.558690  2.513071
          59    40   220  4.220272  6.544266  2.323994
          46    36   200  4.074753  6.389627  2.314874
          55    40   180  4.574979  6.857989  2.283010
          70    44   220  4.220272  6.469843  2.249571
         101    56   200  4.074753  6.319524  2.244772
```

According to the brute force–based optimization, SMA1=40 and SMA2=190 are the optimal parameters, leading to an outperformance of some 230 percentage points. However, this result is heavily dependent on the data set used and is prone to overfitting. A more rigorous approach would be to implement the optimization on one data set, the in-sample or training data set, and test it on another one, the out-of-sample or testing data set.

Overfitting

In general, any type of optimization, fitting, or training in the context of algorithmic trading strategies is prone to what is called *overfitting*. This means that parameters might be chosen that perform (exceptionally) well for the used data set but might perform (exceptionally) badly on other data sets or in practice.

Random Walk Hypothesis

The previous section introduces vectorized backtesting as an efficient tool to backtest algorithmic trading strategies. The single strategy backtested based on a single financial time series, namely historical end-of-day prices for the Apple stock, outperforms the benchmark investment of simply going long on the Apple stock over the same period.

Although rather specific in nature, these results are in contrast to what the *random walk hypothesis* (RWH) predicts, namely that such predictive approaches should not yield any outperformance at all. The RWH postulates that prices in financial markets follow a random walk, or, in continuous time, an arithmetic Brownian motion without drift. The expected value of an arithmetic Brownian motion without drift at any point in the future equals its value today.[6] As a consequence, the best predictor for tomorrow's price, in a least-squares sense, is today's price if the RWH applies.

The consequences are summarized in the following quote:

> For many years, economists, statisticians, and teachers of finance have been interested in developing and testing models of stock price behavior. One important model that has evolved from this research is the theory of random walks. This theory casts serious doubt on many other methods for describing and predicting stock price behavior— methods that have considerable popularity outside the academic world. For example, we shall see later that, if the random-walk theory is an accurate description of reality, then the various "technical" or "chartist" procedures for predicting stock prices are completely without value.
>
> —Eugene F. Fama (1965)

The RWH is consistent with the *efficient markets hypothesis* (EMH), which, non-technically speaking, states that market prices reflect "all available information." Different degrees of efficiency are generally distinguished, such as *weak, semi-strong*, and *strong*, defining more specifically what "all available information" entails. Formally, such a definition can be based on the concept of an information set in theory and on a data set for programming purposes, as the following quote illustrates:

> A market is efficient with respect to an information set S if it is impossible to make economic profits by trading on the basis of information set S.
>
> —Michael Jensen (1978)

Using Python, the RWH can be tested for a specific case as follows. A financial time series of historical market prices is used for which a number of *lagged* versions are created—say, five. OLS regression is then used to predict the market prices based on the lagged market prices created before. The basic idea is that the market prices from yesterday and four more days back can be used to predict today's market price.

The following Python code implements this idea and creates five lagged versions of the historical end-of-day closing levels of the S&P 500 stock index:

```
In [26]: symbol = '.SPX'

In [27]: data = pd.DataFrame(raw[symbol])

In [28]: lags = 5
         cols = []
         for lag in range(1, lags + 1):
             col = 'lag_{}'.format(lag)      ❶
             data[col] = data[symbol].shift(lag)  ❷
```

---

6 For a formal definition and deeper discussion of random walks and Brownian motion–based processes, refer to Baxter and Rennie (1996).

```
            cols.append(col)  ❸
```

```
In [29]: data.head(7)
Out[29]:              .SPX     lag_1     lag_2     lag_3     lag_4     lag_5
         Date
         2010-01-01    NaN       NaN       NaN       NaN       NaN       NaN
         2010-01-04  1132.99       NaN       NaN       NaN       NaN       NaN
         2010-01-05  1136.52  1132.99       NaN       NaN       NaN       NaN
         2010-01-06  1137.14  1136.52  1132.99       NaN       NaN       NaN
         2010-01-07  1141.69  1137.14  1136.52  1132.99       NaN       NaN
         2010-01-08  1144.98  1141.69  1137.14  1136.52  1132.99       NaN
         2010-01-11  1146.98  1144.98  1141.69  1137.14  1136.52  1132.99
```

```
In [30]: data.dropna(inplace=True)
```

❶ Defines a column name for the current lag value.

❷ Creates the lagged version of the market prices for the current lag value.

❸ Collects the column names for later reference.

Using NumPy, the OLS regression is straightforward to implement. As the optimal regression parameters show, lag_1 indeed is the most important one in predicting the market price based on OLS regression. Its value is close to 1. The other four values are rather close to 0. Figure 15-4 visualizes the optimal regression parameter values.

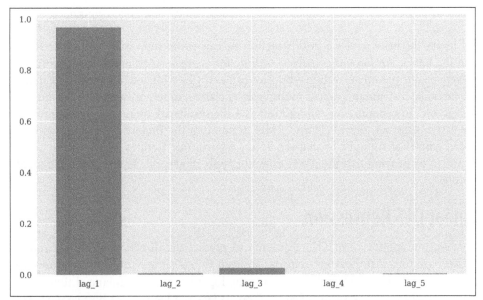

Figure 15-4. Optimal regression parameters from OLS regression for price prediction

When using the optimal results to visualize the prediction values as compared to the original index values for the S&P 500, it becomes obvious from Figure 15-5 that indeed lag_1 is basically what is used to come up with the prediction value. Graphically speaking, the prediction line in Figure 15-5 is the original time series shifted by one day to the right (with some minor adjustments).

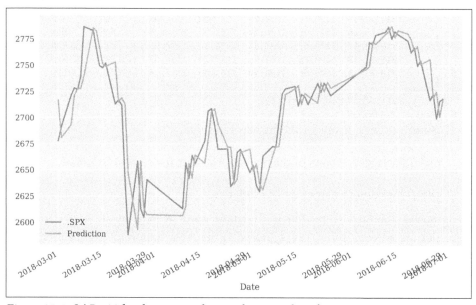

Figure 15-5. S&P 500 levels compared to prediction values from OLS regression

All in all, the brief analysis in this section reveals some support for both the RWH and the EMH. For sure, the analysis is done for a single stock index only and uses a rather specific parameterization—but this can easily be widened to incorporate multiple financial instruments across multiple asset classes, different values for the number of lags, etc. In general, one will find out that the results are qualitatively more or less the same. After all, the RWH and EMH are among the financial theories that have broad empirical support. In that sense, any algorithmic trading strategy must prove its worth by proving that the RWH does not apply in general. This for sure is a tough hurdle.

Linear OLS Regression

This section applies *linear OLS regression* to predict the direction of market movements based on historical log returns. To keep things simple, only two features are used. The first feature (lag_1) represents the log returns of the financial time series lagged by *one day*. The second feature (lag_2) lags the log returns by *two days*. Log returns—in contrast to prices—are *stationary* in general, which often is a necessary condition for the application of statistical and ML algorithms.

The basic idea behind the usage of lagged log returns as features is that they might be informative in predicting future returns. For example, one might hypothesize that after two downward movements an upward movement is more likely ("mean reversion"), or, to the contrary, that another downward movement is more likely ("momentum" or "trend"). The application of regression techniques allows the formalization of such informal reasonings.

The Data

First, the importing and preparation of the data set. Figure 15-6 shows the frequency distribution of the daily historical log returns for the EUR/USD exchange rate. They are the basis for the features as well as the labels to be used in what follows:

```
In [3]: raw = pd.read_csv('../../source/tr_eikon_eod_data.csv',
                          index_col=0, parse_dates=True).dropna()

In [4]: raw.columns
Out[4]: Index(['AAPL.O', 'MSFT.O', 'INTC.O', 'AMZN.O', 'GS.N', 'SPY', '.SPX',
               '.VIX', 'EUR=', 'XAU=', 'GDX', 'GLD'],
              dtype='object')

In [5]: symbol = 'EUR='

In [6]: data = pd.DataFrame(raw[symbol])

In [7]: data['returns'] = np.log(data / data.shift(1))

In [8]: data.dropna(inplace=True)

In [9]: data['direction'] = np.sign(data['returns']).astype(int)

In [10]: data.head()
Out[10]:                 EUR=   returns  direction
         Date
         2010-01-05  1.4368 -0.002988         -1
         2010-01-06  1.4412  0.003058          1
         2010-01-07  1.4318 -0.006544         -1
         2010-01-08  1.4412  0.006544          1
         2010-01-11  1.4513  0.006984          1

In [11]: data['returns'].hist(bins=35, figsize=(10, 6));
```

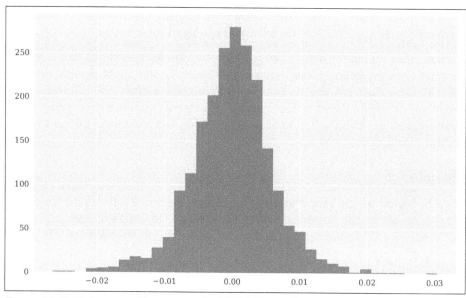

Figure 15-6. Histogram of log returns for EUR/USD exchange rate

Second, the code that creates the features data by lagging the log returns and visual-izes it in combination with the returns data (see Figure 15-7):

```
In [12]: lags = 2

In [13]: def create_lags(data):
             global cols
             cols = []
             for lag in range(1, lags + 1):
                 col = 'lag_{}'.format(lag)
                 data[col] = data['returns'].shift(lag)
                 cols.append(col)

In [14]: create_lags(data)

In [15]: data.head()
Out[15]:                  EUR=   returns  direction      lag_1       lag_2
         Date
         2010-01-05  1.4368 -0.002988         -1        NaN         NaN
         2010-01-06  1.4412  0.003058          1  -0.002988         NaN
         2010-01-07  1.4318 -0.006544         -1   0.003058   -0.002988
         2010-01-08  1.4412  0.006544          1  -0.006544    0.003058
         2010-01-11  1.4513  0.006984          1   0.006544   -0.006544

In [16]: data.dropna(inplace=True)

In [17]: data.plot.scatter(x='lag_1', y='lag_2', c='returns',
                           cmap='coolwarm', figsize=(10, 6), colorbar=True)
```

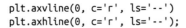

```
plt.axvline(0, c='r', ls='--')
plt.axhline(0, c='r', ls='--');
```

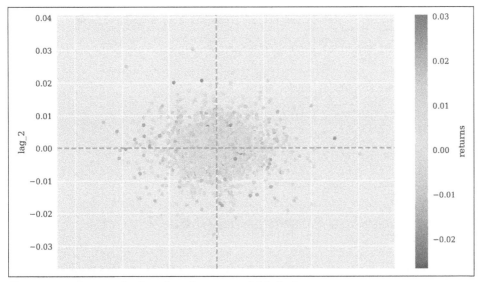

Figure 15-7. Scatter plot based on features and labels data

Regression

With the data set completed, linear OLS regression can be applied to learn about any potential (linear) relationships, to predict market movement based on the features, and to backtest a trading strategy based on the predictions. Two basic approaches are available: using the *log returns* or only the *direction data* as the dependent variable during the regression. In any case, predictions are real-valued and therefore transformed to either +1 or -1 to only work with the direction of the prediction:

```
In [18]: from sklearn.linear_model import LinearRegression    ❶

In [19]: model = LinearRegression()    ❶

In [20]: data['pos_ols_1'] = model.fit(data[cols],
                                        data['returns']).predict(data[cols])    ❷

In [21]: data['pos_ols_2'] = model.fit(data[cols],
                                        data['direction']).predict(data[cols])    ❸

In [22]: data[['pos_ols_1', 'pos_ols_2']].head()
Out[22]:             pos_ols_1  pos_ols_2
         Date
         2010-01-07  -0.000166  -0.000086
         2010-01-08   0.000017   0.040404
         2010-01-11  -0.000244  -0.011756
         2010-01-12  -0.000139  -0.043398
```

```
            2010-01-13   -0.000022    0.002237
```

```
In [23]: data[['pos_ols_1', 'pos_ols_2']] = np.where(
                 data[['pos_ols_1', 'pos_ols_2']] > 0, 1, -1)  ❹
```

```
In [24]: data['pos_ols_1'].value_counts()  ❺
Out[24]: -1    1847
          1     288
         Name: pos_ols_1, dtype: int64
```

```
In [25]: data['pos_ols_2'].value_counts()  ❺
Out[25]:  1    1377
         -1     758
         Name: pos_ols_2, dtype: int64
```

```
In [26]: (data['pos_ols_1'].diff() != 0).sum()  ❻
Out[26]: 555
```

```
In [27]: (data['pos_ols_2'].diff() != 0).sum()  ❻
Out[27]: 762
```

❶ The linear OLS regression implementation from scikit-learn is used.

❷ The regression is implemented on the *log returns* directly …

❸ … and on the *direction data* which is of primary interest.

❹ The real-valued predictions are transformed to directional values (+1, -1).

❺ The two approaches yield different directional predictions in general.

❻ However, both lead to a relatively large number of trades over time.

Equipped with the directional prediction, vectorized backtesting can be applied to judge the performance of the resulting trading strategies. At this stage, the analysis is based on a number of simplifying assumptions, such as "zero transaction costs" and the usage of the same data set for both training and testing. Under these assumptions, however, both regression-based strategies outperform the benchmark passive investment, while only the strategy trained on the direction of the market shows a positive overall performance (Figure 15-8):

```
In [28]: data['strat_ols_1'] = data['pos_ols_1'] * data['returns']
```

```
In [29]: data['strat_ols_2'] = data['pos_ols_2'] * data['returns']
```

```
In [30]: data[['returns', 'strat_ols_1', 'strat_ols_2']].sum().apply(np.exp)
Out[30]: returns        0.810644
         strat_ols_1    0.942422
         strat_ols_2    1.339286
```

```
         dtype: float64

In [31]: (data['direction'] == data['pos_ols_1']).value_counts()  ❶
Out[31]: False    1093
         True     1042
         dtype: int64

In [32]: (data['direction'] == data['pos_ols_2']).value_counts()  ❶
Out[32]: True     1096
         False    1039
         dtype: int64

In [33]: data[['returns', 'strat_ols_1', 'strat_ols_2']].cumsum(
             ).apply(np.exp).plot(figsize=(10, 6));
```

❶ Shows the number of correct and false predictions by the strategies.

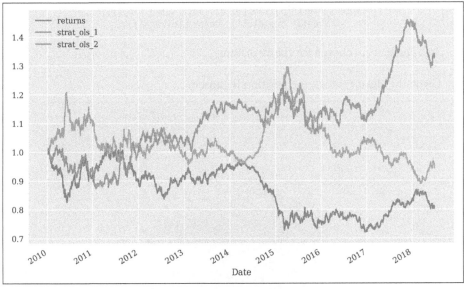

Figure 15-8. Performance of EUR/USD and regression-based strategies over time

Clustering

This section applies *k*-means clustering, as introduced in "Machine Learning" on page 444, to financial time series data to automatically come up with clusters that are used to formulate a trading strategy. The idea is that the algorithm identifies two clusters of feature values that predict either an upward movement or a downward movement.

The following code applies the *k*-means algorithm to the two features as used before. Figure 15-9 visualizes the two clusters:

```
In [34]: from sklearn.cluster import KMeans

In [35]: model = KMeans(n_clusters=2, random_state=0)  ❶

In [36]: model.fit(data[cols])
Out[36]: KMeans(algorithm='auto', copy_x=True, init='k-means++', max_iter=300,
               n_clusters=2, n_init=10, n_jobs=None, precompute_distances='auto',
               random_state=0, tol=0.0001, verbose=0)

In [37]: data['pos_clus'] = model.predict(data[cols])

In [38]: data['pos_clus'] = np.where(data['pos_clus'] == 1, -1, 1)  ❷

In [39]: data['pos_clus'].values
Out[39]: array([-1,  1, -1, ...,  1,  1, -1])

In [40]: plt.figure(figsize=(10, 6))
         plt.scatter(data[cols].iloc[:, 0], data[cols].iloc[:, 1],
                     c=data['pos_clus'], cmap='coolwarm');
```

❶ Two clusters are chosen for the algorithm.

❷ Given the cluster values, the position is chosen.

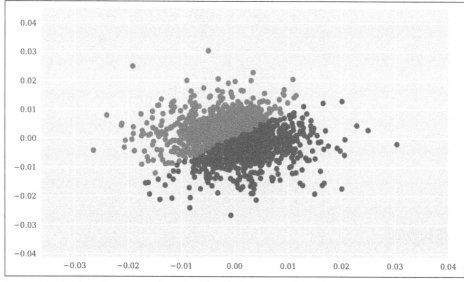

Figure 15-9. Two clusters as identified by the k-means algorithm

Admittedly, this approach is quite arbitrary in this context—after all, how should the
algorithm know what one is looking for? However, the resulting trading strategy
shows a slight outperformance at the end compared to the benchmark passive investment (see Figure 15-10). It is noteworthy that no guidance (supervision) is given and

that the *hit ratio*—i.e., the number of correct predictions in relationship to all predictions made—is less than 50%:

```
In [41]: data['strat_clus'] = data['pos_clus'] * data['returns']

In [42]: data[['returns', 'strat_clus']].sum().apply(np.exp)
Out[42]: returns        0.810644
         strat_clus     1.277133
         dtype: float64

In [43]: (data['direction'] == data['pos_clus']).value_counts()
Out[43]: True     1077
         False    1058
         dtype: int64

In [44]: data[['returns', 'strat_clus']].cumsum(
                    ).apply(np.exp).plot(figsize=(10, 6));
```

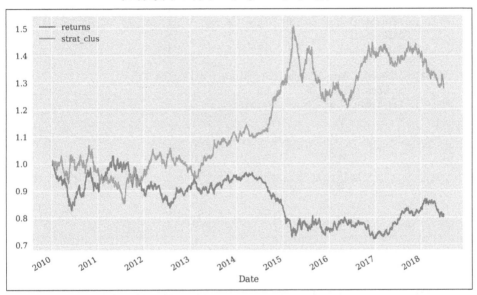

Figure 15-10. Performance of EUR/USD and k-means-based strategy over time

Frequency Approach

Beyond more sophisticated algorithms and techniques, one might come up with the
idea of just implementing a *frequency approach* to predict directional movements in
financial markets. To this end, one might transform the two real-valued features to
binary ones and assess the probability of an upward and a downward movement,
respectively, from the historical observations of such movements, given the four possible combinations for the two binary features ((0, 0), (0, 1), (1, 0), (1, 1)).

Making use of the data analysis capabilities of pandas, such an approach is relatively easy to implement:

```
In [45]: def create_bins(data, bins=[0]):
             global cols_bin
             cols_bin = []
             for col in cols:
                 col_bin = col + '_bin'
                 data[col_bin] = np.digitize(data[col], bins=bins)    ❶
                 cols_bin.append(col_bin)

In [46]: create_bins(data)

In [47]: data[cols_bin + ['direction']].head()    ❷
Out[47]:            lag_1_bin  lag_2_bin  direction
         Date
         2010-01-07         1          0         -1
         2010-01-08         0          1          1
         2010-01-11         1          0          1
         2010-01-12         1          1         -1
         2010-01-13         0          1          1

In [48]: grouped = data.groupby(cols_bin + ['direction'])
         grouped.size()    ❸
Out[48]: lag_1_bin  lag_2_bin  direction
         0          0          -1          239
                                0            4
                                1          258
                    1          -1          262
                                1          288
         1          0          -1          272
                                0            1
                                1          278
                    1          -1          278
                                0            4
                                1          251
         dtype: int64

In [49]: res = grouped['direction'].size().unstack(fill_value=0)    ❹

In [50]: def highlight_max(s):
             is_max = s == s.max()
             return ['background-color: yellow' if v else '' for v in is_max]    ❺

In [51]: res.style.apply(highlight_max, axis=1)    ❻
Out[51]: <pandas.io.formats.style.Styler at 0x1a194216a0>
```

❶ Digitizes the feature values given the bins parameter.

❷ Shows the digitized feature values and the label values.

---

❸ Shows the frequency of the possible movements conditional on the feature value combinations.

❹ Transforms the DataFrame object to have the frequencies in columns.

❺ Highlights the highest-frequency value per feature value combination.

Given the frequency data, three feature value combinations hint at a downward movement while one lets an upward movement seem more likely. This translates into a trading strategy the performance of which is shown in Figure 15-11:

```
In [52]: data['pos_freq'] = np.where(data[cols_bin].sum(axis=1) == 2, -1, 1)  ❶

In [53]: (data['direction'] == data['pos_freq']).value_counts()
Out[53]: True     1102
         False    1033
         dtype: int64

In [54]: data['strat_freq'] = data['pos_freq'] * data['returns']

In [55]: data[['returns', 'strat_freq']].sum().apply(np.exp)
Out[55]: returns       0.810644
         strat_freq    0.989513
         dtype: float64

In [56]: data[['returns', 'strat_freq']].cumsum(
                 ).apply(np.exp).plot(figsize=(10, 6));
```

❶ Translates the findings given the frequencies to a trading strategy.

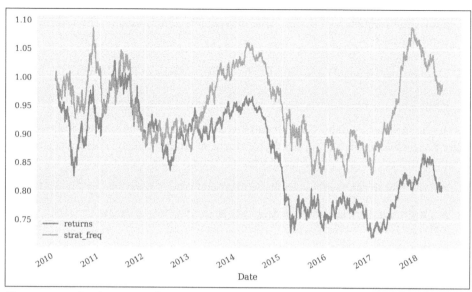

Figure 15-11. Performance of EUR/USD and frequency-based trading strategy over time

Classification

This section applies the classification algorithms from ML (as introduced in "Machine Learning" on page 444) to the problem of predicting the direction of price movements in financial markets. With that background and the examples from previous sections, the application of the logistic regression, Gaussian Naive Bayes, and support vector machine approaches is as straightforward as applying them to smaller sample data sets.

Two Binary Features

First, a fitting of the models based on the binary feature values and the derivation of the resulting position values:

```
In [57]: from sklearn import linear_model
         from sklearn.naive_bayes import GaussianNB
         from sklearn.svm import SVC

In [58]: C = 1

In [59]: models = {
             'log_reg': linear_model.LogisticRegression(C=C),
             'gauss_nb': GaussianNB(),
             'svm': SVC(C=C)
         }

In [60]: def fit_models(data):    ❶
```

```
           mfit = {model: models[model].fit(data[cols_bin],
                                              data['direction'])
                   for model in models.keys()}

In [61]: fit_models(data)

In [62]: def derive_positions(data):   ❷
             for model in models.keys():
                 data['pos_' + model] = models[model].predict(data[cols_bin])

In [63]: derive_positions(data)
```

❶ A function that fits all models.

❷ A function that derives all position values from the fitted models.

Second, the vectorized backtesting of the resulting trading strategies. Figure 15-12 visualizes the performance over time:

```
In [64]: def evaluate_strats(data):   ❶
             global sel
             sel = []
             for model in models.keys():
                 col = 'strat_' + model
                 data[col] = data['pos_' + model] * data['returns']
                 sel.append(col)
             sel.insert(0, 'returns')

In [65]: evaluate_strats(data)

In [66]: sel.insert(1, 'strat_freq')

In [67]: data[sel].sum().apply(np.exp)   ❷
Out[67]: returns            0.810644
         strat_freq         0.989513
         strat_log_reg      1.243322
         strat_gauss_nb     1.243322
         strat_svm          0.989513
         dtype: float64

In [68]: data[sel].cumsum().apply(np.exp).plot(figsize=(10, 6));
```

❶ A function that evaluates all resulting trading strategies.

❷ Some strategies might show the exact same performance.

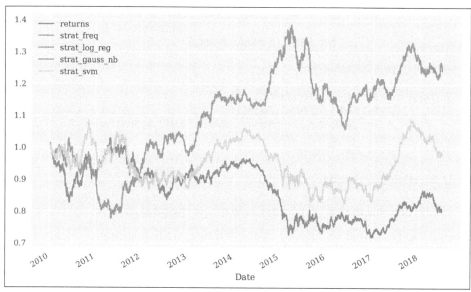

Figure 15-12. Performance of EUR/USD and classification-based trading strategies (two binary lags) over time

Five Binary Features

In an attempt to improve the strategies' performance, the following code works with five binary lags instead of two. In particular, the performance of the SVM-based strategy is significantly improved (see Figure 15-13). On the other hand, the performance of the LR- and GNB-based strategies is worse:

```
In [69]: data = pd.DataFrame(raw[symbol])

In [70]: data['returns'] = np.log(data / data.shift(1))

In [71]: data['direction'] = np.sign(data['returns'])

In [72]: lags = 5    ❶
         create_lags(data)
         data.dropna(inplace=True)

In [73]: create_bins(data)    ❷
         cols_bin
Out[73]: ['lag_1_bin', 'lag_2_bin', 'lag_3_bin', 'lag_4_bin', 'lag_5_bin']

In [74]: data[cols_bin].head()
Out[74]:             lag_1_bin  lag_2_bin  lag_3_bin  lag_4_bin  lag_5_bin
         Date
         2010-01-12          1          1          0          1          0
         2010-01-13          0          1          1          0          1
         2010-01-14          1          0          1          1          0
```

2010-01-15	0	1	0	1	1
2010-01-19	0	0	1	0	1

```
In [75]: data.dropna(inplace=True)

In [76]: fit_models(data)

In [77]: derive_positions(data)

In [78]: evaluate_strats(data)

In [79]: data[sel].sum().apply(np.exp)
Out[79]: returns           0.805002
         strat_log_reg     0.971623
         strat_gauss_nb    0.986420
         strat_svm         1.452406
         dtype: float64

In [80]: data[sel].cumsum().apply(np.exp).plot(figsize=(10, 6));
```

❶ Five lags of the log returns series are now used.

❷ The real-valued features data is transformed to binary data.

Figure 15-13. Performance of EUR/USD and classification-based trading strategies (five binary lags) over time

Five Digitized Features

Finally, the following code uses the first and second moment of the historical log returns to digitize the features data, allowing for more possible feature value combinations. This improves the performance of all classification algorithms used, but for SVM the improvement is again most pronounced (see Figure 15-14):

```
In [81]: mu = data['returns'].mean()   ❶
         v = data['returns'].std()   ❷

In [82]: bins = [mu - v, mu, mu + v]   ❸
         bins   ❸
Out[82]: [-0.006033537040418665, -0.00010174015279231306, 0.005830056734834039]

In [83]: create_bins(data, bins)

In [84]: data[cols_bin].head()
Out[84]:             lag_1_bin  lag_2_bin  lag_3_bin  lag_4_bin  lag_5_bin
         Date
         2010-01-12         3          3          0          2          1
         2010-01-13         1          3          3          0          2
         2010-01-14         2          1          3          3          0
         2010-01-15         1          2          1          3          3
         2010-01-19         0          1          2          1          3

In [85]: fit_models(data)

In [86]: derive_positions(data)

In [87]: evaluate_strats(data)

In [88]: data[sel].sum().apply(np.exp)
Out[88]: returns          0.805002
         strat_log_reg    1.431120
         strat_gauss_nb   1.815304
         strat_svm        5.653433
         dtype: float64

In [89]: data[sel].cumsum().apply(np.exp).plot(figsize=(10, 6));
```

❶ The mean log return and …

❷ … the standard deviation are used …

❸ … to digitize the features data.

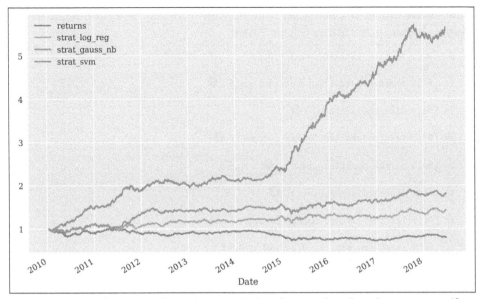

Figure 15-14. Performance of EUR/USD and classification-based trading strategies (five digitized lags) over time

Types of Features

This chapter exclusively works with lagged return data as features data, mostly in binarized or digitized form. This is mainly done for convenience, since such features data can be derived from the financial time series itself. However, in practical applications the features data can be gained from a wealth of different data sources and might include other financial time series and statistics derived thereof, macroeconomic data, company financial indicators, or news articles. Refer to López de Prado (2018) for an in-depth discussion of this topic. There are also Python packages for automated time series feature extraction available, such as tsfresh (*https://github.com/blue-yonder/tsfresh*).

Sequential Train-Test Split

To better judge the performance of the classification algorithms, the code that follows implements a *sequential* train-test split. The idea here is to simulate the situation where only data up to a certain point in time is available on which to train an ML algorithm. During live trading, the algorithm is then faced with data it has never seen before. This is where the algorithm must prove its worth. In this particular case, all classification algorithms outperform—under the simplified assumptions from before

—the passive benchmark investment, but only the GNB and LR algorithms achieve a positive absolute performance (Figure 15-15):

```
In [90]: split = int(len(data) * 0.5)

In [91]: train = data.iloc[:split].copy()   ❶

In [92]: fit_models(train)   ❶

In [93]: test = data.iloc[split:].copy()   ❷

In [94]: derive_positions(test)   ❷

In [95]: evaluate_strats(test)   ❷

In [96]: test[sel].sum().apply(np.exp)
Out[96]: returns          0.850291
         strat_log_reg    0.962989
         strat_gauss_nb   0.941172
         strat_svm        1.048966
         dtype: float64

In [97]: test[sel].cumsum().apply(np.exp).plot(figsize=(10, 6));
```

❶ Trains all classification algorithms on the training data.

❷ Tests all classification algorithms on the test data.

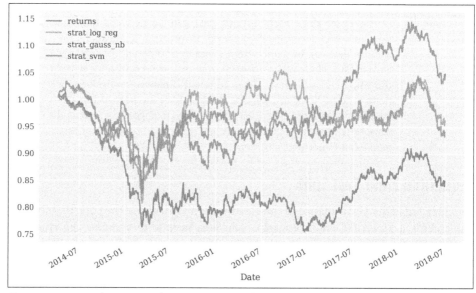

Figure 15-15. Performance of EUR/USD and classification-based trading strategies (sequential train-test split)

Randomized Train-Test Split

The classification algorithms are trained and tested on binary or digitized features data. The idea is that the feature value patterns allow a prediction of future market movements with a better hit ratio than 50%. Implicitly, it is assumed that the patterns' predictive power persists over time. In that sense, it shouldn't make (too much of) a difference on which part of the data an algorithm is trained and on which part of the data it is tested—implying that one can break up the temporal sequence of the data for training and testing.

A typical way to do this is a *randomized* train-test split to test the performance of the classification algorithms out-of-sample—again trying to emulate reality, where an algorithm during trading is faced with new data on a continuous basis. The approach used is the same as that applied to the sample data in "Train-test splits: Support vector machines" on page 459. Based on this approach, the SVM algorithm shows again the best performance out-of-sample (see Figure 15-16):

```
In [98]: from sklearn.model_selection import train_test_split

In [99]: train, test = train_test_split(data, test_size=0.5,
                                         shuffle=True, random_state=100)

In [100]: train = train.copy().sort_index()   ❶

In [101]: train[cols_bin].head()
Out[101]:             lag_1_bin  lag_2_bin  lag_3_bin  lag_4_bin  lag_5_bin
          Date
          2010-01-12          3          3          0          2          1
          2010-01-13          1          3          3          0          2
          2010-01-14          2          1          3          3          0
          2010-01-15          1          2          1          3          3
          2010-01-20          1          0          1          2          1

In [102]: test = test.copy().sort_index()   ❶

In [103]: fit_models(train)

In [104]: derive_positions(test)

In [105]: evaluate_strats(test)

In [106]: test[sel].sum().apply(np.exp)
Out[106]: returns          0.878078
          strat_log_reg    0.735893
          strat_gauss_nb   0.765009
          strat_svm        0.695428
          dtype: float64

In [107]: test[sel].cumsum().apply(np.exp).plot(figsize=(10, 6));
```

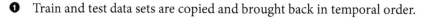 Train and test data sets are copied and brought back in temporal order.

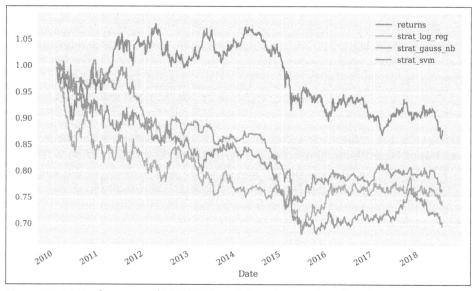

Figure 15-16. Performance of EUR/USD and classification-based trading strategies (randomized train-test split)

Deep Neural Networks

Deep neural networks (DNNs) try to emulate the functioning of the human brain. They are in general composed of an input layer (the features), an output layer (the labels), and a number of hidden layers. The presence of hidden layers is what makes a neural network *deep*. It allows it to learn more complex relationships and to perform better on a number of problem types. When applying DNNs one generally speaks of *deep learning* instead of machine learning. For an introduction to this field, refer to Géron (2017) or Gibson and Patterson (2017).

DNNs with scikit-learn

This section applies the MLPClassifier algorithm from scikit-learn, as introduced in "Deep neural networks" on page 454. First, it is trained and tested on the whole data set, using the digitized features. The algorithm achieves exceptional performance in-sample (see Figure 15-17), which illustrates the power of DNNs for this type of problem. It also hints at strong overfitting, since the performance indeed seems unrealistically good:

```
In [108]: from sklearn.neural_network import MLPClassifier

In [109]: model = MLPClassifier(solver='lbfgs', alpha=1e-5,
```

```
                              hidden_layer_sizes=2 * [250],
                              random_state=1)

In [110]: %time model.fit(data[cols_bin], data['direction'])
          CPU times: user 16.1 s, sys: 156 ms, total: 16.2 s
          Wall time: 9.85 s

Out[110]: MLPClassifier(activation='relu', alpha=1e-05, batch_size='auto',
              beta_1=0.9,
                      beta_2=0.999, early_stopping=False, epsilon=1e-08,
                      hidden_layer_sizes=[250, 250], learning_rate='constant',
                      learning_rate_init=0.001, max_iter=200, momentum=0.9,
                      n_iter_no_change=10, nesterovs_momentum=True, power_t=0.5,
                      random_state=1, shuffle=True, solver='lbfgs', tol=0.0001,
                      validation_fraction=0.1, verbose=False, warm_start=False)

In [111]: data['pos_dnn_sk'] = model.predict(data[cols_bin])

In [112]: data['strat_dnn_sk'] = data['pos_dnn_sk'] * data['returns']

In [113]: data[['returns', 'strat_dnn_sk']].sum().apply(np.exp)
Out[113]: returns          0.805002
          strat_dnn_sk    35.156677
          dtype: float64

In [114]: data[['returns', 'strat_dnn_sk']].cumsum().apply(
                      np.exp).plot(figsize=(10, 6));
```

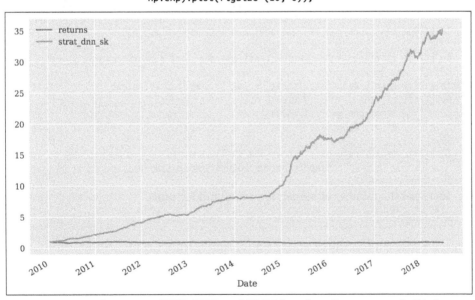

Figure 15-17. Performance of EUR/USD and DNN-based trading strategy (scikit-learn, in-sample)

To avoid overfitting of the DNN model, a randomized train-test split is applied next. The algorithm again outperforms the passive benchmark investment and achieves a positive absolute performance (Figure 15-18). However, the results seem more realistic now:

```
In [115]: train, test = train_test_split(data, test_size=0.5,
                                          random_state=100)

In [116]: train = train.copy().sort_index()

In [117]: test = test.copy().sort_index()

In [118]: model = MLPClassifier(solver='lbfgs', alpha=1e-5, max_iter=500,
                                hidden_layer_sizes=3 * [500], random_state=1)  ❶

In [119]: %time model.fit(train[cols_bin], train['direction'])
          CPU times: user 2min 26s, sys: 1.02 s, total: 2min 27s
          Wall time: 1min 31s

Out[119]: MLPClassifier(activation='relu', alpha=1e-05, batch_size='auto',
                beta_1=0.9,
                    beta_2=0.999, early_stopping=False, epsilon=1e-08,
                    hidden_layer_sizes=[500, 500, 500], learning_rate='constant',
                    learning_rate_init=0.001, max_iter=500, momentum=0.9,
                    n_iter_no_change=10, nesterovs_momentum=True, power_t=0.5,
                    random_state=1, shuffle=True, solver='lbfgs', tol=0.0001,
                    validation_fraction=0.1, verbose=False, warm_start=False)

In [120]: test['pos_dnn_sk'] = model.predict(test[cols_bin])

In [121]: test['strat_dnn_sk'] = test['pos_dnn_sk'] * test['returns']

In [122]: test[['returns', 'strat_dnn_sk']].sum().apply(np.exp)
Out[122]: returns          0.878078
          strat_dnn_sk     1.242042
          dtype: float64

In [123]: test[['returns', 'strat_dnn_sk']].cumsum(
                      ).apply(np.exp).plot(figsize=(10, 6));
```

❶ Increases the number of hidden layers and hidden units.

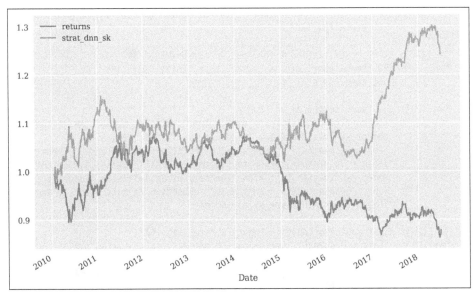

Figure 15-18. Performance of EUR/USD and DNN-based trading strategy (scikit-learn, randomized train-test split)

DNNs with TensorFlow

`TensorFlow` has become a popular package for deep learning. It is developed and supported by Google Inc. and applied there to a great variety of machine learning problems. Zedah and Ramsundar (2018) cover `TensorFlow` for deep learning in depth.

As with `scikit-learn`, the application of the `DNNClassifier` algorithm from `Tensor Flow` to derive an algorithmic trading strategy is straightforward given the background from "Deep neural networks" on page 454. The training and test data is the same as before. First, the training of the model. In-sample, the algorithm outperforms the passive benchmark investment and shows a considerable absolute return (see Figure 15-19), again hinting at overfitting:

```
In [124]: import tensorflow as tf
          tf.logging.set_verbosity(tf.logging.ERROR)

In [125]: fc = [tf.contrib.layers.real_valued_column('lags', dimension=lags)]

In [126]: model = tf.contrib.learn.DNNClassifier(hidden_units=3 * [500],
                                                  n_classes=len(bins) + 1,
                                                  feature_columns=fc)

In [127]: def input_fn():
              fc = {'lags': tf.constant(data[cols_bin].values)}
              la = tf.constant(data['direction'].apply(
                        lambda x: 0 if x < 0 else 1).values,
```

```
                                shape=[data['direction'].size, 1])
                return fc, la

In [128]: %time model.fit(input_fn=input_fn, steps=250)  ❶
          CPU times: user 2min 7s, sys: 8.85 s, total: 2min 16s
          Wall time: 49 s

Out[128]: DNNClassifier(params={'head':
          <tensorflow.contrib.learn.python.learn.estimators.head._MultiClassHead
          object at 0x1a19acf898>, 'hidden_units': [500, 500, 500],
          'feature_columns': (_RealValuedColumn(column_name='lags', dimension=5,
          default_value=None, dtype=tf.float32, normalizer=None),), 'optimizer':
          None, 'activation_fn': <function relu at 0x1161441e0>, 'dropout':
          None, 'gradient_clip_norm': None, 'embedding_lr_multipliers': None,
          'input_layer_min_slice_size': None})

In [129]: model.evaluate(input_fn=input_fn, steps=1)  ❷
Out[129]: {'loss': 0.6879357, 'accuracy': 0.5379925, 'global_step': 250}

In [130]: pred = np.array(list(model.predict(input_fn=input_fn)))  ❷
          pred[:10]  ❷
Out[130]: array([0, 0, 0, 0, 0, 1, 0, 1, 1, 0])

In [131]: data['pos_dnn_tf'] = np.where(pred > 0, 1, -1)  ❸

In [132]: data['strat_dnn_tf'] = data['pos_dnn_tf'] * data['returns']

In [133]: data[['returns', 'strat_dnn_tf']].sum().apply(np.exp)
Out[133]: returns          0.805002
          strat_dnn_tf     2.437222
          dtype: float64

In [134]: data[['returns', 'strat_dnn_tf']].cumsum(
                        ).apply(np.exp).plot(figsize=(10, 6));
```

❶ The time needed for training might be considerable.

❷ The binary predictions (0, 1) …

❸ … need to be transformed to market positions (-1, +1).

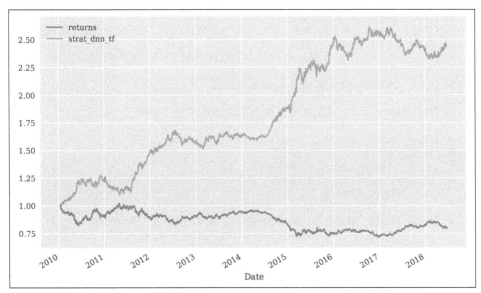

Figure 15-19. Performance of EUR/USD and DNN-based trading strategy (TensorFlow, in-sample)

The following code again implements a randomized train-test split to get a more realistic view of the performance of the DNN-based algorithmic trading strategy. The performance is, as expected, worse out-of-sample (see Figure 15-20). In addition, given the specific parameterization the TensorFlow DNNClassifier underperforms the scikit-learn MLPClassifier algorithm by quite few percentage points:

```
In [135]: model = tf.contrib.learn.DNNClassifier(hidden_units=3 * [500],
                                                  n_classes=len(bins) + 1,
                                                  feature_columns=fc)

In [136]: data = train

In [137]: %time model.fit(input_fn=input_fn, steps=2500)
          CPU times: user 11min 7s, sys: 1min 7s, total: 12min 15s
          Wall time: 4min 27s

Out[137]: DNNClassifier(params={'head':
          <tensorflow.contrib.learn.python.learn.estimators.head._MultiClassHead
          object at 0x116828cc0>, 'hidden_units': [500, 500, 500],
          'feature_columns': (_RealValuedColumn(column_name='lags', dimension=5,
          default_value=None, dtype=tf.float32, normalizer=None),), 'optimizer':
          None, 'activation_fn': <function relu at 0x1161441e0>, 'dropout':
          None, 'gradient_clip_norm': None, 'embedding_lr_multipliers': None,
          'input_layer_min_slice_size': None})

In [138]: data = test
```

```
In [139]: model.evaluate(input_fn=input_fn, steps=1)
Out[139]: {'loss': 0.82882184, 'accuracy': 0.48968107, 'global_step': 2500}

In [140]: pred = np.array(list(model.predict(input_fn=input_fn)))

In [141]: test['pos_dnn_tf'] = np.where(pred > 0, 1, -1)

In [142]: test['strat_dnn_tf'] = test['pos_dnn_tf'] * test['returns']

In [143]: test[['returns', 'strat_dnn_sk', 'strat_dnn_tf']].sum().apply(np.exp)
Out[143]: returns        0.878078
          strat_dnn_sk   1.242042
          strat_dnn_tf   1.063968
          dtype: float64

In [144]: test[['returns', 'strat_dnn_sk', 'strat_dnn_tf']].cumsum(
                      ).apply(np.exp).plot(figsize=(10, 6));
```

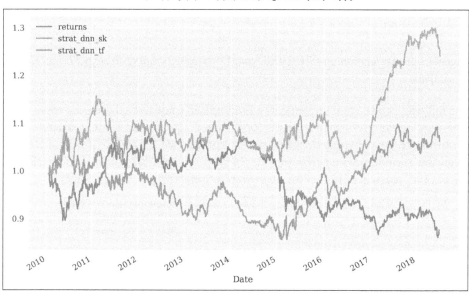

Figure 15-20. Performance of EUR/USD and DNN-based trading strategy (TensorFlow, randomized train-test split)

Performance Results

All performance results shown for the different algorithmic trading strategies from vectorized backtesting so far are illustrative only. Beyond the simplifying assumption of no transaction costs, the results depend on a number of other (mostly arbitrarily chosen) parameters. They also depend on the relative small end-of-day price data set used throughout for the EUR/USD exchange rate. The focus lies on illustrating the application of different approaches and ML algorithms to financial data, not on deriving a robust algorithmic trading strategy to be deployed in practice. The next chapter addresses some of these issues.

Conclusion

This chapter is about algorithmic trading strategies and judging their performance based on vectorized backtesting. It starts with a rather simple algorithmic trading strategy based on two simple moving averages, a type of strategy known and used in practice for decades. This strategy is used to illustrate vectorized backtesting, making heavy use of the vectorization capabilities of NumPy and pandas for data analysis.

Using OLS regression, the chapter also illustrates the random walk hypothesis on the basis of a real financial time series. This is the benchmark against which any algorithmic trading strategy must prove its worth.

The core of the chapter is the application of machine learning algorithms, as introduced in "Machine Learning" on page 444. A number of algorithms, the majority of which are of classification type, are used and applied based on mostly the same "rhythm." As features, lagged log returns data is used in a number of variants—although this is a restriction that for sure is not necessary. It is mostly done for convenience and simplicity. In addition, the analysis is based on a number of simplifying assumptions since the focus is mainly on the technical aspects of applying machine learning algorithms to financial time series data to predict the direction of financial market movements.

Further Resources

The papers referenced in this chapter are:

- Brock, William, Josef Lakonishok, and Blake LeBaron (1992). "Simple Technical Trading Rules and the Stochastic Properties of Stock Returns." *Journal of Finance*, Vol. 47, No. 5, pp. 1731–1764.
- Fama, Eugene (1965). "Random Walks in Stock Market Prices." Selected Papers, No. 16, Graduate School of Business, University of Chicago.

- Jensen, Michael (1978). "Some Anomalous Evidence Regarding Market Efficiency." *Journal of Financial Economics*, Vol. 6, No. 2/3, pp. 95–101.

Finance books covering topics relevant to this chapter include:

- Baxter, Martin, and Andrew Rennie (1996). *Financial Calculus*. Cambridge, England: Cambridge University Press.
- Chan, Ernest (2009). *Quantitative Trading*. Hoboken, NJ: John Wiley & Sons.
- Chan, Ernest (2013). *Algorithmic Trading*. Hoboken, NJ: John Wiley & Sons.
- Chan, Ernest (2017). *Machine Trading*. Hoboken, NJ: John Wiley & Sons.
- López de Prado, Marcos (2018). *Advances in Financial Machine Learning*. Hoboken, NJ: John Wiley & Sons.

Technology books covering topics relevant to this chapter include:

- Albon, Chris (2018). *Machine Learning with Python Cookbook*. Sebastopol, CA: O'Reilly.
- Géron, Aurélien (2017). *Hands-On Machine Learning with Scikit-Learn and Tensorflow*. Sebastopol, CA: O'Reilly.
- Gibson, Adam, and Josh Patterson (2017). *Deep Learning*. Sebastopol, CA: O'Reilly.
- VanderPlas, Jake (2016). *Python Data Science Handbook*. Sebastopol, CA: O'Reilly.
- Zadeh, Reza Bosagh, and Bharath Ramsundar (2018). *TensorFlow for Deep Learning*. Sebastopol, CA: O'Reilly.

For a comprehensive online training program covering Python for algorithmic trading, see *http://certificate.tpq.io*.

## CHAPTER 16

Automated Trading

People worry that computers will get too smart and take over the world, but the real problem is that they're too stupid and they've already taken over the world.

—Pedro Domingos

"Now what?" one might think. A trading platform is available that allows one to retrieve historical data and streaming data, to place buy and sell orders, and to check the account status. A number of different methods have been introduced to derive algorithmic trading strategies by predicting the direction of market price movements. How can this all be put together to work in automated fashion? This question cannot be answered in any generality. However, this chapter addresses a number of topics that are important in this context. The chapter assumes that a single automated algorithmic trading strategy only shall be deployed. This simplifies, among others, aspects like capital and risk management.

The chapter covers the following topics:

"Capital Management" on page 522
> As this section demonstrates, depending on the strategy characteristics and the trading capital available, the Kelly criterion helps with sizing the trades.

"ML-Based Trading Strategy" on page 532
> To gain confidence in an algorithmic trading strategy, the strategy needs to be backtested thoroughly both with regard to performance and risk characteristics; the example strategy used is based on a classification algorithm from machine learning as introduced in Chapter 15.

"Online Algorithm" on page 544
> To deploy the algorithmic trading strategy for automated trading, it needs to be translated into an online algorithm that works with incoming streaming data in real time.

"Infrastructure and Deployment" on page 546

To run automated algorithmic trading strategies robustly and reliably, deployment in the cloud is the preferred option from an availability, performance, and security point of view.

"Logging and Monitoring" on page 547

To be able to analyze the history and certain events during the deployment of an automated trading strategy, logging plays an important role; monitoring via socket communication allows one to observe events (remotely) in real time.

Capital Management

A central question in algorithmic trading is how much capital to deploy to a given algorithmic trading strategy given the total available capital. The answer to this question depends on the main goal one is trying to achieve by algorithmic trading. Most individuals and financial institutions will agree that the *maximization of long-term wealth* is a good candidate objective. This is what Edward Thorpe had in mind when he derived the *Kelly criterion* for investing, as described in the paper by Rotando and Thorp (1992).

The Kelly Criterion in a Binomial Setting

The common way of introducing the theory of the Kelly criterion for investing is on the basis of a coin tossing game, or more generally a binomial setting (where only two outcomes are possible). This section follows that route. Assume a gambler is playing a coin tossing game against an infinitely rich bank or casino. Assume further that the probability for heads is some value p for which $\frac{1}{2} < p < 1$ holds. Probability for tails is defined by $q = 1 - p < \frac{1}{2}$. The gambler can place bets $b > 0$ of arbitrary size, whereby the gambler wins the same amount if right and loses it all if wrong. Given the assumptions about the probabilities, the gambler would of course want to bet on heads. Therefore, the expected value for this betting game B (i.e., the random variable representing this game) in a one-shot setting is:

$$\mathbf{E}[B] = p \cdot b - q \cdot b = (p - q) \cdot b > 0$$

A risk-neutral gambler with unlimited funds would like to bet as large an amount as possible since this would maximize the expected payoff. However, trading in financial markets is not a one-shot game in general. It is a repeated one. Therefore, assume that b_i represents the amount that is bet on day i and that c_0 represents the initial capital. The capital c_1 at the end of day one depends on the betting success on that day and might be either $c_0 + b_1$ or $c_0 - b_1$. The expected value for a gamble that is repeated n times then is:

$$E[B^n] = c_0 + \sum_{i=1}^{n} (p - q) \cdot b_i$$

In classical economic theory, with risk-neutral, expected utility-maximizing agents, a gambler would try to maximize this expression. It is easily seen that it is maximized by betting all available funds—i.e., $b_i = c_{i-1}$—like in the one-shot scenario. However, this in turn implies that a single loss will wipe out all available funds and will lead to ruin (unless unlimited borrowing is possible). Therefore, this strategy does not lead to a maximization of long-term wealth.

While betting the maximum capital available might lead to sudden ruin, betting nothing at all avoids any kind of loss but does not benefit from the advantageous gamble either. This is where the Kelly criterion comes into play, since it derives the *optimal fraction* f^* of the available capital to bet per round of betting. Assume that $n = h + t$, where h stands for the number of heads observed during n rounds of betting and where t stands for the number of tails. With these definitions, the available capital after n rounds is:

$$c_n = c_0 \cdot (1 + f)^h \cdot (1 - f)^t$$

In such a context, long-term wealth maximization boils down to maximizing the average geometric growth rate per bet, which is given as:

$$
\begin{aligned}
r^g &= \log \left(\frac{c_n}{c_0} \right)^{1/n} \\
&= \log \left(\frac{c_0 \cdot (1 + f)^h \cdot (1 - f)^t}{c_0} \right)^{1/n} \\
&= \log \left((1 + f)^h \cdot (1 - f)^t \right)^{1/n} \\
&= \frac{h}{n} \log (1 + f) + \frac{t}{n} \log (1 - f)
\end{aligned}
$$

The problem then formally is to maximize the *expected* average rate of growth by choosing f optimally. With $E[h] = n \cdot p$ and $E[t] = n \cdot q$, one gets:

$$
\begin{aligned}
E[r^g] &= E\left[\frac{h}{n} \log (1 + f) + \frac{t}{n} \log (1 - f) \right] \\
&= E[p \log (1 + f) + q \log (1 - f)] \\
&= p \log (1 + f) + q \log (1 - f) \\
&\equiv G(f)
\end{aligned}
$$

One can now maximize the term by choosing the optimal fraction f^* according to the first-order condition. The first derivative is given by:

$$G'(f) = \frac{p}{1+f} - \frac{q}{1-f}$$
$$= \frac{p - pf - q - qf}{(1+f)(1-f)}$$
$$= \frac{p - q - f}{(1+f)(1-f)}$$

From the first-order condition, one gets:

$$G'(f) \overset{!}{=} 0 \Rightarrow f^* = p - q$$

If one trusts this to be the maximum (and not the minimum), this result implies that it is optimal to invest a fraction $f^* = p - q$ per round of betting. With, for example, $p = 0.55$ one has $f^* = 0.55 - 0.45 = 0.1$, indicating that the optimal fraction is 10%.

The following Python code formalizes these concepts and results through simulation. First, some imports and configurations:

```
In [1]: import math
        import time
        import numpy as np
        import pandas as pd
        import datetime as dt
        import cufflinks as cf
        from pylab import plt
In [2]: np.random.seed(1000)
        plt.style.use('seaborn')
        %matplotlib inline
```

The idea is to simulate, for example, 50 series with 100 coin tosses per series. The Python code for this is straightforward:

```
In [3]: p = 0.55    ❶

In [4]: f = p - (1 - p)    ❷

In [5]: f    ❷
Out[5]: 0.10000000000000009

In [6]: I = 50    ❸

In [7]: n = 100    ❹
```

❶ Fixes the probability for heads.

---

❷ Calculates the optimal fraction according to the Kelly criterion.

❸ The number of series to be simulated.

❹ The number of trials per series.

The major part is the Python function `run_simulation()`, which achieves the simulation according to the prior assumptions. Figure 16-1 shows the simulation results:

```
In [8]: def run_simulation(f):
            c = np.zeros((n, I))   ❶
            c[0] = 100   ❷
            for i in range(I):   ❸
                for t in range(1, n):   ❹
                    o = np.random.binomial(1, p)   ❺
                    if o > 0:   ❻
                        c[t, i] = (1 + f) * c[t - 1, i]   ❼
                    else:   ❽
                        c[t, i] = (1 - f) * c[t - 1, i]   ❾
            return c

In [9]: c_1 = run_simulation(f)   ❿

In [10]: c_1.round(2)
Out[10]: array([[100.  , 100.  , 100.  , ..., 100.  , 100.  , 100.  ],
                [ 90.  , 110.  ,  90.  , ..., 110.  ,  90.  , 110.  ],
                [ 99.  , 121.  ,  99.  , ..., 121.  ,  81.  , 121.  ],
                ...,
                [226.35, 338.13, 413.27, ..., 123.97, 123.97, 123.97],
                [248.99, 371.94, 454.6 , ..., 136.37, 136.37, 136.37],
                [273.89, 409.14, 409.14, ..., 122.73, 150.01, 122.73]])

In [11]: plt.figure(figsize=(10, 6))
         plt.plot(c_1, 'b', lw=0.5)   ⓫
         plt.plot(c_1.mean(axis=1), 'r', lw=2.5);   ⓬
```

❶ Instantiates an ndarray object to store the simulation results.

❷ Initializes the starting capital with 100.

❸ Outer loop for the series simulations.

❹ Inner loop for the series itself.

❺ Simulates the tossing of a coin.

❻ If 1, i.e., heads …

❼ … then add the win to the capital.

❽ If 0, i.e., tails ...

❾ ... then subtract the loss from the capital.

❿ Runs the simulation.

⓫ Plots all 50 series.

⓬ Plots the average over all 50 series.

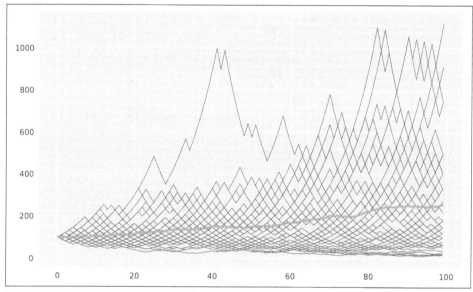

Figure 16-1. 50 simulated series with 100 trials each (red line = average)

The following code repeats the simulation for different values of f. As shown in Figure 16-2, a lower fraction leads to a lower growth rate on average. Higher values might lead to a higher average capital at the end of the simulation ($f = 0.25$) or to a much lower average capital ($f = 0.5$). In both cases where the fraction f is higher, the volatility increases considerably:

```
In [12]: c_2 = run_simulation(0.05)  ❶

In [13]: c_3 = run_simulation(0.25)  ❷

In [14]: c_4 = run_simulation(0.5)   ❸

In [15]: plt.figure(figsize=(10, 6))
         plt.plot(c_1.mean(axis=1), 'r', label='$f^*=0.1$')
         plt.plot(c_2.mean(axis=1), 'b', label='$f=0.05$')
         plt.plot(c_3.mean(axis=1), 'y', label='$f=0.25$')
```

```
plt.plot(c_4.mean(axis=1), 'm', label='$f=0.5$')
plt.legend(loc=0);
```

❶ Simulation with $f = 0.05$.

❷ Simulation with $f = 0.25$.

❸ Simulation with $f = 0.5$.

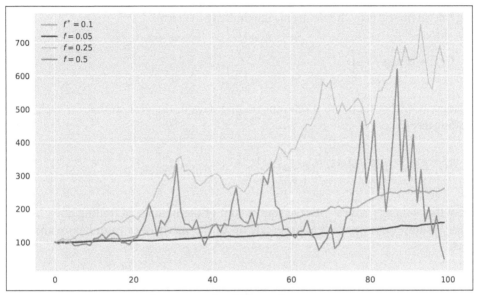

Figure 16-2. Average capital over time for different fractions

The Kelly Criterion for Stocks and Indices

Assume now a stock market setting in which the relevant stock (index) can take on only two values after a period of one year from today, given its known value today. The setting is again binomial, but this time a bit closer on the modeling side to stock market realities.[1] Specifically, assume that:

$$P\left(r^S = \mu + \sigma\right) = P\left(r^S = \mu - \sigma\right) = \frac{1}{2}$$

---

1 The exposition follows Hung (2010).

---

with $\mathrm{E}\left[r^S\right] = \mu > 0$ being the expected return of the stock over one year and $\sigma > 0$ being the standard deviation of returns (volatility). In a one-period setting, one gets for the available capital after one year (with c_0 and f defined as before):

$$c(f) = c_0 \cdot \left(1 + (1 - f) \cdot r + f \cdot r^S\right)$$

Here, r is the constant short rate earned on cash not invested in the stock. Maximizing the geometric growth rate means maximizing the term:

$$G(f) = \mathrm{E}\left[\log \frac{c(f)}{c_0}\right]$$

Assume now that there are n relevant trading days in the year so that for each such trading day i:

$$P\left(r_i^S = \frac{\mu}{n} + \frac{\sigma}{\sqrt{n}}\right) = P\left(r_i^S = \frac{\mu}{n} - \frac{\sigma}{\sqrt{n}}\right) = \frac{1}{2}$$

Note that volatility scales with the square root of the number of trading days. Under these assumptions, the daily values scale up to the yearly ones from before and one gets:

$$c_n(f) = c_0 \cdot \prod_{i=1}^{n} \left(1 + (1 - f) \cdot \frac{r}{n} + f \cdot r_i^S\right)$$

One now has to maximize the following quantity to achieve maximum long-term wealth when investing in the stock:

$$G_n(f) = \mathrm{E}\left[\log \frac{c_n(f)}{c_0}\right]$$

$$= \mathrm{E}\left[\sum_{i=1}^{n} \log\left(1 + (1 - f) \cdot \frac{r}{n} + f \cdot r_i^S\right)\right]$$

$$= \frac{1}{2}\sum_{i=1}^{n} \log\left(1 + (1 - f) \cdot \frac{r}{n} + f \cdot \left(\frac{\mu}{n} + \frac{\sigma}{\sqrt{n}}\right)\right)$$

$$+ \log\left(1 + (1 - f) \cdot \frac{r}{n} + f \cdot \left(\frac{\mu}{n} - \frac{\sigma}{\sqrt{n}}\right)\right)$$

$$= \frac{n}{2} \log\left(\left(1 + (1 - f) \cdot \frac{r}{n} + f \cdot \frac{\mu}{n}\right)^2 - \frac{f^2\sigma^2}{n}\right)$$

Using a Taylor series expansion, one finally arrives at:

$$G_n(f) = r + (\mu - r) \cdot f - \frac{\sigma^2}{2} \cdot f^2 + \mathscr{O}\left(\frac{1}{\sqrt{n}}\right)$$

or for infinitely many trading points in time—i.e., for continuous trading—at:

$$G_\infty(f) = r + (\mu - r) \cdot f - \frac{\sigma^2}{2} \cdot f^2$$

The optimal fraction f^* then is given through the first-order condition by the expression:

$$f^* = \frac{\mu - r}{\sigma^2}$$

I.e., the expected excess return of the stock over the risk-free rate divided by the variance of the returns. This expression looks similar to the Sharpe ratio (see "Portfolio Optimization" on page 415) but is different.

A real-world example shall illustrate the application of these formulae and their role in leveraging equity deployed to trading strategies. The trading strategy under consideration is simply a *passive long position in the S&P 500 index*. To this end, base data is quickly retrieved and required statistics are easily derived:

```
In [16]: raw = pd.read_csv('../../source/tr_eikon_eod_data.csv',
                           index_col=0, parse_dates=True)

In [17]: symbol = '.SPX'

In [18]: data = pd.DataFrame(raw[symbol])

In [19]: data['returns'] = np.log(data / data.shift(1))

In [20]: data.dropna(inplace=True)

In [21]: data.tail()
Out[21]:                  .SPX    returns
         Date
         2018-06-25  2717.07  -0.013820
         2018-06-26  2723.06   0.002202
         2018-06-27  2699.63  -0.008642
         2018-06-28  2716.31   0.006160
         2018-06-29  2718.37   0.000758
```

The statistical properties of the S&P 500 index over the period covered suggest an optimal fraction of about 4.5 to be invested in the long position in the index. In other words, for every dollar available 4.5 dollars shall be invested—implying a *leverage ratio* of 4.5, in accordance with the optimal Kelly "fraction" (or rather "factor" in this case). *Ceteris paribus*, the Kelly criterion implies a higher leverage the higher the expected return and the lower the volatility (variance):

```
In [22]: mu = data.returns.mean() * 252    ❶

In [23]: mu    ❶
Out[23]: 0.09898579893004976

In [24]: sigma = data.returns.std() * 252 ** 0.5    ❷

In [25]: sigma    ❷
Out[25]: 0.1488567510081967

In [26]: r = 0.0    ❸

In [27]: f = (mu - r) / sigma ** 2    ❹

In [28]: f    ❹
Out[28]: 4.4672043679706865
```

❶ Calculates the annualized return.

❷ Calculates the annualized volatility.

❸ Sets the risk-free rate to 0 (for simplicity).

❹ Calculates the optimal Kelly fraction to be invested in the strategy.

The following code simulates the application of the Kelly criterion and the optimal leverage ratio. For simplicity and comparison reasons, the initial equity is set to 1 while the initially invested total capital is set to $1 \cdot f^*$. Depending on the performance of the capital deployed to the strategy, the total capital itself is adjusted daily according to the available equity. After a loss, the capital is reduced; after a profit, the capital is increased. The evolution of the equity position compared to the index itself is shown in Figure 16-3:

```
In [29]: equs = []

In [30]: def kelly_strategy(f):
             global equs
             equ = 'equity_{:.2f}'.format(f)
             equs.append(equ)
             cap = 'capital_{:.2f}'.format(f)
             data[equ] = 1    ❶
             data[cap] = data[equ] * f    ❷
```

```
            for i, t in enumerate(data.index[1:]):
                t_1 = data.index[i]   ❸
                data.loc[t, cap] = data[cap].loc[t_1] * \
                                    math.exp(data['returns'].loc[t])   ❹
                data.loc[t, equ] = data[cap].loc[t] - \
                                    data[cap].loc[t_1] + \
                                    data[equ].loc[t_1]   ❺
                data.loc[t, cap] = data[equ].loc[t] * f   ❻

In [31]: kelly_strategy(f * 0.5)   ❼

In [32]: kelly_strategy(f * 0.66)   ❽

In [33]: kelly_strategy(f)   ❾

In [34]: print(data[equs].tail())
                        equity_2.23   equity_2.95   equity_4.47
         Date
         2018-06-25       4.707070      6.367340      8.794342
         2018-06-26       4.730248      6.408727      8.880952
         2018-06-27       4.639340      6.246147      8.539593
         2018-06-28       4.703365      6.359932      8.775296
         2018-06-29       4.711332      6.374152      8.805026

In [35]: ax = data['returns'].cumsum().apply(np.exp).plot(legend=True,
                                                   figsize=(10, 6))
         data[equs].plot(ax=ax, legend=True);
```

❶ Generates a new column for equity and sets the initial value to 1.

❷ Generates a new column for capital and sets the initial value to $1 \cdot f^*$.

❸ Picks the right DatetimeIndex value for the previous values.

❹ Calculates the new capital position given the return.

❺ Adjusts the equity value according to the capital position performance.

❻ Adjusts the capital position given the new equity position and the fixed leverage ratio.

❼ Simulates the Kelly criterion–based strategy for half of f…

❽ … for two-thirds of f…

❾ … and for f itself.

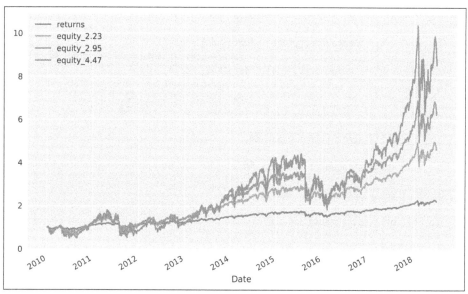

Figure 16-3. Cumulative performance of S&P 500 compared to equity position given different values of f

As Figure 16-3 illustrates, applying the optimal Kelly leverage leads to a rather erratic evolution of the equity position (high volatility) which is—given the leverage ratio of 4.47—intuitively plausible. One would expect the volatility of the equity position to increase with increasing leverage. Therefore, practitioners often reduce the leverage to, for example, "half Kelly"—i.e., in the current example to $\frac{1}{2} \cdot f^* \approx 2.23$. Therefore, Figure 16-3 also shows the evolution of the equity position of values lower than "full Kelly." The risk indeed reduces with lower values of f.

ML-Based Trading Strategy

Chapter 14 introduces the FXCM trading platform, its REST API, and the Python wrapper package fxcmpy. This section combines an ML-based approach for predicting the direction of market price movements with historical data from the FXCM REST API to backtest an algorithmic trading strategy for the EUR/USD currency pair. It uses vectorized backtesting, taking into account this time the bid-ask spread as proportional transaction costs. It also adds, compared to the plain vectorized backtesting approach as introduced in Chapter 15, a more in-depth analysis of the risk characteristics of the trading strategy tested.

Vectorized Backtesting

The backtest is based on intraday data, more specifically on bars of length five minutes. The following code connects to the FXCM REST API and retrieves five-minute bar data for a whole month. Figure 16-4 visualizes the mid close prices over the period for which data is retrieved:

```
In [36]: import fxcmpy

In [37]: fxcmpy.__version__
Out[37]: '1.1.33'

In [38]: api = fxcmpy.fxcmpy(config_file='../fxcm.cfg')    ❶

In [39]: data = api.get_candles('EUR/USD', period='m5',
                                start='2018-06-01 00:00:00',
                                stop='2018-06-30 00:00:00')    ❶

In [40]: data.iloc[-5:, 4:]
Out[40]:                       askopen  askclose  askhigh   asklow  tickqty
         date
         2018-06-29 20:35:00   1.16862   1.16882  1.16896  1.16839      601
         2018-06-29 20:40:00   1.16882   1.16853  1.16898  1.16852      387
         2018-06-29 20:45:00   1.16853   1.16826  1.16862  1.16822      592
         2018-06-29 20:50:00   1.16826   1.16836  1.16846  1.16819      842
         2018-06-29 20:55:00   1.16836   1.16861  1.16876  1.16834      540

In [41]: data.info()
         <class 'pandas.core.frame.DataFrame'>
         DatetimeIndex: 6083 entries, 2018-06-01 00:00:00 to 2018-06-29 20:55:00
         Data columns (total 9 columns):
         bidopen    6083 non-null float64
         bidclose   6083 non-null float64
         bidhigh    6083 non-null float64
         bidlow     6083 non-null float64
         askopen    6083 non-null float64
         askclose   6083 non-null float64
         askhigh    6083 non-null float64
         asklow     6083 non-null float64
         tickqty    6083 non-null int64
         dtypes: float64(8), int64(1)
         memory usage: 475.2 KB

In [42]: spread = (data['askclose'] - data['bidclose']).mean()    ❷
         spread    ❷
Out[42]: 2.6338977478217845e-05

In [43]: data['midclose'] = (data['askclose'] + data['bidclose']) / 2    ❸

In [44]: ptc = spread / data['midclose'].mean()    ❹
         ptc    ❹
Out[44]: 2.255685318140426e-05
```

```
In [45]: data['midclose'].plot(figsize=(10, 6), legend=True);
```

❶ Connects to the API and retrieves the data.

❷ Calculates the average bid-ask spread.

❸ Calculates the mid close prices from the ask and bid close prices.

❹ Calculates the average proportional transaction costs given the average spread
   and the average mid close price.

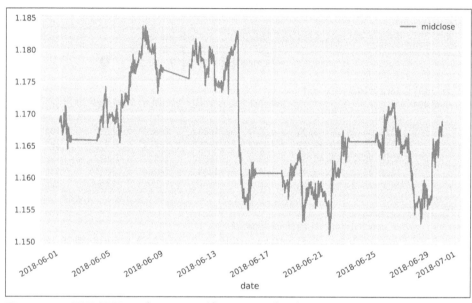

Figure 16-4. EUR/USD exchange rate (five-minute bars)

The ML-based strategy is based on lagged return data that is binarized. In other
words, the ML algorithm learns from historical patterns of upward and downward
movements whether another upward or downward movement is more likely. Accordingly, the following code creates features data with values of 0 and 1 as well as labels
data with values of +1 and -1 indicating the observed market direction in all cases:

```
In [46]: data['returns'] = np.log(data['midclose'] / data['midclose'].shift(1))
```

```
In [47]: data.dropna(inplace=True)
```

```
In [48]: lags = 5
```

```
In [49]: cols = []
         for lag in range(1, lags + 1):
```

```
              col = 'lag_{}'.format(lag)
              data[col] = data['returns'].shift(lag)  ❶
              cols.append(col)

In [50]: data.dropna(inplace=True)

In [51]: data[cols] = np.where(data[cols] > 0, 1, 0)  ❷

In [52]: data['direction'] = np.where(data['returns'] > 0, 1, -1)  ❸

In [53]: data[cols + ['direction']].head()
Out[53]:                      lag_1  lag_2  lag_3  lag_4  lag_5  direction
         date
         2018-06-01 00:30:00      1      0      1      0      1          1
         2018-06-01 00:35:00      1      1      0      1      0          1
         2018-06-01 00:40:00      1      1      1      0      1          1
         2018-06-01 00:45:00      1      1      1      1      0          1
         2018-06-01 00:50:00      1      1      1      1      1         -1
```

❶ Creates the lagged return data given the number of lags.

❷ Transforms the feature values to binary data.

❸ Transforms the returns data to directional label data.

Given the features and label data, different supervised learning algorithms can now be applied. In what follows, a support vector machine algorithm for classification is used from the scikit-learn ML package. The code trains and tests the algorithmic trading strategy based on a sequential train-test split. The accuracy scores of the model for the training and test data are slightly above 50%, while the score is even a bit higher on the test data. Instead of accuracy scores, one would also speak in a financial trading context of the *hit ratio* of the trading strategy; i.e., the number of winning trades compared to all trades. Since the hit ratio is greater than 50%, this might indicate—in the context of the Kelly criterion—a slight edge compared to a random walk setting:

```
In [54]: from sklearn.svm import SVC
         from sklearn.metrics import accuracy_score

In [55]: model = SVC(C=1, kernel='linear', gamma='auto')

In [56]: split = int(len(data) * 0.80)

In [57]: train = data.iloc[:split].copy()

In [58]: model.fit(train[cols], train['direction'])
Out[58]: SVC(C=1, cache_size=200, class_weight=None, coef0=0.0,
             decision_function_shape='ovr', degree=3, gamma='auto', kernel='linear',
               max_iter=-1, probability=False, random_state=None, shrinking=True,
               tol=0.001, verbose=False)
```

```
In [59]: accuracy_score(train['direction'], model.predict(train[cols]))  ❶
Out[59]: 0.5198518823287389

In [60]: test = data.iloc[split:].copy()

In [61]: test['position'] = model.predict(test[cols])

In [62]: accuracy_score(test['direction'], test['position'])  ❷
Out[62]: 0.5419407894736842
```

❶ The accuracy of the predictions from the trained model *in-sample* (training data).

❷ The accuracy of the predictions from the trained model *out-of-sample* (test data).

It is well known that the hit ratio is only one aspect of success in financial trading. Also crucial are, among other things, the transaction costs implied by the trading strategy and getting the important trades right.[2] To this end, only a formal vectorized backtesting approach allows judgment of the quality of the trading strategy. The following code takes into account the proportional transaction costs based on the average bid-ask spread. Figure 16-5 compares the performance of the algorithmic trading strategy (without and with proportional transaction costs) to the performance of the passive benchmark investment:

```
In [63]: test['strategy'] = test['position'] * test['returns']  ❶

In [64]: sum(test['position'].diff() != 0)  ❷
Out[64]: 660

In [65]: test['strategy_tc'] = np.where(test['position'].diff() != 0,
                                        test['strategy'] - ptc,   ❸
                                        test['strategy'])

In [66]: test[['returns', 'strategy', 'strategy_tc']].sum(
                 ).apply(np.exp)
Out[66]: returns        0.999324
         strategy       1.026141
         strategy_tc    1.010977
         dtype: float64

In [67]: test[['returns', 'strategy', 'strategy_tc']].cumsum(
                 ).apply(np.exp).plot(figsize=(10, 6));
```

❶ Derives the log returns for the ML-based algorithmic trading strategy.

---

2 It is a stylized empirical fact that it is of paramount importance for investment and trading performance to get the largest market movements right—i.e., the biggest upward *and* downward movements. This aspect is neatly illustrated in Figures 16-5 and 16-7, which show that the trading strategy gets a large upward movement in the underlying instrument wrong, leading to a large dip for the trading strategy.

❷ Calculates the number of trades implied by the trading strategy based on changes in the position.

❸ Whenever a trade takes place, the proportional transaction costs are subtracted from the strategy's log return on that day.

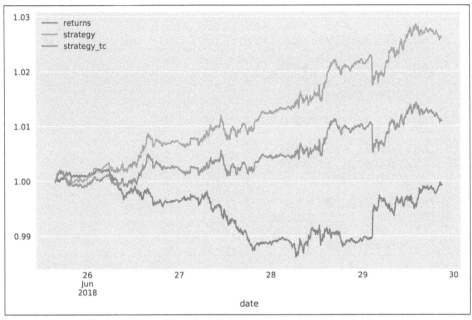

Figure 16-5. Performance of EUR/USD exchange rate and algorithmic trading strategy

Limitations of Vectorized Backtesting

Vectorized backtesting has its limits with regard to how closely to market realities strategies can be tested. For example, it does not allow direct inclusion of fixed transaction costs per trade. One could, as an approximation, take a multiple of the average proportional transaction costs (based on average position sizes) to account indirectly for fixed transactions costs. However, this would not be precise in general. If a higher degree of precision is required other approaches, such as *event-based backtesting* with explicit loops over every bar of the price data, need to be applied.

Optimal Leverage

Equipped with the trading strategy's log returns data, the mean and variance values can be calculated in order to derive the optimal leverage according to the Kelly criterion. The code that follows scales the numbers to annualized values, although this does not change the optimal leverage values according to the Kelly criterion since the mean return and the variance scale with the same factor:

```
In [68]: mean = test[['returns', 'strategy_tc']].mean() * len(data) * 12  ❶
         mean
Out[68]: returns       -0.040535
         strategy_tc    0.654711
         dtype: float64

In [69]: var = test[['returns', 'strategy_tc']].var() * len(data) * 12  ❷
         var
Out[69]: returns        0.007861
         strategy_tc    0.007837
         dtype: float64

In [70]: vol = var ** 0.5  ❸
         vol
Out[70]: returns        0.088663
         strategy_tc    0.088524
         dtype: float64

In [71]: mean / var  ❹
Out[71]: returns       -5.156448
         strategy_tc   83.545792
         dtype: float64

In [72]: mean / var * 0.5  ❺
Out[72]: returns       -2.578224
         strategy_tc   41.772896
         dtype: float64
```

❶ Annualized mean returns.

❷ Annualized variances.

❸ Annualized volatilities.

❹ Optimal leverage according to the Kelly criterion ("full Kelly").

❺ Optimal leverage according to the Kelly criterion ("half Kelly").

Using the "half Kelly" criterion, the optimal leverage for the trading strategy is about 40. With a number of brokers, such as FXCM, and financial instruments, such as foreign exchange and contracts for difference (CFDs), such leverage ratios are feasible, even for retail traders.[3] Figure 16-6 shows in comparison the performance of the trading strategy with transaction costs for different leverage values:

```
In [73]: to_plot = ['returns', 'strategy_tc']

In [74]: for lev in [10, 20, 30, 40, 50]:
             label = 'lstrategy_tc_%d' % lev
             test[label] = test['strategy_tc'] * lev   ❶
             to_plot.append(label)

In [75]: test[to_plot].cumsum().apply(np.exp).plot(figsize=(10, 6));
```

❶ Scales the strategy returns for different leverage values.

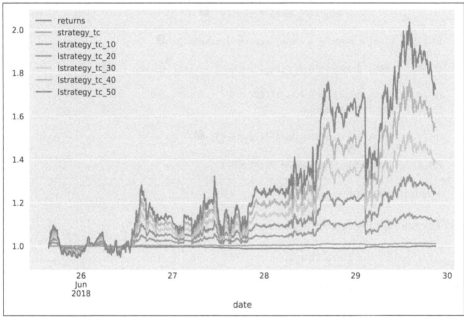

Figure 16-6. Performance of algorithmic trading strategy for different leverage values

Risk Analysis

Since leverage increases the risk associated with a trading strategy, a more in-depth risk analysis seems in order. The risk analysis that follows assumes a leverage ratio of

---

3 Leverage increases risks associated with trading strategies significantly. Traders should read the risk disclaimers and regulations carefully. A positive backtesting performance is also no guarantee whatsoever of future performance. All results shown are illustrative only and are meant to demonstrate the application of programming and analytics approaches. In some jurisdictions, such as in Germany, leverage ratios are capped for retail traders based on different groups of financial instruments.

30. First, the maximum drawdown and the longest drawdown period are calculated. *Maximum drawdown* is the largest loss (dip) after a recent high. Accordingly, the *longest drawdown period* is the longest period that the trading strategy needs to get back to a recent high. The analysis assumes that the initial equity position is 3,333 EUR, leading to an initial position size of 100,000 EUR for a leverage ratio of 30. It also assumes that there are no adjustments with regard to the equity over time, no matter what the performance is:

```
In [76]: equity = 3333   ❶

In [77]: risk = pd.DataFrame(test['lstrategy_tc_30'])   ❷

In [78]: risk['equity'] = risk['lstrategy_tc_30'].cumsum(
                 ).apply(np.exp) * equity   ❸

In [79]: risk['cummax'] = risk['equity'].cummax()   ❹

In [80]: risk['drawdown'] = risk['cummax'] - risk['equity']   ❺

In [81]: risk['drawdown'].max()   ❻
Out[81]: 781.7073602069818

In [82]: t_max = risk['drawdown'].idxmax()   ❼
             t_max   ❼
Out[82]: Timestamp('2018-06-29 02:45:00')
```

❶ The initial equity.

❷ The relevant log returns time series …

❸ … scaled by the initial equity.

❹ The cumulative maximum values over time.

❺ The drawdown values over time.

❻ The maximum drawdown value.

❼ The point in time when it happens.

Technically a (new) high is characterized by a drawdown value of 0. The drawdown period is the time between two such highs. Figure 16-7 visualizes both the maximum drawdown and the drawdown periods:

```
In [83]: temp = risk['drawdown'][risk['drawdown'] == 0]   ❶

In [84]: periods = (temp.index[1:].to_pydatetime() -
                    temp.index[:-1].to_pydatetime())   ❷

In [85]: periods[20:30]   ❷
Out[85]: array([datetime.timedelta(seconds=68700),
                datetime.timedelta(seconds=72000),
          datetime.timedelta(seconds=1800), datetime.timedelta(seconds=300),
          datetime.timedelta(seconds=600), datetime.timedelta(seconds=300),
                datetime.timedelta(seconds=17400),
          datetime.timedelta(seconds=4500), datetime.timedelta(seconds=1500),
                datetime.timedelta(seconds=900)], dtype=object)

In [86]: t_per = periods.max()   ❸

In [87]: t_per   ❸
Out[87]: datetime.timedelta(seconds=76500)

In [88]: t_per.seconds / 60 / 60   ❹
Out[88]: 21.25

In [89]: risk[['equity', 'cummax']].plot(figsize=(10, 6))
         plt.axvline(t_max, c='r', alpha=0.5);
```

❶ Identifies highs for which the drawdown must be 0.

❷ Calculates the `timedelta` values between all highs.

❸ The longest drawdown period in seconds …

❹ … and hours.

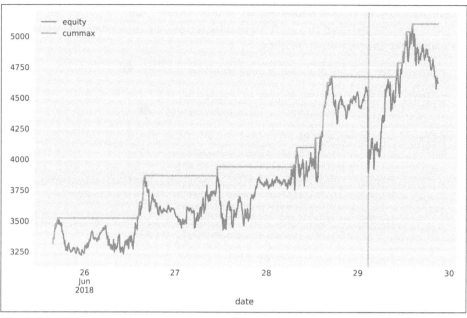

Figure 16-7. Maximum drawdown (vertical line) and drawdown periods (horizontal lines)

Another important risk measure is value-at-risk (VaR). It is quoted as a currency amount and represents the maximum loss to be expected given both a certain time horizon and a confidence level. The code that follows derives VaR values based on the log returns of the equity position for the leveraged trading strategy over time for different confidence levels. The time interval is fixed to the bar length of five minutes:

```
In [91]: import scipy.stats as scs

In [92]: percs = np.array([0.01, 0.1, 1., 2.5, 5.0, 10.0])    ❶

In [93]: risk['returns'] = np.log(risk['equity'] /
                                  risk['equity'].shift(1))

In [94]: VaR = scs.scoreatpercentile(equity * risk['returns'], percs)    ❷

In [95]: def print_var():
             print('%16s %16s' % ('Confidence Level', 'Value-at-Risk'))
             print(33 * '-')
             for pair in zip(percs, VaR):
                 print('%16.2f %16.3f' % (100 - pair[0], -pair[1]))    ❸

In [96]: print_var()    ❸
         Confidence Level    Value-at-Risk
         ---------------------------------
                    99.99          400.854
```

```
            99.90              175.932
            99.00               88.139
            97.50               60.485
            95.00               45.010
            90.00               32.056
```

❶ Defines the percentile values to be used.

❷ Calculates the VaR values given the percentile values.

❸ Translates the percentile values into confidence levels and the VaR values (negative values) to positive values for printing.

Finally, the following code calculates the VaR values for a time horizon of one hour by resampling the original DataFrame object. In effect, the VaR values are increased for all confidence levels but the highest one:

```
In [97]: hourly = risk.resample('1H', label='right').last()   ❶

In [98]: hourly['returns'] = np.log(hourly['equity'] /
                                    hourly['equity'].shift(1))

In [99]: VaR = scs.scoreatpercentile(equity * hourly['returns'], percs)   ❷

In [100]: print_var()
          Confidence Level    Value-at-Risk
          --------------------------------
                     99.99          389.524
                     99.90          372.657
                     99.00          205.662
                     97.50          186.999
                     95.00          164.869
                     90.00          101.835
```

❶ Resamples the data from five-minute to one-hour bars.

❷ Recalculates the VaR values for the resampled data.

Persisting the Model Object

Once the algorithmic trading strategy is "accepted" based on the backtesting, leveraging, and risk analysis results, the model object might be persisted for later use in deployment. It embodies now *the* ML-based trading strategy or *the* trading algorithm:

```
In [101]: import pickle

In [102]: pickle.dump(model, open('algorithm.pkl', 'wb'))
```

Online Algorithm

The trading algorithm tested so far is an *offline algorithm*. Such algorithms use a complete data set to solve a problem at hand. The problem has been to train an SVM algorithm based on binarized features data and directional label data. In practice, when deploying the trading algorithm in financial markets, it must consume data piece-by-piece as it arrives to predict the direction of the market movement for the next time interval (bar). This section makes use of the persisted model object from the previous section and embeds it into a streaming data environment.

The code that transforms the offline trading algorithm into an online trading algorithm mainly addresses the following issues:

Tick data
    Tick data arrives in real time and is to be processed in real time

Resampling
    The tick data is to be resampled to the appropriate bar size given the trading algorithm

Prediction
    The trading algorithm generates a prediction for the direction of the market movement over the relevant time interval that by nature lies in the future

Orders
    Given the current position and the prediction ("signal") generated by the algorithm, an order is placed or the position is kept

"Retrieving Streaming Data" on page 477 shows how to retrieve tick data from the FXCM REST API in real time. The basic approach is to subscribe to a market data stream and pass a callback function that processes the data.

First, the persisted trading algorithm is loaded—it represents the trading logic to be followed. It might also be useful to define a helper function to print out the open position(s) while the trading algorithm is trading:

```
In [103]: algorithm = pickle.load(open('algorithm.pkl', 'rb'))

In [104]: algorithm
Out[104]: SVC(C=1, cache_size=200, class_weight=None, coef0=0.0,
              decision_function_shape='ovr', degree=3, gamma='auto',
              kernel='linear', max_iter=-1, probability=False,
              random_state=None, shrinking=True, tol=0.001, verbose=False)

In [105]: sel = ['tradeId', 'amountK', 'currency',
                 'grossPL', 'isBuy']  ❶

In [106]: def print_positions(pos):
              print('\n\n' + 50 * '=')
```

```
print('Going {}.\n'.format(pos))
time.sleep(1.5)  ❷
print(api.get_open_positions()[sel])  ❸
print(50 * '=' + '\n\n')
```

❶ Defines the `DataFrame` columns to be shown.

❷ Waits a bit for the order to be executed and reflected in the open positions.

❸ Prints the open positions.

Before the online algorithm is defined and started, a few parameter values are set:

```
In [107]: symbol = 'EUR/USD'  ❶
          bar = '15s'  ❷
          amount = 100  ❸
          position = 0  ❹
          min_bars = lags + 1  ❺
          df = pd.DataFrame()  ❻
```

❶ Instrument symbol to be traded.

❷ Bar length for resampling; for easier testing, the bar length might be shortened compared to the real deployment length (e.g., 15 seconds instead of 5 minutes).

❸ The amount, in thousands, to be traded.

❹ The initial position ("neutral").

❺ The minimum number of resampled bars required for the first prediction and trade to be possible.

❻ An empty `DataFrame` object to be used later for the resampled data.

Following is the callback function `automated_strategy()` that transforms the trading algorithm into a real-time context:

```
In [108]: def automated_strategy(data, dataframe):
              global min_bars, position, df
              ldf = len(dataframe)  ❶
              df = dataframe.resample(bar, label='right').last().ffill()  ❷
              if ldf % 20 == 0:
                  print('%3d' % len(dataframe), end=',')

              if len(df) > min_bars:
                  min_bars = len(df)
                  df['Mid'] = df[['Bid', 'Ask']].mean(axis=1)
                  df['Returns'] = np.log(df['Mid'] / df['Mid'].shift(1))
                  df['Direction'] = np.where(df['Returns'] > 0, 1, -1)
                  features = df['Direction'].iloc[-(lags + 1):-1]  ❸
```

```
        features = features.values.reshape(1, -1)  ❹
        signal = algorithm.predict(features)[0]  ❺

        if position in [0, -1] and signal == 1:  ❻
            api.create_market_buy_order(
                symbol, amount - position * amount)
            position = 1
            print_positions('LONG')

        elif position in [0, 1] and signal == -1:  ❼
            api.create_market_sell_order(
                symbol, amount + position * amount)
            position = -1
            print_positions('SHORT')

    if len(dataframe) > 350:  ❽
        api.unsubscribe_market_data('EUR/USD')
        api.close_all()
```

❶ Captures the length of the `DataFrame` object with the tick data.

❷ Resamples the tick data to the defined bar length.

❸ Picks the relevant feature values for all lags …

❹ … and reshapes them to a form that the model can use for prediction.

❺ Generates the prediction value (either +1 or -1).

❻ The conditions to enter (or keep) a *long* position.

❼ The conditions to enter (or keep) a *short* position.

❽ The condition to stop trading and close out any open positions (arbitrarily defined based on the number of ticks retrieved).

Infrastructure and Deployment

Deploying an automated algorithmic trading strategy with real funds requires an appropriate infrastructure. Among others, the infrastructure should satisfy the following conditions:

Reliability
>   The infrastructure on which to deploy an algorithmic trading strategy should allow for high availability (e.g., > 99.9%) and should otherwise take care of reliability (automatic backups, redundancy of drives and web connections, etc.).

Performance

Depending on the amount of data being processed and the computational demand the algorithms generate, the infrastructure must have enough CPU cores, working memory (RAM), and storage (SSD); in addition, the web connections should be sufficiently fast.

Security

The operating system and the applications run on it should be protected by strong passwords as well as SSL encryption; the hardware should be protected from fire, water, and unauthorized physical access.

Basically, these requirements can only be fulfilled by renting appropriate infrastructure from a professional data center or a cloud provider. Investments in the physical infrastructure to satisfy the aforementioned requirements can in general only be justified by the bigger or even biggest players in the financial markets.

From a development and testing point of view, even the smallest Droplet (cloud instance) from DigitalOcean is enough to get started. At the time of this writing such a Droplet costs 5 USD per month; usage is billed by the hour and a server can be created within minutes and destroyed within seconds.[4]

How to set up a Droplet with DigitalOcean is explained in detail in the section "Using Cloud Instances" on page 50, with bash scripts that can be adjusted to reflect individual requirements regarding Python packages, for example.

Operational Risks

Although the development and testing of automated algorithmic trading strategies is possible from a local computer (desktop, notebook, etc.), it is not appropriate for the deployment of live strategies trading real money. A simple loss of the web connection or a brief power outage might bring down the whole algorithm, leaving, for example, unintended open positions in the portfolio or causing data set corruption (due to missing out on real-time tick data), potentially leading to wrong signals and unintended trades/positions.

Logging and Monitoring

Let's assume that the automated algorithmic trading strategy is to be deployed on a remote server (cloud instance, leased server, etc.), that all required Python packages have been installed (see "Using Cloud Instances" on page 50), and that, for instance,

---

4 Use the link *http://bit.ly/do_sign_up* to get a 10 USD bonus on DigitalOcean when signing up for a new account.

Jupyter Notebook is running securely (*http://bit.ly/2A8jkDx*). What else needs to be considered from the algorithmic trader's point of view if they do not want to sit all day in front of the screen while logged in to the server?

This section addresses two important topics in this regard: *logging* and *real-time monitoring*. Logging persists information and events on disk for later inspection. It is standard practice in software application development and deployment. However, here the focus might be put rather on the financial side, logging important financial data and event information for later inspection and analysis. The same holds true for real-time monitoring making use of socket communication. Via sockets a constant real-time stream of important financial aspects can be created that can be retrieved and processed on a local computer, even if the deployment happens in the cloud.

"Automated Trading Strategy" on page 550 presents a Python script implementing all these aspects and making use of the code from "Online Algorithm" on page 544. The script puts the code in a shape that allows, for example, the *deployment* of the algorithmic trading strategy—based on the persisted algorithm object—on a remote server. It adds both *logging* and *monitoring* capabilities based on a custom function that, among others, makes use of ZeroMQ (*http://zeromq.org*) for socket communication. In combination with the short script from "Strategy Monitoring" on page 553, this allows for remote real-time monitoring of the activity on a remote server.

When the script from "Automated Trading Strategy" on page 550 is run, either locally or remotely, the output that is logged and sent via the socket looks as follows:

```
2018-07-25 09:16:15.568208
================================================================
NUMBER OF BARS: 24


================================================================
MOST RECENT DATA
                         Mid    Returns  Direction
2018-07-25 07:15:30  1.168885 -0.000009        -1
2018-07-25 07:15:45  1.168945  0.000043         1
2018-07-25 07:16:00  1.168895 -0.000051        -1
2018-07-25 07:16:15  1.168895 -0.000009        -1
2018-07-25 07:16:30  1.168885 -0.000017        -1


================================================================
features: [[ 1 -1  1 -1 -1]]
position: -1
signal:   -1


2018-07-25 09:16:15.581453
================================================================
no trade placed

****END OF CYCLE***
```

```
2018-07-25 09:16:30.069737
================================================================
NUMBER OF BARS: 25


================================================================
MOST RECENT DATA
                          Mid    Returns  Direction
2018-07-25 07:15:45  1.168945  0.000043          1
2018-07-25 07:16:00  1.168895 -0.000051         -1
2018-07-25 07:16:15  1.168895 -0.000009         -1
2018-07-25 07:16:30  1.168950  0.000034          1
2018-07-25 07:16:45  1.168945 -0.000017         -1


================================================================
features: [[-1  1 -1 -1  1]]
position: -1
signal:   1


2018-07-25 09:16:33.035094
================================================================


=========================================================
Going LONG.

    tradeId  amountK currency  grossPL  isBuy
0  61476318      100  EUR/USD       -2   True
=========================================================
```

****END OF CYCLE***

Running the script from "Strategy Monitoring" on page 553 locally then allows the real-time retrieval and processing of such information. Of course, it is easy to adjust the logging and streaming data to one's own requirements.[5] Similarly, one can also, for example, persist DataFrame objects as created during the execution of the trading script. Furthermore, the trading script and the whole logic can be adjusted to include such elements as stop losses or take profit targets programmatically. Alternatively,

---

5 Note that the socket communication as implemented in the two scripts is not encrypted and is sending plain text over the web, which might represent a security risk in production.

one could make use of more sophisticated order types available via the FXCM trading API (*http://fxcmpy.tpq.io*).

Consider All Risks

Trading currency pairs and/or CFDs is associated with a number of financial risks. Implementing an algorithmic trading strategy for such instruments automatically leads to a number of additional risks. Among them are flaws in the trading and/or execution logic. as well as technical risks such as problems with socket communications or delayed retrieval or even loss of tick data during the deployment. Therefore, before one deploys a trading strategy in automated fashion one should make sure that all associated market, execution, operational, technical, and other risks have been identified, evaluated, and addressed. The code presented in this chapter is intended only for technical illustration purposes.

Conclusion

This chapter is about the deployment of an algorithmic trading strategy—based on a classification algorithm from machine learning to predict the direction of market movements—in automated fashion. It addresses such important topics as capital management (based on the Kelly criterion), vectorized backtesting for performance and risk, the transformation of offline to online trading algorithms, an appropriate infrastructure for deployment, as well as logging and monitoring during deployment.

The topic of this chapter is complex and requires a broad skill set from the algorithmic trading practitioner. On the other hand, having a REST API for algorithmic trading available, such as the one from FXCM, simplifies the automation task considerably since the core part boils down mainly to making use of the capabilities of the Python wrapper package fxcmpy for tick data retrieval and order placement. Around this core, elements to mitigate operational and technical risks as far as possible have to be added.

Python Scripts

Automated Trading Strategy

The following is the Python script to implement the algorithmic trading strategy in automated fashion, including logging and monitoring.

```
#
# Automated ML-Based Trading Strategy for FXCM
# Online Algorithm, Logging, Monitoring
#
```

```
# Python for Finance, 2nd ed.
# (c) Dr. Yves J. Hilpisch
#
import zmq
import time
import pickle
import fxcmpy
import numpy as np
import pandas as pd
import datetime as dt

sel = ['tradeId', 'amountK', 'currency',
       'grossPL', 'isBuy']

log_file = 'automated_strategy.log'

# loads the persisted algorithm object
algorithm = pickle.load(open('algorithm.pkl', 'rb'))

# sets up the socket communication via ZeroMQ (here: "publisher")
context = zmq.Context()
socket = context.socket(zmq.PUB)

# this binds the socket communication to all IP addresses of the machine
socket.bind('tcp://0.0.0.0:5555')


def logger_monitor(message, time=True, sep=True):
    ''' Custom logger and monitor function.
    '''
    with open(log_file, 'a') as f:
        t = str(dt.datetime.now())
        msg = ''
        if time:
            msg += '\n' + t + '\n'
        if sep:
            msg += 66 * '=' + '\n'
        msg += message + '\n\n'
        # sends the message via the socket
        socket.send_string(msg)
        # writes the message to the log file
        f.write(msg)


def report_positions(pos):
    ''' Prints, logs and sends position data.
    '''
    out = '\n\n' + 50 * '=' + '\n'
    out += 'Going {}.\n'.format(pos) + '\n'
    time.sleep(2)  # waits for the order to be executed
    out += str(api.get_open_positions()[sel]) + '\n'
    out += 50 * '=' + '\n'
```

```
        logger_monitor(out)
        print(out)


    def automated_strategy(data, dataframe):
        ''' Callback function embodying the trading logic.
        '''
        global min_bars, position, df
        # resampling of the tick data
        df = dataframe.resample(bar, label='right').last().ffill()

        if len(df) > min_bars:
            min_bars = len(df)
            logger_monitor('NUMBER OF TICKS: {} | '.format(len(dataframe)) +
                           'NUMBER OF BARS: {}'.format(min_bars))
            # data processing and feature preparation
            df['Mid'] = df[['Bid', 'Ask']].mean(axis=1)
            df['Returns'] = np.log(df['Mid'] / df['Mid'].shift(1))
            df['Direction'] = np.where(df['Returns'] > 0, 1, -1)
            # picks relevant points
            features = df['Direction'].iloc[-(lags + 1):-1]
            # necessary reshaping
            features = features.values.reshape(1, -1)
            # generates the signal (+1 or -1)
            signal = algorithm.predict(features)[0]

            # logs and sends major financial information
            logger_monitor('MOST RECENT DATA\n' +
                           str(df[['Mid', 'Returns', 'Direction']].tail()),
                           False)
            logger_monitor('features: ' + str(features) + '\n' +
                           'position: ' + str(position) + '\n' +
                           'signal:   ' + str(signal), False)

            # trading logic
            if position in [0, -1] and signal == 1:  # going long?
                api.create_market_buy_order(
                    symbol, size - position * size)  # places a buy order
                position = 1  # changes position to long
                report_positions('LONG')

            elif position in [0, 1] and signal == -1:  # going short?
                api.create_market_sell_order(
                    symbol, size + position * size)  # places a sell order
                position = -1  # changes position to short
                report_positions('SHORT')
            else:  # no trade
                logger_monitor('no trade placed')

            logger_monitor('****END OF CYCLE***\n\n', False, False)

        if len(dataframe) > 350:  # stopping condition
```

```
    api.unsubscribe_market_data('EUR/USD')  # unsubscribes from data stream
    report_positions('CLOSE OUT')
    api.close_all()  # closes all open positions
    logger_monitor('***CLOSING OUT ALL POSITIONS***')


if __name__ == '__main__':
    symbol = 'EUR/USD'  # symbol to be traded
    bar = '15s'  # bar length; adjust for testing and deployment
    size = 100  # position size in thousand currency units
    position = 0  # initial position
    lags = 5  # number of lags for features data
    min_bars = lags + 1  # minimum length for resampled DataFrame
    df = pd.DataFrame()
    # adjust configuration file location
    api = fxcmpy.fxcmpy(config_file='../fxcm.cfg')
    # the main asynchronous loop using the callback function
    api.subscribe_market_data(symbol, (automated_strategy,))
```

Strategy Monitoring

The following is the Python script to implement a local or remote monitoring of the
automated algorithmic trading strategy via socket communication.

```
#
# Automated ML-Based Trading Strategy for FXCM
# Strategy Monitoring via Socket Communication
#
# Python for Finance, 2nd ed.
# (c) Dr. Yves J. Hilpisch
#
import zmq

# sets up the socket communication via ZeroMQ (here: "subscriber")
context = zmq.Context()
socket = context.socket(zmq.SUB)

# adjust the IP address to reflect the remote location
socket.connect('tcp://REMOTE_IP_ADDRESS:5555')

# configures the socket to retrieve every message
socket.setsockopt_string(zmq.SUBSCRIBE, '')

while True:
    msg = socket.recv_string()
    print(msg)
```

Further Resources

The papers cited in this chapter are:

- Rotando, Louis, and Edward Thorp (1992). "The Kelly Criterion and the Stock Market." *The American Mathematical Monthly*, Vol. 99, No. 10, pp. 922–931.

- Hung, Jane (2010): "Betting with the Kelly Criterion." *http://bit.ly/betting_with_kelly*.

For a comprehensive online training program covering Python for algorithmic trading see *http://certificate.tpq.io*.

## PART V

Derivatives Analytics

This part of the book is concerned with the development of a smaller, but nevertheless still powerful, real-world application for the pricing of options and derivatives by Monte Carlo simulation.[1] The goal is to have, in the end, a set of Python classes—a *pricing library* called DX, for Derivatives analytiX—that allows for the following:

Modeling
> To model short rates for discounting purposes; to model European and American options, including their underlying risk factors as well as their relevant market environments; to model even complex portfolios consisting of multiple options with multiple (possibly correlated) underlying risk factors

Simulation
> To simulate risk factors based on geometric Brownian motion and jump diffusions as well as on square-root diffusions, and to simulate a number of such risk factors simultaneously and consistently, whether they are correlated or not

Valuation
> To value, by the risk-neutral valuation approach, European and American options with arbitrary payoffs; to value portfolios composed of such options in a consistent, integrated fashion ("global valuation")

---

1 See Bittman (2009) for an introduction to options trading and related topics like market fundamentals and the role of the so-called Greeks in options risk management.

Risk management
> To estimate numerically the most important Greeks—i.e., the delta and the vega of an option/derivative—independent of the underlying risk factor or the exercise type

Application
> To use the package to value and manage a portfolio of non-traded American options on the DAX 30 stock index in market-consistent fashion; i.e., based on a calibrated model for the DAX 30 index

The material presented in this part of the book relies on the DX analytics package (*http://dx-analytics.com*), which is developed and maintained by the author and The Python Quants GmbH (and available, e.g., via the Quant Platform (*http://pqp.io*)). The full-fledged version allows, for instance, the modeling, pricing, and risk management of complex multi-risk derivatives and trading books composed thereof.

This part is divided into the following chapters:

- Chapter 17 presents the valuation framework in both theoretical and technical form. Theoretically, the Fundamental Theorem of Asset Pricing and the risk-neutral valuation approach are central. Technically, the chapter presents Python classes for risk-neutral discounting and for market environments.

- Chapter 18 is concerned with the simulation of risk factors based on geometric Brownian motion, jump diffusions, and square-root diffusion processes; a generic class and three specialized classes are discussed.

- Chapter 19 addresses the valuation of single derivatives with European or American exercise based on a single underlying risk factor; again, a generic and two specialized classes represent the major building blocks. The generic class allows the estimation of the delta and the vega independent of the option type.

- Chapter 20 is about the valuation of possibly complex derivatives portfolios with multiple derivatives based on multiple possibly correlated underlyings; a simple class for the modeling of a derivatives position is presented as well as a more complex class for a consistent portfolio valuation.

- Chapter 21 uses the DX library developed in the other chapters to value and risk-manage a portfolio of American put options on the DAX 30 stock index.

## CHAPTER 17

Valuation Framework

Compound interest is the greatest mathematical discovery of all time.

—Albert Einstein

This chapter provides the framework for the development of the DX library by introducing the most fundamental concepts needed for such an undertaking. It briefly reviews the Fundamental Theorem of Asset Pricing, which provides the theoretical background for the simulation and valuation. It then proceeds by addressing the fundamental concepts of *date handling* and *risk-neutral discounting*. This chapter considers only the simplest case of constant short rates for the discounting, but more complex and realistic models can be added to the library quite easily. This chapter also introduces the concept of a *market environment*—i.e., a collection of constants, lists, and curves needed for the instantiation of almost any other class to come in subsequent chapters.

The chapter comprises the following sections:

"Fundamental Theorem of Asset Pricing" on page 558
   This section introduces the Fundamental Theorem of Asset Pricing, which provides the theoretical background for the library to be developed.

"Risk-Neutral Discounting" on page 560
   This section develops a class for the risk-neutral discounting of future payoffs of options and other derivative instruments.

"Market Environments" on page 565
   This section develops a class to manage market environments for the pricing of single instruments and portfolios composed of multiple instruments.

Fundamental Theorem of Asset Pricing

The *Fundamental Theorem of Asset Pricing* is one of the cornerstones and success stories of modern financial theory and mathematics.[1] The central notion underlying the theorem is the concept of a *martingale* measure; i.e., a probability measure that removes the drift from a discounted risk factor (stochastic process). In other words, under a martingale measure, all risk factors drift with the risk-free short rate—and not with any other market rate involving some kind of risk premium over the risk-free short rate.

A Simple Example

Consider a simple economy at the dates today and tomorrow with a risky asset, a "stock," and a riskless asset, a "bond." The bond costs 10 USD today and pays off 10 USD tomorrow (zero interest rates). The stock costs 10 USD today and, with a probability of 60% and 40%, respectively, pays off 20 USD or 0 USD tomorrow. The riskless return of the bond is 0. The expected return of the stock is $\frac{0.6 \cdot 20 + 0.4 \cdot 0}{10} - 1 = 0.2$, or 20%. This is the risk premium the stock pays for its riskiness.

Consider now a call option with strike price of 15 USD. What is the fair value of such a contingent claim that pays 5 USD with 60% probability and 0 USD otherwise? One can take the expectation, for example, and discount the resulting value back (here with zero interest rates). This approach yields a value of $0.6 \cdot 5 = 3$ USD, since the option pays 5 USD in the case where the stock price moves up to 20 USD and 0 USD otherwise.

However, there is another approach that has been successfully applied to option pricing problems like this: *replication* of the option's payoff through a portfolio of traded securities. It is easily verified that buying 0.25 of the stock perfectly replicates the option's payoff (in the 60% case one then has $0.25 \cdot 20 = 5$ USD). A quarter of the stock only costs 2.5 USD and *not* 3 USD. Taking expectations under the real-world probability measure *overvalues* the option.

Why is this the case? The real-world measure implies a risk premium of 20% for the stock since the risk involved in the stock (gaining 100% or losing 100%) is "real" in the sense that it cannot be diversified or hedged away. On the other hand, there is a portfolio available that replicates the option's payoff without any risk. This also implies that someone writing (selling) such an option can completely hedge away any

---

1 Refer to Delbaen and Schachermayer (2004) for a comprehensive review and details of the mathematical machinery involved. See also Chapter 4 of Hilpisch (2015) for a shorter introduction, in particular for the discrete time version.

risk.[2] Such a perfectly hedged portfolio of an option and a hedge position must yield the riskless rate in order to avoid arbitrage opportunities (i.e., the opportunity to make some money out of no money with a positive probability).

Can one save the approach of taking expectations to value the call option? Yes, it is possible. One "only" has to change the probability in such a way that the risky asset, the stock, drifts with the riskless short rate of zero. Obviously, a (martingale) measure giving equal mass of 50% to both scenarios accomplishes this; the calculation is $\frac{0.5 \cdot 20 + 0.5 \cdot 0}{10} - 1 = 0$. Now, taking expectations of the option's payoff under the new martingale measure yields the correct (arbitrage-free) fair value: $0.5 \cdot 5 + 0.5 \cdot 0 = 2.5$ USD.

The General Results

The beauty of this approach is that it carries over to even the most complex economies with, for example, continuous time modeling (i.e., a continuum of points in time to consider), large numbers of risky assets, complex derivative payoffs, etc.

Therefore, consider a general market model in discrete time:[3]

A *general market model* $\mathcal{M}$ in discrete time is a collection of:

- A finite state space Ω
- A filtration $\mathbb{F}$
- A strictly positive probability measure P defined on $\wp(\Omega)$
- A terminal date $T \in \mathbb{N}, T < \infty$
- A set $\mathbb{S} \equiv \left\{ \left(S_t^k \right)_{t \in \{0, \ldots, T\}} : k \in \{0, \ldots, K\} \right\}$ of $K+1$ strictly positive security price processes

Together one has $\mathcal{M} = \{(\Omega, \wp(\Omega), \mathbb{F}, P), T, \mathbb{S}\}$.

Based on such a general market model, one can formulate the Fundamental Theorem of Asset Pricing as follows:[4]

---

2 The strategy would involve selling an option at a price of 2.5 USD and buying 0.25 stocks for 2.5 USD. The payoff of such a portfolio is 0 no matter what scenario plays out in the simple economy.

3 See Williams (1991) on the probabilistic concepts.

4 See Delbaen and Schachermayer (2004).

Consider the general market model $\mathcal{M}$. According to the *Fundamental Theorem of Asset Pricing*, the following three statements are equivalent:

- There are no arbitrage opportunities in the market model $\mathcal{M}$.
- The set $\mathbb{Q}$ of P-equivalent martingale measures is nonempty.
- The set $\mathbb{P}$ of consistent linear price systems is nonempty.

When it comes to valuation and pricing of contingent claims (i.e., options, derivatives, futures, forwards, swaps, etc.), the importance of the theorem is illustrated by the following corollary:

If the market model $\mathcal{M}$ is arbitrage-free, then there exists a *unique price* V_0 associated with any attainable (i.e., replicable) contingent claim (option, derivative, etc.) V_T. It satisfies $\forall Q \in \mathbb{Q}: V_0 = \mathbf{E}_0^Q\!\left(e^{-rT} V_T\right)$, where e^{-rT} is the relevant risk-neutral discount factor for a constant short rate r.

This result illustrates the importance of the theorem, and shows that our simple reasoning from earlier indeed carries over to the general market model.

Due to the role of the martingale measure, this approach to valuation is also often called the *martingale approach*, or—since under the martingale measure all risky assets drift with the riskless short rate—the *risk-neutral valuation approach*. The second term might, for our purposes, be the better one because in numerical applications, one "simply" lets the risk factors (stochastic processes) drift by the risk-neutral short rate. One does not have to deal with the probability measures directly for our applications—they are, however, what theoretically justifies the central theoretical results applied and the technical approach implemented.

Finally, consider market completeness in the general market model:

The market model $\mathcal{M}$ is *complete* if it is arbitrage-free and if every contingent claim (option, derivative, etc.) is attainable (i.e., replicable).

Suppose that the market model $\mathcal{M}$ is arbitrage-free. The market model is complete if and only if $\mathcal{M}$ is a singleton; i.e., if there is a unique P-equivalent martingale measure.

This mainly completes the discussion of the theoretical background for what follows. For a detailed exposition of the concepts, notions, definitions, and results, refer to Chapter 4 of Hilpisch (2015).

Risk-Neutral Discounting

Obviously, risk-neutral discounting is central to the risk-neutral valuation approach. This section therefore develops a Python class for risk-neutral discounting. However, it pays to first have a closer look at the modeling and handling of *relevant dates* for a valuation.

Modeling and Handling Dates

A necessary prerequisite for discounting is the modeling of dates (see also Appendix A). For valuation purposes, one typically divides the time interval between today and the final date of the general market model T into discrete time intervals. These time intervals can be homogeneous (i.e., of equal length), or they can be heterogeneous (i.e., of varying length). A valuation library should be able to handle the more general case of heterogeneous time intervals, since the simpler case is then automatically included. Therefore, the code works with lists of dates, assuming that the smallest relevant time interval is *one day*. This implies that intraday events are considered irrelevant, for which one would have to model *time* (in addition to dates).[5]

To compile a list of relevant dates, one can basically take one of two approaches: constructing a list of concrete *dates* (e.g., as datetime objects in Python) or of *year fractions* (as decimal numbers, as is often done in theoretical works).

Some imports first:

```
In [1]: import numpy as np
        import pandas as pd
        import datetime as dt
```

```
In [2]: from pylab import mpl, plt
        plt.style.use('seaborn')
        mpl.rcParams['font.family'] = 'serif'
        %matplotlib inline
```

```
In [3]: import sys
        sys.path.append('../dx')
```

For example, the following two definitions of dates and fractions are (roughly) equivalent:

```
In [4]: dates = [dt.datetime(2020, 1, 1), dt.datetime(2020, 7, 1),
                 dt.datetime(2021, 1, 1)]
```

```
In [5]: (dates[1] - dates[0]).days / 365.
Out[5]: 0.4986301369863014
```

```
In [6]: (dates[2] - dates[1]).days / 365.
Out[6]: 0.5041095890410959
```

```
In [7]: fractions = [0.0, 0.5, 1.0]
```

---

5 Adding a time component is actually a straightforward undertaking, which is nevertheless not done here for the ease of the exposition.

They are only *roughly* equivalent since year fractions seldom lie on the beginning (0 a.m.) of a certain day. Just consider the result of dividing a year by 50.

Sometimes it is necessary to get year fractions out of a list of dates. The function get_year_deltas() does the job:

```
#
# DX Package
#
# Frame -- Helper Function
#
# get_year_deltas.py
#
# Python for Finance, 2nd ed.
# (c) Dr. Yves J. Hilpisch
#
import numpy as np


def get_year_deltas(date_list, day_count=365.):
    ''' Return vector of floats with day deltas in year fractions.
    Initial value normalized to zero.

    Parameters
    ==========
    date_list: list or array
        collection of datetime objects
    day_count: float
        number of days for a year
        (to account for different conventions)

    Results
    =======
    delta_list: array
        year fractions
    '''

    start = date_list[0]
    delta_list = [(date - start).days / day_count
                  for date in date_list]
    return np.array(delta_list)
```

This function can then be applied as follows:

```
In [8]: from get_year_deltas import get_year_deltas

In [9]: get_year_deltas(dates)
Out[9]: array([0.       , 0.49863014, 1.00273973])
```

When modeling the short rate, it becomes clear what the benefit of this conversion is.

Constant Short Rate

The exposition to follow focuses on the simplest case for discounting by the short rate; namely, the case where the short rate is *constant through time*. Many option pricing models, like the ones of Black-Scholes-Merton (1973), Merton (1976), or Cox-Ross-Rubinstein (1979), make this assumption.[6] Assume continuous discounting, as is usual for option pricing applications. In such a case, the general discount factor as of today, given a future date t and a constant short rate of r, is then given by $D_0(t) = e^{-rt}$. Of course, for the end of the economy the special case $D_0(T) = e^{-rT}$ holds true. Note that here both t and T are in year fractions.

The discount factors can also be interpreted as the value of a *unit zero-coupon bond* (ZCB) as of today, maturing at t and T, respectively.[7] Given two dates $t \geq s \geq 0$, the discount factor relevant for discounting from t to s is then given by the equation $D_s(t) = D_0(t)/D_0(s) = e^{-rt}/e^{-rs} = e^{-rt} \cdot e^{rs} = e^{-r(t-s)}$.

The following translates these considerations into Python code in the form of a class:[8]

```
#
# DX Library
#
# Frame -- Constant Short Rate Class
#
# constant_short_rate.py
#
# Python for Finance, 2nd ed.
# (c) Dr. Yves J. Hilpisch
#
from get_year_deltas import *


class constant_short_rate(object):
    ''' Class for constant short rate discounting.

    Attributes
    ==========
    name: string
        name of the object
    short_rate: float (positive)
```

---

6 For the pricing of, for example, short-dated options, this assumption seems satisfied in many circumstances.

7 A unit zero-coupon bond pays exactly one currency unit at its maturity and no coupons between today and maturity.

8 See Chapter 6 for the basics of object-oriented programming (OOP) in Python. Here, and for the rest of this part, the naming deviates from the standard PEP 8 conventions with regard to Python class names. PEP 8 recommends using "CapWords" or "CamelCase" convention in general for Python class names. The code in this part rather uses the *function name* convention as mentioned in PEP 8 as a valid alternative "in cases where the interface is documented and used primarily as a callable."

```
            constant rate for discounting

        Methods
        =======
        get_discount_factors:
            get discount factors given a list/array of datetime objects
            or year fractions
        '''

        def __init__(self, name, short_rate):
            self.name = name
            self.short_rate = short_rate
            if short_rate < 0:
                raise ValueError('Short rate negative.')
                # this is debatable given recent market realities

        def get_discount_factors(self, date_list, dtobjects=True):
            if dtobjects is True:
                dlist = get_year_deltas(date_list)
            else:
                dlist = np.array(date_list)
            dflist = np.exp(self.short_rate * np.sort(-dlist))
            return np.array((date_list, dflist)).T
```

The application of the class dx.constant_short_rate is best illustrated by a simple, concrete example. The main result is a two-dimensional ndarray object containing pairs of a datetime object and the relevant discount factor. The class in general and the object csr in particular work with year fractions as well:

```
In [10]: from constant_short_rate import constant_short_rate

In [11]: csr = constant_short_rate('csr', 0.05)

In [12]: csr.get_discount_factors(dates)
Out[12]: array([[datetime.datetime(2020, 1, 1, 0, 0), 0.9510991280247174],
                [datetime.datetime(2020, 7, 1, 0, 0), 0.9753767163648953],
                [datetime.datetime(2021, 1, 1, 0, 0), 1.0]], dtype=object)

In [13]: deltas = get_year_deltas(dates)
         deltas
Out[13]: array([0.        , 0.49863014, 1.00273973])

In [14]: csr.get_discount_factors(deltas, dtobjects=False)
Out[14]: array([[0.        , 0.95109913],
                [0.49863014, 0.97537672],
                [1.00273973, 1.        ]])
```

This class will take care of all discounting operations needed in other classes.

Market Environments

Market environment is "just" a name for a collection of other data and Python objects. However, it is rather convenient to work with this abstraction since it simplifies a number of operations and also allows for a consistent modeling of recurring aspects.[9] A market environment mainly consists of three dictionaries to store the following types of data and Python objects:

Constants

These can be, for example, model parameters or option maturity dates.

Lists

These are collections of objects in general, like a `list` of objects modeling (risky) securities.

Curves

These are objects for discounting; e.g., an instance of the `dx.con stant_short_rate` class.

Following is the code for the `dx.market_environment` class. Refer to Chapter 3 for details on the handling of `dict` objects:

```
#
# DX Package
#
# Frame -- Market Environment Class
#
# market_environment.py
#
# Python for Finance, 2nd ed.
# (c) Dr. Yves J. Hilpisch
#

class market_environment(object):
    ''' Class to model a market environment relevant for valuation.

    Attributes
    ==========
    name: string
        name of the market environment
    pricing_date: datetime object
        date of the market environment

    Methods
    =======
    add_constant:
```

---

9 On this concept see also Fletcher and Gardner (2009), who use market environments extensively.

```
            adds a constant (e.g. model parameter)
get_constant:
            gets a constant
add_list:
            adds a list (e.g. underlyings)
get_list:
            gets a list
add_curve:
            adds a market curve (e.g. yield curve)
get_curve:
            gets a market curve
add_environment:
            adds and overwrites whole market environments
            with constants, lists, and curves
    '''

    def __init__(self, name, pricing_date):
        self.name = name
        self.pricing_date = pricing_date
        self.constants = {}
        self.lists = {}
        self.curves = {}

    def add_constant(self, key, constant):
        self.constants[key] = constant

    def get_constant(self, key):
        return self.constants[key]

    def add_list(self, key, list_object):
        self.lists[key] = list_object

    def get_list(self, key):
        return self.lists[key]

    def add_curve(self, key, curve):
        self.curves[key] = curve

    def get_curve(self, key):
        return self.curves[key]

    def add_environment(self, env):
        # overwrites existing values, if they exist
        self.constants.update(env.constants)
        self.lists.update(env.lists)
        self.curves.update(env.curves)
```

Although there is nothing really special about the dx.market_environment class, a simple example shall illustrate how convenient it is to work with instances of the class:

```
In [15]: from market_environment import market_environment

In [16]: me = market_environment('me_gbm', dt.datetime(2020, 1, 1))

In [17]: me.add_constant('initial_value', 36.)

In [18]: me.add_constant('volatility', 0.2)

In [19]: me.add_constant('final_date', dt.datetime(2020, 12, 31))

In [20]: me.add_constant('currency', 'EUR')

In [21]: me.add_constant('frequency', 'M')

In [22]: me.add_constant('paths', 10000)

In [23]: me.add_curve('discount_curve', csr)

In [24]: me.get_constant('volatility')
Out[24]: 0.2

In [25]: me.get_curve('discount_curve').short_rate
Out[25]: 0.05
```

This illustrates the basic handling of this rather generic "storage" class. For practical applications, market data and other data as well as Python objects are first collected, then a dx.market_environment object is instantiated and filled with the relevant data and objects. This is then delivered in a single step to other classes that need the data and objects stored in the respective dx.market_environment object.

A major advantage of this object-oriented modeling approach is, for example, that instances of the dx.constant_short_rate class can live in multiple environments (see the topic of *aggregation* in Chapter 6). Once the instance is updated—for example, when a new constant short rate is set—all the instances of the dx.market_envi ronment class containing that particular instance of the discounting class will be updated automatically.

Flexibility

The market environment class as introduced in this section is a flexible means to model and store any quantities and input data relevant to the pricing of options and derivatives and portfolios composed thereof. However, this flexibility also leads to operational risks in that it is easy to pass nonsensical data, objects, etc. to the class during instantiation, which might or might not be captured during instantiation. In a production context, a number of checks need to be added to at least capture obviously wrong cases.

Conclusion

This chapter provides the basic framework for the larger project of building a Python package to value options and other derivatives by Monte Carlo simulation. The chapter introduces the Fundamental Theorem of Asset Pricing, illustrating it by a rather simple numerical example. Important results in this regard are provided for a general market model in discrete time.

The chapter also develops a Python class for risk-neutral discounting purposes to make numerical use of the mathematical machinery of the Fundamental Theorem of Asset Pricing. Based on a list object of either Python datetime objects or float objects representing year fractions, instances of the class dx.constant_short_rate provide the appropriate discount factors (present values of unit zero-coupon bonds).

The chapter concludes with the rather generic dx.market_environment class, which allows for the collection of relevant data and Python objects for modeling, simulation, valuation, and other purposes.

To simplify future imports, a wrapper module called *dx_frame.py* is used:

```
#
# DX Analytics Package
#
# Frame Functions & Classes
#
# dx_frame.py
#
# Python for Finance, 2nd ed.
# (c) Dr. Yves J. Hilpisch
#
import datetime as dt

from get_year_deltas import get_year_deltas
from constant_short_rate import constant_short_rate
from market_environment import market_environment
```

A single import statement like the following then makes all framework components available in a single step:

```
import dx_frame
```

Thinking of a Python package of modules, there is also the option to store all relevant Python modules in a (sub)folder and to put in that folder a special __init__.py file that does all the imports. For example, when storing all modules in a folder called *dx*, say, the file presented next does the job. However, notice the naming convention for this particular file:

```
#
# DX Package
# packaging file
# __init__.py
#
import datetime as dt

from get_year_deltas import get_year_deltas
from constant_short_rate import constant_short_rate
from market_environment import market_environment
```

In that case you can just use the folder name to accomplish all the imports at once:

```
from dx import *
```

Or, via the alternative approach:

```
import dx
```

Further Resources

Useful references in book form for the topics covered in this chapter are:

- Bittman, James (2009). *Trading Options as a Professional*. New York: McGraw Hill.
- Delbaen, Freddy, and Walter Schachermayer (2004). *The Mathematics of Arbitrage*. Berlin, Heidelberg: Springer-Verlag.
- Fletcher, Shayne, and Christopher Gardner (2009). *Financial Modelling in Python*. Chichester, England: Wiley Finance.
- Hilpisch, Yves (2015). *Derivatives Analytics with Python* (*http://dawp.tpq.io*). Chichester, England: Wiley Finance.
- Williams, David (1991). *Probability with Martingales*. Cambridge, England: Cambridge University Press.

For the original research papers defining the models cited in this chapter, refer to the "Further Resources" sections in subsequent chapters.

## CHAPTER 18

Simulation of Financial Models

> The purpose of science is not to analyze or describe but to make useful models of the world.
>
> —Edward de Bono

Chapter 12 introduces in some detail the Monte Carlo simulation of stochastic processes using Python and NumPy. This chapter applies the basic techniques presented there to implement simulation classes as a central component of the DX package. The set of stochastic processes is restricted to three widely used ones. In particular, the chapter comprises the following sections:

"Random Number Generation" on page 572
    This section develops a function to generate standard normally distributed random numbers using variance reduction techniques.[1]

"Generic Simulation Class" on page 574
    This section develops a generic simulation class from which the other specific simulatation classes inherit fundamental attributes and methods.

"Geometric Brownian Motion" on page 577
    This section is about the geometric Brownian motion (GBM) that was introduced to the option pricing literature through the seminal works of Black and Scholes (1973) and Merton (1973); it is used several times throughout this book and still represents—despite its known shortcomings and given the mounting empirical evidence against it—a benchmark process for option and derivative valuation purposes.

---

1 The text speaks of "random" numbers knowing that they are in general "pseudo-random" only.

"Jump Diffusion" on page 582

The jump diffusion, as introduced to finance by Merton (1976), adds a log-normally distributed jump component to the GBM. This allows one to take into account that, for example, short-term out-of-the-money (OTM) options often seem to have priced in the possibility of larger jumps; in other words, relying on GBM as a financial model often cannot explain the market values of such OTM options satisfactorily, while a jump diffusion may be able to do so.

"Square-Root Diffusion" on page 587

The square-root diffusion, popularized in finance by Cox, Ingersoll, and Ross (1985), is used to model mean-reverting quantities like interest rates and volatility; in addition to being mean-reverting, the process stays positive, which is generally a desirable characteristic for those quantities.

For further details on the simulation of the models presented in this chapter, refer also to Hilpisch (2015). In particular, that book contains a complete case study based on the jump diffusion model of Merton (1976).

Random Number Generation

Random number generation is a central task of Monte Carlo simulation.[2] Chapter 12 shows how to use Python and subpackages such as numpy.random to generate random numbers with different distributions. For the project at hand, *standard normally distributed* random numbers are the most important ones. That is why it pays off to have the convenience function sn_random_numbers(), defined here, available for generating this particular type of random numbers:

```
#
# DX Package
#
# Frame -- Random Number Generation
#
# sn_random_numbers.py
#
# Python for Finance, 2nd ed.
# (c) Dr. Yves J. Hilpisch
#
import numpy as np


def sn_random_numbers(shape, antithetic=True, moment_matching=True,
                      fixed_seed=False):
    ''' Returns an ndarray object of shape shape with (pseudo)random numbers
    that are standard normally distributed.
```

---

2 See Glasserman (2004), Chapter 2, on generating random numbers and random variables.

```
Parameters
==========
shape: tuple (o, n, m)
    generation of array with shape (o, n, m)
antithetic: Boolean
    generation of antithetic variates
moment_matching: Boolean
    matching of first and second moments
fixed_seed: Boolean
    flag to fix the seed

Results
=======
ran: (o, n, m) array of (pseudo)random numbers
'''
if fixed_seed:
    np.random.seed(1000)
if antithetic:
    ran = np.random.standard_normal(
        (shape[0], shape[1], shape[2] // 2))
    ran = np.concatenate((ran, -ran), axis=2)
else:
    ran = np.random.standard_normal(shape)
if moment_matching:
    ran = ran - np.mean(ran)
    ran = ran / np.std(ran)
if shape[0] == 1:
    return ran[0]
else:
    return ran
```

The variance reduction techniques used in this function, namely *antithetic paths* and *moment matching*, are also illustrated in Chapter 12.[3] The application of the function is straightforward:

```
In [26]: from sn_random_numbers import *

In [27]: snrn = sn_random_numbers((2, 2, 2), antithetic=False,
                                   moment_matching=False, fixed_seed=True)
         snrn
Out[27]: array([[[-0.8044583 ,  0.32093155],
                 [-0.02548288,  0.64432383]],

                [[-0.30079667,  0.38947455],
                 [-0.1074373 , -0.47998308]]])

In [28]: round(snrn.mean(), 6)
```

---

3 Glasserman (2004) presents in Chapter 4 an overview and theoretical details of different variance reduction techniques.

```
Out[28]:  -0.045429

In [29]: round(snrn.std(), 6)
Out[29]: 0.451876

In [30]: snrn = sn_random_numbers((2, 2, 2), antithetic=False,
                                   moment_matching=True, fixed_seed=True)
         snrn
Out[30]: array([[[-1.67972865,  0.81075283],
                 [ 0.04413963,  1.52641815]],

                [[-0.56512826,  0.96243813],
                 [-0.13722505, -0.96166678]]])

In [31]: round(snrn.mean(), 6)
Out[31]: -0.0

In [32]: round(snrn.std(), 6)
Out[32]: 1.0
```

This function will prove a workhorse for the simulation classes to follow.

Generic Simulation Class

Object-oriented modeling—as introduced in Chapter 6—allows inheritance of attributes and methods. This is what the following code makes use of when building the simulation classes: one starts with a *generic* simulation class containing those attributes and methods that all other simulation classes share and can then focus with the other classes on specific elements of the stochastic process to be simulated.

Instantiating an object of any simulation class happens by providing three attributes only:

name
    A str object as a name for the model simulation object

mar_env
    An instance of the dx.market_environment class

corr
    A flag (bool) indicating whether the object is correlated or not

This again illustrates the role of a *market environment*: to provide in a single step all data and objects required for simulation and valuation. The methods of the generic class are:

generate_time_grid()
    This method generates the time grid of relevant dates used for the simulation; this task is the same for every simulation class.

```
get_instrument_values()
```
> Every simulation class has to return the ndarray object with the simulated instrument values (e.g., simulated stock prices, commodities prices, volatilities).

The code for the generic model simulation class follows. The methods make use of other methods that the model-tailored classes will provide, like self.gener ate_paths(). The details in this regard become clear when one has the full picture of a specialized, nongeneric simulation class. First, the base class:

```python
#
# DX Package
#
# Simulation Class -- Base Class
#
# simulation_class.py
#
# Python for Finance, 2nd ed.
# (c) Dr. Yves J. Hilpisch
#
import numpy as np
import pandas as pd


class simulation_class(object):
    ''' Providing base methods for simulation classes.

    Attributes
    ==========
    name: str
        name of the object
    mar_env: instance of market_environment
        market environment data for simulation
    corr: bool
        True if correlated with other model object

    Methods
    =======
    generate_time_grid:
        returns time grid for simulation
    get_instrument_values:
        returns the current instrument values (array)
    '''

    def __init__(self, name, mar_env, corr):
        self.name = name
        self.pricing_date = mar_env.pricing_date
        self.initial_value = mar_env.get_constant('initial_value')
        self.volatility = mar_env.get_constant('volatility')
        self.final_date = mar_env.get_constant('final_date')
        self.currency = mar_env.get_constant('currency')
        self.frequency = mar_env.get_constant('frequency')
```

```python
        self.paths = mar_env.get_constant('paths')
        self.discount_curve = mar_env.get_curve('discount_curve')
        try:
            # if time_grid in mar_env take that object
            # (for portfolio valuation)
            self.time_grid = mar_env.get_list('time_grid')
        except:
            self.time_grid = None
        try:
            # if there are special dates, then add these
            self.special_dates = mar_env.get_list('special_dates')
        except:
            self.special_dates = []
        self.instrument_values = None
        self.correlated = corr
        if corr is True:
            # only needed in a portfolio context when
            # risk factors are correlated
            self.cholesky_matrix = mar_env.get_list('cholesky_matrix')
            self.rn_set = mar_env.get_list('rn_set')[self.name]
            self.random_numbers = mar_env.get_list('random_numbers')

    def generate_time_grid(self):
        start = self.pricing_date
        end = self.final_date
        # pandas date_range function
        # freq = e.g. 'B' for Business Day,
        # 'W' for Weekly, 'M' for Monthly
        time_grid = pd.date_range(start=start, end=end,
                                  freq=self.frequency).to_pydatetime()
        time_grid = list(time_grid)
        # enhance time_grid by start, end, and special_dates
        if start not in time_grid:
            time_grid.insert(0, start)
            # insert start date if not in list
        if end not in time_grid:
            time_grid.append(end)
            # insert end date if not in list
        if len(self.special_dates) > 0:
            # add all special dates
            time_grid.extend(self.special_dates)
            # delete duplicates
            time_grid = list(set(time_grid))
            # sort list
            time_grid.sort()
        self.time_grid = np.array(time_grid)

    def get_instrument_values(self, fixed_seed=True):
        if self.instrument_values is None:
            # only initiate simulation if there are no instrument values
            self.generate_paths(fixed_seed=fixed_seed, day_count=365.)
        elif fixed_seed is False:
```

```
    # also initiate resimulation when fixed_seed is False
    self.generate_paths(fixed_seed=fixed_seed, day_count=365.)
  return self.instrument_values
```

Parsing of the market environment is embedded in the special method __init__(), which is called during instantiation. To keep the code concise, there are *no* sanity checks implemented. For example, the following line of code is considered a "success," no matter if the content is indeed an instance of a discounting class or not. Therefore, one has to be rather careful when compiling and passing dx.market_envi ronment objects to any simulation class:

```
self.discount_curve = mar_env.get_curve('discount_curve')
```

Table 18-1 shows all components a dx.market_environment object must contain for the generic and therefore for all other simulation classes.

Table 18-1. Elements of the market environment for all simulation classes

Element	Type	Mandatory	Description
initial_value	Constant	Yes	Initial value of process at pricing_date
volatility	Constant	Yes	Volatility coefficient of process
final_date	Constant	Yes	Simulation horizon
currency	Constant	Yes	Currency of the financial entity
frequency	Constant	Yes	Date frequency, as pandas freq parameter
paths	Constant	Yes	Number of paths to be simulated
discount_curve	Curve	Yes	Instance of dx.constant_short_rate
time_grid	List	No	Time grid of relevant dates (in portfolio context)
random_numbers	List	No	Random number np.ndarray object (for correlated objects)
cholesky_matrix	List	No	Cholesky matrix (for correlated objects)
rn_set	List	No	dict object with pointer to relevant random number set

Everything that has to do with the correlation of model simulation objects is explained in subsequent chapters. In this chapter, the focus is on the simulation of single, uncorrelated processes. Similarly, the option to pass a time_grid is only relevant in a portfolio context, something also explained later.

Geometric Brownian Motion

Geometric Brownian motion is a stochastic process, as described in Equation 18-1 (see also Equation 12-2 in Chapter 12, in particular for the meaning of the parameters and variables). The drift of the process is already set equal to the riskless, constant short rate r, implying that one operates under the equivalent martingale measure (see Chapter 17).

Equation 18-1. Stochastic differential equation of geometric Brownian motion

$$dS_t = rS_t dt + \sigma S_t dZ_t$$

Equation 18-2 presents an Euler discretization of the stochastic differential equation for simulation purposes (see also Equation 12-3 in Chapter 12 for further details). The general framework is a discrete time market model, such as the general market model $\mathcal{M}$ from Chapter 17, with a finite set of relevant dates $0 < t_1 < t_2 < \ldots < T$.

Equation 18-2. Difference equation to simulate the geometric Brownian motion

$$S_{t_{m+1}} = S_{t_m} \exp\left(\left(r - \frac{\sigma^2}{2}\right)(t_{m+1} - t_m) + \sigma\sqrt{t_{m+1} - t_m}z_t\right)$$
$$0 \le t_m < t_{m+1} \le T$$

The Simulation Class

Following is the specialized class for the GBM model:

```
#
# DX Package
#
# Simulation Class -- Geometric Brownian Motion
#
# geometric_brownian_motion.py
#
# Python for Finance, 2nd ed.
# (c) Dr. Yves J. Hilpisch
#
import numpy as np

from sn_random_numbers import sn_random_numbers
from simulation_class import simulation_class


class geometric_brownian_motion(simulation_class):
    ''' Class to generate simulated paths based on
    the Black-Scholes-Merton geometric Brownian motion model.

    Attributes
    ==========
    name: string
        name of the object
    mar_env: instance of market_environment
        market environment data for simulation
```

```
corr: Boolean
    True if correlated with other model simulation object

Methods
=======
update:
    updates parameters
generate_paths:
    returns Monte Carlo paths given the market environment
'''


def __init__(self, name, mar_env, corr=False):
    super(geometric_brownian_motion, self).__init__(name, mar_env, corr)

def update(self, initial_value=None, volatility=None, final_date=None):
    if initial_value is not None:
        self.initial_value = initial_value
    if volatility is not None:
        self.volatility = volatility
    if final_date is not None:
        self.final_date = final_date
    self.instrument_values = None

def generate_paths(self, fixed_seed=False, day_count=365.):
    if self.time_grid is None:
        # method from generic simulation class
        self.generate_time_grid()
    # number of dates for time grid
    M = len(self.time_grid)
    # number of paths
    I = self.paths
    # ndarray initialization for path simulation
    paths = np.zeros((M, I))
    # initialize first date with initial_value
    paths[0] = self.initial_value
    if not self.correlated:
        # if not correlated, generate random numbers
        rand = sn_random_numbers((1, M, I),
                                 fixed_seed=fixed_seed)
    else:
        # if correlated, use random number object as provided
        # in market environment
        rand = self.random_numbers
    short_rate = self.discount_curve.short_rate
    # get short rate for drift of process
    for t in range(1, len(self.time_grid)):
        # select the right time slice from the relevant
        # random number set
        if not self.correlated:
            ran = rand[t]
        else:
            ran = np.dot(self.cholesky_matrix, rand[:, t, :])
```

```
            ran = ran[self.rn_set]
        dt = (self.time_grid[t] - self.time_grid[t - 1]).days / day_count
        # difference between two dates as year fraction
        paths[t] = paths[t - 1] * np.exp((short_rate - 0.5 *
                                         self.volatility ** 2) * dt +
                                         self.volatility * np.sqrt(dt) * ran)
        # generate simulated values for the respective date
    self.instrument_values = paths
```

In this particular case, the dx.market_environment object has to contain only the data and objects shown in Table 18-1—i.e., the minimum set of components.

The method update() does what its name suggests: it allows the updating of selected important parameters of the model. The method generate_paths() is, of course, a bit more involved. However, it has a number of inline comments that should make clear the most important aspects. Some complexity is brought into this method by, in principle, allowing for the correlation between different model simulation objects—the purpose of which will become clearer later, especially in Chapter 20.

A Use Case

The following interactive IPython session illustrates the use of the GBM simulation class. First, one has to generate a dx.market_environment object with all the mandatory elements:

```
In [33]: from dx_frame import *

In [34]: me_gbm = market_environment('me_gbm', dt.datetime(2020, 1, 1))

In [35]: me_gbm.add_constant('initial_value', 36.)
         me_gbm.add_constant('volatility', 0.2)
         me_gbm.add_constant('final_date', dt.datetime(2020, 12, 31))
         me_gbm.add_constant('currency', 'EUR')
         me_gbm.add_constant('frequency', 'M')   ❶
         me_gbm.add_constant('paths', 10000)

In [36]: csr = constant_short_rate('csr', 0.06)

In [37]: me_gbm.add_curve('discount_curve', csr)
```

❶ Monthly frequency with *month end* as default.

Second, one instantiates a model simulation object to work with:

```
In [38]: from geometric_brownian_motion import geometric_brownian_motion

In [39]: gbm = geometric_brownian_motion('gbm', me_gbm)   ❶

In [40]: gbm.generate_time_grid()   ❷

In [41]: gbm.time_grid   ❸
```

```
Out[41]: array([[datetime.datetime(2020, 1, 1, 0, 0),
                 datetime.datetime(2020, 1, 31, 0, 0),
                 datetime.datetime(2020, 2, 29, 0, 0),
                 datetime.datetime(2020, 3, 31, 0, 0),
                 datetime.datetime(2020, 4, 30, 0, 0),
                 datetime.datetime(2020, 5, 31, 0, 0),
                 datetime.datetime(2020, 6, 30, 0, 0),
                 datetime.datetime(2020, 7, 31, 0, 0),
                 datetime.datetime(2020, 8, 31, 0, 0),
                 datetime.datetime(2020, 9, 30, 0, 0),
                 datetime.datetime(2020, 10, 31, 0, 0),
                 datetime.datetime(2020, 11, 30, 0, 0),
                 datetime.datetime(2020, 12, 31, 0, 0)], dtype=object)

In [42]: %time paths_1 = gbm.get_instrument_values()   ❹
         CPU times: user 21.3 ms, sys: 6.74 ms, total: 28.1 ms
         Wall time: 40.3 ms

In [43]: paths_1.round(3)   ❹
Out[43]: array([[36.    , 36.    , 36.    , ..., 36.    , 36.    , 36.    ],
                [37.403, 38.12 , 34.4  , ..., 36.252, 35.084, 39.668],
                [39.562, 42.335, 32.405, ..., 34.836, 33.637, 37.655],
                ...,
                [40.534, 33.506, 23.497, ..., 37.851, 30.122, 30.446],
                [42.527, 36.995, 21.885, ..., 36.014, 30.907, 30.712],
                [43.811, 37.876, 24.1  , ..., 36.263, 28.138, 29.038]])

In [44]: gbm.update(volatility=0.5)   ❺

In [45]: %time paths_2 = gbm.get_instrument_values()   ❺
         CPU times: user 27.8 ms, sys: 3.91 ms, total: 31.7 ms
         Wall time: 19.8 ms
```

❶ Instantiates the simulation object.

❷ Generates the time grid …

❸ … and shows it; note that the initial date is added.

❹ Simulates the paths given the parameterization.

❺ Updates the volatility parameter and repeats the simulation.

Figure 18-1 shows 10 simulated paths for the two different parameterizations. The effect of increasing the volatility parameter value is easy to see:

```
In [46]: plt.figure(figsize=(10, 6))
         p1 = plt.plot(gbm.time_grid, paths_1[:, :10], 'b')
         p2 = plt.plot(gbm.time_grid, paths_2[:, :10], 'r-.')
         l1 = plt.legend([p1[0], p2[0]],
                         ['low volatility', 'high volatility'], loc=2)
```

```
plt.gca().add_artist(l1)
plt.xticks(rotation=30);
```

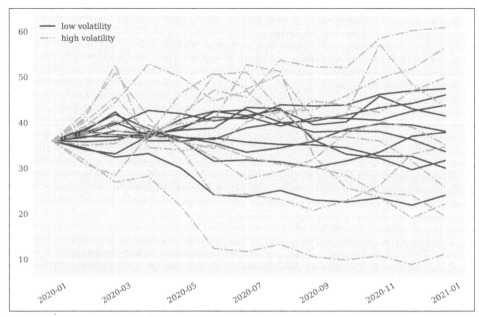

Figure 18-1. Simulated paths from GBM simulation class

Vectorization for Simulation

As argued and shown already in Chapter 12, vectorization approaches using NumPy and pandas are well suited to writing concise and performant simulation code.

Jump Diffusion

Equipped with the background knowledge from the dx.geometric_brownian_motion class, it is now straightforward to implement a class for the jump diffusion model described by Merton (1976). The stochastic differential equation for the jump diffusion model is shown in Equation 18-3 (see also Equation 12-8 in Chapter 12, in particular for the meaning of the parameters and variables).

Equation 18-3. Stochastic differential equation for Merton jump diffusion model

$$dS_t = (r - r_J)S_t dt + \sigma S_t dZ_t + J_t S_t dN_t$$

An Euler discretization for simulation purposes is presented in Equation 18-4 (see also Equation 12-9 in Chapter 12 and the more detailed explanations given there).

Equation 18-4. Euler discretization for Merton jump diffusion model

$$S_{t_{m+1}} = S_{t_m}\left(\exp\left(\left(r - r_J - \frac{\sigma^2}{2} \right)(t_{m+1} - t_m) + \sigma\sqrt{t_{m+1} - t_m}z_t^1 \right) + \left(e^{\mu_J + \delta z_t^2} - 1 \right)y_t \right)$$

$$0 \le t_m < t_{m+1} \le T$$

The Simulation Class

The Python code for the dx.jump_diffusion simulation class follows. This class should by now contain no surprises. Of course, the model is different, but the design and the methods are essentially the same:

```
#
# DX Package
#
# Simulation Class -- Jump Diffusion
#
# jump_diffusion.py
#
# Python for Finance, 2nd ed.
# (c) Dr. Yves J. Hilpisch
#
import numpy as np

from sn_random_numbers import sn_random_numbers
from simulation_class import simulation_class


class jump_diffusion(simulation_class):
    ''' Class to generate simulated paths based on
    the Merton (1976) jump diffusion model.

    Attributes
    ==========
    name: str
        name of the object
    mar_env: instance of market_environment
        market environment data for simulation
    corr: bool
        True if correlated with other model object

    Methods
    =======
    update:
        updates parameters
    generate_paths:
```

```
            returns Monte Carlo paths given the market environment
    '''

    def __init__(self, name, mar_env, corr=False):
        super(jump_diffusion, self).__init__(name, mar_env, corr)
        # additional parameters needed
        self.lamb = mar_env.get_constant('lambda')
        self.mu = mar_env.get_constant('mu')
        self.delt = mar_env.get_constant('delta')

    def update(self, initial_value=None, volatility=None, lamb=None,
               mu=None, delta=None, final_date=None):
        if initial_value is not None:
            self.initial_value = initial_value
        if volatility is not None:
            self.volatility = volatility
        if lamb is not None:
            self.lamb = lamb
        if mu is not None:
            self.mu = mu
        if delta is not None:
            self.delt = delta
        if final_date is not None:
            self.final_date = final_date
        self.instrument_values = None

    def generate_paths(self, fixed_seed=False, day_count=365.):
        if self.time_grid is None:
            # method from generic simulation class
            self.generate_time_grid()
        # number of dates for time grid
        M = len(self.time_grid)
        # number of paths
        I = self.paths
        # ndarray initialization for path simulation
        paths = np.zeros((M, I))
        # initialize first date with initial_value
        paths[0] = self.initial_value
        if self.correlated is False:
            # if not correlated, generate random numbers
            sn1 = sn_random_numbers((1, M, I),
                                    fixed_seed=fixed_seed)
        else:
            # if correlated, use random number object as provided
            # in market environment
            sn1 = self.random_numbers

        # standard normally distributed pseudo-random numbers
        # for the jump component
        sn2 = sn_random_numbers((1, M, I),
                                fixed_seed=fixed_seed)
```

```
rj = self.lamb * (np.exp(self.mu + 0.5 * self.delt ** 2) - 1)

short_rate = self.discount_curve.short_rate
for t in range(1, len(self.time_grid)):
    # select the right time slice from the relevant
    # random number set
    if self.correlated is False:
        ran = sn1[t]
    else:
        # only with correlation in portfolio context
        ran = np.dot(self.cholesky_matrix, sn1[:, t, :])
        ran = ran[self.rn_set]
    dt = (self.time_grid[t] - self.time_grid[t - 1]).days / day_count
    # difference between two dates as year fraction
    poi = np.random.poisson(self.lamb * dt, I)
    # Poisson-distributed pseudo-random numbers for jump component
    paths[t] = paths[t - 1] * (
        np.exp((short_rate - rj -
                0.5 * self.volatility ** 2) * dt +
               self.volatility * np.sqrt(dt) * ran) +
        (np.exp(self.mu + self.delt * sn2[t]) - 1) * poi)
self.instrument_values = paths
```

Of course, since this is a different model, it needs a different set of elements in the dx.market_environment object. In addition to those for the generic simulation class (see Table 18-1), there are three parameters required, as outlined in Table 18-2: namely, the parameters of the log-normal jump component, lambda, mu, and delta.

Table 18-2. Specific elements of the market environment for dx.jump_diffusion class

Element	Type	Mandatory	Description
lambda	Constant	Yes	Jump intensity (probability p.a.)
mu	Constant	Yes	Expected jump size
delta	Constant	Yes	Standard deviation of jump size

For the generation of the paths, this class needs further random numbers because of the jump component. Inline comments in the method generate_paths() highlight the two spots where these additional random numbers are generated. For the generation of Poisson-distributed random numbers, see also Chapter 12.

A Use Case

The following interactive session illustrates how to use the simulation class dx.jump_diffusion. The dx.market_environment object defined for the GBM object is used as a basis:

```
In [47]: me_jd = market_environment('me_jd', dt.datetime(2020, 1, 1))
```

```
In [48]: me_jd.add_constant('lambda', 0.3)  ❶
         me_jd.add_constant('mu', -0.75)  ❶
         me_jd.add_constant('delta', 0.1)  ❶

In [49]: me_jd.add_environment(me_gbm)  ❷

In [50]: from jump_diffusion import jump_diffusion

In [51]: jd = jump_diffusion('jd', me_jd)

In [52]: %time paths_3 = jd.get_instrument_values()  ❸
         CPU times: user 28.6 ms, sys: 4.37 ms, total: 33 ms
         Wall time: 49.4 ms

In [53]: jd.update(lamb=0.9)  ❹

In [54]: %time paths_4 = jd.get_instrument_values()  ❺
         CPU times: user 29.7 ms, sys: 3.58 ms, total: 33.3 ms
         Wall time: 66.7 ms
```

❶ The three additional parameters for the dx.jump_diffusion object. These are specific to the simulation class.

❷ Adds a complete environment to the existing one.

❸ Simulates the paths with the base parameters.

❹ Increases the jump intensity parameters.

❺ Simulates the paths with the updated parameter.

Figure 18-2 compares a couple of simulated paths from the two sets with low and high intensity (jump probability), respectively. It is easy to spot several jumps for the low-intensity case and the multiple jumps for the high-intensity case in the figure:

```
In [55]: plt.figure(figsize=(10, 6))
         p1 = plt.plot(gbm.time_grid, paths_3[:, :10], 'b')
         p2 = plt.plot(gbm.time_grid, paths_4[:, :10], 'r-.')
         l1 = plt.legend([p1[0], p2[0]],
                         ['low intensity', 'high intensity'], loc=3)
         plt.gca().add_artist(l1)
         plt.xticks(rotation=30);
```

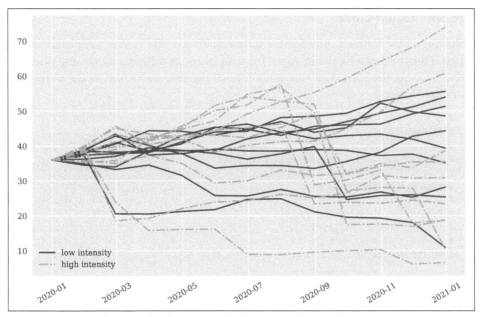

Figure 18-2. Simulated paths from jump diffusion simulation class

Square-Root Diffusion

The third stochastic process to be simulated is the square-root diffusion as used, for example, by Cox, Ingersoll, and Ross (1985) to model stochastic short rates. Equation 18-5 shows the stochastic differential equation of the process (see also Equation 12-4 in Chapter 12 for further details).

Equation 18-5. Stochastic differential equation of square-root diffusion

$$dx_t = \kappa(\theta - x_t)dt + \sigma\sqrt{x_t}dZ_t$$

The code uses the discretization scheme as presented in Equation 18-6 (see also Equation 12-5 in Chapter 12, as well as Equation 12-6 for an alternative, exact scheme).

Equation 18-6. Euler discretization for square-root diffusion (full truncation scheme)

$$\tilde{x}_{t_{m+1}} = \tilde{x}_{t_m} + \kappa(\theta - \tilde{x}_s^+)(t_{m+1} - t_m) + \sigma\sqrt{\tilde{x}_s^+}\sqrt{t_{m+1} - t_m}z_t$$
$$x_{t_{m+1}} = \tilde{x}_{t_{m}\,1}$$

The Simulation Class

Following is the Python code for the dx.square_root_diffusion simulation class, which is the third and final one. Apart from, of course, a different model and discretization scheme, the class does not contain anything new compared to the other two specialized classes:

```
#
# DX Package
#
# Simulation Class -- Square-Root Diffusion
#
# square_root_diffusion.py
#
# Python for Finance, 2nd ed.
# (c) Dr. Yves J. Hilpisch
#
import numpy as np

from sn_random_numbers import sn_random_numbers
from simulation_class import simulation_class


class square_root_diffusion(simulation_class):
    ''' Class to generate simulated paths based on
    the Cox-Ingersoll-Ross (1985) square-root diffusion model.

    Attributes
    ==========
    name : string
        name of the object
    mar_env : instance of market_environment
        market environment data for simulation
    corr : Boolean
        True if correlated with other model object

    Methods
    =======
    update :
        updates parameters
    generate_paths :
        returns Monte Carlo paths given the market environment
    '''

    def __init__(self, name, mar_env, corr=False):
        super(square_root_diffusion, self).__init__(name, mar_env, corr)
        # additional parameters needed
        self.kappa = mar_env.get_constant('kappa')
        self.theta = mar_env.get_constant('theta')

    def update(self, initial_value=None, volatility=None, kappa=None,
                  theta=None, final_date=None):
```

```
        if initial_value is not None:
            self.initial_value = initial_value
        if volatility is not None:
            self.volatility = volatility
        if kappa is not None:
            self.kappa = kappa
        if theta is not None:
            self.theta = theta
        if final_date is not None:
            self.final_date = final_date
        self.instrument_values = None

    def generate_paths(self, fixed_seed=True, day_count=365.):
        if self.time_grid is None:
            self.generate_time_grid()
        M = len(self.time_grid)
        I = self.paths
        paths = np.zeros((M, I))
        paths_ = np.zeros_like(paths)
        paths[0] = self.initial_value
        paths_[0] = self.initial_value
        if self.correlated is False:
            rand = sn_random_numbers((1, M, I),
                                     fixed_seed=fixed_seed)
        else:
            rand = self.random_numbers

        for t in range(1, len(self.time_grid)):
            dt = (self.time_grid[t] - self.time_grid[t - 1]).days / day_count
            if self.correlated is False:
                ran = rand[t]
            else:
                ran = np.dot(self.cholesky_matrix, rand[:, t, :])
                ran = ran[self.rn_set]

            # full truncation Euler discretization
            paths_[t] = (paths_[t - 1] + self.kappa *
                        (self.theta - np.maximum(0, paths_[t - 1, :])) * dt +
                        np.sqrt(np.maximum(0, paths_[t - 1, :])) *
                        self.volatility * np.sqrt(dt) * ran)
            paths[t] = np.maximum(0, paths_[t])
        self.instrument_values = paths
```

Table 18-3 lists the two elements of the market environment that are specific to this class.

Table 18-3. Specific elements of the market environment for dx.square_root_diffusion class

Element	Type	Mandatory	Description
kappa	Constant	Yes	Mean reversion factor
theta	Constant	Yes	Long-term mean of process

A Use Case

A rather brief example illustrates the use of the simulation class. As usual, one needs a market environment, for example, to model a volatility (index) process:

```
In [56]: me_srd = market_environment('me_srd', dt.datetime(2020, 1, 1)) ❶

In [57]: me_srd.add_constant('initial_value', .25)
         me_srd.add_constant('volatility', 0.05)
         me_srd.add_constant('final_date', dt.datetime(2020, 12, 31))
         me_srd.add_constant('currency', 'EUR')
         me_srd.add_constant('frequency', 'W')
         me_srd.add_constant('paths', 10000)

In [58]: me_srd.add_constant('kappa', 4.0)
         me_srd.add_constant('theta', 0.2)

In [59]: me_srd.add_curve('discount_curve', constant_short_rate('r', 0.0)) ❷

In [60]: from square_root_diffusion import square_root_diffusion

In [61]: srd = square_root_diffusion('srd', me_srd) ❸

In [62]: srd_paths = srd.get_instrument_values()[:, :10] ❹
```

❶ Additional parameters for the dx.square_root_diffusion object.

❷ The discount_curve object is required by default but not needed for the simulation.

❸ Instantiates the object ...

❹ ... simulates the paths, and selects 10.

Figure 18-3 illustrates the mean-reverting characteristic by showing how the simulated paths on average revert to the long-term mean theta (dashed line), which is assumed to be 0.2:

```
In [63]: plt.figure(figsize=(10, 6))
         plt.plot(srd.time_grid, srd.get_instrument_values()[:, :10])
         plt.axhline(me_srd.get_constant('theta'), color='r',
                     ls='--', lw=2.0)
         plt.xticks(rotation=30);
```

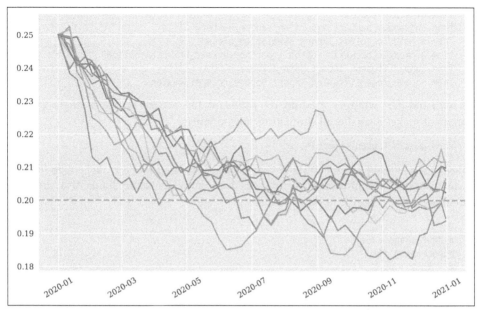

Figure 18-3. Simulated paths from square-root diffusion simulation class (dashed line = long-term mean theta)

Conclusion

This chapter develops all the tools and classes needed for the simulation of the three stochastic processes of interest: geometric Brownian motion, jump diffusions, and square-root diffusions. The chapter presents a function to conveniently generate standard normally distributed random numbers. It then proceeds by introducing a generic model simulation class. Based on this foundation, the chapter introduces three specialized simulation classes and presents use cases for these classes.

To simplify future imports one can again use a wrapper module, this one called *dx_simulation.py*:

```
#
# DX Package
#
# Simulation Functions & Classes
#
# dx_simulation.py
#
# Python for Finance, 2nd ed.
# (c) Dr. Yves J. Hilpisch
#
import numpy as np
import pandas as pd
```

```
from dx_frame import *
from sn_random_numbers import sn_random_numbers
from simulation_class import simulation_class
from geometric_brownian_motion import geometric_brownian_motion
from jump_diffusion import jump_diffusion
from square_root_diffusion import square_root_diffusion
```

As with the first wrapper module, *dx_frame.py*, the benefit is that a single import statement makes available all simulation components:

```
from dx_simulation import *
```

Since *dx_simulation.py* also imports everything from *dx_frame.py*, this single import in fact exposes *all functionality* developed so far. The same holds true for the enhanced *__init__.py* file in the *dx* folder:

```
#
# DX Package
# packaging file
# __init__.py
#
import numpy as np
import pandas as pd
import datetime as dt

# frame
from get_year_deltas import get_year_deltas
from constant_short_rate import constant_short_rate
from market_environment import market_environment

# simulation
from sn_random_numbers import sn_random_numbers
from simulation_class import simulation_class
from geometric_brownian_motion import geometric_brownian_motion
from jump_diffusion import jump_diffusion
from square_root_diffusion import square_root_diffusion
```

Further Resources

Useful references in book form for the topics covered in this chapter are:

- Glasserman, Paul (2004). *Monte Carlo Methods in Financial Engineering*. New York: Springer.
- Hilpisch, Yves (2015): *Derivatives Analytics with Python (http://dawp.tpq.io/)*. Chichester, England: Wiley Finance.

Original papers cited in this chapter are:

- Black, Fischer, and Myron Scholes (1973). "The Pricing of Options and Corporate Liabilities." *Journal of Political Economy*, Vol. 81, No. 3, pp. 638–659.

- Cox, John, Jonathan Ingersoll, and Stephen Ross (1985). "A Theory of the Term Structure of Interest Rates." *Econometrica*, Vol. 53, No. 2, pp. 385–407.
- Merton, Robert (1973). "Theory of Rational Option Pricing." *Bell Journal of Economics and Management Science*, Vol. 4, pp. 141–183.
- Merton, Robert (1976). "Option Pricing When the Underlying Stock Returns Are Discontinuous." *Journal of Financial Economics*, Vol. 3, No. 3, pp. 125–144.

## CHAPTER 19

Derivatives Valuation

Derivatives are a huge, complex issue.

—Judd Gregg

Options and derivatives valuation has long been the domain of the so-called *rocket scientists* on Wall Street—i.e., people with a PhD in physics or a similarly demanding discipline when it comes to the mathematics involved. However, the application of the models by the means of numerical methods like Monte Carlo simulation is generally a little less involved than the theoretical models themselves.

This is particularly true for the valuation of options and derivatives with *European exercise*—i.e., where exercise is only possible at a certain predetermined date. It is a bit less true for options and derivatives with *American exercise*, where exercise is allowed at any point over a prespecified period of time. This chapter introduces and uses the *Least-Squares Monte Carlo* (LSM) algorithm, which has become a benchmark algorithm when it comes to American options valuation based on Monte Carlo simulation.

The current chapter is similar in structure to Chapter 18 in that it first introduces a generic valuation class and then provides two specialized valuation classes, one for European exercise and another for American exercise. The generic valuation class contains methods to numerically estimate the most important Greeks of an option: the *delta* and the *vega*. Therefore, the valuation classes are important not only for valuation purposes, but also for *risk management* purposes.

The chapter is structured as follows:

"Generic Valuation Class" on page 596
> This section introduces the *generic* valuation class from which the specific ones inherit.

"European Exercise" on page 600
> This section is about the valuation class for options and derivatives with *European* exercise.

"American Exercise" on page 607
> This section covers the valuation class for options and derivatives with *American* exercise.

Generic Valuation Class

As with the generic simulation class, one instantiates an object of the valuation class by providing only a few inputs (in this case, four):

name
> A `str` object, as a name for the model simulation object

underlying
> An instance of a simulation class representing the underlying

mar_env
> An instance of the `dx.market_environment` class

payoff_func
> A Python `str` object containing the payoff function for the option/derivative

The generic class has three methods:

update()
> Updates selected valuation parameters (attributes)

delta()
> Calculates a numerical value for the delta of an option/derivative

vega()
> Calculates the vega of an option/derivative

Equipped with the background knowledge from the previous chapters about the DX package, the generic valuation class as presented here should be almost self-explanatory; where appropriate, inline comments are also provided. Again, the class is presented in its entirety first, then discussed in more detail:

```
#
# DX Package
#
# Valuation -- Base Class
#
# valuation_class.py
#
```

```
# Python for Finance, 2nd ed.
# (c) Dr. Yves J. Hilpisch
#


class valuation_class(object):
    ''' Basic class for single-factor valuation.

    Attributes
    ==========
    name: str
        name of the object
    underlying: instance of simulation class
        object modeling the single risk factor
    mar_env: instance of market_environment
        market environment data for valuation
    payoff_func: str
        derivatives payoff in Python syntax
        Example: 'np.maximum(maturity_value - 100, 0)'
        where maturity_value is the NumPy vector with
        respective values of the underlying
        Example: 'np.maximum(instrument_values - 100, 0)'
        where instrument_values is the NumPy matrix with
        values of the underlying over the whole time/path grid

    Methods
    =======
    update:
        updates selected valuation parameters
    delta:
        returns the delta of the derivative
    vega:
        returns the vega of the derivative
    '''

    def __init__(self, name, underlying, mar_env, payoff_func=''):
        self.name = name
        self.pricing_date = mar_env.pricing_date
        try:
            # strike is optional
            self.strike = mar_env.get_constant('strike')
        except:
            pass
        self.maturity = mar_env.get_constant('maturity')
        self.currency = mar_env.get_constant('currency')
        # simulation parameters and discount curve from simulation object
        self.frequency = underlying.frequency
        self.paths = underlying.paths
        self.discount_curve = underlying.discount_curve
        self.payoff_func = payoff_func
        self.underlying = underlying
        # provide pricing_date and maturity to underlying
```

```python
            self.underlying.special_dates.extend([self.pricing_date,
                                                   self.maturity])

    def update(self, initial_value=None, volatility=None,
               strike=None, maturity=None):
        if initial_value is not None:
            self.underlying.update(initial_value=initial_value)
        if volatility is not None:
            self.underlying.update(volatility=volatility)
        if strike is not None:
            self.strike = strike
        if maturity is not None:
            self.maturity = maturity
            # add new maturity date if not in time_grid
            if maturity not in self.underlying.time_grid:
                self.underlying.special_dates.append(maturity)
                self.underlying.instrument_values = None

    def delta(self, interval=None, accuracy=4):
        if interval is None:
            interval = self.underlying.initial_value / 50.
        # forward-difference approximation
        # calculate left value for numerical delta
        value_left = self.present_value(fixed_seed=True)
        # numerical underlying value for right value
        initial_del = self.underlying.initial_value + interval
        self.underlying.update(initial_value=initial_del)
        # calculate right value for numerical delta
        value_right = self.present_value(fixed_seed=True)
        # reset the initial_value of the simulation object
        self.underlying.update(initial_value=initial_del - interval)
        delta = (value_right - value_left) / interval
        # correct for potential numerical errors
        if delta < -1.0:
            return -1.0
        elif delta > 1.0:
            return 1.0
        else:
            return round(delta, accuracy)

    def vega(self, interval=0.01, accuracy=4):
        if interval < self.underlying.volatility / 50.:
            interval = self.underlying.volatility / 50.
        # forward-difference approximation
        # calculate the left value for numerical vega
        value_left = self.present_value(fixed_seed=True)
        # numerical volatility value for right value
        vola_del = self.underlying.volatility + interval
        # update the simulation object
        self.underlying.update(volatility=vola_del)
        # calculate the right value for numerical vega
        value_right = self.present_value(fixed_seed=True)
```

```
# reset volatility value of simulation object
self.underlying.update(volatility=vola_del - interval)
vega = (value_right - value_left) / interval
return round(vega, accuracy)
```

One topic covered by the generic dx.valuation_class class is the estimation of Greeks. This is worth taking a closer look at. To this end, assume that a continuously differentiable function $V(S_0, \sigma_0)$ is available that represents the present value of an option. The *delta* of the option is then defined as the first partial derivative with respect to the current value of the underlying S_0; i.e., $\Delta = \frac{\partial V(\cdot)}{\partial S_0}$.

Suppose now that from Monte Carlo valuation (see Chapter 12 and subsequent sections in this chapter) there is a numerical Monte Carlo estimator $\bar{V}(S_0, \sigma_0)$ available for the option value. A numerical approximation for the delta of the option is then given in Equation 19-1.[1] This is what the delta() method of the generic valuation class implements. The method assumes the existence of a present_value() method that returns the Monte Carlo estimator given a certain set of parameter values.

Equation 19-1. Numerical delta of an option

$$\bar{\Delta} = \frac{\bar{V}(S_0 + \Delta S, \sigma_0) - \bar{V}(S_0, \sigma_0)}{\Delta S}, \Delta S > 0$$

Similarly, the *vega* of the instrument is defined as the first partial derivative of the present value with respect to the current (instantaneous) volatility σ_0, i.e., $V = \frac{\partial V(\cdot)}{\partial \sigma_0}$.

Again assuming the existence of a Monte Carlo estimator for the value of the option, Equation 19-2 provides a numerical approximation for the vega. This is what the vega() method of the dx.valuation_class class implements.

Equation 19-2. Numerical vega of an option

$$V = \frac{\bar{V}(S_0, \sigma_0 + \Delta\sigma) - \bar{V}(S_0, \sigma_0)}{\Delta\sigma}, \Delta\sigma > 0$$

Note that the discussion of delta and vega is based only on the *existence* of either a differentiable function or a Monte Carlo estimator for the present value of an option. This is the very reason why one can define methods to numerically estimate these

---

1 For details on how to estimate Greeks numerically by Monte Carlo simulation, refer to Chapter 7 of Glasserman (2004). The code uses *forward-difference* schemes only since this leads to only *one* additional simulation and revaluation of the option. For example, a *central-difference* approximation would lead to *two* option revaluations and therefore a higher computational burden.

quantities without knowledge of the exact definition and numerical implementation of the Monte Carlo estimator.

European Exercise

The first case to which the generic valuation class is specialized is the case of European exercise. To this end, consider the following simplified recipe to generate a Monte Carlo estimator for an option value:

1. Simulate the relevant underlying risk factor S under the risk-neutral measure I times to come up with as many simulated values of the underlying at the maturity of the option T—i.e., $\bar{S}_T(i), i \in \{1, 2, ..., I\}$.

2. Calculate the payoff h_T of the option at maturity for every simulated value of the underlying—i.e., $h_T(\bar{S}_T(i)), i \in \{1, 2, ..., I\}$.

3. Derive the Monte Carlo estimator for the option's present value as
$$\bar{V}_0 \equiv e^{-rT} \frac{1}{I} \Sigma_{i=1}^{I} h_T(\bar{S}_T(i)).$$

The Valuation Class

The following code shows the class implementing the present_value() method based on this recipe. In addition, it contains the method generate_payoff() to generate the simulated paths and the payoff of the option given the simulated paths. This, of course, builds the very basis for the Monte Carlo estimator:

```
#
# DX Package
#
# Valuation -- European Exercise Class
#
# valuation_mcs_european.py
#
# Python for Finance, 2nd ed.
# (c) Dr. Yves J. Hilpisch
#
import numpy as np

from valuation_class import valuation_class


class valuation_mcs_european(valuation_class):
    ''' Class to value European options with arbitrary payoff
    by single-factor Monte Carlo simulation.

    Methods
    =======
```

```
generate_payoff:
    returns payoffs given the paths and the payoff function
present_value:
    returns present value (Monte Carlo estimator)
'''

def generate_payoff(self, fixed_seed=False):
    '''
    Parameters
    ==========
    fixed_seed: bool
        use same/fixed seed for valuation
    '''
    try:
        # strike is optional
        strike = self.strike
    except:
        pass
    paths = self.underlying.get_instrument_values(fixed_seed=fixed_seed)
    time_grid = self.underlying.time_grid
    try:
        time_index = np.where(time_grid == self.maturity)[0]
        time_index = int(time_index)
    except:
        print('Maturity date not in time grid of underlying.')
    maturity_value = paths[time_index]
    # average value over whole path
    mean_value = np.mean(paths[:time_index], axis=1)
    # maximum value over whole path
    max_value = np.amax(paths[:time_index], axis=1)[-1]
    # minimum value over whole path
    min_value = np.amin(paths[:time_index], axis=1)[-1]
    try:
        payoff = eval(self.payoff_func)
        return payoff
    except:
        print('Error evaluating payoff function.')

def present_value(self, accuracy=6, fixed_seed=False, full=False):
    '''
    Parameters
    ==========
    accuracy: int
        number of decimals in returned result
    fixed_seed: bool
        use same/fixed seed for valuation
    full: bool
        return also full 1d array of present values
    '''
    cash_flow = self.generate_payoff(fixed_seed=fixed_seed)
    discount_factor = self.discount_curve.get_discount_factors(
        (self.pricing_date, self.maturity))[0, 1]
```

```
            result = discount_factor * np.sum(cash_flow) / len(cash_flow)
            if full:
                return round(result, accuracy), discount_factor * cash_flow
            else:
                return round(result, accuracy)
```

The generate_payoff() method provides some special objects to be used for the definition of the payoff of the option:

- strike is the *strike* of the option.

- maturity_value represents the 1D ndarray object with the simulated values of the *underlying at maturity* of the option.

- mean_value is the *average* of the underlying over a whole path from today until maturity.

- max_value is the *maximum value* of the underlying over a whole path.

- min_value gives the *minimum value* of the underlying over a whole path.

The last three allow for the efficient handling of options with Asian (i.e., lookback or path-dependent) features.

Flexible Payoffs

The approach taken for the valuation of options and derivatives with European exercise is quite flexible in that arbitrary payoff functions can be defined. This allows, among other things, modeling of derivatives with conditional exercise (e.g., options) as well as unconditional exercise (e.g., forwards). It also allows the inclusion of exotic payoff elements, such as lookback features.

A Use Case

The application of the valuation class dx.valuation_mcs_european is best illustrated by a specific use case. However, before a valuation class can be instantiated, an instance of a simulation object—i.e., an underlying for the option to be valued—is needed. From Chapter 18, the dx.geometric_brownian_motion class is used to model the underlying:

```
In [64]: me_gbm = market_environment('me_gbm', dt.datetime(2020, 1, 1))

In [65]: me_gbm.add_constant('initial_value', 36.)
         me_gbm.add_constant('volatility', 0.2)
         me_gbm.add_constant('final_date', dt.datetime(2020, 12, 31))
         me_gbm.add_constant('currency', 'EUR')
         me_gbm.add_constant('frequency', 'M')
         me_gbm.add_constant('paths', 10000)
```

```
In [66]: csr = constant_short_rate('csr', 0.06)

In [67]: me_gbm.add_curve('discount_curve', csr)

In [68]: gbm = geometric_brownian_motion('gbm', me_gbm)
```

In addition to a simulation object, one needs to define a market environment for the option itself. It has to contain at least a `maturity` and a `currency`. Optionally, a value for the `strike` parameter can be included as well:

```
In [69]: me_call = market_environment('me_call', me_gbm.pricing_date)

In [70]: me_call.add_constant('strike', 40.)
         me_call.add_constant('maturity', dt.datetime(2020, 12, 31))
         me_call.add_constant('currency', 'EUR')
```

A central element, of course, is the payoff function, provided here as a `str` object containing Python code that the `eval()` function can evaluate. A European *call* option shall be modeled. Such an option has a payoff of $h_T = \max(S_T - K, 0)$, with S_T being the value of the underlying at maturity and K being the strike price of the option. In Python and NumPy—with vectorized storage of all simulated values—this takes on the following form:

```
In [71]: payoff_func = 'np.maximum(maturity_value - strike, 0)'
```

Having all the ingredients together, one can then instantiate an object from the `dx.valuation_mcs_european` class. With the valuation object available, all quantities of interest are only one method call away:

```
In [72]: from valuation_mcs_european import valuation_mcs_european

In [73]: eur_call = valuation_mcs_european('eur_call', underlying=gbm,
                           mar_env=me_call, payoff_func=payoff_func)

In [74]: %time eur_call.present_value()  ❶
         CPU times: user 14.8 ms, sys: 4.06 ms, total: 18.9 ms
         Wall time: 43.5 ms

Out[74]: 2.146828

In [75]: %time eur_call.delta()  ❷
         CPU times: user 12.4 ms, sys: 2.68 ms, total: 15.1 ms
         Wall time: 40.1 ms

Out[75]: 0.5155

In [76]: %time eur_call.vega()  ❸
         CPU times: user 21 ms, sys: 2.72 ms, total: 23.7 ms
         Wall time: 89.9 ms

Out[76]: 14.301
```

❶ Estimates the present value of the European call option.

❷ Estimates the delta of the option numerically; the delta is positive for calls.

❸ Estimates the vega of the option numerically; the vega is positive for both calls and puts.

Once the valuation object is instantiated, a more comprehensive analysis of the present value and the Greeks is easily implemented. The following code calculates the present value, delta, and vega for initial values of the underlying ranging from 34 to 46 EUR. The results are presented graphically in Figure 19-1:

```
In [77]: %%time
         s_list = np.arange(34., 46.1, 2.)
         p_list = []; d_list = []; v_list = []
         for s in s_list:
             eur_call.update(initial_value=s)
             p_list.append(eur_call.present_value(fixed_seed=True))
             d_list.append(eur_call.delta())
             v_list.append(eur_call.vega())
         CPU times: user 374 ms, sys: 8.82 ms, total: 383 ms
         Wall time: 609 ms

In [78]: from plot_option_stats import plot_option_stats

In [79]: plot_option_stats(s_list, p_list, d_list, v_list)
```

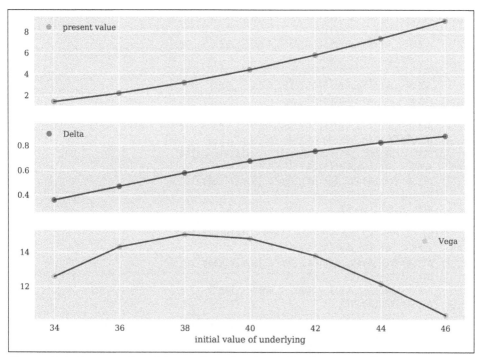

Figure 19-1. Present value, delta, and vega estimates for European call option

The visualization makes use of the helper function `plot_option_stats()`:

```
#
# DX Package
#
# Valuation -- Plotting Options Statistics
#
# plot_option_stats.py
#
# Python for Finance, 2nd ed.
# (c) Dr. Yves J. Hilpisch
#
import matplotlib.pyplot as plt


def plot_option_stats(s_list, p_list, d_list, v_list):
    ''' Plots option prices, deltas, and vegas for a set of
    different initial values of the underlying.

    Parameters
    ==========
    s_list: array or list
        set of initial values of the underlying
    p_list: array or list
        present values
```

```
d_list: array or list
    results for deltas
v_list: array or list
    results for vegas
'''

plt.figure(figsize=(10, 7))
sub1 = plt.subplot(311)
plt.plot(s_list, p_list, 'ro', label='present value')
plt.plot(s_list, p_list, 'b')
plt.legend(loc=0)
plt.setp(sub1.get_xticklabels(), visible=False)
sub2 = plt.subplot(312)
plt.plot(s_list, d_list, 'go', label='Delta')
plt.plot(s_list, d_list, 'b')
plt.legend(loc=0)
plt.ylim(min(d_list) - 0.1, max(d_list) + 0.1)
plt.setp(sub2.get_xticklabels(), visible=False)
sub3 = plt.subplot(313)
plt.plot(s_list, v_list, 'yo', label='Vega')
plt.plot(s_list, v_list, 'b')
plt.xlabel('initial value of underlying')
plt.legend(loc=0)
```

This illustrates that working with the DX package—despite the fact that heavy numerics are involved—boils down to an approach that is comparable to having a closed-form option pricing formula available. However, this approach does not only apply to such simple or "plain vanilla" payoffs as the one considered so far. With exactly the same approach, one can handle more complex payoffs.

To this end, consider the following payoff, a mixture of a *regular* and an *Asian payoff*. The handling and the analysis are the same and are mainly independent of the type of payoff defined. Figure 19-2 shows that delta becomes 1 when the initial value of the underlying reaches the strike price of 40 in this case. Every (marginal) increase of the initial value of the underlying leads to the same (marginal) increase in the option's value from this particular point on:

```
In [80]: payoff_func = 'np.maximum(0.33 * '
         payoff_func += '(maturity_value + max_value) - 40, 0)'  ❶

In [81]: eur_as_call = valuation_mcs_european('eur_as_call', underlying=gbm,
                                    mar_env=me_call, payoff_func=payoff_func)

In [82]: %%time
         s_list = np.arange(34., 46.1, 2.)
         p_list = []; d_list = []; v_list = []
         for s in s_list:
             eur_as_call.update(s)
             p_list.append(eur_as_call.present_value(fixed_seed=True))
             d_list.append(eur_as_call.delta())
             v_list.append(eur_as_call.vega())
         CPU times: user 319 ms, sys: 14.2 ms, total: 333 ms
```

```
Wall time: 488 ms

In [83]: plot_option_stats(s_list, p_list, d_list, v_list)
```

❶ Payoff dependent on both the simulated maturity value and the maximum value over the simulated path.

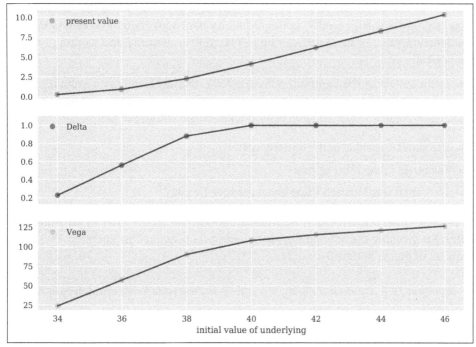

Figure 19-2. Present value, delta, and vega estimates for option with Asian feature

American Exercise

The valuation of options with American exercise or Bermudan exercise is much more involved than with European exercise.[2] Therefore, a bit more valuation theory is needed before proceeding to the valuation class.

---

2 *American* exercise refers to a situation where exercise is possible at every instant of time over a fixed time interval (at least during trading hours). *Bermudan* exercise generally refers to a situation where there are multiple discrete exercise dates. In numerical applications, American exercise is approximated by Bermudan exercise, and maybe letting the number of exercise dates go to infinity in the limit.

Least-Squares Monte Carlo

Although Cox, Ross, and Rubinstein (1979) presented with their binomial model a simple numerical method to value European and American options in the same framework, only with the Longstaff-Schwartz (2001) approach was the valuation of American options by Monte Carlo simulation (MCS) satisfactorily solved. The major problem is that MCS per se is a forward-moving algorithm, while the valuation of American options is generally accomplished by backward induction, estimating the continuation value of the American option starting at maturity and working *back* to the present.

The major insight of the Longstaff-Schwartz (2001) model is to use an ordinary least-squares regression to estimate the continuation value based on the cross section of all available simulated values.[3] The algorithm takes into account, per path:

- The simulated value of the underlying(s)
- The inner value of the option
- The actual continuation value given the specific path

In discrete time, the value of a Bermudan option (and in the limit of an American option) is given by the *optimal stopping problem*, as presented in Equation 19-3 for a finite set of points in time $0 < t_1 < t_2 < \ldots < T$.[4]

Equation 19-3. Optimal stopping problem in discrete time for Bermudan option

$$V_0 = \sup_{\tau \in \{0, t_1, t_2, \ldots, T\}} e^{-r\tau} \mathbf{E}_0^Q(h_\tau(S_\tau))$$

Equation 19-4 presents the continuation value of the American option at date $0 \le t_m < T$. It is the risk-neutral expectation at date t_m under the martingale measure of the value of the American option $V_{t_{m+1}}$ at the subsequent date.

Equation 19-4. Continuation value for the American option

$$C_{t_m}(s) = e^{-r(t_{m+1} - t_m)} \mathbf{E}_{t_m}^Q \left(V_{t_{m`1}}(S_{t_{m`1}}) \middle| S_{t_m} = s \right)$$

---

3 That is why their algorithm is generally abbreviated as LSM, for *Least-Squares Monte Carlo*.

4 Kohler (2010) provides a concise overview of the theory of American option valuation in general and the use of regression-based methods in particular.

The value of the American option V_{t_m} at date t_m can be shown to equal the formula in Equation 19-5—i.e., the maximum of the payoff of immediate exercise (inner value) and the expected payoff of not exercising (continuation value).

Equation 19-5. Value of American option at any given date

$$V_{t_m} = \max\left(h_{t_m}(s), C_{t_m}(s)\right)$$

In Equation 19-5, the inner value is of course easily calculated. The continuation value is what makes it a bit trickier. The Longstaff-Schwartz (2001) algorithm approximates this value by a regression, as presented in Equation 19-6. There, i stands for the current simulated path, D is the number of basis functions for the regression used, α^* are the optimal regression parameters, and b_d is the regression function with number d.

Equation 19-6. Regression-based approximation of continuation value

$$\bar{C}_{t_m, i} = \sum_{d=1}^{D} \alpha^*_{d, t_m} \cdot b_d\left(S_{t_m, i}\right)$$

The optimal regression parameters are the result of the solution of the least-squares regression problem presented in Equation 19-7. Here, $Y_{t_m, i} \equiv e^{-r\left(t_{m+1} - t_m\right)} V_{t_{m+1}, i}$ is the actual continuation value at date t_m for path i (and not a regressed/estimated one).

Equation 19-7. Ordinary least-squares regression

$$\min_{\alpha_{1, t_m}, \ldots, \alpha_{D, t_m}} \frac{1}{I} \sum_{i=1}^{I} \left(Y_{t_m, i} - \sum_{d=1}^{D} \alpha_{d, t_m} \cdot b_d\left(S_{t_m, i}\right)\right)^2$$

This completes the basic (mathematical) tool set to value an American option by MCS.

The Valuation Class

The code that follows represents the class for the valuation of options and derivatives with American exercise. There is one noteworthy step in the implementation of the LSM algorithm in the `present_value()` method (which is also commented on inline): the *optimal decision step*. Here, it is important that, based on the decision that is made, the LSM algorithm takes either the inner value or the *actual* continuation value, and *not* the estimated continuation value:[5]

```
#
# DX Package
#
# Valuation -- American Exercise Class
#
# valuation_mcs_american.py
#
# Python for Finance, 2nd ed.
# (c) Dr. Yves J. Hilpisch
#
import numpy as np

from valuation_class import valuation_class


class valuation_mcs_american(valuation_class):
    ''' Class to value American options with arbitrary payoff
    by single-factor Monte Carlo simulation.

    Methods
    =======
    generate_payoff:
        returns payoffs given the paths and the payoff function
    present_value:
        returns present value (LSM Monte Carlo estimator)
        according to Longstaff-Schwartz (2001)
    '''

    def generate_payoff(self, fixed_seed=False):
        '''
        Parameters
        ==========
        fixed_seed:
            use same/fixed seed for valuation
        '''
        try:
            # strike is optional
            strike = self.strike
        except:
            pass
        paths = self.underlying.get_instrument_values(fixed_seed=fixed_seed)
        time_grid = self.underlying.time_grid
        time_index_start = int(np.where(time_grid == self.pricing_date)[0])
        time_index_end = int(np.where(time_grid == self.maturity)[0])
        instrument_values = paths[time_index_start:time_index_end + 1]
        payoff = eval(self.payoff_func)
```

---

5 See also Chapter 6 of Hilpisch (2015).

```
        return instrument_values, payoff, time_index_start, time_index_end

    def present_value(self, accuracy=6, fixed_seed=False, bf=5, full=False):
        '''
        Parameters
        ==========
        accuracy: int
            number of decimals in returned result
        fixed_seed: bool
            use same/fixed seed for valuation
        bf: int
            number of basis functions for regression
        full: bool
            return also full 1d array of present values
        '''
        instrument_values, inner_values, time_index_start, time_index_end = \
            self.generate_payoff(fixed_seed=fixed_seed)
        time_list = self.underlying.time_grid[
            time_index_start:time_index_end + 1]
        discount_factors = self.discount_curve.get_discount_factors(
            time_list, dtobjects=True)
        V = inner_values[-1]
        for t in range(len(time_list) - 2, 0, -1):
            # derive relevant discount factor for given time interval
            df = discount_factors[t, 1] / discount_factors[t + 1, 1]
            # regression step
            rg = np.polyfit(instrument_values[t], V * df, bf)
            # calculation of continuation values per path
            C = np.polyval(rg, instrument_values[t])
            # optimal decision step:
            # if condition is satisfied (inner value > regressed cont. value)
            # then take inner value; take actual cont. value otherwise
            V = np.where(inner_values[t] > C, inner_values[t], V * df)
        df = discount_factors[0, 1] / discount_factors[1, 1]
        result = df * np.sum(V) / len(V)
        if full:
            return round(result, accuracy), df * V
        else:
            return round(result, accuracy)
```

A Use Case

As has become by now the means of choice, a use case shall illustrate how to work with the dx.valuation_mcs_american class. The use case replicates all American option values as presented in Table 1 of the seminal paper by Longstaff and Schwartz (2001). The underlying is the same as before, a dx.geometric_brownian_motion object. The initial parameterization is as follows:

```
In [84]: me_gbm = market_environment('me_gbm', dt.datetime(2020, 1, 1))

In [85]: me_gbm.add_constant('initial_value', 36.)
```

```
me_gbm.add_constant('volatility', 0.2)
me_gbm.add_constant('final_date', dt.datetime(2021, 12, 31))
me_gbm.add_constant('currency', 'EUR')
me_gbm.add_constant('frequency', 'W')
me_gbm.add_constant('paths', 50000)

In [86]: csr = constant_short_rate('csr', 0.06)

In [87]: me_gbm.add_curve('discount_curve', csr)

In [88]: gbm = geometric_brownian_motion('gbm', me_gbm)

In [89]: payoff_func = 'np.maximum(strike - instrument_values, 0)'

In [90]: me_am_put = market_environment('me_am_put', dt.datetime(2020, 1, 1))

In [91]: me_am_put.add_constant('maturity', dt.datetime(2020, 12, 31))
         me_am_put.add_constant('strike', 40.)
         me_am_put.add_constant('currency', 'EUR')
```

The next step is to instantiate the valuation object based on the numerical assumptions and to initiate the valuations. The valuation of the American put option can take quite a bit longer than the same task for the European options. Not only is the number of paths and time intervals increased, but the algorithm is also more computationally demanding due to the backward induction and the regression per induction step. The numerical estimate obtained for the first option considered is close to the correct one reported in the original paper of 4.478:

```
In [92]: from valuation_mcs_american import valuation_mcs_american

In [93]: am_put = valuation_mcs_american('am_put', underlying=gbm,
                           mar_env=me_am_put, payoff_func=payoff_func)

In [94]: %time am_put.present_value(fixed_seed=True, bf=5)
         CPU times: user 1.57 s, sys: 219 ms, total: 1.79 s
         Wall time: 2.01 s

Out[94]: 4.472834
```

Due to the very construction of the LSM Monte Carlo estimator, it represents a *lower bound* of the mathematically correct American option value.[6] Therefore, one expects the numerical estimate to lie under the true value in any numerically realistic case. Alternative dual estimators can provide *upper bounds* as well.[7] Taken together, two such different estimators then define an interval for the true American option value.

---

6 The main reason is that the "optimal" exercise policy based on the regression estimates for the continuation values is in fact "suboptimal."

7 See Chapter 6 in Hilpisch (2015) for a dual algorithm leading to an upper bound and a Python implementation thereof.

The main stated goal of this use case is to replicate all American option values of Table 1 in the original paper. To this end, one only needs to combine the valuation object with a nested loop. During the innermost loop, the valuation object has to be updated according to the then-current parameterization:

```
In [95]: %%time
         ls_table = []
         for initial_value in (36., 38., 40., 42., 44.):
             for volatility in (0.2, 0.4):
                 for maturity in (dt.datetime(2020, 12, 31),
                                  dt.datetime(2021, 12, 31)):
                     am_put.update(initial_value=initial_value,
                                   volatility=volatility,
                                   maturity=maturity)
                     ls_table.append([initial_value,
                                      volatility,
                                      maturity,
                                      am_put.present_value(bf=5)])
         CPU times: user 41.1 s, sys: 2.46 s, total: 43.5 s
         Wall time: 1min 30s

In [96]: print('S0  | Vola | T | Value')
         print(22 * '-')
         for r in ls_table:
             print('%d  | %3.1f  | %d | %5.3f' %
                   (r[0], r[1], r[2].year - 2019, r[3]))
         S0  | Vola | T | Value
         ----------------------
         36  | 0.2  | 1 | 4.447
         36  | 0.2  | 2 | 4.773
         36  | 0.4  | 1 | 7.006
         36  | 0.4  | 2 | 8.377
         38  | 0.2  | 1 | 3.213
         38  | 0.2  | 2 | 3.645
         38  | 0.4  | 1 | 6.069
         38  | 0.4  | 2 | 7.539
         40  | 0.2  | 1 | 2.269
         40  | 0.2  | 2 | 2.781
         40  | 0.4  | 1 | 5.211
         40  | 0.4  | 2 | 6.756
         42  | 0.2  | 1 | 1.556
         42  | 0.2  | 2 | 2.102
         42  | 0.4  | 1 | 4.466
         42  | 0.4  | 2 | 6.049
         44  | 0.2  | 1 | 1.059
         44  | 0.2  | 2 | 1.617
         44  | 0.4  | 1 | 3.852
         44  | 0.4  | 2 | 5.490
```

These results are a simplified version of Table 1 in the paper by Longstaff and Schwartz (2001). Overall, the numerical values come close to those reported in the paper, where some different parameters have been used (they use, for example, double the number of paths).

To conclude the use case, note that the estimation of Greeks for American options is formally the same as for European options—a major advantage of the implemented approach over alternative numerical methods (like the binomial model):

```
In [97]: am_put.update(initial_value=36.)
         am_put.delta()
Out[97]: -0.4631

In [98]: am_put.vega()
Out[98]: 18.0961
```

 Least-Squares Monte Carlo

The LSM valuation algorithm of Longstaff and Schwartz (2001) is a numerically efficient algorithm to value options and even complex derivatives with American or Bermudan exercise features. The OLS regression step allows the approximation of the optimal exercise strategy based on an efficient numerical method. Since OLS regression can easily handle high-dimensional data, it makes it a flexible method in derivatives pricing.

Conclusion

This chapter is about the numerical valuation of European and American options based on Monte Carlo simulation. The chapter introduces a generic valuation class, called dx.valuation_class. This class provides methods, for example, to estimate the most important Greeks (delta, vega) for both types of options, independent of the simulation object (i.e., the risk factor or stochastic process) used for the valuation.

Based on the generic valuation class, the chapter presents two specialized classes, dx.valuation_mcs_european and dx.valuation_mcs_american. The class for the valuation of European options is mainly a straightforward implementation of the risk-neutral valuation approach presented in Chapter 17 in combination with the numerical estimation of an expectation term (i.e., an integral by Monte Carlo simulation, as discussed in Chapter 11).

The class for the valuation of American options needs a certain kind of regression-based valuation algorithm, called Least-Squares Monte Carlo (LSM). This is due to the fact that for American options an optimal exercise policy has to be derived for a valuation. This is theoretically and numerically a bit more involved. However, the respective present_value() method of the class is still concise.

The approach taken with the DX derivatives analytics package proves to be beneficial. Without too much effort one is able to value a relatively large class of options with the following features:

- Single risk factor
- European or American exercise
- Arbitrary payoff

In addition, one can estimate the most important Greeks for this class of options. To simplify future imports, again a wrapper module is used, this time called *dx_valuation.py*:

```
#
# DX Package
#
# Valuation Classes
#
# dx_valuation.py
#
# Python for Finance, 2nd ed.
# (c) Dr. Yves J. Hilpisch
#
import numpy as np
import pandas as pd

from dx_simulation import *
from valuation_class import valuation_class
from valuation_mcs_european import valuation_mcs_european
from valuation_mcs_american import valuation_mcs_american
```

The *__init__.py* file in the *dx* folder is updated accordingly:

```
#
# DX Package
# packaging file
# __init__.py
#
import numpy as np
import pandas as pd
import datetime as dt

# frame
from get_year_deltas import get_year_deltas
from constant_short_rate import constant_short_rate
from market_environment import market_environment
from plot_option_stats import plot_option_stats

# simulation
from sn_random_numbers import sn_random_numbers
from simulation_class import simulation_class
```

```
from geometric_brownian_motion import geometric_brownian_motion
from jump_diffusion import jump_diffusion
from square_root_diffusion import square_root_diffusion

# valuation
from valuation_class import valuation_class
from valuation_mcs_european import valuation_mcs_european
from valuation_mcs_american import valuation_mcs_american
```

Further Resources

References for the topics of this chapter in book form are:

- Glasserman, Paul (2004). *Monte Carlo Methods in Financial Engineering*. New York: Springer.
- Hilpisch, Yves (2015). *Derivatives Analytics with Python* (*http://dawp.tpq.io/*). Chichester, England: Wiley Finance.

Original papers cited in this chapter are:

- Cox, John, Stephen Ross, and Mark Rubinstein (1979). "Option Pricing: A Simplified Approach." *Journal of Financial Economics*, Vol. 7, No. 3, pp. 229–263.
- Kohler, Michael (2010). "A Review on Regression-Based Monte Carlo Methods for Pricing American Options." In Luc Devroye et al. (eds.): *Recent Developments in Applied Probability and Statistics* (pp. 37–58). Heidelberg: Physica-Verlag.
- Longstaff, Francis, and Eduardo Schwartz (2001). "Valuing American Options by Simulation: A Simple Least Squares Approach." *Review of Financial Studies*, Vol. 14, No. 1, pp. 113–147.

## CHAPTER 20

Portfolio Valuation

Price is what you pay. Value is what you get.

—Warren Buffet

By now, the whole approach for building the DX derivatives analytics package—and its associated benefits—should be clear. By strictly relying on Monte Carlo simulation as the only numerical method, the approach accomplishes an almost complete modularization of the analytics package:

Discounting
The relevant risk-neutral discounting is taken care of by an instance of the `dx.constant_short_rate` class.

Relevant data
Relevant data, parameters, and other input are stored in (several) instances of the `dx.market_environment` class.

Simulation objects
Relevant risk factors (underlyings) are modeled as instances of one of three simulation classes:

- `dx.geometric_brownian_motion`
- `dx.jump_diffusion`
- `dx.square_root_diffusion`

Valuation objects

Options and derivatives to be valued are modeled as instances of one of two valuation classes:

- `dx.valuation_mcs_european`
- `dx.valuation_mcs_american`

One last step is missing: the valuation of possibly complex *portfolios* of options and derivatives. To this end, the following requirements shall be satisfied:

Nonredundancy

Every risk factor (underlying) is modeled only once and potentially used by multiple valuation objects.

Correlations

Correlations between risk factors have to be accounted for.

Positions

An option position, for example, consists of a certain number of option contracts.

However, although it is in principle allowed (it is in fact even required) to provide a currency for both simulation and valuation objects, the following code assumes that portfolios are denominated in a *single currency* only. This simplifies the aggregation of values within a portfolio significantly, because one can abstract from exchange rates and currency risks.

The chapter presents two new classes: a simple one to model a *derivatives position*, and a more complex one to model and value a *derivatives portfolio*. It is structured as follows:

"Derivatives Positions" on page 618

This section introduces the class to model a single derivatives position.

"Derivatives Portfolios" on page 622

This section introduces the core class to value a portfolio of potentially many derivatives positions.

Derivatives Positions

In principle, a *derivatives position* is nothing more than a combination of a valuation object and a quantity for the instrument modeled.

The Class

The code that follows presents the class to model a derivatives position. It is mainly a container for data and objects. In addition, it provides a get_info() method, printing the data and object information stored in an instance of the class:

```
#
# DX Package
#
# Portfolio -- Derivatives Position Class
#
# derivatives_position.py
#
# Python for Finance, 2nd ed.
# (c) Dr. Yves J. Hilpisch
#


class derivatives_position(object):
    ''' Class to model a derivatives position.

    Attributes
    ==========

    name: str
        name of the object
    quantity: float
        number of assets/derivatives making up the position
    underlying: str
        name of asset/risk factor for the derivative
    mar_env: instance of market_environment
        constants, lists, and curves relevant for valuation_class
    otype: str
        valuation class to use
    payoff_func: str
        payoff string for the derivative

    Methods
    =======
    get_info:
        prints information about the derivatives position
    '''

    def __init__(self, name, quantity, underlying, mar_env,
                 otype, payoff_func):
        self.name = name
        self.quantity = quantity
        self.underlying = underlying
        self.mar_env = mar_env
        self.otype = otype
        self.payoff_func = payoff_func
```

```
def get_info(self):
    print('NAME')
    print(self.name, '\n')
    print('QUANTITY')
    print(self.quantity, '\n')
    print('UNDERLYING')
    print(self.underlying, '\n')
    print('MARKET ENVIRONMENT')
    print('\n**Constants**')
    for key, value in self.mar_env.constants.items():
        print(key, value)
    print('\n**Lists**')
    for key, value in self.mar_env.lists.items():
        print(key, value)
    print('\n**Curves**')
    for key in self.mar_env.curves.items():
        print(key, value)
    print('\nOPTION TYPE')
    print(self.otype, '\n')
    print('PAYOFF FUNCTION')
    print(self.payoff_func)
```

To define a derivatives position the following information is required, which is almost the same as for the instantiation of a valuation class:

name
:   Name of the position as a `str` object

quantity
:   Quantity of options/derivatives

underlying
:   Instance of simulation object as a risk factor

mar_env
:   Instance of `dx.market_environment`

otype
:   `str`, either `"European"` or `"American"`

payoff_func
:   Payoff as a Python `str` object

A Use Case

The following interactive session illustrates the use of the class. However, first a definition of a simulation object is needed (but not in full; only the most important, object-specific information is required):

```
In [99]: from dx_valuation import *

In [100]: me_gbm = market_environment('me_gbm', dt.datetime(2020, 1, 1))  ❶

In [101]: me_gbm.add_constant('initial_value', 36.)  ❶
          me_gbm.add_constant('volatility', 0.2)  ❶
          me_gbm.add_constant('currency', 'EUR')  ❶

In [102]: me_gbm.add_constant('model', 'gbm')  ❷
```

❶ The dx.market_environment object for the underlying.

❷ The model type needs to be specified here.

Similarly, for the definition of the derivatives position, one does not need a "complete" dx.market_environment object. Missing information is provided later (during the portfolio valuation), when the simulation object is instantiated:

```
In [103]: from derivatives_position import derivatives_position

In [104]: me_am_put = market_environment('me_am_put', dt.datetime(2020, 1, 1))  ❶

In [105]: me_am_put.add_constant('maturity', dt.datetime(2020, 12, 31))  ❶
          me_am_put.add_constant('strike', 40.)  ❶
          me_am_put.add_constant('currency', 'EUR')  ❶

In [106]: payoff_func = 'np.maximum(strike - instrument_values, 0)'  ❷

In [107]: am_put_pos = derivatives_position(
                        name='am_put_pos',
                        quantity=3,
                        underlying='gbm',
                        mar_env=me_am_put,
                        otype='American',
                        payoff_func=payoff_func)  ❸

In [108]: am_put_pos.get_info()
          NAME
          am_put_pos

          QUANTITY
          3

          UNDERLYING
          gbm

          MARKET ENVIRONMENT

          **Constants**
          maturity 2020-12-31 00:00:00
          strike 40.0
```

```
currency EUR

**Lists**

**Curves**

OPTION TYPE
American

PAYOFF FUNCTION
np.maximum(strike - instrument_values, 0)
```

❶ The dx.market_environment object for the derivative.

❷ The payoff function of the derivative.

❸ The instantiation of the derivatives_position object.

Derivatives Portfolios

From a portfolio perspective, a *relevant market* is mainly composed of the relevant risk factors (underlyings) and their correlations, as well as the derivatives and derivatives positions, respectively, to be valued. Theoretically, the analysis to follow now deals with a general market model $\mathcal{M}$ as defined in Chapter 17, and applies the Fundamental Theorem of Asset Pricing (with its corollaries) to it.[1]

The Class

A somewhat complex Python class implementing a *portfolio valuation* based on the Fundamental Theorem of Asset Pricing—taking into account multiple relevant risk factors and multiple derivatives positions—is presented next. The class is documented inline, especially during passages that implement functionality specific to the purpose at hand:

```
#
# DX Package
#
# Portfolio -- Derivatives Portfolio Class
#
# derivatives_portfolio.py
#
# Python for Finance, 2nd ed.
# (c) Dr. Yves J. Hilpisch
#
```

---

1 In practice, the approach chosen here is sometimes called *global valuation* instead of *instrument-specific valuation*. See Albanese, Gimonet, and White (2010a).

```python
import numpy as np
import pandas as pd

from dx_valuation import *

# models available for risk factor modeling
models = {'gbm': geometric_brownian_motion,
          'jd': jump_diffusion,
          'srd': square_root_diffusion}

# allowed exercise types
otypes = {'European': valuation_mcs_european,
          'American': valuation_mcs_american}


class derivatives_portfolio(object):
    ''' Class for modeling and valuing portfolios of derivatives positions.

    Attributes
    ==========
    name: str
        name of the object
    positions: dict
        dictionary of positions (instances of derivatives_position class)
    val_env: market_environment
        market environment for the valuation
    assets: dict
        dictionary of market environments for the assets
    correlations: list
        correlations between assets
    fixed_seed: bool
        flag for fixed random number generator seed

    Methods
    =======
    get_positions:
        prints information about the single portfolio positions
    get_statistics:
        returns a pandas DataFrame object with portfolio statistics
    '''

    def __init__(self, name, positions, val_env, assets,
                 correlations=None, fixed_seed=False):
        self.name = name
        self.positions = positions
        self.val_env = val_env
        self.assets = assets
        self.underlyings = set()
        self.correlations = correlations
        self.time_grid = None
        self.underlying_objects = {}
        self.valuation_objects = {}
```

```python
        self.fixed_seed = fixed_seed
        self.special_dates = []
        for pos in self.positions:
            # determine earliest starting_date
            self.val_env.constants['starting_date'] = \
                min(self.val_env.constants['starting_date'],
                    positions[pos].mar_env.pricing_date)
            # determine latest date of relevance
            self.val_env.constants['final_date'] = \
                max(self.val_env.constants['final_date'],
                    positions[pos].mar_env.constants['maturity'])
            # collect all underlyings and
            # add to set (avoids redundancy)
            self.underlyings.add(positions[pos].underlying)

        # generate general time grid
        start = self.val_env.constants['starting_date']
        end = self.val_env.constants['final_date']
        time_grid = pd.date_range(start=start, end=end,
                                  freq=self.val_env.constants['frequency']
                                  ).to_pydatetime()
        time_grid = list(time_grid)
        for pos in self.positions:
            maturity_date = positions[pos].mar_env.constants['maturity']
            if maturity_date not in time_grid:
                time_grid.insert(0, maturity_date)
                self.special_dates.append(maturity_date)
        if start not in time_grid:
            time_grid.insert(0, start)
        if end not in time_grid:
            time_grid.append(end)
        # delete duplicate entries
        time_grid = list(set(time_grid))
        # sort dates in time_grid
        time_grid.sort()
        self.time_grid = np.array(time_grid)
        self.val_env.add_list('time_grid', self.time_grid)

        if correlations is not None:
            # take care of correlations
            ul_list = sorted(self.underlyings)
            correlation_matrix = np.zeros((len(ul_list), len(ul_list)))
            np.fill_diagonal(correlation_matrix, 1.0)
            correlation_matrix = pd.DataFrame(correlation_matrix,
                                              index=ul_list, columns=ul_list)
            for i, j, corr in correlations:
                corr = min(corr, 0.999999999999)
                # fill correlation matrix
                correlation_matrix.loc[i, j] = corr
                correlation_matrix.loc[j, i] = corr
            # determine Cholesky matrix
            cholesky_matrix = np.linalg.cholesky(np.array(correlation_matrix))
```

```python
        # dictionary with index positions for the
        # slice of the random number array to be used by
        # respective underlying
        rn_set = {asset: ul_list.index(asset)
                    for asset in self.underlyings}

        # random numbers array, to be used by
        # all underlyings (if correlations exist)
        random_numbers = sn_random_numbers((len(rn_set),
                                            len(self.time_grid),
                                            self.val_env.constants['paths']),
                                            fixed_seed=self.fixed_seed)

        # add all to valuation environment that is
        # to be shared with every underlying
        self.val_env.add_list('cholesky_matrix', cholesky_matrix)
        self.val_env.add_list('random_numbers', random_numbers)
        self.val_env.add_list('rn_set', rn_set)

    for asset in self.underlyings:
        # select market environment of asset
        mar_env = self.assets[asset]
        # add valuation environment to market environment
        mar_env.add_environment(val_env)
        # select right simulation class
        model = models[mar_env.constants['model']]
        # instantiate simulation object
        if correlations is not None:
            self.underlying_objects[asset] = model(asset, mar_env,
                                                    corr=True)
        else:
            self.underlying_objects[asset] = model(asset, mar_env,
                                                    corr=False)

    for pos in positions:
        # select right valuation class (European, American)
        val_class = otypes[positions[pos].otype]
        # pick market environment and add valuation environment
        mar_env = positions[pos].mar_env
        mar_env.add_environment(self.val_env)
        # instantiate valuation class
        self.valuation_objects[pos] = \
            val_class(name=positions[pos].name,
                    mar_env=mar_env,
                    underlying=self.underlying_objects[
                positions[pos].underlying],
                payoff_func=positions[pos].payoff_func)

def get_positions(self):
    ''' Convenience method to get information about
    all derivatives positions in a portfolio. '''
```

```
        for pos in self.positions:
            bar = '\n' + 50 * '-'
            print(bar)
            self.positions[pos].get_info()
            print(bar)

    def get_statistics(self, fixed_seed=False):
        ''' Provides portfolio statistics. '''
        res_list = []
        # iterate over all positions in portfolio
        for pos, value in self.valuation_objects.items():
            p = self.positions[pos]
            pv = value.present_value(fixed_seed=fixed_seed)
            res_list.append([
                p.name,
                p.quantity,
                # calculate all present values for the single instruments
                pv,
                value.currency,
                # single instrument value times quantity
                pv * p.quantity,
                # calculate delta of position
                value.delta() * p.quantity,
                # calculate vega of position
                value.vega() * p.quantity,
            ])
        # generate a pandas DataFrame object with all results
        res_df = pd.DataFrame(res_list,
                              columns=['name', 'quant.', 'value', 'curr.',
                                       'pos_value', 'pos_delta', 'pos_vega'])
        return res_df
```

Object Orientation

The class dx.derivatives_portfolio illustrates a number of benefits of object orientation as mentioned in Chapter 6. At first inspection, it might look like a complex piece of Python code. However,
the financial problem that it solves is a pretty complex one and it
provides the flexibility to address a large number of different use
cases. It is hard to imagine how all this could be achieved without
the use of object-oriented programming and Python classes.

A Use Case

In terms of the DX analytics package, the modeling capabilities are, on a high level,
restricted to a combination of a simulation and a valuation class. There are a total of
six possible combinations:

```
models = {'gbm' : geometric_brownian_motion,
          'jd' : jump_diffusion
          'srd': square_root_diffusion}

otypes = {'European' : valuation_mcs_european,
          'American' : valuation_mcs_american}
```

The interactive use case that follows combines selected elements to define two different derivatives positions that are then combined into a portfolio.

Recall the `derivatives_position` class with the `gbm` and `am_put_pos` objects from the previous section. To illustrate the use of the `derivatives_portfolio` class, we'll define both an additional underlying and an additional options position. First, a `dx.jump_diffusion` object:

```
In [109]: me_jd = market_environment('me_jd', me_gbm.pricing_date)
```

```
In [110]: me_jd.add_constant('lambda', 0.3)  ❶
          me_jd.add_constant('mu', -0.75)
          me_jd.add_constant('delta', 0.1)
          me_jd.add_environment(me_gbm)  ❷
```

```
In [111]: me_jd.add_constant('model', 'jd')  ❸
```

❶ Adds jump diffusion-specific parameters.

❷ Adds other parameters from `gbm`.

❸ Needed for portfolio valuation.

Second, a European call option based on this new simulation object:

```
In [112]: me_eur_call = market_environment('me_eur_call', me_jd.pricing_date)
```

```
In [113]: me_eur_call.add_constant('maturity', dt.datetime(2020, 6, 30))
          me_eur_call.add_constant('strike', 38.)
          me_eur_call.add_constant('currency', 'EUR')
```

```
In [114]: payoff_func = 'np.maximum(maturity_value - strike, 0)'
```

```
In [115]: eur_call_pos = derivatives_position(
                    name='eur_call_pos',
                    quantity=5,
                    underlying='jd',
                    mar_env=me_eur_call,
                    otype='European',
                    payoff_func=payoff_func)
```

From a portfolio perspective, the relevant market now is as shown in the following in `underlyings` and `positions`. For the moment, the definitions do not include correlations between the underlyings. Compiling a `dx.market_environment` for the portfolio valuation is the last step before the instantiation of a `derivatives_portfolio` object:

```
In [116]: underlyings = {'gbm': me_gbm, 'jd' : me_jd}    ❶
          positions = {'am_put_pos' : am_put_pos,
                       'eur_call_pos' : eur_call_pos}    ❷

In [117]: csr = constant_short_rate('csr', 0.06)    ❸

In [118]: val_env = market_environment('general', me_gbm.pricing_date)
          val_env.add_constant('frequency', 'W')
          val_env.add_constant('paths', 25000)
          val_env.add_constant('starting_date', val_env.pricing_date)
          val_env.add_constant('final_date', val_env.pricing_date)    ❹
          val_env.add_curve('discount_curve', csr)    ❸

In [119]: from derivatives_portfolio import derivatives_portfolio

In [120]: portfolio = derivatives_portfolio(
                          name='portfolio',
                          positions=positions,
                          val_env=val_env,
                          assets=underlyings,
                          fixed_seed=False)    ❺
```

❶ Relevant risk factors.

❷ Relevant portfolio postions.

❸ Unique discounting object for the portfolio valuation.

❹ `final_date` is not yet known; therefore, set `pricing_date` as preliminary value.

❺ Instantiation of the `derivatives_portfolio` object.

Now one can harness the power of the valuation class and easily get important statistics for the `derivatives_portfolio` object just defined. The *sum* of the position values, deltas, and vegas is also easily calculated. This portfolio is slightly long delta (almost neutral) and long vega:

```
In [121]: %time portfolio.get_statistics(fixed_seed=False)
          CPU times: user 4.68 s, sys: 409 ms, total: 5.09 s
          Wall time: 14.5 s

Out[121]:
                 name  quant.    value curr.  pos_value  pos_delta  pos_vega
          0   am_put_pos      3  4.458891  EUR  13.376673    -2.0430   31.7850
          1  eur_call_pos     5  2.828634  EUR  14.143170     3.2525   42.2655

In [122]: portfolio.get_statistics(fixed_seed=False)[
```

```
              ['pos_value', 'pos_delta', 'pos_vega']].sum()   ❶
Out[122]: pos_value      27.502731
          pos_delta       1.233500
          pos_vega       74.050500
          dtype: float64

In [123]: portfolio.get_positions()   ❷


              ...


In [124]: portfolio.valuation_objects['am_put_pos'].present_value()   ❸
Out[124]: 4.453187

In [125]: portfolio.valuation_objects['eur_call_pos'].delta()   ❹
Out[125]: 0.6514
```

❶ Aggregation of single position values.

❷ This method call would create a rather lengthy output about all positions.

❸ The present value estimate for a single position.

❹ The delta estimate for a single position.

The derivatives portfolio valuation is conducted based on the assumption that the risk factors are *not* correlated. This is easily verified by inspecting two simulated paths (see Figure 20-1), one for each simulation object:

```
In [126]: path_no = 888
          path_gbm = portfolio.underlying_objects[
              'gbm'].get_instrument_values()[:, path_no]
          path_jd = portfolio.underlying_objects[
              'jd'].get_instrument_values()[:, path_no]

In [127]: plt.figure(figsize=(10,6))
          plt.plot(portfolio.time_grid, path_gbm, 'r', label='gbm')
          plt.plot(portfolio.time_grid, path_jd, 'b', label='jd')
          plt.xticks(rotation=30)
          plt.legend(loc=0)
```

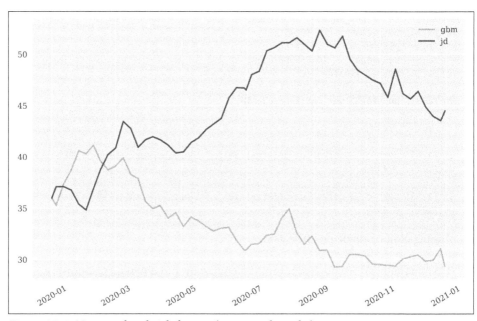

Figure 20-1. Noncorrelated risk factors (two sample paths)

Now consider the case where the two risk factors are highly positively correlated. In this case, there is no direct influence on the values of the single positions in the portfolio:

```
In [128]: correlations = [['gbm', 'jd', 0.9]]

In [129]: port_corr = derivatives_portfolio(
                          name='portfolio',
                          positions=positions,
                          val_env=val_env,
                          assets=underlyings,
                          correlations=correlations,
                          fixed_seed=True)

In [130]: port_corr.get_statistics()
Out[130]:
              name   quant.     value curr.  pos_value  pos_delta  pos_vega
          0  am_put_pos       3  4.458556   EUR  13.375668    -2.0376   30.8676
          1  eur_call_pos      5  2.817813   EUR  14.089065     3.3375   42.2340
```

However, the correlation takes place behind the scenes. The graphical illustration in Figure 20-2 takes the same combination of paths as before. The two paths now almost move in parallel:

```
In [131]: path_gbm = port_corr.underlying_objects['gbm'].\
                          get_instrument_values()[:, path_no]
          path_jd = port_corr.underlying_objects['jd'].\
```

```
                    get_instrument_values()[:, path_no]

In [132]: plt.figure(figsize=(10, 6))
          plt.plot(portfolio.time_grid, path_gbm, 'r', label='gbm')
          plt.plot(portfolio.time_grid, path_jd, 'b', label='jd')
          plt.xticks(rotation=30)
          plt.legend(loc=0);
```

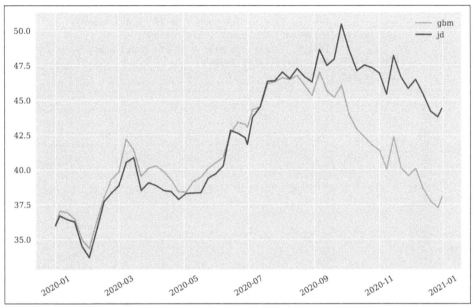

Figure 20-2. Correlated risk factors (two sample paths)

As a last numerical and conceptual example, consider the *frequency distribution of the
portfolio present value*. This is something impossible to generate in general with other
approaches, like the application of analytical formulae or the binomial option pricing
model. Setting the parameter full=True causes the complete set of present values per
option position to be returned after the present value estimation:

```
In [133]: pv1 = 5 * port_corr.valuation_objects['eur_call_pos'].\
                    present_value(full=True)[1]
          pv1
Out[133]: array([ 0.        , 39.71423714, 24.90720272, ...,  0.        ,
                  6.42619093,  8.15838265])

In [134]: pv2 = 3 * port_corr.valuation_objects['am_put_pos'].\
                    present_value(full=True)[1]
          pv2
Out[134]: array([21.31806027, 10.71952869, 19.89804376, ..., 21.39292703,
                  17.59920608,  0.        ])
```

First, compare the frequency distribution of the two positions. The payoff profiles of
the two positions, as displayed in Figure 20-3, are quite different. Note that the values
for both the x- and y-axes are limited for better readability:

```
In [135]: plt.figure(figsize=(10, 6))
          plt.hist([pv1, pv2], bins=25,
                   label=['European call', 'American put']);
          plt.axvline(pv1.mean(), color='r', ls='dashed',
                      lw=1.5, label='call mean = %4.2f' % pv1.mean())
          plt.axvline(pv2.mean(), color='r', ls='dotted',
                      lw=1.5, label='put mean = %4.2f' % pv2.mean())
          plt.xlim(0, 80); plt.ylim(0, 10000)
          plt.legend();
```

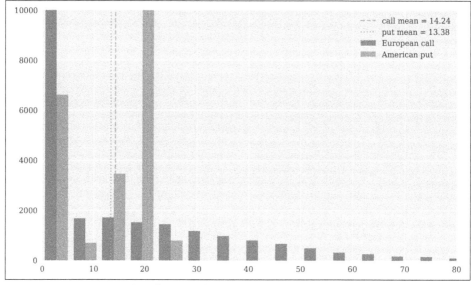

Figure 20-3. Frequency distribution of present values of the two positions

Figure 20-4 finally shows the full frequency distribution of the portfolio present values. One can clearly see the offsetting diversification effects of combining a call with a
put option:

```
In [136]: pvs = pv1 + pv2
          plt.figure(figsize=(10, 6))
          plt.hist(pvs, bins=50, label='portfolio');
          plt.axvline(pvs.mean(), color='r', ls='dashed',
                      lw=1.5, label='mean = %4.2f' % pvs.mean())
          plt.xlim(0, 80); plt.ylim(0, 7000)
          plt.legend();
```

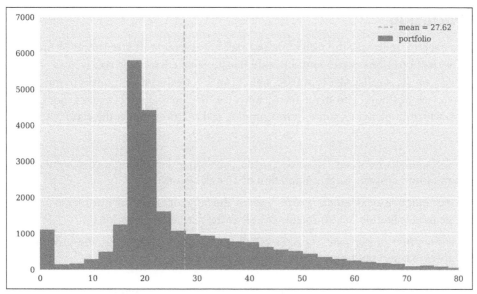

Figure 20-4. Portfolio frequency distribution of present values

What impact does the correlation between the two risk factors have on the risk of the portfolio, measured in the standard deviation of the present values? This can be answered by the following two estimations:

```
In [137]: pvs.std()  ❶
Out[137]: 16.723724772741118

In [138]: pv1 = (5 * portfolio.valuation_objects['eur_call_pos'].
                     present_value(full=True)[1])
          pv2 = (3 * portfolio.valuation_objects['am_put_pos'].
                     present_value(full=True)[1])
          (pv1 + pv2).std()  ❷
Out[138]: 21.80498672323975
```

❶ Standard deviation of portfolio values *with* correlation.

❷ Standard deviation of portfolio values *without* correlation.

Although the mean value stays constant (ignoring numerical deviations), correlation obviously significantly decreases the portfolio risk when measured in this way. Again, this is an insight that it is not really possible to gain when using alternative numerical methods or valuation approaches.

Conclusion

This chapter addresses the valuation and risk management of a portfolio of multiple derivatives positions dependent on multiple (possibly correlated) risk factors. To this end, a new class called `derivatives_position` is introduced to model an options or derivatives position. The main focus, however, lies on the `derivatives_portfolio` class, which implements some more complex tasks. For example, the class takes care of:

- *Correlations* between risk factors (the class generates a single consistent set of random numbers for the simulation of all risk factors)
- *Instantiation of simulation objects* given the single market environments and the general valuation environment, as well as the derivatives positions
- *Generation of portfolio statistics* based on all the assumptions, the risk factors involved, and the terms of the derivatives positions

The examples presented in this chapter can only show some simple versions of derivatives portfolios that can be managed and valued with the DX package developed so far and the `derivatives_portfolio` class. Natural extensions to the DX package would be the addition of more sophisticated financial models, like a stochastic volatility model, and multi-risk valuation classes to model and value derivatives dependent on multiple risk factors (like a European basket option or an American maximum call option, to name just two). At this stage, the modular modeling using OOP and the application of a valuation framework as general as the Fundamental Theorem of Asset Pricing (or "global valuation") play out their strengths: the nonredundant modeling of the risk factors and the accounting for the correlations between them will then also have a direct influence on the values and Greeks of multi-risk derivatives.

The following is a final wrapper module bringing all the components of the DX analytics package together for a single `import` statement:

```
#
# DX Package
#
# All components
#
# dx_package.py
#
# Python for Finance, 2nd ed.
# (c) Dr. Yves J. Hilpisch
#
from dx_valuation import *
from derivatives_position import derivatives_position
from derivatives_portfolio import derivatives_portfolio
```

And here is the now-complete ___init___.py file for the *dx* folder:

```
#
# DX Package
# packaging file
# __init__.py
#
import numpy as np
import pandas as pd
import datetime as dt

# frame
from get_year_deltas import get_year_deltas
from constant_short_rate import constant_short_rate
from market_environment import market_environment
from plot_option_stats import plot_option_stats

# simulation
from sn_random_numbers import sn_random_numbers
from simulation_class import simulation_class
from geometric_brownian_motion import geometric_brownian_motion
from jump_diffusion import jump_diffusion
from square_root_diffusion import square_root_diffusion

# valuation
from valuation_class import valuation_class
from valuation_mcs_european import valuation_mcs_european
from valuation_mcs_american import valuation_mcs_american

# portfolio
from derivatives_position import derivatives_position
from derivatives_portfolio import derivatives_portfolio
```

Further Resources

As for the preceding chapters on the DX derivatives analytics package, Glasserman (2004) is a comprehensive resource for Monte Carlo simulation in the context of financial engineering and applications. Hilpisch (2015) also provides Python-based implementations of the most important Monte Carlo algorithms:

- Glasserman, Paul (2004). *Monte Carlo Methods in Financial Engineering*. New York: Springer.
- Hilpisch, Yves (2015). *Derivatives Analytics with Python* (*http://dawp.tpq.io*). Chichester, England: Wiley Finance.

However, there is hardly any research available when it comes to the valuation of (complex) portfolios of derivatives in a consistent, nonredundant fashion by Monte Carlo simulation. A notable exception, at least from a conceptual point of view, is the brief article by Albanese, Gimonet, and White (2010a). There is a bit more detail in the working paper by the same team of authors:

- Albanese, Claudio, Guillaume Gimonet and Steve White (2010a). "Towards a Global Valuation Model" (*http://bit.ly/risk_may_2010*). *Risk Magazine*, Vol. 23, No. 5, pp. 68–71.

- Albanese, Claudio, Guillaume Gimonet and Steve White (2010b). "Global Valuation and Dynamic Risk Management" (*http://bit.ly/global_valuation*). Working paper.

## CHAPTER 21

Market-Based Valuation

We are facing extreme volatility.

—Carlos Ghosn

A major task in derivatives analytics is the *market-based valuation of options and derivatives* that are not liquidly traded. To this end, one generally calibrates a pricing model to market quotes of liquidly traded options and uses the calibrated model for the pricing of the non-traded options.[1]

This chapter presents a case study based on the DX package and illustrates that this package, as developed step-by-step in the previous four chapters, is suited to implement a market-based valuation. The case study is based on the DAX 30 stock index, which is a blue chip stock market index consisting of stocks of 30 major German companies. On this index, liquidly traded European call and put options are available.

The chapter is divided into sections that implement the following major tasks:

"Options Data" on page 638
> One needs two types of data, namely for the DAX 30 stock index itself and for the liquidly traded European options on the index.

"Model Calibration" on page 641
> To value the non-traded options in a market-consistent fashion, one generally first calibrates the chosen model to quoted option prices in such a way that the model based on the optimal parameters replicates the market prices as well as possible.

---

1 For details, refer to Hilpisch (2015).

"Portfolio Valuation" on page 651

Equipped with the data and a market-calibrated model for the DAX 30 stock index, the final task then is to model and value the non-traded options; important risk measures are also estimated on a position and portfolio level.

The index and options data used in this chapter are from the Thomson Reuters Eikon Data API (see "Python Code" on page 654).

Options Data

To get started, here are the required imports and customizations:

```
In [1]: import numpy as np
        import pandas as pd
        import datetime as dt
```

```
In [2]: from pylab import mpl, plt
        plt.style.use('seaborn')
        mpl.rcParams['font.family'] = 'serif'
        %matplotlib inline
```

```
In [3]: import sys
        sys.path.append('../')
        sys.path.append('../dx')
```

Given the data file as created in "Python Code" on page 654, the options data is read with pandas and processed such that date information is given as pd.Timestamp objects:

```
In [4]: dax = pd.read_csv('../../source/tr_eikon_option_data.csv',
                          index_col=0)  ❶
```

```
In [5]: for col in ['CF_DATE', 'EXPIR_DATE']:
            dax[col] = dax[col].apply(lambda date: pd.Timestamp(date))  ❷
```

```
In [6]: dax.info()  ❸
        <class 'pandas.core.frame.DataFrame'>
        Int64Index: 115 entries, 0 to 114
        Data columns (total 7 columns):
        Instrument     115 non-null object
        CF_DATE        115 non-null datetime64[ns]
        EXPIR_DATE     114 non-null datetime64[ns]
        PUTCALLIND     114 non-null object
        STRIKE_PRC     114 non-null float64
        CF_CLOSE       115 non-null float64
        IMP_VOLT       114 non-null float64
        dtypes: datetime64[ns](2), float64(3), object(2)
        memory usage: 7.2+ KB
```

```
In [7]: dax.set_index('Instrument').head(7)  ❸
Out[7]:
```

```
                    CF_DATE EXPIR_DATE PUTCALLIND  STRIKE_PRC  CF_CLOSE  \
Instrument
.GDAXI              2018-04-27        NaT         NaN         NaN  12500.47
GDAX105000G8.EX 2018-04-27 2018-07-20       CALL     10500.0   2040.80
GDAX105000S8.EX 2018-04-27 2018-07-20        PUT     10500.0     32.00
GDAX108000G8.EX 2018-04-27 2018-07-20       CALL     10800.0   1752.40
GDAX108000S8.EX 2018-04-26 2018-07-20        PUT     10800.0     43.80
GDAX110000G8.EX 2018-04-27 2018-07-20       CALL     11000.0   1562.80
GDAX110000S8.EX 2018-04-27 2018-07-20        PUT     11000.0     54.50

                    IMP_VOLT
Instrument
.GDAXI                   NaN
GDAX105000G8.EX        23.59
GDAX105000S8.EX        23.59
GDAX108000G8.EX        22.02
GDAX108000S8.EX        22.02
GDAX110000G8.EX        21.00
GDAX110000S8.EX        21.00
```

❶ Reads the data with pd.read_csv().

❷ Processes the two columns with date information.

❸ The resulting DataFrame object.

The following code stores the relevant index level for the DAX 30 in a variable and creates two new DataFrame objects, one for calls and one for puts. Figure 21-1 presents the market quotes for the calls and their implied volatilities:[2]

```
In [8]: initial_value = dax.iloc[0]['CF_CLOSE']  ❶

In [9]: calls = dax[dax['PUTCALLIND'] == 'CALL'].copy()  ❷
        puts = dax[dax['PUTCALLIND'] == 'PUT '].copy()   ❷

In [10]: calls.set_index('STRIKE_PRC')[['CF_CLOSE', 'IMP_VOLT']].plot(
             secondary_y='IMP_VOLT', style=['bo', 'rv'], figsize=(10, 6));
```

❶ Assigns the relevant index level to the initial_value variable.

❷ Separates the options data for calls and puts into two new DataFrame objects.

---

2 The *implied volatility* of an option is the volatility value that gives, *ceteris paribus*, when put into the Black-Scholes-Merton (1973) option pricing formula, the market quote of the option.

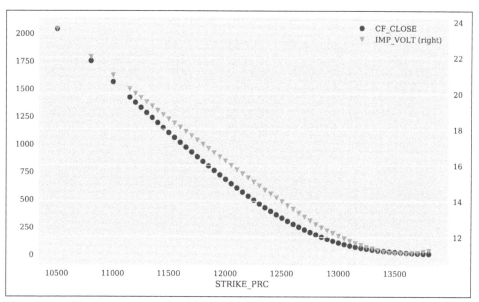

Figure 21-1. Market quotes and implied volatilities for European call options on the DAX 30

Figure 21-2 presents the market quotes for the puts and their implied volatilities:

```
In [11]: ax = puts.set_index('STRIKE_PRC')[['CF_CLOSE', 'IMP_VOLT']].plot(
             secondary_y='IMP_VOLT', style=['bo', 'rv'], figsize=(10, 6))
         ax.get_legend().set_bbox_to_anchor((0.25, 0.5));
```

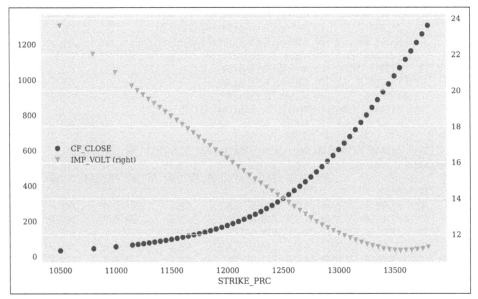

Figure 21-2. Market quotes and implied volatilities for European put options on the DAX 30

Model Calibration

This section selects the relevant market data, models the European options on the DAX 30 index, and implements the calibration procedure itself.

Relevant Market Data

Model calibration generally takes place based on a smaller subset of the available option market quotes.[3] To this end, the following code selects only those European call options whose strike price is relatively close to the current index level (see Figure 21-3). In other words, only those European call options are selected that are not too far in-the-money or out-of-the-money:

```
In [12]: limit = 500   ❶

In [13]: option_selection = calls[abs(calls['STRIKE_PRC'] - initial_value)
                                  < limit].copy()   ❷

In [14]: option_selection.info()   ❸
         <class 'pandas.core.frame.DataFrame'>
         Int64Index: 20 entries, 43 to 81
         Data columns (total 7 columns):
```

---

3 See Hilpisch (2015), Chapter 11, for more details.

```
Instrument     20 non-null object
CF_DATE        20 non-null datetime64[ns]
EXPIR_DATE     20 non-null datetime64[ns]
PUTCALLIND     20 non-null object
STRIKE_PRC     20 non-null float64
CF_CLOSE       20 non-null float64
IMP_VOLT       20 non-null float64
dtypes: datetime64[ns](2), float64(3), object(2)
memory usage: 1.2+ KB
```

```
In [15]: option_selection.set_index('Instrument').tail()    ❸
Out[15]:
                        CF_DATE EXPIR_DATE PUTCALLIND  STRIKE_PRC  CF_CLOSE  \
Instrument
GDAX128000G8.EX     2018-04-27 2018-07-20       CALL     12800.0     182.4
GDAX128500G8.EX     2018-04-27 2018-07-20       CALL     12850.0     162.0
GDAX129000G8.EX     2018-04-25 2018-07-20       CALL     12900.0     142.9
GDAX129500G8.EX     2018-04-27 2018-07-20       CALL     12950.0     125.4
GDAX130000G8.EX     2018-04-27 2018-07-20       CALL     13000.0     109.4

                    IMP_VOLT
Instrument
GDAX128000G8.EX        12.70
GDAX128500G8.EX        12.52
GDAX129000G8.EX        12.36
GDAX129500G8.EX        12.21
GDAX130000G8.EX        12.06
```

```
In [16]: option_selection.set_index('STRIKE_PRC')[['CF_CLOSE', 'IMP_VOLT']].plot(
             secondary_y='IMP_VOLT', style=['bo', 'rv'], figsize=(10, 6));
```

❶ Sets the limit value for the derivation of the strike price from the current index level (*moneyness* condition).

❷ Selects, based on the limit value, the European call options to be included for the calibration.

❸ The resulting DataFrame with the European call options for the calibration.

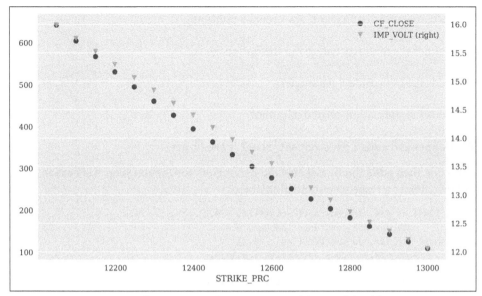

Figure 21-3. European call options on the DAX 30 used for model calibration

Option Modeling

Having the relevant market data defined, the DX package can now be used to model the European call options. The definition of the dx.market_environment object to model the DAX 30 index follows, along the lines of the examples in previous chapters:

```
In [17]: import dx

In [18]: pricing_date = option_selection['CF_DATE'].max()    ❶

In [19]: me_dax = dx.market_environment('DAX30', pricing_date)    ❷

In [20]: maturity = pd.Timestamp(calls.iloc[0]['EXPIR_DATE'])    ❸

In [21]: me_dax.add_constant('initial_value', initial_value)    ❹
         me_dax.add_constant('final_date', maturity)    ❹
         me_dax.add_constant('currency', 'EUR')    ❹

In [22]: me_dax.add_constant('frequency', 'B')    ❺
         me_dax.add_constant('paths', 10000)    ❺

In [23]: csr = dx.constant_short_rate('csr', 0.01)    ❻
         me_dax.add_curve('discount_curve', csr)    ❻
```

❶ Defines the initial or pricing date given the options data.

❷ Instantiates the dx.market_environment object.

❸ Defines the maturity date given the options data.

❹ Adds the basic model parameters.

❺ Adds the simulation-related parameters.

❻ Defines and adds a dx.constant_short_rate object.

This code then adds the model-specific parameters for the dx.jump_diffusion class and instantiates a respective simulation object:

```
In [24]: me_dax.add_constant('volatility', 0.2)
         me_dax.add_constant('lambda', 0.8)
         me_dax.add_constant('mu', -0.2)
         me_dax.add_constant('delta', 0.1)

In [25]: dax_model = dx.jump_diffusion('dax_model', me_dax)
```

As an example for a European call option, consider the following parameterization for which the strike is set equal to the current index level of the DAX 30. This allows for a first value estimation based on Monte Carlo simulation:

```
In [26]: me_dax.add_constant('strike', initial_value)   ❶
         me_dax.add_constant('maturity', maturity)

In [27]: payoff_func = 'np.maximum(maturity_value - strike, 0)'   ❷

In [28]: dax_eur_call = dx.valuation_mcs_european('dax_eur_call',
                            dax_model, me_dax, payoff_func)   ❸

In [29]: dax_eur_call.present_value()   ❹
Out[29]: 654.298085
```

❶ Sets the value for strike equal to the initial_value.

❷ Defines the payoff function for a European call option.

❸ Instantiates the valuation object.

❹ Initiates the simulation and value estimation.

Similarly, valuation objects can be defined for all relevant European call options on the DAX 30 index. The only parameter that changes is the strike price:

```
In [30]: option_models = {}   ❶
         for option in option_selection.index:
             strike = option_selection['STRIKE_PRC'].loc[option]   ❷
             me_dax.add_constant('strike', strike)   ❷
```

```
option_models[strike] = dx.valuation_mcs_european(
                        'eur_call_%d' % strike,
                        dax_model,
                        me_dax,
                        payoff_func)
```

❶ The valuation objects are collected in a dict object.

❷ Selects the relevant strike price and (re)defines it in the dx.market_environment object.

Now, based on the valuation objects for all relevant options, the function calcu late_model_values() returns the model values for all options given a set of the model-specific parameter values p0:

```
In [32]: def calculate_model_values(p0):
             ''' Returns all relevant option values.

             Parameters
             ==========
             p0: tuple/list
                 tuple of kappa, theta, volatility

             Returns
             =======
             model_values: dict
                 dictionary with model values
             '''
             volatility, lamb, mu, delta = p0
             dax_model.update(volatility=volatility, lamb=lamb,
                              mu=mu, delta=delta)
             return {
                     strike: model.present_value(fixed_seed=True)
                     for strike, model in option_models.items()
                 }

In [33]: calculate_model_values((0.1, 0.1, -0.4, 0.0))
Out[33]: {12050.0: 611.222524,
          12100.0: 571.83659,
          12150.0: 533.595853,
          12200.0: 496.607225,
          12250.0: 460.863233,
          12300.0: 426.543355,
          12350.0: 393.626483,
          12400.0: 362.066869,
          12450.0: 331.877733,
          12500.0: 303.133596,
          12550.0: 275.987049,
          12600.0: 250.504646,
          12650.0: 226.687523,
          12700.0: 204.550609,
```

```
12750.0: 184.020514,
12800.0: 164.945082,
12850.0: 147.249829,
12900.0: 130.831722,
12950.0: 115.681449,
13000.0: 101.917351}
```

The function `calculate_model_values()` is used during the calibration procedure, as described next.

Calibration Procedure

Calibration of an option pricing model is, in general, a convex optimization problem. The most widely used function for the calibration—i.e., the minimization of some error function value—is the *mean-squared error* (MSE) for the model option values given the market quotes of the options.[4] Assume there are N relevant options, and also model and market quotes. The problem of calibrating an option pricing model to the market quotes based on the MSE is then given in Equation 21-1. There, C_n^* and C_n^{mod} are the market price and the model price of the nth option, respectively. p is the parameter set provided as input to the option pricing model.

Equation 21-1. Mean-squared error for model calibration

$$\min_{p} \frac{1}{N} \sum_{n=1}^{N} \left(C_n^* - C_n^{mod}(p) \right)^2$$

The Python function `mean_squared_error()` implements this approach to model calibration technically. A global variable `i` is used to control the output of intermediate parameter `tuple` objects and the resulting MSE:

```
In [34]: i = 0
         def mean_squared_error(p0):
             ''' Returns the mean-squared error given
             the model and market values.

             Parameters
             ===========
             p0: tuple/list
                 tuple of kappa, theta, volatility

             Returns
             =======
             MSE: float
```

---

4 There are multiple alternatives to define the target function for the calibration procedure. See Hilpisch (2015), Chapter 11, for a discussion of this topic.

```
      mean-squared error
    '''
    global i
    model_values = np.array(list(
            calculate_model_values(p0).values())))   ❶
    market_values = option_selection['CF_CLOSE'].values   ❷
    option_diffs = model_values - market_values   ❸
    MSE = np.sum(option_diffs ** 2) / len(option_diffs)   ❹
    if i % 75 == 0:
        if i == 0:
            print('%4s  %6s  %6s  %6s  %6s --> %6s' %
                    ('i', 'vola', 'lambda', 'mu', 'delta', 'MSE'))
        print('%4d  %6.3f  %6.3f  %6.3f  %6.3f --> %6.3f' %
                (i, p0[0], p0[1], p0[2], p0[3], MSE))
    i += 1
    return MSE

In [35]: mean_squared_error((0.1, 0.1, -0.4, 0.0))   ❺
            i    vola  lambda     mu   delta -->    MSE
            0   0.100   0.100  -0.400   0.000 --> 728.375

Out[35]: 728.3752973715275
```

❶ Estimates the set of model values.

❷ Picks out the market quotes.

❸ Calculates element-wise the differences between the two.

❹ Calculates the mean-squared error value.

❺ Illustrates such a calculation based on sample parameters.

Chapter 11 introduces the two functions (spo.brute() and spo.fmin()) that are
used to implement the calibration procedure. First, the global minimization based on
ranges for the four model-specific parameter values. The result is an optimal parameter combination given all the parameter combinations checked during the *brute force
minimization*:

```
In [36]: import scipy.optimize as spo

In [37]: %%time
         i = 0
         opt_global = spo.brute(mean_squared_error,
                         ((0.10, 0.201, 0.025),   # range for volatility
                          (0.10, 0.80, 0.10),     # range for jump intensity
                          (-0.40, 0.01, 0.10),    # range for average jump size
                          (0.00, 0.121, 0.02)),   # range for jump variability
                         finish=None)
            i    vola  lambda     mu   delta -->    MSE
```

```
   0   0.100   0.100  -0.400   0.000 --> 728.375
  75   0.100   0.300  -0.400   0.080 --> 5157.513
 150   0.100   0.500  -0.300   0.040 --> 12199.386
 225   0.100   0.700  -0.200   0.000 --> 6904.932
 300   0.125   0.200  -0.200   0.100 --> 855.412
 375   0.125   0.400  -0.100   0.060 --> 621.800
 450   0.125   0.600   0.000   0.020 --> 544.137
 525   0.150   0.100   0.000   0.120 --> 3410.776
 600   0.150   0.400  -0.400   0.080 --> 46775.769
 675   0.150   0.600  -0.300   0.040 --> 56331.321
 750   0.175   0.100  -0.200   0.000 --> 14562.213
 825   0.175   0.300  -0.200   0.100 --> 24599.738
 900   0.175   0.500  -0.100   0.060 --> 19183.167
 975   0.175   0.700   0.000   0.020 --> 11871.683
1050   0.200   0.200   0.000   0.120 --> 31736.403
1125   0.200   0.500  -0.400   0.080 --> 130372.718
1200   0.200   0.700  -0.300   0.040 --> 126365.140
CPU times: user 1min 45s, sys: 7.07 s, total: 1min 52s
Wall time: 1min 56s

In [38]: mean_squared_error(opt_global)
Out[38]: 17.946670038040985
```

The opt_global values are intermediate results only. They are used as starting values for the *local minimization*. Given the parameterization used, the opt_local values are final and optimal given certain assumed tolerance levels:

```
In [39]: %%time
         i = 0
         opt_local = spo.fmin(mean_squared_error, opt_global,
                              xtol=0.00001, ftol=0.00001,
                              maxiter=200, maxfun=550)
           i    vola lambda      mu   delta -->     MSE
           0   0.100   0.200  -0.300   0.000 --> 17.947
          75   0.098   0.216  -0.302  -0.001 -->  7.885
         150   0.098   0.216  -0.300  -0.001 -->  7.371
         Optimization terminated successfully.
                  Current function value: 7.371163
                  Iterations: 100
                  Function evaluations: 188
         CPU times: user 15.6 s, sys: 1.03 s, total: 16.6 s
         Wall time: 16.7 s

In [40]: i = 0
         mean_squared_error(opt_local)    ❶
           i    vola lambda      mu   delta -->     MSE
           0   0.098   0.216  -0.300  -0.001 -->  7.371

Out[40]: 7.371162645265256

In [41]: calculate_model_values(opt_local)    ❷
Out[41]: {12050.0: 647.428189,
```

```
12100.0: 607.402796,
12150.0: 568.46137,
12200.0: 530.703659,
12250.0: 494.093839,
12300.0: 458.718401,
12350.0: 424.650128,
12400.0: 392.023241,
12450.0: 360.728543,
12500.0: 330.727256,
12550.0: 302.117223,
12600.0: 274.98474,
12650.0: 249.501807,
12700.0: 225.678695,
12750.0: 203.490065,
12800.0: 182.947468,
12850.0: 163.907583,
12900.0: 146.259349,
12950.0: 129.909743,
13000.0: 114.852425}
```

❶ The mean-squared error given the optimal parameter values.

❷ The model values given the optimal parameter values.

Next, we compare the model values for the optimal parameters with the market quotes. The pricing errors are calculated as the absolute differences between the model values and market quotes and as the deviation in percent from the market quotes:

```
In [42]: option_selection['MODEL'] = np.array(list(calculate_model_values(
                                      opt_local).values()))
         option_selection['ERRORS_EUR'] = (option_selection['MODEL'] -
                                      option_selection['CF_CLOSE'])
         option_selection['ERRORS_%'] = (option_selection['ERRORS_EUR'] /
                                      option_selection['CF_CLOSE']) * 100

In [43]: option_selection[['MODEL', 'CF_CLOSE', 'ERRORS_EUR', 'ERRORS_%']]
Out[43]:          MODEL  CF_CLOSE  ERRORS_EUR  ERRORS_%
         43   647.428189     642.6    4.828189  0.751352
         45   607.402796     604.4    3.002796  0.496823
         47   568.461370     567.1    1.361370  0.240058
         49   530.703659     530.4    0.303659  0.057251
         51   494.093839     494.8   -0.706161 -0.142716
         53   458.718401     460.3   -1.581599 -0.343602
         55   424.650128     426.8   -2.149872 -0.503719
         57   392.023241     394.4   -2.376759 -0.602627
         59   360.728543     363.3   -2.571457 -0.707805
         61   330.727256     333.3   -2.572744 -0.771900
         63   302.117223     304.8   -2.682777 -0.880176
         65   274.984740     277.5   -2.515260 -0.906400
         67   249.501807     251.7   -2.198193 -0.873338
         69   225.678695     227.3   -1.621305 -0.713289
```

```
71  203.490065     204.1    -0.609935  -0.298841
73  182.947468     182.4     0.547468   0.300147
75  163.907583     162.0     1.907583   1.177520
77  146.259349     142.9     3.359349   2.350839
79  129.909743     125.4     4.509743   3.596286
81  114.852425     109.4     5.452425   4.983935
```

```
In [44]: round(option_selection['ERRORS_EUR'].mean(), 3)   ❶
Out[44]: 0.184
```

```
In [45]: round(option_selection['ERRORS_%'].mean(), 3)   ❷
Out[45]: 0.36
```

❶ The average pricing error in EUR.

❷ The average pricing error in percent.

Figure 21-4 visualizes the valuation results and errors:

```
In [46]: fix, (ax1, ax2, ax3) = plt.subplots(3, sharex=True, figsize=(10, 10))
         strikes = option_selection['STRIKE_PRC'].values
         ax1.plot(strikes, option_selection['CF_CLOSE'], label='market quotes')
         ax1.plot(strikes, option_selection['MODEL'], 'ro', label='model values')
         ax1.set_ylabel('option values')
         ax1.legend(loc=0)
         wi = 15
         ax2.bar(strikes - wi / 2., option_selection['ERRORS_EUR'], width=wi)
         ax2.set_ylabel('errors [EUR]')
         ax3.bar(strikes - wi / 2., option_selection['ERRORS_%'], width=wi)
         ax3.set_ylabel('errors [%]')
         ax3.set_xlabel('strikes');
```

Calibration Speed

The calibration of an option pricing model to market data in general requires the recalculation of hundreds or even thousands of option values. This is therefore typically done based on analytical pricing formulae. Here, the calibration procedure relies on Monte Carlo simulation as the pricing method, which is computationally more demanding compared to analytical methods. Nevertheless, the calibration procedure does not take "too long" even on a typical notebook. The use of parallelization techniques, for instance, can speed up the calibration considerably.

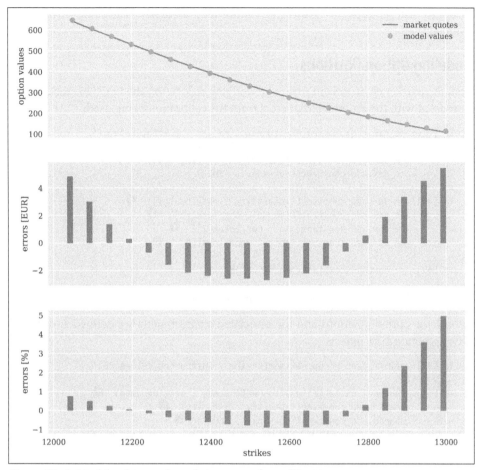

Figure 21-4. Model values and market quotes after calibration

Portfolio Valuation

Being equipped with a calibrated model reflecting realities in the financial markets as represented by market quotes of liquidly traded options enables one to model and value non-traded options and derivatives. The idea is that calibration "infuses" the correct risk-neutral martingale measure into the model via optimal parameters. Based on this measure, the machinery of the Fundamental Theorem of Asset Pricing can then be applied to contingent claims beyond those used for the calibration.

This section considers a portfolio of American put options on the DAX 30 index. There are no such options available that are liquidly traded on exchanges. For simplicity, it is assumed that the American put options have the same maturity as the

European call options used for the calibration. Similarly, the same strikes are assumed.

Modeling Option Positions

First, the market environment for the underlying risk factor, the DAX 30 stock index, is modeled with the optimal parameters from the calibration being used:

```
In [47]: me_dax = dx.market_environment('me_dax', pricing_date)
         me_dax.add_constant('initial_value', initial_value)
         me_dax.add_constant('final_date', pricing_date)
         me_dax.add_constant('currency', 'EUR')

In [48]: me_dax.add_constant('volatility', opt_local[0])    ❶
         me_dax.add_constant('lambda', opt_local[1])    ❶
         me_dax.add_constant('mu', opt_local[2])    ❶
         me_dax.add_constant('delta', opt_local[3])    ❶

In [49]: me_dax.add_constant('model', 'jd')
```

❶ This adds the optimal parameters from the calibration.

Second, the option positions and the associated environments are defined and stored in two separate dict objects:

```
In [50]: payoff_func = 'np.maximum(strike - instrument_values, 0)'

In [51]: shared = dx.market_environment('share', pricing_date)    ❶
         shared.add_constant('maturity', maturity)    ❶
         shared.add_constant('currency', 'EUR')    ❶

In [52]: option_positions = {}
         option_environments = {}
         for option in option_selection.index:
             option_environments[option] = dx.market_environment(
                 'am_put_%d' % option, pricing_date)    ❷
             strike = option_selection['STRIKE_PRC'].loc[option]    ❸
             option_environments[option].add_constant('strike', strike)    ❸
             option_environments[option].add_environment(shared)    ❹
             option_positions['am_put_%d' % strike] = \
                         dx.derivatives_position(
                             'am_put_%d' % strike,
                             quantity=np.random.randint(10, 50),
                             underlying='dax_model',
                             mar_env=option_environments[option],
                             otype='American',
                             payoff_func=payoff_func)    ❺
```

❶ Defines a shared dx.market_environment object as the basis for all option-specific environments.

❷ Defines and stores a new dx.market_environment object for the relevant American put option.

❸ Defines and stores the strike price parameter for the option.

❹ Adds the elements from the shared dx.market_environment object to the option-specific one.

❺ Defines the dx.derivatives_position object with a randomized quantity.

The Options Portfolio

To value the portfolio with all the American put options, a valuation environment is needed. It contains the major parameters for the estimation of position values and risk statistics:

```
In [53]: val_env = dx.market_environment('val_env', pricing_date)
         val_env.add_constant('starting_date', pricing_date)
         val_env.add_constant('final_date', pricing_date)   ❶
         val_env.add_curve('discount_curve', csr)
         val_env.add_constant('frequency', 'B')
         val_env.add_constant('paths', 25000)

In [54]: underlyings = {'dax_model' : me_dax}   ❷

In [55]: portfolio = dx.derivatives_portfolio('portfolio', option_positions,
                                              val_env, underlyings)   ❸

In [56]: %time results = portfolio.get_statistics(fixed_seed=True)
         CPU times: user 1min 5s, sys: 2.91 s, total: 1min 8s
         Wall time: 38.2 s

In [57]: results.round(1)
Out[57]:              name  quant.  value  curr.  pos_value  pos_delta  pos_vega
         0    am_put_12050      33  151.6   EUR     5002.8       -4.7   38206.9
         1    am_put_12100      38  161.5   EUR     6138.4       -5.7   51365.2
         2    am_put_12150      20  171.3   EUR     3426.8       -3.3   27894.5
         3    am_put_12200      12  183.9   EUR     2206.6       -2.2   18479.7
         4    am_put_12250      37  197.4   EUR     7302.8       -7.3   59423.5
         5    am_put_12300      37  212.3   EUR     7853.9       -8.2   65911.9
         6    am_put_12350      36  228.4   EUR     8224.1       -9.0   70969.4
         7    am_put_12400      16  244.3   EUR     3908.4       -4.3   32871.4
         8    am_put_12450      17  262.7   EUR     4465.6       -5.1   37451.2
         9    am_put_12500      16  283.4   EUR     4534.8       -5.2   36158.2
         10   am_put_12550      38  305.3   EUR    11602.3      -13.3   86869.9
         11   am_put_12600      10  330.4   EUR     3303.9       -3.9   22144.5
         12   am_put_12650      38  355.5   EUR    13508.3      -16.0   89124.8
         13   am_put_12700      40  384.2   EUR    15367.5      -18.6   90871.2
         14   am_put_12750      13  413.5   EUR     5375.7       -6.5   28626.0
         15   am_put_12800      49  445.0   EUR    21806.6      -26.3  105287.3
```

```
16  am_put_12850      30  477.4   EUR   14321.8   -17.0   60757.2
17  am_put_12900      33  510.3   EUR   16840.1   -19.7   69163.6
18  am_put_12950      40  544.4   EUR   21777.0   -24.9   80472.3
19  am_put_13000      35  582.3   EUR   20378.9   -22.9   66522.6

In [58]: results[['pos_value','pos_delta','pos_vega']].sum().round(1)
Out[58]: pos_value       197346.2
         pos_delta         -224.0
         pos_vega       1138571.1
         dtype: float64
```

❶ The final_date parameter is later reset to the final maturity date over all options in the portfolio.

❷ The American put options in the portfolio are all written on the same underlying risk factor, the DAX 30 stock index.

❸ This instantiates the dx.derivatives_portfolio object.

The estimation of all statistics takes a little while, since it is all based on Monte Carlo simulation and such estimations are particularly compute-intensive for American options due to the application of the Least-Squares Monte Carlo (LSM) algorithm. Because we are dealing with long positions of American put options only, the portfolio is short delta and long vega.

Python Code

The following presents code to retrieve options data for the German DAX 30 stock index from the Eikon Data API:

```
In [1]: import eikon as ek   ❶
        import pandas as pd
        import datetime as dt
        import configparser as cp

In [2]: cfg = cp.ConfigParser()   ❷
        cfg.read('eikon.cfg')   ❷
Out[2]: ['eikon.cfg']

In [3]: ek.set_app_id(cfg['eikon']['app_id'])   ❷

In [4]: fields = ['CF_DATE', 'EXPIR_DATE', 'PUTCALLIND',
                  'STRIKE_PRC', 'CF_CLOSE', 'IMP_VOLT']   ❸

In [5]: dax = ek.get_data('0#GDAXN8*.EX', fields=fields)[0]   ❹

In [6]: dax.info()   ❹

        <class 'pandas.core.frame.DataFrame'>
```

```
RangeIndex: 115 entries, 0 to 114
Data columns (total 7 columns):
Instrument     115 non-null object
CF_DATE        115 non-null object
EXPIR_DATE     114 non-null object
PUTCALLIND     114 non-null object
STRIKE_PRC     114 non-null float64
CF_CLOSE       115 non-null float64
IMP_VOLT       114 non-null float64
dtypes: float64(3), object(4)
memory usage: 6.4+ KB
```

```
In [7]: dax['Instrument'] = dax['Instrument'].apply(
            lambda x: x.replace('/', ''))  ❺
```

```
In [8]: dax.set_index('Instrument').head(10)
Out[8]:                    CF_DATE  EXPIR_DATE PUTCALLIND  STRIKE_PRC  CF_CLOSE  \
        Instrument
        .GDAXI          2018-04-27        None       None         NaN  12500.47
        GDAX105000G8.EX 2018-04-27  2018-07-20       CALL     10500.0   2040.80
        GDAX105000S8.EX 2018-04-27  2018-07-20        PUT     10500.0     32.00
        GDAX108000G8.EX 2018-04-27  2018-07-20       CALL     10800.0   1752.40
        GDAX108000S8.EX 2018-04-26  2018-07-20        PUT     10800.0     43.80
        GDAX110000G8.EX 2018-04-27  2018-07-20       CALL     11000.0   1562.80
        GDAX110000S8.EX 2018-04-27  2018-07-20        PUT     11000.0     54.50
        GDAX111500G8.EX 2018-04-27  2018-07-20       CALL     11150.0   1422.50
        GDAX111500S8.EX 2018-04-27  2018-07-20        PUT     11150.0     64.30
        GDAX112000G8.EX 2018-04-27  2018-07-20       CALL     11200.0   1376.10

                         IMP_VOLT
        Instrument
        .GDAXI                NaN
        GDAX105000G8.EX     23.59
        GDAX105000S8.EX     23.59
        GDAX108000G8.EX     22.02
        GDAX108000S8.EX     22.02
        GDAX110000G8.EX     21.00
        GDAX110000S8.EX     21.00
        GDAX111500G8.EX     20.24
        GDAX111500S8.EX     20.25
        GDAX112000G8.EX     19.99
```

```
In [9]: dax.to_csv('../../source/tr_eikon_option_data.csv')  ❻
```

❶ Imports the eikon Python wrapper package.

❷ Reads the login credentials for the Eikon Data API.

❸ Defines the data fields to be retrieved.

❹   Retrieves options data for the July 2018 expiry.

❺   Replaces the slash character / in the instrument names.

❻   Writes the data set as a CSV file.

Conclusion

This chapter presents a larger, realistic use case for the application of the DX analytics package to the valuation of a portfolio of non-traded American options on the German DAX 30 stock index. The chapter addresses three main tasks typically involved in any real-world derivatives analytics application:

Obtaining data
> Current, correct market data builds the basis of any modeling and valuation effort in derivatives analytics; one needs index data as well as options data for the DAX 30.

Model calibration
> To value, manage, and hedge non-traded options and derivatives in a market-consistent fashion, one has to calibrate the parameters of an appropriate model (simulation object) to the relevant option market quotes (relevant with regard to maturity and strikes). The model of choice is the jump diffusion model, which is in some cases appropriate for modeling a stock index; the calibration results are quite good although the model only offers three degrees of freedom (lambda as the jump intensity, mu as the expected jump size, and delta as the variability of the jump size).

Portfolio valuation
> Based on the market data and the calibrated model, a portfolio with the American put options on the DAX 30 index was modeled and major statistics (position values, deltas, and vegas) were estimated.

The realistic use case in this chapter shows the flexibility and the power of the DX package; it essentially allows one to address the major analytical tasks with regard to derivatives. The very approach and architecture make the application largely comparable to the benchmark case of a Black-Scholes-Merton analytical formula for European options. Once the valuation objects are defined, one can use them in a similar way as an analytical formula—despite the fact that under the hood, computationally demanding and memory-intensive algorithms are applied.

Further Resources

As for previous chapters, the following book is a good general reference for the topics covered in this chapter, especially when it comes to the calibration of option pricing models:

- Hilpisch, Yves (2015). *Derivatives Analytics with Python* (*http://dawp.tpq.io*). Chichester, England: Wiley Finance.

With regard to the consistent valuation and management of derivatives portfolios, see also the resources at the end of Chapter 20.

Dates and Times

As in the majority of scientific disciplines, dates and times play an important role in finance. This appendix introduces different aspects of this topic when it comes to Python programming. It cannot, of course, be exhaustive. However, it provides an introduction to the main areas of the Python ecosystem that support the modeling of date and time information.

Python

The `datetime` module (*https://docs.python.org/3/library/datetime.html*) from the Python standard library allows for the implementation of the most important date and time–related tasks:

```
In [1]: from pylab import mpl, plt
        plt.style.use('seaborn')
        mpl.rcParams['font.family'] = 'serif'
        %matplotlib inline

In [2]: import datetime as dt

In [3]: dt.datetime.now()  ❶
Out[3]: datetime.datetime(2018, 10, 19, 15, 17, 32, 164295)

In [4]: to = dt.datetime.today()  ❶
        to
Out[4]: datetime.datetime(2018, 10, 19, 15, 17, 32, 177092)

In [5]: type(to)
Out[5]: datetime.datetime

In [6]: dt.datetime.today().weekday()  ❷
Out[6]: 4
```

❶ Returns the exact date and system time.

❷ Returns the day of the week as a number, where 0 = Monday.

Of course, datetime objects can be defined freely:

```
In [7]: d = dt.datetime(2020, 10, 31, 10, 5, 30, 500000)  ❶
        d
Out[7]: datetime.datetime(2020, 10, 31, 10, 5, 30, 500000)

In [8]: str(d)  ❷
Out[8]: '2020-10-31 10:05:30.500000'

In [9]: print(d)  ❸
        2020-10-31 10:05:30.500000

In [10]: d.year  ❹
Out[10]: 2020

In [11]: d.month  ❺
Out[11]: 10

In [12]: d.day  ❻
Out[12]: 31

In [13]: d.hour  ❼
Out[13]: 10
```

❶ Custom datetime object.

❷ String representation.

❸ Printing such an object.

❹ The year ...

❺ ... month ...

❻ ... day ...

❼ ... and hour attributes of the object.

Transformations and split-ups are easily accomplished:

```
In [14]: o = d.toordinal()  ❶
         o
Out[14]: 737729

In [15]: dt.datetime.fromordinal(o)  ❷
Out[15]: datetime.datetime(2020, 10, 31, 0, 0)
```

```
In [16]: t = dt.datetime.time(d)   ❸
         t
Out[16]: datetime.time(10, 5, 30, 500000)

In [17]: type(t)
Out[17]: datetime.time

In [18]: dd = dt.datetime.date(d)   ❹
         dd
Out[18]: datetime.date(2020, 10, 31)

In [19]: d.replace(second=0, microsecond=0)   ❺
Out[19]: datetime.datetime(2020, 10, 31, 10, 5)
```

❶ Transformation *to* ordinal number.

❷ Transformation *from* ordinal number.

❸ Splitting up the time component.

❹ Splitting up the date component.

❺ Setting selected values to 0.

timedelta objects result from, among other things, arithmetic operations on date time objects (i.e., finding the difference between two such objects):

```
In [20]: td = d - dt.datetime.now()   ❶
         td
Out[20]: datetime.timedelta(days=742, seconds=67678, microseconds=169720)

In [21]: type(td)   ❷
Out[21]: datetime.timedelta

In [22]: td.days
Out[22]: 742

In [23]: td.seconds
Out[23]: 67678

In [24]: td.microseconds
Out[24]: 169720

In [25]: td.total_seconds()   ❸
Out[25]: 64176478.16972
```

❶ The difference between two datetime objects …

❷ … gives a timedelta object.

❸ The difference in seconds.

There are multiple ways to transform a datetime object into different representations, as well as to generate datetime objects out of, say, str objects. Details are
found in the documentation of the datetime module. Here are a few examples:

```
In [26]: d.isoformat()  ❶
Out[26]: '2020-10-31T10:05:30.500000'

In [27]: d.strftime('%A, %d. %B %Y %I:%M%p')  ❷
Out[27]: 'Saturday, 31. October 2020 10:05AM'

In [28]: dt.datetime.strptime('2017-03-31', '%Y-%m-%d')  ❸
Out[28]: datetime.datetime(2017, 3, 31, 0, 0)

In [29]: dt.datetime.strptime('30-4-16', '%d-%m-%y')  ❸
Out[29]: datetime.datetime(2016, 4, 30, 0, 0)

In [30]: ds = str(d)
         ds
Out[30]: '2020-10-31 10:05:30.500000'

In [31]: dt.datetime.strptime(ds, '%Y-%m-%d %H:%M:%S.%f')  ❸
Out[31]: datetime.datetime(2020, 10, 31, 10, 5, 30, 500000)
```

❶ ISO format string representation.

❷ Exact template for string representation.

❸ datetime object from str object based on template.

In addition to the now() and today() functions, there is also the utcnow() function,
which gives the exact date and time information in UTC (Coordinated Universal
Time, formerly known as Greenwich Mean Time, or GMT). This represents a one-
hour or two-hour difference from the author's time zone (Central European Time,
CET, or Central European Summer Time, CEST):

```
In [32]: dt.datetime.now()
Out[32]: datetime.datetime(2018, 10, 19, 15, 17, 32, 438889)

In [33]: dt.datetime.utcnow()  ❶
Out[33]: datetime.datetime(2018, 10, 19, 13, 17, 32, 448897)

In [34]: dt.datetime.now() - dt.datetime.utcnow()  ❷
Out[34]: datetime.timedelta(seconds=7199, microseconds=999995)
```

❶ Returns the current UTC time.

❷ Returns the difference between local time and UTC time.

Another class of the datetime module is the tzinfo class, a generic time zone class with methods utcoffset(), dst(), and tzname(). A definition for UTC and CEST time might look as follows:

```
In [35]: class UTC(dt.tzinfo):
             def utcoffset(self, d):
                 return dt.timedelta(hours=0)  ❶
             def dst(self, d):
                 return dt.timedelta(hours=0)  ❶
             def tzname(self, d):
                 return 'UTC'

In [36]: u = dt.datetime.utcnow()

In [37]: u
Out[37]: datetime.datetime(2018, 10, 19, 13, 17, 32, 474585)

In [38]: u = u.replace(tzinfo=UTC())  ❷

In [39]: u
Out[39]: datetime.datetime(2018, 10, 19, 13, 17, 32, 474585, tzinfo=<__main__.UTC
         object at 0x11c9a2320>)

In [40]: class CEST(dt.tzinfo):
             def utcoffset(self, d):
                 return dt.timedelta(hours=2)  ❸
             def dst(self, d):
                 return dt.timedelta(hours=1)  ❸
             def tzname(self, d):
                 return 'CEST'

In [41]: c = u.astimezone(CEST())  ❹
         c
Out[41]: datetime.datetime(2018, 10, 19, 15, 17, 32, 474585,
         tzinfo=<__main__.CEST object at 0x11c9a2cc0>)

In [42]: c - c.dst()  ❺
Out[42]: datetime.datetime(2018, 10, 19, 14, 17, 32, 474585,
         tzinfo=<__main__.CEST object at 0x11c9a2cc0>)
```

❶ No offsets for UTC.

❷ Attaches the dt.tzinfo object via the replace() method.

❸ Regular and DST (Daylight Saving Time) offsets for CEST.

❹ Transforms the UTC time zone to the CEST time zone.

❺ Gives the DST time for the transformed datetime object.

There is a Python module available called `pytz` (*http://pytz.sourceforge.net*) that implements the most important time zones from around the world:

```
In [43]: import pytz

In [44]: pytz.country_names['US']  ❶
Out[44]: 'United States'

In [45]: pytz.country_timezones['BE']  ❷
Out[45]: ['Europe/Brussels']

In [46]: pytz.common_timezones[-10:]  ❸
Out[46]: ['Pacific/Wake',
          'Pacific/Wallis',
          'US/Alaska',
          'US/Arizona',
          'US/Central',
          'US/Eastern',
          'US/Hawaii',
          'US/Mountain',
          'US/Pacific',
          'UTC']
```

❶ A single country.

❷ A single time zone.

❸ Some common time zones.

With `pytz`, there is generally no need to define custom `tzinfo` objects:

```
In [47]: u = dt.datetime.utcnow()

In [48]: u = u.replace(tzinfo=pytz.utc)  ❶

In [49]: u
Out[49]: datetime.datetime(2018, 10, 19, 13, 17, 32, 611417, tzinfo=<UTC>)

In [50]: u.astimezone(pytz.timezone('CET'))  ❷
Out[50]: datetime.datetime(2018, 10, 19, 15, 17, 32, 611417, tzinfo=<DstTzInfo
         'CET' CEST+2:00:00 DST>)

In [51]: u.astimezone(pytz.timezone('GMT'))  ❷
Out[51]: datetime.datetime(2018, 10, 19, 13, 17, 32, 611417, tzinfo=<StaticTzInfo
         'GMT'>)

In [52]: u.astimezone(pytz.timezone('US/Central'))  ❷
Out[52]: datetime.datetime(2018, 10, 19, 8, 17, 32, 611417, tzinfo=<DstTzInfo
         'US/Central' CDT-1 day, 19:00:00 DST>)
```

❶ Defining the `tzinfo` object via `pytz`.

❷ Transforming a `datetime` object to different time zones.

NumPy

NumPy also provides functionality to deal with date and time information:

```
In [53]: import numpy as np

In [54]: nd = np.datetime64('2020-10-31')   ❶
         nd
Out[54]: numpy.datetime64('2020-10-31')

In [55]: np.datetime_as_string(nd)   ❶
Out[55]: '2020-10-31'

In [56]: np.datetime_data(nd)   ❷
Out[56]: ('D', 1)

In [57]: d
Out[57]: datetime.datetime(2020, 10, 31, 10, 5, 30, 500000)

In [58]: nd = np.datetime64(d)   ❸
         nd
Out[58]: numpy.datetime64('2020-10-31T10:05:30.500000')

In [59]: nd.astype(dt.datetime)   ❹
Out[59]: datetime.datetime(2020, 10, 31, 10, 5, 30, 500000)
```

❶ Construction from `str` object and string representation.

❷ Metainformation about the data itself (type, size).

❸ Construction from `datetime` object.

❹ Conversion to `datetime` object.

Another way to construct such an object is by providing a `str` object, e.g., with the year and month and the frequency information. Note that the object value then defaults to the first day of the month. The construction of `ndarray` objects based on `list` objects also is possible:

```
In [60]: nd = np.datetime64('2020-10', 'D')
         nd
Out[60]: numpy.datetime64('2020-10-01')

In [61]: np.datetime64('2020-10') == np.datetime64('2020-10-01')
Out[61]: True

In [62]: np.array(['2020-06-10', '2020-07-10', '2020-08-10'], dtype='datetime64')
```

```
Out[62]: array(['2020-06-10', '2020-07-10', '2020-08-10'], dtype='datetime64[D]')

In [63]: np.array(['2020-06-10T12:00:00', '2020-07-10T12:00:00',
                   '2020-08-10T12:00:00'], dtype='datetime64[s]')
Out[63]: array(['2020-06-10T12:00:00', '2020-07-10T12:00:00',
                '2020-08-10T12:00:00'], dtype='datetime64[s]')
```

One can also generate ranges of dates by using the function `np.arange()`. Different frequencies (e.g., days, weeks, or seconds) are easily taken care of:

```
In [64]: np.arange('2020-01-01', '2020-01-04', dtype='datetime64')  ❶
Out[64]: array(['2020-01-01', '2020-01-02', '2020-01-03'], dtype='datetime64[D]')

In [65]: np.arange('2020-01-01', '2020-10-01', dtype='datetime64[M]')  ❷
Out[65]: array(['2020-01', '2020-02', '2020-03', '2020-04', '2020-05',
                '2020-06', '2020-07', '2020-08', '2020-09'],
               dtype='datetime64[M]')

In [66]: np.arange('2020-01-01', '2020-10-01', dtype='datetime64[W]')[:10]  ❸
Out[66]: array(['2019-12-26', '2020-01-02', '2020-01-09', '2020-01-16',
                '2020-01-23', '2020-01-30', '2020-02-06', '2020-02-13',
                '2020-02-20', '2020-02-27'], dtype='datetime64[W]')

In [67]: dtl = np.arange('2020-01-01T00:00:00', '2020-01-02T00:00:00',
                         dtype='datetime64[h]')  ❹
         dtl[:10]
Out[67]: array(['2020-01-01T00', '2020-01-01T01', '2020-01-01T02',
                '2020-01-01T03', '2020-01-01T04', '2020-01-01T05', '2020-01-01T06',
                '2020-01-01T07', '2020-01-01T08', '2020-01-01T09'],
               dtype='datetime64[h]')

In [68]: np.arange('2020-01-01T00:00:00', '2020-01-02T00:00:00',
                   dtype='datetime64[s]')[:10]  ❺
Out[68]: array(['2020-01-01T00:00:00', '2020-01-01T00:00:01',
                '2020-01-01T00:00:02', '2020-01-01T00:00:03',
                '2020-01-01T00:00:04', '2020-01-01T00:00:05',
                '2020-01-01T00:00:06', '2020-01-01T00:00:07',
                '2020-01-01T00:00:08', '2020-01-01T00:00:09'],
               dtype='datetime64[s]')

In [69]: np.arange('2020-01-01T00:00:00', '2020-01-02T00:00:00',
                   dtype='datetime64[ms]')[:10]  ❻
Out[69]: array(['2020-01-01T00:00:00.000', '2020-01-01T00:00:00.001',
                '2020-01-01T00:00:00.002', '2020-01-01T00:00:00.003',
                '2020-01-01T00:00:00.004', '2020-01-01T00:00:00.005',
                '2020-01-01T00:00:00.006', '2020-01-01T00:00:00.007',
                '2020-01-01T00:00:00.008', '2020-01-01T00:00:00.009'],
               dtype='datetime64[ms]')
```

❶ Daily frequency.

❷ Monthly frequency.

❸ Weekly frequency.

❹ Hourly frequency.

❺ Second frequency.

❻ Millisecond frequency.

Plotting date-time and/or time series data can sometimes be tricky. matplotlib has support for standard datetime objects. Transforming NumPy datetime64 information into Python datetime information generally does the trick, as the following example, whose result is shown in Figure A-1, illustrates:

```
In [70]: import matplotlib.pyplot as plt
         %matplotlib inline

In [71]: np.random.seed(3000)
         rnd = np.random.standard_normal(len(dtl)).cumsum() ** 2

In [72]: fig = plt.figure(figsize=(10, 6))
         plt.plot(dtl.astype(dt.datetime), rnd)   ❶
         fig.autofmt_xdate();   ❷
```

❶ Uses the datetime information as *x* values.

❷ Autoformats the datetime ticks on the x-axis.

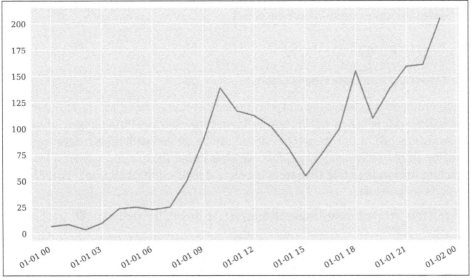

Figure A-1. Plot with datetime x-ticks autoformatted

pandas

The pandas package was designed, at least to some extent, with time series data in mind. Therefore, the package provides classes that are able to efficiently handle date and time information, like the DatetimeIndex class for time indices (see the documentation at *http://bit.ly/timeseries_doc*).

pandas introduces the Timestamp object as a further alternative to datetime and datetime64 objects:

```
In [73]: import pandas as pd

In [74]: ts = pd.Timestamp('2020-06-30')   ❶
         ts
Out[74]: Timestamp('2020-06-30 00:00:00')

In [75]: d = ts.to_pydatetime()   ❷
         d
Out[75]: datetime.datetime(2020, 6, 30, 0, 0)

In [76]: pd.Timestamp(d)   ❸
Out[76]: Timestamp('2020-06-30 00:00:00')

In [77]: pd.Timestamp(nd)   ❹
Out[77]: Timestamp('2020-10-01 00:00:00')
```

❶ Timestamp object from str object.

❷ datetime object from Timestamp object.

❸ Timestamp from datetime object.

❹ Timestamp from datetime64 object.

Another important class is the aforementioned DatetimeIndex class (*http://bit.ly/datetimeindex_doc*), which is a collection of Timestamp objects with a number of helpful methods attached. A DatetimeIndex object can be created with the pd.date_range() function (*http://bit.ly/date_range_doc*), which is rather flexible and powerful for constructing time indices (see Chapter 8 for more details on this function). Typical conversions are possible:

```
In [78]: dti = pd.date_range('2020/01/01', freq='M', periods=12)   ❶
         dti
Out[78]: DatetimeIndex(['2020-01-31', '2020-02-29', '2020-03-31', '2020-04-30',
                        '2020-05-31', '2020-06-30', '2020-07-31', '2020-08-31',
                        '2020-09-30', '2020-10-31', '2020-11-30', '2020-12-31'],
                       dtype='datetime64[ns]', freq='M')

In [79]: dti[6]
```

```
Out[79]: Timestamp('2020-07-31 00:00:00', freq='M')

In [80]: pdi = dti.to_pydatetime()  ❷
         pdi
Out[80]: array([datetime.datetime(2020, 1, 31, 0, 0),
                 datetime.datetime(2020, 2, 29, 0, 0),
                 datetime.datetime(2020, 3, 31, 0, 0),
                 datetime.datetime(2020, 4, 30, 0, 0),
                 datetime.datetime(2020, 5, 31, 0, 0),
                 datetime.datetime(2020, 6, 30, 0, 0),
                 datetime.datetime(2020, 7, 31, 0, 0),
                 datetime.datetime(2020, 8, 31, 0, 0),
                 datetime.datetime(2020, 9, 30, 0, 0),
                 datetime.datetime(2020, 10, 31, 0, 0),
                 datetime.datetime(2020, 11, 30, 0, 0),
                 datetime.datetime(2020, 12, 31, 0, 0)], dtype=object)

In [81]: pd.DatetimeIndex(pdi)  ❸
Out[81]: DatetimeIndex(['2020-01-31', '2020-02-29', '2020-03-31', '2020-04-30',
                        '2020-05-31', '2020-06-30', '2020-07-31', '2020-08-31',
                        '2020-09-30', '2020-10-31', '2020-11-30', '2020-12-31'],
                       dtype='datetime64[ns]', freq=None)

In [82]: pd.DatetimeIndex(dtl)  ❹
Out[82]: DatetimeIndex(['2020-01-01 00:00:00', '2020-01-01 01:00:00',
                        '2020-01-01 02:00:00', '2020-01-01 03:00:00',
                        '2020-01-01 04:00:00', '2020-01-01 05:00:00',
                        '2020-01-01 06:00:00', '2020-01-01 07:00:00',
                        '2020-01-01 08:00:00', '2020-01-01 09:00:00',
                        '2020-01-01 10:00:00', '2020-01-01 11:00:00',
                        '2020-01-01 12:00:00', '2020-01-01 13:00:00',
                        '2020-01-01 14:00:00', '2020-01-01 15:00:00',
                        '2020-01-01 16:00:00', '2020-01-01 17:00:00',
                        '2020-01-01 18:00:00', '2020-01-01 19:00:00',
                        '2020-01-01 20:00:00', '2020-01-01 21:00:00',
                        '2020-01-01 22:00:00', '2020-01-01 23:00:00'],
                       dtype='datetime64[ns]', freq=None)
```

❶ DatetimeIndex object with monthly frequency for 12 periods.

❷ DatetimeIndex object converted to ndarray objects with datetime objects.

❸ DatetimeIndex object from ndarray object with datetime objects.

❹ DatetimeIndex object from ndarray object with datetime64 objects.

pandas takes care of proper plotting of date-time information (see Figure A-2 and also Chapter 8):

```
In [83]: rnd = np.random.standard_normal(len(dti)).cumsum() ** 2
```

```
In [84]: df = pd.DataFrame(rnd, columns=['data'], index=dti)

In [85]: df.plot(figsize=(10, 6));
```

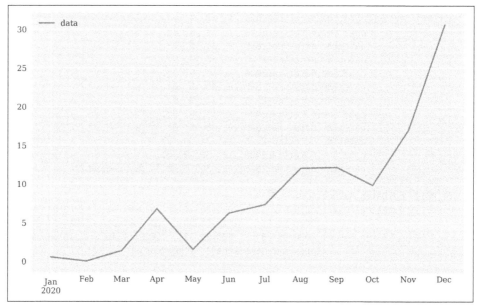

Figure A-2. pandas plot with Timestamp x-ticks autoformatted

pandas also integrates well with the `pytz` module to manage time zones:

```
In [86]: pd.date_range('2020/01/01', freq='M', periods=12,
                        tz=pytz.timezone('CET'))
Out[86]: DatetimeIndex(['2020-01-31 00:00:00+01:00', '2020-02-29
         00:00:00+01:00',
         '2020-03-31 00:00:00+02:00', '2020-04-30 00:00:00+02:00',
         '2020-05-31 00:00:00+02:00', '2020-06-30 00:00:00+02:00',
         '2020-07-31 00:00:00+02:00', '2020-08-31 00:00:00+02:00',
         '2020-09-30 00:00:00+02:00', '2020-10-31 00:00:00+01:00',
         '2020-11-30 00:00:00+01:00', '2020-12-31 00:00:00+01:00'],
                        dtype='datetime64[ns, CET]', freq='M')

In [87]: dti = pd.date_range('2020/01/01', freq='M', periods=12, tz='US/Eastern')
         dti
Out[87]: DatetimeIndex(['2020-01-31 00:00:00-05:00', '2020-02-29
         00:00:00-05:00',
         '2020-03-31 00:00:00-04:00', '2020-04-30 00:00:00-04:00',
         '2020-05-31 00:00:00-04:00', '2020-06-30 00:00:00-04:00',
         '2020-07-31 00:00:00-04:00', '2020-08-31 00:00:00-04:00',
         '2020-09-30 00:00:00-04:00', '2020-10-31 00:00:00-04:00',
         '2020-11-30 00:00:00-05:00', '2020-12-31 00:00:00-05:00'],
                        dtype='datetime64[ns, US/Eastern]', freq='M')
```

```
In [88]: dti.tz_convert('GMT')
Out[88]: DatetimeIndex(['2020-01-31 05:00:00+00:00', '2020-02-29
         05:00:00+00:00',
         '2020-03-31 04:00:00+00:00', '2020-04-30 04:00:00+00:00',
         '2020-05-31 04:00:00+00:00', '2020-06-30 04:00:00+00:00',
         '2020-07-31 04:00:00+00:00', '2020-08-31 04:00:00+00:00',
         '2020-09-30 04:00:00+00:00', '2020-10-31 04:00:00+00:00',
         '2020-11-30 05:00:00+00:00', '2020-12-31 05:00:00+00:00'],
                       dtype='datetime64[ns, GMT]', freq='M')
```

BSM Option Class

Class Definition

The following presents a class definition for a European call option in the Black-Scholes-Merton (1973) model. The class-based implementation is an alternative to the one based on functions as presented in "Python Script" on page 392:

```
#
# Valuation of European call options in Black-Scholes-Merton model
# incl. vega function and implied volatility estimation
# -- class-based implementation
#
# Python for Finance, 2nd ed.
# (c) Dr. Yves J. Hilpisch
#
from math import log, sqrt, exp
from scipy import stats


class bsm_call_option(object):
    ''' Class for European call options in BSM model.

    Attributes
    ==========
    S0: float
        initial stock/index level
    K: float
        strike price
    T: float
        maturity (in year fractions)
    r: float
        constant risk-free short rate
    sigma: float
        volatility factor in diffusion term
```

```
Methods
=======
value: float
    returns the present value of call option
vega: float
    returns the vega of call option
imp_vol: float
    returns the implied volatility given option quote
'''

def __init__(self, S0, K, T, r, sigma):
    self.S0 = float(S0)
    self.K = K
    self.T = T
    self.r = r
    self.sigma = sigma

def value(self):
    ''' Returns option value.
    '''
    d1 = ((log(self.S0 / self.K) +
          (self.r + 0.5 * self.sigma ** 2) * self.T) /
          (self.sigma * sqrt(self.T)))
    d2 = ((log(self.S0 / self.K) +
          (self.r - 0.5 * self.sigma ** 2) * self.T) /
          (self.sigma * sqrt(self.T)))
    value = (self.S0 * stats.norm.cdf(d1, 0.0, 1.0) -
            self.K * exp(-self.r * self.T) * stats.norm.cdf(d2, 0.0, 1.0))
    return value

def vega(self):
    ''' Returns vega of option.
    '''
    d1 = ((log(self.S0 / self.K) +
          (self.r + 0.5 * self.sigma ** 2) * self.T) /
          (self.sigma * sqrt(self.T)))
    vega = self.S0 * stats.norm.pdf(d1, 0.0, 1.0) * sqrt(self.T)
    return vega

def imp_vol(self, C0, sigma_est=0.2, it=100):
    ''' Returns implied volatility given option price.
    '''
    option = bsm_call_option(self.S0, self.K, self.T, self.r, sigma_est)
    for i in range(it):
        option.sigma -= (option.value() - C0) / option.vega()
    return option.sigma
```

Class Usage

This class can be used in an interactive Jupyter Notebook session as follows:

```
In [1]: from bsm_option_class import *

In [2]: o = bsm_call_option(100., 105., 1.0, 0.05, 0.2)
        type(o)
Out[2]: bsm_option_class.bsm_call_option

In [3]: value = o.value()
        value
Out[3]: 8.021352235143176

In [4]: o.vega()
Out[4]: 39.67052380842653

In [5]: o.imp_vol(C0=value)
Out[5]: 0.2
```

The option class can also be used to visualize, for example, the value and vega of the option for different strikes and maturities. It is, in the end, one of the major advantages of having an analytical option pricing formula available. The following Python code generates the option statistics for different maturity-strike combinations:

```
In [6]: import numpy as np
        maturities = np.linspace(0.05, 2.0, 20)
        strikes = np.linspace(80, 120, 20)
        K, T = np.meshgrid(strikes, maturities)
        C = np.zeros_like(K)
        V = np.zeros_like(C)
        for t in enumerate(maturities):
            for k in enumerate(strikes):
                o.T = t[1]
                o.K = k[1]
                C[t[0], k[0]] = o.value()
                V[t[0], k[0]] = o.vega()
```

First, a look at the option values. Figure B-1 presents the value surface for the European call option:

```
In [7]: from pylab import cm, mpl, plt
        from mpl_toolkits.mplot3d import Axes3D
        mpl.rcParams['font.family'] = 'serif'
        %matplotlib inline

In [8]: fig = plt.figure(figsize=(12, 7))
        ax = fig.gca(projection='3d')
        surf = ax.plot_surface(K, T, C, rstride=1, cstride=1,
                    cmap=cm.coolwarm, linewidth=0.5, antialiased=True)
        ax.set_xlabel('strike')
```

```
ax.set_ylabel('maturity')
ax.set_zlabel('European call option value')
fig.colorbar(surf, shrink=0.5, aspect=5);
```

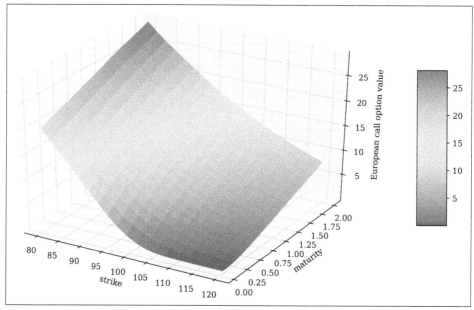

Figure B-1. Value surface for European call option

Second, a look at the vega values. Figure B-2 presents the vega surface for the European call option:

```
In [9]: fig = plt.figure(figsize=(12, 7))
        ax = fig.gca(projection='3d')
        surf = ax.plot_surface(K, T, V, rstride=1, cstride=1,
                cmap=cm.coolwarm, linewidth=0.5, antialiased=True)
        ax.set_xlabel('strike')
        ax.set_ylabel('maturity')
        ax.set_zlabel('Vega of European call option')
        fig.colorbar(surf, shrink=0.5, aspect=5);
```

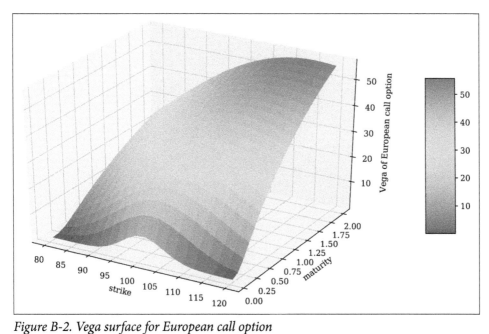

Figure B-2. Vega surface for European call option

Index

Symbols

% character, 71
%time function, 276
%timeit function, 276
* (multiplication) operator, 150, 161
+ (addition) operator, 150, 161
2D plotting
    interactive, 195-203
    matplotlib import and customization, 168
    one-dimensional data sets, 169-176
    other plot styles, 183-191
    two-dimensional data sets, 176-183
3D plotting, 191-194
__abs__ method, 160
__add__ method, 161
__bool__ method, 160
__getitem__ method, 161
__init__ method, 155, 159
__iter__ method, 162
__len__ method, 161
__mul__ method, 161
__repr__ method, 160
__sizeof__ method, 150
{} (curly braces), 71

A

absolute differences, calculating, 212
absolute price data, 442
abstraction, 147
acknowledgments, xviii
adaptive quadrature, 336
addition (+) operator, 150, 161
aggregation, 148, 158
AI-first finance, 28

algorithmic trading
    automated trading, 521-554
    FXCM trading platform, 467-481
    trading strategies, 483-520
algorithms (see also financial algorithms)
    Fibonacci numbers, 286-290
    for supervised learning, 448
    for unsupervised learning, 444
    prime numbers, 282-286
    the number pi, 290-294
Amazon Web Services (AWS), 50
American options, 376, 380, 607-614
anonymous functions, 80
antithetic paths, 573
antithetic variates, 373
append() method, 136
appending, using pandas, 136
apply() method, 142, 218
approximation
    interpolation technique, 324-328
    main focus of, 312
    package imports and customizations, 312
    regression technique, 313-324
arbitrary-precision floats, 65
array module, 88
arrays (see also NumPy)
    handling with pure Python code, 86-90
    I/O with PyTables, 263
    Python array class, 88-90
    writing and reading NumPy arrays, 242
artificial intelligence (AI), 28
Asian payoff, 606
attributes, in object-oriented programming, 145

individual basis functions, 317
least-squares approach, 321
linear regression, 314
monomials as basis functions, 313
multiple dimensions and, 321
noisy data and, 319
np.polyval() function, 314
ordinary least-squares (OLS) regression, 226, 494-498
parameters of polyfit() function, 314
task of, 313
unsorted data, 320
regular expressions, 74
relational databases, 239
relative return data, 442
Relative Strength Index (RSI), 199
relevant markets, 622
replace() method, 70
resampling, 215
reusability, 148
Reuters Instrument Codes (RICs), 209
risk management
automated trading, 547
credit valuation adjustments (CVA), 388
FXCM trading platform, 468
minimizing portfolio risk, 416
valuation classes for, 595
value-at-risk (VaR), 383
risk-neutral discounting
constant short rate, 563
modeling and handling dates, 560
risk-neutral investors, 523
risk-neutral valuation approach, 560
riskless assets, 426
rolling statistics
deriving using pandas, 218
financial time series example, 217
technical analysis example, 220
Romberg integration, 336
RSA public and private keys, 51

S

sample() function, 432
sampling error, 356
scaling out versus scaling up, 274
scatter plots, 184, 247
scatter_matrix() function, 225
sci.fixed_quad(), 336
sci.quad(), 336

sci.romberg(), 336
sci.splev() function, 325
sci.splrep() function, 325
scientific method, 25
scientific stack, 8
scikit-learn
basics of, 8
benefits of for machine learning, 444
DNNs with, 454, 512-514
predicting market price movements, 28
SciPy
basics of, 8, 40
documentation, 343, 463
scipy.integrate package, 334
scipy.integrate subpackage, 336
scipy.optimize.minimize() function, 333
scipy.stats subpackage, 355, 402
sco.fmin() function, 331
sco.fsolve() function, 427
scs.describe() function, 356, 402
scs.scoreatpercentile() function, 385
Secure Shell (SSH), 50
Secure Sockets Layer (SSL), 50
self.generate_paths(), 575
sequential train-test split, 509
serialization, 233, 236
Series class, 128
sets, 82
set_price() method, 156
Sharpe ratio, 421
short rates, 359, 563
simple moving averages (SMAs), 220, 484-491
simulation
dynamic simulation, 356
random variables, 353
stochastic processes, 356
value of in finance, 352
variance reduction, 372
simulation classes
generic simulation class, 574-577
geometric Brownian motion, 577-582
jump diffusion, 582-586
overview of, 614
random number generation, 572
square-root diffusion, 587-590
wrapper module for, 591
skewness test, 405
slicing, 77
sn_random_numbers() function, 572

solid state disks (SSDs), 231
SQLAlchemy, 239
SQLite3, 239
square-root diffusion, 359, 587-590
stacking, 99
standard normally distributed random numbers, 572
static coupling, 276
statically typed languages, 62
statistical learning, 398
statistics
    Bayesian statistics, 429-443
    machine learning (ML), 444-461
    normality tests, 398-409
    portfolio optimization, 415-428
    value of in finance, 397
stochastic differential equation (SDE), 299, 356
stochastic processes
    definition of, 356
    geometric Brownian motion, 356, 399
    jump diffusion, 369
    square-root diffusion, 359
    stochastic volatility, 365
stochastic volatility models, 365
stochastics
    Python script, 392
    random numbers, 346-352
    risk measures, 383-391
    simulation, 352-375
    use cases for, 345
    valuation, 375-382
str() function, 69
streaming data, 477
strike values, 191, 376
strings
    parsing date-time information, 74
    printing and string replacements, 71
    string methods, 69
    text representation with, 69
    Unicode strings, 71
Structured Query Language (SQL) databases
    from SQL to pandas, 247
    working with in pandas, 246
    working with in Python, 239
sum() method, 142
summary statistics, 210-212
supervised learning
    classification versus estimation problems, 448

data for, 448
decision trees (DTs), 452
deep neural networks (DNNs), 454-461
definition of, 448
Gaussian Naive Bayes (GNB), 449, 504
logistic regression (LR), 451, 504
support vector machine (SVM) algorithm, 29, 460, 504
sy.diff() function, 341
Symbol class, 338
symbolic computation
    differentiation, 341
    equations, 340
    integration and differentiation, 340
    Symbol class, 338
    SymPy library for, 337
SymPy, 337-343

T

tables
    compressed tables with PyTables, 261
    data retrieval with TsTables, 271
    data storage with TsTables, 270
    I/O with PyTables, 254
tail risk, 383
technical analysis, rolling statistics using pandas, 220
technology in finance
    advances in speed and frequency, 11
    potential of, 9
    real-time analytics, 13
    technology and talent as barriers to entry, 11
    technology as enabler, 10
    technology spending, 9
TensorFlow, 28, 455, 515-519
Terminal, 50
text files
    compatibility issues, 236
    I/O with Python, 232
    reading and writing with Python, 236
text/code editors, 7, 50
tick data, 228, 470
time indices, 120
time-to-results, improved with Python, 19
timedelta objects, 661
times-to-maturity, 191
Timestamp object, 668
today() function, 662

.to_csv() method, 251
trace plots, 433
trading strategies
    algorithmic trading, defined, 483
    classification, 504-511
    deep neural networks (DNNs) and, 512-519
    frequency approach, 501-503
    k-means clustering algorithm, 499-501
    linear OLS regression, 494-498
    ML-based trading strategy, 532-543
    random walk hypothesis, 491-494
    simple moving averages (SMAs), 484-491
    vectorized backtesting approach, 483
train_test_split() function, 460
ts.read_range() function, 272
TsTables
    data retrieval, 271
    data storage, 270
    sample data, 268
tuples, 75
type function, 62
typographical conventions, xv
tzinfo class, 663
tzname() method, 663

U

Unicode strings, 71
unit zero-coupon bond (ZCB), 563
unsorted data, 320
unsupervised learning
    algorithms performing, 444
    data for, 445
    Gaussian mixture, 447
    k-means clustering algorithm, 446
update() method, 580
user-defined functions, 477
UTC (Coordinated Universal Time), 662
utcnow() function, 662
utcoffset() method, 663

V

valuation
    American options, 380
    derivatives valuation, 595-616
    European options, 14, 376
    market-based valuation, 637-657
    portfolio valuation, 617-636
    valuation of contingent claims, 375
valuation framework
    Fundamental Theorem of Asset Pricing,
        558-560
    market environments, 565-567
    risk-neutral discounting, 560-564
value-at-risk (VaR), 383, 542
van Rossum, Guido, 5
variance of the returns, 398
variance reduction, 372, 573
vectorization of code
    benefits of, 309
    increased memory footprint with, 279
    speeding up typical tasks with, 275
    with NumPy, 106-112
    with NumPy looping, 278
vectorized backtesting approach, 483, 487,
    533-537
vega, 599
view_init() method, 194
Vim, 7
virtual environment managers, 34, 41-44
volatility clusters, spotting, 224
volatility processes, 359
volatility surfaces, 191

Z

Zen of Python, 4
zero-based numbering, 76

About the Author

Dr. Yves J. Hilpisch is founder and managing partner of The Python Quants (*http://tpq.io*), a group focusing on the use of open source technologies for financial data science, artificial intelligence, algorithmic trading, and computational finance. He is also founder and CEO of The AI Machine (*http://aimachine.io*), a company focused on harnessing the power of artificial intelligence for algorithmic trading via a proprietary strategy execution platform. He is the author of two other books (*http://books.tpq.io*):

- *Derivatives Analytics with Python* (Wiley, 2015)
- *Listed Volatility and Variance Derivatives* (Wiley, 2017)

Yves lectures on computational finance at the CQF Program (*http://cqf.com*). He is also the director of the first online training program leading to a University Certificate in Python for Algorithmic Trading and/or Computational Finance (*http://certificate.tpq.io*).

Yves wrote the financial analytics library DX Analytics (*http://dx-analytics.com*) and organizes meetups (*http://pqf.tpq.io*), conferences, and bootcamps (*http://fpq.io*) about artificial intelligence, quantitative finance and algorithmic trading in London, Frankfurt, Berlin, Paris, and New York. He has given keynote speeches at technology conferences in the United States, Europe, and Asia.

Colophon

The animal on the cover of *Python for Finance* is a Hispaniolan solenodon. The Hispaniolan solenodon (*Solenodon paradoxus*) is an endangered mammal that lives on the Caribbean island of Hispaniola, which comprises Haiti and the Dominican Republic. It's particularly rare in Haiti and a bit more common in the Dominican Republic.

Solenodons are known to eat arthropods, worms, snails, and reptiles. They also consume roots, fruit, and leaves on occasion. A solenodon weighs a pound or two and has a foot-long head and body plus a ten-inch tail, give or take. This ancient mammal looks somewhat like a big shrew. It's quite furry, with reddish-brown coloring on top and lighter fur on its undersides, while its tail, legs, and prominent snout lack hair.

It has a rather sedentary lifestyle and often stays out of sight. When it does come out, its movements tend to be awkward, and it sometimes trips when running. However, being a night creature, it has developed an acute sense of hearing, smell, and touch. Its own distinctive scent is said to be "goatlike."

It excretes toxic saliva from a groove in the second lower incisor and uses it to paralyze and attack its invertebrate prey. As such, it is one of few venomous mammals.

Sometimes the venom is released when fighting among each other, and can be fatal to the solenodon itself. Often, after initial conflict, they establish a dominance relationship and get along in the same living quarters. Families tend to live together for a long time. Apparently, it only drinks while bathing.

Many of the animals on O'Reilly covers are endangered; all of them are important to the world. To learn more about how you can help, go to *animals.oreilly.com*.

The cover image is from Wood's *Illustrated Natural History*. The cover fonts are URW Typewriter and Guardian Sans. The text font is Adobe Minion Pro; the heading font is Adobe Myriad Condensed; and the code font is Dalton Maag's Ubuntu Mono.

Milton Keynes UK
Ingram Content Group UK Ltd.
UKHW021300240624
444522UK00010BA/6

9 781492 024330